Parallel Logic Programming

Logic Programming

Ehud Shapiro, editor
Koichi Furukawa, Jean-Louis Lassez, Fernando Pereira, and David H. D. Warren, associate editors

The Art of Prolog: Advanced Programming Techniques, Leon Sterling and Ehud Shapiro, 1986

Logic Programming: Proceedings of the Fourth International Conference (volumes 1 and 2), edited by Jean-Louis Lassez, 1987

Concurrent Prolog: Collected Papers (volumes 1 and 2), edited by Ehud Shapiro, 1987

Logic Programming: Proceedings of the Fifth International Conference and Symposium (volumes 1 and 2), edited by Robert A. Kowalski and Kenneth A. Bowen, 1988

Constraint Satisfaction in Logic Programming, Pascal Van Hentenryck, 1989

Logic-Based Knowledge Representation, edited by Peter Jackson, Han Reichgelt, and Frank van Harmelen, 1989

Logic Programming: Proceedings of the Sixth International Conference, edited by Giorgio Levi and Maurizio Martelli, 1989

Meta-Programming in Logic Programming, edited by Harvey Abramson and M. H. Rogers, 1989

Logic Programming: Proceedings of the North American Conference 1989 (volumes 1 and 2), edited by Ewing L. Lusk and Ross A. Overbeek, 1989

Logic Programming: Proceedings of the 1990 North American Conference, edited by Saumya Debray and Manuel Hermenegildo, 1990

Logic Programming: Proceedings of the Seventh International Conference, edited by David H. D. Warren and Peter Szeredi, 1990

Prolog VLSI Implementations, Pierluigi Civera, Gianluca Piccinini, and Maurizio Zamboni, 1990

The Craft of Prolog, Richard A. O'Keefe, 1990

The Practice of Prolog, edited by Leon S. Sterling, 1990

Eco-Logic: Logic-Based Approaches to Ecological Modelling, David Robertson, Alan Bundy, Robert Muetzelfeldt, Mandy Haggith, and Michael Uschold, 1991

Warren's Abstract Machine: A Tutorial Reconstruction, Hassan Aït Kaci, 1991

Parallel Logic Programming, Evan Tick, 1991

Parallel Logic Programming

Evan Tick

The MIT Press
Cambridge, Massachusetts
London, England

This book was printed and bound in the United States of America.

Library of Congress Cataloging-in-Publication Data

Tick, Evan, 1959–
    Parallel logic programming / Evan Tick.
       p.   cm. — (Logic programming)
    Includes bibliographical references and index.
    ISBN 0-262-20087-2
    1. Parallel programming (Computer science) 2. Logic programming. I. Title. II. Series.
QA76.642.T53 1991
004'.35—dc20

91-2963
CIP

For N.M.

Contents

Series Foreword

Preface

Acknowledgments

1   Introduction   **1**

1.1   Some Pragmatics   4

    1.1.1   Programming in UNIX   4
    1.1.2   Programming With Monitors   4
    1.1.3   Programming in Parallel Lisp   11

1.2   Parallelism and Concurrency   12

1.3   Measuring Parallel Performance   14

2   Prolog and FGHC   **19**

2.1   Prolog   19

    2.1.1   Programming Objects   19
    2.1.2   Informal Semantics   21
    2.1.3   Extra-Logical Features and Builtins   25
    2.1.4   OR-Parallel Execution Model   28
    2.1.5   Programming Paradigms: Difference Lists   29

2.2   Flat Guarded Horn Clauses   33

    2.2.1   Programming Objects   33
    2.2.2   Informal Semantics   34
    2.2.3   Extra-Logical Features and Builtins   40
    2.2.4   Programming Paradigms   42
    2.2.5   Other Committed-Choice Languages   45

2.3   Programming Style   49

    2.3.1   Converting Nondeterminate into Determinate Code   49
    2.3.2   Generic Procedures and Modularity   51
    2.3.3   Order of Evaluation and Speculative Parallelism   53

2.4   Architectures   56

    2.4.1   Overview of Aurora and Panda   57
    2.4.2   Statistics   64

2.5   Summary   66

3   Small Programs   **71**

3.1   Appending   71

3.2   Reversing   75

3.3   Sorting   77

3.4   Stacking and Queueing   81

3.5   Filtering   84

3.6   Summary   87

4   More Small Programs   **91**

4.1   Permuting and Combining   91

    4.1.1   Permuting in OR-Parallel Prolog   91
    4.1.2   Combining in FGHC: Eager Evaluation   92
    4.1.3   Bounded-Buffer Communication   97
    4.1.4   Lazy Evaluation   99
    4.1.5   Prolog Revisited   102

4.2   Merging   104

    4.2.1   Simple Merge   105
    4.2.2   Splitting   106
    4.2.3   Cross Products   108

4.3   Summary   109

5   N-Queens   **117**

5.1   Prolog Versions   119

    5.1.1   Naive Generate & Test   119
    5.1.2   Fused Generate & Test   122
    5.1.3   Constraints   124
    5.1.4   More Constraints   127

5.2	FGHC Versions		129
	5.2.1	Candidates and Noncandidates	129
	5.2.2	Continuation-Based Machine Translation	133
	5.2.3	Distributed Process Structure	139
	5.2.4	Pipelined Filters	143
	5.2.5	Layered Streams	147
	5.2.6	Throttling Eager Evaluation in Layered Streams	150
5.3	Single and Multiple Solution Search		151
	5.3.1	Parallel Cut in OR-Prolog	151
	5.3.2	Termination Flags and Lazy Evaluation in FGHC	152
5.4	Discussion		158
5.5	Summary		165
6	**Isomorphic Trees and NAND Circuits**		**169**
6.1	Isomorphic Trees		169
	6.1.1	Nondeterminate Algorithms in Prolog	170
	6.1.2	Determinate Algorithm in FGHC	172
	6.1.3	Prolog Revisited: Determinate Algorithm	175
	6.1.4	Discussion: Complexity	175
6.2	NAND-Gate Circuit Designer		178
	6.2.1	Nondeterminate Algorithm in Prolog	179
	6.2.2	Determinate Algorithm in FGHC	184
	6.2.3	Discussion	187
6.3	Summary		190
7	**Triangle and MasterMind**		**197**
7.1	Triangle		197
	7.1.1	Structure Copying	199
	7.1.2	List Copying	200
	7.1.3	Discussion	202
7.2	MasterMind		205
	7.2.1	Naive Generate & Test	207
	7.2.2	Fused Generate & Test	209
	7.2.3	Discussion	211
7.3	Summary		214

8   Zebra, Salt and Mustard   **219**

8.1   Zebras   219

8.2   Salt and Mustard   229

8.3   Summary   236

9   Instant Insanity and Turtles   **241**

9.1   Instant Insanity   241

    9.1.1   Fused Generate & Test   243

    9.1.2   Naive Generate & Test   246

    9.1.3   Serialization by Short-Circuit Chain   248

    9.1.4   Bounded-Buffer Communication   250

    9.1.5   Pipelined Filters   251

    9.1.6   Layered Streams   256

    9.1.7   Degenerate Candidates & Noncandidates   259

    9.1.8   Complexity   259

    9.1.9   Discussion   263

9.2   Turtles   266

    9.2.1   Fused Generate & Test   266

    9.2.2   Candidates & Noncandidates   269

    9.2.3   Pipelined Filters   272

    9.2.4   Layered Streams   275

    9.2.5   Discussion   277

9.3   Summary   281

10   Puzzle and Waltz   **285**

10.1   Puzzle   286

    10.1.1   List Representation: Board Copying in Prolog   287

    10.1.2   Structure Representation: Constraints in Prolog   289

    10.1.3   Board Copying in FGHC   292

    10.1.4   Discussion   299

10.2   Waltz   300

    10.2.1   Logical Constraints   302

    10.2.2   Layered Streams   305

    10.2.3   Discussion   312

10.3   Summary   314

Contents

11   Semigroup and Pascal's Triangle   **323**

11.1 Semigroup   324

      11.1.1   Sequential Prolog   325
      11.1.2   Granularity Collection   330
      11.1.3   Pipelined Generator/Filters   334
      11.1.4   Improving the Pipeline Throughput   337
      11.1.5   Binary Hash Tree Filter   338
      11.1.6   Discussion   342

11.2 Pascal's Triangle   344

      11.2.1   Sequential Prolog   345
      11.2.2   Pairwise Addition   349
      11.2.3   AND-in-OR Parallelism   350
      11.2.4   Granularity Collection   353
      11.2.5   Discussion   356

11.3 Summary   359

12   BestPath   **365**

12.1 Johnson-Dijkstra in Prolog   367

12.2 How Not to Program in FGHC   374

12.3 Dijkstra's Algorithm with an Active Heap   376

12.4 Monitor Evaluation   381

12.5 Distributed Nearest Neighbors   384

12.6 Mergers Revisited   388

12.7 Partitioned Moore   390

12.8 Discussion and Summary   396

13   Summary and Conclusions   **405**

13.1 Programming Techniques   405

      13.1.1   OR-Parallel Prolog   405
      13.1.2   AND-Parallel FGHC   407

13.2 How Easy Was it to Write These Programs?   411

13.3 Empirical Results   413

13.4 Directions in Parallel Logic Programming   423

     13.4.1   A'UM   424

     13.4.2   Pandora   427

     13.4.3   Andorra   431

A   **Aurora and Panda Instruction Sets**   **435**

B   **Programming Projects**   **451**

C   **Glossary**   **465**

     Bibliography   471

     Index   481

Series Foreword

The logic programming approach to computing investigates the use of logic as a programming language and explores computational models based on controlled deduction.

The field of logic programming has seen a tremendous growth in the last several years, both in depth and scope. This growth is reflected in the number of articles, journals, theses, books, workshops, and conferences devoted to the subject. The MIT Press Series in Logic Programming was created to accommodate this development and to nurture it. It is dedicated to the publication of high-quality textbooks, monographs, collections, and proceedings in logic programming.

Ehud Shapiro
The Weizmann Institute of Science
Rehovot, Israel

Preface

People have been parallel programming for years on a wide variety of dual-processor mainframes, loosely-coupled distributed multiprocessors, array processors, vector machines, dataflow machines, shared-memory multiprocessors, etc. Yet in all these years, some of us found it hard to get excited about parallelism because there were few if any *high-class* parallel programming languages implemented on these machines. The lack of such languages was not completely due to lack of technology—the push to parallelize FORTRAN and other algorithmic languages was and still is very strong. What is a high-class language? It is a language that is *natural for programming*, all considerations of parallelism aside. We do not wish to trade away anything to gain performance improvement in exploiting parallelism: not declarativity, not clean semantics, not modularity, not correctness, not conciseness, nothing.

This book is an introduction to parallel logic programming languages, one (but not the only) family of high-class languages. The key development that inspired this book was the implementation of parallel logic programming languages on commercial shared-memory multiprocessors. Without the ability to measure actual performance tradeoffs, there is little point in writing a textbook about parallel processing as opposed to concurrent programming. Discussions of the beauty of concurrent semantics or the abundance of theoretical parallelism are only precursors to the acid test: the ability to achieve absolute performance improvement over the best sequential algorithms, as proved by timing statistics on real machines.

This book began at the Institute of New Generation Computer Technology (ICOT) as a series of performance benchmarks. The material was further developed concurrently with teaching the subject as a semester graduate course at the University of Tokyo during Spring 1989, and a quarter course at the University of Oregon during Summer 1990. The main purpose of these courses was to give the students experience in programming multiprocessors. Within two weeks students, many of whom had little experience with logic programming, were writing parallel programs and getting real speedups. This book should aid in developing a course wherein substantial parallel programming projects can be tackled by the students. Several such projects are suggested here. Prior knowledge of logic programming is not required; however, a strong programming background is desirable. The software systems used in this book, or ones similar to them, are available on a variety of multiprocessors.

It is time to make parallel programming as exciting as it should have been from the beginning.

Acknowledgments

Part of this book was written while I was a visiting researcher at the Institute of New Generation Computer Technology (ICOT) supported by a grant from the U.S. National Science Foundation. I thank Director Kazuhiro Fuchi and Dr. Sunichi Uchida of ICOT for their support of this work. I greatly enjoyed both working and socializing with the many researchers of ICOT's Fourth Research Laboratory. Especially helpful was Masatoshi Sato from the Oki Electric Industry Co. Ltd. who developed the real-parallel FGHC system on the Sequent multiprocessor. I apologize to him for taking the liberty of renaming his KL1PS system to Panda! Stimulating looks at the "big picture" with Manuel Hermenegildo, now at the University of Madrid, and Jim Crammond, now at Quintus Computer Systems Inc., were made possible by their separate visits to ICOT. I also thank Ewing Lusk and Ross Overbeek from the Argonne National Laboratory, and Andrzej Ciepielewski from the Swedish Institute of Computer Science, for their help with the Aurora system.

The remainder of this book was written at the University of Tokyo and at the University of Oregon. At Todai I was supported by a chair in Information Science endowed by the CSK Corporation. I thank my graduate students at Todai who overcame their public-university morass and worked quite hard. During summer 1990, Andrzej Ciepielewski visited the University of Oregon and used the text in his course. Andrzej and his students, notably Peter Adamson and Dae Yeon Park, were of invaluable assistance in correcting the text.

I thank Mark Korsloot from the Delft University of Technology, Kish Shen from Cambridge University, and Tim Lindholm from Quintus for their extensive comments on early drafts of this book. Sections 13.4 and Appendix B were greatly aided by help from Reem Bahgat from Imperial College, Daniel Dure from the French Ministry of Industry (on leave from Ecole Normale Supérieure), Rong Yang from Bristol University, and Kaoru Yoshida from ICOT. Lisa James, from the University of Oregon, did excellent copy editing of the book.

Parallel Logic Programming

1 Introduction

"Two things, however, are impressed on novices: that all experiences are of
equal spiritual significance (drudgery is divine); and that reasoning is futile.
Zen holds that nobody can actually think himself into a state of
enlightenment, still less depend on the logical arguments of others."
R.H.P. Mason and J.G. Caiger
A History of Japan
C.E. Tuttle Co., Inc. 1973

One of the most difficult problems with developing parallel processing systems
is the job of parallel programming. By parallel programming we mean the programming of a single application to execute efficiently on multiple processors. The
problem with parallel programming has been finessed, to some degree, by implementing sequential languages like FORTRAN on suitable multiprocessors, such
as pipelined machines (e.g., CDC 6600), vector machines (e.g., CRAY-1), MIMD
(multiple-instruction stream multiple-data stream) shared-memory machines (e.g.,
Alliant FX/8), and even MIMD pipelined machines (e.g., Denelcor HEP). The main
reason for using sequential languages is the massive amount of code already written
in those languages, as well as offloading the responsibility for "thinking in parallel"
from the programmer to the compiler. The problem with sequential languages of
the FORTRAN generation is that insufficient parallelism can be exploited from
automatic translation alone [97].

From the genes of FORTRAN and ALGOL came families of *imperative* (procedural) parallel programming languages, e.g., Pascal Plus, Modula-2, Ada, and occam;
and *applicative* parallel programming languages, e.g., SISAL, VAL, and ID. These
languages use various methods of implementing parallel tasks, for example, the
mutual exclusion of shared data updates and synchronization between tasks. The
families were developed primarily to fill the need for design languages that could
easily and clearly express parallelism.

While these families were being developed, and even earlier, other language designers were more concerned with designing languages that could easily and clearly
express *the problem to be solved*. Examples of this latter family of languages are
Lisp, Prolog, APL, and Smalltalk. Only recently have the two directions in language research met. Two major developments have been the implementation of
parallel Lisp-like languages, e.g., Qlisp, MultiLisp, and MultiScheme, and parallel
Prolog-like languages, e.g., Restricted AND-Parallel Prolog, OR-Parallel Prolog,
Flat Guarded Horn Clauses (FGHC), Flat Concurrent Prolog (FCP), and Parlog.

This book is about how to program in two of these languages: OR-parallel Prolog
and AND-parallel FGHC. Mastery of these two languages should easily facilitate

the grasp of others. In addition, as Prolog offers a logical and clean approach to
understanding programming in general, parallel Prolog-like languages (i.e., parallel
Horn-clause logic-programming languages) offer a logical and clean approach to
understanding the requirements of mutual exclusion and synchronization required
by asynchronous parallel programming in general. Thus this book is an introduction
both to logic programming and to parallel programming. Extensive programming
examples are given, and their performance is analyzed using data collected on
real shared-memory multiprocessor implementations. Performance data, although
specific to these implementations and hardware hosts, is critical to understanding
the tradeoffs in parallel programming. In many cases, we can abstract away the
specific details of the system implementations and make concrete statements about
efficient techniques for programming in these languages.

Logic programming, the paradigm of using first-order logic as the foundation of a
programming language, is most popularly espoused in the form of Prolog. Prolog is
a sequential language based on Horn-clause logic.[1] Prolog differs from procedural
languages because it uses backtracking and unification, and is single assignment
(within the scope of a clause). Prolog differs from functional languages in that
Prolog has two-way unification, allowing a procedure to be executed in alternative
modes. For example, a sorting program can be "run backwards" to produce permutations. Logic programming languages are distinct from almost all other languages
in that logic programming languages naturally express a large number of different
types of parallelism. The most renowned types are AND and OR parallelism. In
general, AND-parallelism is the ability to execute two conjunctive tasks in parallel; OR-parallelism is the ability to execute two disjunctive tasks in parallel. In
terms of logic programming, the task has the *granularity* of a goal execution, i.e.,
a procedure call and execution.

A goal execution is also called a reduction or logical inference.[2] The most promis-
ing types of AND-parallelism are *restricted* (sometimes called *independent*) and
stream. Restricted-AND-parallelism avoids binding conflicts by guaranteeing, before spawning parallel goals, that the goals will not attempt to bind the same variable. Stream AND parallelism is the ability to 'stream' partially instantiated data
structures from one conjunctive goal to the next. Binding conflicts are avoided by

---

[1]Objections that Prolog is *not* sequential should be saved until Section 1.2. To avoid ambiguity
we sometimes write "sequential Prolog" meaning Prolog, as opposed to "AND-parallel Prolog" or
"OR-parallel Prolog."

[2]Thus many systems claim performance figures in terms of KLIPS – thousands of logic inferences per second or KRPS – thousands of reductions per second. Beware however: not all logical
inferences are equal because different goals may require different amounts of computation. Thus
KLIPS is a very gross and often misleading metric.

suspending a goal when an input is unbound, and explicitly locking variables when binding them. In addition to these major types of parallelism, there are several other types, such as those described in Conery [33], Gregory [57], and Hermenegildo [62].

Although the theoretical importance of the presence of these various types of parallelism in logic programming languages is important, without practical implementations these results will not produce realistic speedups on multiprocessors. If programming becomes complex during the drive to efficiently implement these various types of parallelism, then sight of the original goal (to provide a *good* programming language that can be executed in parallel) will be lost. Thus logic programming language designers have been walking a fine line over the past several years — trying to exploit parallelism efficiently without weakening language semantics to the point of making programming impossible.

This book analyzes two vastly different approaches to this problem: OR-parallel Prolog and stream-AND-parallel FGHC (Flat Guarded Horn Clauses). Together, these languages represent the current state-of-the-art in parallel logic programming language design, in terms of both technology and programming methodologies.

On one hand, OR-parallel Prolog (also called "OR-Prolog" in this book) retains all the power of sequential Prolog, but exploits only the OR-parallel execution of nondeterminate clauses. OR-parallel execution involves running completely independent processes that cannot communicate with each other in any way. Any interrelated analysis of the solutions must be conducted on the group of solutions *after* the solutions have been constructed. Collection of independent solutions is performed in this book with the **findall** procedure. This builtin is an example of an *aggregation operator* that evaluates a goal for all its possible solutions [86].

On the other hand, FGHC sacrifices the ability to backtrack, i.e., to produce multiple solutions to nondeterminate problems, but exploits stream-AND-parallel execution of all goals. FGHC allows communication between processes, which permits the processes to collaborate during the search for solutions. However, the added burden of specifying communication often gives a program the characteristics of an intricate control structure. The program control structure is thus given the euphemism "the process reading," rather than the logical declarative reading. FGHC can be considered in some sense representative of a class of *committed-choice languages* including FCP [116], FLENG [89], Parlog [57, 35], Strand [49] and others.

This book is written as a programming primer, giving a progressive selection of annotated programs written in both OR-parallel Prolog and FGHC. The programs are used to expound certain programming techniques and pitfalls. In addition, performance timings are presented as evidence of why one type of programming methodology is better than another. These timings were collected from real parallel implementations of the languages on the Sequent Symmetry [95] and Encore Multimax [46] shared-memory multiprocessors. The programs given in this book progress from a trivial list-appending program, to variations of the classics, such as placing N queens on an $N \times N$ chessboard, to more advanced problems in semigroup theory and graph theory.

The importance of parallel processing is generally accepted in both the computer engineering community and the scientific (number-crunching) community. However, the importance of high-level programming languages is often neglected. Even within the so-called centers of logic programming research, little emphasis has been placed on developing sophisticated parallel debuggers or efficient optimizing compilers. One reason is that the research field is still young. The lack of tools puts greater emphasis on careful and efficient programming style. This book is meant as a guide to help "get it right the first time," because it may be some time before parallel programming environments approach those of sequential languages.

1.1   Some Pragmatics

Before eagerly jumping into the book, which is filled with possibly uncommon terms such as *clauses*, *guards*, *logical variables*, and *streams*, let us first consider (with tongue firmly in cheek) some examples of programming a multiprocessor in *the conventional way*. The three examples given, in increasing order of sophistication, speak for themselves.

1.1.1   Programming in UNIX

Figure 1.1 shows a manual page taken verbatim from the operating system of the Encore Multimax (UMAX 4.2) [46]. This particular page is concerned with spawning a parallel task from within a 'C' program. Especially amusing is the restriction concerning `printf`.

1.1.2   Programming With Monitors

Lusk *et al.* [77] give a clean, hierarchical approach to writing programs, for commercially available shared-memory multiprocessors, with *monitors*. Even though the 'C' language is used, the hierarchical use of macros keeps the programs uncluttered and portable. To explain the use of monitors, we review an example taken from Lusk *et al.*: a program which adds two vectors of integers (what could be simpler?). We present the 'C' program below without detailed explanation in order to give

TASK_START(3P)

NAME
   task_start - initiating a parallel action

SYNOPSIS
   #include <parallel.h>
   task_start(p, stacksize, argc, arg0, ..., argn)
   void (*proc)();
   int stacksize, argc;

DESCRIPTION
   The task_start function, a part of the multitasking library, creates a
   thread of control (a parallel activity) that is separately scheduled by
   the multitask scheduler. A stack of size stack_size 32-bit integers is
   allocated, the arguments, arg0...argn are copied onto the stack, and the
   task with this stack and procedure _p is created and placed in the
   scheduler queue. The task will begin execution as soon as there is a
   process available to execute it (possibly immediately). A task identifier is returned; NULL is returned on error (for example, failed to allocate stack space).

   The argc parameter is the size of the parameter list to be passed to the
   task. To pass floats, doubles, or structures requires that argc does
   not equal the number of arguments.

FILES
   /usr/lib/libpp.a   library archive, compile with -lpp switch
   /usr/include/parallel.h   header file

SEE ALSO
   sigpause(2), intro(3P), multitask(3P), printf(3S), spin(3P), share(3P)

RESTRICTIONS
   There is no run time detection of stack overflow.

   The printf (3S) routine requires a large stack. Try to print only from a
   few tasks and give those tasks stacks of size at least 1000.

   Since the multitasking environment is trying to schedule tasks to maximize processor use, tasks that block by spinlocks, sigpause(2), and so
   on, will have a negative effect on performance.

   Tasks can block using either TASK_BLOCK or PROCESS_BLOCK. Using
   PROCESS_BLOCK, however, makes an entire process block so that it is not
   available for use by any tasks.

Figure 1.1
UMAX 4.2 Programmer's Reference Manual Page for task-start

only a taste of this method.[3] Note that, although we show vector addition (which suffers from low granularity,), the granularity of the computation can be increased by assuming that some arbitrarily complex function is performed on pairs of vector elements.

System-defined macros INITENV, GSINIT, CREATE, WAIT_FOR_END, and GETSUB are built for and from monitors. The key portion of the program in Figure 1.2 is the work function. Here the GETSUB monitor delivers a vector index, i, to the process executing work. The process uses i to add two elements together, then requests another index.

The full macro expansion for GETSUB on the Sequent Balance is given in Figure 1.3 (taken from Lusk *et al.* p.28). The programmer rarely needs to examine the program at this level of detail, except possibly during debugging. But this program has been included here to illustrate one simple point:

> Parallel programming in monitors with a procedural language is best left for system programmers only — application programmers should not have to wade through this.

But that point is moot *if all there is* is parallel programming with monitors. Certainly that is *more* than you get when you buy a standard shared-memory multiprocessor. And this does not imply that programming with monitors is considered low-level programming. To the contrary, many people consider monitors (and their equivalents in other languages, such as Ada's *rendezvous*) to be a perfectly acceptable level of abstraction with which to program. However, not *all* people agree, and the logic programming systems described in this book offer much higher-level alternatives.

To illustrate the higher-level alternatives, consider the pseudo-FGHC version of the vector addition program shown in Figure 1.4. (The reader need not, and *should not* understand the precise meaning of FGHC semantics to appreciate this example. In fact, Figure 1.4 is only pseudo-code. As coded, the output of the final vector is not guaranteed to be ordered.) This program is written to mimic the general style of the 'C' program; however, a critical change has been made: *the FGHC program does not do self-scheduling.* Instead, a new process is spawned for each pair of vector elements. Inefficiency in this policy can be prevented by an independent scheduler which attempts to distribute a fair amount of work among all the real processors, and then efficiently execute the subsequently spawned processes locally.

---

[3]The code is taken directly from Lusk *et al.* [77], where there is an excellent derivation.

```
#include <stdio.h>
#define MAXLEN 1000

ENV

struct globmem {
    int length, a[MAXLEN], b[MAXLEN], c[MAXLEN], nprocs;
    GSDEC(GS)
} *glob;

main(argc,argv)
    int argc;      char *argv[];
{   int i,j;

    INITENV
    glob = (struct globmem *) G_MALLOC(sizeof(struct globmem));
    GSINIT(glob->GS)

    scanf(''%d'',&glob->nproc);        /* read in number of processes */
    scanf(''%d'',&glob->length);       /* read in length and two vectors */
    for (i=0; i<glob->length; i++) scanf(''%d'',&glob->a[i]);
    for (i=0; i<glob->length; i++) scanf(''%d'',&glob->b[i]);

    for (i=1; i<glob->nprocs; i++) { /* create the other processes */
        CREATE(slave)
    }
    work();
    WAIT_FOR_END(glob->nprocs - 1)

    for (i=0; i<glob->length;) {       /* print the answer */
        for (j=0; (j < 9) && (i<glob->length; j++)
            printf(''%d\t'', glob->c[i++]);
        printf(''\n'');
} }

slave()
{   work();    }

work()
{   int i,j;
    GETSUB(glob->GS,i,glob->length-1,glob->nprocs)
    while (i >= 0) {
        for (j=0; j<10000; j++)
            glob->c[i] = glob->a[i] + glob->b[i];
        GETSUB(glob->GS,i,glob->length-1,glob->nprocs)
} }
```

Figure 1.2
Parallel-'C' Program for Adding Two Integer Vectors

```
    {
        p_lock((glob->GS.lock));
    }

    if (glob->GS.sub <= glob->length - 1) {
        i = glob->GS.sub++;
    }
    else {
        i = -1;
        if (glob->GS.count[0] < (glob->nprocs - 1)) {
            glob->GS.count[0]++;
            p_unlock(glob->GS.lock);
            p_lock((glob->GS.queue[0]));
        }
        else
            glob->GS.sub = 0;
        if (glob->GS.count[0] == 0) {
                p_unlock(glob->GS.lock);
            }
            else {
                (glob->GS.count[0])--;
                p_unlock(glob->GS.queue[0]);
            }
            goto L5283;
        }
    p_unlock(glob->GS.lock);
    L5283: ;
```

Figure 1.3
GETSUB Monitor for Sequent Balance

```
main :-
    read(N), % size of vector
    readv(N,A),
    readv(N,B),
    master(A,B,C),
    writev(10,C).

readv(0,A) :- A=[].
readv(N,A) :- read(X), A=[X|As], N1 is N+1, readv(N1,As).

writev(_,[]).
writev(0,[X|Xs]) :- writenl(X), writev(Xs).
writev(N,[X|Xs]) :- N1 is N-1, write(X), writev(N1,Xs).

master([],[],C) :- C=[].
master([A|As],[B|Bs],C) :-
    C = [X|Xs],
    slave(A,B,X),
    master(As,Bs,Xs).

slave(A,B,C) :- work(A,B,C).
work(A,B,C) :- C is A+B.
```

Figure 1.4
FGHC Version of the Vector Addition Program

PEs†	'C'			FGHC			FGHC/'C'
	sec.	speedup	eff.	sec.	speedup	eff.	
1	5.15	1.0	1.00	173.2	1.0	1.00	33.6
2	2.68	1.9	0.96	91.7	1.9	0.95	34.2
4	1.44	3.6	0.90	49.9	3.5	0.87	34.7
8	0.83	6.2	0.78	29.7	5.8	0.73	35.8

† PE is processing element

Table 1.1
Vector Addition Performance Measurements (Multimax)

But what about performance? We have introduced the simpler FGHC program, casually mentioning that self-scheduling is not used. Certainly there will be some expense for this omission. The burden of scheduling, falling upon the underlying system, will have some overhead. The 'C' measurements made on the Encore Multimax (with NS32032 processors) by Lusk *et al.* are compared to our own FGHC measurements[4] in Table 1.1. This table shows the execution time (in seconds), speedup, efficiency, and execution time ratio of each program. Throughout this book *efficiency* (sometimes called *utilization*) is calculated as the speedup divided by the number of PEs. Both programs achieve somewhat efficient speedups, keeping the execution time ratio constant at around 35. This high ratio is more a problem with compiler technology and emulation overheads (in the FGHC system) than with the overhead of exploiting parallelism although, on eight PEs, the FGHC program is 5% less efficient than the 'C' program. Native code parallel logic programming systems and state-of-the-art compiler technology are expected to bridge much of the gap of 35. For example, JAM Parlog is a committed-choice system that executes programs 20%–40% faster than the system measured in Table 1.1 [131].

As another data point, we compared the OR-parallel Prolog system to a self-scheduling 'C' program, in their performance at solving the N-Queens problem discussed in Chapter 5. Both programs used the same fused generate & test algorithm. As shown in Table 1.2, the 'C' program executed about six times faster than OR-parallel Prolog on the Sequent Symmetry, with slightly lower speedups [2]. The execution time ratio is narrowed further by advanced Prolog compilation — an advanced OR-parallel system executes this program 40% faster than the measurements in Table 1.2. The main reason that the ratio is closer than in the previous

---

[4]These measurements are of Panda, the parallel FGHC architecture, discussed fully in the next chapters.

PEs	'C'			Prolog			Prolog/'C'
	sec.	speedup	eff.	sec.	speedup	eff.	
1	17.0	1.0	1.00	112.9	1.0	1.00	6.6
2	8.5	2.0	1.00	58.1	1.9	0.95	6.8
4	5.1	3.3	0.83	31.3	3.6	0.90	6.1
8	3.3	5.2	0.65	17.6	6.4	0.80	5.3

Table 1.2
N-Queens Performance Measurements (Symmetry)

FGHC comparison is because the large granularity of the N-Queens problem is well suited for logic programming.

In our opinion, the FGHC and Prolog programs are easier to write, maintain, extend, and understand than the 'C' programs.[5] In addition, as the application problem gets larger, the advantage of using high-level logic programming languages becomes even stronger. There is no doubt that more and more applications will be implemented on multiprocessors once friendly languages and environments become available to the application programmer. Similarly, there is no doubt that logic programming languages will increase in popularity when their strengths in the arena of parallel programming are proved.

This book is not meant to be "religious" or chauvinistic with respect to applicative vs. imperative parallel programming. Obviously the marketplace speaks. However, an accurate analysis of paradigms within parallel logic programming requires a controlled experiment. In the rest of the book, performance results are not compared with parallel 'C' programs (or Lisp programs for that matter) in order to concentrate the analysis on logic programming. An interesting "symbiotic" approach is *bilingual* programming, for example, Strand [49] which combines procedural and logic programming.

1.1.3 Programming in Parallel Lisp

The following excerpt is taken from Gabriel and McCarthy's original paper describing Qlisp [54]:

> "Because a closure is already a lot like a separate process, it could be
> used as a means for expressing less regular parallel computations.
>
> (**QLAMBDA** *pred* (*lambda-list*) . *body*)

---

[5]We haven't said anything about debugging — debugging tools in current committed-choice language systems are not yet up to par with even `pdbx` under UNIX, which itself isn't so friendly.

creates a closure. *Pred* is a predicate that is evaluated before any other action regarding this form is taken. It is assumed to evaluate to either (), **EAGER**, or something else. If *pred* evaluates to (), then the **QLAMBDA** acts exactly as a **LAMBDA**. That is, a closure is created; applying this closure is exactly the same as applying a normal closure.

"If *pred* evaluates to something other than **EAGER**, the **QLAMBDA** creates a closure that, when applied, is run as a separate process. Creating the closure by evaluating the **QLAMBDA** expression is called *spawning*; the process that evaluates the **QLAMBDA** is called the *spawning process*; and the process that is created by the **QLAMBDA** is called the *spawned process*. When a closure running as a separate process is applied, the separate process is started, the arguments are evaluated by the spawning process, and a message is sent to the spawned process containing the evaluated arguments and a return address. The spawned process does the appropriate lambda-binding, evaluates its body, and finally returns the results to the spawning process. We call a closure that will run or is running in its own process a *process closure*. In short, the expression (**QLAMBDA** non-() ...) returns a process closure as its value.

"If *pred* evaluates to **EAGER**, then a closure is created which is immediately spawned. It lambda-binds empty binding cells as described earlier, and evaluation of its body starts immediately. When an argument is needed, the process either has had it supplied or it blocks. Similarly, if the process completes before the return address has been supplied, the process blocks."

'Nuf said.[6]

1.2   Parallelism and Concurrency

Parallelism and concurrency are different, although parallel and concurrent computer languages are often confused. A parallel language is a language that can be executed in parallel, i.e., parallelism is the ability to gain speedup by executing

---

[6]Since 1984 there has been a great deal of research and advancement in parallel Lisp at both the language and implementation levels. This section obviously does not treat this major topic seriously and is meant only as a joke! See, for example, Kogge [74].

actions simultaneously. A concurrent language is a language that can express simultaneous actions, for example, a language where processes can be created and can communicate. Parallelism does not imply concurrency, nor does concurrency imply parallelism. There are sequential languages, i.e., languages with sequential constructs and semantics, that can be executed in parallel while retaining the strict sequential semantics. There are also concurrent languages that have been implemented only sequentially!

The goals of parallel and concurrent languages are subtly different. The design of a parallel language, i.e., the exploitation of parallelism in a language, has only one purpose: to gain execution speed. Concurrent languages represent a programming paradigm in which certain algorithms can be expressed more clearly than sequential languages. In addition, concurrent languages have the (not necessarily primary) goal of parallel execution. The two languages discussed in this book, OR-parallel Prolog and FGHC, are good examples of the differences between parallelism and concurrency.

Prolog is a sequential language and OR-parallel Prolog is a parallel language with sequential semantics. In other words, the programming paradigm is good old Prolog, and parallelism is "hidden" from the user (although, as we shall see, this is not quite true in practice). In OR-parallel Prolog, the programmer can completely debug a program on a uniprocessor, as in Prolog, and be guaranteed correctness on multiple PEs (although no guarantee of speedups is given!). In contrast, FGHC is a concurrent language with the semantics of communicating processes. The programmer writes programs within this paradigm and cannot escape from it, even if the program is inherently sequential. Debugging a program often requires checking its correctness on one PE, then two PEs, and so on (although it is rare to design a program that runs correctly on two PEs and not on eight PEs). Speedup of FGHC programs again is not guaranteed even if the program is correct — that is the job of the implementation. Because FGHC has fine-grained processes, we find that, in practice, when executing a problem with inherent parallelism on successively larger numbers of PEs, speedups are exhibited.

Taking another view, Prolog is considered a sequential language because it is deterministic,[7] whereas FGHC is not. A Prolog program will always execute its procedures in exactly the same sequence. The semantics of FGHC allow truly nondeterministic procedures, therefore a valid FGHC program may even return different results for different runs.

There is a great debate among researchers as to the utility of parallel languages

---

[7]This should not be confused with nondeterminate procedures in Prolog, which return multiple solutions, but always the *same* solutions and always in the *same order*.

where parallelism is hidden from the programmer. On one hand, thinking sequentially, exploiting very efficient sequential algorithms, and sequential debugging are great advantages. On the other hand, the main purpose of these languages is to gain speedup, yet the programmer has no control over parallel execution and no direct ability to specify *concurrent* algorithms. The hope here is that advanced compilers and dynamic schedulers can extract and exploit parallelism efficiently. If this scheme fails to reduce execution time for a given problem, there is little the programmer can do.

The utility of concurrent languages, where concurrency is forced upon the programmer, raises a similar question. On one hand, thinking about concurrency can facilitate new, efficient algorithms and model certain real-world problems quite well. In addition, the concurrent processes may be directly implemented as parallel processes, thus gaining speedup. On the other hand, thinking about concurrency can be a headache, and well-known efficient sequential algorithms must be rethought and reprogrammed, often with some overhead.

The jury is still out on the utility of parallel and concurrent languages. A conclusion from this book is that a concurrent language with simple semantics, such as FGHC, is not much more difficult to program than sequential Prolog. It often *looks* like Prolog at the end of the day. However, the day is much longer, as debugging is at present a burden. We must await more sophisticated debuggers before passing judgment.

Perhaps a point more vital than parallelism vs. concurrency is whether we have given anything up to go from a sequential to a concurrent language. In the case of FGHC, the answer is, unfortunately, yes — we give up backtracking over full unification. The cost of this sacrifice will haunt us later in this book, as we try to develop equally efficient algorithms for OR-parallel Prolog and FGHC. Thus another conclusion of the book is that, ideally, we would like a strong concurrent language which offers all the power of its sequential ancestors without inflated overhead.

1.3   Measuring Parallel Performance

The problems described in this book are toy problems that, in general, require a great deal of brute force searching. In multiple-solution problems there are many cases where the solutions exhibit symmetry. Yet the programs described do *searches*, not *reasoning*, to find solutions. Programs that reason about symmetries among solutions will have significantly different performance characteristics than the programs presented here. However, a "reasoning" program may be simply too difficult to write. Certainly all successful chess-playing programs to date use brute-force search, and do no reasoning about symmetries. An example of a program given in this book that makes use of a very simple symmetry is Pascal's Triangle. Only half of each row of Pascal's Triangle is computed because the other half is a mirror image. Such simple symmetries are easy to exploit (however, we don't use binomial coefficients, which are simplest to compute!). Nevertheless, symmetries in a problem as simple as N-Queens (Chapter 5) are rather difficult to exploit.

The problems presented here can be categorized as "single-solution" and "all-solution" problems. By "single solution" we mean a *determinate* computation that has only one result. By "all solutions" we mean a *nondeterminate* problem in which we exhaustively search for all solutions. In the literature, "nondeterminate" and "nondeterministic" have subtle nuances. In this book, a "nondeterminate" procedure is a procedure in a Horn-clause logic program that can be satisfied in more than one way. We reserve the word "nondeterministic" to describe a process (in the most general sense) the behavior of which cannot be predicted exactly, e.g., successive readings of a thermometer. We consider execution times of programs on multiprocessors to be nondeterministic, although highly predictable. In the systems studied in this book, nondeterminate problems are solved without *a priori* knowledge of how many solutions exist.

Exhaustive search is not a realistic model of symbolic processing applications. However, exhaustive search is a good teaching and benchmarking vehicle. The performance results of speedups of exhaustive search are likely to be better than other more intelligent search strategies, such as alpha-beta pruning [146, 16]. Certainly the logic programming languages described in this book are general enough to describe any search strategy. The techniques given here for increasing performance and speedup can be applied to more sophisticated algorithms as well.

If we know *a priori* that there are only n solutions, then (in some cases) the search can be discontinued when the nth solution is found. Thus the amount of work performed by an all-solutions program, compared to an n-solutions program, can be quite different. The difference is especially large for $n = 1$. Unfortunately, a *pure* OR-parallel system cannot search for an arbitrary n solutions because the search processes cannot communicate. In the case of $n = 1$, the first independent process to find a solution can terminate the entire program, but for $n > 1$, how can the program determine the nth process for which to do the termination? In fact, OR-Prolog allows limited communication between parallel search processes to the extent that one process can terminate all other processes belonging to the same nondeterminate procedure. This communication still is not powerful enough to allow searching for arbitrary n solutions. In FGHC, given n, in some cases the program can be modified to efficiently search for only n solutions.

For real applications, we would probably wish to search for n (but then again, in real applications, do we know n?). Although it complicates the code, using *a priori* information can drastically reduce the execution time of the program. However, for the purposes of measuring execution efficiency in this book, we do *not* make use of such information. *All* measured programs search for *all* solutions, i.e., the programs evaluate the entire search space. This procedure facilitates evaluating the characteristics of one program executing on a varying number of processors. It also aids in comparing programs to other programs. When we evaluate the entire search space, every path must be computed by some group of processor(s) in some order. Thus all program executions do roughly the same amount of work, independent of the number of processors. However, if one searches for only n solutions, the search space evaluated to reach those n may depend on the number of processors, the timing of the schedulers, etc. By measuring the evaluation of an entire search space, we may be doing extra work, but at least we know what we are doing.

That discussion brings up the issue of *repeatability* and *variance* of measurements. That is, precisely how much does program performance depend on system timing? For sequential machines and languages, performance timing is highly repeatable with low variance once operating system effects are controlled. Here we present measurements taken on both Encore Multimax and Sequent Symmetry multiprocessors. The Symmetry has 16 processing elements (PEs). Each is Intel 80386 microprocessor-based and runs at 16 MHz. The Multimax has eight PEs, each NS32032 microprocessor-based, running at 6 MHz. Programs execute about 4–5 times faster on the Symmetry than on the Multimax. An important factor in this disparity is clock speed (16 vs. 6 MHz), followed by physical memory size (80 vs. 25 Mbytes), and disk space for paging (240 vs. 66 Mbytes). Both machines run versions of the UNIX operating system with extensions for shared-memory multiprocessing [95, 46].

The Symmetry and Multimax experiments were measured on 1–15 PEs and 1–8 PEs respectively. Many attributes of parallel execution do not become apparent on such a small number of PEs, so the results presented here paint an incomplete picture. Nevertheless we point out some important overheads that present themselves even on a few PEs. The empirical results are important not so much to claim the precise execution speed limits of parallel logic programming languages as to give ballpark figures of merit to these approaches.

The Prolog and FGHC systems studied here, as their implementations improve and other similar systems are developed, will no doubt narrow the gap with procedural language execution speed. For example, the JAM Parlog system executes a group of the programs presented from 15%–70% faster than the FGHC system. This speed is due mainly to a lower overhead scheduler [131]. In addition, the OR-parallel Prolog system measured here has since been improved; the latest version executes the programs presented in this book up to 50% faster than the system measured here. This improvement is due primarily to an improved compiler and engine/scheduler interface.

The timing measurements on Symmetry vary because of nondeterministic factors such as scheduling and system load. Nondeterministic hardware events, such as bus arbitration or memory interference, have less effect. The measurement error is highly program-dependent, and somewhat worse for FGHC than for OR-parallel Prolog for two reasons. First, stream AND-parallelism may involve a complex series of synchronizing processes. Second, the FGHC system requires frequent garbage collections which vary greatly in time. Even the OR-parallel scheduler, which is usually stable, sometimes displays timing fluctuations due to time-critical decisions. System load was kept very low, so timing variations which resulted from a changing system load were much less significant than the variations caused by the scheduler of the programming language itself. Overall, we do not attempt to analyze these fluctuations in detail because, given another host and/or scheduler, the variations will change.

It is worth emphasizing that the programs presented in this book are a result of painstaking writing and rewriting. The programs are efficient. In many cases several alternatives are given. Often these alternatives, or the original programs we started with, came from the logic programming literature, and can be seen to be quite inefficient. *It cannot be stressed enough that there is no point in speeding up a seriously ill algorithm.* At the very least, speedups with respect to the most efficient sequential algorithms must be shown to illustrate the benefit of parallel processing. In addition, one can view the shared-memory testbed used in this study as a best-case assumption, i.e., if you can't get speedups on a shared-memory machine, where can you get them?

Moreover, parallel algorithms must be shown to have complexity comparable to that of the most efficient sequential algorithms. In other words, a hidden factor in an empirical study is the problem sizes tested. Small problems may lie at the elbow of a complexity curve, making parallel algorithms appear competitive where in reality, for larger problems, sequential algorithms are superior. Complexity analysis, which is especially difficult for nondeterminate algorithms, is touched on here for a few programs but is mainly beyond the scope of this book. Several of the problems examined here can be solved with algorithms of severely reduced complexity in sequential constraint logic programming languages such as CHIP [140]. These languages have potential for parallelism; however, their architectures, performance characteristics, and comparisons warrant another entire book. Readers must accept this exposition as a first step in the quantitative evaluation of parallel logic programming languages.

Concerning the relevance of specific performance results for Sequent Symmetry and Encore Multimax, it suffices to say that, although future multiprocessors will have different execution and communication speeds, the measurements collected here still give us useful insights into parallel logic programming execution characteristics. For example, the ICOT MultiPsi/V2 multiprocessor has a single PE (Psi-II) execution speed about 9–14 times faster than an Intel 80386 Symmetry PE for a subset of the FGHC programs studied here. The MultiPsi achieves this performance by executing the underlying FGHC emulator in microcode, whereas the Symmetry implementation studied here is an emulator written in 'C'. One is tempted to conclude that there is no need to use a Symmetry at all if a single Psi-II machine is available with the appropriate microcode! However, to achieve speedups on MultiPsi, the same problems encountered on Symmetry will have to be tackled again. There is no doubt that this struggle will be ongoing as technology improves.

2 Prolog and FGHC

"This soul—to an outside observer who has a view into the machine world
(by means of a special installation, an auxiliary module that is a type of
probe, built into the computer)—appears as a 'coherent cloud of processes,'
as a functional aggregate with a kind of 'center' that can be isolated fairly
precisely, i.e., delimited within the machine network."

Stanislaw Lem
A Perfect Vacuum: Perfect Reviews of Nonexistent Books
Harcourt Brace Jovanovich, Inc., 1979

This chapter gives a full introduction to both Prolog and Flat Guarded Horn
Clauses (FGHC) languages. Prolog is the premiere example of a *noncommitted-choice logic programming language*, i.e., it backtracks over clauses within a nonde-terminate procedure in an attempt to satisfy a proof. FGHC is an excellent example
of a *committed-choice concurrent logic programming language*, i.e., a procedure call
either *commits to* a clause or *suspends* until a clause can be committed. A full
explanation of these distinctions is given in this chapter.

2.1   Prolog

Prolog was the first practical logic programming language, designed by A. Colmer-auer in 1973 [108], with its theoretical groundwork laid by R. Kowalski in 1974 [75].
Prolog is the most widely known representative of logic programming languages;
most other logic programming languages are derivatives of the Prolog computa-tion model. To the first order, Prolog execution characteristics can be extended to
Prolog-like languages and moreover to logic programming languages. Care must be
taken because backtracking in Prolog, if not efficiently compiled, can lead to exe-cution characteristics that are vastly different from characteristics of, for example,
committed-choice languages.

2.1.1   Programming Objects

Prolog programs and data are composed of *terms*. Terms are either *simple* or
compound (also called a *complex term* or *structure*). A simple term is either a
constant or a *variable*. A structure consists of a *functor* and *arguments*. The
functor is composed of a *name* and *arity* (this is usually written as *name/arity*).
The name is the symbolic identifier of the structure, the arity is the number of
arguments, and the arguments themselves are terms. An example of a structure is
`tree(1,void,Subtree)`, with functor `tree/3`. A constant may be a number or an

atomic identifier. Examples of constants are 1 and void.[1] A (logical) variable is an
object which can be bound, only once, to another term. Prolog uses a capitalized
identifier to represent a variable, e.g., Subtree. Prolog also uses underscore, '_',
to represent an *anonymous* or *"don't care"* variable, i.e., a unique variable that
cannot be shared or accessed elsewhere in the program. The use of anonymous
variables will become clear from later examples.

A Prolog *program* consists of collections of *clauses*. Each collection is known as
a *procedure*. A procedure implements a relation known as a predicate in first-order
logic. A clause is a term consisting of a functor :-/2, where the *head* and *body* are
the two arguments. In general a clause appears as follows

$$H :- B_1, B_2, ..., B_n.$$

where H is the head, containing the formal parameters of the procedure definition.
The body consists of a (possibly empty) set of *goals*, B_i, for $0 \geq i \geq n$. A goal is
a procedural invocation with its corresponding passed parameters. A procedure is
uniquely specified by the name and arity of the head of each of its clauses. The
arity of a procedure represents the (fixed) number of arguments it must receive
when invoked.

A Prolog program which determines if two binary trees are *isomorphic* is given
below. Two trees are isomorphic if the set of paths, from the root to every leaf,
is identical in both trees. In other words, the set of nodes at each level of the two
trees are identical, although possibly out of order. The branch from the root to a
given leaf will pass through the same nodes, in the same order, in both trees.

The Prolog program (from Sterling and Shapiro [119]) consists of a single recursive procedure, isotree/2, which has three clauses.

```
isotree(void,void).
isotree(tree(X,Left1,Right1),
        tree(X,Left2,Right2)) :-
    isotree(Left1,Left2),
    isotree(Right1,Right2).
isotree(tree(X,Left1,Right1),
        tree(X,Left2,Right2)) :-
    isotree(Left1,Right2),
    isotree(Right1,Left2).
```

The first clause has an empty body and is called a *unit clause* or *fact*. The second

---

[1]In most tagged Prolog architectures, including the ones considered in this book, the constant
tag is distinct from the structure tag. In simpler systems, atomic constants may be implemented
as structures of zero arity. Numbers have their own tag to facilitate arithmetic, comparison, and
conversion.

two clauses are called *conjunctive clauses*, *non-unit clauses*, or *rules* because they define relations between facts and/or other rules.

A third necessary program construct is a *query*, e.g.,

```
?- isotree(tree(1,tree(2,tree(4,void,void),
                        tree(5,void,void)),
                   tree(3,void,void)),
           tree(1,tree(3,void,void),
                   tree(2,tree(4,void,void),
                        tree(5,void,void)))).
```

In its simplest form, a query is a procedure invocation with external input, i.e., a request to execute a program with given data.

2.1.2 Informal Semantics

Prolog semantics can be viewed declaratively or procedurally. The *declarative view* treats a procedure as a logical disjunction of its clauses and a clause as a logical conjunction of its goals.[2] This view benefits programmers because it is independent of program control. The *procedural view* is similar to the semantics of ordinary procedural languages. In this section we review both.

Declarative Semantics

The following Prolog clause

$$H :- B_1, B_2, ..., B_n.$$

is read declaratively as "Head H is true if body goals B_i are all true." Within this statement, variables appearing in the head of a rule are universally quantified over the clause in which they appear. Variables appearing only in the body of a rule are existentially quantified over the clause in which they appear.

For instance, the second clause of `isotree/2` has an informal declarative reading: "*Any* two trees are isomorphic *if* they both have the same root value and the left subtree of one is isomorphic to the left subtree of the other and the right subtree of one is isomorphic to the right subtree of the other."

A query, being a clause with a body but no head, has the declarative reading: "All body goals are true." Since there is no head, all variables in the query are existentially quantified. For instance, the query in the previous section asks: "Are the two trees in Figure 2.1 isomorphic?" This invocation of `isotree` is often represented as `isotree(+,+)` signifying that both arguments are instantiated.

---

[2]The semantics described in this book rest on the operational model defined by van Emden and Kowalski [139].

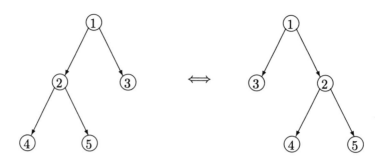

Figure 2.1
Are These Trees Isomorphic?

As another example, the query

```
?- isotree(tree(1,tree(2,tree(4,void,void),
                             tree(5,void,void)),
                    tree(3,void,void)),
           X).
```

is read: "Does there *exist* a tree X such that the tree shown in Figure 2.2 is isomorphic to it?" This invocation of isotree is often denoted isotree(+,-) signifying that the first argument is instantiated and the second argument is unbound when the procedure is initially invoked. In general, the symbols '+', '-', and '?' denote *argument modes*. The mode '?' represents an argument which can act either as an input or output. In this book this notation is used to clarify, for a given invocation, which arguments are used as inputs and which arguments are used as outputs. [3]

There are four solutions to the previous query: [4]

```
[tree(1,tree(3,void,void),
        tree(2,tree(4,void,void),
                tree(5,void,void))),
```

---

[3]In some logic programming systems, knowledge of which modes are used can facilitate code optimization. The more precise the knowledge, the more efficient the code, e.g., isotree(+,+) will run faster than isotree(?,?). Usually the programmer specifies the modes, if optimization is desired. In more sophisticated systems the compiler itself *derives* the modes!

[4]Actually this program is only correct for queries isotree(+,+) under the stronger condition that both inputs are *fully ground*, i.e., the data structures are completely instantiated and no logical variables exist anywhere within the structures. Consider an isotree(+,-) query that produces the *wrong* answer. Let T = tree(2,void,void), then "?- isotree(tree(1,T,T),X)" erroneously has *two* solutions, both the *same*! We need additional clauses to check for isomorphic subtrees to avoid this. In any case, we return to this example in Chapter 6.

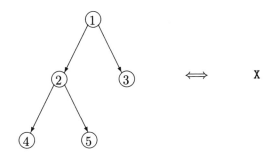

Figure 2.2
Are These Trees Isomorphic?

```
tree(1,tree(2,tree(4,void,void),
              tree(5,void,void)),
       tree(3,void,void)),

tree(1,tree(3,void,void),
       tree(2,tree(5,void,void),
              tree(4,void,void)))),

tree(1,tree(2,tree(5,void,void),
              tree(4,void,void)),
       tree(3,void,void))]
```

Procedural Semantics

The *procedural view* treats a procedure as an ordered sequence of entry points (clauses) which must be executed until one succeeds. A clause is treated as an ordered sequence of procedure calls (goals), all of which must be executed successfully in order for the clause to succeed. Upon failure of any goal, the computation is backed up to the entry of the most recently invoked procedure with unattempted clauses. That procedure is re-entered at its next clause, and the computation continues. The main implementation distinction between Prolog and procedural languages is that Prolog programs *backtrack* in this manner.

The procedural semantics are derived from the observation that, to solve an existential query Q with a universal fact P, one finds a *common instance* C, i.e., two *substitutions*, τ_1 and τ_2, such that

$$C = P\tau_1 = Q\tau_2.$$

Two deduction rules are in effect here. *Generalization* — an existential query is a logical consequence of an instance of that query; and *instantiation* — an instance of a universally quantified fact is a logical consequence of that fact. The combination of these two rules is called *resolution*.

Generalizing, the query Q is a logical consequence of program P with the universal rule

$$H :- B_1, B_2, ..., B_n.$$

if H and Q have a common instance and $B_1, B_2, ..., B_n$ are also logical consequences of P. This is called *Horn-clause resolution* and was developed by J. A. Robinson [106]. In other words, a goal is executed by attempting resolution with the heads of the clauses of the procedure of the same name and arity as the goal. Successful resolution involves successfully *unifying* each goal argument to each corresponding head argument. Unification finds a *most general* common instance of its input terms to avoid specializing the proof more than necessary.

> If the goal cannot unify with any clause of its associated procedure, the goal fails. When the goal unifies with a clause and it can be determined that no other clauses can unify, the procedure entry is called *determinate*. When the goal unifies with a clause and other (untried) clauses also possibly can unify, the procedure entry is called *nondeterminate*.

The *scope* of a variable is a clause; therefore the occurrences of X in the second and third clauses of `isotree/2` are unrelated. The goal `isotree(tree(X,void,void), Y)` can successfully resolve with the heads of either the second or third clauses. Note again that the scopes of the X in the goal `isotree(tree(X,void,void),Y)` and the X in the clause heads are independent, and therefore these two variables are unique and can be bound to distinct objects. The goal `isotree(void,void)` can unify with only the first clause and the goal `isotree(X,Y)` can unify with any clause.

Resolution is the key mechanism in Prolog procedure invocation. Prolog program execution consists of a sequence of resolutions, sometimes called *reductions*. Initially the query specifies a sequence of goals, called the *resolvent*, to be reduced. In general, a reduction entails resolving one of the goals in the resolvent against a clause in the program. The goal within the resolvent is replaced with the body goals of the unifying clause. The substitution created when unifying the goal and clause is applied to the entire resolvent (this is an automatic side-effect of unification in most Prolog systems).

The resolvent is continually reduced until it is either empty or no goal can be resolved. In the former case, the program has succeeded. In the latter case, execution must backtrack to a previous resolvent, the one associated with the last nondeterminate resolution. An alternative clause is picked for this resolution and reduction continues. If there have been no nondeterminate resolutions, or if no alternative clauses exist for any nondeterminate resolution (i.e., all alternatives have all been attempted), then the program fails.

For Prolog, the execution model just described is constrained to perform goal reductions from left-to-right in the resolvent, and to attempt clause resolutions in the textual clause order specified by the program. This execution model is known as *SLD resolution*. The program execution, if successful, results in the bindings of the existential variables in the query (if there are any) created by the substitutions made during resolution. If the program fails, no bindings are created, i.e., a Prolog program cannot produce "partial" answers.

Two excellent logic programming textbooks are Robinson [107] on proof theory and Lloyd [76] on formal semantics.

2.1.3   Extra-Logical Features and Builtins

For convenience and efficiency, Prolog has been given additional support, above and beyond vanilla logic programming, for:

- **numbers** — As mentioned previously, numbers are considered a special type of constant. This definition facilitates efficient arithmetic. Different systems support different types of numbers: the programs in this book use only integers.

- **lists** — A list, which is a structure with functor ./2, is given a special syntax in Prolog. The list '.'(X,Y) can be written as [X|Y]. A list of two objects, '.'(1,'.'(2,[])) can be written as [1,2]. Note that [] is a special constant representing nil (end-of-list).[5]

- **builtins** — Many procedures are predefined in Prolog. The most frequently used of these include arithmetic, construction and decomposition of terms, conditional tests for types of terms, and strict equality (wherein no unification is allowed to take place). See the next section for a description of the builtins used in this book.

---

[5]In most tagged Prolog architectures, including the ones considered in this book, the list data type is given a unique tag. Thus a list pair requires only two words of storage, in contrast to three words of storage required for a standard structure of arity two.

Predicate	Meaning
triadic	
findall	collect all solutions
functor	create a structure
arg	access a structure argument
diadic	
=:=	arithmetic equal
=\=	arithmetic not-equal
<	arithmetic less-than
>	arithmetic greater-than
<=	arithmetic less-than-or-equal-to
>=	arithmetic greater-than-or-equal-to
@>	symbolic greater-than
=	term unification
\=	term not-unification
is	arithmetic assignment
monadic	
call	meta-call
\+	not
var	test if unbound
nonvar	test if bound
singleton	
!	cut
true	trivially true

Table 2.1
Prolog Builtin Predicates Used in this Book

- **cut** — Cut is an extra-logical control feature, represented by '!', used to prevent undesired backtracking. As a goal in a clause of a procedure, cut always succeeds, a side effect is that goals textually preceding the cut or subsequent clauses of that procedure cannot be tried in the event of backtracking.

The builtin procedures used in the Prolog programs throughout this book are summarized in Table 2.1. All solutions to nondeterminate procedures are collected in only one way in this book: findall/3. The builtin findall(V,G,L) collects all values of variable V that satisfy goal G. The values are stored in list L. In general, V can be replaced by a term containing multiple variables, although we do not make use of this facility. As an example, consider the database of facts:

```
color(red).
color(blue).
color(yellow).
```

Then `findall(V,color(V),L)` will bind `L = [red,blue,yellow]`.

The builtins `functor/3` and `arg/3` are used to create and access data structures. The builtin `functor(F,N,A)` unifies F with a structure with name N and arity A. In this book, only `functor(-,+,+)` is used. Recall that these argument modes indicate that the first argument is output, and the latter two arguments are input, i.e., we create a structure from a name and arity.

The builtin `arg(I,F,V)` unifies V with the Ith argument of structure F. This builtin must be called as `arg(+,+,?)`, i.e., the index and structure must be specified but the final argument may be either bound or unbound. These builtins are used in several of the Prolog programs in the book, always for the purpose of allowing constant-time access to data. Structures are not strictly necessary in logic programming because their functor can be simulated with lists. The penalty, however, is one of performance — a list has linear time access to data. A further point is that a structure initially filled with unbound logical variables can be used to efficiently simulate a write-once array. One example of write-once arrays is in the N-Queens program given in Section 5.1.4.

Of the diadic builtins, the arithmetic comparison predicates either succeed or fail, but cannot make bindings. The unification operator can make bindings if successful. However, if unification fails, no bindings are made. The builtin `\=` succeeds if unification fails, therefore bindings are never made.

Arithmetic is performed by the `is/2` operator. For example "X is 1+4" binds X to 5. Arithmetic operators permissible in the right-hand side include `+`, `-`, `*`, `/` (real division), `//` (integer division), and `mod` (remainder).

The extra-logical predicates are used sparingly in Prolog programs. The builtin `call(G)` succeeds if goal G succeeds. Otherwise it fails. The builtin `\+(G)` succeeds if goal G fails. Otherwise `\+(G)` fails. Success of `\+(G)` does *not* mean that G is false — it simply means that G cannot be proved. In most Prolog systems, there is no stronger method of negation than by failure.

The builtins `var(X)` and `nonvar(X)` succeed if X is bound or unbound respectively. Testing whether a variable is instantiated is meta-logical because success of `var(X)` or failure of `nonvar(X)` can be contradicted by a subsequent binding of X. In the former case, the program may succeed even though there is a logical contradiction. In the latter case, not all solutions to the program may be generated.

Cut is meta-logical for the same reason — it can prevent solutions from being generated in a nondeterminate program. As a goal in a clause of a procedure, cut always succeeds; the side effect is that previous goals and subsequent clauses cannot be tried in the event of backtracking. Most cuts in Prolog programs do *not* affect the completeness of solutions, but only the efficiency of finding solutions.

Builtins `call`, `var`/`nonvar`, and `\+` are each used in two or three programs in this book. In addition, `assert` and `retract` are used in one program to implement a garbage collector, because the OR-parallel Prolog system measured here has none. Cut is used moderately in this book — about 100 instances in source code given here. However, almost all instances are "safe," i.e., they affect efficiency, not logical completeness. Although cuts of any kind are evil, they are a necessary evil. It is better to learn how to use them correctly than to accept the programming style of textbooks which avoid using them, then endlessly puzzle over programs that cause memory overflow.

Refer to the SICStus Prolog User's Manual [19], Quintus Prolog User's Manual [101], etc., for the complete semantics of the builtins of a large Prolog system.

2.1.4   OR-Parallel Execution Model

At this point we wish to briefly and informally discuss the potential for executing Prolog programs in OR-parallel. This section is meant only to whet the appetite of the reader. Consider the previous `isotree` query which is nondeterminate with four solutions. Intuitively, we can explore all clauses of `isotree/2` in parallel. This exploration amounts to reducing a goal in the resolvent against *multiple clauses in parallel, effectively creating alternative resolvents, i.e., independent proofs.*

In sequential Prolog, the resolvents associated with reductions form a linear sequence. In OR-parallel Prolog, however, parallel reductions form a *tree* of resolvents, i.e., each node in the tree is a resolvent. The root of this OR-tree is the query, i.e., the initial resolvent. The resolvents emanating from a parent node were generated from that parent node by resolution with alternative clauses of some procedure. Note that strict Prolog semantics constrain the next reduction so that it always involves the leftmost goal in the resolvent, leaving no ambiguity as to which goal is involved in the reduction from parent to child node. Therefore the overall composition of the OR-tree is determinate; however, the parallel growth of the tree is nondeterministic, depending on the allocation of processors for performing parallel reductions.[6]

Considering `isotree`, the biggest payoff for parallel execution will occur in the second and third clauses where recursion extends the computation. If the system attempts to execute each recursive call by evaluating all its solutions in parallel, then the granularity of the tasks eventually decreases. In other words, the number of reductions within a subtree becomes limited as we approach the OR-tree leaves.

---

[6]We are simplifying the model by saying that the OR-tree composition is determinate. There are in fact variations of *cut* that can nondeterministically prune the tree (discussed in Section 5.3.1).

Granularity will decrease to the point where the overheads of parallel computation outweigh the benefits. At that point the best strategy is to *throttle* the
parallelism, i.e., avoid it and execute sequentially. Complete analysis of `isotree`'s
parallelism is given in Chapter 6.

The Or-Parallel Prolog considered in this book includes the following extensions:

- **parallel declaration** — This static declaration indicates which procedures
  should be evaluated in OR-parallel. All nondeterminate clauses in such a procedure potentially can be evaluated in parallel. For example, by declaring ":-
  parallel isotree/2.", we enable the isomorphic tree program to execute
  in OR-parallel.

- **cavalier commit** — Commit is an extra-logical control feature, represented
  by '/', similar to cut. Cut guarantees commitment to the *leftmost* derivation
  of the procedure containing the cut; all other derivations will be disallowed.
  Cavalier commit accepts the *first* derivation completed and all others are
  disallowed. These two results are equivalent in a sequential Prolog system but,
  in a parallel Prolog, cavalier commit will in general select the first solution
  found and kill all others. See Section 5.3.1 for more details.

The abstract reduction-level semantics of OR-parallel Prolog is given by D. H.
D. Warren [145] and further detailed by Carlsson and Szeredi [21]. In this book we
continue no further with abstract semantics, but rather plunge into the pragmatic
semantics of OR-parallel Prolog programming.

2.1.5   Programming Paradigms: Difference Lists

Difference lists are *the* most important data structure in logic programming languages and therefore deserve special mention. Both Prolog and FGHC use the same
difference list construct. A difference list or D-list, often denoted by X-Y,[7] is a list
X with tail Y. For example, as illustrated in Figure 2.3, the list

```
[1,2,3,4|T]
```

can be expressed as

```
X-Y
```

where

```
X = [1,2,3,4|T]
Y = T
```

---

[7]The operator -/2 is arbitrary but we will conform to using it throughout this book.

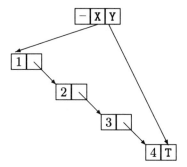

Figure 2.3
Example of a Difference List

The above is an example of an *incomplete list*, i.e., a list that has an unbound tail.
Consider that a completed list

    [1,2,3,4]

can be expressed as a completed D-list X-Y, where

    X = [1,2,3,4]
    Y = []

D-lists are primarily used to efficiently manipulate incomplete lists. Essentially, the
D-list gives direct access to the unbound tail. To illustrate the immense power of
obtaining access to the tail of a list, consider that we can append two D-lists for
free! For example, as shown in Figure 2.4, assuming

    X = [1,2,3,4|T]
    Y = T

    A = [5,6,7,8|S]
    B = S

we can append X-Y with A-B by unifying Y with A, giving D-list X-B:

    X = [1,2,3,4|[5,6,7,8|S]] = [1,2,3,4,5,6,7,8|S]
    B = S

The unification of Y with A involves a single assignment, i.e., constant time complexity (for all practical purposes, "no cost"). Thus we can express dappend/3 in
Prolog as a simple fact:

    dappend(X-Y,Y-Z,X-Z).

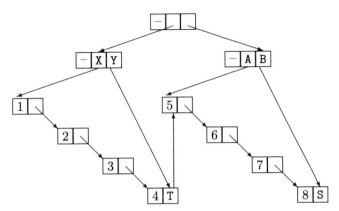

Figure 2.4
Example of Appending Two Difference Lists

As another example, a tree-flattening program is given below.

```
flattenTree(void,L-L) :- !.
flattenTree((Seq1,Seq2),L0-L2) :- !,
    flattenTree(Seq1,L0-L1),
    flattenTree(Seq2,L1-L2).
flattenTree(E,[E|L]-L).
```

The `flattenTree/3` procedure flattens a binary tree structure into a list, removing empty sequences represented by the atom `void`, e.g., the query[8]

```
?- flattenTree(((1,2),((3,void),(4,5),void)),L-[]).
```

representing the binary tree

instantiates L to the list `[1,2,3,4,5]`. Note that here only the leaves have values, in contrast to the previous `isotree` example.

---

[8]Note that ','/2 is a right-associative infix operator.

Read procedurally, `flattenTree/2` recursively processes the left and right branches of a subtree, with a difference list to collect the resulting leaves. The second and third subterms of the second procedure argument represent the difference list as an answer list and the tail of the answer list, facilitating efficient concatenation of the resulting sublists from the left and right branches. This method of concatenation is illustrated in the second clause, where the answer is composed by instantiating the tail of the first sequence's flattened list, L1, to the second sequence's flattened list.

Read declaratively, `flattenTree/2` specifies three rules concerning flattening. The result of flattening an empty sequence is an empty difference list. The result of flattening a binary tree, `(Seq1,Seq2)`, is L0 (with tail L2), if flattening the left subtree, `Seq1`, results in L0 (with tail L1) and flattening the right subtree, `Seq2`, results in L1 (with tail L2). The result of flattening anything else (presumably a value), E, is a list with head E and tail L. The dual recursion coupled with the wiring of the D-list in the second clause gives a depth-first, left-to-right traversal of the tree. Modifying this to traverse right-to-left is easy. To traverse any way other than depth-first, however, is troublesome because of the way reduction is implemented in most logic programming systems.

An important use of difference lists is the representation of strings of words. Most Prolog systems exploit this representation for implementing *definite clause grammars* (DCGs).[9] In fact, one of the primary motivations for developing Prolog was for nondeterminate parsing of natural language. An excellent introduction to Prolog, from within the framework of natural-language analysis, is given by Pereira and Shieber [98].

---

[9]We shall examine DCGs in Exercise 103.

2.2 Flat Guarded Horn Clauses

Flat Guarded Horn Clauses (FGHC) is a *committed-choice logic programming language* designed by K. Ueda [137]. FGHC is a restricted form of Ueda's original Guarded Horn Clauses (GHC), which derives in a general sense from Prolog. However, committed-choice languages differ significantly from Prolog, as will be shown in this section, in that they do not backtrack, i.e., a predicate with multiple clauses will "commit" to a single choice never to be undone. In other words, Prolog can use multiple program clauses to (nondeterminately) reduce a goal in a resolvent, whereas committed-choice languages can use only a single clause.

GHC/FGHC are closely related to other committed-choice languages, such as Concurrent Prolog and Flat Concurrent Prolog (CP/FCP) [116], Parlog/Flat Parlog [57, 48, 35], Strand [49], and FLENG [89]. The common ancestor of the committed-choice languages is the Relational Language of Clark and Gregory [27]. These alternative languages are discussed briefly in Section 2.2.5. In general, FGHC program characteristics are identical to those of the other languages.

An added confusion to this already confusing group of languages is the relationship between FGHC and the Fifth Generation Computer System (FGCS) project at ICOT [51]. The KL (Kernel Language) family used for the FGCS is based on logic programming. KL0 is a Prolog-like language (also called ESP) [24]. KL1 is an FGHC-like language. KL1 differs most from FGHC in that meta-control has been introduced to control program failure. These additions are useful for writing operating-systems code and do not concern us here. The programs presented here are given in "pure" FGHC (although there is really no FGHC standard, as there is a *de facto* for Prolog — Edinburgh DEC10 Prolog). The FGCS terminology complicates the situation further by having KL1-B, KL1-P, KL1-U, etc. These variations of KL1 represent different levels of implementation, e.g., KL1-U is a higher-level language than FGHC, and KL1-B is a lower-level language. Since the precise definitions of these levels is continually in flux, this notation is not used here. We simply talk about "FGHC."

2.2.1 Programming Objects

FGHC inherits its data types and program structure from Prolog. Simple and complex terms and logical variables are defined as in Prolog. FGHC programs are also collections of Horn clauses, known as procedures. Each clause is a term consisting of the the functor :-/2, separating the clause into a head and a body. Unlike Prolog, however, the body may be *guarded*. In general, an FGHC program is a set of guarded Horn clauses of the following form:

$$H :- G_1, G_2, ..., G_m | B_1, B_2, ..., B_n.$$

where m and n are zero or positive integers. H is the clause head, G_i is a guard goal, and B_i is a body goal. The commit operator '|' divides the clause into a passive part (the *guard*) and active part (the *body*). As in Prolog, if the head is missing, the clause forms a query, i.e., a program invocation. The head and goals in the clauses can have arguments. For clauses with a body, there can be either an empty guard or a guard containing only certain builtin goals, such as arithmetic comparison (see Section 2.2.3). Clauses with empty guards omit the commit operator.

User-defined goals cannot occur in the guard of an FGHC program. Thus the language is called "flat" (not unlike stale club soda). GHC, without the flat restriction, is somewhat more powerful because guards may be arbitrarily complex; however, this drastically complicates the implementation. We will discuss only flat committed-choice languages in this book.

2.2.2 Informal Semantics

FGHC semantics can be viewed declaratively and procedurally, as in Prolog. The declarative view treats a procedure as a set of clauses, only one of which can satisfy its truth value. A clause is considered a logical conjunction of its goals. If the set of clauses comprising a procedure are mutually exclusive (to be defined later), then the semantics are a simple logical disjunction. This closely corresponds to a determinate Prolog procedure.

If the set of clauses are *not* mutually exclusive, then the procedure is nondeterministic in a strong sense. In this case, we cannot always logically relate the procedure's truth value to the truth values of its clauses. In practice, however, well-written nondeterministic procedures (we shall see some as early as Section 4.2) do not affect the logical reading of a program, only its execution time.

The procedural view is similar to the semantics of ordinary functional languages. The execution model is based on Horn-clause resolution, with the appropriate modifications and additions to enable parallel reduction. In fact, we often think of FGHC semantics in terms of a third view: the *process reading*. The process reading considers the goals comprising the resolvent as communicating processes.

Declarative Semantics

Because FGHC, like Prolog, is based on Horn-clause logic, the declarative semantics are similar. Two flies in the ointment are guards and nondeterministic procedures which make the declarative semantics weaker and less useful than those of Prolog.

The following FGHC clause

$$H : - G_1, G_2, ..., G_m | B_1, B_2, ..., B_n.$$

is read declaratively as "Head H is true if guards G_i are all true and body goals B_j are all true." Within this statement, variables appearing in the head of a rule are universally quantified over the clause in which they appear. Variables appearing only in the guard and body of a rule are existentially quantified over the clause in which they appear.

Consider the following procedure for the Boolean OR function of two variables. Procedure or(X,Y,S) binds S=yes if (X OR Y) is true. Otherwise S is bound to no.

```
or(yes,  _,S)  :- S=yes.
or( _,yes,S)  :- S=yes.
or( no, no,S)  :- S=no.
```

As in Prolog, a singleton variable (often denoted with an underscore) can unify with any input argument. The first clause has the declarative reading: "The value of yes OR'ed with anything is yes."

Taken together, the declarative semantics of the individual clauses form the declarative reading for or/3. However, the semantics of the procedure is not the *disjunction* of its clauses, but rather the meaning of its single *committed* clause. It is therefore more intuitive to describe the declarative semantics of a committed-choice procedure as a *set* of all its successful executions.

In the case of or/3, the three clauses' heads are effectively mutually exclusive (although the first two clauses have ambiguous heads, their bodies are identical). Therefore or/3 is a determinate procedure that cannot return more than one answer for a given query. The set of all successful executions is a singleton, and we can say that the declarative meaning of or/3 is in fact the disjunction of its individual clause readings: "*Either* the value of yes OR'ed with anything (or vice versa) is yes *or* the value of no OR'ed with no is no."

Guards were originally introduced into committed-choice languages to help the programmer to form concise, mutually exclusive clauses. By "mutually exclusive clauses" we mean that, for any argument value combination seen by that procedure, no more than one head and guard can succeed, i.e., there is no ambiguity. The declarative semantics break down if the clauses are not mutually exclusive, and we lose the ability to express the outcome of the program logically. For example, consider the following program:

```
die(X) :- X=1.      die(X) :- X=4.
die(X) :- X=2.      die(X) :- X=5.
die(X) :- X=3.      die(X) :- X=6.

unlucky(A,B) :- die(A), die(B), A=B.
```

The Prolog semantics of unlucky/2 is "Doubles are unlucky." Procedure unlucky can be executed in four alternative modes. In FGHC, unlucky has no declarative semantics. The program can fail or succeed — we cannot predict which. It is truly a crap shoot.

As in Prolog, an FGHC query has the declarative reading: "All body goals are true." Since there is no head, all variables in the query are existentially quantified. For instance, the query

```
?- or(no,yes,S).
```

asks what binding of S will satisfy this goal, i.e., "What is the value of no OR'ed with yes?"

Procedural Semantics and Process Reading

As in Prolog, FGHC clauses with the same name and arity form procedures. Execution proceeds as a set of reductions of the initial query. A successful reduction entails the unification of a goal to a clause head and subsequent successful evaluation of the guard. If the unification or guard evaluation fails, other candidate clauses are attempted. If all clauses fail, then the reduction fails. Unlike Prolog, a failed reduction is fatal in a flat committed-choice language, i.e., if any reduction fails then the entire program fails. Correctly-written FGHC programs do not fail, which may at first seem strange to a Prolog programmer who is familiar (maybe *too* familiar) with shallow backtracking. The key point is that a reduction may also *suspend*. Suspension occurs when unification attempts to bind an input argument. For example, consider the following procedure:

```
color(red) :- ...
color(blue) :- ...
color(yellow) :- ...
```

with the query "?- color(X), X=blue." Suppose that we attempt reduction of the query by first reducing the color(X) goal. Goal color(X) will suspend because we attempt to unify X with some atom (first red, then blue, etc.). None of the clauses in color/1 successfully commit. If we then bind X in the query, then the suspended goal will be resumed, i.e., re-executed. When the color(X) goal is resumed, X will already be bound (to blue), so that the second clause matches and commits, and the query successfully reduces.

Consider the previous procedure for the Boolean-OR function of two variables. The query

```
?- or(X,Y,S), X=no, Y=yes.
```

if reduced in the goal order shown, will first attempt to reduce or(X,Y,S). The first clause cannot commit because of the attempted output binding of X. Similarly, the second clause cannot commit because of the attempted output binding of Y. The third clause attempts output bindings of both variables. The goal or(X,Y,S) therefore suspends on *both* input arguments X and Y (but not S). When the binding of X=no is made in the query, the or(X,Y,S) goal will be resumed. Suppose that the resumed goal is reduced next (before the Y=yes goal in the query). The first clause cannot commit because of input unification failure of the first argument. However, the second and third clauses still cannot commit because of attempted output bindings of Y, therefore the or(X,Y,S) goal suspends again. When the binding of Y=yes is made in the query, the or(X,Y,S) goal is again resumed, and when reduced will finally succeed in clause two.

When we say "a goal is suspended on a variable," we mean that the variable is linked with that goal, allowing a binding of the variable to resume the goal. The various implementation techniques for linking a variable to a suspended goal do not concern us here. However, it is critically important that, for a given goal invocation, if none of the clauses of the corresponding procedure can commit, then the goal is suspended on *at least one* variable per clause that did not fail. Suppose the query

```
?- or(X,Y,S), Y=yes.
```

is reduced in the goal order shown. Consider a faulty system wherein the goal or(X,Y,S) suspends on variable X only. Binding Y in the query would not trigger resumption and *deadlock* would ensue. Deadlock is a state wherein all processes are suspended. In a correct system, or(X,Y,S) suspends on both X and Y.

The process reading of FGHC is the procedural interpretation of how programs execute. The *process structure* of an FGHC program refers to the goals in the resolvent and their data dependencies. Interestingly, whereas in a procedural language, program and data are clearly separated in form and function, data structures in committed-choice languages can be implemented as process structures. For example, a list can be implemented as a group of communicating processes, one for each element of the list. This type of *active* data structure is attractive because concurrent, multiple accesses to the data can be made, with the usual suspension mechanism enforcing synchronization if necessary.

As another example of FGHC programming, the `isotree` program is now given.
For FGHC, a determinate programming language, we must in fact write two programs to match the single Prolog definition. This is because, whereas procedure
arguments in Prolog can handle both input and output, FGHC arguments are restricted to one or the other. We categorize these two programs as: `isotree(+,+)`
and `isotree(+,-)`.[10] This notation is identical to the *argument modes* introduced
for Prolog. An input argument, i.e., an instantiated variable, is denoted by '+'. An
output argument, i.e., an unbound variable, is denoted by '-'. Argument mode declarations are not a part of the FGHC language, and we use them only as a notation
for the intended meanings of procedures. In committed-choice languages such as
Parlog, mode declarations are mandatory. Although FGHC argument modes are
implicit, we still refer to procedure arguments as either "input" or "output."

The `isotree(+,+)` procedure is described here using the tree data structure from
the previous Prolog program (this problem is revisited in Chapter 6). The top-level
procedure must have an *additional* argument signifying whether the two trees are
isomorphic or not. This practice of *reifying* Prolog's failure action into a status
argument is common in committed-choice languages (discussed further in Section
2.3.1).

```
isotree(void,void,S)  :- S=yes.
isotree(tree(X,L1,R1),tree(X,L2,R2),S)  :-
    or(A,B,S),
    isotree(L1,L2,S1),    \
    isotree(R1,R2,S2),     > disjunctive subrule 1
    and(S1,S2,A),         /
    isotree(L1,R2,S3),    \
    isotree(R1,L2,S4),     > disjunctive subrule 2
    and(S3,S4,B).         /
isotree(_,_,S) :- otherwise | S=no.

and( no,  _,S) :- S=no.
and(  _, no,S) :- S=no.
and(yes,yes,S) :- S=yes.

or(yes,  _,S)  :- S=yes.
or(  _,yes,S)  :- S=yes.
or( no, no,S)  :- S=no.
```

The program is quite declarative. The first rule states that two void trees are
isomorphic. The second rule states that two trees are isomorphic if the trees have

---

[10]In general, a procedure with n arguments has 2^n input/output argument mode combinations.
Therefore Prolog `isotree/2` corresponds to four FGHC procedures. We describe `isotree(+,+)`
here, and `isotree(+,-)` in Chapter 6. The `isotree(-,+)` procedure is identical to `isotree(+,-)`
with the arguments reversed. In addition, `isotree(-,-)` is not very useful!

the same root value X and if *either* the left subtrees are isomorphic and the right subtrees are isomorphic (status S1 and S2) *or* the corresponding left and right subtrees are isomorphic (status S3 and S4). The third rule states that if the previous two rules do not hold, then the trees are *not* isomorphic. The precise semantics of otherwise is given in the next section.

As in the Prolog program, the two disjunctive subrules for isomorphism, as stated in the second clause, have the greatest potential for OR-parallel execution. Furthermore, unlike the Prolog program, the two conjunctive goals comprising each subrule *also* have potential for AND-parallel execution. In other words, all four recursive calls to isotree/3 can be executed in parallel in FGHC.

However, the benefits of exploiting all that parallelism are not clear. The problem raised by this simple program is fundamental: the parallel execution of the two disjunctive subrules is *speculative*, i.e., usually only one will succeed, but we don't know *a priori* which one. The parallel execution of the two conjunctive goals comprising a subrule is *constructive*, i.e., both goals are *required* to formulate the answer (A and B in this case).

Notice that the disjunctive subrules race to bind their status variables. The or/3 predicate is written to allow a yes answer from either subrule to determine the status of the tree. In reality, program behavior is up to the whim of the scheduler that schedules each goal for execution. If one of the subrules completes, but the or/3 process is not immediately scheduled, then the overall status S of tree isomorphism may not be quickly determined. In any case, the scheduler has no information pertaining to the intended disjunctive meaning of the subrules, and may continue to execute the remaining subrule! The intended meaning is hidden in or/3, above the level of the abstract architecture. This process is in stark contrast to OR-parallel Prolog, where parallel disjunction is implemented in the abstract architecture and, as a result, the intended Prolog meaning is clear (i.e., find one solution or find all solutions).

So we have a tradeoff to make. On one hand, OR-parallel Prolog will blindly set forth, attempting both disjunctive rules in parallel — true speculation. As soon as a solution is found, the searches are suspended. OR-parallel Prolog cannot, however, take advantage of constructive (AND) parallelism.

On the other hand, FGHC will also blindly set forth, attempting all goals in parallel no matter what their intended meaning. The programmer is responsible for crafting the program to explicitly contain this parallelism, or the program may end up doing pointless work. In Chapter 6 we rewrite the isotree program with this fact in mind.

In FGHC, as defined here, notice that execution can proceed by attempting reduction of *any* goal with *any* clause. More importantly, *any number of goals can be reduced in parallel.* It is the suspension rule that guarantees consistency between results. However, somewhat controversially, we abandon this definition in this early chapter, and take a more restricted, realistic view of FGHC in the remainder of the book. It is simply not efficient to try to execute all the guards of a procedure in OR-parallel. Since the guards are flat, there is little computation in them, and the synchronization necessary for OR-parallel execution far outweighs any benefit. Moreover, current logic programming compiler technology makes great use of *indexing* to efficiently select the subgroup of clauses that can unify with a given goal. We can assist the compiler in generating efficient code by constraining the clauses to be attempted in their textual order, sequentially.[11] Again, the amount of parallelism to be exploited here, for flat languages, is microscopic and not worth the overhead.

Other arguments against an implied textual order stem from reduced declarativity of the code; we disagree with these arguments. Two common situations are apparently encountered by a programmer writing a procedure definition. The first is when the procedure definition is simple enough to be clear with or without an implied order. The second is when the procedure definition is complex enough to be *impossible to write without assuming an implied order.* Thus either way, given that we are not going to exploit OR-parallel execution of guards, an implied sequential semantics is best.

Our hats are off to those futurists who argue that smart compilers will be able to *transform* naive programs into efficient programs, and that an implied order makes it harder to *verify* programs, or to write correct programs. At this time we can only say that the issue is as fundamental as a procedural language IF-THEN-ELSE construct: of course no one inserts the negation of the condition in the ELSE part! Such negation simply does not clarify the program, and is also quite difficult within nested IF statements.

2.2.3   Extra-Logical Features and Builtins

In this book we use a very simple dialect of FGHC that should facilitate programming all examples in just about any committed-choice language. In this simple dialect, guards can contain any conjunction of the operators shown in Table 2.2. An `otherwise` guard implicitly partitions the clauses of a procedure into two groups; the first (textually) must be tried before the second. If all clauses preceding

---

[11]To be fair, constraining clause order may hinder an optimizing compiler that creates a decision graph for the clause heads.

Operator	Meaning
diadic	
=:=	arithmetic equal
=\=	arithmetic not-equal
<	arithmetic less-than
>	arithmetic greater-than
<=	arithmetic less-than-or-equal-to
>=	arithmetic greater-than-or-equal-to
=	term unification
\=	term not-unification
singleton	
otherwise	partition clauses
true	trivially true

Table 2.2
Subset of FGHC Builtin Guard Operators Used in this Book

the clause containing the `otherwise` fail, then the `otherwise` will succeed. If no clause preceding the clause containing the `otherwise` succeeds and some clause(s) suspend, then the procedure suspends (i.e., it is as if the `otherwise` guard and all succeeding guards fail). More than one clause within a single procedure may contain `otherwise` guards.

Arithmetic is performed by `is/2`, where the second argument can be an arithmetic expression using the usual Prolog operators (+, -, *, /, //, mod). In Prolog the infamous semantics of `is/2` are well known — for example "X is Y-Z" can only be executed if Y and Z are bound to numbers. In most Prologs (including the system measured here), if Y or Z is unbound, then `is/2` gives a runtime error. The `is/2` semantics in FGHC are lenient: suspension occurs in "X is Y-Z" if either Y or Z is unbound.[12]

In the particular implementation of FGHC used in this book, `is/2` is actually restricted to use in the guard, although we have listed it as a body builtin. We have exercised our artistic license in the programs presented here in that, if `is/2` *cannot* suspend (i.e., if we can guarantee that its arguments are bound), then we may place the statement in the body. This placement makes the code prettier. Another alternative is to spawn an arithmetic goal (as in FLENG, for instance), but we have shied away from this alternative for efficiency reasons.

---

[12]Note that FGHC does *not* execute "2 is 3-Z" by evaluating 3−2, binding Z=1, as do constraint logic programming languages. In FGHC, this goal will suspend, and if another goal binds Z=1, then the suspended arithmetic goal will resume and succeed.

2.2.4   Programming Paradigms

In this section we examine three fundamental data structures for committed-choice
languages: streams, layered streams, and buffers. Other data structures can of
course be created in FGHC — the language is fully general. We specifically review
these structures because they represent the core of our tool set.

Streams

A stream is an incomplete list. Reading elements from a stream is equivalent
to reading a list, with suspension occurring if the unbound tail is encountered.
Although Prolog and FGHC use the same difference-list construct, in FGHC it is
with difference lists that we can write to *streams*, and hence exploit stream-AND
parallelism. Recall from Section 2.1.5 that a difference list, often denoted by X-Y, is
a list X with tail Y. For example, we can express a constant-time dappend(+,+,-)
in FGHC as:

```
dappend(X-Y,A-B,Result) :- Y=A, Result=X-B.
```

Lists X and A are considered streams with tails Y and B respectively. We sometimes
informally refer to X-Y as a stream; however, precisely the stream itself is X.

In general, we often see FGHC code with D-lists running through the goals in
a clause body. We can best think of these D-lists as representing a *stream* of
data flowing between the goals. For example, reconsider the previous flattenTree
example (this time in FGHC for variety):

```
?- flattenTree(((1,2),((3,void),(4,5),void)),L-[]).

flattenTree(void, L0-L1) :- L0=L1.
flattenTree((Seq1,Seq2), L0-L2) :-
    flattenTree(Seq1, L0-L1),
    flattenTree(Seq2, L1-L2).
flattenTree(E, L0-L1) :- otherwise | L0=[E|L1].
```

The declarative semantics of the procedure are identical to the Prolog version. A
more procedural explanation is now given. In the first clause, an empty D-list is
created by binding output stream L0 to its own tail L1. In other words, the D-list
L0-L1 is *shorted* because we do not wish to insert a void leaf in the flattened list.
In the third clause, a non-void element E is inserted into output stream L0.

In the second clause, streams L0 and L1 are appended by cleverly reusing variable
L1 as the tail of the first D-list L0-L1. Thus the dappend procedure has been
effectively fused into flattenTree/2.

Often D-lists are specified as two procedure arguments, rather than with the
operator -/2. This saves execution time for decomposing and composing structures,

and avoids creation of garbage. For example, the previous code is:

```
?- flattenTree(((1,2),((3,void),(4,5),void)),L,[]).

flattenTree(void, L0, L1) :- L0=L1.
flattenTree((Seq1,Seq2), L0, L2) :-
    flattenTree(Seq1, L0, L1),
    flattenTree(Seq2, L1, L2).
flattenTree(E, L0, L1) :- otherwise | L0=[E|L1].
```

The meaning and execution of this code are identical to the previous version.

Layered Streams

A layered stream is to a stream as a stream is to a list. A layered stream is a (possibly empty) list of elements of the form H*Ts,[13] where Ts is a list of all possible tails for head H. Each of the tails themselves can be layered streams. For example, the layered stream:

```
[1*[2*[],
    3*[4*[],
      5*[]],
    6*[]]]
```

can represent the list:

```
[[1,2],[1,3,4],[1,3,5],[1,6]]
```

In most programs that use layered streams, we extend the above definition of a layered stream as follows. A layered stream can also be the atom **begin**. All valid layered streams end with **begin** and all invalid (or incomplete) layered streams end with []. Thus the layered stream

```
[1*[2*begin,
    3*[4*[],
      5*begin],
    6*[]]]
```

represents the list:

```
[[1,2],[1,3,5]]
```

In other words, the layered stream above contains both valid and invalid data. We defer, until Section 5.2.5, explaining the advantages of layered streams and the utility of validating layered-stream data with **begin**. For now, we introduce layered streams simply as a curious data structure.

To convert a layered stream, defined in the previous manner, into its constituent lists we use the following program:

---

[13]The operator */2 is arbitrary but we will conform to using it throughout this book.

```
fromLStoL(LayeredStream,List) :-
    fromLStoS(LayeredStream,[],List-[]).

fromLStoS(begin,        Stack,L0-L1) :- L0=[Stack|L1].
fromLStoS([],                _,L0-L1) :- L0=L1.
fromLStoS([A*LS1|Rest],Stack,L0-L2) :-
    fromLStoS(LS1,[A|Stack], L0-L1),
    fromLStoS(Rest,Stack,    L1-L2).
```

The program removes all layered streams that do not terminate with **begin**. This converter is rather sloppy and its output, **List**, is reversed from the definition previously given. The delimiter **begin** is so named because the programs discussed in this book construct layered streams from the inside out. The converter's reverse order is irrelevant for these programs. One further note: often layered stream elements **H*Ts** are specified as **[H|Ts]** rather than with the operator ***/2**, to take advantage of a common storage optimization (see Exercise 22).

Buffers

A buffer is a fixed-size stream, i.e., a fixed-size list with an unbound tail. We represent a buffer as B/E[14] where E is the buffer tail. For example, the buffer

```
    [_,_,_,_|T]
```

can be expressed as

```
    B/E
```

where

```
    B = [_,_,_,_|T]
    E = T
```

Thus a buffer is essentially a difference list. However, *a buffer always retains the same fixed number of slots*, whereas a D-list can grow and shrink arbitrarily. The purpose of the buffer is to constrain the size of a stream. A buffer can be created as

```
    buffer(0,B/E) :- B=E.
    buffer(N,B/E) :- N>0 | N1 is N-1, B=[_|T], buffer(N1,T/E).
```

where N is the number of slots. We will assume a protocol wherein the final valid piece of datum in a buffer is always followed by the special atom: **stop**. Thus a buffer consumer has the general form:

---

[14]The operator '/'/2 is arbitrary but we will conform to using it throughout this book.

```
consume([stop|_]/_,...) :- ...
consume([A|As]/E,...) :- A \= stop |
    E = [_|Es],
    %      ^ new slot here
    ...
    consume(As/Es,...).
```

When an item A is read from the buffer, a new slot is inserted at the tail E. To write
to a buffer,

```
producer([A|As]/_,...) :-  ... A=stop.
producer([A|As]/_,...) :-
    A = ...
    ...
    producer(As/_,...).
```

When the buffer has been filled up the producer will suspend because argument As
in its recursion will become unbound. The producer will be resumed when/if the
consumer accepts another datum and creates a new slot. The first clause above
represents the end of production when the last buffer datum written is stop.

Note that this implementation of a buffer, in FGHC, has space complexity $O(n)$
where n is the number of buffer writes. A more space-efficient implementation
with a fixed-sized array would require either a very sophisticated compiler or the
introduction of a *buffer type* into FGHC. Often buffers, like D-lists, are specified
in FGHC as two procedure arguments rather than with the operator '/'/2. This
technique decreases the space complexity by a constant factor, and saves execution
time for decomposing and composing '/'/2 structures.

The uses and advantages of buffers will be fully explained in later chapters by
way of example programs.

2.2.5 Other Committed-Choice Languages

FGHC is quite similar to several committed-choice languages. In this section we
outline the major differences between FGHC and Parlog, Flat Concurrent Prolog
(FCP), GHC, KL1, Strand, and FLENG. The differences are informative if only to
dispel the misconception that one language holds a clear advantage over the others.
In fact, the committed-choice family is closely knit, with equal expressive power
and performance *for everyday programming*. The languages do differ, however,
with respect to meta-programming and systems programming, for instance. After
outlining these characteristics here, we discuss only applications programming in
this book.

Guarded Horn Clauses (GHC) is the parent language of Flat GHC (FGHC).
GHC allows user-defined procedure calls in a guard. Such a feature is nice for

the programmer who can define test predicates for synchronization. For example, colors may be defined as an abstract data type with a group of facts, color/1. To test if an input argument, X, in a clause is a color, the test predicate color(X) can be included in the guard.

The inclusion of "deep guards" implies that, during evaluation of such guards, some number of recursive reductions might be necessary. Because GHC does not permit output bindings in the head and guard (an attempt to do so causes suspension), a deep reduction within a guard might need to suspend because it attempts to make an output binding. However, the definition of "output binding" is complex because it does *not* refer to *any* binding, only to a binding that appears in the outermost scope of the initial guard. In addition to this complexity, GHC, like FGHC, does not specify any order in evaluating the guards in a procedure with multiple clauses. Thus implementation of OR-parallel evaluation of guards is difficult because each guard may be a group of nested and suspended procedure invocations.

FGHC permits only certain builtin predicates in the guard, thus guaranteeing that a guard can be evaluated with a "flat" sequence of procedure reductions. The suspension rule is simplified because the guard's goals all execute directly within the environment of their clause, with no intervening levels of procedure invocation. Thus suspension occurs only if a binding is attempted to an incoming procedure argument. Guard predicates simply check that their input arguments are instantiated to the correct type. In addition, weakening the guards lessens their granularity, and therefore it is no longer beneficial to evaluate the guards in OR-parallel.

KL1 is a superset of FGHC including powerful meta-logical builtin procedures facilitating the implementation of operating systems, modules, prioritizing goals, user-assisted scheduling via *pragma*, etc. KL1 has no fixed definition and is currently implemented on UNIX machines in the sequential PDSS system [65], and in parallel on the MultiPsi/V2 multiprocessor [66].

Two important meta-logical KL1 builtin procedures are unbound/2 and wait/1. Builtin unbound(V,S) which binds S = yes if V is unbound, otherwise binds S = no. Builtin wait(V) succeeds if V is bound, and otherwise suspends until V becomes bound. These test predicates are useful for controlling synchronization. Similar builtins are given in Parlog (var/1 and data/1), Strand (unknown/1 and data/1), and other languages. Several other builtin procedures, of course, are defined in all these languages.

FLENG [89] is a child of FGHC wherein there are no guards at all! In an effort to simplify the language to its bare essentials to promote efficient compilation and execution, guards have been banned. One clear observation concerning logic programs (see those in this book as examples) is that most clauses have no guard. In the instances where a guard is needed, it can be moved to the caller. Thus the integer generator in FGHC

```
gen(0,X) :- X=[].
gen(N,X) :- N>0 | M is N-1, X=[N|Xs], gen(M,Xs).

?- gen(5,L).
   L = [5,4,3,2,1]
```

can be written in FLENG as

```
gen(N,L) :- gt(N,1,S), gen(S,N,L).

gen(no,_,X) :- X=[].
gen(yes,N,X) :- gt(N,1,S), M is N-1, X=[N|Xs], gen(S,M,Xs).
```

where gt(I,J,S) is a builtin predicate that tests if I is greater than J and if so binds S = yes, otherwise binds S = no. This programming style is bothersome, but note that even in FGHC similar machinations are needed to simulate user-defined guard predicates. In any case, FLENG can only suspend in the head, thus simplifying execution.

Parlog, and its children Flat Parlog and Strand, are similar to GHC and FGHC. Parlog's synchronization method is subtly different than that of GHC. In Parlog, each procedure must be given a *mode declaration* indicating the mode of each of its arguments. There are two possible modes: input ('+') and output ('−'), retaining the notation introduced earlier for Prolog to avoid confusion. Whereas the GHC programmer implicitly indicates output modes by placing bindings after the guard, in Parlog this is not necessary. For example, the integer generator in Parlog is:

```
mode gen(+,-).

gen(0,[]).
gen(N,[N|Xs]) :- N>0 | M is N-1, gen(M,Xs).
```

Theoretically, GHC has greater flexibility than Parlog because each clause in a procedure can specify different modes of the arguments! In practice this specification is almost never done. In some dialects of FLENG, output bindings can be specified in the head with special notation:

```
gen(no,0,![]).
gen(yes,N,![N|Xs]) :- gt(N,1,S), M is N-1, gen(S,M,Xs).
```

These are expanded by the compiler into bindings placed after the commit.

Parlog provides the synchronization primitives ';' and '&'. The former is analogous to `otherwise` in GHC (as defined in this book). The latter guarantees that the execution of two body goals proceeds sequentially.

Parlog, as originally specified, consisted of both a committed-choice component, as discussed above, and a noncommitted-choice component similar to Prolog! Prolog procedures could be invoked by a `set/3` builtin, similar to the familiar `findall/3` builtin in Prolog. However, `set/3` issued bindings down its output stream as a producer, thus allowing attached consumer processes to work concurrently. As specified, this part of the Parlog language proved difficult to implement. As we shall examine in Chapter 13, merging committed-choice and nondeterminate computation within a single framework is the basis of two recent parallel logic programming languages, Andorra and Pandora.

Flat Parlog is Parlog with flat guards. Strand [49] is essentially Flat Parlog, and as with its parent, mode declarations can be used to specify procedure synchronization constraints. However, a more common method of synchronization in Strand is with *assignment* (`:=/2`) in the body, as in GHC. Assignment is output unification where one of the variables is guaranteed to be unbound. Thus in Strand, the integer generator can be written as in Parlog, or as:

```
gen(0,X) :- X := [].
gen(N,X) :- N>0 | M is N-1, X := [N|Xs], gen(M,Xs).
```

There is little practical distinction between the use of assignment in Strand and the more flexible output unification in FGHC. Output unification can make programs prettier. For example, in FGHC, `gen/2` can be executed as either `gen(+,-)` or `gen(+,+)`. This is not the case in Strand: a different procedure must be written to check `gen(+,+)`. Thus output arguments are strictly output, and cannot be partially instantiated by the caller, as in FGHC. As a final note, Strand defines `otherwise`, but not sequential '&'.

Concurrent Prolog (CP) [116] and its child Flat Concurrent Prolog (FCP) are the final committed-choice languages we consider here.[15] We saved CP for last because it most differs from FGHC. The synchronization method of CP is a data-level representation, rather than procedure-level as in the previous languages. Among the arguments passed to a body goal, annotation is permitted to specify that an argument is "read-only." This annotation means that, when the goal is reduced, if a binding is attempted to that variable the goal is suspended. Thus not only can different clauses of a procedure have different synchronization specifications (as in

---

[15] An interesting paper by Codish and Shapiro [30] describes various `isotree/3` programs in CP and FCP.

GHC), but different *invocations* of a procedure can also have different synchronization specifications! This added power permits meta-level programming and systems programming that cannot be achieved within the GHC or Parlog families.[16]

CP also specifies *atomic unification* that is missing from the other committed-choice languages. Atomic unification is the protected action of unifying two terms in the head of clause, i.e., before committing. If the unification fails, then any temporary bindings made are discarded. If the unification succeeds, then the clause is committed and the bindings are exported. Since synchronization is conducted on read-only variables, unification can entail binding variables in the passed argument without causing suspension. Atomic unification allows certain abstract data types, such as *channels* [116], to be implemented in CP. Moreover, atomic unification can reduce structure copying because logical variables can be conditionally bound in the head, regaining some of the power of Prolog's ability to rebind logical variables upon backtracking. Unfortunately, atomic unification is expensive to implement.

The purpose of this section was to briefly sketch the committed-choice languages, emphasizing that they are all basically the same with respect to applications programming.

> All FGHC programs presented in this book can be easily converted to related committed-choice languages with little more than syntax substitutions. The least powerful intersection of the languages was used here to increase the relevance and generality of the analysis presented.

2.3 Programming Style

In this section we discuss various points about Prolog and FGHC programming style. This book by no means eschews good programming style! It is assumed that the reader has learned programming style already, and is comfortable and confident enough to treat the programs given here as sketches of more robust programs. We do note various style issues specific to logic programming languages in this section.

2.3.1 Converting Nondeterminate into Determinate Code

Programmers, especially Prolog programmers, may initially use inefficient methods of converting nondeterminate procedures into determinate procedures. A naive

---

[16]By including certain meta-logical builtins in GHC and Parlog, one can achieve some or all of the power of CP. Each language makes different tradeoffs between expressiveness and ease of implementation. Often these languages come in flavors: a version with powerful builtins for systems programmers, and a safer, vanilla version for applications programmers.

method is the use of an additional *status* variable that returns **true** if the procedure
succeeded or **false** if the procedure "failed." For instance, in Prolog the two-input
Boolean AND function is defined with a single clause that fails unless both of its
arguments are **yes**.

```
and(yes,yes).
```

In FGHC, as shown in the **isotree** example, **and** is defined with a third argument
returning the status.

```
and(  _,  no,S)  :- S=no.
and( no,   _,S)  :- S=no.
and(yes,yes,S)  :- S=yes.
```

Such a status variable must be placed in every clause in the procedure, then interpreted by the caller. This method is simple but not always efficient. A more
sophisticated method uses a *continuation*, i.e., a set of variables that are required
for the goals occurring *after* the nondeterminate goal. The continuation can be
passed into the nondeterminate goal, and it is the responsibility of the nondeterminate procedure to call these continuation goals. For example, the previous **isotree**
procedure was

```
isotree(void,void,S)  :- S=yes.
isotree(tree(X,L1,R1),tree(X,L2,R2),S)  :-
    or(A,B,S),
    isotree(L1,L2,S1),
    isotree(R1,R2,S2),
    and(S1,S2,A),
    isotree(L1,R2,S3),
    isotree(R1,L2,S4),
    and(S3,S4,B).
isotree(_,_,S)  :- otherwise | S=no.
```

We can rewrite this with a continuation as

```
isotree(void,void,S)  :- S=yes.
isotree(tree(X,L1,R1),tree(X,L2,R2),S)  :-
    isotree(L1,L2,S1),
    isotree(R1,R2,S2),
    and(S1,S2,A),
    isotree1(A,cont(L1,R1,L2,R2),S).
isotree(_,_,S)  :- otherwise | S=no.

isotree1(yes,_,S)  :- S=yes.
isotree1(no,cont(L1,R1,L2,R2),S)  :-
    isotree(L1,R2,S3),
    isotree(R1,L2,S4),
    and(S3,S4,S).
```

The continuation consists of the variables wrapped up in `cont/5`. We obviated the need for `or/3` by essentially folding the disjunctive function into `isotree1`.

In essence, we have sequentialized the two disjunctive subrules by synchronizing the second subrule, now in `isotree1`, with the result `A` of the first subrule. The continuation method is more efficient in cases when the first subrule succeeds, obviating the need to perform computation in the second subrule (`isotree1` clause 2). In other words, continuations can avoid computation during speculative search, at the price of sequentializing the search.

The use of continuations lessens modularity of a program. For instance, by folding `or/3` into `isotree1` we have in a sense overspecialized and complicated the code. A more general form of a continuation is the set of the *actual goals* following the call, rather than just their variables. To invoke the continuation, the callee executes the goals with a meta-call builtin, available in many committed-choice languages.

We shy away from using continuations in this book when it obscures the program. It is important to preserve modularity of useful library procedures, such as managers for 2–3 trees, heaps, and arrays. Thus introducing continuations into these functions would be harmful.

In general, continuations are more powerful in FGHC than in Prolog. Prolog execution already utilizes continuations at the architecture level, in the sense that a body goal is executed only after all preceding body goals complete (see Section A.1). However, in FGHC, *goal records* are created for all the body goals but one, which is immediately reduced. The goal records are queued, to be reduced at some later time. Use of continuations *delays* the decision to call a given procedure, thus saving reductions (goal-record space and execution time) during speculative computation.

2.3.2 Generic Procedures and Modularity

Most programs presented in this book would receive rather poor grades in an undergraduate course, "Introduction to Programming." Often key parts of the input data describing a specific instance of the problem are hardwired into the programs presented. This practice is condoned because of the following considerations.

- It is helpful to keep the programs terse to facilitate visualization of all interacting procedures.

- A zealous attempt is made to exploit the compiler's ability to generate efficient code when unifying ground data structures [143, 128].

- Use of meta-functions is avoided to simplify the language kernels. For example, one can run most of these programs with even the simplest Prolog or committed-choice system. We avoided using language-specific builtins as much as possible to allow readers to type these programs, as is, into their own systems.

- To increase program efficiency and efficiently exploit parallelism, it is often best to explicitly encode the problem.

This problematic style exposes itself at many levels. Most Prolog programmers feel justified to include specific input data as facts in a program. Yet this practice will require recompiling the database of facts for each new instance of the problem. Less justified are practices of incorporating specific problem data directly into the program rule base. An extreme example of this is a constraints problem where the program consists entirely of recodified constraints between pieces of the input data. This programming style is quite elegant and we shall show examples in later chapters.

The most valid criticism of the programming styles presented in this book is that they are "programming in the small" rather than "programming in the large." By this distinction we mean that great attention is paid to the fine details of small programs. These details may affect the execution performance of the particular programs, but may also be irrelevant

- if the input data set is enlarged many times, creating different bottlenecks, such as garbage collection, serial input/output transformations, etc.

- if the algorithm has much higher than linear complexity. For large, complex problems, even perfect speedup on a shared-memory multiprocessor will not allow us to execute the problem in a reasonable amount of time. For example, the all-solutions fused generate & test algorithms given in this book all have exponential complexity. Thus if we wish to solve big problems, speeding them up is irrelevant — we really need new algorithms.

- if the primary target of the program is extensibility and not speed. In this case, modular, object-oriented programming styles are needed.

- if the programming task becomes hopelessly complex with increasing problem size.

We acknowledge these important criticisms. The issues raised above are not addressed in this book, yet they are vitally important. In fact, for any programming project, parallel or sequential, one must carefully prioritize goals: performance, extensibility, ease of prototyping, portability, etc. Parallel logic programming languages do not compare well to more mature languages, such as Ada, in these regards. Yet even among the logic programming languages, the problems presented in this book can be formulated in easier to understand, more modular and extensible implementations. Here we assume the reader knows the importance of such lessons and present only bare-bones high-performance programs. Perhaps surprisingly to a procedural programmer, the programs are not at all primitive.

2.3.3 Order of Evaluation and Speculative Parallelism

What can we safely assume about the *order* or *scheduling* of OR-Parallel Prolog and FGHC execution? This question is more than an exercise in theoretical semantics because, in general, the more one can assume about execution behavior, the more optimized an architecture one can build.

Very little can be assumed about FGHC execution. For example, the clauses of a procedure can be evaluated concurrently or in any order, as can the goals in the guard and in the body. Arguments may be passed before they are instantiated. As architects we would like to constrain the order of clause evaluation only in the interest of efficiency. For this purpose, otherwise can be used to avoid redundant evaluation of guard conditions.

otherwise in a guard implicitly partitions the clauses of a procedure into two groups, the first (textually) must be tried before the second. In some architectures, this choice of semantics may cause a loss of efficiency, e.g., FLENG executing on a SIMD (single-instruction, multiple-data stream) computer, such as a vector machine [88, 90], or an optimizing compiler that needs to rearrange clauses.

OR-Parallel Prolog should support the evaluation order of sequential Prolog to retain Prolog's full semantics. These semantics include evaluation of clauses and goals in their textual order. We shall see in later chapters that these strict semantics are not always necessary to ensure program correctness. In fact, the strict evaluation order of sequential Prolog can lead to inefficient execution of OR-parallel Prolog, so as architects we wish to "liberate" these semantics. One such idea, that of cavalier commit, '/'/0, was introduced in Section 2.1.4.

A related point concerns *speculative parallelism*. Consider a program in which we try, in parallel, two (or more) methods to solve a given problem. Both methods will, if successful, return an answer, but usually we care only about the faster method. The slower method should be cancelled as soon as the faster method returns.

In OR-parallel Prolog, speculative parallelism is always exploited when searching the parallel branches of the OR-tree. Cavalier commit can be used to select the

first solution and cancel all other searches. A simple example is the isomorphic-tree
program:

```
isotree(void,void) :- /.
isotree(tree(X,Left1,Right1),
        tree(X,Left2,Right2)) :-
    isotree(Left1,Left2),
    isotree(Right1,Right2), /.
isotree(tree(X,Left1,Right1),
        tree(X,Left2,Right2)) :-
    isotree(Left1,Right2),
    isotree(Right1,Left2), /.
```

The cavalier commits guarantee that any successful path in the OR-tree will terminate alternative paths emanating from each branchpoint on that path, i.e., the
entire tree. When invoked as `isotree(+,+)`, although there is only one solution
(either success or failure), the cavalier commits increase efficiency by early removal
of paths that will eventually fail.

In FGHC, the speculative isomorphic-tree program is:

```
isotree(Tree1,Tree2,S) :- isotree(_,Tree1,Tree2,S).

isotree(yes,_,_,S) :- S=no.
isotree(_,void,void,S) :- S=yes.
isotree(F,tree(X,L1,R1),tree(X,L2,R2),S) :-
    or(A,B,S),
    isotree(F1,L1,L2,S1),      \
    isotree(F1,R1,R2,S2),       >disjunctive subrule 1
    and(S1,S2,A),              /
    or(F,A,F2),
    isotree(F2,L1,R2,S3),      \
    isotree(F2,R1,L2,S4),       >disjunctive subrule 2
    and(S3,S4,B),              /
    or(F,B,F1).
isotree(_,_,_,S) :- otherwise | S=no.

and( _, no,S) :- S=no.
and( no, _,S) :- S=no.
and(yes,yes,S) :- S=yes.

or(yes, _,S)  :- S=yes.
or( _,yes,S)  :- S=yes.
or( no, no,S) :- S=no.
```

An isomorphic tree is determined by two disjunctive subrules, each composed of two
conjunctive goals. If either subrule finds that the subtrees are isomorphic (variables
A or B) then the trees themselves are isomorphic. Thus both subrules race to find
the answer. Status variables A and B signify if/when either subrule finds a solution.

When A is bound to **yes**, the processes in the subrule computing B should be killed (in the first clause) and vice versa. Another occasion to kill both subrules is if an ancestor subrule has terminated successfully, indicated by flag F. Thus the logical OR of F with either A or B form new flags, F1 and F2, for the recursive descent.

In the example, timing is not critical because the status flags do not affect correctness. Here the granularity of subrules killed is very small. Most practical uses of this technique involve large granularity subrules, such as multiple, alternative methods of solving sets of complex mathematical equations.

The scheme requires an implicit order of clause evaluation, namely the textual order. If this order is not guaranteed by the language (for instance, if the first clause is continually checked *last*) then the slower subrule will not kill itself at the proper time. In fact, FGHC does *not* make this guarantee. In some committed-choice languages, this order requirement can be avoided by the introduction of meta-logical builtin predicates. Consider a guard predicate var(X) which succeeds if X is unbound at the time of evaluation, otherwise it fails. This predicate would allow us to rewrite the above code as follows:

```
isotree(yes,_,_,S) :- S=no.
isotree(F,void,void,S) :- var(F) | S=yes.
isotree(F,tree(X,L1,R1),tree(X,L2,R2),S) :- var(F) |
    or(A,B,S),
    isotree(F1,L1,L2,S1),
    isotree(F1,R1,R2,S2),
    and(S1,S2,A),
    or(F,A,F2),
    isotree(F2,L1,R2,S3),
    isotree(F2,R1,L2,S4),
    and(S3,S4,B),
    or(F,B,F1).
isotree(F,_,_,S) :- otherwise, var(F) | S=no.
```

Syntactically, the program above is similar to the previous program, differing only in the treatment of the first argument. Semantically, the two programs are vastly different. The use of var/1 in the last three guards enables the clauses to be evaluated in any order, guaranteeing correctness. Most critically, if F is bound (to **yes**) then the last three guards fail, guaranteeing that the first clause is attempted. Thus introduction of var/1 guarantees that the slower method will kill itself once the faster method has found a solution and has bound F.

The builtin var/1, however, is not logically correct. The var(X) builtin is true if X is unbound *at the instant of evaluation*, but no guarantee is given about any subsequent time. Consider the following degenerate example:

```
f(Y) :- var(Y) | Y=2.
?- f(X), X=3.
```

Process `f(Y)` may commit before `X=3` is executed. At this point both `X=3` and `Y=2` will race to bind the same data cell (variables `X` and `Y` are aliased by the procedure call). The loser will perform a failing unification and the query will fail. Considering a naive point of view from `f(Y)`, program failure is logically incorrect because the `var(Y)` guard should have ensured that `Y` was unbound and able to be privately bound to anything desired. Yet `var(Y)` only guarantees that `Y` is unbound at the instant `Y` is checked. Although the validity or logical correctness of `var/1` cannot be guaranteed by the system, the programmer can make this guarantee. A simple rule to follow is never to attempt to bind `Y` in the body of a goal with guard `var(Y)`, although weaker conditions apply in many instances.

In summary, FGHC constrains the order of program execution very little and must be constrained by the architect to achieve efficiency. Conversely, Prolog constrains the order of program execution a great deal and must be made more flexible in OR-parallel Prolog to achieve efficiency. We have briefly introduced the techniques of clause ordering by meta-logical predicates in FGHC and by efficient selection of any solution by cavalier commit in OR-parallel Prolog. These methods are used to control speculative parallelism, and our discussion of them continues in later chapters.

2.4   Architectures

With the introduction to program construction presented in the previous sections, we have set the stage for delving into the details of systems that execute the programs: the architectures. This section gives a brief overview of two implementations for the OR-parallel Prolog and FGHC languages studied in this book. We sketch the components of the systems, including the instruction sets, compilers, engines, and schedulers. For readers especially interested in instruction-set architecture, a detailed exposition is given in Appendix A.

Shared-memory multiprocessors, in their current and near-future realizations as shared-bus machines, are ultimately bus-bandwidth limited. In other words, one can add memories and processors but eventually the bus will limit performance. The primary function of shared-bus machine architectures is to reduce the bus-bandwidth requirement. A good *architecture* accomplishes this in diverse ways: efficient instruction encoding, reduced branching frequency, high temporal and spatial locality of data and instruction memory references,[17] powerful instructions,[18] instruction-set facility for optimization, etc. Often these goals are at odds; creating an architecture with optimal tradeoffs is still very much an art.

The bus-bandwidth requirement is a metaphor for the communication-bandwidth requirement that threatens to bottleneck any multiprocessor organization. The characteristics of message traffic in a nonshared-memory organization will differ greatly from shared-bus traffic. However, the bottom line is still the required bandwidth. The architectures described in the next section have been designed with reduced bandwidth very much in mind.

2.4.1 Overview of Aurora and Panda

The Aurora research project [78, 21] is a joint effort by Argonne National Laboratories (ANL), University of Bristol,[19] and the Swedish Institute of Computer Science (SICS). Aurora is an OR-parallel implementation of Prolog currently available on some shared-memory multiprocessors. Since the original system was released, an AND/OR-parallel system called Andorra is currently being developed [58].

The Parallel Inference Machine (PIM) project is being conducted at the Institute of New Generation Computer Technology (ICOT). PIM is a special-purpose multiprocessor for executing KL1 programs. The PIM organization is a group of clusters, each of which is a shared-memory multiprocessor. In the interest of comparison between the systems, only a single PIM cluster is discussed in this chapter. Panda[20] is an AND-parallel implementation of FGHC (a subset of KL1) on shared-memory multiprocessors [113, 112]. Details of each project are given here.

The Aurora system[21] runs on the Sequent Balance and Symmetry, Encore Multimax, Alliant FX/8, and other machines. The system is quite robust, built on top of SICStus Prolog [19] which has a top-level interpreter loop, compiler, and debugger. Low-level parallel constructs are implemented by calls to macros defined in a monitor toolkit [77]. The toolkit can be rewritten for specific machine architectures,

---

[17]Anticipating that the processors utilize local memory of some kind.

[18]The more powerful the instructions, the fewer instructions are needed to execute a given task. However, this potency must not come at an excessive price of instruction complexity (in decoding and interpretation overheads).

[19]with the original work done at the University of Manchester.

[20]originally called KL1-PS in the literature. I have taken the liberty of moving away from the Japanese overuse of acronyms, and renamed this system Panda. Thus the systems are calibrated not only in terms of instruction-set efficiency (see Appendix A), but also in terms of pun content. Note that the market is getting crowded in this department, what with Andorra [58], Pandora [11], Sandra [45], and Agora [13].

[21]Measurements of the "Delta" version are given in this book. The system has since been upgraded. For example the "Foxtrot" version has an improved compiler and executes significantly faster than the system measured for this book.

thus facilitating Aurora ports to a wide variety of multiprocessors.

The Panda system runs on the Sequent Balance and Symmetry and Encore Multimax. The system lacks a proper top-level interpreter, but can accept a user query to a preloaded, precompiled user program. Panda has no user debugger; however, programs can be debugged by the user on alternative systems. For example, PDSS [65] and Strand [49], although they offer supersets of Panda-supported FGHC (functionally they are supersets — syntactically these languages are different), have good debugging environments.

To calibrate the two systems, Kumon's N-Queens algorithm (discussed in Section 5.2.1) was chosen because the program is the same in both Prolog and FGHC. The program was executed for 8-Queens on a single Symmetry 80386 processing element (PE), resulting in 13.0 sec (Panda) and 13.8 sec (Aurora Delta). SICStus Prolog V0.5 ran in 8.0 sec, showing Aurora overheads degraded performance over 40%. Larger benchmarks measured by Lusk *et al.* [78] indicate an average of 20% overhead. These overheads are caused by an earlier version of the Aurora compiler.

Note that, as these and other logic programming systems evolve, their performances will improve. For example, JAM Parlog executes Kumon's Queens 25% faster than Panda and executes other programs from 20%–40% faster [131]. This performance gap is due to less memory traffic and lower suspension overhead in the JAM-Parlog system. In addition, the Foxtrot version of Aurora executes Kumon's Queens 53% faster than the Delta version and executes other Queens programs from 10%–16% faster. This gap is due mainly to an improved compiler.

The most important design considerations in these systems concerning performance are listed below. These interrelated issues are quite difficult to analyze individually.

- **engine architecture** — the instruction-set design is important with respect to the instruction execution times, the required instruction memory bandwidth, and the possible compiler optimizations. The Aurora system uses Carlsson's (SICStus) version of the Warren Abstract Machine (WAM) [143] instruction set. Modifications were made to implement binding, dereferencing, and trailing with respect to binding arrays (see next item). The Panda system uses Kimura and Chikayama's version of the WAM, called KL1-B [71]. KL1-B is both simpler than the WAM because backtracking has been removed, and more complex than the WAM because suspension and locking mechanisms have been integrated. Both Aurora and Panda use the compilation technique of clause indexing.

- **storage model** — memory management is important to retain the spatial

locality needed to make efficient use of local memory, a processor component
in most high-performance computers. In addition, efficient memory management creates less garbage, therefore, garbage collection will be less frequent.
For example, a stack can be managed more efficiently than a heap implemented with a free list. The heap will get fragmented as data words are
deallocated; these words cannot be reused for allocation of larger structures.

In Aurora, groups of intertwined stacks are used. A stack group, similar to
that of the WAM, is allocated to each processor. A single OR-tree grows
as the program executes — this tree is mapped onto the stack groups in
the following manner. Initially the root of the OR-tree is the program query,
allocated to a given processor. The processor can execute the query in a depth-
first manner, like a WAM engine, on its stack group. However, procedures
enabled to be evaluated with an OR-parallel search for multiple solutions will
create branchpoints in the stack. An idle processor can form a branch of the
OR-tree emanating from a branchpoint in another processor's stack group.
The branch extension is allocated in the stack group of the idle processor. In
other words, the branch, from root to leaf, passing through the branchpoint,
will extend through two stack groups.

As a program executes, processors periodically become idle and, as a result,
switch tasks. The new task might be an extension of a branch "sprouting"
from another processor. Thus the intertwined stacks may be thought of as a
type of "cactus stack." A branch from root to leaf may extend through any
number of stack groups. The intertwining can even be "incestuous," i.e., a
branch may extend through the same stack group more than once.

Holes may form in the stack groups when a branch "dies back," i.e., when
backtracking fails through the branchpoints of the branch. Suppose a portion
of the branch extended through a given stack group, and that stack group
has since grown further with the extension of another (independent) branch.
If the first branch dies back, then the area allocated to that branch on the
given stack group becomes a hole, i.e., garbage that cannot be immediately
reclaimed. The hole cannot be immediately reused because another branch
is allocated above it in the same stack group. Eventually the hole will be
reclaimed when the covering branch dies back, exposing the hole to the top
of the stack group.

In Panda, each processor has a storage group consisting of goal and suspension
record lists. These lists are allocated from a larger group of free lists, which
is split among the processors to avoid contention. One can consider all the

free lists as residing in a heap, i.e., the Panda storage model is a heap. In general, Panda storage management is simpler than Aurora's. But FGHC programs create garbage, i.e., memory locations that are no longer referenced, at a significantly faster rate than OR-parallel Prolog programs. Memory fragmentation is reduced by allocating different sizes of records from a group of free lists, each specializing in objects of a given size. However, garbage can be reallocated to a free list by explicit collection only.

- **binding mechanism** — in parallel systems, bindings are the means by which processes communicate among each other and with the outside world. In Aurora, parallel processes executing a nondeterminate procedure create independent solutions, i.e., the processes can potentially produce conflicting, but valid, bindings. To implement multiple valid bindings, the Aurora system uses a *binding array* per processor, wherein bindings to variables shared among branches reside (i.e., bindings to variables that may potentially differ among the processors).

Any branch, from leaf to root in the OR-tree, defines an independent parallel computation. Two branches that emanate from a given branchpoint will share the portion of the OR-tree from the root to that branchpoint. Logical variables residing in this shared portion can potentially be given different bindings by each branch. Thus the value of such a binding cannot be stored in the logical variable itself. Each branch must cache these values and reference them indirectly. The binding array is essentially a software cache of logical variables and their values. Referencing a variable (either reading it or binding it) is a bit more expensive in Aurora than in sequential Prolog, but the overhead is constant.

In sequential Prolog, failure restores the state of computation at the most recently invoked nondeterminate procedure with potential multiple solutions. This is called *backtracking*. State restoration may involve *unbinding* variables bound by descendents of the nondeterminate procedure. In OR-parallel Prolog, backtracking proceeds similarly, where unbinding a shared variable involves removing its value from the binding array.

Backtracking may return the state to the entry point of a nondeterminate procedure that has already spawned multiple, independent, yet incomplete branches in the OR-tree. The Aurora scheduler may choose to extend one of these incomplete branches or to extend the branchpoint itself if the branchpoint is still pregnant (i.e., has additional clauses to explore). In the former case, extension of the incomplete branch may begin at any of its pregnant branchpoints. Thus the branch must be traversed downwards (away from the root) to another branchpoint. All bindings made on this portion of the branch are loaded into the binding array, restoring the computation state at the destination node.

In summary, traversal of the OR-tree from one node to another, via the combined action of backtracking (up) and restoring (down), requires that bindings in the binding array be discarded and reloaded. This action defines a "task switch" in standard operating-systems terminology. Thus binding arrays facilitate task switching, but the task-switch overhead is not constant. Compared to conventional architectures, the Aurora task-switch has significant overhead.

In Panda, AND-parallel execution implies that all processes have equal authority to bind any variable at any time. Thus the binding problem becomes a locking problem. The binding (in the active part of a clause) of variables transferred from the passive part of the clause must be locked. Consider binding an input variable to a newly-created structure. The Panda compiler first builds the structure completely, then binds the variable to it. Only the final binding operation needs to be locked. An alternative would be first to bind the variable to a location in the heap and then to build the structure incrementally from this location. This method would require locking the entire structure-creation operation. The first scheme minimizes the locking periods of variables, but the code that is required first to create a structure and then to bind it is often less concise than code that incrementally builds a structure.

In a clause head, an attempt to bind a variable that is passed as an argument to the procedure, can potentially suspend the procedure call. If no clause can commit and one or more clauses can suspend, then the call suspends. The suspension overhead, proportional in some sense to the number of procedure clauses, can be considered part of the binding cost.

Goal resumption causes further binding cost. Binding a variable will trigger the resumption of all goals suspended on that variable. The resumption overhead is proportional to the number of goals suspended on the variable.

- **scheduler** — the process scheduler must be efficient in two major respects. First, the work must be evenly distributed among the processors (good load balancing, preferably dynamic). Second, the overheads of process spawning, suspending, resuming, and switching must be low.

The Aurora system we measured uses an advanced version of the Argonne

scheduler described by Butler *et al.* [17]. Scheduling decisions are made locally by the processors, called workers,[22] with a distributed algorithm. This
strategy stresses low overhead, at the cost of less coordination between workers, than other schedulers for Aurora [18, 15]. In Panda, each PE schedules
goals on demand from local goal queues [113, 112]. If a PE's goal queue
empties, then the idle PE sends a message to a busy PE, requesting a goal.

The Argonne scheduler has larger overheads than the Panda scheduler when
scheduling small granule tasks, because an Aurora task switch involves more
work than a Panda task switch. An Aurora worker must traverse the OR
tree and update its binding array. A Panda worker need only access a new
goal from its local goal queue. When attempting to exploit small granularity parallelism on many PEs, the Argonne scheduler often will thrash, i.e.,
idle workers will traverse the OR-tree in competition for finding work. The
Manchester scheduler [18] lessens this contention, but we do not present its
measurements in this book.

The Panda scheduler is potentially less efficient than the Aurora schedulers for
large granule tasks, because the Panda scheduler cannot distinguish between
goals of different granularity. Thus an idle PE is just as likely to receive a
small goal as a large goal when requesting work from a busy PE. When an
Aurora worker becomes idle, one of a few Argonne scheduler heuristics prefers
choosing a task closer, to the OR-tree root, to choosing the node where the
idle worker is currently located. In general, a task closer to the root contains
more work (although not always). The sequential '&' operator can be used
in Parlog to explicitly collect larger granules, however, FGHC does not have
this feature.

- **garbage collection** — all languages that dynamically create structures require some form of garbage collection (GC). In Aurora, the WAM performs
  two major optimizations that reduce garbage creation. Tail-recursion optimization (or last-call optimization) deallocates a procedure's stack frame
  before the call to the last body goal in a clause. Thus the frame is reused
  and, for instance, a recursive procedure that simply calls itself will not access
  the stack (the single frame will be allocated in the WAM register set).

  Another WAM optimization is automatic memory recovery on backtracking.
  Thus when searching for all solutions to a nondeterminate problem, memory

---

[22]In general, a worker is a meta-process that executes logic programming processes. However,
the systems discussed in this book statically allocate one worker per processor, so we equate the
terms.

used to explore bad paths is easily recovered. However, the determinate portions of programs can still produce garbage (in the form of temporary data structures used to get from one intermediate point to another, and then discarded).

Committed-choice languages naturally can exploit tail-recursion optimization because, after a goal is reduced, no references to that goal record remain. Therefore the goal record can be reused for one of the body goals — in fact for any of the body goals. Committed-choice languages, however, generate more garbage than Prolog because lack of backtracking means lack of automatic memory recovery. Panda has a parallel stop & copy garbage collector. Aurora (Delta) has no garbage collector.

Although the Aurora and Panda systems may be handicapped, they are still calibrated in their present state for the Kumon's N-Queens benchmark. In general, however, we believe that the Panda engine is slower than the Aurora engine for the following reasons (in order of their perceived impact):

- **memory bandwidth** — the Panda emulator uses *two* 32-bit words to represent one data item. Aurora uses one 32-bit word. Note that a 64-bit data item is *not* a fundamental requirement of FGHC nor of committed-choice languages in general. For example JAM-Parlog uses a 32-bit data word. Word size is independent of the abstract architecture and programming language, but it affects Panda's performance.

- **compiler technology** — the FGHC compiler is less sophisticated than the SICStus Prolog compiler [19], as used in the Aurora system. In particular, the FGHC compiler has inefficient register allocation and often builds unnecessary data structures, increasing the frequency of garbage collection.

- **emulator technology** — the Panda emulator frequently uses indirect structure referencing to access fields of an eight-byte data cell. In general, the Aurora engine is better crafted and great attention is paid to the mapping of abstract machine (WAM) registers to 'C' registers.

- **language differences** — since FGHC is completely AND-parallel, its locking problems are more severe than those of Aurora Prolog, which is only OR-parallel. To ease the locking problem, the compiler generates code that is somewhat roundabout and not truly efficient when executed sequentially.

Descriptions of the Aurora and Panda instruction sets are given in Appendix A.

2.4.2   Statistics

At the outset, we need to offer a disclaimer concerning the completeness of performance analysis presented in this book. Garbage collection (GC), a significant subsystem in any declarative architecture, has not been analyzed. The Panda system has parallel stop & copy GC, but the Aurora system studied has no GC. In addition, different memory allocations and partitions make comparison difficult. Even the *definition of garbage* is somewhat different in the systems, since Aurora, like all WAMs, cleans up its heap upon backtracking. To equalize GC as much as possible on the two systems, large memory spaces were used when necessary to minimize GC.

Most of the measurements presented here were made on a Sequent Symmetry [95] with 16 processing elements (PEs), each an Intel 80386. At most, 15 PEs were used to execute the measured programs. A few measurements were made on an Encore Multimax [46] with eight PEs, each an NS32032. The execution times given are minima from a group of measurements made on an unloaded host. Because timing measurements had some variance, we felt that the minimum observed execution time gives the programmer or architecture designer more information than an average execution time.

The programs listed in this book, although correct and executable, are not *exactly* the programs executed to collect the measurements. The main differences, listed below, simply reduce memory usage:

- difference lists, denoted in the program listings as S0-S1, were expanded into two variables, S0 and S1 in the actual code.

- layered streams, denoted in the program listings as H*Ts, were represented in the actual code as [H|Ts].

- buffers, denoted in the program listings as B/E, were expanded into two variables, B and E in the actual code.

We mention these details because we believe that in a book about parallel programming, reproducible performance results are as important as reproducible solutions!

Execution of builtin Prolog and FGHC procedures are *not* counted as reductions. Some types of shallow backtracking are not counted as backtracking because the compiler indexes to avoid creating a *choicepoint*. A choicepoint is a stack object similar to the aforementioned branchpoint, except that a choicepoint can only produce alternative clauses sequentially via backtracking. Shallow backtracking results when failure occurs in the head of a clause, causing execution of an alternative clause (in contrast to deep backtracking, triggered by failure in a body goal). A naive execution model for Prolog attempts all clauses of a procedure by shallow backtracking among them. Indexing is a more sophisticated execution method, wherein only a predetermined subset of potentially unifying clauses are attempted (see Appendix A).

For example, the SICStus Prolog compiler obviates backtracking in the following procedure gen(+,-) by clever indexing:

```
gen(0,[]) :- !.
gen(N,[N|X]) :- M is N-1, gen(M,X).
```

Thus well-indexed determinate programs have no backtracking. However, some other types of shallow backtracking *are* counted. An example is:

```
anySame([X|_],[X|_]).
anySame([_|Xs],[_|Ys]) :- anySame(Xs,Ys).
```

When invoked determinately as anySame(+,+), the above procedure backtracks once per failure of the first clause.

Prolog systems have a variety of aggregation operations for collecting all solutions to a query [86]. These builtins often differ in whether they return a list of solutions in the order specified by the strict Prolog backtracking semantics, and whether they return duplications of solutions. Because these builtins have no standard semantics, especially among parallel Prologs, we avoid rigorously defining any here. However, the programmer must be aware of the different execution-time overheads of the different builtins.

In this book we use only findall/3, as defined in Section 2.1.3. In most of the programs in this book, order of solutions is unimportant, so that any aggregation operator could be used. We chose findall because it has the least overhead in Aurora (Delta). However, findall is not without cost, as indicated in Table 2.3. Procedures bagof and setof are two common Prolog aggregation builtins, shown for comparison.

Rare cases where a program requires ordered solutions are explicitly discussed in the text. To avoid confusion (we hope), we distinguish between an ordered and unordered findall although, in reality, these functions may be best performed by different builtins on different systems. An ordered collection requires synchronization between workers performing the OR-parallel search. Hence for the same data, an ordered findall is generally slower than an unordered findall.

query	reductions	backtracks
del(3,[1,2,3],_)	3	2
findall(X,del(X,[],_),L)	9	3
findall(X,del(X,[1,2,3],_),L)	48	6
bagof(X,del(X,[1,2,3],_),L)	91	19
setof(X,del(X,[1,2,3],_),L)	97	19

Table 2.3
Reduction and Backtrack Overheads in Aurora Prolog (Delta Version)

2.5 Summary

Both Prolog and Flat Guarded Horn Clauses (FGHC) were introduced in this chapter. Prolog is a sequential logic programming language that can be parallelized, almost (but not quite) below the perception level of the programmer. FGHC is a concurrent logic programming language that can also be parallelized. In general, OR-parallel Prolog exploits large-grain tasks and stream-AND parallel FGHC exploits finer-grained tasks. As discussed, FGHC is representative of a family of committed-choice languages. In applications programming, there is little difference between our choice of FGHC and other members of the family.

With regard to Prolog, the reader is referred to various textbooks: Sterling and Shaprio [119], Clocksin and Mellish [29], Bratko [16], and Pereira and Shieber [98]. With regard to committed-choice languages, the reader is referred to books on Concurrent Prolog [116, 127], Strand [49] and Parlog [57, 35].

In the next chapter, Prolog and FGHC are further introduced by means of very simple examples. This exposition does not emphasize parallelism *per se*, but rather gives a more in-depth look at how programs are constructed.

Exercises

Exercise 1 What will happen for the following Prolog queries? Justify your answers. Do not execute these on a Prolog system; thinking is far more valuable.

```
?- alpha = beta.
?- X = Y.
?- f(X) = X.
?- [a,b] = [a,b,c].
?- [1,2,3] = [1|X].
?- a \= 1.
?- f(X) \= f(a).
```

Exercise 2 Consider the following FGHC program:

```
same(X,X,S) :- S=yes.
same(X,Y,S) :- X \= Y | S=no.
```

What will happen for the following queries? Justify your answers. Again, think before you type.

```
?- same(alpha,beta,S).
?- same(X,X,S).
?- same([1,2,3],[1,2,X],S).
?- same([1,2],[1,2,3],S).
?- same([1,2],[1,2,X],S).
?- same([1,2],[1,X,3],S).
```

Exercise 3 Write an FGHC procedure, not/2, implementing the Boolean NOT function. Using only and/3 and not/2 define procedures for Boolean NAND, NOR, and XOR functions of two variables.

Exercise 4 Similar to the and/2 predicate given in Section 2.3.1, write Prolog predicates for Boolean OR, NOT, NAND, NOR, and XOR functions.

Exercise 5 Builtin comparison functions differ subtly among various logic programming systems. Experiment with the following builtin functions in a variety of systems to ensure that you understand their semantics. Not all systems support all of these builtins.

```
X = Y        X \= Y        X := Y
X == Y       X \== Y       X is Y
X =:= Y      X =/= Y
```

Exercise 6 Prolog procedures are not always declarative and are sometimes quite confusing. Consider the flattenTree/2 procedure given in Section 2.1.5:

```
flattenTree(void,L-L) :- !.
flattenTree((Seq1,Seq2),L0-L2) :- !,
    flattenTree(Seq1,L0-L1),
    flattenTree(Seq2,L1-L2).
flattenTree(E,[E|L]-L).
```

Can this program execute correctly in the mode flattenTree(-,+)? If not, can you modify the program to enable its execution? Hint: what answers would you expect from flattenTree(-,+)?

Exercise 7 In Section 2.3.3 the isotree(+,-) OR-parallel Prolog procedure has been modified with cavalier commit to select a single solution. Consider an alternative formulation with the original Prolog procedure given in Section 2.1.1:

```
?- In = ..., isotree(In,Out), /.
```
What is the difference in meaning between having the cavalier commit in the top-level query, as opposed to having it within the `isotree` procedure? Qualitatively, what is the expected difference in performance of these two approaches?

Exercise 8 Convert the data in Table 2.4 into Prolog facts. Make top-level queries, with `findall/3` and `setof/3`, for collecting:

- the names of all the kings.
- the names of all the queens.
- all the houses.
- all the monarchs of a given house.
- all the monarchs of a given century.

Exercise 9 Why is it so difficult to efficiently exploit both AND parallelism and backtracking within the same logic programming system? Address the issues of binding, task switching, scheduling, and garbage collection.

Exercise 10 Why is it so difficult to efficiently exploit both AND parallelism and OR parallelism within the same logic programming system? Address the issues of binding, task switching, scheduling, and garbage collection.

2.5. Summary69

Monarch	House	Reign	Monarch	House	Reign
William-I	Norman	1066–1087	Jane	Tudor	1553–1553
William-II	Norman	1087–1100	Mary-I	Tudor	1553–1558
Henry-I	Norman	1100–1135	Elizabeth-I	Tudor	1558–1603
Stephen	Norman	1135–1154	James-I	Stuart	1603–1625
Henry-II	Plantagenet	1154–1189	Charles-I	Stuart	1625–1649†
Richard-I	Plantagenet	1189–1199	Charles-II	Stuart	1660–1685
John	Plantagenet	1199–1216	James-II	Stuart	1685–1688
Henry-III	Plantagenet	1216–1272	Mary-II	Stuart	1689–1694
Edward-I	Plantagenet	1272–1307	William-III	Stuart	1689–1702
Edward-II	Plantagenet	1307–1327	Anne	Stuart	1702–1714
Edward-III	Plantagenet	1327–1377	George-I	Hanover	1714–1727
Richard-II	Plantagenet	1377–1399	George-II	Hanover	1727–1760
Henry-IV	Lancaster	1399–1413	George-III	Hanover	1760–1820
Henry-IV	Lancaster	1413–1422	George-IV	Hanover	1820–1830
Henry-VI	Lancaster	1422–1461	William-IV	Hanover	1830–1837
Edward-IV	York	1461–1483	Victoria	Hanover	1837–1901
Edward-V	York	1483–1483	Edward-VII	Saxe-Coburg	1901–1910
Richard-III	York	1483–1485	George-V	Windsor	1910–1936
Henry-VII	Tudor	1485–1509	Edward-VIII	Windsor	1936–1936
Henry-VIII	Tudor	1509–1547	George-VI	Windsor	1936–1952
Edward-VI	Tudor	1547–1553	Elizabeth-II	Windsor	1952–

† Cromwell ruled as dictator from 1649–1660.

Table 2.4
British Monarchs

3 Small Programs

"I don't know what's the matter with people: they don't learn by understanding; they learn by some other way — by rote, or something. Their knowledge is so fragile!"

Richard P. Feynman
Surely You're Joking, Mr. Feynman
Bantam Books, 1985.

In this chapter, Prolog and FGHC are introduced by means of simple examples of list-manipulation procedures. Lists are easy to understand and form the basis for streams, layered streams, and buffers. In later chapters, we expand the use of data structures to balanced and unbalanced binary trees, self-balancing 2–3 trees, hash trees, graphs, arrays, and various interconnected arrays of two and three dimensions.

We also introduce the various statistics measured to analyze the performance of parallel logic programs. A few Encore Multimax measurements are presented to sketch simple program characteristics. The Multimax measurements should not be given too much weight, because the machine used is an old version that is limited (even on few numbers of PEs) by hardware factors that have since been improved. Nevertheless, these preliminary results help our intuition about later, more complex programs.

3.1 Appending

Append (also called concatenate) is *the* classic Prolog example because it is easy to type into vendor systems on display at logic programming conferences *and* it manages to do something meaningful (append one list to another in the most commonly used determinate mode of execution). The Prolog **append** procedure, shown below, consists of two clauses.

```
append([], L, L).
append([X|L1], L2, [X|L3]) :- append(L1, L2, L3).
```

The first clause states that appending any list to the empty list results in the original list. The second clause states that appending a list L2 to a list with head X and tail L1 results in a list with head X and tail L3 if list L3 is the result of appending L2 to L1. When executed determinately, e.g.,

```
?- append([1,2,3],[4,5],A).
A = [1,2,3,4,5]
```

the pattern of reductions is quite easy to follow. The second clause is repeatedly invoked, each time tail-recursing. For each invocation of the second clause, the head of the first argument list is extracted and used to build a new list element for the third argument, the result list. When the first list is used up, i.e., the first argument is the empty list [], then the first clause matches. The first clause attaches the second argument list at the end of the result. The time complexity is $O(N)$ where N is the length of the first list.

The above explanation comprises a procedural semantics for append when its first two arguments are bound inputs. The append procedure can also be "run in the reverse direction," e.g.,

```
?- append(L1, L2, [1,2,3]).
```

In this case, the procedural semantics are more difficult to state clearly. Therein lies one of the great advantages of Prolog — that the declarative semantics allow a clean reading of program behavior independent of the "direction" or mode of execution. In the reverse direction, append will produce four answers:

```
L1 = [],       L2 = [1,2,3]
L1 = [1],      L2 = [2,3]
L1 = [1,2],    L2 = [3]
L1 = [1,2,3],  L2 = []
```

The order of the answers is fixed by the execution semantics of Prolog, i.e., clauses are selected in their textual order. All solutions can be collected with a findall/3, for instance, preserving that order.

The informal specification of append is given in Figure 3.1, along with some other procedures we will soon define. Throughout this book, such specifications are given to clarify the intended meanings of programs. In general, a procedure is characterized by:

- the modes and types of the procedure's arguments.

- the relation that the procedure satisfies.

- any preconditions that the arguments must satisfy before initial invocation of the procedure. Self-recursive calls to the procedure do not satisfy these conditions.

- any postconditions or invariants that the arguments satisfy after execution of the procedure.

Figure 3.1
Informal Specification of Prolog Append, Reverse, and Qsort

<u>Procedure</u>: `append(L1, L2, L3)`
    ? L1: list   ? L2: list   ? L3: list

<u>Relation</u>: List L3 is list L1 concatenated to list L2.

<u>Procedure</u>: `nrev(L1, L2)`
    ? L1: list   ? L2: list

<u>Relation</u>: List L2 is the reverse of list L1.

<u>Procedure</u>: `rev(L1, L2, L3)`
    ? L1: list   ? L2: list   ? L3: list

<u>Relation</u>: List L3 is the reverse of list L1, appended to list L2.

<u>Procedure</u>: `qsort(In, Out)`
    + In: list of numbers   − Out: D-list of numbers

<u>Relation</u>: Out is a D-list X-Y where list X holds the sorted values of In.

<u>Procedure</u>: `split(In, Pivot, Out1, Out2)`
    + In: list of numbers   − Out1: list of numbers
    + Pivot: number   − Out2: list of numbers

<u>Relation</u>: Out1 holds all values from In less than or equal to Pivot and Out2
holds all values from In greater than Pivot.

This characterization is *very* informal, especially concerning argument types. Abstract types are introduced without formal definition. For example, the type **solution** may be equated with the type "list of integers." If the meaning is not immediately obvious from the procedure relation, then the abstract types are made explicit. In most cases, "a list of integers" means "a *ground* list of integers." However, in certain cases it may mean "a list of unbound variables that *will be* bound to integers," because the logical variable subsumes all types. This distinction cannot be indicated by the argument mode, since both lists are '+' input mode, i.e., the argument is instantiated to a list. Therefore the latter distinction is made explicit in the rare cases where it is used.

The FGHC version of determinate **append**, shown below,

```
append([], L1, L2) :- L1 = L2.
append([X|L1], L2, L4) :- L4 = [X|L3], append(L1, L2, L3).
```

is quite similar to the Prolog version with the following important distinctions. Since output unification is not permitted in the head (i.e., *passive part*), the first clause must perform the output unification explicitly in the body, i.e., in the *active part*. A similar action is performed in the second clause.[1]

Note that no guards appear, i.e., they are assumed to be trivially true. There is no ambiguity when selecting between the two clauses because the first argument, if bound, will unify with only one of the clauses. We call such clauses *mutually exclusive*. In this particular case, for both Prolog and FGHC, a sophisticated architecture and compiler should implement indexing, wherein a simple tag check is made to determine which of the two clauses to select (see Appendix A).

Consider writing append(+,-) in FGHC to simulate append(-,-,+) in Prolog, for instance:

```
?- append([1,2,3], S).
   S = [([],[1,2,3]), ([1],[2,3]), ([1,2],[3]), ([1,2,3],[])]
```

Here the second argument of **append/2** is an output stream containing pairs of lists that, when appended, form the input list.

```
append(L, S) :- ap(L, [], S).

ap([], P, S) :- S=[(P,[])].
ap([E|Es], P, S) :-
    S = [(P,[E|Es])|S1],
    append(P, [E], P1),
    ap(Es, P1, S1).
```

The second argument of **ap/3** is often called an accumulator. The accumulator is initialized to [] and holds the first append list. In each recursion, the accumulator P is extended by the head E of the second append list to form P1. Thus as the accumulator grows, the second append list shrinks. Eventually the loop terminates and the last pair is sent down the output stream. The informal specification of the program is given in Figure 3.2.

One can see that the "reverse direction" (multiple-solution) FGHC program is significantly more complex than the "forward direction" (single-solution) FGHC program. In Prolog both programs are identical. An interesting alternative to writing multiple-solution programs in FGHC, or in any committed-choice language

---

[1]In some committed-choice languages, *argument modes* can be declared for a procedure, thus obviating the need to move output unification into the body. For example we may declare ":- mode append(+,-)," where '+' is input mode and '-' is output mode. Then we can use the same **append** definition as in Prolog.

Figure 3.2
Informal Specification of FGHC Append

Procedure: `append(L, S)`
    + L: list   − S: stream

Relation: S contains all pairs of lists that when appended form L.

Procedure: `ap(L1, L2, S)`
    + L1: list   + L2: list   −S: stream

Relation: S contains all pairs of lists that when appended form the concatenation of L2 followed by L1.

Preconditions: Initially L2 is empty.

---

for that matter, is to automatically translate Prolog programs into these languages. Consider the advantages: programming is simplified and the original Prolog programs, once translated, will execute in AND parallel. We discuss translation in detail in Section 5.2.2.

3.2 Reversing

Naive reverse is another classic Prolog example. In fact, it has unfortunately gained status as a classic Prolog *benchmark* with which to measure execution performance. Like **append**, it is terse yet performs a concrete function, that of reversing a list. Naive reverse is a bad (if not terrible) benchmark, however, because it exhibits no characteristics of typical Prolog programs [128]. It has also misled many architecture and system designers into thinking that an efficient implementation of naive reverse was equivalent, to the first order, to an efficient implementation of Prolog. This is not true, for the primary reason that naive reverse does no backtracking of any kind, neither shallow nor deep. Real Prolog programs typically perform backtracking of both kinds.

The naive reverse Prolog program, **nrev**, uses **append**.

```
nrev([], []).
nrev([X|L0], L2) :-
    nrev(L0, L1),
    append(L1, [X], L2).
```

The first clause states that the reverse of the empty list is the empty list. The second clause states that the reverse of a list with head X and tail L0 is a list L2, if

the reverse of L0 is a list L1 and L2 is the concatenation of a list L1 with element X.
Note that the declarativity of Prolog shines through in this particular case — if the
goals in the second clause are reversed, the procedure still runs correctly (although
the procedural semantics in this case are complex).

The FGHC version of nrev(+,-) below is quite similar to the Prolog version; the
only difference is the explicit output unification in the first clause.

```
nrev([], X) :- X = [].
nrev([X|L0], L2) :-
    nrev(L0, L1),
    append(L1, [X], L2).
```

It is easy to see why this algorithm is naive. To reverse a list of length N, append
is called N times from nrev, appending lists varying in size from 0 to $N-1$. Thus
the complexity order is $O(N^2)$. This can be reduced to linear complexity by *fusing*
append into nrev with the help of an additional argument. We can write this code
in both Prolog and FGHC as follows:

```
rev(X,Y)  :-  rev(X,[],Y).
rev([],    Y,Z) :- Z=Y.
rev([A|X],Y,Z) :- rev(X,[A|Y],Z).
```

The second argument of rev/3 is a partial solution or accumulator, initialized to
[]. The elements of the input list are peeled off, one by one, and deposited in the
accumulator. When the input list has been emptied, the accumulator is returned
as the final solution, by binding it to the last argument of rev/3. The astute
reader will have discovered the declarative semantics for rev(L1,L2,L3): "L3 is
the reversed list of L1, appended to L2!"

As a final note, the fused algorithm presented has no parallelism. However, the
naive algorithm potentially has exploitable stream-AND parallelism! This parallelism stems from spawning multiple append processes. Although the appends are
serialized by synchronization on their first arguments, stream-AND communication
can allow a subsequent append to begin computing as soon as the previous append
starts to produce an answer incrementally. Exploiting this parallelism efficiently
is difficult, because suspensions will be quite frequent possibly outweighing the
benefit of parallel computation. In any case, even with linear speedup, the naive
algorithm cannot win asymptotically (i.e., for arbitrarily large lists) against the
linear-complexity algorithm.

3.3 Sorting

The QuickSort algorithm is a famous programming example in every language. In Prolog, QuickSort is an interesting example of the use of *difference lists* and *cut*. The Prolog version of QuickSort is shown below.

```
sort(In,Out) :- qsort(In,Out-[]).

qsort([],R-R).
qsort([X|L],R0-R) :-
    split(L,X,L1,L2),
    qsort(L1,R0-[X|R1]),
    qsort(L2,R1-R).

split([],_,[],[]).
split([X|Xs],A,S,[X|L]) :- X>A,  split(Xs,A,S,L).
split([X|Xs],A,[X|S],L) :- X=<A, split(Xs,A,S,L).
```

The top-level `sort` has input and output arguments for the unsorted and sorted lists. The auxiliary procedure `qsort` initializes the output in the form of a difference list (D-list), `Out-[]`.

In the top-level call, the D-list is closed by instantiating the tail to `[]`. The first clause of `qsort` can be read declaratively as "the sorted empty list is the empty D-list." An empty D-list is represented by two identical variables, i.e., the D-list has no contents. The D-lists are represented with the `-/2` structure, e.g., `X-Y`. In this case, an empty D-list is `R-R`. Review Section 2.1.5 for more details about D-lists.

The second clause of `qsort` has three body goals. The first, `split`, splits the tail of the input list, L, into two lists, L1 and L2. The split is performed on the pivot, X, taken from the head of the input list. The second and third clauses, `qsort`, recursively sort the two split lists. Procedure `qsort` creates the sorted answer in the form of a D-list. This allows the two sub-answers to be concatenated at *no cost*. In addition, it allows the pivot X to be inserted between the combined sub-answers.

Perhaps an easier way to view the second clause of `qsort` is as follows:

```
qsort([X|L],Out) :-
    split(L,X,L1,L2),
    qsort(L1,D1),
    qsort(L2,D2),
    dappend(D1,[X|T]-T,D3),
    dappend(D3,D2,Out).
```

where the two explicit `dappend` goals (Section 2.1.5) concatenate the results from the recursive calls.

There is no OR-parallelism in QuickSort because the algorithm is determinate.
Although the `split/4` procedure has three clauses, they are mutually exclusive, i.e.,
they produce only one solution. One of the three can be selected either through
indexing or through immediate arithmetic comparison. It is impossible to execute
efficiently, in parallel, both comparisons (essentially guards) in the second and third
clauses. Reasonable OR-parallel implementations perform no parallel execution for
this program.

Given that we choose to execute `split/4` sequentially, a slightly more optimized
version of the code uses cut:

```
split([],_,[],[]).
split([X|Xs],A,S,[X|L]) :- X>A, !, split(Xs,A,S,L).
split([X|Xs],A,[X|S],L) :-         split(Xs,A,S,L).
```

The cut is used in this instance as both a time and a space optimization. The
comparison can be removed from the third clause, saving time, because the cut
guarantees that if `X>A` then the third clause will not be executed, i.e., the third
clause will only be executed if `X=<A`. Space is saved if the second clause is selected,
because the cut removes the choicepoint associated with `split/4`.

In any case, QuickSort contains AND parallelism. The second and third recursive
goals of `qsort` are independent, as can be seen most easily in the previous version
with explicit `dappend` goals. Even in the original program, although the two goals
share variable R1, R1 will be bound by the third goal and never read by the second goal. Potentially the goals can execute quite nicely in parallel. Independent
AND-parallel Prolog exploits such parallelism where goals can be shown to make
independent bindings. To exploit this type of parallelism, either programmer annotation of independent goals or extensive compiler analysis is required. Another
alternative is to implement the program in a stream AND-parallel language, as
shown next.

The FGHC version of QuickSort directly corresponds to the Prolog version, with
the necessary modifications to move output unification from the head to the body.

```
sort(In, Out) :- qsort(In,Out-[]).

qsort([],R-A) :- R=A.
qsort([X|L],R0-R) :-
    split(L,X,L1,L2),
    qsort(L1,R0-[X|R1]),
    qsort(L2,R1-R).

split([]    ,_,S,L) :- S=[], L=[].
split([X|Xs],A,S,L) :- A>X  | L=[X|L1], split(Xs,A,S,L1).
split([X|Xs],A,S,L) :- A=<X | S=[X|S1], split(Xs,A,S1,L).
```

In addition, the second and third clauses of split/4 *both* have arithmetic comparisons in their guards, because FGHC theoretically allows all clause head/guards to be attempted in parallel. As discussed in the previous chapter, we can replace the arithmetic comparison in the last clause with otherwise.

```
split([]     ,_,S,L) :- S=[], L=[].
split([X|Xs],A,S,L) :- A>X  | L=[X|L1], split(Xs,A,S,L1).
split([X|Xs],A,S,L) :- otherwise | S=[X|S1], split(Xs,A,S1,L).
```

The semantics of otherwise is that, if all clauses preceding the clause containing the otherwise fail, then the otherwise will succeed. If no clause preceding the clause containing the otherwise succeeds and some clause(s) suspend, then the procedure suspends (i.e., it is as if the otherwise guard and all succeeding guards fail).

The interesting thing about FGHC QuickSort is that it is truly parallel, i.e., speedups can be obtained with ease. The reason is that FGHC is AND-parallel, so that the body goals in the second clause of qsort/2 can run in parallel. The split/4 process feeds the streams L1 and L2 to the two children qsort/2 processes. This use of stream-AND parallelism allows the sorting of sublists that have not yet been completed. Since this process structure is applied recursively, the list to be sorted naturally expands into a large process tree of incomplete streams of sublists.

On a multiprocessor with a limited number of PEs, the additional parallelism inherent in the tree eventually is not exploited when entire subtrees of processes are executed on a single PE. However, if the implementation executes in a depth-first manner, then this phase of "saturation" is efficiently managed in terms of memory usage and speed. In other words, when qsort/3 is executing within a single PE because all other PEs are busy, the body goals are reduced depth first. First split/4 is completely reduced, then the first qsort/3, and then the second qsort/3. Thus there are no suspensions.

An efficiency problem occurs when the scheduler cannot exploit the hierarchical granularity inherent in the QuickSort process structure. If goals near the leaves of the process tree are spawned on different PEs, then the overhead of parallel goal management can overtake the advantage of parallel execution. Table 3.1 shows the execution time of the FGHC QuickSort program sorting a list of 800 pseudo-random integers (with period of 200).[2] Figure 3.3 is a utilization (efficiency) vs. time plot illustrating the same data. Throughout the book we plot utilization vs. time to compare the base and parallelization overheads of alternative systems.

---

[2]OR-parallel Prolog is not compared in this table because there is no exploitable OR-parallelism in QuickSort.

PEs	Random			Degenerate		
	seconds	speedup	efficiency	seconds	speedup	efficiency
1	8.4	1.0	1.00	262.6	1.0	1.00
2	4.5	1.9	0.94	139.9	1.9	0.94
3	3.4	2.5	0.82	149.2	1.8	0.59
4	2.6	3.2	0.81	147.5	1.8	0.45

Table 3.1
Quick-Sorting Lists of 800 Elements in FGHC on Multimax (Panda)

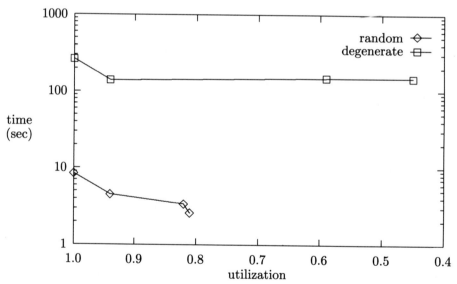

Figure 3.3
Quick-Sorting Lists of 800 Elements in FGHC on Multimax (Panda)

> The *naive speedup* of a program for N PEs is defined as the total execution time of the program on one PE divided by the total execution time of the same program on N PEs. The *real speedup* of a given program for N PEs is the execution time of the fastest sequential program (in the same language) on a single PE divided by the execution time of the given program on N PEs. The *efficiency* of a program for N PEs is defined as the speedup divided by N.

The statistics in Table 3.1 and Figure 3.3 show the effect of inefficient spawning near the leaves — efficiency is limited to about 80% on three or more PEs. Other causes of this efficiency peak are the limited theoretical parallelism in the random data and the limited bus bandwidth on Multimax.

Another way to view the effects of inefficient spawning near the leaves and lack of theoretical parallelism is to sort a degenerate list. In a list that is precisely in reverse order, each pivot chosen will split the list into grossly unequal portions. Table 3.1 also shows the execution time of the FGHC QuickSort program sorting a reverse-ordered list of 800 integers. Here the granularity is abysmal and the efficiency continues to decline with increasing numbers of PEs.

3.4   Stacking and Queueing

Stacks and queues are handy abstract data types. The simple procedures needed to implement these objects illustrate the ease and elegance of data abstraction in Prolog and FGHC. The languages differ in that FGHC spawns a perpetual process to act as the object manager. Clients communicate with the manager by sending messages on a stream. These messages are incomplete, i.e., they contain one or more unbound variables wherein the manager binds the result. Prolog has no perpetual processes and so all permanent state information must be passed back and forth between the client and manager. Consider a FILO (First In Last Out) stack manager in Prolog:

```
stackEmpty([]).

stackOp([],empty,[]).
stackOp(Ss,X,[X|Ss]).
```

The client executes three types of commands. Procedure `stackEmpty(S)` is true if stack `S` is empty. Procedure `stackOp(+In,+X,-Out)` returns a new stack `Out` which is the old stack `In` with element `X` pushed onto the top. Procedure `stackOp(-Out,`

Figure 3.4
Informal Specification of Prolog Stacks and Queues

Procedure: `stackEmpty(S)`
    ? S: list

Relation: Stack S is empty.

Procedure: `stackOp(S0, X, S1)`
    ? S0: list   ? X: atom   ? S1: list

Relation: Element X is the top, and S0 is the remainder, of stack S1. However, if S1 is empty then S0 is also empty and X is bound to `empty`.

Procedure: `queueEmpty(Q)`
    ? Q: difference list

Relation: Q is an empty queue.

Procedure: `queuePush(Qin, X, Qout)`
    +`Qin`: difference list   +X: atom   −Qout: difference list

Relation: X is the tail element, and `Qin` is the preceeding elements, of `Qout`.

Procedure: `queuePop(Qin, X, Qout)`
    +`Qin`: difference list   +X: atom   −Qout: difference list

Relation: X is the head and `Qout` is the remainder, of queue `Qin`. If `Qin` is empty then X is the unbound head of `Qout`.

-X, +In) returns a new stack Out which is the old stack In with its top element X removed. The `empty` keyword is reserved for the error condition when trying to pop an empty stack.

The informal specification of stacks and queues (to be described next) are given in Figure 3.4. An example of stack management follows:

```
?- stackEmpty(S0),stackOp(S0,1,S1),stackOp(S1,2,S2),
   stackOp(S3,A,S2),stackOp(S4,B,S3),stackOp(S5,C,S4).

   S0 = []
   S1 = [1]
   S2 = [2,1]        A = 2
   S3 = [1]          B = 1
   S4 = []           C = empty
   S5 = []
```

In FGHC we spawn a stack manager communicating with a client via a stream:

```
?- stack(Ms),client(Ms).
```

The manager initializes the stack and then calls stack/2. Here the client's messages are serviced in the obvious manner.

```
stack(Ms) :- stack(Ms,[]).

stack([],_).
stack([push(X)|Ms],Ss) :- stack(Ms,[X|Ss]).
stack([pop(X)|Ms],[]) :- X=empty, stack(Ms,[]).
stack([pop(X)|Ms],[S|Ss]) :- X=S, stack(Ms,Ss).
```

An example follows:

```
?- stack(Ms), Ms = [push(1),push(2),pop(A),pop(B),pop(C)].

    A = 2        B = 1        C = empty
```

As a further example of these programming styles, a FIFO (First In First Out) queue manager is given below. Both the Prolog version,

```
queueEmpty(X-X).
queuePush(Q0-[X|Q1],X,Q0-Q1).
queuePop([X|Q0]-Q1,X,Q0-Q1).
```

and the FGHC version,

```
queue(Ms) :- queue(Ms,Q-Q).

queue([],_).
queue([push(X)|Ms],Q0-Q1) :- Q1=[X|Q2], queue(Ms,Q0-Q2).
queue([pop(X)|Ms],[Y|Q0]-Q1) :- X=Y, queue(Ms,Q0-Q1).
queue([pop(X)|Ms],Q) :- otherwise | X=empty, queue(Ms,Q).
```

use D-lists to implement the queue. The Prolog queue manager can service a pop request even if the queue is empty, whereas the FGHC manager does not. For example, consider the Prolog query:

```
?- queueEmpty(Q0),queuePush(Q0,1,Q1),queuePush(Q1,2,Q2),
   queuePop(Q2,A,Q3),queuePop(Q3,B,Q4),queuePop(Q4,C,Q5),
   queuePush(Q5,3,Q6).

Q0 = [1,2,3|X]-[1,2,3|X]
Q1 = [1,2,3|X]-[2,3|X]
Q2 = [1,2,3|X]-[3|X]
Q3 = [2,3|X]-[3|X]              A = 1
Q4 = [3|X]-[3|X]               B = 2
Q5 = X-[3|X]
Q6 = X-X                        C = 3
```

The third pop is satisfied by creating an unbound logical variable in the queue. The subsequent push binds this slot instead of creating another. Thus the client can borrow against the queue.

3.5 Filtering

The Sieve of Eratosthenes [14] is an ancient algorithm for generating prime numbers. Although the algorithm is rather inefficient, it is elegant, and is therefore used to teach computer programming. The algorithm is especially suited to illustrate stream-AND parallelism, as first done by Ueda in his classic paper [137]. There is no OR-parallelism in the algorithm; however, the Prolog version is used as an introduction to the FGHC version.

Prolog Version

A Prolog prime-number generator implementing the Sieve of Eratosthenes is shown below. The top-level procedure, `prime(Limit,Ps)`, produces all primes greater than one and less than `Limit` in the list `Ps`. The procedure first creates a list of integers, `Is`, and then sifts `Is` with the Sieve of Eratosthenes. Each sift is done by removing the head of the integer list (the pivot), and filtering the tail of the list with that head integer. The filter checks each successive element and, if it is a multiple of the pivot P, then it is discarded. If the element is *not* a multiple, then it is retained in the list. Successive sifts are conducted until no pivots remain. By this method, each pivot encountered is prime, and after each sift all factors of that prime are removed.

```
prime(Limit,Ps) :-
    gen(2,Limit,Is),
    sift(Is,Ps).

gen(N,Max,[N|Ns]) :- N =< Max, !, N1 is N+1, gen(N1,Max,Ns).
gen(_,_,[]).

sift([],[]).
sift([P|Ns],[P|Ps]) :-
    filter(Ns,P,Ns1),
    sift(Ns1,Ps).

filter([],P,[]).
filter([N|Ns],P,Out) :- 0 is N mod P,!,
    filter(Ns,P,Out).
filter([N|Ns],P,[N|Out]) :-
    filter(Ns,P,Out).
```

Figure 3.5
Informal Specification of Prolog Primes

    <u>Procedure</u>: `prime(N, Ps)`
       + N: integer $(N > 1)$ $-$ Ps: list of primes

    <u>Relation</u>: `Ps` contains sorted primes from 2 to maximum prime less than `N`.
       If $N < 2$ then `Ps` is empty.

    <u>Procedure</u>: `gen(N, Max, Ns)`
       + N: integer   + Max: integer $-$ Ns: list of integers

    <u>Relation</u>: List `Ns` is an ordered list of consecutive integers from `N` to `Max`. If
       $N > Max$ then `Ns` is empty.

    <u>Procedure</u>: `sift(In, Out)`
       + In: list of integers $-$ Out: list of primes

    <u>Relation</u>: `Out` contains those values of `In` that are prime.

    <u>Postconditions</u>: The values in `Out` are in the same order as `In`.

    <u>Procedure</u>: `filter(In, Prime, Out)`
       + In: list of integers $-$ Out: list of primes
       + Prime: prime

    <u>Relation</u>: `Out` contains those values of `In` that are not multiples of `Prime`.

    <u>Postconditions</u>: The values in `Out` are in the same order as `In`.

The informal specification of the program is given in Figure 3.5.

The program has no OR-parallelism because the algorithm is completely determinate. The selection of `filter` clauses causes shallow backtracking at worst, when selecting between the second and third clauses. Such selection cannot efficiently exploit OR-parallelism. In fact, there is no *independent* AND-parallelism either. The second clause of `sift/2` has two body goals that *seem* likely candidates for AND-in-OR parallelism (later discussed in Chapter 11), or some other form of independent AND-parallelism, like RAP [62]. However, the two goals are dependent, communicating via variable `Ns1`. Notice `Ns1` is "more" dependent than `R1` in the Quicksort Prolog program in Section 3.3. Variable `Ns1` is a list produced by one goal for consumption by the other goal. This is a good example of a *very sequential* algorithm in strictly independent-AND and OR parallel languages.

FGHC Version: Pipelined Filters

The FGHC program is a direct translation of the Prolog version, with the necessary modifications to avoid output unification in the head, etc. When specified in a committed-choice language such as FGHC, dependent stream-AND parallelism can be exploited!

```
prime(Limit,Ps) :-
    gen(2,Limit,Is),
    sift(Is,Ps).

gen(N,Max,Ns) :- N =< Max | N1 is N+1, Ns=[N|Ns1], gen(N1,Max,Ns1).
gen(N,Max,Ns) :- N > Max | Ns=[].

sift([],Ps) :- Ps=[].
sift([P|Ns],Ps) :-
    Ps=[P|Ps1],
    filter(Ns,P,Ns1),
    sift(Ns1,Ps1).

filter([],_,Out) :- Out=[].
filter([N|Ns],P,Out) :- N mod P =:= 0 |
    filter(Ns,P,Out).
filter([N|Ns],P,Out) :- otherwise |
    Out=[N|Out1],
    filter(Ns,P,Out1).
```

Stream-AND parallelism is exploited by the generator, **gen**, sending a stream of integers to the sifter, **sift**. Each **sift** spawns a **filter** to do its work, then spawns another **sift** for the next level of filtering. The stream of integers can therefore pass from one level of filtering to the next, with fewer and fewer surviving deeper levels of filtering. Each **sift** process represents the finding of one prime, which it dutifully passes along to the output stream, **Ps**. Communication between the filters is controlled by synchronization of the streams. This synchronization is performed by suspending on unbound input variables, i.e., when a stream from one filter to the next "runs dry," the second filter suspends because it attempts to make an output unification in the head. For example, suspension occurs when the first argument, **X**, of **filter** is unbound, and output unification is attempted in the first clause (**X=[]**) or the second and third clauses (**X=[N|Ns]**).

Table 3.2 shows the timing results for calculating 1229 primes, on Multimax. Speedup is poor because the pipeline of filters limits parallelism. Algorithms with much greater parallelism exist for this problem. In general, it is a bad idea to constrain the process structure in the form of a single pipeline, although many problems are naturally mapped onto pipelines (as we shall see in later chapters).

PEs	seconds	speedup	efficiency
1	773.5	1.0	1.00
2	393.0	2.0	0.99
4	331.2	2.3	0.59
8	220.4	3.5	0.44

Table 3.2
Filtering 1229 Primes From 1 to 10,000 in FGHC on Multimax (Panda)

3.6 Summary

In this chapter we introduced Prolog and FGHC through a series of simple list-manipulation programs. We do not place much importance on gaining speedups on such small programs. However, it is important to note, as these examples illustrated, that the parallel execution characteristics of OR-parallel Prolog and FGHC are vastly different. In the next chapter, additional small programs are discussed, introducing the more sophisticated issues of the granularity of parallel tasks, eager vs. lazy computation, garbage production, buffered communication, and the nondeterministic merging of streams.

Exercises

Exercise 11 Write Prolog and FGHC procedures to determine if an input element is a member of a given list.

Exercise 12 Write an FGHC program for append(-,+,-). First we suggest you test this mode of execution in Prolog to determine the correct behavior. The program should generate an infinite stream of solutions.

Exercise 13 Write an FGHC program for append(-,-,+) (collecting all solutions) with $O(N)$ time complexity where N is the length of the input list. If you cannot achieve this complexity, then give an argument as to why it is theoretically impossible (in FGHC).

Exercise 14 Write a Prolog procedure del(X,L1,L2) to delete the first occurrence of an element X from a list L1 to produce a list L2. If the element is not a member of L1, then the procedure should fail. Be sure that your procedure can execute in both modes (+,+,-) and (-,+,-).

Exercise 15 Write FGHC procedures for list deletion in both modes mentioned in the previous exercise.

Exercise 16 Write Prolog and FGHC procedures to delete all occurrences (if any) of an element from a list.

Exercise 17 Write Prolog and FGHC procedures to delete all occurrences (if any) of all members of one list from another list.

Exercise 18 Write Prolog and FGHC procedures to take the intersection and difference of two lists.

Exercise 19 What does the following FGHC program compute?

```
f([C|Cs],Out) :- Out=[C|Os], f(Cs,C,Os).

f([],_,S) :- S=[].
f([C|Cs],C,S) :- f(Cs,C,S).
f([C|Cs],X,SO) :- C\=X |
    SO = [C|S1],
    f(Cs,X,T),
    f(T,C,S1).
```

Rewrite the program to perform the same computation in a more efficient manner.

Exercise 20 Write a queue manager in FGHC that can service a pop request even if the queue is empty, similar to the Prolog procedure given in Section 3.4.

Exercise 21 Implement an assortment of list-sorting algorithms in Prolog and FGHC. Try bubble sort, insertion sort, and merge sort.

Exercise 22 Write Prolog and FGHC programs that calculate the total size of a layered stream. Recall from Section 2.2.4 that a layered stream is either the special atom **begin** or a (possibly empty) list of elements H*Ts where Ts is the layered stream of all tails of head H. To optimize space we usually represent H*Ts as [H|Ts]. For example:

```
[[1],[2,[4,[1,[3|begin]]]],[3,[1,[4,[2|begin]]]],[4]]
```

is a layered stream wherein the data are integers. The total size of this structure, illustrated in Figure 3.6, is 40 cells, assuming that integers, list pointers, and atoms each occupy a single cell.

Exercise 23 Derive an analytical expression for the execution-time complexity of converting a layered stream into a list with the FGHC procedure fromLStoL/2 given in Section 2.2.4. Sometimes the overhead of conversion is a significant portion of total program execution time. Can you write a converter that has lower complexity order?

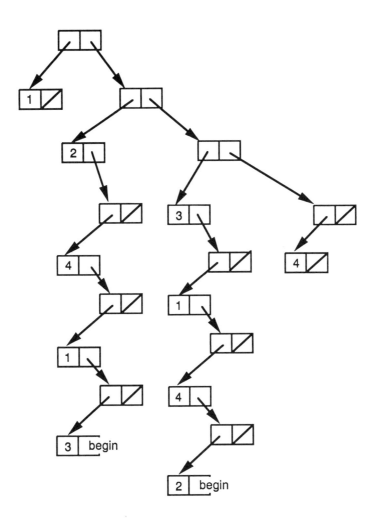

Figure 3.6
Storage Cells Implementing a Layered Stream

4 More Small Programs

In this chapter we shall use small programs to introduce more advanced topics concerning execution performance, garbage collection, and nondeterminism. The programs include calculating all combinations of a set of elements, with and without replacement, merging and splitting streams, and calculating the cross product of two streams. The issues of controlling the granularity of tasks, controlling garbage production (with buffers), controlling resource starvation by lazy computation, and guaranteeing fairness of goal scheduling are discussed. Correct logic programs are not necessarily fast or memory-efficient. When executed by an unfair or eager scheduler, correct programs may be grossly inefficient, to the point of effectively not terminating. We introduce programming methods to avoid or assuage some of these problems.

4.1 Permuting and Combining

4.1.1 Permuting in OR-Parallel Prolog

The classic permutation program, perm(L,P), nondeterminately produces all permutations P of list L. A permutation P is a combination choosing from the set of all members of L without replacement. To collect all permutations, one can use findall, for example:

```
?- findall(X,perm([1,2,3],X),L).
   L = [[1,2,3],[2,1,3],[1,3,2],[2,3,1],[3,1,2],[3,2,1]]
```

The program's declarative semantics are as follows. The permutation of a list [H|T], is a list [A|P], where an element A is nondeterminately deleted (selected) from the input list, and list P is the permutation of the resulting list L.

```
perm([],[]).
perm([H|T],[A|P]) :- del(A,[H|T],L), perm(L,P).

:- parallel del/3.

del(X,[X|Y],Y).
del(X,[Y|Z],[Y|W]) :- del(X,Z,W).
```

Note that this version of del/3 is nondeterminate and declared **parallel**. In nondeterminate mode del(-,+,-) deletion is equivalent to selection. For example:

```
?- del(X,[1,2,3],Y).
   X = 1   Y = [2,3]
   X = 2   Y = [1,3]
   X = 3   Y = [1,2]
```

Figure 4.1
Informal Specification of Prolog Permute

    Procedure: del(X, L1, L2)
        ? X: atom   ? L1: list   ? L2: list

    Relation: X is an element of L1. L2 holds the remaining elements of L1.

    Postconditions: The values in L1 are in the same order as in L2.

    Procedure: perm(L1, L2)
        ? L1: list   ? L2: list

    Relation: List L1 and L2 are permutations of each other.

---

where X is a selected element from the input list. The informal specification of the
program is given in Figure 4.1.

It often helps to annotate the procedure definition with modes for better understanding:

```
            +   -
     perm([],[]).
            +        -            -   +   -        + -
     perm([H|T],[A|P]) :- del(A,[H|T],L), perm(L,P).
```

In this annotation a '−' output argument of one body goal will both feed '+' input
arguments of other body goals and '−' output arguments of the procedure head.
For example, L is produced by del and consumed by perm. List P is produced by
perm for export in the output argument of the procedure.

Creating a permutation involves selection of elements *with no replacement* from
the original list. The number of permutations of n items is $n!$ of course. The
OR-tree of a permutation of a 4-element list is sketched in Figure 4.2. The entire
OR-tree (with 24 solutions) is not illustrated, but subtrees of equal granularity
are indicated by similarly shaded areas. Table 4.1 shows the timing results for
collecting all 5040 permutations of a 7-element list, on the Symmetry. The problem
has considerable parallelism that can be exploited in OR-parallel Prolog. Still, the
OR-tree is only of height seven, so that scheduling many PEs near the leaves is
inefficient. The rapid decrease in efficiency on four and eight PEs confirms this.

4.1.2 Combining in FGHC: Eager Evaluation

For variety, the FGHC program presented here calculates not permutations, but
rather combinations *with replacement*. Both combinations and permutations play

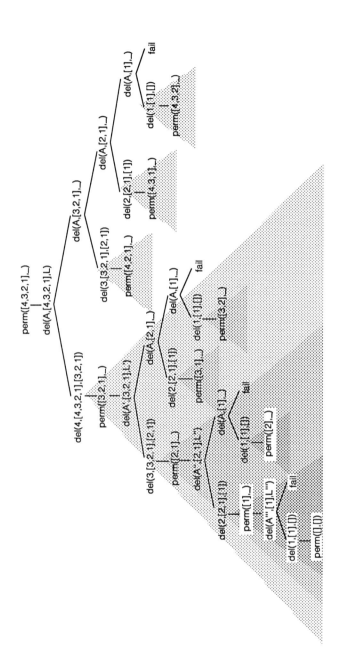

Figure 4.2
OR-Tree of the Permutation of a List $[1, 2, 3, 4]$

PEs	seconds	speedup	efficiency
1	11.2	1.0	1.00
2	7.0	1.6	0.80
4	4.9	2.3	0.58
8	3.7	3.0	0.38

Table 4.1
Calculating 5040 Permutations of 7-Element List in OR-Prolog on Symmetry
(Aurora Foxtrot)

similar roles as generators in generate & test algorithms. Moreover, generating combinations incrementally in a pipeline is similar to the computation in layered-streams algorithms, discussed in great detail in later chapters.

Procedure `combo(L,N,A)` produces a list `A` of all unique lists of length `N` consisting of elements selected from list `L`. For example:

```
?- combo([a,b],3,A).
   A = [[a,a,a],[a,a,b],[a,b,a],[a,b,b],
        [b,a,a],[b,a,b],[b,b,a],[b,b,b]]
```

This program spawns `N` **add** processes that form a *pipeline* for producing combinations. Each **add** process accepts partial combinations on its input stream and *expands* those partial combinations. A new list is created for each element of input list `L`, formed by prepending that element to a partial combination. Thus at each stage of the pipeline, every input combination is expanded into m output combinations, where m is the length of list `L`.

```
combo(L,N,Out) :- combo(N,[[]],L,Out).

combo(0,In,_,Out) :- Out=In.
combo(N,In,L,Out) :- N>0 |
    N1 is N-1,
    add(In,L,T),
    combo(N1,T,L,Out).

add([],_,S)  :- S=[].
add([I|Is],L,S0) :-
    combo1(L,I,S0-S1),
    add(Is,L,S1).

combo1([],_,O1-O2)  :- O1=O2.
combo1([C|Cs],I,O1-O3) :-
    O1 = [[C|I]|O2],
    combo1(Cs,I,O2-O3).
```

The informal specification of the program is given in Figure 4.3.

<u>Procedure</u>: combo(L, N, Out)
  + L: list   − Out: list of combinations
  + N: integer

<u>Relation</u>: Out contains all combinations of length N of elements from L. A combination is a list of elements. If $N < 1$ then Out is a list of the empty list.

<u>Procedure</u>: combo(N, In, L, Out)
  + N: integer   + L: list
  + In: list of combinations   − Out: list of combinations

<u>Relation</u>: Out contains expanded combinations from In. The combinations are expanded by the values in L, taken N times. If $N < 1$ then Out=In.

<u>Postconditions</u>: For a list L of k elements, each combination from In expands into k^N new combinations.

<u>Procedure</u>: add(In, L, Out)
  + In: list of combinations   − Out: list of combinations
  + L: list

<u>Relation</u>: Out contains expanded combinations from In. The combinations are expanded by the values in L, taken once.

<u>Postconditions</u>: For a list L of k elements, each combination from In expands into k new combinations.

<u>Procedure</u>: combo1(L, C, Out)
  + L: list   − Out: difference list of combinations
  + C: combination

<u>Relation</u>: Out contains expanded combinations of C. The combinations are expanded by the values in L, taken once.

<u>Postconditions</u>: For a list L of k elements, combination C expands into k new combinations. The new elements are added to the head of C.

Figure 4.3
Informal Specification of FGHC Combinations

PEs	seconds	speedup	efficiency
1	60.0	1.0	1.00
2	33.7	1.8	0.89
3	24.8	2.4	0.81
4	20.6	2.9	0.73

Table 4.2
Calculating 46,656 Combinations of a 6-Element List in FGHC on Multimax
(Panda)

Table 4.2 shows the timing results for calculating all 46,656 combinations of a
6-element list chosen from six items, on the Multimax. Although there are six
pipeline stages, it should not be surprising that efficiency is only 73% on four PEs.
The stages involve exponentially increasing amounts of computation, so the last
stages account for most of the work. Moreover, the stages are synchronized in that,
unless stage i produces partial combinations, stage $i + 1$ cannot execute. For this
program, it is advantageous that Panda dynamically allocates goals among PEs.
If goals were explicitly allocated, for instance as one stage per PE, then most PEs
would soon become idle.

This raises the issue of interpreting speedup: are inefficiencies due to overheads
of exploiting parallelism, or simply to lack of inherent parallelism? The empirical
definition of speedup as used throughout the book is somewhat orthogonal to the
simple classical model summarized by "Amdahl's Law:"

$$speedup = \frac{1}{(1 - f) + f/s}$$

where f is the fraction of the program that contains inherent parallelism and s is
the real speedup achieved on the parallel code, producing an overall *speedup* for the
program in total. In our programs it is difficult if not impossible to characterize f
because parallelism is implicit, often fine-grained, and nondeterministic. Thus our
speedup measurements mix both the effects of implementation overheads, s, with
lack of theoretical parallelism, f. Amdahl's Law should be kept in mind, however,
because it reminds us that a program with poor speedup may not be the fault of
the system. The algorithm itself might be inherently synchronous.

Although the combinations program achieves fairly good speedup, it has a fundamental flaw — the program has profligate memory consumption. Creating a
combination involves selection of elements *with replacement* from the original list.
Thus the number of list combinations of length N with elements selected from a
list of length m is m^N. It is possible that m^N words of memory are required for

this computation, for instance, if the client who plans to consume the combinations is suspended for some reason. In other words, `combo/3` uses as much memory as necessary without regard for the complications if m and N are large. This is called *eager evaluation*.

In the next two sections we explore methods of throttling `combo/3`'s eagerness, thereby constraining its use of resources. The first method constrains memory usage by a self-disciplined use of *bounded buffers*. In a second, similar method called *lazy evaluation*, the consumer, instead of the producer, drives the computation.

4.1.3 Bounded-Buffer Communication

Recall from Section 2.2.4 that a buffer is a fixed-size list B with an unbound tail E, represented as B/E. To fix the combinations program, we insert a buffer between each **add** process. This constrains the number of partial combinations that can be in transit in the pipeline. If each buffer has a fixed size of K words, then the total memory used by the program is only $N \times K$. The rate at which the client consumes the combinations at the output of the pipeline regulates the flow through the pipe. In general, this paradigm is called *bounded-buffer communication*.

For the new program we define a top-level `combo(N,M,L,Out)`, where M is the buffer size in words and `Out` is the output buffer (cf., previous program where `Out` is a *stream*). A buffer can be created with `buffer/2`.

```
buffer(0,B/E) :- B=E.
buffer(N,B/E) :- N>0 | N1 is N-1, B=[_|T], buffer(N1,T/E).
```

We will assume a protocol wherein the final valid piece of datum in a buffer is always followed by the special `stop` atom. For example, a client might use `combo/4` as follows.

```
?- combo(2,10,[a,b],Buffer),consume(Buffer,Out).
   Out = [[a,a],[a,b],[b,a],[b,b]]
```

where the client is defined as:

```
consume([stop|_]/_,Out) :- Out=[].
consume([A|As]/E,Out) :- A \= stop |
    Out = [A|Os],
    E = [_|Es],
    consume(As/Es,Os).
```

Procedure `combo` initializes the input buffer to `[[],stop]/_`. The first element is the seed for generating the combinations. The second element is the stop code necessary for termination. Note that we don't care about the tail of the input buffer since it is given as a complete list.

```
combo(N,M,L,Bout) :-
    Bin = [[],stop]/_,
    top(N,M,L,Bin,Bout).
```

Procedure `top/5` spawns N `combo2` processes, forming the pipeline. Note the buffer wiring: the output buffer of pipeline stage i is the input buffer of stage $i + 1$. The output buffer at the end of the pipeline is the final output buffer of the program, to be handed off to a client.

```
top(0,_,_,Bin,Bout) :- Bout=Bin.
top(N,M,L,Bin,Bout) :- N>0 |
    N1 is N-1,
    combo2(M,L,Bin,Buff),
    top(N1,M,L,Buff,Bout).
```

Procedure `combo2` creates a buffer of size M. This output buffer, `Bout`, is handed to the next pipeline stage as input. The output buffer is passed to an `add` process, as an output receptacle (note that `add` does not need the tail).

```
combo2(M,L,Bin,Bout) :-
    Bout = OutBuff/_,
    buffer(M,Bout),
    add(Bin,L,OutBuff).
```

The key to the program lies in `add/3` and its subprocedure `combo1`. Here bounded-buffer communication takes place. The `add` procedure needs to do two types of communication. First, it needs to take a partial combination from its input buffer. Second, it needs to expand that combination into m combinations, putting the new items into its output buffer. In the previous FGHC program, these actions were not constrained. Now we constrain the input and output such that *if a buffer slot is not available for input or output then the procedures suspend.*

If the input message to `add` is the `stop` code then we simply output `stop` (first clause). Otherwise, if an input message exists, we expand it with `combo1` (second clause). Note that, if the input buffer has been temporarily exhausted, then the first argument is unbound and thus `add` will suspend, waiting for input. The second clause carefully *creates a new buffer slot* (`_NewSlot`) to replace the slot just consumed. This is the crux of the biscuit.

```
add([stop|_]/_,_,[B|_]) :- B=stop.
add([I|Is]/InEnd,L,Buff) :- I\=stop |
    InEnd = [_NewSlot|NewInEnd],
    combo1(L,I,Buff,NewBuff),
    add(Is/NewInEnd,L,NewBuff).
```

To expand the combination in `combo1` we recursively prepend list elements to it. Note that each new combination is assigned to B, the first element of the output buffer. If that slot is not free then the second clause of `combo1` will suspend, waiting for later stages in the pipeline (or the consumer client) to make some space.

```
combo1([],_,B0,B1) :- B0=B1.
combo1([C|Cs],I,[B|B0],B1) :-
    B = [C|I],
    combo1(Cs,I,B0,B1).
```

The informal specification of the program is given in Figure 4.4.

This program has a major flaw — it is a profligate garbage producer. The reason is that buffers are implemented explicitly in FGHC with no system support. Although the buffers are of a *fixed size*, their implementation causes them to creep through memory. Whenever the head buffer element is consumed, a new tail spot is created. In the FGHC system used in this book, the tail spot will *not* reuse the memory cell freed by the head element.

This is a specific instance of a more general problem in most implementations of committed-choice languages: any clause that consumes elements from an input stream, and passes them on to an output stream, cannot immediately reuse the input stream list memory cell. The general problem is hard to solve because a stream may be shared by multiple consumers. Thus only the *last* consumer to read can reuse an input element's memory cell. The case of buffers is easier to analyze because a buffer conventionally has only one consumer.

The general problem can be solved by incremental garbage collection schemes integrated within the instruction-set architecture, compile-time dataflow analysis, or language semantics. The Multiple Reference Bit (MRB) scheme [25] is an example of incremental garbage collection. Abstract interpretation [114] is one method of compile-time analysis that can detect variables to reuse. Janus [111] is an example of a logic programming language which allows only single-consumer streams, facilitating reuse. The details of these interesting schemes are beyond the scope of this book; suffice it to say that, with each, a buffer really does occupy the same fixed sized area in memory!

The evolution from excess memory consumption (in our first version of `combo`) to excess garbage production (in our second version of `combo`) is considered a step in the right direction. With no bounds on the active memory required, we cannot be guaranteed that a program will execute at all. Once bounds are established, the issue becomes how fast we can clean up the garbage!

4.1.4 Lazy Evaluation

Similar to the use of bounded buffers in the previous section, lazy evaluation (sometimes called data-driven computation) limits the system resources used by a pro-

<u>Procedure</u>: buffer(M, B)
   + M: positive integer   − B: difference list (buffer)

<u>Relation</u>: B is an empty buffer of length M, i.e., a difference list with exactly
   M unbound elements.

<u>Procedure</u>: combo(N, M, L, B)
   + N: positive integer   + L: list
   + M: positive integer   − B: buffer of combinations

<u>Relation</u>: B buffers all combinations of length N of elements selected from L.
   B contains at most M combinations at any one time.

<u>Procedure</u>: top(N, M, L, Bin, Bout)
   + N: positive integer   + Bin: buffer of combinations
   + M: positive integer   − Bout: buffer of combinations
   + L: list

<u>Relation</u>: Bout contains expanded combinations from Bin. The combinations
   are expanded by the values in L, taken N times. M is the buffer size.

<u>Procedure</u>: combo2(M, L, Bin, Bout)
   + M: positive integer   + Bin: buffer of combinations
   + L: list   − Bout: buffer of combinations

<u>Relation</u>: Bout contains expanded combinations from buffer Bin. The com-
   binations are expanded by the values in L, taken once.

<u>Procedure</u>: add(Bin, L, Bout)
   + Bin: buffer of combinations   − Bout: list of combinations
   + L: list

<u>Relation</u>: Bout contains expanded combinations from buffer Bin. The com-
   binations are expanded by the values in L, taken once. The stop message
   is not expanded and terminates the computation.

<u>Procedure</u>: combo1(L, C, Buff, NewBuff)
   + L: list of atoms   + Buff: list of combinations
   + C: combination   − NewBuff: list of combinations

<u>Relation</u>: Slots in Buff are bound with expanded combinations of C. The
   combinations are expanded by the values in L, taken once. NewBuff is
   the remainder of Buff after the combinations are bound.

Figure 4.4
Informal Specification of FGHC Buffered Combinations

ducer. The reasoning is the same: let the consumer specify how much data it wants
by instantiating a producer's output stream with unbound variables, i.e., slots. The
producer is thus held by this reign and cannot overrun production.

In general, an eager producer appears as follows:

```
producer(S) :- produce(P), S=[P|Ps], producer(Ps).

?- producer(S), consumer(S).
```

The signature of the eager producer is the insertion of a product P into output
stream S. A lazy producer appears as follows:

```
producer([P|Ps]) :- produce(P), producer(Ps).
```

Here the slot P is generated by the consumer, i.e., the producer will suspend until
a slot appears. To make this technique more concrete, we now describe a lazy
combinations program.

Consider the situation where the consumer of a long series of combinations can
only decide how many combinations it needs during the computation itself. We
initially spawn a producer that begins creating an infinite sequence of combinations.
To prevent the producer from running ahead and starving the consumer, [1] we desire
a *lazy evaluation* of combo. Lazy evaluation is driven by the size of the desired
output, cf., the previous *eager evaluation* scheme which is a default for FGHC and
other committed-choice languages.

At the top level, lazy evaluation appears as follows. Notice that an argument
limiting the number of combinations is *not* given.

```
?- combo([a,b,c,d],Xs), consumer(Xs).
```

The consumer begins to incrementally bind stream Xs to slots, enabling the producer to generate combinations. To introduce the program, recall the operation of
add/3 in Section 4.1.2:

```
?- add([[a],[b]],[a,b],X).
   X = [[a,a],[a,b],[b,a],[b,b]]
```

The lazy program below uses add/3. Each reduction of combo/8 invokes add/3 to
extend the combinations once more. Procedure combo/8 continues to recurse until
the output stream Out is *closed by the consumer*.

---

[1] Although there may be an inundation of data combinations, we say the consumer process is
starved if it does not receive execution cycles.

```
combo(L,Out) :-
    length(L,Lsize),
    combo(ok,Lsize,Lsize,Lsize,[[]],L,Out,As),
    unify(Out,As).

combo(ok,_,_,_,In,_,[],As) :- As=In.
combo(ok,Extra,Size,Lsize,In,L,Out,As) :-
    add(In,L,T),
    accept(Out,Extra,NewOut,Synch),
    NewSize is Lsize*Size,
    NewExtra is NewSize-Size,
    combo(Synch,NewExtra,NewSize,Lsize,T,L,NewOut,As).

accept(Xs,0,Out,Synch) :- Out=Xs, Synch=ok.
accept([],_,Out,Synch) :- Out=[], Synch=ok.
accept([X|Xs],N,Out,Synch) :- N>0 |
    N1 is N-1,accept(Xs,N1,Out,Synch).

unify([],_).
unify([X|Xs],[A|As]) :- X=A, unify(Xs,As).
```

Each iteration of **combo/8** produces **Extra** *additional* combinations. The total number of combinations is **Size**, calculated as powers of the size of the original input
list. The output stream driving the computation is checked for **Extra** additional
slots. If the output stream is not yet long enough, then **accept/4** will suspend. If
accept suspends, then the synchronization variable **Synch** will not be bound to **ok**,
and therefore, the recursion will suspend. The informal specification of the program
is given in Figure 4.5.

The lazy combinations program given above is inefficient because none of the
output-stream variables are bound until the consumer closes the stream! This
situation would lead to an immediate deadlock if the consumer were using the
combinations to decide to terminate or not. The problem stems not from the
general technique of transforming eager into lazy programs, but rather from how the
combinations are generated. The combinations cannot be generated incrementally;
instead they are generated in groups as a function of the previous combinations.
Thus the producer never has even a single correct combination until it is told to
stop. A more "classic" example of lazy evaluation (that doesn't have this quirk) is
the lazy prime-number generator given by Clark and Gregory [26].

4.1.5 Prolog Revisited

Although much of this chapter has been devoted to FGHC, Prolog also has memory
problems. Consider the eager combinations program, which can be directly trans-

<u>Procedure</u>: combo(L, Out)
      + L: list   + Out: list of slots

<u>Relation</u>: Each unbound element (slot) of Out is bound to a combination
      created by selections from L.

<u>Postconditions</u>: For a list L of length k, a list Out of length n can hold
      combinations of length p, for the maximum p such that $k^{p-1} < n$.

<u>Procedure</u>: combo(Synch, Extra, Size, Lsize, In, L, Out, As)
      + Synch: atom   + In: list of combinations
      + Extra: integer   + L: list
      + Size: integer   + Out: list of slots
      + LSize: integer   − As: list of combinations

<u>Relation</u>: If Synch = ok and Out has a total of Extra or less unbound slots,
      then As contains combinations from In expanded by the values in L, taken
      once. If Out has more than Extra slots, then As contains combinations
      from In expanded by values in L, taken multiple times.

<u>Preconditions</u>: Size is the length of In and LSize is the length of L. Initially
      Extra is the length of L.

<u>Procedure</u>: accept(Xs, N, Out, Synch)
      + Xs: list of slots   − Out: list of slots
      + N: integer   − Synch: atom

<u>Relation</u>: If stream Xs has N or more unbound variables then Synch = ok
      and Out is the rest of stream Xs. Otherwise this procedure suspends,
      waiting for slots to appear on Xs.

<u>Procedure</u>: unify(X, A)
      + X: list of slots   + A: list

<u>Relation</u>: List X is bound to the elements of A, in order. If X is shorter than
      A, the last elements of A do not appear in X.

Figure 4.5
Informal Specification of FGHC Lazy Combinations

lated into Prolog from FGHC. Since the program is determinate, the heap grows monotonically in either language. In fact, the Aurora system measured cannot compute the 49,656 combinations of a six-element list chosen from six items — the heap overflows with garbage.

There are fewer programming methods for reducing resource consumption in Prolog than there are in FGHC. When searching for all solutions in a nondeterminate program, Prolog systems can automatically recover those portions of the search space that are freed upon backtracking. However, to recover space in a determinate program, an explicit garbage collector is needed. For sequential Prolog, explicit garbage collection can be simulated with failure — we call this "home-brew garbage collection." The technique is inelegant and is better left as a last resort (an example is given in Section 11.2.1). Techniques such as bounded buffers and lazy evaluation are not applicable to standard Prologs. However these techniques are applicable to Prolog systems with coroutining, such as NU-Prolog [87] and Quintus Multiprocessing Prolog [102].

4.2 Merging

A fundamental operation in stream-AND parallel committed-choice languages is merge. Merge joins multiple input streams in some *nondeterministic* manner and sends the data through to one or more output streams. A standard merge should service incoming data in a timely and approximately first-come, first-served manner. This behavior will, in general, increase the potential for parallel execution of the program.

Ordering of data, as in appending multiple difference lists into a single stream, usually decreases potential parallelism. Consider two goals that independently produce data on two streams that are appended for a single consumer:

```
?- g1(S1), g2(S2), append(S1,S2,S3), consumer(S3).
```

Recall that, with streams implemented as difference lists, **append** is reduced to a constant time operation:

```
?- g1(X-Y), g2(Y-Z), consumer(X-Z).
```

There is a potential problem, however! The consumer cannot begin reading data from stream X-Z until goal **g1** starts to produce data. The data produced by **g2** are delayed from appearing on the stream until **g1** shorts its difference list. Our motivation in developing a merge is to exploit *all* the potential parallelism:

```
?- g1(S1), g2(S2), merge(S1,S2,S3), consumer(S3).
```

We stipulate that S3 can merge data from S1 and S2 nondeterministically so that neither goal is delayed by the other, and so that the consumer can proceed with minimal delay.

4.2.1 Simple Merge

The simplest formulation, of a binary merge, joins two input streams into one output stream:

```
merge([X|Xs], Ys, Z) :- Z = [X|Zs], merge(Xs, Ys, Zs).
merge(Xs, [Y|Ys], Z) :- Z = [Y|Zs], merge(Xs, Ys, Zs).
merge([],       Y, Z) :- Z = Y.
merge(X,       [], Z) :- Z = X.
```

This program is truly nondeterministic, i.e., if messages arrive on both inputs (first two arguments) simultaneously, either of the first two clauses can commit. Thus the order of messages on the two inputs and the output have no fixed relationship. In fact, if the system were not *fair*, then one input stream might be favored above the other. Most systems *are* unfair, for instance, the FGHC system used in this book checks most clauses in their textual order. Thus it favors the first stream.

Hypothetically, in an extreme case one stream could be continually favored above the other, i.e., all messages from one stream would be merged before the other. In fact, in this case, the above **merge** degenerates to **append(+,+,-)**! In some programs, where a process is waiting for an important message (delayed on the neglected stream), this effect can be disastrous.

One implementation of a fair merge in FGHC follows:

```
merge([X|Xs],Ys,Z) :- Z = [X|Zs], merge(Ys,Xs,Zs).
merge(Xs,[Y|Ys],Z) :- Z = [Y|Zs], merge(Ys,Xs,Zs).
merge([],       Y,Z) :- Z = Y.
merge(X,       [],Z) :- Z = X.
```

The two streams are switched in the recursive invocation of **merge**. The switch ensures that, even if one of the first two clauses is favored over the other, neither stream can exploit this to the exclusion of the other stream. However, one or both of the last two clauses may still be neglected. This neglect will not affect fairness, but may delay shorting the **merge**, prolonging the use of the first two clauses and therefore slowing down the program.

To solve this problem, another implementation of a fair merge (on the next page) requires the use of meta-logical **var/1**. Guard predicate **var(X)** succeeds if **X** is unbound; otherwise it fails.

```
merge([X|Xs],[Y|Ys],Z)  :- Z = [X,Y|Zs], merge(Xs,Ys,Zs).
merge([X|Xs],    Ys,Z)  :- var(Ys) | Z = [X|Zs], merge(Xs, Ys, Zs).
merge(Xs,    [Y|Ys],Z)  :- var(Xs) | Z = [Y|Zs], merge(Xs, Ys, Zs).
merge([],         Y,Z)  :- Z = Y.
merge(X,          [],Z) :- Z = X.
```

Notice that, although var(X) is meta-logical (i.e., the variable X may not remain
unbound for the entire computation, thus contradicting the proof), in this case var
is quite acceptable.

N-way mergers accept several streams as messages and combine them into a single
stream. For instance, in Strand the builtin merger/2 can be used as:

```
?- merger([1,2,merge(S1),3,merge(S2),4],Out).
```

which nondeterminately combines the elements 1,2,3,4 and streams S1 and S2
into a single stream. The design of fair and efficient n-way mergers is an ongoing
research topic (e.g., [116, 66]). One simple way to implement an n-way merger is
in FGHC itself, from binary components:

```
merger([],Out) :- Out=[].
merger([merge(S)|Ms],Out) :-
    merger(Ms,T),
    merge(S,T,Out).
merger([M|Ms],Out) :- otherwise |
    Out = [M|Os],
    merger(Ms,Os).
```

For n input streams, this naive implementation has a worst-case delay of $n - 1$
reductions for messages emanating from the first input stream. A better idea
would be to create a binary tree of binary merges, giving a worst-case delay of
$log(n)$ reductions. We defer further discussion of n-way mergers until Chapter 12,
where we encounter our first need for quickly merging multiple streams.

The informal specification of the binary merge and merger are given in Figure
4.6. In the next two sections we discuss two additional uses of merging. The first
is a *lazy merge* that is demand-driven, instead of the standard version given above
which is data-driven or eager. Another name for lazy merging is simply *splitting!*
The second use of merging is the incorporation of additional computation within
the merge process itself. This technique allows filtering, combining, comparing, etc.
of messages en route.

4.2.2   Splitting

If we execute a binary merge in a demand-driven manner, we effectively create a
splitter that routes a single stream of data nondeterminately between two outputs
[26]. Ideally we desire a program with the following behavior:

Procedure: merge(Xs, Ys, Zs)
    + Xs: stream   + Ys: stream   – Zs: stream

Relation: Zs contains partially-ordered elements from streams Xs and Ys. In other words, the elements from Xs appear in the same order in Zs, similarly for Ys. However, Xs and Ys elements have no fixed order with respect to each other.

Procedure: merger(In, Out)
    + In: stream   – Out: stream

Relation: Out contains all the merged data represented on stream In. Messages on In of the form merge(S) have stream S merged into Out. Other messages are individual data that are also merged into Out.

Procedure: split(Xs, Ys, Zs)
    – Xs: stream   – Ys: stream   + Zs: stream

Relation: Streams Xs and Ys contain all data from stream Zs, nondeterministically split between the two. The element order on either output stream is the same as the order in Zs.

Procedure: cross(Xs, Ys, Zs)
    + Xs: stream   + Ys: stream   – Zs: stream

Relation: Zs contains the cross products of every element of stream Xs with every element of stream Ys.

Procedure: cross(Xs, Ys, Sx, Sy, Zs)
    + Xs: stream   + Sx: list (stack)   – Zs: difference list
    + Ys: stream   + Sy: list (stack)

Relation: Zs contains the cross products (calculated by send/3) of every element from stream Xs with elements from stack Sy and stream Ys. Similarly for every element from stream Ys with elements from stack Sx and stream Xs.

Preconditions: Stacks Sx and Sy are empty.

Procedure: send(Ls, R, Out)
    + Ls: stack   + R: atom   – Out: difference list

Relation: Out contains products of R with every element in Ls.

Figure 4.6
Informal Specification of FGHC Merge(r), Split, and Cross

```
?- split(X,Y,Z), Z = [1,2,3,4,5...]
   X = [1,2,4,...]
   Y = [3,5,...]
```

Streams X and Y would be chosen randomly for a truly nondeterministic splitter. A naive splitter can be implemented as follows:

```
split(X,Y,[Z|Zs]) :- X = [Z|Xs], split(Xs,Y,Zs).
split(X,Y,[Z|Zs]) :- Y = [Z|Ys], split(X,Ys,Zs).
split(X,Y,[]   ) :- X = [], Y = [].
```

Unless the scheduler randomly chooses between the first two clauses, this program will not be fair. On the FGHC system used in this book the naive program will certainly *not* be fair! To partially fix this we can ping-pong between the two output streams:

```
split(X,Y,[Z|Zs]) :- X = [Z|Xs], split(Y,Xs,Zs).
split(X,Y,[])      :- X = [], Y = [].
```

Although the selection is not random, it is determinately fair, which suffices for most applications. The informal specification of the splitter is given in Figure 4.6.

4.2.3   Cross Products

Another programming practice is to fuse more functionality into the merge. For example, the merger could do a bit of processing or filtering of the messages it receives. One useful example is taking a cross-product of the messages arriving on two input streams. Assume the cross-product operator is #/2. For example,

```
?- cross([1,2],[a,b,c],S).
   S = [1#a,1#b,1#c,2#a,2#b,2#c]
```

The top-level procedure, cross(In1, In2, Out), crosses each pair of messages on input streams In1 and In2, and issues the pairs on output stream Out.

```
cross(In1,In2,Out) :-
    cross(In1,In2,[],[],Out-[]).

cross([],     [],_,_,     S0-S1) :- S0=S1.
cross([L|Ls],R,LS,RS,     S0-S2) :-
    send(RS,L,             S0-S1),
    cross(Ls,R,[L|LS],RS,S1-S2).
cross(L,[R|Rs],LS,RS,     S0-S2) :-
    send(LS,R,             S0-S1),
    cross(L,Rs,LS,[R|RS],S1-S2).

send([],_,S0-S1) :- S0=S1.
send([L|Ls],R,S0-S2) :-
    S0=[L#R|S1],
    send(Ls,R,S1-S2).
```

The third and fourth arguments of **cross/5** are stacks for storing the messages from the input streams. Initially the stacks are empty. When a message arrives on the right-hand stream, it is crossed with all messages stored in the left-hand stack, then the new message is pushed onto the right-hand stack. The process is similar for an incoming left-hand stream message.

This method has the advantage that the cross-product is performed symmetrically, i.e., whenever a message arrives, its cross-products are calculated and shipped out. A severe disadvantage, however, is that a great deal of storage is required. The space complexity is $O(n)$ where n is the total number of messages arriving on the streams. Thus this scheme is impractical if the input streams are very long. The informal specification of this program is given in Figure 4.6.

We can trade time for space and lessen the disadvantage of the previous program by using only a single stack. In the following program, the entire left-hand input stream must be received before the cross-product is performed.

```
cross(In1,In2,Out) :- cross1(In1,In2,[],Out-[]).

cross1([],    R,LS,S) :- cross2(R,LS,S).
cross1([L|Ls],R,LS,S) :- cross1(Ls,R,[L|LS],S).

cross2([],     _,S0-S1) :- S0=S1.
cross2([R|Rs],LS,S0-S2) :-
    send(LS,R,    S0-S1),
    cross2(Rs,LS,S1-S2).
```

Another example of a custom merge is given in Chapter 12, where two input messages from dual streams are compared arithmetically and the minimum is passed through on the output stream. Analogs of **merge** and **merger** in OR-parallel Prolog do not exist, because independent-OR processes do not communicate.

4.3   Summary

Given our initial experience with the small programs here and in Chapter 3, we can summarize the architectures in gross terms as follows.

The OR-Prolog architecture is a large-grain parallel architecture and without sufficiently large independent tasks, parallelism cannot be exploited efficiently. The method of collecting parallel solutions, via a **findall** or similar builtin, entails significant overhead. Therefore the parallel execution of many "lightweight" procedures cannot be exploited to any advantage. The programmer need not be concerned with parallel control or synchronization *per se*, but still must keep in mind the cost associated with executing a given procedure in parallel, i.e., creating a parallel branchpoint.

The FGHC architecture is a small-grain parallel architecture wherein streams allow sequential bottlenecks in a computation to be "broken through." By this we mean that the computation naturally (with no explicit help from the programmer) "seeps" through bottlenecks, from one region of high parallelism to another. The mechanism facilitating this is the synchronization on unbound shared variables. Still, the scheduler plays a crucial role and, without the ability to detect large granules of computation, efficiency often degrades as the computation approaches the boundaries of the search space.

Committed-choice languages, because of the inherent parallelism in all tasks, can suffer from resource starvation in many forms. The default execution paradigm of eager evaluation can cause a producer to starve a consumer. Unfair stream merging can cause processes to starve while waiting for delayed messages. More generally, an unfair scheduler can inadvertently starve some goals by continually (re)scheduling other goals.

In general, communicating processes create a lot of garbage, more than do independent processes like those in OR-parallel Prolog. Each stream element requires a list cell that will be discarded once all recipients have accepted the message. Object-oriented programming involves many processes that wait for messages, act on them and then suspend, waiting for more messages. Such processes can create a lot of garbage if the system is not careful to fully reuse the storage already allocated for the process. In simple cases, such as merge, simple tail-recursion optimization can prevent most garbage production.

We have discussed several programming methods and styles that promote efficient execution. These ideas are further developed in subsequent chapters, in the context of larger programs.

Exercises

Exercise 24 The FGHC combination program introduced in Section 4.1 computes all selections of a given number (N) of elements from a given list (of length M). Modify the program so that given N lists, all selections of N elements (choosing one element from each list) are computed.

Exercise 25 Write an FGHC program to compute all the permutations of a given list. Note that a permutation is simply a combination of the list elements without replacement.

Exercise 26 Consider *unrolling* the `del/3` procedure, analogous to unrolling a loop in a procedural language to reduce the overhead of iterating. Unrolling (3x) is illustrated below:

```
del(X,[X|Y],Y).
del(X,[A,X|Y],[A|Y]).
del(X,[A,B,X|Y],[A,B|Y]).
del(X,[A,B,C|Z],[A,B,C|W]) :- del(X,Z,W).
```

The purpose of unrolling is to increase the efficiency of the branchpoint created for `del/3` by increasing the number of nondeterminate clauses that can match without an intervening reduction. Write the following permute programs in OR-parallel Prolog:

- standard two-clause `del/3`, declared parallel, as given in text.

- `del/3` is *fully unrolled* and parallel, i.e., it has no recursive clause.

- the first call to `del/3` is fully unrolled and parallel, and subsequent calls are to a standard two-clause sequential version.

For each program, sketch the OR-tree for all permutations of a 4-element list and measure the speedup for all permutations of a 7-element list. In this case does unrolling help improve speedup?

Exercise 27 Devise an Aurora experiment to determine quantitatively the increase in branchpoint efficiency as a function of the degree of unrolling. By branchpoint efficiency we mean the overhead of initially spawning all branches from a parallel nondeterminate procedure.

Exercise 28 (Shuffles) A *shuffle* of two lists is a combination of their elements with arbitrary interleaving, while retaining the order of elements within the original lists. For example:

```
?- shuffle([1,2,3],[a,b,c],L).
   L = [1,2,3,a,b,c] ;
   L = [1,a,2,b,3,c] ;
   L = [a,1,b,2,c,3] ;
   ...
```

Write efficient Prolog and FGHC programs to generate all shuffles of two input lists. The order of the solutions is unimportant. Do not use **append**!

Exercise 29 (The Grep Problem) Write Prolog and FGHC procedures, `grep(String,Pattern,N)` to find N occurrences of `Pattern` within `String`. Your programs should execute in mode `grep(+,+,-)`. A string is represented by a list of characters. First define patterns as strings. Then extend your program to accept *wildcards* in the patterns. For example a*b should match 'a' followed by any characters followed by 'b'.

Exercise 30 Write a lazy append(-,+) FGHC program. For example,

```
?- S = [_,_,_], append(S,[1,2,3,4]).
   S = [([],[1,2,3,4]),
        ([1],[2,3,4]),
        ([1,2],[3,4])]
```

Be careful that the program can handle the cases when the output list is too short (as shown above) and when the output list is too long. Be wary of deadlocks!

Exercise 31 Implement trinary (3-way) and ternary (4-way) merge procedures in FGHC in the same fashion as the binary merge.

Exercise 32 Implement an efficient *n*-way merger in FGHC from binary merge procedures.

Exercise 33 Implement an efficient *n*-way merger in FGHC from the binary and trinary merge procedure designed in Exercise 31.

Exercise 34 Develop an experiment to determine the average time delay through a merge network for a set of randomly generated input sources. Use this testbed to compare the *n*-way mergers developed in the previous two exercises. Explain your empirical results.

Exercise 35 Write Prolog and FGHC programs to convert a list into a layered stream.

Exercise 36 A converter from layered streams into lists is given in Section 2.2.4. This program actually produces each of the constituent lists in reverse. A naive way to fix this is to reverse each list after conversion. Can you write a program that generates the answer correctly in the first place?

Exercise 37 (Maximum Number Problem) Write OR-Prolog and FGHC programs to find the maxima of a large set of integers. Test your programs on a list of thousands of randomly-generated integers. You may simplify the problem and assume all integers are distinct.

One idea for the FGHC program is to create a circular pipeline (a "ring") of processes, one for each integer. A stage in the pipeline issues messages to its right and receives messages from its left. Initially every stage issues a message containing its value. The idea is to short-out any stage that receives a message value greater than its own value or discard any message that is less than its own value. The algorithm terminates when a process receives a message with its own value (assuming no duplications of the maxima).

One idea for OR-Prolog is to use nondeterminate **member** to select groups of integers to compare. For each group, a maximum is computed. The list of maxima is then similarly reduced.

Which language is better suited to this problem and why?

Exercise 38 Write Prolog and FGHC managers for read-only balanced binary trees. The manager performs two functions: create a tree from a list of data and read an element from the tree. Assume a data item is in the form Key-Data where Key is used for balancing and read access. If the read operation is given instantiated Data, then a check is performed. You may assume that the keys are consecutive integers to allow a perfectly balanced tree to be created.

Exercise 39 Write Prolog and FGHC managers for read/write unbalanced binary trees. The manager performs three functions: initialize an empty tree, write an element in the tree, and read an element from the tree. Assume a data item is in the form Key-Data. Choose either integers or strings (list of characters or ascii codes) for the keys. Both operations are passed data items as input. You may assume that Key is always given as a ground input. If unbound Data is passed to the read operation, the manager will bind Data to the proper value, or fail if no corresponding Key exists. If bound Data is passed to the read operation, the manager will perform a check.

Exercise 40 (Horner's Rule) Write Prolog and FGHC programs to evaluate an nth–order polynomial of the form:

$$a_n x^n + a_{n-1} x^{n-1} + ... + a_1 x + a_0$$

for a given x by computing

$$(...(a_n x + a_{n-1})x + ... + a_1)x + a_0.$$

Is there any available AND or OR parallelism in this algorithm? Develop an algorithm with more parallelism and compare the complexity of your new algorithm with the previous one. A good estimate of complexity is the number of multiplications and additions executed.

Exercise 41 (Hamming's Problem) Generate all positive integers less than some N with no prime factors other than 2, 3, or 5. There may be no repetitions. Two ways to solve this problem come to mind. First, we could modify the prime-number generator from Section 3.5 by removing the filters corresponding to 2, 3, and 5. This would allow multiples of 2, 3, and 5 to pass through untouched. Another idea is generate three independent streams of the multiples of 2, 3, and 5. These streams can then be merged, removing duplications. Note that the merger must be deterministic and the streams must be ordered to allow us to check for duplications.

Implement both algorithms and measure their performance for some large N. Estimate the time complexity of programs. Check your complexity model against the timing statistics for different N.

Exercise 42 Generalize Exercise 41 to accept an input list of prime factors. A stream of positive integers composed only of those prime factors is generated.

Exercise 43 (Ramanujan Numbers) Generate all positive integers less than some N that are the sum of two cubes (i.e., $i^3 + j^3$ for integers i, j) in *two different ways*. The first such number is $1729 = 1^3 + 12^3 = 9^3 + 10^3$. What is the complexity of your algorithm in terms of numbers of multiplications and additions?

Exercise 44 Consider the following Prolog program due to L. Baxter:

```
half(0,[],[]).
half(C,[A|X],[B|Y]) :- h(C,A,B,C1), half(C1,X,Y).

h(0,0,0,0).    h(0,5,2,1).    h(1,0,5,0).    h(1,5,7,1).
h(0,1,0,1).    h(0,6,3,0).    h(1,1,5,1).    h(1,6,8,0).
h(0,2,1,0).    h(0,7,3,1).    h(1,2,6,0).    h(1,7,8,1).
h(0,3,1,1).    h(0,8,4,0).    h(1,3,6,1).    h(1,8,9,0).
h(0,4,2,0).    h(0,9,4,1).    h(1,4,7,0).    h(1,9,9,1).
```

The procedure h(C,A,B,C1) is true when, with a carry-in of C, half of A equals B with a remainder of C1. This is radix-10 arithmetic where the arguments are digits. For instance, h(1,7,8,1) means that $(10 + 7)/2 = 8$ with a remainder of one. The purpose of h/4 becomes apparent when viewing half/3. Procedure half(C,X,Y) is true when, with a carry-in of C, of half of X equals Y. Both X and Y are radix-10 integers with equal numbers of digits.

This program can be used to solve simple criptarithmetic problems with radix-10 numbers of the form $d_k...d_2 d_1 d_0$, where d_i is the ith digit. For example, to solve $35a2b_{10}/2 = 1ab64_{10}$ for a and b:

```
?- half(0,[3,5,A,2,B],[1,A,B,6,4]).

   A = 7
   B = 8
```

Now solve the following problem concerning an n-digit number (with $d_0 = 5$) multiplied by five: $d_{n-1}...d_2d_15 \times 5 = 5d_{n-1}...d_2d_1$. Hint: $5 = 10/2$.

5 N-Queens

"We managed to produce the first transistorized radio in 1955 and our first
tiny 'pocketable' transistor radio in 1957. It was the world's smallest, but
actually it was a bit bigger than a standard men's shirt pocket, and that
gave us a problem for a while, even though we never said which pocket we
had in mind when we said 'pocketable.' We liked the idea of a salesman
being able to demonstrate how simple it would be to drop it into a shirt
pocket. We came up with a simple solution — we had some shirts made for
our salesman with slightly larger than normal pockets, just big enough to
slip the radio into."

Akio Morita
Made In Japan
Signet 1986

The N-Queens problem is a classic example for procedural, functional, and logic
programming languages. The problem is to place N queens on an $N \times N$ chessboard
so that no queen can attack another queen. A queen can attack any piece on its
diagonals, horizontal row or vertical column. An example of a solution to 20-Queens
is shown in Figure 5.1, where the list elements represent columns and the indices of
the elements represent rows. For example, in this solution, there is a queen placed
at row 3, column 5.

In the logic-programming community, the problem most often measured, when
discussing Prolog and FGHC implementations, is the 8-Queen problem, indicating
the current state of garbage collection technology (measurements of the slightly
bigger 9-Queens are presented here). N-Queens is a rich enough problem to allow
a variety of different solutions.[1] It is no secret that the large number of N-Queens
programs is driven by the desire of each group of logic programming system implementors to find the fastest algorithm for their particular language.

The number of solutions of N-Queens as a function of N is given in Table 5.1.
The OR-trees produced by the algorithms discussed here are much larger than
the number of solutions. For example, in 9-Queens, a naive search space consists of all possible queen placements, giving $9! = 362,880$ branchpoints in the
OR-tree. A more sophisticated search technique called "fused generate & test"
can avoid many placements by exploiting early failure — 9-Queens builds 22,335
branchpoints. Since 9-Queens has 352 solutions, the solution paths comprise 3168
branchpoints in the OR-tree, less than 1% of the naive OR-tree.

Like naive reverse, N-Queens has taken on the role of the classic parallel logic
programming language benchmark. Again, this choice is unfortunate, because N-

---

[1] including constrained logic-programming language solutions [140, 11] somewhat related to two
of the Prolog programs presented here.

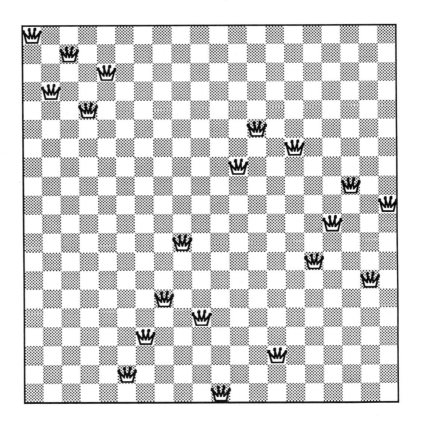

[1,3,5,2,4,13,15,12,18,20,17,9,16,19,8,10,7,14,6,11]

Figure 5.1
A Solution to the 20-Queens Problem

N	solutions	N	solutions
4	2	8	92
5	10	9	352
6	4	10	724
7	40	11	2680

Table 5.1
N-Queens: N vs. Number of Solutions

Queens does not share the characteristics of real parallel applications. One major flaw is that it requires only very simple data structures, thus inter-goal communication costs and garbage collection costs are not adequately reflected. Another major flaw is that the OR-tree is rather regular, making load balancing easy, i.e., distributing the goals evenly among the multiple processing elements. One would *not* expect a complex application program to create a single uniform OR-tree.

5.1 Prolog Versions

In this section, we present four Prolog algorithms for solving the N-Queens problem. Each program is invoked by a top-level call to queen(N,A), to find a single solution A for N queens. A findall is used in go(N,As) to collect all solutions As. This choice illustrates the ease with which OR-parallel Prolog can collect either one or all solutions. However, Aurora cannot collect m solutions for arbitrary m. In addition, we have no control over the search strategy: depth-first search is used to abide by sequential Prolog semantics.

Descriptions of the programs are given in the following sections, followed by analysis of performance results. In general, the remaining chapters in this book abide by this format: program descriptions preceding in-depth analysis.

5.1.1 Naive Generate & Test

A "classic" version of N-Queens, attributed to M. Bruynooghe [31], is given below. This is a generate & test program where queens are placed without regard and then checked by an independent procedure. The failure of the check causes the generator to produce yet another placement. In detail, first an integer list of N rows is generated with **gen/2**. The solution to the problem is produced by **queen/2** as a list of columns corresponding to the rows. The list of all solutions is collected with a findall.

```
:- parallel del/3.

go(N,As) :- findall(A,queen(N,A),As).

gen(0,[]) :- !.
gen(N,[N|T]) :- N>0, N1 is N-1, gen(N1,T).

queen(N,A) :- gen(N,L), perm(L,A), test(A).

perm([],[]).
perm([H|T],[A|P]) :- del(A,[H|T],L), perm(L,P).
```

```
del(X,[X|Y],Y).
del(X,[Y|Z],[Y|W]) :- del(X,Z,W).
```

Procedure **perm/2** (see Section 4.1) simply generates permutations of the row list.
Each permutation is a potential solution. A queen within the solution is represented
by a value (the column) and its implied index within the list (the row). In this and
in fact *all* of the Prolog versions of N-Queens, nondeterminate **del/3** is used as
the source of OR-parallelism. In other words, the generator creates an OR-tree of
potential solutions, where each leaf is a tester.

The tester of the program is done by **test/1**, which fails if its argument is
not a valid solution, otherwise it succeeds. A solution is valid if it is either the
empty list or if it is a non-empty list [H|T], such that for each queen H there is no
conflict with queens in the remainder of the board T. This solution is checked with
safe(T,H,1). Two queens conflict when the difference between their row numbers
is equal to the difference between their column numbers, i.e., $X_i - X_j = Y_i - Y_j$
or $X_i - X_j = Y_j - Y_i$. In the code below, H corresponds to Y_i, U corresponds to
Y_j, and D corresponds to $X_i - X_j$. The clever calculation of the row difference by
incrementing a counter is valid because for each **safe/3** recursion, the head queen
is compared to a queen one row further away. Thus the row difference increases by
one. In fact, this comparison is used in most of the algorithms presented in this
chapter.

```
test([]).
test([H|T]) :- safe(T,H,1), test(T).

safe([],_,_).
safe([H|T],U,D) :-
    H-U=\=D,
    U-H=\=D,
    D1 is D+1,
    safe(T,U,D1).
```

The informal specification of the program is given in Figure 5.2.

This method is simplistic (for example, it does not take advantage of symmetry
the way a human does), but it is declarative and easy to understand. A naive hope is
that parallelization will improve the algorithm's performance to an acceptable level.
OR-parallelism is exploitable in that each permutation can be checked in parallel.
If the safety check has insufficient work to outweigh the cost of spawning another
process, exploiting OR-parallelism will fail to produce speedups for this program.
For the all-solutions 9-Queens problem, this is not the case — relative speedup
of 7.5 on eight PEs (Symmetry) was measured. Unrolling the **del** procedure is
not necessary to attain high speedup, because the Aurora scheduler can exploit

<u>Procedure</u>: `go(N, As)`
    + `N`: integer $(N > 0)$ − `As`: list of boards

<u>Relation</u>: `As` contains all board solutions to the N-Queens problem. A board
    is a list of queens. A queen is represented by an integer column number
    from 1 to `N`. A solution is a board wherein no two queens can attack one
    another.

<u>Procedure</u>: `queen(N, A)`
    + `N`: integer   − `A`: list of queens

<u>Relation</u>: `A` is a single solution to the N-Queens problem.

<u>Procedure</u>: `gen(N, Is)`
    + `N`: integer   − `Is`: list of integers

<u>Relation</u>: `Is` is a list of consecutive integers from `N` to 1.

<u>Procedure</u>: `test(A)`
    + `A`: list of queens

<u>Relation</u>: `A` is a consistent board wherein no two queens can attack one
    another.

<u>Procedure</u>: `safe(Qs, Q, D)`
    + `Qs`: list of queens   + `Q`: queen   + `D`: integer

<u>Relation</u>: `Q` is consistent with `Qs`, the head of which is `D` rows from `Q`.

<u>Preconditions</u>: Initially `D=1` when comparing a newly chosen queen against
    previously placed queens.

Figure 5.2
Informal Specification of Bruynooghe's Queens

large-granule parallelism near the root of the OR-tree.

We mentioned a "naive hope" because this is a naive algorithm. Naive generate & test has complexity $O(N!)$ for N-Queens, in both execution time and (OR-tree) space. The 4-Queens OR-tree is sketched in Figure 5.3, similar to the illustration given in Figure 4.2 in Section 4.1. The complexity explodes for large N and no amount of speedup can cure this explosion. Thus we need a better algorithm, as discussed in the next section.

5.1.2 Fused Generate & Test

In an effort to damp the explosive complexity, a variant of the previous program, attributed to L. Pereira [31], is shown below. Here the generator and tester are fused. The fused program is significantly faster for both sequential and parallel executions. Note that the fused program produces the list of answers in reverse order to the naive version.

```
queen(N,A) :- gen(N,L), queen(L,[],A).

queen([],R,R).
queen([H|T],R,P) :-
    del(A,[H|T],L),
    safe(R,A,1),
    queen(L,[A|R],P).
```

Perhaps the annotated version of this program is easier to understand:

```
        + -          + -        + + -
queen(N,A) :- gen(N,L), queen(L,[],A).
        + + -
queen([],R,R).
        +  + -        - + -       + + +      +   +   -
queen([H|T],R,P) :- del(A,[H|T],L),safe(R,A,1),queen(L,[A|R],P).
```

Fusion works by minimizing the number of calls to `safe/3` by immediately testing each new choice against the partial answer (in R). The technique of fusing tester into generator is valuable; we shall encounter it again in many programs. The informal specification of the program is given in Figure 5.4. Refer to previous program specifications for procedures already defined.

For 9-Queens, the fused program executes 21 times faster than the naive version on eight Symmetry PEs but attains a speedup of only 4.6. We encounter this phenomenon throughout this book: that of decreasing the complexity of an algorithm at the expense of decreasing the available parallelism.

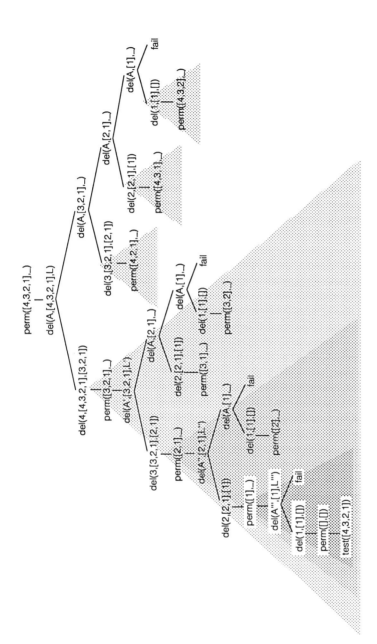

Figure 5.3
4-Queens Naive Generate & Test OR-Tree

Figure 5.4
Informal Specification of Pereira's Queens

Procedure: `queen(L, R, P)`
  + L: list of columns   – P: final solution
  + R: partial solution

Relation: P is a complete board solving the Queens problem, extending the
  partially complete board R by placing queens on columns specified in L. If
  R and L cannot be extended into a complete solution then this call fails.

Procedure: `del(X, L1, L2)`
  ? X: atom   ? L1: list   ? L2: list

Relation: X is an element of L1. L2 holds the remaining elements of L1.

Postconditions: The values in L1 are in the same order as in L2.

The full OR-tree for 4-Queens is illustrated in Figure 5.5. Darkened squares represent queen placements. Each leaf is either a failure or a solution. The branching factor decreases as depth increases. The complexity analysis of this type of search is left as an Exercise in this chapter, with discussion deferred until Section 9.1.8.

5.1.3   Constraints

Kondo's queens, given below, uses logical variables to enforce constraints that prevent queens from attacking one another. Most of the program code is devoted to creating the complex board, so we begin by showing a 7x7 board:

```
[b(a(X7,Yd),a(X8,Yc),a(X9,Yb),a(Xa,Ya),a(Xb,Y9),a(Xc,Y8),a(Xd,Y7)),
 b(a(X6,Yc),a(X7,Yb),a(X8,Ya),a(X9,Y9),a(Xa,Y8),a(Xb,Y7),a(Xc,Y6)),
 b(a(X5,Yb),a(X6,Ya),a(X7,Y9),a(X8,Y8),a(X9,Y7),a(Xa,Y6),a(Xb,Y5)),
 b(a(X4,Ya),a(X5,Y9),a(X6,Y8),a(X7,Y7),a(X8,Y6),a(X9,Y5),a(Xa,Y4)),
 b(a(X3,Y9),a(X4,Y8),a(X5,Y7),a(X6,Y6),a(X7,Y5),a(X8,Y4),a(X9,Y3)),
 b(a(X2,Y8),a(X3,Y7),a(X4,Y6),a(X5,Y5),a(X6,Y4),a(X7,Y3),a(X8,Y2)),
 b(a(X1,Y7),a(X2,Y6),a(X3,Y5),a(X4,Y4),a(X5,Y3),a(X6,Y2),a(X7,Y1))]
```

Each row of the board is represented by a `b/7` structure wherein each element `a/2` represents a square. A square contains two logical variables representing the two diagonals passing through the square. The key is that all squares along the same diagonal share the same logical variable. Thus binding any square with a queen will automatically bind all the squares sharing the two diagonals of that square. The procedure to create the board is shown below without explanation (it is standard Prolog).

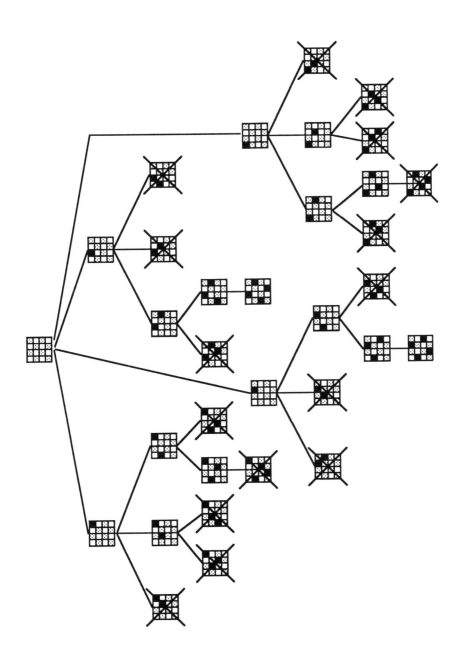

Figure 5.5
4-Queens Fused Generate & Test OR-Tree

```
board(N,B) :-
    M is N*2-1,
    functor(X,x,M),
    functor(Y,y,M),
    make(N,M,N,N,B,X,Y).

make(0,_,_,_,[],_,_) :- !.
make(M,X,Y,N,[Row|Rows],Nx,Ny) :- M>0,
    functor(Row,b,N),
    row(N,Row,X,Y,Nx,Ny),
    X1 is X-1, Y1 is Y+1, M1 is M-1,
    make(M1,X1,Y1,N,Rows,Nx,Ny).

row(0,_,_,_,_,_) :- !.
row(N,S,X,Y,Nx,Ny) :- N>0,
    X1 is X-1, Y1 is Y-1, N1 is N-1,
    arg(X,Nx,A),
    arg(Y,Ny,B),
    arg(N,S,a(A,B)),
    row(N1,S,X1,Y1,Nx,Ny).
```

The main body of the algorithm is quite simple. Again, we use a parallel delete procedure, del/3, as previously defined. Initially queen/3 is passed the board, a list of column positions for queens, and an unbound variable for the final answer. The queens are placed row by row, starting with the first row. The procedural semantics of queen/3 begins by nondeterminately deleting a column number E from the list L. The next row of the board is indexed by E to produce a square, which is bound to a(E,E). This binding ensures that all other squares sharing this square's diagonals are also bound, preventing their later selection. Procedure queen/3 then recurses with the rest of the board, the remaining available columns, and the partial answer.

```
go(N,As) :- findall(A,queen(N,A),As).

queen(N,A) :-
    gen(N,L),
    board(N,P),
    queen(P,L,A).

queen([],_,[]).
queen([H|T],L,[E|Z]) :-
    del(E,L,L1),
    arg(E,H,a(E,E)),
    queen(T,L1,Z).
```

Kondo's algorithm is one of the fastest Prolog N-Queens programs. Shared logical variables enable enforcing constraints along the diagonal with constant overhead (essentially for free).

5.1.4 More Constraints

Bratko's queens, given below, uses a pseudo-constraint method [16] similar to Kondo's queens. Each queen is characterized by a unique integer that represents its row, column, left diagonal, and right diagonal. These constraints are placed in four lists, and successively removed when a queen is placed. An example of the constraint lists for an 8x8 board are:

```
Dxy = [1,2,3,4,5,6,7,8]
 Du = [-7,-6,-5,-4,-3,-2,-1,0,1,2,3,4,5,6,7]
 Dv = [2,3,4,5,6,7,8,9,10,11,12,13,14,15,16]
```

Although the algorithm is elegant and parallel, removing the constraints is slow, causing rather poor performance.

```
:- parallel del/3.

go(N,As) :- findall(A,queen(N,A),As).

queen(N,A) :-
    gen(1, N, Dxy),
    Nu1 is 1-N, Nu2 is N-1,
    gen(Nu1, Nu2, Du),
    Nv2 is N+N,
    gen(2, Nv2, Dv),
    sol(Dxy, A, Dxy, Du, Dv).

sol([],[],Dy,Du,Dv).
sol([X|Dx1],[Y|Ylist],Dy,Du,Dv) :-
    del(Y,Dy,Dy1),
    U is X-Y,
    sdel(U,Du,Du1),
    V is X+Y,
    sdel(V,Dv,Dv1),
    sol(Dx1,Ylist,Dy1,Du1,Dv1).

% identical to del/3, but determinate and sequential
sdel(X, [X|T], T) :- !.
sdel(X, [H|T], [H|R]) :- sdel(X, T, R).

del(X, [X|T], T).
del(X, [H|T], [H|R]) :- del(X, T, R).

gen(N,N,[N]) :- !.
gen(N1,N2,[N1|L]) :- N1 < N2, M is N1+1, gen(M,N2,L).
```

The diagonal constraints Du and Dv essentially encode the relationships checked by test/1 in the fused generate & test program. The informal specification of the program is given in Figure 5.6.

Figure 5.6
Informal Specification of Bratko's Queens

Procedure: sol(Dx, A, Dy, Du, Dv)
   + Dx: row constraints   + Du: diagonal constraints
   − A: partial solution   + Dv: diagonal constraints
   + Dy: column constraints

Relation: A contains a partial board solving the Queens problem if the remaining rows in Dx can be assigned columns in Dy, consistent with the constraints in Du and Dv. Otherwise the call to this procedure fails.

Preconditions: All constraint lists hold increasing, consecutive integers. Initially Dx = Dy are lists from 1 to N, where N the number of queens. Du is a list from $1 - N$ to $N - 1$. Dv is a list from 2 to 2N.

The original Bratko's queens, as given above, suffers from slow deletion from the constraint lists. The following version solves this problem by implementing the constraints in structures. Here a constraint is implicitly represented by a structure index.

```
queen(N,A) :-
    gen(1, N, Dxy),
    N2 is (N*2)-1,
    functor(Du,du,N2),
    functor(Dv,dv,N2),
    sol(Dxy, A, Dxy, Du, Dv, N).

sol([],[],_,_,_,_).
sol([X|Dx1],[Y|Ylist],Dy,Du,Dv,N) :-
    del(Dy,Y,Dy1),
    U is X-Y+N,
    arg(U,Du,X),
    V is X+Y-1,
    arg(V,Dv,X),
    sol(Dx1,Ylist,Dy1,Du,Dv,N).
```

This small improvement in mechanics reduces execution time by a factor of five on 8 PEs for 9-Queens (Symmetry), at the expense of reducing speedup from 6.5 (list version) to 5.6 (structure version). The algorithm is one of the fastest Prolog N-Queens programs, performing as well as Kondo's queens.

5.2 FGHC Versions

In this section, we present five FGHC algorithms for solving the N-Queens problem. Each program is invoked by a top-level call to queen(N,As) to find all solutions As for N queens. Each program uses a stream (in the form of a difference list) to collect the solutions. The wiring of the D-list implies that the solutions are ordered in the same order as sequential Prolog semantics.

To find a single solution or m solutions for arbitrary m, we must rewrite the programs to allow early termination. This method is illustrated in Section 5.3.

5.2.1 Candidates and Noncandidates

Kumon's N-Queens algorithm explicitly builds an OR-tree of processes with the *(non)candidates method*. The queen/4 procedure represents a node in the OR-tree, similar to a branchpoint in Aurora. Procedure queen(Cs,NCs,L,S) contains a partial solution L and an output stream S. The combination of the candidate list, Cs, and the noncandidate list, NCs, hold the columns not yet chosen in the partial solution. A queen is represented by a column — the corresponding row is implicit. For example, the row corresponding to the current candidate (the head of the candidate list) could be calculated from the length of the candidate list. Similarly, the row of any queen in the partial solution could be calculated from its position in the partial solution.

```
queen(N,A) :-
    gen(N,L),
    queen(L,[],[],A-[]).

queen([C|Cs],NCs,L,S0-S2) :-
    check(C,Cs,NCs,L,S0-S1),
    queen(Cs,[C|NCs],L,S1-S2).
queen([],[],L,S0-S1) :- S0=[L|S1].
queen([],[_|_],_,S0-S1) :- S0=S1.

gen(0, X) :- X=[].
gen(N, X) :- N>0 | M is N-1, X=[N|Xs], gen(M,Xs).
```

The first clause of queen/4 represents the action of spawning a new child branch (check/5) from the OR-node. For each child branch, the current candidate C is checked against the partial solution L. The "process reading" is that check/5 generates all solutions *including* C, whereas the queen/4 child generates all solutions *not* including C. If C is a faulty choice, then check/5 catches this fault and shorts out its portion of the answer stream, S0-S1.

The second argument of queen/4 is a noncandidate list, i.e., a list of columns that cannot be used for placement in the current row. The noncandidate list is necessary to prevent the queen/4 child process from choosing the same placement as the one being explored by check/5.

The final two clauses in queen/4 deal with the cases when the candidate list is empty. If the candidate and noncandidate lists are *both* empty (second clause) then the partial solution L is complete and is inserted into the answer stream. The second clause represents a successful leaf node of the OR-tree, i.e., a solution! If the candidate list is empty but the noncandidate list is *not* empty (third clause) then the partial solution cannot be extended and the OR-branch is pruned, i.e., the answer stream is shorted. The third clause represents a failing leaf node of the OR-tree.

The check procedure is shown below. The first argument of check/7 holds the partial solution of queens. This list is examined during the check: each queen is compared with the current queen placement to determine if it is correct (the same criteria used in the Prolog programs is used again here). The partial solution is also passed as the sixth argument to be either discarded (if the new queen is bad), or to be used to compose the new partial solution, [C|L], for the call to queen/4 in the first clause.

```
check(C,Cs,NCs,L,S) :- check(L,C,1,NCs,Cs,L,S).

check([],C,_,NCs,Cs,L,S) :-
    append(NCs,Cs,Ps),
    queen(Ps,[],[C|L],S).
check([P|Ps],C,D,NCs,Cs,L,S) :-
    P-C =\= D, C-P =\= D |
    D1 is D+1,
    check(Ps,C,D1,NCs,Cs,L,S).
check(_,_,_,_,_,_,S0-S1) :- otherwise | S0=S1.
```

If the check succeeds (clause 1), then the noncandidates and candidates are appended together to form a new list of candidates Ps for queen/4. The new list of noncandidates is initially empty, and the new partial solution prepends the current candidate C to the previous partial solution L.

The informal specification of the program is given in Figure 5.7. The full 4-Queens process structure is illustrated in Figure 5.8. Each node in the tree represents a queen/4 process, with the first three arguments shown: candidates, noncandidates, and the partial solution. The call to check/5 spawns the left child and the recursive call to queen/4 spawns the right child. Each leaf is either a failure (queen/4 clause 3) or a solution (clause 2). The process structure can be viewed as an OR-tree.

Figure 5.7
Informal Specification of Kumon's Queens

    <u>Procedure</u>: `queen(Cs, NCs, L, S)`
      + `Cs`: list of candidates   + `L`: partial solution
      + `NCs`: list of noncandidates   − `S`: stream of solutions

    <u>Relation</u>: Stream `S` contains all extensions of partial solution `L` completed
      with the queen positions (columns) given in `Cs` and `NCs`.

    <u>Preconditions</u>: Initially `Cs` is a list of all columns, and `NCs` and `L` are empty.

    <u>Procedure</u>: `check(C, Cs, NCs, L, S)`
      + `C`: chosen candidate   + `L`: partial solution
      + `Cs`: list of candidates   − `S`: stream of solutions
      + `NCs`: list of noncandidates

    <u>Relation</u>: Stream `S` contains all partial solutions `L` extended by queen `C` and
      completed with the queen positions given in `Cs` and `NCs`.

This method of simulating an OR-parallel search with an AND-parallel system requires that `queen/4` make N recursions to spawn N branches from a branchpoint node. Each recursion requires a reduction that creates two goals. Exploiting a form of tail-recursion optimization, only one new goal record need be created for each reduction (see Appendix A.2) but the overhead is still N goal records to emulate N branches (in this particular case).

The OR-parallel Prolog queens programs suffer from the same overheads: N backtracks over N `del/3` branchpoints are needed to spawn N branches. For both systems, these overheads can be reduced by variations of *code unrolling*. We introduced branchpoint unrolling in Exercise 26 in the previous chapter. For example, if `del/3` is unrolled twice:

```
del(X,[X|Y],Y).
del(X,[A,X|Y],[A|Y]).
del(X,[A,B|Z],[A,B|W]) :- del(X,Z,W).
```

then only $N/2$ branchpoints are needed to spawn N branches (although N backtracks are still necessary). A similar FGHC technique is feasible, although messy, in a procedure such as `queen/4`. We defer discussion of the FGHC optimization until Section 9.1.9 where there is a more appropriate program.

Kumon's Queens is efficient because it *rarely suspends*. The spawning of the child OR-branches in `queen/4` proceeds without any synchronization. In fact, only

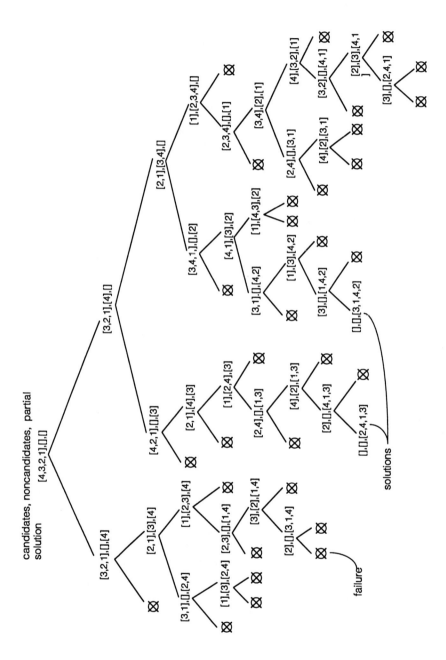

Figure 5.8
4-Queens (Non)Candidates Process Structure: queen/4 Process at Each Node

one producer-consumer relationship exists in any clause body: between **append** and **queen/4** in **check/7** (via **Ps**). In practice, the other FGHC algorithms, Okumura's Queens and Tick's Queens (discussed later in this chapter), suspend about 90 and 2700 times as frequently as Kumon's Queens, respectively, for the 9-Queens problem.

Kumon's Queens, unlike the other N-Queens programs, can be executed in both FGHC and Prolog. In general, most candidates/noncandidates programs have this characteristic because they exploit neither shared logical variables (which FGHC cannot implement) nor producer-consumer synchronization (which OR-Prolog cannot implement).

5.2.2 Continuation-Based Machine Translation

Recall from Section 3.1 that FGHC **append**

```
append([], L1, L2) :- L1 = L2.
append([X|L1], L2, L4) :- L4 = [X|L3], append(L1, L2, L3).
```

assumes a determinate mode of execution wherein the first two arguments are bound input arguments and the third argument is an unbound output argument. The common notation for this mode of execution is **append(+,+,-)**. This information was implicit when we wrote the code. If we desire a different mode of execution, e.g., **append(-,-,+)**, then we must write a different FGHC program.

Ueda [136, 138] discusses how to generate FGHC programs automatically from Prolog programs for a restricted subset of programs, such as **append**. A nondeterminate Prolog program may be satisfied in more than one way, i.e., multiple solutions may exist. The translation of such a program into a committed-choice language is a form of *OR-in-AND parallelism*. Whereas OR-parallel Prolog can produce the multiple solutions in OR-parallel, FGHC can produce the multiple solutions in AND-parallel. In essence, the FGHC program *simulates* the OR-parallel search conducted by OR-parallel Prolog, hence the name OR-in-AND parallelism.

In this section, we will analyze an OR-in-AND parallel implementation of N-Queens. By way of introduction, however, we first tackle a more modest problem. Ueda's *continuation method* is illustrated below for **append(-,-,+)**.

```
append(Z, X) :-
    ap(Z, c0, X-[]).

ap(Z, Cont, S0-S2) :-
    ap1(Z, Cont, S0-S1),
    ap2(Z, Cont, S1-S2).

ap1(Z, Cont, S) :- cont(Cont, [], Z, S).
```

```
ap2([A|Z], Cont, S) :- ap(Z, c1(A, Cont), S).
ap2([], _, S0-S1)    :- S0=S1.

cont(c1(A, Cont), X, Z, S) :-
    cont(Cont, [A|X], Z, S).
cont(c0, X, Z, S0-S1) :-
    S0 = [(X,Z)|S1].
```

In this case, execution produces the same result as nondeterminate Prolog execution. We call `append(Z,X)` where Z is the input argument and X is a list of output pairs. For example:

```
?- append([1,2,3], X).
    X = [([],[1,2,3]), ([1],[2,3]), ([1,2],[3]), ([1,2,3],[])]
```

Procedure `append/2` calls `ap/3` with the input list as the first argument, an initial "continuation" c0, and the difference list representing the output stream, X-[]. Procedure `ap/3` builds the answer stream by spawning two processes: `ap1/3` and `ap2/3`, corresponding to the two original clauses of `append`. Procedure `ap1/3` simply calls `cont/4`, which is a continuation "unraveller," as will be discussed shortly. Procedure `ap2/3` recurses on `ap/3`, building up the nested continuation with the head of the list. When the input list has been exhausted, the output D-list is closed.

For each `ap1(Z,Cont,S)` process, the continuation unraveller is invoked to unravel the continuation Cont into a list X. At the end of unraveling, an answer is composed as (X,Z) and sent down the answer stream S.

This example gives a bite-sized taste of how Prolog programs can be *automatically* translated into FGHC programs with the continuation methodology. It is safe to say that larger translated programs are impossible to understand, i.e., from an FGHC perspective, even by the experts. This program, however, is small enough to illustrate how the continuation is built up, holding the information necessary to construct the stream of answers later. In addition, the process tree described by this example, although automatically generated, can be viewed independently as a general all-solutions-search programming method in FGHC.

The key point is that ap spawns two children, ap1 and ap2. We can view process ap1 as generating all solutions that have Z as the second element of the answer pair. Likewise, process ap2 generates all solutions *without* Z as the second element of the answer pair. Dividing a nondeterminate problem as a binary process tree is a quick and easy way to program a great deal of problems. In the last section, we saw a general form of this candidate/noncandidate method.

It seems appropriate at this point to talk a bit about optimizing FGHC programs. Certainly the previous machine-generated code is ripe for optimization. We

will proceed by incrementally improving the program. First, a procedure with a
singleton clause can easily be placed in-line. In the case of ap1, there is no serious
loss of modularity:

```
ap(Z, Cont, S0-S2) :-
    cont(Cont, [], Z, S0-S1),
    ap2(Z, Cont, S1-S2).
```

The purpose of in-line insertion is to reduce the number of procedure calls. Next,
we can *fold* ap2 into ap [52] because the two procedures are mutually recursive:

```
ap([], Cont, S0-S2) :-
    cont(Cont, [], [], S0-S1),
    S1=S2.
ap([A|Z], Cont, S0-S2) :-
    cont(Cont, [], [A|Z], S0-S1),
    ap(Z, c1(A,Cont), S1-S2).
```

The purpose of folding is, again, to reduce the number of procedure calls. The code
above can be slightly simplified:

```
ap([], Cont, S) :-
    cont(Cont, [], [], S).
ap([A|Z], Cont, S0-S2) :-
    cont(Cont, [], [A|Z], S0-S1),
    ap(Z, c1(A,Cont), S1-S2).
```

Here we *shorted-out* a section of the answer stream D-list in the first clause. This
choice doesn't buy us much in terms of performance, but it makes the code prettier.
Now we focus our attention on cont/4. The continuation structure is of the form:

```
c1(An, ..., c1(A1, c1(A0, c0)))
```

where Ai is the ith element in the original list. A more efficient representation is
with a list: [An,...,A1,A0].

```
append(Z, X) :-
    ap(Z, [], X-[]).

ap([], Cont, S) :-
    cont(Cont, [], [], S).
ap([A|Z], Cont, S0-S2) :-
    cont(Cont, [], [A|Z], S0-S1),
    ap(Z, [A|Cont], S1-S2).

cont([A|Cont], X, Z, S) :-
    cont(Cont, [A|X], Z, S).
cont([], X, Z, S0-S1) :-
    S0 = [(X,Z)|S1].
```

Notice we changed c1(H,T) into [H|T] and c0 into []. Again, this modification saves us little (one word per list element), but helps clarify what is happening — we are simply *reversing* the list! Procedure cont/4 is a reverse procedure fused with answer stream output. A more modular program is:

```
ap([], Cont, S0-S1) :-
    rev(Cont, R),
    S0 = [(R,[])|S1].
ap([A|Z], Cont, S0-S2) :-
    rev(Cont, R),
    S0 = [(R,[A|Z])|S1],
    ap(Z, [A|Cont], S1-S2).
```

assuming some predefined rev/2 procedure (see the next section). In comparing this program with the version given in Section 3.1, we see that, whereas previously append/3 was used, now rev/2 is used as an auxiliary procedure. The structure and time complexity of both programs are equivalent, although one might argue that collecting a continuation and then reversing it is less intuitive than simply appending.

It is interesting to compare the complexity of the nondeterminate Prolog append/3 with that of the continuation-based FGHC append/2. The Prolog program has complexity $O(N)$ where N is the length of the input list. The FGHC program has complexity $O(N^2)$ because we must reverse each of $N + 1$ answers, where the complexity of reversal is $O(N)$ for a list of length N, i.e.,

$$\sum_{i=1}^{N+1} i = \frac{N(N+1)}{2}.$$

Both the Prolog and FGHC programs display parallelism for append(-,-,+). In OR-parallel Prolog, parallelism can be exploited by the findall in a search for independent solutions. In FGHC, each solution Cont can be reversed independently of the next solution. Note, however, that all this parallelism is "false" because it derives from the increased complexity of the algorithm. This pitfall awaits the unwary programmer. Often the unnecessarily high complexity of subordinate functions of an algorithm (e.g., initialization, sorting final solutions, etc.), can produce excellent, but meaningless, speedups. When debugging one of the problems in this book, for the longest time we unwittingly used an algorithm that displayed superlinear speedups (i.e., a speedup *greater* than the number of PEs used to execute the program). Fantastic! Finally the truth dawned that most of the speedup came from an $O(N^2)$ initialization procedure that could be rewritten to be $\sim O(N)$. Then our superlinear speedup disappeared.

```
queen(N,A) :- gen(N,L), queen(L,[],e1,A-[]).

queen([H|T],R,Cont,S) :-
    select([H|T],e2(Cont,R),e2,S).
queen([],R,Cont,S0-S1) :- S0=[R|S1].

select(HT,Cont,Conts,S0-S2) :-
    d1(HT,Cont,Conts,S0-S1),
    d2(HT,Cont,Conts,S1-S2).

d1([D|L],e2(Cont,R),Conts,S) :-
    check(R,D,1,e4(Cont,R,D,L,Conts),S).
d1([], Cont,Conts,S0-S1) :- S0=S1.

d2([H|T],Cont,Conts,S) :-
    select(T,Cont,e5(Conts,H),S).
d2([], Cont,Conts,S0-S1) :- S0=S1.

check([],_,_,e4(Cont,R,A,L,Conts),S) :-
    cont(Conts,e3(Cont,R,A),L,S).
check([H|_],U,D,_,S0-S1) :- H-U =:= D | S0=S1.
check([H|_],U,D,_,S0-S1) :- U-H =:= D | S0=S1.
check([H|T],U,D,Cont,S) :- H-U =\= D, U-H =\= D |
    D1 is D+1,
    check(T,U,D1,Cont,S).

cont(e5(Conts,A),Cont,T,S) :- cont(Conts,Cont,[A|T],S).
cont(e2,e3(Cont,R,A),L,S) :- queen(L,[A|R],Cont,S).
```

Figure 5.9
Ueda's Queens (Translated from Prolog Fused Generate & Test)

Now let us proceed with Ueda's version of N-Queens [138], shown in Figure 5.9. This code is generated by a program, not written by a programmer. The program is translated from the fused Prolog program given in Section 5.1.2. The translation is semi-automatic, but the resulting FGHC code is unfortunately difficult to understand.[2] The program is interesting to examine for various reasons. An estimation of the execution efficiency compared to other queen programs can be obtained by examining the circuity of the control flow. Another issue is how one would debug this program — in its original Prolog, or in FGHC.

We now discuss optimizing the above machine translation by hand with folding-unfolding rules [52]. The resulting program, shown in Figure 5.10, is 34% faster

---

[2]Prolog procedure safe/3 becomes check/5, renamed to mimic Kumon's Queens. Prolog procedure del/3 indirectly becomes select/4 with subprocedures d1 and d2.

```
queen(N,A) :- gen(N,L), queen(L,[],A-[]).

queen([],L,S0-S1) :- S0=[L|S1].
queen( Q,L,S0-S2) :- otherwise |
    d1(Q,[],L,S0-S1),
    d2(Q,[],L,S1-S2).

d1(   [],_,_,S0-S1) :- S0=S1.
d1([P|N],C,L,S) :- check(L,P,1,N,L,C,S).

d2(   [],_,_,S0-S1) :- S0=S1.
d2([P|U],C,L,S0-S2) :-
    d1(U,[P|C],L,S0-S1),
    d2(U,[P|C],L,S1-S2).

check([],_,D,N,L,NCs,S) :- cont(NCs,L,D,N,S).
check([P|Ps],C,D,N,L,NCs,S) :- C-P =\= D, P-C =\= D |
    D1 is D+1,
    check(Ps,C,D1,N,L,NCs,S).
check(_,_,_,_,_,_,S0-S1) :- otherwise | S0=S1.

cont(    [],B,D,N,S) :- queen(N,[D|B],S).
cont([C|Cs],B,D,N,S) :- cont(Cs,B,D,[C|N],S).
```

Figure 5.10
Optimized Ueda's Queens (Translated from Prolog Fused Generate & Test)

(on Symmetry) and easier to understand. Note that the variable `Cont` has been completely removed from the code! It serves no purpose. By unwrapping the continuations, we can remove the redundant passing of two copies of D to `check`. Procedure `check` can be reduced to three clauses by combining the second and third clauses and moving them last, with an `otherwise` guard.

The program in Figure 5.10 is basically the same as Kumon's Queens! Program variables have been renamed and rearranged to match Kumon's Queens, to clarify the similarities. There is only one major difference — the process structure involving `d1` and `d2`. The translation mechanism is not clever enough to have the candidates C as an argument of `queen`. The candidates, and how they are created by appending, are obscurely hidden within `cont/5`. At this point in optimization, nothing less than major restructuring of the program (for which we have no mechanized rules) can produce Kumon's more efficient code. On eight Symmetry PEs, Kumon's 9-Queens executes 14% faster than the optimized Ueda's Queens in Figure 5.10.

5.2.3 Distributed Process Structure

In the optimized FGHC N-Queens implementations previously discussed, the programmers' goal was to make N-Queens run as quickly as possible. When such a program is used as a benchmark for performance measurements, the analyst may lose sight of the fact that N-Queens execution entails passing a trivially simple data structure around a symmetrical proof tree. As a result, information gathered about N-Queens execution does not have much bearing on more meaty applications, e.g., game-playing programs that must pass a game board around the tree. Our objective was to write N-Queens with an incredibly strong/general skeleton (process tree) so that the basic framework could be mapped onto other applications. As far as N-Queens itself is concerned, however, the algorithm we present (Tick's distributed Queens!) has a process tree that is too bulky for the trivial composition of the leaves. As a result, it came as no surprise that this program performed significantly worse than the other FGHC versions.

Tick's Queens is based on Kumon's process structure; however, this is a fully distributed version, i.e., the partial solution is represented solely by a group of `piece` processes. Each `piece` process, representing a placed queen, can respond to the following commands: `echo(I,O)` returns a D-list `I,O` of Y representing the queen's column (the row is implicit in the list order) and `check(X,Y,A)` — check the queen represented by the row,column pair `X,Y` with the internal queen for safety: if safe, return `A=yes`, otherwise `A=no`.

A `queen/5` process first selects a queen `X,Y` for the next placement. The selection

algorithm will never choose a previously selected row and column, so subsequent
checking for this need not done. The queen is sent to a checker which checks for
correctness (i.e., consistency with previous choices). If the queen is consistent,
the checker will spawn a `queen` process to find all solutions including this queen.
Whether the queen is correct or incorrect, another `queen` process is spawned to find
all solutions without the queen.

```
queen(N,A) :- gen(N,L), top(Snd), queen(L,Snd,A).

queen(L,Snd,A) :-
    queen(L,L,[],Snd,A-[]).

queen([C|Cs], [R|Rs], NCs, Snd, S0-S2) :-
    Snd = [check(R,C,Reply)|SndT],
    check(Reply, Rs, R, C, NCs, Cs, SndR, SndT, S0-S1),
    queen(Cs, [R|Rs], [C|NCs], SndR, S1-S2).
queen([], _, [_|_], Snd, S0-S1) :- Snd=[], S0=S1.
queen([], _, [],    Snd, S0-S1) :- Snd=[echo(L,[])], S0=[L|S1].

check(no, _, _, _, _, _, SndR, Snd, S0-S1) :- SndR=Snd, S0=S1.
check(yes, Rs, R, C, NCs, Cs, SndR, Snd, S) :-
    append(NCs, Cs, N),
    merge(SndL, SndR, Snd),
    piece(Snd1, SndL, R, C),
    queen(N, Rs, [], Snd1, S).
```

The `piece`, `top`, and `merge` processes are perpetual, i.e., they act as objects, re-
ceiving a message, acting on it, then calling themselves in anticipation of another
message. Eventually, they kill themselves when a [] message instructs them to
do so. These AND-parallel processes form a virtual OR-tree that is incrementally
pruned as good solutions are found and bad partial solutions are discarded. The
largest execution overhead of Tick's Queens are frequent suspensions, 30 times
Okumura's queens and 2700 times Kumon's Queens for 9-Queens!

```
piece([], Snd, _, _) :- Snd=[].
piece([echo(A,B)|Rcv], Snd, X, Y) :-
    A = [Y|C],
    Snd = [echo(C,B)|Snd0],
    piece(Rcv, Snd0, X, Y).
piece([check(X1,Y1,A)|Rcv], Snd, X2, Y2) :-
    X2-X1 =\= Y2-Y1, X2-X1 =\= Y1-Y2 |
    Snd = [check(X1,Y1,A)|Snd0],
    piece(Rcv, Snd0, X2, Y2).
piece([check(_,_,A)|Rcv], Snd, X, Y) :- otherwise |
    A = no,
    piece(Rcv, Snd, X, Y).
```

```
top([check(_,_,A)|Rcv]) :- A=yes, top(Rcv). % always answer yes
top([echo(A,B)   |Rcv]) :- A=B,   top(Rcv). % finish echo
top([]).                                    % kill yourself
```

The program is fully distributed, so that both the row and column of each queen must be stored and compared in the `piece/4` process. A lazy strategy of checking a new piece is incorporated above. The path from leaf to root must be checked for consistency, but the check is done sequentially by passing the `check/3` message from piece to piece. Another scheme is to eagerly perform the check, broadcasting the message to all pieces in the path to the root. Problems with such a method are that extra work is done, and there is additional overhead combining the replies (**yes** or **no**) from all pieces. Eager evaluation of the check is a form of *speculative parallelism* (see Section 2.3.3) that is quite difficult to execute efficiently for small granularity processes. The specification of the program is given in Figure 5.11.

Since we have chosen to serialize the consistency check, it is possible to simplify the above program by exploiting the fact that the difference in row positions is the distance from the leaf. This version is shown below.

```
queen(N,A) :- gen(N,L), top(Snd), queen(L,[],Snd,A-[]).

queen([C|Cs], NCs, Snd, S0-S2) :-
    Snd = [check(1,C,Reply)|SndT],
    check(Reply, C, NCs, Cs, SndR, SndT, S0-S1),
    queen(Cs, [C|NCs], SndR, S1-S2).
queen([], [_|_], Snd, S0-S1) :- Snd=[], S0=S1.
queen([], [],    Snd, S0-S1) :- Snd=[echo(L,[])], S0=[L|S1].

check( no, _, _, _, SndR, Snd, S0-S1) :- SndR=Snd, S0=S1.
check(yes, C, NCs, Cs, SndR, Snd, S) :-
    append(NCs, Cs, N),
    merge(SndL, SndR, Snd),
    piece(Snd1, SndL, C),
    queen(N, [], Snd1, S).

piece([], Snd, _) :- Snd=[].
piece([echo(A,B)|Rcv], Snd, Y) :-
    A = [Y|C],
    Snd = [echo(C,B)|Snd0],
    piece(Rcv, Snd0, Y).
piece([check(D,Y1,Answer)|Rcv], Snd, Y2) :-
    D =\= Y2-Y1, D =\= Y1-Y2 |
    D1 is D+1,
    Snd = [check(D1,Y1,Answer)|Snd0],
    piece(Rcv, Snd0, Y2).
piece([check(_,_,A)|Rcv], Snd, Y) :- otherwise | A = no,
    piece(Rcv, Snd, Y).
```

<u>Procedure</u>: queen(Cs, Rs, NCs, SndT, S)
  + Cs: list of candidates (columns)   −SndT: stream to top/1
  + Rs: list of rows   − S: stream of solutions
  + NCs: list of noncandidates

<u>Relation</u>: S contains all extensions of the partial solution represented by the
  piece/4 processes connected to communication stream SndT. A partial
  solution is completed with the positions given in Rs and Cs, NCs. If a
  partial solution cannot be completed then SndT is closed.

<u>Preconditions</u>: Initially Cs is a list of all columns, Rs is a list of all rows, and
  NCs is empty. Initially SndT communicates to process top/1.

<u>Postconditions</u>: Upon completion of the search, the top process and all piece
  processes are terminated.

<u>Procedure</u>: check(Reply, Rs, R, C, NCs, Cs, SndR, SndT, S)
  +Reply: atom (yes/no)   +NCs: noncandidate list
  +Rs: list of rows   +Cs: candidate list
  +R: row number   −SndR: stream from sibling
  +C: column number   −SndT: stream towards top/1
                            − S: stream of solutions

<u>Relation</u>: If Reply=yes then S contains all partial solutions represented by
  the piece processes connected to communication stream SndT. A partial
  solution is extended by the queen placed at (R,C) and completed with
  the queen positions given in Rs and Cs, NCs. The completed queens
  communicate via a stream merged with SndR into SndT. Otherwise if
  Reply=no then the partial solution cannot be extended.

<u>Procedure</u>: top(In)
  + In: stream of queries

<u>Relation</u>: For query check/3 answer affirmative. For query echo/2 short the
  D-list. For query [] terminate.

<u>Procedure</u>: piece(In, Out, X, Y)
  + In: stream of queries   + X: row number
  − Out: stream of queries   + Y: column number

<u>Relation</u>: For query check/3, if locally consistent then pass message up,
  otherwise answer negative. For query echo/2, partially bind D-list to
  local queen, and pass message up. For query [] terminate.

Figure 5.11
Informal Specification of Tick's Queens

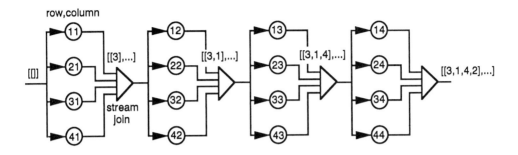

Figure 5.12
Pipelined Filters Process Structure of 4-Queens

This program looks similar to Kumon's program. Kumon's 9-Queens is 3–4 times faster, however, primarily due to the overhead of checking constraints by message passing. Speedup is comparable: on eight Symmetry PEs, Tick's (distributed) 9-Queens has a speedup of 6.9 and Kumon's 9-Queens has a speedup of 7.7.

5.2.4 Pipelined Filters

Pipelined filters in FGHC are akin to the fused generate & test paradigm in sequential Prolog. We have seen that, by Ueda's continuation-based method, the fused generate & test program can be transformed into a non/candidates program. Pipelined filters differs primarily in that the process structure is a linear pipeline of processes, not an OR-tree. The pipelined filters mimic the Prolog program structure: each stage of the pipeline corresponds to a fused generator/tester pair. A pipeline stage is composed of multiple `filter` processes that implement the nondeterminism inherent in the Prolog program.

The FGHC program spawns a "column" of N `filter/4` processes for every column in the chessboard. Thus N^2 filters are spawned, as illustrated in Figure 5.12 for 4-Queens. Filters belonging to the same column share a single input stream (broadcast to the filters). The filters of the column have their outputs linked together in an output stream.

```
queen(N,A) :- queen(1,N,[[]],A).

queen(I,N,In,Out) :- I =< N |
    I1 is I+1,
    column(1,N,In,In1),
    queen(I1,N,In1,Out).
queen(I,N,In,Out) :- I > N | Out=In.

column(I,N,In,Out) :- I =< N |
    I1 is I+1,
    filter(In,I,Out-Out1),
    column(I1,N,In,Out1).
column(I,N,_,Out) :- I > N | Out=[].
```

Initially a seed input of [] is given to the **filter** process structure. The job of
a filter is to determine if the incoming message, representing a partial solution,
is compatible with the square represented by that filter. If the incoming partial
solution is *not* compatible (clause 3 of **check**), then the solution is discarded. If
the incoming partial solution *is* compatible (**check** recursive terminates in clause 1
when all queens in the first argument are tested), then the square is prepended to
the partial solution.[3]

```
filter([],     _,S0-S1) :- S0=S1.
filter([P|Ps],I,S0-S2) :-
    filter(Ps,I,S1-S2),
    check(P,I,1,P,S0-S1).

check([],I,_,P,S0-S1) :- S0=[[[I|P]]|S1].
check([J|Js],I,D,P,S) :-
    J =\= I, D =\= I-J, D =\= J-I |
    D1 is D+1,
    check(Js,I,D1,P,S).
check(_,_,_,_,S0-S1) :- otherwise | S0=S1.
```

The output stream from the final column of filters will contain only complete, valid
solutions. The informal specification of this program is given in Figure 5.13.

In the pipelined filters program we get pipeline parallelism, i.e., concurrent computation in different filters in the pipeline. Initially the computation "spreads"
through the pipe from the leftmost column of the board (given the seed). "Spread-
ing" is a natural result of process scheduling and automatic producer-consumer
stream communication. The parallelism is limited by the startup time to fill the
pipeline and the wind-down time to empty the pipeline. In addition, when **check**

---

[3]Unlike the previous N-Queens programs, we are now considering partial solutions containing
queens specified by row number, where column number is implicit. The pipelined filters program
has a different orientation because usually pipelines are drawn from horizontally, i.e., as a row of
columns. Since rows and columns are interchangeable, this distinction is unimportant.

Procedure: `queen(I, N, In, Out)`
  + `I`: column number   + `In`: partial solution stream
  + `N`: number of rows   − `Out`: solution stream

Relation: `Out` contains all extensions of the partial solutions from `In`, solving the N-Queens problem. Partial solutions are of length I-1.

Preconditions: Initially `I=1` and `In = [[]]`.

Procedure: `column(I, N, In, Out)`
  + `I`: row number   + `In`: partial solution stream
  + `N`: number of rows   − `Out`: partial solution stream

Relation: `Out` contains all extensions of the partial solutions from `In`, solving the N-Queens problem. Partial solutions are of length I-1.

Preconditions: Initially `I=1`.

Procedure: `filter(In, I, Out)`
  + `In`: partial solution stream   − `Out`: partial solution stream
  + `I`: row number

Relation: Stream `Out` contains all partial solutions incoming on stream `In` that can be extended by row `I`, for the implicit column of this `filter` process.

Procedure: `check(Js, I, D, Ps, Out)`
  + `Js`: list of queens (rows)   + `Ps`: list of queens
  + `I`: row number   − `Out`: stream of partial solutions
  + `D`: integer

Relation: If queen `I` is consistent with remaining partial solution `Js` at column distance `D`, then partial solution `Ps` is extended by `I` and sent down `Out`.

Preconditions: Initially `D=1`.

Figure 5.13
Informal Specification of Pipelined-Filters Queens

starts to check partial solution P against queen I, no output is made until the check is complete. Notice that later columns will also have to check P, but cannot begin until the previous check is finished. We can envision a type of speculative parallelism wherein later columns can begin checking P even *before* previous columns have completed their check (more on this idea later).

In addition to limited parallelism, the pipelined filters method has another great disadvantage. Communication between columns of filters via streams, i.e., D-lists, creates a tremendous amount of garbage. Specifically, problems lie in two places in the above program. The second clause of `filter/4` contains the input argument `[P|Ps]`, where the next partial solution P is read. The list is decomposed into its head and tail. The list will in fact be decomposed in this fashion in each filter of the column. When the last filter to decompose the list has completed, the list is no longer referenced, i.e., the list pointer becomes garbage.

This concern may seem a small, but consider that 50% of the storage required for this stream is occupied by list pointers (tails). In this program, each stage of the pipeline essentially rebuilds its input stream, leaving all the list pointers and the filtered-away partial solutions as garbage. The stream is rebuilt in the first clause of `check/5` with the goal `S0=[[I|P]|S1]` where the partial solution is extended by queen I. Here the new list pointer is `S0=[_|S1]`. Since there are N stages, there is about N times as much list-pointer garbage as in a single stage (although the size of stream fluctuates for each stage).

The previous analysis condemns not only pipelined filters, but in fact *any* program with stream communication! Let us return even to the very first program in the book, `append`.

```
append([],L1,L2) :- L1=L2.
append([X|L1],L2,L4) :- L4=[X|L3], append(L1,L2,L3).
```

Here we see the same problem. The arguments can be considered streams and the input stream is decomposed in the head of the second clause. The output stream is constructed in the goal `L4=[X|L3]`. Again, for each iteration, the list pointer of the input stream is left as garbage.

For `append` we could imagine a sophisticated compiler that would reuse the tails. But such sophistication would require doing dataflow analysis to determine that no other process shares the input list. Another idea is to implement incremental garbage collection, and a prime spot for reclaiming and reusing a storage cell is in the second clause of `append` above. For example, the MRB scheme [25] generates code to check if the list pointer is in fact no longer referenced once the second clause commits. If so, then the tail is reused (overwritten) during list construction in the first goal. Otherwise new storage is allocated and garbage is generated. However, stream input and output (list decomposition and construction) rarely occur in the same clause! Glancing at the many FGHC programs in this book, one can surmise that the `append` case is a fluke.[4] Reducing garbage in the pipelined filters N-Queens program would be next to impossible because decomposition is of the list [P|Ps]. Only the *last* filter within a column to decompose the list would be permitted to reuse it, and only if both P and Ps were no longer referenced. But Ps is clearly in use until *all* filters in the next pipeline stage finish reading!

Perhaps it is mysterious that the candidates program, which solves the same N-Queens problem and also uses streams to some extent, does not share these problems. The reason is that the candidates program creates a process tree, not pipeline. Each branch in the tree corresponds to a partial solution. Thus no stream communication is used for *building* partial solutions. We write only final solutions to an output stream.

> In summary, pipelined filters correspond closely to sequential fused generate & test. Unlike (non)candidates, which also can be derived from fused generate & test (by automatic translation from Prolog), pipelined filters has many problems stemming from its linear process structure. These problems include sequentiality of the pipeline, stream synchronization, and heavy garbage production.

The pipelined filters program was introduced as a precursor to the following *layered-stream* program. In essence, layered streams reduce pipeline startup and wind-down times and exploit the speculative parallelism mentioned. Stream synchronization and garbage production are drastically reduced.

5.2.5 Layered Streams

Recall from Section 2.2.4 that a layered stream is either the special atom `begin` or a (possibly empty) list of structures H*Ts, where H is a head of a list and Ts is a set of all possible tails of H. Argument Ts is itself represented with a layered stream. This style of programming exploits a great amount of parallelism because a producer can send an element through a layered stream before its tail has been constructed.

The layered-streams N-Queens program was written by A. Okumura [94]. The `queen/4` and `column/4` processes (identical to those in the previous pipelined filters

---

[4]and a further reason for disbelieving any performance figures concerning the speed of `append` or naive reverse.

program) create a grid of processes that initially consists of one `filter` process per
square of the board.

```
queen(N,A) :- queen(1,N,begin,LS), fromLStoL(LS,A).

queen(I,N,In,Out) :- I =< N |
    I1 is I+1,
    column(1,N,In,In1),
    queen(I1,N,In1,Out).
queen(I,N,In,Out) :- I > N | Out=In.

column(I,N,In,Out) :- I =< N |
    I1 is I+1,
    filter(In,I,Out-Out1),
    column(I1,N,In,Out1).
column(I,N,_,Out) :- I > N | Out=[].
```

Initially a seed of the atom `begin` is input to the first column of filters, and each
column independently seeds its successor column with a partial solution, `I*In1` in
`filter/3`, shown below. Procedure `filter/4` encapsulates the queen check. For
an input layered stream `J*In`, if queen J at depth D is compatible with the filter's
queen I, then the partial solution `J*NewIn` is issued down the output stream (clause
3). Two filters are then spawned. The first filter checks the sub-layers of solution
J and creates `NewIn`. The second filter checks remaining solutions at the current
level, `Ins`, and creates `Out1`. If the check fails, then the remaining partial solutions
are checked (clause 4).

```
filter(In,I,S0-S1) :- S0=[I*In1|S1], filter(In,I,1,In1).

filter(begin,_,_,Out) :- Out = begin.
filter([],_,_,Out) :- Out = [].
filter([J*In|Ins],I,D,Out) :-
    J =\= I, D =\= I-J, D =\= J-I |
    D1 is D+1,
    Out = [J*NewIn|Out1],
    filter(In,I,D1,NewIn),
    filter(Ins,I,D,Out1).
filter([_|Ins],I,D,Out) :- otherwise | filter(Ins,I,D,Out).
```

Filter `fromLStoL(LS,L)` converts a layered stream LS into a list L (Section 2.2.4).

```
fromLStoL(LS,L) :- fromLStoS(LS,[],L-[]).

fromLStoS(begin,        Stack,L0-L1) :- L0=[Stack|L1].
fromLStoS([],             _,L0-L1) :- L0=L1.
fromLStoS([A*LS1|Rest],Stack,L0-L2) :-
    fromLStoS(LS1,[A|Stack], L0-L1),
    fromLStoS(Rest,Stack,     L1-L2).
```

```
    [1*[3*[5*[2*[4*[]]]],           ┌──▶ 4*[1*[3*[5*[2*[]],
            6*[2*[]]],                      6*[2*[]]],
        4*[2*[5*[3*[]]]],                 5*[2*[6*[3*begin]]]],
            6*[3*[]]],                 2*[5*[3*[1*[],
        5*[2*[6*[3*[]]]]],                    6*[]]]],
        6*[2*[5*[]],                   6*[1*[3*[5*[]],
            4*[2*[]]]],                     5*[2*[]]],
    2*[4*[1*[3*[5*[]]]],               3*[5*[2*[]]]]],
            6*[1*[3*[5*begin],     5*[1*[4*[6*[3*[]]],
                5*[]],                     6*[4*[2*[]]]],
            3*[5*[]]]],                2*[4*[1*[3*[],
        5*[1*[4*[],                        6*[3*[]]],
            6*[4*[]]],                 6*[1*[3*[],
        3*[1*[4*[]],                        3*[]]],
            6*[4*[]]]],                3*[1*[4*[2*[]],
        6*[1*[3*[5*[]]],                    6*[2*[],
            3*[1*[4*[]]]]],                     4*[2*begin]]],
    3*[1*[4*[2*[5*[]]],                6*[4*[2*[]]]]],
            6*[2*[5*[]],           6*[1*[3*[5*[]],
                4*[2*[]]]],                5*[2*[]]],
        5*[2*[4*[1*[],                 2*[5*[1*[4*[]]]],
                6*[]]]],               3*[1*[4*[],
        6*[2*[5*[1*[4*begin]]],             5*[2*[4*[]]]],
            4*[1*[5*[]],               4*[1*[5*[]],
                2*[5*[]]]]],   ───┘        2*[5*[3*[]]]]]]]]
```

Figure 5.14
Layered Stream Produced by Okumura's 6-Queens

To increase the efficiency of this program, the layered-stream representation of X*Y
can be changed to [X|Y]. This optimization reduces the storage requirement of the
layered stream, thereby increasing program speed.

To further understand how Okumura's queens works, consider the layered stream
LS produced for 6-Queens, shown in Figure 5.14. Note that the structure of the
layered stream is a list of elements, H*Ts, where H is an integer (queen placement)
and Ts is a layered stream of all possible tails. Thus the layered stream is actually
a tree, where the leaves are either **begin** or []. A **begin** leaf represents a solution,
found by traversing from root to leaf. In Figure 5.14 the four solutions are easily
seen — the first is [2,4,6,1,3,5]. A [] leaf represents a dead branch, i.e., all N
queens could not be placed because in some row (given by the depth of the [] leaf)
all previous queens attacked every position.

5.2.6   Throttling Eager Evaluation in Layered Streams

We can use a *nil check* [94] to avoid the production of most invalid layered streams. A modification is required in the last clause of `filter/4`:

```
filter([J*In|Ins],I,D,Out) :-
    J =\= I, D =\= I-J, D =\= J-I |
    D1 is D+1,
    filter(In,I,D1,NewIn),
    send(NewIn,J,Out-Out1),
    filter(Ins,I,D,Out1).

send( [],_,S0-S1) :- S0=S1.
send(Out,Q,S0-S1) :- Out\=[] | S0=[Q*Out|S1].
```

The idea behind the nil check, `send/3`, is to throttle speculative parallelism. We do not allow the partial solution to be sent down the output stream unless we are sure that at least the next layer is not totally incompatible. This process kills some of the eager evaluation in the algorithm, preventing subsequent filters from executing unnecessary work.

   We can also insert a nil check in `filter/3`, where the initial seeds are planted at the beginning of the computation. This check has little effect because most seeds will be compatible with at least one following constraint. In all the nil-check programs given in this book, we include the check only in the critical filter split.

   With the nil check the layered stream is almost minimal in size:

```
[1*[],
 2*[4*[6*[1*[3*[5*begin]]]]],
 3*[6*[2*[5*[1*[4*begin]]]]],
 4*[1*[5*[2*[6*[3*begin]]]]],
 5*[3*[1*[6*[4*[2*begin]]]]]]
 6*[]]
```

There is no sharing among the answers in 6-Queens, but application of the nil check does not prevent such sharing. As another example, consider 9-Queens with 352 solutions. In a standard stream representation, each solution is a list of nine integers, requiring 20 data words per solution (the extra two words are the stream storage overhead). A layered stream program without nil checks produces solutions that are an average of 95 words long. With nil checks a solution is on average 25 words. Note that, to exploit structure sharing, layered streams have inherent space overhead. Thus even with no garbage in the layered stream, the average of 25 words per solution is *higher* than the standard representation. This finding is usually the case, but not always. If the solutions share enough common structure, the average size may be *lower* than in a standard representation. The N-Cubes problem (Chapter 9) is one such example.

The synchronization overhead of the nil check makes itself felt by an increase in suspensions, thereby reducing parallelism. However, because the layered-stream program without nil checks is overeager, it suspends more frequently. For example, in Panda on eight Symmetry PEs, the 10-Queens layered-stream program achieves 6.9 speedup with 111,000 suspensions compared to a speedup of 6.5 with 26,000 suspensions with the nil check. The nil-check version executed in 13.4 seconds compared to 13.7 seconds without the nil check. Although the difference in these statistics is below the variance of the measurements, the statistics tend to support the hypothesis that a nil check benefits performance by throttling harmful eager evaluation.

5.3   Single and Multiple Solution Search

5.3.1   Parallel Cut in OR-Prolog

In any of the OR-parallel Prolog Queens programs discussed, the query

```
?- queen(8, A).
```

will find a solution to 8-Queens; however, workers will proceed searching for multiple solutions, building the OR-tree in anticipation of backtracking. Although A has been bound to a single solution, it is not guaranteed that the work expended was proportional to finding only a single solution. To ensure this proportion, the first worker (i.e., processor) to find a solution needs to cut all remaining workers.

Aurora offers two types of cut in this regard. A *strict cut* will enforce that the solution found is in fact the leftmost in the OR-tree, i.e., sequential Prolog semantics are guaranteed. This cut is indicated in the standard way:

```
?- queen(8,A), !.
```

To avoid limiting parallelism in this manner, if any solution will suffice, a *cavalier commit* is offered. Cavalier commit, '/'/0 can be executed by the first arriving worker, i.e., the quickest solution cuts out the others. The query

```
?- queen(8,A), /.
```

signifies that the first worker to find an answer should cut the search space, i.e., terminate all other workers.

In general, cuts can be used anywhere in an OR-Prolog program, just like Prolog. The *scope* of a cut is the lexical procedure containing the cut, and all the procedures it calls before the cut. Thus the portion of the search space created by these subprocedures will be removed. We say the scope is non-parallel if none of the subprocedures are declared as **parallel**. In a non-parallel scope, there are no branchpoints (only choicepoints) and a cut acts like a normal Prolog cut, removing a portion of the OR-tree branch private to the worker executing the cut. *All the cuts encountered in programs given in this book act in non-parallel scopes.*

If the scope of the cut is parallel, then the cut may need to operate over a portion of the OR-tree containing branchpoints and multiple branches. The cut may affect workers other than the one executing the cut. These mechanics are quite complex [59]; however, the user view is as described above. A clean and self-documenting way to use parallel cuts is to wrap them up so that they become evident in the code:

```
oneof(P) :- call(P), /.

?- oneof(queen(8, A)).
```

We can thus search for one or all solutions, but we cannot search for some intermediate number of solutions with Aurora (Delta version). To implement multiple-solution search, some type of semaphore machinery must be built into each parallel cut, for instance as !(N) or /(N). Each worker executing the cut would essentially decrement the semaphore. The worker that decremented the semaphore to zero could then cut the remaining workers. This cut could be hidden inside a generalized **findsome** procedure:

```
someof(P,N) :- call(P), /(N).
findsome(N,A,P,L) :- findall(A, someof(P,N), L).

?- findsome(N, A, queen(8,A), As).
```

5.3.2   Termination Flags and Lazy Evaluation in FGHC

Kumon's Queens is a good candidate (argghhh...) for illustrating how to conduct an OR-parallel search *for a fixed number of solutions* in an AND-parallel system. We present four versions of Kumon's algorithm in this section. The algorithms progress from naive and slow (send all solutions to a filter which counts down only the ones needed and then kills the OR-parallel search) to sophisticated and fast (true lazy evaluation driven by unbound variables in the output stream).

Figure 5.15 shows a naive version of the candidate/noncandidate queens program that is modified to find M solutions. If less than M solutions exist then all solutions are returned. The key to the program is the **filter/4** procedure which counts down the first M solutions and binds the Stop flag when the Mth is found. The Stop flag

```
queen(N,M,B) :- M>0 |
    gen(N,L),
    queen(L,[],[],A-[],Stop),
    filter(A,B,M,Stop).

filter([],    B,_,_  ) :- B=[].
filter([A| _],B,1,Stop) :- Stop=stop, B=[A].
filter([A|As],B,M,Stop) :- B=[A|Bs],
    M1 is M-1, filter(As,Bs,M1,Stop).

queen(_,_,_,S0-S1,stop) :- S0=S1.
queen([C|Cs],NCs,L,S0-S2,Stop) :-
    check(C,Cs,NCs,L,S0-S1,Stop),
    queen(Cs,[C|NCs],L,S1-S2,Stop).
queen([],[],L,S0-S1,_) :- S0=[L|S1].
queen([],[_|_],_,S0-S1,_) :- S0=S1.

check(C,Cs,NCs,L,S,Stop) :- check(L,C,1,NCs,Cs,L,S,Stop).

check([],C,_,NCs,Cs,L,S,Stop) :-
    append(NCs,Cs,Ps),
    queen(Ps,[],[C|L],S,Stop).
check([P|Ps],C,D,NCs,Cs,L,S,Stop) :-
    P-C =\= D,  C-P =\= D |
    D1 is D+1,
    check(Ps,C,D1,NCs,Cs,L,S,Stop).
check(_,_,_,_,_,_,S0-S1,_) :- otherwise | S0=S1.
```

Figure 5.15
M Solutions (Non)Candidates N-Queens (Depth-First Search, FGHC)

```
queen(N,M,B) :- M>0 |
    gen(N,L),
    queen(L,[],[],A,Stop),
    filter(A,B,M,Stop).

queen(_,_,_,S,stop) :- S=[].
queen([C|Cs],NCs,L,S,Stop) :-
    check(C,Cs,NCs,L,S1,S,Stop),
    queen(Cs,[C|NCs],L,S2,Stop).
queen([],    [],L,S,_) :- S=[L].
queen([],[_|_],_,S,_) :- S=[].

check(C,Cs,NCs,L,S1,S,Stop) :-
    check(L,C,1,NCs,Cs,L,S1,S,Stop).

check([],C,_,NCs,Cs,L,S1,S,Stop) :-
    append(NCs,Cs,Ps),
    merge(S1,S2,S),
    queen(Ps,[],[C|L],S2,Stop).
check([P|Ps],C,D,NCs,Cs,L,S1,S,Stop) :-
    P-C =\= D,  C-P =\= D |
    D1 is D+1,
    check(Ps,C,D1,NCs,Cs,L,S1,S,Stop).
check(_,_,_,_,_,_,S1,S,_) :- otherwise | S=S1.
```

Figure 5.16
M Quickest Solutions (Non)Candidates N-Queens (FGHC)

is passed through queen/5. The first clause of queen/5 checks if Stop is bound, in which case the process is terminated. This encoding assumes that the clauses in queen/5 are evaluated in their textual order.[5]

As written, the program finds solutions in the same order as the all-solutions search. In some cases this method is not beneficial because we may wish to find the M quickest solutions and any solutions will suffice. Thus a stream cannot be used for collecting the answers, because that fixes the order to a depth-first search. Instead the solutions must be sent to the filter via a merge tree (see Section 4.2).

Figure 5.16 shows the new version of Kumon's Queens that finds the M quickest solutions. Note the use of the binary merge in the first clause of check/9 for routing solutions sent from the two child processes. This delayed use of merge avoids spawning when the check fails.

There are some serious cautions concerning these M-solution programs. First, if

---

[5]In some languages a more robust version of this program can be written with extra-logical builtin guards such as var/2 (see Section 2.2.5).

the problem has a fairly uniform search space, i.e., all solutions require about the same amount of computation and are distributed within the OR-tree uniformly, then searching for a few solutions on a large number of PEs probably will not achieve efficient speedups. The PEs may begin to explore more independent solution paths (in the OR-tree) than the desired number of solutions. Note that the filter only stops the computation *after* the solutions are produced.

In general, we have difficulty controlling the allocation of PEs to branches of the OR-tree. Panda uses, by and large, a depth-first scheduler. By this we mean that scheduling decisions favor exploration of the leftmost part of the search space. This policy can be overcome by explicit synchronization encoded in the user program. Algorithmically, Kumon's Queens is a breadth-first search but, local to a PE, Panda executes depth-first. Thus a hybrid effect is achieved. It is difficult to predict and impossible to guarantee that "quick" solutions on the right side of the OR-tree will be found before slower solutions to the left.

Third, and most serious, it is possible that the scheduler *cannot be trusted at all* to schedule goals fairly. Thus all solutions may be computed, even in a single-solution program! Consider what will happen in the previous programs if the `filter` process is not scheduled fairly. For instance, `filter` suspends waiting for a solution and is not immediately resumed by the scheduler when a solution appears. If this happens, then the search processes (`queen` and `check`) will continue producing solutions even though the solutions are not needed. This unnecessary production can have a detrimental feedback effect on the scheduler, causing the search processes to multiply, *starving* the filter. Starvation is in general the hogging of some resource by a process or set of processes to the detriment of other processes.

One way to fix these problems is to allow the programmer to assign *priorities* to goals. Because Panda does not have the capability of priorities, we cannot comment on their utility. In general, it would appear difficult to determine a good set of priorities in a complex program. However, in some cases, priorities can be used cleverly to drastically reduce the complexity of a nondeterminate algorithm. We discuss this further in the context of the BestPath Problem in Chapter 12. An alternative, considered next, is to sequentialize the search. This alternative may seem drastic but, in most cases, it is better to have a slow program that executes than a potentially fast program that doesn't execute!

Figure 5.17 shows a version of Kumon's Queens that is strictly sequential. The program searches for M solutions[6] one at a time, enforcing sequentiality by a short-circuit chain KO-K in `queen/5`. The chain is initialized to M-_. Procedure `queen/5` is

---

[6] If M is greater than the number of available solutions then this program will deadlock. Additional checks to avoid this have been left as an exercise.

```
go(M,N,A) :-
    gen(N,L),
    queen(L,[],[],A-[],M-_).

queen(_,_,_,S0-S1,0-K) :- S0=S1, K=0.
queen([C|Cs],NCs,L,S0-S2,K0-K) :- integer(K0) |
    check(L,C,1,NCs,Cs,L,S0-S1,K0-K1),
    queen(Cs,[C|NCs],L,S1-S2,K1-K).
queen([],[],L,S0-S1,K0-K) :- K is K0-1, S0=[L|S1].
queen([],[_|_],_,S0-S1,K0-K) :- S0=S1, K=K0.

check([],C,_,NCs,Cs,L,S,K) :-
    append(NCs,Cs,Ps),
    queen(Ps,[],[C|L],S,K).
check([P|Ps],C,D,NCs,Cs,L,S,K) :-
    P-C =\= D, C-P =\= D |
    D1 is D+1,
    check(Ps,C,D1,NCs,Cs,L,S,K).
check(_,_,_,_,_,_,S0-S1,K0-K) :- otherwise | S0=S1, K=K0.
```

Figure 5.17
Serialized M Solutions (Non)Candidates N-Queens (FGHC)

synchronized on K0 in the chain K0-K and will suspend unless K0 is an integer. In the second clause, where the OR-tree is split into two parallel branches, the right branch (**queen**) is synchronized on K1. This trick enforces pure depth-first evaluation of the search space. If a solution is found (clause 3) then K0 is decremented. If K0=0 (first clause) then the desired number of solutions have all been found. In the last clause, this branch of the OR-tree is abandoned because it offers no valid solutions. In both cases, the answer stream and short-circuit chain are shorted.

The previous algorithm assumes that we know M, the number of desired solutions, ahead of time. Often this is not the case, and we wish to drive the computation from the output. Such demand-driven or lazy evaluation was introduced in Section 4.1.4. Figure 5.18 shows a lazy candidates/noncandidates N-Queens program (**check/8** is identical to that of the previous program). The top-level query assumes that both arguments are instantiated — the output **A** must be bound by the consumer to a list of unbound variables. The instantiation of **A** drives the computation. The program is remarkably similar to the previous program. Instead of having the short-circuit chain constructed of integer counters, a simple **ok** flag suffices. Procedure **queen/5** is synchronized on **ok** and will compute the solutions sequentially.

```
go(N,A) :-
    gen(N,L),
    queen(L,[],[],A-_,ok-_).

queen(_,_,_,[]-As,ok-K) :- As=[], K=ok.
queen([C|Cs],NCs,L,S0-S2,ok-K) :-
    check(L,C,1,NCs,Cs,L,S0-S1,ok-K1),
    queen(Cs,[C|NCs],L,S1-S2,K1-K).
queen([],[],L,[A|As]-Out,ok-K) :- A=L, Out=As, K=ok.
queen([],[_|_],_,S0-S1,ok-K) :- S1=S0, K=ok.
```

Figure 5.18
Lazy (Non)Candidates N-Queens (FGHC)

The key difference in the programs is the third clause of `queen/5`. Here the output stream must have an answer slot A to avoid suspension. If the slot exists, then it is bound to a solution L[7] and computation proceeds by binding Out to the tail of the output stream As, and shorting the synchronization chain. This action allows the *next* solution to be computed *before* the request (the next A slot) has been verified. If the consumer is late in terminating the output stream, then the producer will have calculated at most one extra solution.

Converting eager programs into lazy programs does not always follow a set pattern. The only general rule is that the output stream becomes an input stream, driving the computation. If the original eager program is an OR-parallel search, then it must be sequentialized. We have seen how searching for solutions in parallel while filtering only those that are desired may not produce demand-driven behavior if the filter is not scheduled with high enough priority.

As a final point, when developing all four of these programs, deadlock was a constant headache. "Lucky deadlock" occurs after the M solutions have been found, and simply means that some leftover goals were not properly terminated. "Unlucky deadlock" occurs in the midst of the computation. When short-circuit chains are used for serialization, as they are here, deadlock is often the result of neglecting to short the chain at the proper juncture.

---

[7]As in the previous program, if no more solutions exist, and a slot is given, then the program will deadlock. Additional checks to avoid this have been left as an exercise.

Author	Method	instr	reduct	back†	entries	sec	KEPS
\multicolumn{8}{c}{**Aurora/Prolog**}							
Bruynooghe	naive gen & test	59087962	5776886	986411	6763297	113.0	60
Bratko	pseudo-constraints	3781143	312168	481020	793188	13.6	58
Pereira	fused gen & test	1708218	138214	24013	162227	5.3	31
Kondo	blackboard	517776	45152	32055	77223	2.7	29
Bratko	with structures	603503	45067	24022	69089	2.6	27
\multicolumn{8}{c}{**Panda/FGHC**}							
Tick	distributed	5771641	319767	222057	541824	13.9	39
Tick	pipelined filters	4274063	287757	559	288316	15.6	18
Ueda	from fused Prolog	3456495	218458	52	218510	6.6	33
Ueda	optimized	2311350	186405	79	186484	4.2	44
Kumon	candidates	2112454	144918	82	145000	4.2	35
Okumura	layered streams ‡	1480037	98731	7523	106254	3.2	33

† backtracks for Prolog, suspensions for FGHC.
‡ with [H|Ts] notation and no nil-check.

Table 5.2
9-Queens High-Level Characteristics (Eight PEs Symmetry)

> Short-circuit chains can be constructed in various ways. To collect M
> solutions in OR-parallel search, where M is known *a priori*, a serial-
> ization chain K0-K can be used. Variable K0 is initialized to M and is
> decremented as each solution is found. When K0=0 the desired solutions
> have been found and the computation must be terminated. To imple-
> ment lazy evaluation, a short-chain K0-K of a single synchronization
> flag can be used. When a solution is found, the consumer synchronizes
> on the unbound head of the output stream. When the output stream
> empties, the computation must be terminated.

5.4   Discussion

In this section we compare the performance of the N-Queens algorithms for all-
solutions search. Table 5.2 gives the high-level characteristics of the various queens
programs. For this and all subsequent programs in the book, the following measurements are given: number of instructions executed, number of reductions, number
of backtracks (for Prolog) or suspensions (for FGHC), number of procedure entries

Author	Method	1 PE	2 PE	4 PE	8 PE	12 PE	15 PE
Aurora/Prolog							
Bruynooghe	naive gen & test	850.0	424.3	217.4	113.0	74.2	59.7
Bratko	pseudo-constraints	88.6	46.3	23.6	13.6	7.0	6.2
Pereira	fused gen & test	24.4	12.4	6.8	5.3	3.0	2.7
Kondo	blackboard	15.0	7.4	4.2	2.7	2.2	2.0
Bratko	with structures	13.4	7.3	4.2	2.6	2.1	2.0
Panda/FGHC							
Tick	distributed	95.8	49.5	26.7	13.9	10.2	7.9
Tick	pipelined filters	58.1	30.6	18.4	15.6	20.2	15.7
Ueda	from fused Prolog	49.7	25.2	12.8	6.4	4.3	3.5
Ueda	optimized	31.8	16.2	8.3	4.2	2.8	2.3
Kumon	candidates	28.3	14.3	7.2	3.7	2.5	2.0
Okumura	layered streams †	21.4	11.2	6.0	3.2	2.3	1.8

† with [H|Ts] notation and no nil-check.

Table 5.3
9-Queens: Execution Time (Seconds) on Symmetry

(reductions plus backtracks or suspensions), and thousands of entries per second (KEPS). Table 5.3 gives the execution time (in seconds) of the programs on Symmetry. Table 5.4 gives both the naive and the real speedups of the programs on Symmetry.

All programs displayed improved performance with increasing numbers of PEs, except the pipelined filters in FGHC. Pipelined filters displayed serious garbage collection overheads on more than eight PEs. Moreover, measurements of GC time varied greatly from run to run, indicating that the algorithm produced highly unbalanced amounts of garbage on the multiple PEs. Since the time to conduct a parallel GC in Panda is the maximum of the times to conduct a GC on each PE, garbage unbalancing causes overheads (other parallel GC algorithms may avoid this problem). Notice that layered streams in FGHC does not have this problem, although the process structure is almost the same. The difference between the two programs is in their dataflow. Layered streams is more balanced because each column of filters begins partial computation at the beginning of program execution.

All the queens programs, except for the layered-streams program, create the same OR-tree process structure when searching for solutions. These programs all test a new queen placement (at a leaf) against all previously placed queens in the partial solution represented by an OR-tree path from root to leaf. Consider the segment of the OR-tree for 6-Queens illustrated in Figure 5.19. When we place the queens in

Author	Method	1 PE	2 PE	4 PE	8 PE	12 PE	15 PE
Aurora/Prolog							
Bruynooghe	naive gen & test	1.0	2.0	3.9	7.5	11	14
		0.02	0.03	0.06	0.12	0.18	0.22
Bratko	pseudo-constraints	1.0	1.9	3.8	6.5	13	14
		0.15	0.29	0.57	0.99	1.9	2.2
Pereira	fused gen & test	1.0	2.0	3.6	4.6	8.1	9.0
		0.55	1.1	2.0	2.5	4.5	5.0
Kondo	blackboard	1.0	2.0	3.6	5.6	6.8	7.5
		0.89	1.8	3.2	5.0	6.1	6.7
Bratko	structures	1.0	1.8	3.2	5.2	6.4	6.7
Panda/FGHC							
Tick	distributed	1.0	1.9	3.6	6.9	9.4	12
		0.22	0.43	0.81	1.6	2.1	2.7
Tick	pipelined filters	1.0	1.9	3.2	3.7	2.9	3.7
		0.37	0.70	1.2	1.4	1.1	1.4
Ueda	from fused Prolog	1.0	2.0	3.9	7.8	12	14
		0.43	0.85	1.7	3.4	5.0	6.1
Ueda	optimized	1.0	2.0	3.8	7.6	11	14
		0.67	1.3	2.6	5.1	7.6	9.3
Kumon	candidates	1.0	2.0	3.9	7.6	11	14
		0.76	1.5	3.0	5.8	8.6	11
Okumura	layered streams †	1.0	1.9	3.6	6.7	9.3	12

† with [H|Ts] notation and no nil-check.

Table 5.4
9-Queens Speedups (Naive/Real) on Symmetry

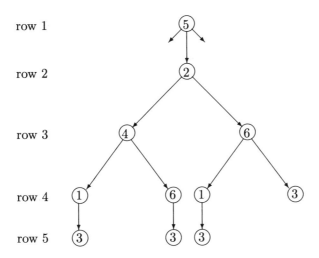

Figure 5.19
Portion of the 6-Queens OR-Tree

row five, each must perform four checks (with the previously placed queens). Note that one of these checks is redundant, namely checking queen (5,3) with queen (4,1) twice. The cause of the redundancy, and the resulting extra computation, is clear: the two solutions in the OR-tree split apart (at row two) and subsequent computations are independent. This is the essence of a naive all-solutions search in OR-parallel, even when implemented in an AND-parallel language such as FGHC.

Okumura's queens avoids this redundancy by virtue of the data-sharing nature of layered streams. One process per board square is initially spawned. Thus we do not represent the OR-tree by processes, as in the other algorithms. Okumura's OR-tree is represented by the layered stream itself. Consider the 6-Queens example. Initially, the sixth-row queen is represented by the layered stream:

        [1*begin,2*begin,3*begin,4*begin,5*begin,6*begin]

because all placements are correct. This layered stream is then broadcast to the next row of filters (row five), and pruned down to:

        [1*[3*begin,4*begin,5*begin,6*begin],
         2*[4*begin,5*begin,6*begin],
         3*[1*begin,5*begin,6*begin],
         4*[1*begin,2*begin,6*begin],
         5*[1*begin,2*begin,3*begin],
         6*[1*begin,2*begin,3*begin,4*begin]]

Thus, for instance, queen (6,3) and queen (5,1) are compatible, as indicated in the first partial solution. This filtering mechanism continues row by row until we finally get the full layered stream as output from the final (row one) filter. Whenever a new queen is incompatible with all incoming sub-layered-stream partial solutions, the mechanism filters them all away, resulting in a [] leaf. Now let us reconsider the previous OR-tree segment, represented in the final layered stream as:

```
5*[...
   2*[4*[1*[3*[]],
         6*[3*[]]],
      6*[1*[3*[]],
         3*[]]],
   ...]
```

This particular segment will be completely removed by the final conversion filter because its paths are incomplete — row six could not be placed. As we saw, the layered-stream queens check for consistency in the reverse order of the stream algorithms. In this segment, the row-two queen (2,2) checks all incoming sub-layered-stream elements for consistency (nine checks). Similarly, queen (3,4) must perform four checks, etc. However, queen (4,1) performs only *one* check against queen (5,3) because, in the process structure, there is only one process representing each board square. Thus we save one check compared to the OR-process-tree algorithms. Although at first glance this savings seems to be insignificant, it turns out to be quite large. Redundant checks are avoided over the full OR-tree, including bad branches (discarded by the filters), incomplete branches (ending in [] leaf), and complete solutions.

Although Kumon's queens and the optimized Ueda's queens algorithms are fundamentally the same, they still differ by 5576 reductions (3%) because of Ueda's program's inefficiencies. A larger difference is between Kumon's queens and Pereira's fused queens. These reduction counts differ by about 40K, an overhead due to the simulation of each k-way OR-branching node with $k-1$ binary nodes. The k-way branch requires Pereira's fused 9-Queens to execute about 13K reductions for del/3. The $k-1$ binary branches require Kumon's 9-Queens to execute about 55K reductions for append/3. When these differences are accounted for the reductions counts match closely.

More pronounced is the difference in reductions between Okumura's queens and Kumon's queens. Having accounted for Kumon's append, the difference still is about 55K reductions, or about 22% of all reductions. This difference is due to the avoidance of redundant checks in the layered-stream algorithm. However, even with this fundamental difference in algorithm, Okumura's queens still executes about

Author	Method	PEs	instr	reduct	susp	entries	sec	KEPS
Sequent Symmetry (Intel 80386)								
Tick	distributed	1	5008943	261540	209065	470605	95.8	5
		8	5771641	319767	222057	541824	13.9	39
Okumura	layered streams †	1	1449257	98731	0	98731	21.5	5
		8	1480037	98731	7523	106254	3.2	33
Encore Multimax (NS32032)								
Tick	distributed	1	6047353	261540	209065	470605	362.0	1
		8	7029455	327196	212641	539837	72.3	7
Okumura	layered streams †	1	1825272	98731	0	98731	82.7	1
		8	1886212	98731	15044	113775	14.0	8

† with [H|Ts] notation and no nil-check.

Table 5.5
FGHC/Panda 9-Queens Characteristics on Symmetry and Multimax

25K more reductions than Kondo's queens and Bratko's queens, which perform all the redundant checks. This difference is due to the *cost* of the check itself, which is higher in Okumura's queens than in these Prolog programs.

Table 5.5 gives the high-level execution characteristics of two of the queens programs on both Symmetry and Multimax. We show representative statistics for the distributed process structure and layered-streams programs, executing on one and eight PEs. Symmetry executes about 4–5 times faster than Multimax.

Table 5.6 shows the characteristics of the superior algorithms for both 9-Queens and 10-Queens. Figure 5.20 illustrates the 10-Queens measurements. [8] The speedups (and efficiency) improve with the larger problem size, although less so for FGHC than for Prolog. Aurora could take better advantage of the increased granularity of 10-Queens than could Panda, because the Aurora scheduler spawns parallel tasks as close to the root of the OR-tree as possible. Thus, for instance, the speedup on 15 PEs of Bratko's queens improved by 18% from 9 to 10-Queens. The Panda scheduler does not explicitly exploit the increased granularity, but fortuitously gains some advantage (9% improvement of speedup on 15 PEs for Okumura's queens without a nil check). Layered streams *with* a nil check was also measured for 10-Queens; as shown, it is superior in speed, but not speedup. These results are as expected: layered-stream size increases as a nonlinear function of problem size. Thus memory management overheads increase and speed suffers. Although the nil check repairs

---

[8]Variance in the measurements and complex scheduler interactions can cause nonmonotonic curves, e.g., Okumura's queens on four PEs.

Author	Method	1 PE	2 PE	4 PE	8 PE	12 PE	15 PE
9-Queens (Aurora/Prolog)							
Pereira	fused gen & test	24.4	12.4	6.8	5.3	3.0	2.7
		1.0	2.0	3.6	4.6	8.1	9.0
Bratko	with structures	13.4	7.3	4.2	2.6	2.1	2.0
		1.0	1.8	3.2	5.2	6.4	6.7
9-Queens (Panda/FGHC)							
Kumon	candidates	28.3	14.3	7.2	3.7	2.5	2.0
		1.0	2.0	3.9	7.6	11	14
Okumura	layered streams †	21.4	11.2	6.0	3.2	2.3	1.8
		1.0	1.9	3.6	6.7	9.3	12
10-Queens (Aurora/Prolog)							
Pereira	fused gen & test	112.9	58.1	31.3	17.6	12.9	11.4
		1.0	1.9	3.6	6.4	8.8	9.9
Bratko	with structures	58.5	30.9	17.3	10.4	8.3	7.4
		1.0	1.9	3.4	5.6	7.0	7.9
10-Queens (Panda/FGHC)							
Kumon	candidates	137.6	70.1	35.2	18.0	12.1	9.7
		1.0	2.0	3.9	7.6	11	14
Okumura	layered streams †	95.1	49.6	26.0	13.8	10.5	7.7
		1.0	1.9	3.7	6.9	9.1	12
	layered streams ‡	86.7	45.7	27.8	13.4	9.1	7.5
		1.0	1.9	3.1	6.5	9.5	12

† without nil check
‡ with nil check

Table 5.6
9+10-Queens Execution Time (Seconds)/Speedup on Symmetry

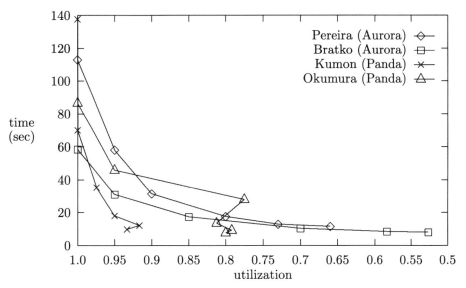

Figure 5.20
10-Queens (724 Solutions): Utilization vs. Time (Symmetry)

these problems, the cost of doing so is increased synchronization and therefore reduced parallelism and speedup. Finally, we note that Bratko's queens consistently outperforms Okumura's queens, although the margin narrows with increasing numbers of PEs.

5.5 Summary

N-Queens illustrates all-solutions search over fairly regular search spaces. The regularity and fullness of the OR-trees enables the systems to achieve high speedups. These searches are constraint problems, wherein constraints are satisfied by simple arithmetic. As such, the programs do not exercise the full capabilities of logic programming languages to express complex logical constraints. On the other hand, the simple construction of solutions in N-Queens fails to exercise memory management ability (or lack thereof) under severe conditions. In fact, we purposely declined to solve greater than 10-Queens because the memory requirement was too great. As the architectures mature, so will their ability to manage memory.

The performance measurements summarize the improvement of the execution time of a given problem on increasing numbers of PEs. This definition of speedup is the primary metric used in this book. An alternative measure of speedup is the increase in problem size that can be solved in constant time on increasing numbers of PEs. For example we saw that Bratko's 9-Queens on two Symmetry PEs and 10-Queens on 15 PEs both execute in about 7.4 seconds. Thus by increasing the number of PEs by a factor of eight, the next larger problem could be solved in constant time. This alternative definition should be kept in mind throughout the book:

> Increases in speed are often less important than increases in the size of the problem that can be solved.

In Chapter 13 we return to the N-Queens problem, to introduce some newer parallel logic programming languages that promise both to exploit additional parallelism and to reduce algorithm complexity by satisfying constraints more efficiently.

Exercises

Exercise 45 Measure the effect of unrolling `del/3` in the various Prolog N-Queens programs. See Exercise 26 in the previous chapter.

Exercise 46 Draw a diagram of the full OR-tree for Kondo's 4-Queens.

Exercise 47 Fix the N-Queens programs given in Figure 5.17 and Figure 5.18 to cope with a request for more solutions than exist. Excess requests for solutions should be bound to the atom `empty`.

Exercise 48 Modify the fastest N-Queens programs to search for a single solution in the most efficient manner (use cavalier commit in Aurora and lazy evaluation for FGHC). Experiment with these programs for large board size N. What is largest N for which you can successfully find a solution? Can you achieve speedup on multiple PEs? What system limitations prevent solving larger problems?

Exercise 49 Derive analytical complexity models for the various N-Queens algorithms. What general conclusions can you draw by looking at the asymptotic (i.e., as N becomes very large) complexity?

Exercise 50 Write a candidates/noncandidates FGHC Queens program to collect M solutions, exploiting symmetry. For example, given a solution, three additional solutions (modulo repeats) can be created by rotating the board 90, 180, and 270 degrees. For each of these, flipping the board around its vertical or horizontal axis may produce two more solutions. Determine the utility of these and other symmetries by measuring 10-Queen execution time for sufficient M, for increasing numbers of PEs. Try to avoid redundant computation (in the OR-tree) of solutions already generated by symmetry transformations.

Exercise 51 Generalize the candidates/noncandidates method to solve a 3-dimensional N-Queens problem in FGHC. In addition, solve the problem in OR-parallel Prolog, with any backtracking algorithm. How do the programs compare in terms of coding and debugging complexity?

Exercise 52 (Knight's Tour) A Knight's Tour is the set of all unique paths of a knight on a chessboard from a starting square to a finishing square. No path may visit the same square more than once and any length path (up to N^2) is acceptable. For an $N \times N$ chessboard, the number of possible paths increases dramatically with N. We will restrict ourselves here to starting at square $(1, 1)$ and finishing at square $(1, N)$. Consider that a 5x5 board has 73,946 solutions!

Write OR-Prolog and FGHC programs to solve a variant of the Knight's Tour, collecting all solutions, when the knight is maimed, i.e., instead of allowing him freedom to move in eight directions from his current square, we limit him to six.

Exercise 53 Write efficient OR-Prolog and FGHC programs to find a single solution to the healthy Knight's Tour. What is the largest board size for which you can successfully find a solution? What speedups do you achieve for this board? What system limitations prevent solving larger problems?

6 Isomorphic Trees and NAND Circuits

> "The way the sun came down through the redwood leaves — trunks and leaves seemed to stretch up for hundreds of feet above your head. It was always sunny and cool at the same time, like a perfect fall day all year around. The sun came down through miles of leaves and got broken up like a pointillist painting, deep green and dapple shadows but brilliant light in a soaring deep green super-bower, a perpetual lime-green light, green-and-gold afternoon, stillness, perpendicular peace, wood-scented..."
>
> Tom Wolfe
> The Electric Kool-Aid Acid Test
> Bantam, 1968

What do isomorphic trees and NAND-gate circuits have in common? A logic circuit with multiple inputs and a single output can be represented as a binary tree, where each node is a dual-input logic gate. The root of the tree is the output of the circuit, and the leaves are inputs. We describe an algorithm whereby, given a desired sequence of output signals, all NAND-gate circuits generating that sequence are created. Due to the NAND gate's logical ambiguity (`1 = X+0 = 0+X`) [1] and commutativity (`X+Y = Y+X`), a naive program may create many isomorphic circuits. The isomorphic tree checker can be used to filter out these redundant solutions.

6.1   Isomorphic Trees

Two trees are isomorphic if the set of paths, from the root to every leaf, is identical in both trees. In other words, the sets of nodes, at each level of the two trees, are identical, but possibly out of order. The branch from the root to a given leaf will pass through the same nodes, in the same order, in both trees. We concentrate on binary trees here, although extensions to general trees are straightforward.

As introduced in Section 2.1, the isomorphic tree problem is to determine if two trees are isomorphic, or to generate all the trees isomorphic to a given tree. We concentrate on the latter problem here. Note that, for a complete binary tree of height n (where root alone is of height one), there are $2^{n-1} - 1$ non-leaf nodes and 2^{n-1} leaves. Each non-leaf node can toggle left and right to create isomorphisms, so that the total number of isomorphic trees is $2^{2^{n-1}-1}$ (assuming each node is uniquely labeled). Generating this many trees is costly, as we shall see. We tackle ground, complete binary trees of the form: `tree(Label,Left,Right)`, where `Label` is an integer identifier, `Left` is the left subtree and `Right` is the right subtree. For example,

---

[1] Here +/2 is the NAND operator and X is a "don't care" logic value.

```
tree(1,tree(2,tree(4,void,void),
            tree(5,void,void)),
      tree(3,void,void))
```

has the following four isomorphic trees:

```
[tree(1,tree(3,void,void),
       tree(2,tree(4,void,void),
             tree(5,void,void))),

 tree(1,tree(2,tree(4,void,void),
             tree(5,void,void)),
       tree(3,void,void)),

 tree(1,tree(3,void,void),
       tree(2,tree(5,void,void),
             tree(4,void,void))),

 tree(1,tree(2,tree(5,void,void),
             tree(4,void,void)),
       tree(3,void,void))]
```

Although this binary tree is of height three, it is incomplete; there are less than $2^{2^{3-1}-1} = 8$ isomorphic trees. Note that the following tree, although a complete binary tree of height three, also has less than eight isomorphic trees because the two subtrees are themselves isomorphic.

```
tree(1,tree(3,tree(4,void,void),
            tree(5,void,void)),
      tree(3,tree(5,void,void),
            tree(4,void,void)))
```

6.1.1 Nondeterminate Algorithms in Prolog

The Prolog program for isotree(+,+), previously given in Section 2.1, is shown below.

```
:- parallel isotree/2.

isotree(void,void).
isotree(tree(X,Left1,Right1),
        tree(X,Left2,Right2)) :-
    isotree(Left1,Left2),
    isotree(Right1,Right2).
isotree(tree(X,Left1,Right1),
        tree(X,Left2,Right2)) :-
    isotree(Left1,Right2),
    isotree(Right1,Left2).
```

Execution time complexity can be approximated as the number of `isotree/2` procedure entries. Consider two complete binary trees that are "maximally" isomorphic, i.e., all children at every level are switched (the trees are mirror images of each other). In checking these trees, the second clause repeatedly fails, succeeding in the third clause. For this worst case scenario, four recursive calls are needed to satisfy the top-level node at depth 1. Each of these recursive calls is similarly satisfied with four calls at depth 2. This process continues until depth $n - 1$, when each leaf call is trivially satisfied in the first clause. Thus the worst-case complexity is $O(4^n)$.

This procedure also can be used in the nondeterminate mode `isotree(+,-)`, with one slight addition. The third clause requires a check to prevent redundant answers, as in the example given previously. We include this check below, renaming the procedure `isotrees/2`. The top-level goal, `go(Tree,Trees)`, generates a list `Trees` of all trees isomorphic to input `Tree`.

```
:- parallel isotrees/2.

go(Tree,Ts) :- findall(T,isotrees(Tree,T),Ts).

isotrees(void,void).
isotrees(tree(X,Left1,Right1),
         tree(X,Left2,Right2)) :-
    isotrees(Left1,Left2),
    isotrees(Right1,Right2).
isotrees(tree(X,Left1,Right1),
         tree(X,Left2,Right2)) :-
    \+(isotree(Left1,Right1)),
    isotrees(Left1,Right2),
    isotrees(Right1,Left2).
```

The `isotree/2` check is expensive, however, there is an even bigger complexity problem! For `isotrees(+,-)` both the second and third clauses above compute the *same* trees in their body goals. The only difference is the assignment of variables `Right2` and `Left2`. Thus, for every backtrack into the third clause, the previous body computation is redone. One way to avoid this redundancy is as follows:

```
isotrees(void,void).
isotrees(tree(X,Left1,Right1),T) :-
    isotrees(Left1,Left),
    isotrees(Right1,Right),
    (T = tree(X,Left,Right)
    ;
     \+(isotree(Left1,Right1)),
     T = tree(X,Right,Left)
    ).
```

This program is no longer OR parallel, and with good reason: the previous parallelism is bogus — it is parallel redundant computation. However, the two recursive isotrees/2 calls are candidates for AND-in-OR parallelism (later discussed in Chapter 11), or some other form of independent AND-parallelism.

Unfortunately the latest program *still* has complexity problems. The backtracking *between* the recursive goals in the second clause causes redundant computation. For every new tree isomorphic to Left1 that is produced by the first goal, all the previously computed trees isomorphic to Right1 are recomputed. This problem is fundamental with noncommitted-choice languages in general — lack of intelligent backtracking can cause extra computation.

However, since this latest Prolog program lacks exploitable OR-parallelism, its nondeterminate backtracking algorithm serves no purpose and should be replaced by a determinate algorithm. A determinate algorithm would solve all complexity problems once and for all. We defer our derivation of the determinate algorithm until the middle of the next section, because the algorithm is most naturally implemented in FGHC.

6.1.2 Determinate Algorithm in FGHC

The FGHC program for isotree(+,+,-), previously given in Section 2.2.2, is shown below.

```
isotree(void,void,S) :- S=yes.
isotree(tree(X,L1,R1),tree(X,L2,R2),S) :-
    or(A,B,S),
    isotree(L1,L2,S1),
    isotree(R1,R2,S2),
    and(S1,S2,A),
    isotree(L1,R2,S3),
    isotree(R1,L2,S4),
    and(S3,S4,B).
isotree(_,_,S) :- otherwise | S=no.

and(  _, no,S) :- S=no.
and( no,  _,S) :- S=no.
and(yes,yes,S) :- S=yes.

or(yes,  _,S)  :- S=yes.
or(  _,yes,S)  :- S=yes.
or( no, no,S)  :- S=no.
```

As mentioned, this program has the disadvantage of fully evaluating both disjunctive subrules concerning isomorphism (second clause of isotree/3). This problem can be avoided by rewriting the program to first check one subrule, and then, if that subrule fails, check the other subrule.

```
isotree(void,void,S) :- S=yes.
isotree(tree(X,L1,R1),tree(X,L2,R2),S) :-
    isotree(L1,L2,S1),
    isotree(R1,R2,S2),
    and(S1,S2,A),
    isotree1(A,cont(L1,R1,L2,R2),S).
isotree(_,_,S) :- otherwise | S=no.

isotree1(yes,_,S) :- S=yes.
isotree1(no,cont(L1,R1,L2,R2),S) :-
    isotree(L1,R2,S3),
    isotree(R1,L2,S4),
    and(S3,S4,S).
```

The or/3 procedure is no longer needed, because the disjunction has been serialized. Thus we have removed parallelism to increase overall efficiency. Another (more elegant?) solution, utilizing speculative parallelism, was also introduced in Section 2.3.3. As reproduced below, one disjunctive subrule explicitly kills the other if it succeeds.

```
isotree(Tree1,Tree2,S) :- isotree(_,Tree1,Tree2,S).

isotree(yes,_,_,S) :- S=no.
isotree(_,void,void,S) :- S=yes.
isotree(F,tree(X,L1,R1),tree(X,L2,R2),S) :-
    or(A,B,S),
    isotree(F1,L1,L2,S1),       \
    isotree(F1,R1,R2,S2),        >disjunctive subrule 1
    and(S1,S2,A),               /
    or(F,A,F2),
    isotree(F2,L1,R2,S3),       \
    isotree(F2,R1,L2,S4),        >disjunctive subrule 2
    and(S3,S4,B),               /
    or(F,B,F1).
isotree(_,_,_,S) :- otherwise | S=no.
```

Note that the new first argument effectively kills an isotree process if bound to yes. Otherwise, if the first argument has no value as yet, computation proceeds. This encoding assumes that the clauses are attempted in their textual order. Notice most importantly that if we use an otherwise in the last clause, FGHC will deadlock. This deadlock occurs because otherwise will suspend until the first argument is bound in order to guarantee mutual exclusion from the first three clauses. In general, one should not attempt to implement a nondeterministic procedure with otherwise. There are "correct" ways to implement nondeterministic procedures in other committed-choice languages with extra-logical guards such as var.

We now define a procedure `isotrees(+,-)` that creates *all* trees isomorphic to
an input tree. This is the determinate algorithm that eluded us in the previous
section because we were thinking in terms of declarative, backtracking programs.

```
isotrees(void, S) :- S=[void].
isotrees(tree(X,L,R),S) :-
    isotree(L,R,Status),
    isotrees(L,Ls),
    isotrees(R,Rs),
    cross(Ls,Rs,X,Status,S).
```

If the tree is `void`, then the answer `void` is output. If the tree is `tree(X,L,R)`, then
three processes are spawned. Two `isotree/2` children produce lists of trees isomorphic to the left and right subtrees, L and R. Procedure `cross(Ls,Rs,X,Status,S)`
merges these two lists, Ls and Rs, by taking their cross-product, and outputs the
answer list to stream S.

The basic cross-product procedure, `cross(Ls,Rs,Out)`, was derived in Section
4.2.3. The additional two arguments here, X and Status, are needed to formulate
the output stream data items, as described below. Recall that the cross-product can
be implemented with one or two stacks, trading time delays for space requirements.
Procedure `cross/5` uses two stacks, causing minimal delays.

```
cross(In1,In2,X,Status,Out) :-
    cross(In1,In2,[],[],X,Status,Out-[]).

cross([],[],_,_,_,_,S0-S1) :- S0=S1.
cross([L|Ls],R,LS,RS,X,T,S0-S2) :-
    send(T,RS,L,X,S0-S1),
    cross(Ls,R,[L|LS],RS,X,T,S1-S2).
cross(L,[R|Rs],LS,RS,X,T,S0-S2) :-
    send(T,LS,R,X,S0-S1),
    cross(L,Rs,LS,[R|RS],X,T,S1-S2).

send(_,[],_,_,S0-S1) :- S0=S1.
send(yes,[L|Ls],R,X,S0-S2) :-
    S0=[tree(X,L,R)|S1],
    send(yes,Ls,R,X,S1-S2).
send(no,[L|Ls],R,X,S0-S2) :-
    S0=[tree(X,L,R),tree(X,R,L)|S1],
    send(no,Ls,R,X,S1-S2).
```

Two cases are differentiated: when the two streams are isomorphic *to each other*
(Status = yes) and when the two streams are *not* isomorphic (Status = no). In
the former case, the streams are combined at a single node X. In the latter case, the
streams are combined twice, switching the polarity of the left and right subtrees at
node X. The one-stack cross-product version is shown below:

```
cross(In1,In2,X,Status,Out) :-
    cross(In1,In2,[],X,Status,Out-[]).

cross(    [],R,LS,X,T,S)  :- cross1(R,LS,X,T,S).
cross([L|Ls],R,LS,X,T,S)  :- cross(Ls,R,[L|LS],X,T,S).

cross1([],_,_,_,S0-S1)  :- S0=S1.
cross1([R|Rs],LS,X,T,S0-S2) :-
    send(T,LS,R,X,S0-S1),
    cross1(Rs,LS,X,T,S1-S2).
```

6.1.3 Prolog Revisited: Determinate Algorithm

A determinate Prolog program can be written as an indirect translation of the previous FGHC program:

```
isotrees(void,[void]).
isotrees(tree(X,L,R),S) :-
    isotrees(L,Ls),
    isotrees(R,Rs),
    (isotree(L,R) ->
        cross1(Rs,Ls,X,yes,S)
    ;
        cross1(Rs,Ls,X,no,S)
    ).
```

Procedures `cross1/5` and `send/5` are identical to the FGHC code. Note that the `isotree(+,+)` check for isomorphic subtrees is included in the conditional. Procedure `cross1/5` is called directly because, in Prolog, both lists `Ls` and `Rs` will be ground. Notice that no choicepoints are built by this program. Since the stacking in `cross/6` can be avoided, we expect the Prolog program to be faster than the FGHC program on a single PE. The Prolog program cannot achieve speedups, however, because there is no OR parallelism.

6.1.4 Discussion: Complexity

Timing measurements are not presented in this section because comparison between Aurora and Panda is not possible — there is no viable OR-Prolog algorithm. Even if there were an OR-Prolog algorithm, this type of problem, with a great number of solutions, taxes `findall/3`, making collection overhead a significant portion of execution time. Consider that a complete binary tree of height five has 32,768 isomorphisms. If each tree occupies 124 words of memory, about 4 million words are needed just for the solutions. In addition, the OR-tree will occupy many times that space.

It is beneficial, however, to derive complexity estimates for the `isotrees/2` pro-

grams. Complexity models help our intuition about why the naive (nondeterminate) algorithm is slower than the determinate algorithm, and how much slower we
should expect it to be.

The nondeterminate Prolog algorithm builds an OR-tree wherein each branch
from root to leaf represents an isomorphic tree. Consider an input tree of height[2]
n. Thus there are $2^{2^{n-1}-1}$ branches in the OR-tree. The OR-tree is also a complete
binary tree, because `isotrees/2` has two nondeterminate clauses, i.e., each branchpoint in the OR-tree has two children corresponding to these recursive clauses. Note
that a complete binary tree of height k has 2^{k-1} branches and $2^k - 1$ nodes. Since
the OR-tree has $2^{2^{n-1}-1}$ branches, then $k = 2^{n-1}$, and the total number of nodes
is $2^{2^{n-1}} - 1$.

We can estimate the space and execution time complexity of the program as the
number of nodes in the OR-tree: $O(2^{2^{n-1}})$. The remaining unknown is the constant
factor, which can be considered as the average computation performed (or space
required) in a node. Because there are determinate reductions (matching the first
clause of `isotrees/2`) embedded in the OR-tree, all nodes are not equal. There
are 2^{n-1} leaves in the data tree and therefore 2^{n-1} determinate reductions in each
branch of the OR-tree. There are $2^{n-1} - 1$ non-leaf nodes in the data tree and
therefore $2^{n-1} - 1$ branchpoints in each branch of the OR-tree. Both types of calls
are shared among branches in the OR-tree, and the occurrence of both types is
equal.

The average computation performed in a node can therefore be approximated as
one nondeterminate procedure call (branchpoint creation), one backtrack (procedure entry into the third clause), and one determinate reduction (procedure call of
first clause). In general, the branchpoint creation and backtrack will far outweigh
the determinate reduction. As an example, consider a data tree of height $n = 4$.
The complexity is $2^{2^{4-1}} = 256$ OR-tree nodes. If we count all entries equally, we get
$3 \times 256 = 768$, approximately equal to the actual number of `isotrees/2` procedure
entries, 684. The discrepancy between these measures is due to the inaccuracy of
assuming three entries per node. In reality, the leaf nodes have two determinate
reductions, but no branchpoint. The nodes near the root have branchpoints but no
determinate reductions. For greater accuracy, nodes at each depth in the OR-tree
must be weighted appropriately.

Now let us analyze the complexity of the determinate algorithm. In this Prolog
program, all procedure calls are determinate, so the analysis is easy. The number

---

[2]A root, `tree(X,void,void)`, has height $n = 2$ because of the `void` leaves. This complexity
can be avoided with a `leaf(X)` data structure, for instance. In this case the analysis presented
here is valid with $n - 1$.

of procedure calls, $P(n)$, invoked when computing all isomorphisms of a complete binary tree of height n is

$$P(n) = \sum_{k=2}^{n} 2^{n-k} g(k-1)^2$$

$$g(k) = 2^{2^{k-1}-1}$$

where $g(k)$ is the number of isomorphic trees of height k. The summation is over the heights k of subtrees within a data tree of height n. In other words, $k = 2$ corresponds to parents of the leaves and $k = n$ corresponds to the root. The first term inside the summation is the number of nodes of height k within a tree of height n. Each such node corresponds to a recursive procedure call to `isotrees/2`. Aside from the recursive descent, the majority of the computation in each `isotrees/2` invocation is a cross-product. The cross-product operates on two lists, each containing $g(k-1)$ isomorphic trees of height $k-1$. The complexity of this cross-product is $O(g(k-1)^2)$. Combining and simplifying:

$$P(n) = 2^{n-3} \sum_{k=1}^{n-1} 2^{2^k - k}.$$

For our purposes, this form of $P(n)$ will suffice to estimate execution time complexity. As an example, consider a data tree of height $n = 4$. The number of procedure calls is

$$P(4) = 2^{4-3} \sum_{k=1}^{3} 2^{2^k - k} = 2(2^1 + 2^2 + 2^5) = 76.$$

Thus we find that the determinate program is at least 10 times faster than the naive program when computing all 128 isomorphic trees of height four. In SICStus Prolog the determinate program executes 13 times faster, confirming our analytical models.

In the asymptotic limit, the execution time complexity of both the determinate and nondeterminate algorithms are *equal!* In the nondeterminate program, the work creating a complete binary OR-tree is asymptotically equal to twice the number of leaves, $2g(n)$. In the determinate program, we can see from $P(n)$ that, for large n, most of the computation is taking the cross-product in the topmost procedure invocation, corresponding to $g(n-1)^2$. In the asymptotic limit, $O(2g(n) = g(n-1)^2 = 2^{2^{n-1}})$. This means that, since the number of solutions explodes double exponentially, no algorithm can successfully compute all solutions for large n.

sel	a	b	out
0	0	0	0
0	0	1	0
0	1	0	1
0	1	1	1
1	0	0	0
1	0	1	1
1	1	0	0
1	1	1	1

Table 6.1
Truth Table for 2–1 Multiplexor

Note that, for finding a *single* solution, the nondeterminate algorithm is superior because only a single branch of the OR-tree is built, requiring $O(2^n - 1)$ procedure calls (nodes in the data tree). The determinate algorithm only produces all solutions, so its complexity remains unchanged.

> The Isomorphic Tree Problem illustrates a classic pitfall wherein a declarative Prolog program is correct, but has high complexity in the nondeterminate mode of operation when finding all solutions. Parallelism can be exploited, but this parallelism is bogus — it consists of redundant computation. The complexity can often be minimized with a determinate algorithm. However, if the problem is *inherently* complex, e.g., the number of solutions is of exponential order, then *no* all-solutions algorithm will do well asymptotically.

6.2   NAND-Gate Circuit Designer

The following programs design a 2–1 multiplexor with three levels of NAND gates. A 2–1 multiplexor has three inputs: data bits a and b and a binary selector flag, sel. These three inputs comprise $2^3 = 8$ different states, thus the output signal is of length eight. The truth table is given in Table 6.1. The predicate output/1 specifies this Boolean function:

```
output(T) :- T=[0,0,1,1,0,1,0,1].
```

There are two unique three-level circuits for this problem:

```
out = ((sel+sel)+a)+(sel+b)
out = ((sel+a)+a)+(sel+b)
```

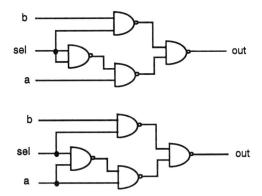

Figure 6.1
Two NAND-Gate Circuits for the 2–1 Multiplexor

where +/2 is the NAND operator. These solutions are illustrated in Figure 6.1.

The NAND-gate circuit design programs are quite inefficient when computing all solutions. It takes a *very* long time to design even the 2–1 multiplexor, because the program first generates many redundant solutions. In addition, without negation, the program must rederive that not(X) = X+X each time it needs the negation of X (or calculate negation in some other strange way, as in the 2–1 multiplexor example). The redundancies do not appear in the output because we filter them away; however, generating redundancies impacts execution time. Also, the actual mechanics of the programs are slow: at each loop through the algorithm, the desired output signal must be compared against all of the given input signals to terminate the design. Note that the programs do not produce *all* existing NAND-gate circuits — a depth-level prevents the design of circuits with greater than a maximum delay.

6.2.1 Nondeterminate Algorithm in Prolog

The Prolog program is based on a version by B. Fagin [47]. The key to the Prolog program is the ngate(Out,In1,In2) procedure, which is given a desired output signal Out in the form of a list of binary digits. Procedure ngate/3 nondeterminately generates the two NAND-gate input signals, In1 and In2, that will produce the desired output signal. For example,

```
?- findall(X-Y,ngate([1,0,1],X,Y),S).
S = [[0,1,0]-[_,1,_],
     [0,1,_]-[_,1,0],
     [_,1,0]-[0,1,_],
     [_,1,_]-[0,1,0]]
```

To generate the output of '0', both inputs must be '1'. However, to generate the
output of '1', either input can be '0'.

```
:- parallel ngate/3.

ngate([], [], []).
ngate([X|T0], [_|T1], [_|T2]) :- var(X), !, ngate(T0,T1,T2).
ngate([0|T0], [1|T1], [1|T2]) :- !,          ngate(T0,T1,T2).
ngate([1|T0], [0|T1], [_|T2]) :-             ngate(T0,T1,T2).
ngate([1|T0], [_|T1], [0|T2]) :-             ngate(T0,T1,T2).
```

The nondeterminism is apparent in the last two clauses, which describe how to
produce a binary output of '1'. A NAND gate can produce this output in two
ways, if either input is '0'. Note the use of var/1 — "don't-care" signals are
represented as unbound logical variables. Thus if the desired NAND-gate output
is don't-care, both inputs are also don't-care.

Procedure t(D,C,T) nondeterminately produces all circuits C of gate depth D
that generate signal T. The first three clauses check if the desired signal is in fact
one of the supplied input signals. The final clause builds a NAND-gate circuit Y+Z
at depth D from two subcircuits, Y and Z at depth D-1.

```
t(_, sel, [0,0,0,0,1,1,1,1]).
t(_,   a, [0,0,1,1,0,0,1,1]).
t(_,   b, [0,1,0,1,0,1,0,1]).
t(D, Y+Z, T) :- D>0,
    D1 is D-1,
    ngate(T, A, B),
    t(D1, Y, A),
    t(D1, Z, B).
```

Note that the first three clauses contain no cuts. The absence of cuts allows the
program to generate all unique circuits that solve the problem. If we prematurely
cut the solution space, certain combinations of gates would not be generated. In
fact, even for the simple 2–1 multiplexor, if cuts are inserted, then the second
solution is not produced because sel is selected before a for the second operand of
the innermost NAND gate.[3] However, the choicepoints produced in ngate/3 and
t/3 create many, many multiple copies of the same circuit.

At the top level, we collect all circuits in a findall and then filter out isomorphic
copies.

```
go(D,U) :-
    output(T),
    findall(C, t(D,C,T), L),
    filter(L,U).
```

---

[3]In fact, sel+a may be the better solution because it puts less of a load on sel.

The filter for isomorphic circuits is based directly on the isomorphic-tree analyzer previously discussed. Here we can optimize things slightly for the case of NAND gates.

```
filter(L,U) :- filter(L,[],U).

filter([],U,U).
filter([C|Cs],U,A) :-
    test(U,C),!,
    filter(Cs,[C|U],A).
filter([_|Cs],U,A) :-
    filter(Cs,U,A).

test([],_).
test([U|Us],C) :-
    \+(isotree(U,C)),
    test(Us,C).

:- parallel isotree/2.

isotree(L1+R1,L2+R2) :-   isotree(L1,L2),isotree(R1,R2).
isotree(L1+R1,L2+R2) :- !,isotree(L1,R2),isotree(R1,L2).
isotree(X,X).
```

Note that the final clause of **isotree/2** catches identical input signals. The complete Prolog NAND-gate circuit design program is summarized in Figure 6.2. The informal specification of the program is given in Figure 6.3.

The code is written to fully backtrack within **t/3**, because we wished to consider all input signals when terminating the circuit design. This decision causes extra work, however, when Prolog backtracks into the last clause of **t/3** after some input signals have been previously matched. With the use of *intelligent backtracking* techniques, **t/3** can be rewritten to avoid this problem.

```
t(D, sel, [0,0,0,0,1,1,1,1]) :-
    (D>0 -> assert(ok(D)); true).
t(D,   a, [0,0,1,1,0,0,1,1]) :-
    (D>0 -> (ok(D)->true; assert(ok(D))) ; true).
t(D,   b, [0,1,0,1,0,1,0,1]) :-
    (D>0 -> (ok(D)->true; assert(ok(D))) ; true).
t(D, Y+Z, T) :- D>0,
    \+(retract(ok(D))),
    D1 is D-1,
    ngate(T, A, B),
    t(D1, Y, A),
    t(D1, Z, B).
```

In this modification, the fact **ok(D)** is asserted (only once) whenever an input signal is used to terminate the design at level D. When the last clause is entered, if **ok(D)**

```
:- parallel ngate/3,isotree/3.

go(D,U) :-
    output(T),
    findall(C, t(D,C,T), L),
    filter(L,U).

output(   [0,0,1,1,0,1,0,1]).
t(_, sel, [0,0,0,0,1,1,1,1]).
t(_,   a, [0,0,1,1,0,0,1,1]).
t(_,   b, [0,1,0,1,0,1,0,1]).
t(D, Y+Z, T) :- D > 0,
    D1 is D-1,
    ngate(T, A, B),
    t(D1, Y, A),
    t(D1, Z, B).

ngate([], [], []).
ngate([X|T0], [_|T1], [_|T2]) :- var(X),!,ngate(T0,T1,T2).
ngate([0|T0], [1|T1], [1|T2]) :- !,      ngate(T0,T1,T2).
ngate([1|T0], [0|T1], [_|T2]) :-         ngate(T0,T1,T2).
ngate([1|T0], [_|T1], [0|T2]) :-         ngate(T0,T1,T2).

filter(L,U) :- filter(L,[],U).
filter(   [],U,U).
filter([C|Cs],U,A) :- test(U,C),!,filter(Cs,[C|U],A).
filter([_|Cs],U,A) :- filter(Cs,U,A).

test([],_).
test([U|Us],C) :- \+(isotree(U,C)),test(Us,C).

isotree(L1+R1,L2+R2) :-   isotree(L1,L2),isotree(R1,R2).
isotree(L1+R1,L2+R2) :- !,isotree(L1,R2),isotree(R1,L2).
isotree(X,X).
```

Figure 6.2
2–1 Multiplexor NAND-Gate Circuit Designer in Prolog

<u>Procedure</u>: `go(D, Cs)`
  + D: positive integer   − Cs: list of circuits

<u>Relation</u>: `Cs` contains all unique circuits of depth D implementing the Boolean function specified by `output/1`. A circuit is a `+/2` structure.

<u>Preconditions</u>: `output(L)` must be defined with list L bound to a sequence of 2^n Boolean digits, representing an n-input function. A unbound variable is considered a valid Boolean digit, representing a "don't care" signal.

<u>Procedure</u>: `t(D, C, T)`
  + D: positive integer   + T: list of Booleans
  − C: circuit

<u>Relation</u>: `C` is a circuit producing the function described by `T`. Backtracking through this call will produce all such circuits, and may produce the same circuit more than once.

<u>Procedure</u>: `ngate(Tout, Tin1, Tin2)`
  + Tout: list of Booleans   − Tin2: list of Booleans
  − Tin1: list of Booleans

<u>Relation</u>: `Tin1` and `Tin2` are two NAND-input signals that produce an output signal `Tout`. Backtracking through this call will produce all such pairs of input signals, and may produce the same pair more than once.

<u>Procedure</u>: `filter(In, Out)`
  + In: list of circuits   − Out: list of circuits

<u>Relation</u>: `Out` contains all and only unique circuits of `In`.

<u>Procedure</u>: `test(Cs, C)`
  + Cs: list of circuits   + C: circuit

<u>Relation</u>: `C` is not isomorphic to any circuit in `Cs`.

<u>Procedure</u>: `isotree(C1, C2)`
  + C1: circuit   + C2: circuit

<u>Relation</u>: Circuits `C1` and `C2` are isomorphic.

Figure 6.3
Informal Specification of Prolog Circuit Designer

exists, then \+retract(ok(D)) fails (after retracting the ok fact). Thus the search
space is intelligently pruned. The modification to the code is not pretty, but it is
somewhat effective. The sequential execution time is reduced by 14% for SICStus
Prolog. The savings is not greater because of the high overhead of implementing
intelligent backtracking with assert and retract. For larger design problems and
more efficient implementations of the ok flag, the savings is expected to be greater.

6.2.2   Determinate Algorithm in FGHC

The FGHC program go(D,U) generates all level-D NAND-gate circuits U for the
Boolean function specified by predicate output/1. We describe the solution of the
2–1 multiplexor here. The circuits are constructed in parallel and streamed into a
pipeline filter to check for isomorphisms.

```
go(D,U) :-
    output(T),
    t(D,T,S-[]),
    filter(S,U).
```

The workhorse of the program is t/3. Procedure t(D,T,S) constructs a stream S
of many D-level circuits producing output signal T. First, we check if the output
signal is simply one of the given input signals (in this case, there are three: sel, a
and b).

```
t(D,T,S0-S4) :-
    check(T,[0,0,0,0,1,1,1,1],sel,S0-S1,C1),
    check(T,[0,0,1,1,0,0,1,1],  a,S1-S2,C2),
    check(T,[0,1,0,1,0,1,0,1],  b,S2-S3,C3),
    design(C1,C2,C3,D,T,S3-S4).
```

If the output signal is not one of the given input signals, then we must design a
circuit with NAND gate(s). Each check/5 procedure returns a status to indicate
if it matched (yes) or failed to match (no). If all checks fail, but the depth has
reached zero, then we must close this branch of the solution space. If all checks fail
and the depth is still positive, then we design all circuits producing output signal
T. Otherwise if one or more checks succeeds, we also short out the solution stream.

```
design(no,no,no,0,_,S0-S1) :- S0=S1.
design(no,no,no,D,Tout,S) :- D>0 |
    D1 is D-1,
    ngate(Tout,Tins),
    spawn(Tins,D1,S).
design(_,_,_,_,_,S0-S1) :- otherwise | S0=S1.
```

The check recursively compares the desired signal with the supplied input signal.
If they match, the check succeeds; otherwise the check fails.

```
check([],_,T,S0-S1,C) :- S0=[T|S1],C=yes.
check([0|T1],[0|T2],T,S,C) :- check(T1,T2,T,S,C).
check([1|T1],[1|T2],T,S,C) :- check(T1,T2,T,S,C).
check([v|T1],[_|T2],T,S,C) :- check(T1,T2,T,S,C).
check(_,_,_,S0-S1,C) :- otherwise | S0=S1,C=no.
```

To create all circuits producing a given output signal, `Tout`, first we generate all
pairs of input signals for a NAND gate, `Tins`, with `ngate/2`. For each pair of
possible input signals, `A-B` in list `Tins`, we design all circuits that can generate
them individually, lists `C1` and `C2`. The lists are then crossed to produce all possible
circuits including the NAND gate we just added.

```
spawn([],_,S0-S1) :- S0=S1.
spawn([A-B|Ts],D,S0-S2) :-
    t(D,A,C1-[]),
    t(D,B,C2-[]),
    cross(C1,C2,S0-S1),
    spawn(Ts,D,S1-S2).

cross(C1,C2,S) :- cross1(C1,C2,S,[]).

cross1([],SR,S,Stack) :-
    filter(Stack,NewStack),
    cross2(SR,NewStack,S).
cross1([SL|SLs],SR,S,Stack) :-
    cross1(SLs,SR,S,[SL|Stack]).

cross2([],    _,S0-S1) :- S0=S1.
cross2([R|Rs],L,S0-S2) :-
    send(L,R,    S0-S1),
    cross2(Rs,L,S1-S2).

send([],    _,S0-S1) :- S0=S1.
send([L|Ls],R,S0-S2) :-
    S0 = [L+R|S1],
    send(Ls,R,S1-S2).
```

Note that the cross-product is taken asymmetrically (see Section 4.2.3) by first
collecting a stack of `C1` circuits. The stack is then filtered, removing isomorphic
circuits. This partial filtering is quite effective in reducing the number of redundant
circuits generated. For the 2–1 multiplexor, 160 circuits are generated without
partial filtering, compared to 21 circuits with filtering. After final filtering, only
two unique circuits remain in either case.

Procedure `ngate(+,-)` returns a list containing all possible NAND-gate inputs
that produce the desired output. For example:

```
?- ngate([0,1,1],X).
X= [[1,0,0]-[1,v,v],[1,v,0]-[1,0,v],[1,0,v]-[1,v,0],[1,v,v]-[1,0,0]]
```

We first reverse the output signal because the inputs are constructed backwards.

```
ngate(In,Out) :-
    rev(In,Rev),
    ngate(Rev,[[]-[]],Out).

ngate([],    In,Out) :- In=Out.
ngate([0|T],In,Out) :- genOne(In,1,Temp), ngate(T,Temp,Out).
ngate([1|T],In,Out) :- genTwo(In,  Temp), ngate(T,Temp,Out).
ngate([v|T],In,Out) :- genOne(In,v,Temp), ngate(T,Temp,Out).

genOne([],_,Out) :- Out=[].
genOne([A-B|Ins],X,Out) :-
    Out = [[X|A]-[X|B]|Outs],
    genOne(Ins,X,Outs).

genTwo([],Out) :- Out=[].
genTwo([A-B|Ins],Out) :-
    Out = [[0|A]-[v|B],[v|A]-[0|B]|Outs],
    genTwo(Ins,Outs).
```

The following filter is based on `isotree(+,+,-)`. Procedure `filter(C,L)` collects all non-isomorphic circuits from C into L, with a pipeline technique (see Section 11.1.3 for a similar pipeline filter in the Semigroup Problem).

```
filter([],S) :- S=[].
filter([C|Cs],S) :-
    S = [C|S1],
    filter(Cs,C,S0),
    filter(S0,S1).

filter([],_,S) :- S=[].
filter([C|Cs],U,S) :-
    isotree(U,C,Status),
    filter(Status,U,C,Cs,S).

filter(yes,U,_,Cs,S) :- filter(Cs,U,S).
filter(no,U,C,Cs,S0) :- S0=[C|S1],filter(Cs,U,S1).

isotree(L1+R1,L2+R2,S) :-
    isotree(L1,L2,S1),
    isotree(R1,R2,S2),
    isotree(S1,S2,L1,R1,L2,R2,S).
isotree(X,X,S) :- otherwise | S=yes.
isotree(X,Y,S) :- X\=Y      | S=no.
```

System	instr	reduct	back/susp	entries	sec	KEPS
Aurora	2052767	110611	151030	261641	9.7	27
Panda	2286667	142398	2811	145209	4.7	31

Table 6.2
NAND-Gate Circuit Designer: High-Level Characteristics (Eight PEs Symmetry)

```
isotree(yes,yes,_,_,_,_,S) :- S=yes.
isotree(_,_,L1,R1,L2,R2,S) :- otherwise |
    isotree(L1,R2,S1),
    isotree(R1,L2,S2),
    and(S1,S2,S).

and( _, no,S) :- S=no.
and( no, _,S) :- S=no.
and(yes,yes,S) :- S=yes.
```

The informal specification of the program is given in Figure 6.4.

6.2.3 Discussion

The 2–1 multiplexor NAND-gate circuit design problem (with two solutions) was measured. The high-level characteristics, Table 6.2, and the timings, Table 6.3, point out the inefficiencies in the Prolog program. The '—' statistics represent no improvement in execution speed with increasing numbers of PEs. Figure 6.5 summarizes the timing measurements.

First, the Prolog program measured does not do intelligent backtracking, thus extra work is performed when backtracking into the last clause of **t/3** after some input signal(s) have been previously matched. The FGHC program avoids this problem by a rather messy use of three status variables. If one or more of the input signals match, a circuit is not designed. The intelligent backtracking Prolog program was not measured, because the **assert/retract** implementation is simply

System	1 PE	2 PE	4 PE	8 PE	12 PE	15 PE
raw execution time (seconds)						
Aurora	42.6	22.4	13.0	9.7	7.0	—
Panda	33.4	17.1	9.1	4.5	3.1	2.6
speedup						
Aurora	1.0	1.9	3.3	4.4	6.1	—
Panda	1.0	2.0	3.7	7.4	11	13

Table 6.3
NAND-Gate Circuit Designer: Execution Time and Speedup (Symmetry)

Procedure: go(D, Cs)
    + D: integer   − Cs: list of circuits

Relation: Cs contains all unique circuits of delay D implementing the Boolean
    function specified by output/1. A circuit is a +/2 structure.

Preconditions: output(L) must be defined with list L bound to a sequence
    of 2^n Boolean digits, representing an n-input function. A Boolean digit
    is either '0', '1' or 'v' (representing a "don't care" signal).

Procedure: t(D, T, S)
    +D: integer   +T: list of Booleans   −S: stream of circuits

Relation: Stream S contains all unique circuits that produce the function
    described by T. Multiple copies of the circuits may be present. Each
    given input signals must be described with a check/5 goal.

Procedure: check(T, Tin, Cin, S, Status)
    + T: list of Booleans   + Cin: atom (input signal)
    + Tin: list of Booleans   − S: stream of circuits
                          − Status: atom (yes/no)

Relation: If T and Tin are consistent then input signal Cin is sent down S
    and Status=yes. Otherwise S is shorted and Status=no.

Precondition: Tin describes the Boolean function of a given input signal.

Procedure: design(C1, C2, C3, D, T, S)
    + C1: atom   + C3: atom   + T: list of Booleans
    + C2: atom   + D: integer   − S: stream of circuits

Relation: If none of C1, C2 or C3 are yes and circuit depth D is greater than
    zero, then stream S contains all unique circuits that produce the function
    T. Otherwise stream S is shorted.

Procedure: ngate(Tout, Tins)
    + Tout: list of Booleans (a signal)   −Tins: list of signal pairs

Relation: Tins contains all pairs of NAND-gate signals that produce an out-
    put signal Tout. There may be redundant pairs in Tins due to the inter-
    pretation of the "don't care" signal 'v'.

Procedure: spawn(Tins, D, S)
    + Tins: list of signal pairs   + D: integer   − S: stream of circuits

Relation: Stream S contains all unique circuits, less than or equal to depth
    D, that produce every pair of signals in Tins, combined at a root NAND
    gate. Multiple copies of the circuits may be present.

Figure 6.4
Informal Specification of FGHC Circuit Designer

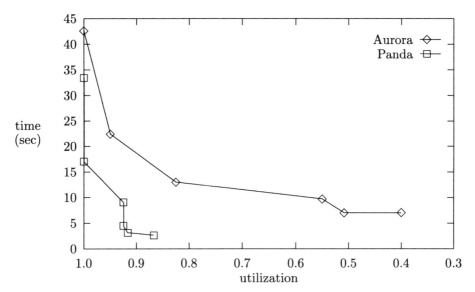

Figure 6.5
NAND-Gate Circuit Designer: Utilization vs. Time (Symmetry)

too inefficient to be informative.

Second, the FGHC program can filter isomorphic circuits at an early stage (during circuit design). The Prolog program, because circuits are designed via backtracking, must filter all the circuits after they have been created.

Third, the Prolog program gets poor speedup, because the design was constrained to a maximum circuit depth of three. Thus the OR-tree branches are too short to achieve high efficiency. Above 12 PEs (with 50% efficiency), Aurora performance degrades. Panda continues to exploit parallelism with 86% efficiency on 15 PEs.

Although Prolog can use backtracking over unbound logical variables to implement **ngate/3** efficiently, this process does not prove to be the bottleneck in the program. The production of excess circuits due to lack of control over automatic OR-parallel search in Prolog has a greater impact than the overheads incurred by FGHC for simulating logical variables (copying in **ngate/3**). Essentially, excess circuit production is exponentially complex, whereas copying is only linear in complexity. For larger design problems, the situation rapidly worsens for this Prolog program. It is difficult to envision how control can be incorporated into the Prolog program to reduce the complexity while exploiting the OR-parallel search.

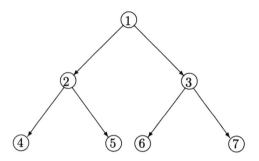

Figure 6.6
Simple Binary Tree

6.3 Summary

The Prolog programs discussed in this chapter suffered significantly more from complexity problems than from system overheads. Both the isomorphic tree program and NAND-gate circuit designer had gross amounts of redundant computation in Prolog. In FGHC, complexity was decreased by use of determinate algorithms. For example, FGHC must simulate the OR-tree to collect all solutions in the circuit design, facilitating placement of a filter to remove redundant computations early on. Explicit manipulation of partial solutions cannot be implemented in OR-parallel Prolog, because all paths are independent in the implicit OR-tree. A lesson here is that an efficient algorithm often is not elegant, and is considerably more important than an algorithm that is simply parallel.

Exercises

Exercise 54 In Chapter 2 we developed a `flattenTree(Tree,List)` procedure that flattened a binary tree into a list. That program uses a tree with values only at the leaves. Rewrite the `flattenTree` program to flatten trees with values at each node, i.e., `node(Left, X, Right)`, as in the isomorphic tree programs. Use a standard depth-first, left-to-right traversal.

Exercise 55 There are various methods of flattening a tree with values at each node. For instance the tree given in Figure 6.6 can be flattened as `[4,2,5,1,6,3,7]` — this is a standard depth-first, left-to-right traversal. Write a program to flatten the tree as follows: `[1,2,3,4,5,6,7]`.

Exercise 56 Generalize both the Prolog and FGHC isomorphic tree programs to handle trees with arbitrary branching factors. One way to represent such a tree is with nodes of the form tree(X,List), where X is the value of the node and List is a list of subtrees, any of which may be void.

Exercise 57 Generalize the Prolog NAND-gate circuit design program to accept a desired signal as input, and automatically generate the appropriate input signals (a, b, and sel in the case of the 2–1 multiplexor).

Exercise 58 As discussed, there are two main bottlenecks in the Prolog NAND-gate circuit designer. The first is the generation of redundant solutions. The second is that t/3 is slow. Is it possible to avoid generating redundant solutions and still guarantee generation of *all* solutions? If not, give an argument as to why not. If it is possible, then implement your idea.

Exercise 59 An idea for speeding up t/3 in the Prolog NAND-gate circuit design program is to generate a hash key from the signal for a quick comparison with the input signals. This hash key is strange: one must hash '+', '0' and '_' (don't care) into a key that can be compared *imprecisely*. Suppose we use a trinary hash, where '_' is given the value two. Then for instance, [0,1,_,1] has the value $0 \cdot 3^0 + 1 \cdot 3^1 + 2 \cdot 3^2 + 1 \cdot 3^3 = 48$. If the hash of the desired output signal is *less than* the hash of the input signal, then the signals are incompatible (this assumes that there are no "don't cares" in the input signals!). Otherwise, the signals must be checked bit-by-bit. The "don't cares" increase the fuzziness (and decrease the usefulness) of the key. Implement this or another hash scheme. Does performance improve for a larger problem?

Exercise 60 Generalize the FGHC NAND-gate circuit design program to accept a desired signal as input, and automatically generate the appropriate input signals (a, b, and sel in the case of the 2–1 multiplexor) (see Exercise 57).

Exercise 61 Implement a hash scheme in the FGHC NAND-gate circuit design program to speedup the signal check (see Exercise 59).

Exercise 62 Rewrite the Prolog NAND-gate circuit design program to mimic the FGHC method of avoiding extra work. Measure and compare the performance of the two versions.

Exercise 63 (Automatic Test Pattern Generation) Write a parallel program to generate test patterns for faulty combinational logic circuits. For simplicity,

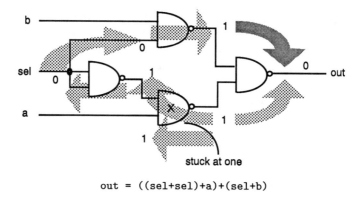

out = ((sel+sel)+a)+(sel+b)

Figure 6.7
2–1 Multiplexor Stuck-at-One Test Generation

consider only NAND-gate circuits. Test for single *stuck-at-one* and *stuck-at-zero* faults, i.e., wherein a single gate is faulty and always produces a logical one or zero, respectively. Consider the 2-1 multiplexor circuit shown in Figure 6.7.

The purpose of the test generator is to specify the three inputs [sel,a,b] and the corresponding outputs [out] for determining if a given gate is stuck at either one or zero. Let's suppose we wish to test if the lower NAND gate (with input a) is stuck-at-one. The test we wish to perform is [sel,a,b]=[0,1,_], where we don't care about input b. If out=0 then the gate *is* stuck-at-one. If out=1 then there is *no* fault.

One way to generate these input values is by propagation. Begin by assuming that the output of the lower gate is stuck-at-one. Propagating backwards, towards the circuit inputs, we choose input values for this gate. We choose both input values to be one because this combination contradicts the error. Thus a=1 and (sel+sel)=1. Propagating backwards again (this time we propagate correctly, since we assume the first gate is not in error) we find that sel=0. Propagating forwards we find that if sel=0 then (sel+b)=1 for any value of b. Thus the output out = 1+1 = 0. If the gate is not stuck-at-one then, given the same test input, the output will be out=1. Thus we can *observe* the fault via an output.

In Prolog, one can write a generate & test program to backtrack through possible input sets until a suitable test pattern is found. As with the NAND-gate circuit design program, the complexity of this method is exponential with respect to the number of gates. Try to write a more clever scheme to reduce this complexity order.

Hex Format	Mnemonic	Type	Meaning
0YYY	PSHC	push constant	$sp := sp - 1; s[sp] := y$
1XXX	PUSH	push direct	$sp := sp - 1; s[sp] := m[x]$
2XXX	POP	pop direct	$m[x] := s[sp]; sp := sp + 1$
3ZZZ	ADD	add indirect	$tmp := s[sp]; sp := sp + 1$ $s[sp] := s[sp] + tmp$
4ZZZ	SUB	subtract indirect	$tmp := s[sp]; sp := sp + 1$ $s[sp] := s[sp] - tmp$
5XXX	JPOS	jump positive	$tmp := s[sp]; sp := sp + 1$ $if\ tmp > 0\ then\ pc := x$
6XXX	JUMP	jump	$pc := x$
7ZZZ	HALT	halt	

Table 6.4
Shapiro's Easy Machine Instruction Set

In FGHC, one can propagate values in almost the same manner as described above. The gates of the circuit itself become processes that perform the backward and forward communication. A gate with insufficient inputs to determine its output should suspend. For additional ideas (including a test generator written in constraint logic programming) and references to the literature, see Simonis [118].

Exercise 64 (Shapiro's Easy Machine)   Write Prolog and FGHC programs to simulate the following computer (Shapiro [116]). The machine consists of a processor connected to a memory. The processor architecture consists of a k-element stack and a program counter pc. There are eight instructions which are listed in Table 6.4. Each instruction occupies one 16-bit word. The opcodes are four bits, however, the high-order bit is not used. The **XXX** and **YYY** fields are 12-bit addresses and non-negative constants, respectively. The **ZZZ** fields are not currently in use. The notation $m[x]$ refers to the contents of memory location x; $s[sp]$ refers to the top of the stack. The stack pointer sp is a mod-k counter, i.e., the stack is circular.

Addresses are 12 bits, therefore, $2^{12} = 4096$ words of memory are addressable. For each simulated machine cycle, the instruction located at the address in pc is fetched, decoded, and executed. Directly addressed operands (in **PUSH** and **POP**) must be fetched from memory.

The critical implementation choice is how to simulate the memory. A well-simulated memory is a fast memory. Ideally, we desire constant time access, which would require a destructable array, something we don't normally have in logic programming systems. A list, with $O(N)$ time complexity to simulate N words of memory, is too slow. Shapiro discusses using a balanced tree of binary distributor processes to route the memory request by peeling off the binary digits in the request address. This has $O(logN)$ time complexity. However, a tree is rather costly in numbers of required processes, and is wasteful if only a small portion of the entire address space is frequently used. Can you improve upon this?

Test your computer simulator by writing a test program in the machine language and loading it into the simulated memory. Then execute the program and dump the contents of memory to ensure that the program executed correctly.

Exercise 65 (Tanenbaum's MAC-1) Write Prolog and FGHC programs to emulate the MAC-1 machine architecture [125]. MAC-1 is meatier than the previous stack architecture, having a program counter *pc*, an accumulator *ac* and a stack pointer *sp*. MAC-1 sports 23 opcodes, performing arithmetic, branching, stack operations, procedure call, and return. Direct, indexed, and indirect addressing are all supported. The instruction set is summarized in Table 6.5 (taken from Tanenbaum [125]). Addresses are 12 bits, i.e., memory consists of 4096 16-bit words. The instruction formats use expanding opcodes of one and two nibbles. The notation $m[x]$ refers to the contents of memory location x. The ZZ fields are not currently in use. The YYY and YY fields are non-negative 12-bit and 8-bit constants, respectively. Note that the stack grows towards low addresses.

Test your computer simulator by writing a test program in the machine language and loading it into the simulated memory. Then execute the program and dump the contents of memory to ensure that the program executed correctly.

Exercise 66 In the previous two emulator exercises, each fetch-decode-execute cycle will be serialized if the stack (Exercise 64) or register set (Exercise 65) is implemented as a "passive" data structure. An example of a passive stack, in Prolog, is given in Section 3.4. A stack is a sequential structure in any case, because each operation is dependent on the previous operation.

Consider, however, a register set. Since the register set is directly addressed, access dependencies are few. For example, a read-after-write (RAW) dependency entails writing a register and then reading the same register. Similarly, there are write-after-read (WAR) and write-after-write (WAW) dependencies. Most instructions, however, will not contain these dependencies. Whereas dependent instructions must be executed sequentially, independent instructions can be overlapped or even executed out of order!

An "active" data structure represents components in the structure with processes. For example, in an active register set a process corresponds to each register. These processes accept access messages from the emulator. Access messages from

Hex Format	Mnemonic	Type	Meaning
0XXX	LODD	load direct	$ac := m[x]$
1XXX	STOD	store direct	$m[x] := ac$
2XXX	ADDD	add direct	$ac := ac + m[x]$
3XXX	SUBD	subtract direct	$ac := ac - m[x]$
4XXX	JPOS	jump positive	$if\ ac \geq 0\ then\ pc := x$
5XXX	JZER	jump zero	$if\ ac = 0\ then\ pc := x$
6XXX	JUMP	jump	$pc := x$
7YYY	LOCO	load constant	$ac := y$
8XXX	LODL	load local	$ac := m[sp + x]$
9XXX	STOL	store local	$m[sp + x] := ac$
AXXX	ADDL	add local	$ac := ac + m[sp + x]$
BXXX	SUBL	subtract local	$ac := ac - m[sp + x]$
CXXX	JNEG	jump negative	$if\ ac < 0\ then\ pc := x$
DXXX	JNZE	jump nonzero	$if\ ac \neq 0\ then\ pc := x$
EXXX	CALL	call	$sp := sp - 1; m[sp] := pc; pc := x$
F0ZZ	PSHI	push indirect	$sp := sp - 1; m[sp] := m[ac]$
F2ZZ	POPI	pop indirect	$m[ac] := m[sp]; sp := sp + 1$
F4ZZ	PUSH	push onto stack	$sp := sp - 1; m[sp] := ac$
F6ZZ	POP	pop from stack	$ac := m[sp]; sp := sp + 1$
F8ZZ	RETN	return	$pc := m[sp]; sp := sp + 1$
FAZZ	SWAP	swap ac,sp	$tmp := ac; ac := sp; sp := tmp$
FCYY	INSP	increment sp	$sp := sp + y$
FEYY	DESP	decrement sp	$sp := sp - y$

Table 6.5
Tanenbaum's MAC-1 Instruction Set

sequential instructions are ordered, so that dependencies are enforced. However, independent accesses proceed concurrently!

Implement the MAC-1 emulator from the previous exercise with an active register set. Craft your emulator to reduce synchronizations between MAC-1 instructions as much as possible. Measure the performance improvement for a test program, compared to the previous implementation. The ratio of execution times indicates the percentage of MAC-1 instruction overlap on the new emulator.

7 Triangle and MasterMind

"Meese in his wisdom somehow managed to give North almost 48 hours to
destroy the evidence—but, even then, there was not enough time, and North
didn't understand the *destructo* function of his computer well enough to
make it eat everything he'd put into it...And when smarter people punched
a different mix of recall buttons, all manner of dark plots and criminal
gibberish came spitting out on the printer, dredged up from some
seldom-used memory chip, deep in the bowels of the mainframe."

Hunter S. Thompson
Generation of Swine
Simon & Schuster Inc., 1988

In this chapter we present programs that play two children's games. Triangle
is a board game wherein pegs are jumped in an effort to create a final board
with only one remaining peg. MasterMind is a guessing game wherein a secret
code is deciphered in successive guesses. The games are not complex enough to
give speedups when searching for single solutions, so we take this opportunity to
search for all solutions. A solution consists of a sequence of winning moves. The
Prolog and FGHC programs displayed speedups from 9–15 on 15 PEs (Sequent
Symmetry), indicating that the problems have reasonable parallelism. These two
problems are especially interesting because whereas Panda has trouble scheduling
Triangle, Aurora has trouble scheduling MasterMind. The reasons for this difference
will be discussed.

7.1 Triangle

Triangle, also called Solitare, is given as a Lisp benchmark in Gabriel [53]; Prolog
versions are given in Coelho [31][1] and a Strand version in Foster and Taylor [49].
The problem is to calculate all winning sequences of moves in a simple board game.
The board is a triangular set of 15 holes, initially filled with pegs ('1'), except for
the center one which is empty ('0'), as illustrated in Figure 7.1.

The goal of this game is to remove all the pegs but one from the board. Any peg
can jump over any other peg along a straight line provided that it lands in an open

---

[1]Coelho discusses two Prolog programs (problem 77 in [31]), both different from the program
presented here. One of the programs uses intelligent backtracking to avoid recomputation when
computing all solutions to the Triangle problem. This raises an interesting point concerning how
to measure the efficiency of parallel programs. OR-parallel search (implemented either in Prolog
or FGHC), cannot easily backtrack intelligently because execution paths are independent. Thus
speedup is attained at the cost of doing extra work (with respect to an intelligent backtracking
program).

```
            1                              1
          1   1                          1   1
        1   0   1        ⟹             1   1   1
      1   1   1   1                   1   0   1   1
    1   1   1   1   1               1   0   1   1   1
```

Table 7.1
Triangle Game: Initial Board and One of Two Symmetrical First Moves

hole. The jumped peg is then removed. The jumping peg, the jumped peg, and the
open hole must be successive neighbors. The board indicates 36 possible moves. A
winning sequence will contain 13 moves. There are two possible symmetrical first
moves, one of which is shown above. The game has 1550 solutions — 775 solutions
for each of the symmetrical first moves.

Prolog Versions

Two Prolog programs were examined: one with lists for the board representation
and the other with structures. The triangle can be flattened onto a list or structure
in a number of ways. As we shall see, the programs do not need to compute peg
indices in order to compute legal moves. Therefore any flattening of the triangle is
sufficient. We choose to pack the rows of the triangle, starting with the apex, into
the list in order. For example, the initial configuration of the board is represented
by the list

        [1,1,1,1,0, 1,1,1,1,1, 1,1,1,1,1]

or by the structure

        b(1,1,1,1,0, 1,1,1,1,1, 1,1,1,1,1).

With our algorithm, the entire board must be copied for each move. The initial
question when writing these implementations was: which is faster, lists or structures? Lists have the apparent advantage that, during board copying, if the tail
of board was left unmodified, the tail could be copied as a pointer. On the other
hand, lists require two words of storage for each list element (no cdr-coding is used
in any of the Prolog or FGHC implementations), whereas structures require only
one. The ability to make random accesses into a structure cannot be exploited in
this problem. In sequential Prolog implementations, the structure implementation
executed about twice as fast as the list representation.

7.1.1 Structure Copying

The top-level query of the Prolog program initializes the board with `board/1` and then collects all winning sequences X in list A with a `findall`. Procedure `play(N,Board,Ms)` computes a list Ms of length N necessary to reduce Board to one remaining peg.

```
go(A) :- board(B), findall(Ms,play(13,B,Ms),A).

board(b(1,1,1,1,0, 1,1,1,1,1, 1,1,1,1,1)).

play(0,_,[]) :- !.
play(N,Board,[M|Ms]) :-
    move(M,Board,NewBoard),
    N1 is N-1,
    play(N1,NewBoard,Ms).
```

The moves are nondeterminately selected from the database of `move/3` facts listed below. The informal specification of the program is given in Figure 7.1.

```
:- parallel move/3.

move(1,b( 1, 1,X3, 0,X5,X6,X7,X8,X9,X10,X11,X12,X13,X14,X15),
       b( 0, 0,X3, 1,X5,X6,X7,X8,X9,X10,X11,X12,X13,X14,X15)).
move(2,b(X1, 1,X3, 1,X5,X6, 0,X8,X9,X10,X11,X12,X13,X14,X15),
       b(X1, 0,X3, 0,X5,X6, 1,X8,X9,X10,X11,X12,X13,X14,X15)).
move(3,b(X1,X2,X3, 1,X5,X6, 1,X8,X9,X10, 0,X12,X13,X14,X15),
       b(X1,X2,X3, 0,X5,X6, 0,X8,X9,X10, 1,X12,X13,X14,X15)).
       .
       .
       .
move(35,b(X1,X2,X3,X4,X5,X6,X7, 0, 1, 1,X11,X12,X13,X14,X15),
        b(X1,X2,X3,X4,X5,X6,X7, 1, 0, 0,X11,X12,X13,X14,X15)).
move(36,b(X1,X2,X3, 0, 1, 1,X7,X8,X9,X10,X11,X12,X13,X14,X15),
        b(X1,X2,X3, 1, 0, 0,X7,X8,X9,X10,X11,X12,X13,X14,X15)).
```

The speed bottleneck in this program is the time needed to copy the board in `move`. For this small board size, the space overhead is not a concern, because Prolog automatically recovers the garbage space of the old board upon backtracking.

The OR-tree is very regular, because the database has 36 possible moves. However, the tree does not grow with a branching factor of 36, because many of these moves fail. A process scheduler's local heuristic of selecting a goal high in the OR-tree (i.e., near the root) will work well for this tree. In normal execution, on a limited number of PEs, the top-level call to `play` will spawn M processes where M is the number of PEs, still without exhausting the number of possible first moves. It is expected that these goals (and the goals in row two of the tree) have very high

---

Figure 7.1
Informal Specification of Prolog Triangle

Procedure: `play(N, Bin, Ms)`
 + N: integer   – Ms: list of moves
 + Bin: board structure

Relation: List `Ms` contains the `N` additional moves needed to complete board `Bin`, solving the Triangle problem. If `Bin` cannot be completed then this procedure call fails, causing backtracking of a previous move.

Preconditions: Initially `N=13` and `Bin` is described by predicate `board/1`.

Procedure: `move(N, Bin, Bout)`
 + N: integer   – Bout: board structure
 + Bin: board structure

Relation: Given board `Bin`, taking move `N` results in board `Bout`.

---

granularity, so that most PEs are steadily working. Scheduling is still required, because there are 775 solutions and numerous failures along the way. As discussed in a later section, we do in fact get almost linear speedup with this program!

7.1.2   List Copying

The list-based version of the program is similar, with the following types of moves.

```
move(1,[ 1, 1,X3, 0|T],
       [ 0, 0,X3, 1|T]).
move(2,[X1, 1,X3, 1,X5,X6, 0|T],
       [X1, 0,X3, 0,X5,X6, 1|T]).
move(3,[X1,X2,X3, 1,X5,X6, 1,X8,X9,X10, 0|T],
       [X1,X2,X3, 0,X5,X6, 0,X8,X9,X10, 1|T]).
       .
       .
       .
move(35,[X1,X2,X3,X4,X5,X6,X7, 0, 1, 1|T],
        [X1,X2,X3,X4,X5,X6,X7, 1, 0, 0|T]).
move(36,[X1,X2,X3, 0, 1, 1|T],
        [X1,X2,X3, 1, 0, 0|T]).
```

FGHC Version

The FGHC AND-tree looks similar to Prolog's OR-tree in that the parallelism is exploited from spawning independent processes for the 36 possible moves. This exploitation occurs in the `play` procedure. The high branching factor gives high speedups. There are 36 `move` procedures, one per unique move. A `move` procedure consists of two clauses. The first clause attempts the move by checking if the board position will allow the move. If so, the board is copied and the move is inserted in the front of the partial answer being built. Otherwise, the second clause short-circuits the answer stream and prunes the branch.

An answer is complete after 13 successful moves, as tested in the first clause of play. When complete, the answer is inserted in the answer stream and the branch is pruned. Termination will occur when all branches are pruned at some level down to 13. Upon termination, all answers will have been inserted into the answer stream. The informal specification of the program is given in Figure 7.2.

```
go(A) :- board(B), play([],0,B,A-[]).

board(b(1,1,1,1,0, 1,1,1,1,1, 1,1,1,1,1)).

play(A,13,_,S0-S1) :- S0 = [A|S1].
play(A,N,B,S00-S36) :- N =\= 13 | N1 is N+1,
    move1( B,S00-S01,A,N1), move2( B,S01-S02,A,N1), move3( B,S02-S03,A,N1),
    move4( B,S03-S04,A,N1), move5( B,S04-S05,A,N1), move6( B,S05-S06,A,N1),
    move7( B,S06-S07,A,N1), move8( B,S07-S08,A,N1), move9( B,S08-S09,A,N1),
    move10(B,S09-S10,A,N1), move11(B,S10-S11,A,N1), move12(B,S11-S12,A,N1),
    move13(B,S12-S13,A,N1), move14(B,S13-S14,A,N1), move15(B,S14-S15,A,N1),
    move16(B,S15-S16,A,N1), move17(B,S16-S17,A,N1), move18(B,S17-S18,A,N1),
    move19(B,S18-S19,A,N1), move20(B,S19-S20,A,N1), move21(B,S20-S21,A,N1),
    move22(B,S21-S22,A,N1), move23(B,S22-S23,A,N1), move24(B,S23-S24,A,N1),
    move25(B,S24-S25,A,N1), move26(B,S25-S26,A,N1), move27(B,S26-S27,A,N1),
    move28(B,S27-S28,A,N1), move29(B,S28-S29,A,N1), move30(B,S29-S30,A,N1),
    move31(B,S30-S31,A,N1), move32(B,S31-S32,A,N1), move33(B,S32-S33,A,N1),
    move34(B,S33-S34,A,N1), move35(B,S34-S35,A,N1), move36(B,S35-S36,A,N1).

move1(b(1,1,B,0,C,D,E,F,G,H,I,J,K,L,M),S,A,N) :-
    play([1|A],N,b(0,0,B,1,C,D,E,F,G,H,I,J,K,L,M),S).
move1(_,S0-S1,_,_) :- otherwise | S0=S1.

move2(b(B,1,C,1,D,E,0,F,G,H,I,J,K,L,M),S,A,N) :-
    play([2|A],N,b(B,0,C,0,D,E,1,F,G,H,I,J,K,L,M),S).
move2(_,S0-S1,_,_) :- otherwise | S0=S1.

move3(b(B,C,D,1,E,F,1,G,H,I,0,J,K,L,M),S,A,N) :-
    play([3|A],N,b(B,C,D,0,E,F,0,G,H,I,1,J,K,L,M),S).
move3(_,S0-S1,_,_) :- otherwise | S0=S1.
  .
  .
  .
move36(b(B,C,D,0,1,1,E,F,G,H,I,J,K,L,M),S,A,N) :-
    play([36|A],N,b(B,C,D,1,0,0,E,F,G,H,I,J,K,L,M),S).
move36(_,S0-S1,_,_) :- otherwise | S0=S1.
```

Figure 7.2
Informal Specification of FGHC Triangle

Procedure: `play(Ms, N, Bin, S)`
+ `Ms`: list of moves   + `Bin`: board structure
+ `N`: integer   − `S`: stream of solutions

Relation: Stream `S` contains all extensions of partial solution `Ms` given that
board `Bin` can be completed in `N` additional moves. If `N=13` then the
partial solution is complete and is sent down stream `S`.

Preconditions: Initially `Ms` is empty, `N=0` and `Bin` is described by predicate
`board/1`.

Procedure: `moveX(Bin, S, Ms, N)`
+ `Bin`: board structure   + `Ms`: list of moves
− `S`: stream of solutions + `N`: integer

Relation: If move X can be made on board `Bin` then stream `S` contains all
extensions of partial solution `Ms` with move X, such that the new board
can be completed in `N` additional moves. Otherwise stream `S` is shorted.

There are three major overheads in this program. The first two are the time
and space necessary to copy the board. The Prolog program has a similar time
overhead, but space is automatically reclaimed by backtracking. In both programs,
the space occupied by the structure representing the old board becomes garbage
once copied into a new board. In Panda, this garbage must be collected by explicit
garbage collection (GC). In the performance measurements discussed in the next
section, GC was not a significant factor because a large memory space was used.
The time overhead is approximately the same as that for the Prolog program. As
we shall see in the next section, the third overhead (that of spawning the 36 `move`
processes) is the most significant.

7.1.3   Discussion

Triangle was measured with three initial moves already taken, as illustrated in Figure 7.2 This board has 133 solutions. High-level characteristics on eight Symmetry
PEs are given in Table 7.3. Table 7.4 gives the raw execution times (in seconds)
and speedups of the programs. A large memory was used for FGHC execution to
avoid GCs. Figure 7.3 summarizes the measurements.

The high-level statistics clearly show the differences between the two Prolog
versions and between Prolog and FGHC. FGHC executes more than twice the

Table 7.2
Triangle Game: Board After Three Initial Moves

System	Method	instr	reduct	back/susp	entries	sec	KEPS
Aurora	lists	8789573	33503	553422	586925	13.0	45
	structures	5496734	33503	553422	586925	8.6	68
Panda		13173858	601123	1	601124	25.7	23

Table 7.3
Triangle (133 Solutions) High-Level Characteristics (eight PEs Symmetry)

System	Method	1 PE	2 PE	4 PE	8 PE	12 PE	15 PE
		raw execution time (seconds)					
Aurora	lists	98.8	50.5	25.5	13.0	8.9	7.2
	structures	68.1	33.6	16.9	8.6	5.9	4.8
Panda		184.2	98.5	52.8	25.7	21.2	16.6
		speedup					
Aurora	structures	1.0	2.0	4.0	7.9	12	14
Panda		1.0	1.9	3.5	7.2	8.7	11

Table 7.4
Triangle (133 Solutions): Total Execution Time and Speedup (Symmetry)

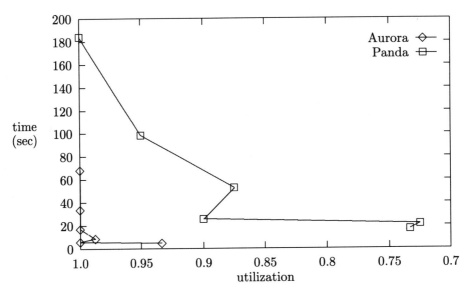

Figure 7.3
Triangle (133 Solutions): Utilization vs. Time (Symmetry)

number of abstract instructions as the structure-based Prolog program. These extra instructions come mainly from the calls to `move1` through `move36`, each of which creates a goal record and loads five arguments. The same function is performed automatically by Prolog backtracking, reusing the information in the branchpoint. In fact, the total number of procedure entries is almost the same in FGHC as in Prolog.

The Triangle program in FGHC, in contrast to the N-Queens (Chapter 5) and Puzzle (Chapter 10) programs, for instance, has a constant branching factor for all nodes in the OR-tree, no matter how far from the root the nodes are. Thus 36 `move` goals are spawned even when the solution is nearly complete and there are few pegs left on the board. The "failure" rate of these goals is astronomically high, causing significant thrashing in local PE memories for eight or more PEs [56]. It is simply not a wise scheduling decision to remotely spawn a `move` goal that is near the leaves of the OR-tree. This is one reason why the FGHC program is more than two times slower than the Prolog program.

If the FGHC program could be rewritten to reduce inefficient branching (i.e., remote spawning) near the leaves, its performance would improve. For example, in Parlog, body goals can be specified as sequential. Although messy, one could spec-

ify a third `play/5` clause for moves near the end of the game that gives all the `move`
goals sequentially. Thus no branching would occur near the leaves. We might envision implementing such an idea in FGHC with explicit serialization, for instance,
using a short-circuit chain (see Section 9.1.3). However, user serialization will not
guarantee that the `move` goals are not spawned remotely by an ignorant scheduler,
thus causing many suspensions. We really need an underlying architecture that
guarantees local execution where we specify it.

Even near the root of the OR-tree, i.e., during the initial moves of the game,
spawning 36 `move` goals is not a good idea. Generally, there appears to be no way
to avoid this in committed-choice languages such as FGHC.

7.2   MasterMind

MasterMind is a guessing game wherein an attempt is made to break a code in the
minimal number of steps. The code consists of any sequence of M colored pegs,
where each peg can be chosen from N possible colors. Once the code is chosen, it
remains fixed throughout the game. Each step of the game consists of a guess and
an answer. The guess is simply a sequence of M colors that might be the code. The
answer consists of two pieces of information: the number of *cows* and the number
of *bulls*. A bull is a correct color in the right position. The number of cows is
the number of pegs that appear in both sequences (the guess and the code) but
not in the same position. For example, encoding colors as integers, the sequences
`[2,1,3,2,3]` and `[3,1,3,3,4]` have two bulls and one cow.

Several strategies may be used for this game (see Coelho [31] and Van Hentenryck
[140] for instance); however, the method introduced by Sterling and Shapiro [119]
is an elegant and efficient algorithm for Prolog. The basic idea is to make each
guess *consistent* with the previous information gathered. Sterling and Shapiro [119]
write: "...a guess is consistent with a set of answers to queries if the answers to
the queries would have remained the same if the guess was the secret code." The
logical construction of that definition is somewhat counter-intuitive, but is quite
acceptable to Prolog.

The MasterMind programs presented here have a programmable number of pegs,
colors, and maximum allowed guesses. We define a "solution" to the game as a
sequence of consistent guesses, as defined above.[2] All programs given generate
guesses out of colors by selecting the combinations of colors *in the same order*.

---

[2]In other words, we choose not to generate "stupid" solutions, e.g., solutions with repeated
guesses, guesses that do not incorporate the knowledge gained by previous guesses, intuitive
guesses, etc. The program will never pass Turing's Test...

Prolog Version

The Prolog program presented here is an optimized version of an original described
in detail in Sterling and Shapiro [119]. The key to the program is **guess(L,G)**, which
generates a new guess, G, compatible with the known facts, L. Procedure **guess/2**
uses **pick/1** to exploit parallelism, i.e., the OR-tree is formed by branchpoints that
choose colors in the guess. The guess is checked with **test/2**. This test is done
by checking each peg in the guess against the known facts. The top-level loop,
solveBody/5, continues to generate guesses until M bulls are detected.

We begin by defining the secret code and possible colors. All the parallelism in
the program comes from the nondeterminancy of **color/1**.

```
code([2,1,3,2]).

:- parallel color/1.

color(1).
color(2).
color(3).
```

At the top-level, for a given maximum number of guesses, NG, we compute all
solutions, A. The main workhorse is **solveBody/5**. Here a valid guess is generated
and the bulls and cows are calculated. If there are only bulls, a solution is found.
Otherwise, if we are still under the maximum number of allowed guesses, we recurse,
adding the new guess to our guess list.

```
go(NG,A) :-
    code(C),
    length(C,CL),
    findall(X, solveBody(NG,CL,X), A).

solveBody(NG,CL,A) :- solveBody(NG,CL,[],0,A).

solveBody(NG,CL,L,N,X) :-
    guess(L,Choice),
    code(Code),
    eval(Choice,Code,Bulls,Cows),
    (Bulls =:= CL ->
        X = L
    ;
        N1 is N+1, N1 < NG,
        solveBody(NG,CL,[p(Bulls,Cows,Choice)|L],N1,X)
    ).
```

Note that the final (correct) guess is *not* included in each solution. The remaining problems are how to write the generator–tester, **guess/2**, and the bull-cow
evaluator, **eval/4**.

Calculating cows and bulls is the job of `eval/4`. An optimized version of the program given in [119] is used here. First, the bulls are calculated by comparing the X and Y guesses. During this check, *the bulls are removed from the lists*. Next, the cows are calculated by deleting each remaining X element from Y. By removing the bulls in the first step, the second deletion step is shortened.

```
eval(X,Y,Bulls,Cows) :-
    exact(X,Y,Bulls,0,X1,Y1),
    inexact(X1,Y1,Cows,0).

exact([],S2,N,N,[],S2).
exact([H|T],[H|T2],N,I,S1,S2) :- !,
    I1 is I+1,
    exact(T,T2,N,I1,S1,S2).
exact([X|T1],[Y|T2],N,I,[X|S1],[Y|S2]) :-
    exact(T1,T2,N,I,S1,S2).

del(X,[X|Y],Y) :- !.
del(X,[X1|Y],[X1|Z]) :- del(X,Y,Z).

inexact([], _,N,N).
inexact([Ht|Tt],Choice,N,I) :-
    (del(Ht,Choice,New_Choice) ->
        J is I+1, inexact(Tt,New_Choice,N,J)
    ;
        inexact(Tt,Choice,N,I)
    ).
```

The informal specification of this program is given in Figure 7.4.

7.2.1 Naive Generate & Test

Our first attempt at `guess/2` is a naive generate & test procedure. Four colors are chosen nondeterminately and the guess P is tested against the previous guesses L.

```
guess(L,P) :-
    P = [P1,P2,P3,P4],
    color(P1),color(P2),color(P3),color(P4),
    test(L,P).

test([],_).
test([p(Bulls,Cows,Tried)|T],Choice) :-
    eval(Choice,Tried,Bulls,Cows),
    test(T,Choice).
```

The consistency check states that if the previous guess *was in fact* the code, then this newest guess would produce the same numbers of bulls and cows as did the previous guess (when compared to the real code).

Procedure: go(NG, A)
    + NG: integer   – A: list of solutions

Relation: A contains all sequences of consistent guesses of length NG or less
    that solve the MasterMind code defined in predicate code/1.

Preconditions: Predicate code/1 must define a list of integers as a codeword.

Procedure: solveBody(NG, CL, L, N, A)
    +NG: integer   +L: list of guesses   –A: list of guesses
    +CL: integer   +N: integer

Relation: A is an extension of partial solution L by less than NG-N additional
    guesses, solving the MasterMind problem. If L cannot be completed in
    less than this number of moves then this call fails. A guess is a p/3
    structure containing a codeword, its bulls and cows.

Preconditions: Initially L is empty and N=0.

Procedure: eval(Guess, Code, Bulls, Cows)
    + Guess: list of integers   – Bulls: integer
    + Code: list of integers   – Cows: integer

Relation: Guess has Bulls and Cows for a given Code.

Procedure: guess(L, Guess)
    + L: list of guesses   – Guess: list of integers

Relation: Guess is "consistent" with history of guesses in L.

Procedure: test(L, N, Guess)
    + L: list of guesses   + Guess: list of integers
    + N: integer

Relation: Partial Guess is "consistent" with history of guesses in L.

Preconditions: N + length of Guess equals length of codeword in code/1.

Figure 7.4
Informal Specification of Prolog MasterMind

7.2.2 Fused Generate & Test

A fused generate & test can be fashioned from the previous code [120]. Again, a guess code of length four is described. Colors are again picked nondeterminately, but a *partial* guess is tested for compatibility with previous guesses.

```
guess(L,[P1,P2,P3,P4]) :-
    color(P1), test(L,3,[P1]),
    color(P2), test(L,2,[P1,P2]),
    color(P3), test(L,1,[P1,P2,P3]),
    color(P4), test(L,0,[P1,P2,P3,P4]).

test([],_,_).
test([p(OldBulls,OldCows,Tried)|T],U,Choice) :-
    eval(Choice,Tried,Bulls,Cows),
    Bulls =< OldBulls,OldBulls =< Bulls+U,
    I is Bulls+Cows,
    S is OldBulls+OldCows,
    I =< S,S =< I+U,
    test(T,U,Choice).
```

The tester has been generalized with an additional argument U, the number of colors as yet unpicked. Here consistency is a bit harder to explain. Two bounds must be established. The number of bulls in each previous guess must be bounded by the number of bulls in the new guess (lower bound) and the bulls plus the number of pegs as yet unchosen (upper bound). The sum of the bulls and cows in each previous guess must be similarly bounded.

The above definition of guess/2, with four tests instead of one, allows early tests to quickly avoid mistaken guesses. For example, if an early peg in the guess contradicts some known information, then the peg, *and all subsequent peg choices*, can be avoided. Without such an optimization, all possible combinations of subsequent pegs will be generated and tested before backtracking finally undoes the early faulty choice. This type of fused generate & test is similar to the fused N-Queens program given in Section 5.1.2.

FGHC Version

The FGHC program described here performs a naive generate & test with combo/3 (see Section 4.1) as the generator. Recall that combo([a,b],3,A), for instance, generates all lists of length three with elements selected from the list [a,b], i.e.,

A = [[a,a,a],[a,a,b],[a,b,a],[a,b,b],[b,a,a],[b,a,b],[b,b,a],[b,b,b]]

The top level of the FGHC program is similar to that of the Prolog code. Procedure spawn(Guesses,Clist,CL,NG,Out) produces all winning sequences on stream Out, from the input list of initial guesses, `Guesses`. Argument `Clist` is a list of colors, of length `NC`. Argument `CL` is the length of the secret code and `NG` is the maximum number of allowed guesses in a solution.

```
code(C) :- C=[2,1,3,2].

go(NG,NC,Out) :-
    code(C),
    length(C,0,CL),
    gen(NC,Clist),
    combo(Clist,CL,Guesses),
    spawn(Guesses,Clist,CL,NG,Out).

length([],X,Y) :- X=Y.
length([_|T],X,Y) :- X1 is X+1, length(T,X1,Y).

gen(0,X) :- X=[].
gen(N,X) :- N>0 | M is N-1, X = [N|Xs], gen(M,Xs).
```

Procedure `spawn/5` easily exploits the OR parallelism in the problem. The branching factor in the OR-tree, generated by `spawn/4`, is equal to the number of possible guesses, i.e., combinations of colors. Many of these branches will soon be pruned by the subsequent `test` which checks for consistency.

```
spawn(Guesses,Clist,CL,NG,Out) :-
    spawn(Guesses,[],c(Clist,CL,0,NG),Out-[]).

spawn([],    _,Cont,S0-S1) :- S0=S1.
spawn([G|Gs],A,Cont,S0-S2) :-
    test(A,G,A,Cont,S0-S1),
    spawn(Gs,A,Cont,S1-S2).

test([p(OldBulls,OldCows,Tried)|Gs],Guess,A,Cont,S) :-
    eval(Guess,Tried,Bulls,Cows),
    check(OldCows,Cows,OldBulls,Bulls,Gs,Guess,A,Cont,S).
test([],Guess,A,Cont,S) :-
    code(Code),
    eval(Guess,Code,Bulls,Cows),
    loop(Bulls,Cows,Guess,A,Cont,S).

check(Cows,Cows,Bulls,Bulls,Gs,Guess,A,Cont,S) :-
    test(Gs,Guess,A,Cont,S).
check(_,_,_,_,_,_,_,S0-S1) :- otherwise | S0=S1.
```

The consistency check is similar to that in the naive generate & test Prolog program. If the check passes, the bulls and cows for the newest guess are calculated and added to the partial solution, in `loop/6`. There are two termination conditions tested for in `loop`. If the number of bulls equals the length of the secret code, the solution is complete (first clause). If the number of guesses exceeds the maximum allowable limit, the solution is discarded (last clause). Otherwise, a new guess is generated (with combo/3) and a new node is spawned in the OR-tree (with spawn/4).

```
loop(CL,_,_,A,c(_,CL,_,_),S0-S1) :- S0=[A|S1].
loop(Bulls,Cows,Guess,A,c(Clist,CL,N,NG),S) :-
    Bulls < CL, N1 is N+1, N1 < NG |
    combo(Clist,CL,Guesses),
    spawn(Guesses,[p(Bulls,Cows,Guess)|A],c(Clist,CL,N1,NG),S).
loop(_,_,_,_,_,S0-S1) :- otherwise | S0=S1.
```

The evaluation of bulls and cows is much the same as in the Prolog code.

```
eval(X,Y,Bulls,Cows) :-
    exact(X,Y,Bulls,0,X1,Y1),
    inexact(X1,Y1,Cows,0).

inexact( _,[],N,I) :- I=N.
inexact([], _,N,I) :- I=N.
inexact([Ht|Tt],Choice,N,I) :- otherwise |
    delete(Choice,Ht,F,F,Choice,Tt,N,I).

delete([],_,_,_,Choice,Tt,N,I) :-
    inexact(Tt,Choice,N,I).
delete([X|Y],X,F,NewChoice,_,Tt,N,I) :-
    I1 is I+1,
    F=Y,
    inexact(Tt,NewChoice,N,I1).
delete([X1|Y],X,F,NewChoice,Choice,Tt,N,I) :- X1=\=X |
    F = [X1|Z],
    delete(Y,X,Z,NewChoice,Choice,Tt,N,I).

exact([],T2,N,I,S1,S2) :- N=I, S2=T2, S1=[].
exact([H|T],[H|T2],N,I,S1,S2) :-
    I1 is I+1,
    exact(T,T2,N,I1,S1,S2).
exact([X|T1],[Y|T2],N,I,X1,Y1) :- X=\=Y |
    X1 = [X|S1],
    Y1 = [Y|S2],
    exact(T1,T2,N,I,S1,S2).
```

The informal specification of this program is given in Figure 7.5.

7.2.3 Discussion

For the measurements presented, we use four pegs, three colors, and a maximum of three guesses (including the final, correct guess), giving a total of 860 solutions. The secret code is [2,1,3,2]. Table 7.5 gives the high-level characteristics of the programs executing on eight Symmetry PEs. Table 7.6 gives the execution time (in

<u>Procedure</u>: go(NG, NC, Out)
    +NG: integer   +NC: integer   −Out: list of solutions

<u>Relation</u>: Out contains all sequences (of length NG or less) of consistent guesses that solve the MasterMind code defined in predicate code/1.

<u>Preconditions</u>: Predicate code/1 defines a list of integers from 1 to NC.

<u>Procedure</u>: combo(L, N, Out)
    +L: list of integers   +N: integer   −Out: list of combinations

<u>Relation</u>: Out contains all combinations of length N of elements from L.

<u>Procedure</u>: spawn(Guesses, A, Cont, S)
    + Guesses: list of guesses   + Cont: continuation
    + A: partial solution   − S: stream of solutions

<u>Relation</u>: S contains all completions of partial solution A extended first with a guess from Guesses. A guess is a p/3 structures containing a codword, its bulls and cows.

<u>Preconditions</u>: Initially A is empty and Cont = c(Clist,CL,0,NG), where Clist is the list of integers, CL is the length of the code and NG is the maximum number of guesses per solution.

<u>Procedure</u>: test(L, G, A, Cont, S)
    + L: list of guesses   + A: partial solution   − S: stream of solutions
    + G: list of integers   + Cont: continuation

<u>Relation</u>: S contains all completions of A extended first with Guess.

<u>Procedure</u>: check(PCow, Cow, PBull, Bull, Gs, G, A, Cont, S)
    +PCow: integer   +Bull: integer   +A: partial solution
    +Cow: integer   +Gs: list of guesses +Cont: continuation
    +PBull: integer   +G: list of integers −S: stream of solutions

<u>Relation</u>: If PCows = Cows and PBulls = Bulls then Guess G is "consistent" with a previous guess, and S contains all completions of partial solution A extended first with Guess. Otherwise stream S is shorted.

<u>Procedure</u>: loop(Bulls, Cows, Guess, A, Cont, S)
    +Bulls: integer   +Guess: list of integers   +Cont: continuation
    + Cows: integer   +A: partial solution   −S: stream of solutions

<u>Relation</u>: If all Bulls then A is a completed solution and is sent down stream S. Otherwise S contains all completions of partial solution A extended first with p(Bulls,Cows,Guess).

Figure 7.5
Informal Specification of FGHC MasterMind

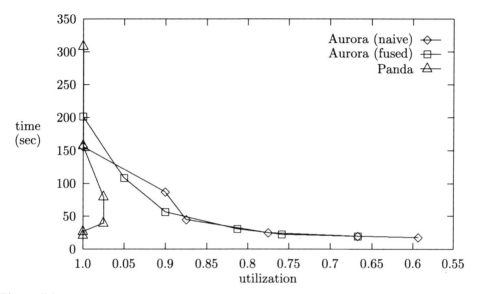

Figure 7.6
MasterMind (860 Solutions): Utilization vs. Time (Symmetry)

seconds) and speedup on Symmetry. Figure 7.6 summarizes the measurements.

GC time in the FGHC programs was insignificant, because a large memory was used. The most curious result is that the naive generate & test in Prolog outperforms the fused generate & test. Apparently the overhead of the more complex test required in the fused version, in addition to the extra number of tests, outweighs the savings in reducing the search space. As the secret-code size increases, one would expect the advantage to switch to the fused program, because the naive search space increases as a faster exponential. In any case, the FGHC program is the slowest of the three programs, but displays the best speedup.

system	method	instr	reduct	back/susp	entries	sec	KEPS
Aurora	naive	8894444	926721	533829	1460550	25.0	58
	fused	10718409	1096844	673638	1770482	30.8	57
Panda	naive	25676344	1509802	15495	1525297	39.5	39

Table 7.5
MasterMind (860 solutions): High-Level Characteristics (eight PEs)

system	method	1 PE	2 PE	4 PE	8 PE	12 PE	15 PE
raw execution time (seconds)							
Aurora	naive	155.9	86.8	45.0	25.0	19.6	17.5
	fused	201.7	108.2	56.3	30.8	22.2	19.5
Panda	naive	307.9	157.1	79.3	39.5	26.6	21.0
speedup							
Aurora	naive	1.0	1.8	3.5	6.2	8.0	8.9
	fused	1.0	1.9	3.6	6.5	9.1	10
Panda	naive	1.0	2.0	3.9	7.8	12	15

Table 7.6
MasterMind (860 solutions): Execution Time and Speedup (Symmetry)

> MasterMind is a good example of Panda's ability to exploit fine-grained
> AND-parallelism, overcoming a 2:1 deficit in sequential execution time
> and achieving within 20% of Aurora's execution time on 15 PEs. For
> larger problems on more PEs, it appears likely that Panda will catch
> and surpass Aurora in execution speed (assuming that Panda overheads
> with respect to Aurora remain constant for larger problems).

Aurora achieves mediocre speedups for these programs. For increasing numbers
of PEs, efficiency degrades rapidly, dropping from 82% on eight PEs to 59% on
15 PEs. This problem is mainly because the input data constrains the search to
solutions containing a maximum of three guesses. This constraint limits the length
of the OR-tree branches, lowering efficiency. We expect better efficiency when more
guesses are allowed.

7.3   Summary

Two game-playing problems with alternative implementations in OR-parallel Prolog
and FGHC were introduced in this chapter. The programs find all solutions, where
a solution consists of a sequence of winning moves. The Prolog programs developed
in this chapter all used a top-level `findall` to collect solutions. This type of problem
is well-suited to OR-parallelism, as attested by the 14.2 and 8.9 speedups attained
by Aurora on 15 Symmetry PEs. MasterMind did not fare well for the given test
data, because the OR-parallel branches were too short. When collecting longer
solutions, program performance is expected to improve. Panda attained speedups
of 11.1 and 14.7 for the same two problems. In this case, Triangle did not fare well

because the nondeterminate selection of the next move caused the indiscriminate spawning of 36 goals, many of which immediately failed. Still, 11.1 speedup on 15 PEs is not bad, and Panda shows that it can achieve as much efficiency as Aurora for all-solutions problems. However, let us examine the raw execution times.

The Aurora/Panda execution-time ratio varied with the benchmarks: 0.43 (Triangle) and 0.83 (MasterMind) on 15 PEs. In the case of Triangle, inefficient goal spawning in FGHC led to slow execution. The FGHC MasterMind program suffered because it uses naive generate & test. With some rewriting (see Exercise 73), MasterMind will probably be a match. Thus neither system displayed overwhelming advantages. Prolog was easier in general to program for these problems, although this too is a close call.

Exercises

Exercise 67 The FGHC Triangle program specifies `play/5` in a manner such that all 36 possible moves are spawned at once. Generalize the program so that `play` accepts an additional input specifying the number of possible moves. Procedure `play/6` will loop around, spawning one move in each iteration. How does this affect parallelism, scheduling, and program execution time? Explain.

Exercise 68 Generalize the given Triangle programs to obviate the need to spell-out each of the 36 moves. For example, legitimate moves could be specified in a list, `[move(A1, B1, C1), ...]` where the first legal move consists of a jump from peg `A1` over peg `B1`, to peg `C1`. The `move` procedure must be rewritten to process this more abstract representation.

Exercise 69 With the representation in Exercise 68, experiment with new rules and board spaces for games similar to Triangle. Invent a game with simple rules that has the same or smaller (with respect to the Triangle game) ratio of the number of solutions to the number of initial pegs.

Exercise 70 Write a more intelligent Triangle program in FGHC that avoids the problem wherein the branching factor of OR-tree nodes near the leaves remain constant. This program must not blindly try all 36 possible moves late in the game.

Exercise 71 The `guess/2` procedure in the Prolog MasterMind program always generates guesses of length four. Rewrite this procedure as `guess/3`, where the additional argument specifies the desired length of guess.

Exercise 72 Experiment with the MasterMind input parameters and illustrate a situation where the fused generate & test Prolog algorithm outperforms the naive version. Analyze the complexity of the two algorithms as a function of the input parameters. Also illustrate that increasing the number of allowable guesses in a solution will increase the efficiency of the Prolog programs.

Exercise 73 Write an FGHC program for MasterMind with a fused generate & test algorithm, as in the Prolog program. The generalized `test/3` procedure from Prolog must be fused into the FGHC `combo/3` procedure. Compare its performance to the other versions.

Exercise 74 (Magic Series) Write programs in OR-parallel Prolog and FGHC to find all magic series of length n. A series $S = (s_0, s_1, ..., s_n)$ is magic if and only if there are s_i occurrences of i in S for each integer $0 \le i \le n$. For example, the two solutions for $n = 3$ are (1,2,1,0) and (2,0,2,0). See Van Hentenryck [140] for a version of this program in CHIP.

Exercise 75 (Latin Squares) Write programs in OR-parallel Prolog and FGHC to find a single $N \times N$ Latin Square. Place the integers 1 to N^2 on an $N \times N$ board so that the sum of numbers in each row, column, and diagonal are equal. Don't even *think* about using any kind of generate & test for this problem!

Exercise 76 (Nim) No textbook would be complete without an exercise in implementing the game of Nim. Two players initially are given the same triangular board as in the Triangle Problem, with all 15 pegs in place. The players take turns removing any number of pegs from a given row. The player to remove the last peg wins. Write Prolog and FGHC versions of Nim for a board of arbitrary size. The program should assume the role of one of the players. The parallelism we wish to exploit is in searching for the next best move to make. This strategy may follow the line of reasoning: "If I move here, then he will move there, then I will..." For general information about such MIN-MAX search strategies, see Winston [146]. Also see Sterling and Shapiro [119] for a version of Nim in Prolog.

Exercise 77 (Tiles) Write programs in OR-parallel Prolog and FGHC to find a solution to the following children's game. You are given an $N \times N$ board filled with tiles marked 1 to $N^2 - 1$, i.e., one tile is missing. The empty square is called the slot. Initially the tiles and slot are randomly placed. A tile adjacent to the slot can be moved into the slot. The objective of the game is to sort the tiles (from top left to bottom right) in the minimum number of moves.

The complexity of this problem is too great to solve with generate & test, or even with simple heuristical search. A common approach is to solve the topmost row, then leftmost column in a $K \times K$ board to create a $(K-1) \times (K-1)$ board. The smaller board is then reduced, keeping the previously solved tiles frozen. If a sub-board cannot be solved, certain tiles bordering the sub-board must be unfrozen to allow more freedom of movement. Unfrozen tiles can be moved under constraints that guarantee their return to their proper spots.

See Coelho [31] for a version of this game in Prolog. Nilsson [92] describes solving the puzzle with the famous A* search algorithm. The game with $N = 4$, often called the 15-Puzzle, is a famous benchmark problem.

Exercise 78 (Mahjong) Write a parallel logic program to evaluate a set of Mahjong tiles. Mahjong plays an even more fundamental role than golf in bonding business and family relationships in East Asia. The game of Mahjong is played by four players with 136 tiles called *pai*'s. The *pai*'s consist of four types: *man-zu*, *pin-zu*, *so-zu*, and *ji-hai*. The first three types are marked with integers 1–9. For instance, we could denote these as *1-man*, *2-man*, ..., *9-so*. The *ji-hai* consist of seven unique kanji characters: *ton*, *nan*, *sha*, *pei*, *haku*, *hatsu*, and *chun*. That gives us $3 \times 9 + 7 = 34$ unique *pai*'s. There are four duplicates of each, giving 136 tiles.

During play each player holds 13 *pai*'s. Play proceeds in some fixed order, each player choosing an additional (as yet unknown) *pai* and then discarding one of his now 14 *pai*'s. Discards are made face up so that all players can see. A player may also choose to end play if he has a winning combination of 14 *pai*'s (or he can continue to play even if he has a winning combination, in an effort to gain a *better* winning combination).

A winning combination is basically a 2–3–3–3–3 grouping of 14 *pai*'s, where the '2' is a pair of identical *pai*'s (*toitsu*) and the '3' is either a triple of identical *pai*'s (*koutsu*) or a set of consecutive *pai*'s of the same type (*shuntsu*). For example, the hand:

    `[ton,haku,4-man,haku,ton,5-man,6-so,9-pin,7-so,9-pin,haku,3-man,9-pin]`

might be grouped as:

```
[ton, ton]
[haku, haku, haku]
[3-man, 4-man, 5-man]
[9-pin, 9-pin, 9-pin]
[6-so, 7-so]
```

If we pick `5-so` or `8-so`, the final *shuntsu* can be completed, forming a winning combination. The scoring of hands is difficult and is unnecessary for this exercise.

Write a program to order a hand of 14 *pai's*. The program should indicate if the hand is a winning combination or not. If not, the program should return one of the *pai's* for discard. Note that alternative combinations can be grouped in OR-parallel, each calculating a heuristic of "best chance to win."

Exercise 79 Incorporate the procedure of the previous exercise into a Mahjong simulator consisting of four players and a dealer. Modify the evaluation procedure to account for the changing probabilities apparent from the discards of other players.

8 Zebra, Salt and Mustard

"It is not easy for me to imagine how someone who was not in the grip of an ideology would find the idea [of strong AI] at all plausible."

J. R. Searle

Minds, Brains, and Programs

from *The Behavioral and Brain Sciences vol. 3*

Cambridge University Press 1980

In this chapter, we present two logic problems for which Prolog is well-suited. Zebra concerns finding the owner of a zebra given various facts about the vices of some *gaijin* living in a row of tenements. Salt and Mustard concerns finding the condiments preferred by a group of Englishmen given a complex set of facts governing their dietary habits. When searching for all solutions, these problems are particularly well-suited to OR-parallel search. It is of interest to see if the OR-parallel Prolog programs truly require little or no modifications to solve the problems efficiently, and if OR-parallel Prolog can attain near-linear speedups. It is important to look at how one would attempt to code these problems in committed-choice languages, or if/how they can be translated into committed-choice languages directly from Prolog.

8.1 Zebras

The Zebra problem is a logical constraint problem derived from the original given in Coelho [31]. The facts of the extended problem follow.

> The Englishman lives in the red house. The Spaniard owns the dog. Coffee is drunk in the green house. The Ukrainian drinks tea. Kools are smoked in the yellow house. The whiskey drinker owns a parrot. Milk is drunk in the middle house. The Norwegian lives in the first house on the left. The man who smokes Chesterfields lives in the house next to the man with the fox. Kools are smoked in the house next to the house where the horse is kept. The Lucky Strike smoker drinks orange juice. The Japanese smokes Parliaments. The Norwegian lives next to the blue house. The Japanese lives next to the purple house. The Winton smoker owns snails. Chesterfields are smoked in the ivory house. Seven-Stars are smoked in the house next to the house where the zebra is kept. The water drinker lives next to the American.

The problem is to associate each nationality, drink, cigarette, house color, house position, and pet. There are $(6!)^5 = 193,491,763,200,000$ combinations, obviously too many for a naive generate & test algorithm. There are four solutions to the problem, all of which have the Ukranian owning the zebra. One of the solutions is shown below:[1]

```
[house(yellow,norwegian,parrot,whiskey,kools),
 house(blue,japanese,horse,water,parliaments),
 house(purple,american,snails,milk,winstons),
 house(green,spanish,dog,coffee,seven_stars),
 house(ivory,ukranian,zebra,tea,chesterfields),
 house(red,english,fox,orange_juice,lucky_strikes)]
```

Prolog Version: Fused Generate & Test

The Prolog program is arranged to incorporate each fact as a constraint, *in the given order*. For comparative timings (with FGHC, for instance), order is important because the size of the OR-tree is dependent on when constraints are satisfied. For example, if the facts about the Norwegian were constrained at the beginning of the program, the search space would be drastically reduced. We take the liberty of incorporating two of the constraints into the initial partial solution:

```
init([house(_,norwegian,_,_,_),
      house(_,_,_,_,_),
      house(_,_,_,milk,_),
      house(_,_,_,_,_),
      house(_,_,_,_,_),
      house(_,_,_,_,_)]).
```

The constraints are easily formulated with two procedures: **member/2** and **next-To/3**, having the obvious meanings. These procedures are nondeterminate, so backtracking from later contradictory facts will cause alternative choices to be made.

```
go(L) :- findall(Z,solve(Z),L).

solve(Houses) :-
    init(Houses),
    member(house(red,english,_,_,_),Houses),
    member(house(_,spanish,dog,_,_),Houses),
    member(house(green,_,_,coffee,_),Houses),
    member(house(_,ukranian,_,tea,_),Houses),
    member(house(yellow,_,_,_,kools),Houses),
    member(house(_,_,parrot,whiskey,_),Houses),
    nextTo(house(_,_,_,_,chesterfields),house(_,_,fox,_,_),Houses),
    nextTo(house(_,_,_,_,kools),house(_,_,horse,_,_),Houses),
    member(house(_,_,_,orange_juice,lucky_strikes),Houses),
    member(house(_,japanese,_,_,parliaments),Houses),
    nextTo(house(_,norwegian,_,_,_),house(blue,_,_,_,_),Houses),
    nextTo(house(_,japanese,_,_,_),house(purple,_,_,_,_),Houses),
    member(house(_,_,snails,_,winstons),Houses),
```

---

[1] Van Hentenryck [140] gives an efficient solution to a version of this problem in CHIP.

```
┌─────────────────────────────────────────────────────────────────────────────┐
│                                                                               │
│  Figure 8.1                                                                   │
│  Informal Specification of Prolog Zebra                                       │
│                                                                               │
│      Procedure: solve(Hs)                                                     │
│         + Hs: list of houses                                                  │
│                                                                               │
│      Relation: Hs is fully instantiated with a solution to the Zebra problem. │
│                                                                               │
│      Preconditions: Initially Hs is described by predicate init/1.            │
│                                                                               │
│                                                                               │
│      Procedure: nextTo(H1, H2, Hs)                                            │
│            ? H1: house    ? H2: house    ? Hs: list of houses                 │
│                                                                               │
│      Relation: Houses H1 and H2 are adjacent within Hs.                       │
│                                                                               │
│                                                                               │
│      Procedure: member(H, Hs)                                                 │
│            ? H: house    ? Hs: list of houses                                 │
│                                                                               │
│      Relation: Hs contains H.                                                 │
│                                                                               │
└─────────────────────────────────────────────────────────────────────────────┘
```

```
        member(house(ivory,_,_,_,chesterfields),Houses),
        nextTo(house(_,_,_,_,seven_stars),house(_,_,zebra,_,_),Houses),
        nextTo(house(_,american,_,_,_),house(_,_,_,water,_),Houses).
```

The only remaining task is to define the procedures used in formulating the constraints.

```
    :- parallel member/2,nextTo/3.

    member(X,[X|_]).
    member(X,[_|Y]) :- member(X,Y).

    nextTo(A,B,[A,B|_]).
    nextTo(A,B,[B,A|_]).
    nextTo(A,B,[_|Y]) :- nextTo(A,B,Y).
```

The informal specification of this program is given in Figure 8.1.

These procedures can be unrolled to increase the efficiency of the branchpoints they create. Below we show both procedures fully unrolled.

```
    member(X,[X|_]).
    member(X,[_,X|_]).
    member(X,[_,_,X|_]).
    member(X,[_,_,_,X|_]).
    member(X,[_,_,_,_,X]).
```

```
nextTo(A,B,[A,B|_]).
nextTo(A,B,[B,A|_]).
nextTo(A,B,[_,A,B|_]).
nextTo(A,B,[_,B,A|_]).
nextTo(A,B,[_,_,A,B|_]).
nextTo(A,B,[_,_,B,A|_]).
nextTo(A,B,[_,_,_,A,B|_]).
nextTo(A,B,[_,_,_,B,A|_]).
nextTo(A,B,[_,_,_,_,A,B]).
nextTo(A,B,[_,_,_,_,B,A]).
```

The purpose of unrolling is to increase the efficiency of the branchpoint created for
nextTo/3 and member/2 by increasing the number of nondeterminate clauses that
can match without an intervening reduction.

The following formulation of the problem reduces the search space by ordering
the facts so that the most severe constraints are executed first.

```
solve(Houses) :-
    init(Houses),
    nextTo(house(ivory,_,_,_,chesterfields),house(_,_,fox,_,_),Houses),
    nextTo(house(_,japanese,_,_,parliaments),house(purple,_,_,_,_),Houses),
    nextTo(house(_,norwegian,_,_,_),house(blue,_,_,_,_),Houses),
    nextTo(house(_,american,_,_,_),house(_,_,_,water,_),Houses),
    nextTo(house(_,_,_,_,kools),house(_,_,horse,_,_),Houses),
    nextTo(house(_,_,_,_,seven_stars),house(_,_,zebra,_,_),Houses),
    member(house(red,english,_,_,_),Houses),
    member(house(_,spanish,dog,_,_),Houses),
    member(house(green,_,_,coffee,_),Houses),
    member(house(_,ukranian,_,tea,_),Houses),
    member(house(yellow,_,_,_,kools),Houses),
    member(house(_,_,parrot,whiskey,_),Houses),
    member(house(_,_,_,orange_juice,lucky_strikes),Houses),
    member(house(_,_,snails,_,winstons),Houses).
```

For SICStus Prolog, this version runs in 80 seconds compared to 180 seconds for the
previous version, a speedup of 2.25. This speedup comes not from parallelism but
from reduction of algorithmic complexity. Unfortunately, one rarely has the luxury
of reducing the search space in this manner; programs are usually too complex to
analyze.

FGHC Version: Pipelined Filters

As we have seen in previous problems, FGHC does not backtrack over logical variables, so this action must be simulated. The automatic rebinding of variables when
attempting to satisfy the constraints in the previous Prolog program must be made

explicit. In the FGHC program presented here, 'v' represents an unbound variable. The initial houses are defined in a structure differently than in the Prolog program:

```
init(Houses) :-
    Houses = [b(h(v,norwegian,v,v,v),
               h(v,v,v,v,v),
               h(v,v,v,milk,v),
               h(v,v,v,v,v),
               h(v,v,v,v,v),
               h(v,v,v,v,v))].
```

A structure b/6 is used because it requires about 23% less storage than a list (for this example), and we anticipate garbage problems. A list is used in the Prolog version because a list lends itself to deconstruction by nondeterminate **member**. A structure can also be deconstructed by nondeterminate application of builtin **arg/3**, but at some overhead. For this problem, Aurora has no garbage problems and therefore we can afford the luxury of lists.

The stream **Houses** contains partial answers to the problem. Initially there is one, albeit ambiguous, solution (shown above). Our strategy will be to further "instantiate" this solution with the given facts.[2] Each fact will be spawned as a filter/generator, forming a linear pipeline. The partial solutions will stream through the pipeline. As a filter, a fact process will discard any partial solutions that contradict its information. As a generator, a fact processor will *expand* each incoming partial solution into a set of further instantiated partial solutions and pass them down the stream.

Top-level procedure **solve/1** forms the pipeline. The pipeline is ordered first with 12 **member** facts and then with six **nextTo** facts. This order is chosen because we have no two-way unification in committed-choice languages, so we must know *a priori* which **HouseList** arguments we are trying to match (input unification) and which arguments we are trying to create (output unification). In the following, **member** facts do output unification and **nextTo** facts do input unification.

```
solve(S18) :-
    init(S0),
    member( S0, 1, S1),    member( S1, 2, S2),    member( S2, 3, S3),
    member( S3, 4, S4),    member( S4, 5, S5),    member( S5, 6, S6),
    member( S6, 7, S7),    member( S7, 8, S8),    member( S8, 9, S9),
    member( S9,10,S10),    member(S10,11,S11),    member(S11,12,S12),
    nextTo(S12,13,S13),    nextTo(S13,14,S14),    nextTo(S14,15,S15),
    nextTo(S15,16,S16),    nextTo(S16,17,S17),    nextTo(S17,18,S18).
```

---

[2]The word "instantiate" does *not* refer to binding logical variables, as in Prolog. More abstractly it refers to increasing the information content of the partial solution. Given more powerful language constructs, we in fact could use logic variables instead of simulating them with 'v'.

Each type of fact has three arguments: the incoming stream, a rule number, and the outgoing stream. A `member/3` fact constrains a single house only. A `nextTo/3` fact constrains two houses to be next to each other.

```
member(    [],_,Out) :- Out=[].
member([B|Bs],I,Out)  :- add(I,B,Out-Out1), member(Bs,I,Out1).

add(I,b(H1,H2,H3,H4,H5,H6),S0-S6) :-
    rule(I,_,H1,N1,b(N1,H2,H3,H4,H5,H6),S0-S1),
    rule(I,_,H2,N2,b(H1,N2,H3,H4,H5,H6),S1-S2),
    rule(I,_,H3,N3,b(H1,H2,N3,H4,H5,H6),S2-S3),
    rule(I,_,H4,N4,b(H1,H2,H3,N4,H5,H6),S3-S4),
    rule(I,_,H5,N5,b(H1,H2,H3,H4,N5,H6),S4-S5),
    rule(I,_,H6,N6,b(H1,H2,H3,H4,H5,N6),S5-S6).

nextTo(    [],_,Out) :- Out=[].
nextTo([B|Bs],I,Out)  :- nadd(I,B,Out-Out1), nextTo(Bs,I,Out1).

nadd(I,b(H1,H2,H3,H4,H5,H6),S0-SA) :-
    rule(I,H1,H2,N1,b(H1,N1,H3,H4,H5,H6),S0-S1),
    rule(I,H2,H1,N2,b(N2,H2,H3,H4,H5,H6),S1-S2),
    rule(I,H2,H3,N3,b(H1,H2,N3,H4,H5,H6),S2-S3),
    rule(I,H3,H2,N4,b(H1,N4,H3,H4,H5,H6),S3-S4),
    rule(I,H3,H4,N5,b(H1,H2,H3,N5,H5,H6),S4-S5),
    rule(I,H4,H3,N6,b(H1,H2,N6,H4,H5,H6),S5-S6),
    rule(I,H4,H5,N7,b(H1,H2,H3,H4,N7,H6),S6-S7),
    rule(I,H5,H4,N8,b(H1,H2,H3,N8,H5,H6),S7-S8),
    rule(I,H5,H6,N9,b(H1,H2,H3,H4,H5,N9),S8-S9),
    rule(I,H6,H5,NA,b(H1,H2,H3,H4,NA,H6),S9-SA).
```

Each fact type processes each incoming partial solution until the end of stream is detected. The `add/3` and `nadd/3` procedures are spawned for each partial solution to filter it away or expand it. These processes are composed of `rule/6` processes, connected with a D-list for generated solutions. If a given rule cannot be satisfied, the D-list is shorted. Otherwise, a further instantiated partial solution is sent down the D-list stream. Note that facts constraining a single house can expand a given solution into a maximum of six solutions (since there are six houses).

The constraint pipeline is constructed so that partial solutions arriving at a constraint dealing with two houses are guaranteed to have the attribute in one of the houses instantiated. Thus two-house constraint filter/generators do *not* expand a solution, only further instantiate it or discard it. For example, to enforce this, we introduced a new fact (number 11), that says "Someone smokes Seven Stars." and placed this constraint *before*[3] the fact (number 18) constraining the Seven Stars

[3]By "before" we mean "earlier in the pipeline," which is not necessarily directly related to the order in which the goals are evaluated.

smoker and the zebra to be in adjacent houses.

The rules are defined below. Rules 1–12 are single-house constraints. Rules 13–18 constrain two houses. Each rule checks if the house in question can be further instantiated to satisfy the constraint. If so, the newly created solution is passed down the stream. Otherwise the solution is discarded and the stream is shorted.

```
rule(1, _,h( v,X2,X3,X4, v),N,B,S0-S1) :-
    N=h(ivory,X2,X3,X4,chesterfields),S0=[B|S1].
rule(2, _,h(X1, v,X3,X4, v),N,B,S0-S1) :-
    N=h(X1,japan,X3,X4,parliments),   S0=[B|S1].
rule(3, _,h( v, v,X3,X4,X5),N,B,S0-S1) :-
    N=h(red,english,X3,X4,X5),        S0=[B|S1].
rule(4, _,h(X1, v, v,X4,X5),N,B,S0-S1) :-
    N=h(X1,spanish,dog,X4,X5),        S0=[B|S1].
rule(5, _,h( v,X2,X3, v,X5),N,B,S0-S1) :-
    N=h(green,X2,X3,coffee,X5),       S0=[B|S1].
rule(6, _,h(X1, v,X3, v,X5),N,B,S0-S1) :-
    N=h(X1,ukranian,X3,tea,X5),       S0=[B|S1].
rule(7, _,h( v,X2,X3,X4, v),N,B,S0-S1) :-
    N=h(yellow,X2,X3,X4,kools),       S0=[B|S1].
rule(8, _,h(X1,X2, v, v,X5),N,B,S0-S1) :-
    N=h(X1,X2,parrot,whiskey,X5),     S0=[B|S1].
rule(9, _,h(X1,X2,X3, v, v),N,B,S0-S1) :-
    N=h(X1,X2,X3,oj,lucky),           S0=[B|S1].
rule(10,_,h(X1,X2, v,X4, v),N,B,S0-S1) :-
    N=h(X1,X2,snails,X4,winstons),    S0=[B|S1].
rule(11,_,h(X1,X2,X3,X4, v),N,B,S0-S1) :-
    N=h(X1,X2,X3,X4,seven_stars),     S0=[B|S1].
rule(12,_,h(X1, v,X3,X4,X5),N,B,S0-S1) :-
    N=h(X1,american,X3,X4,X5),        S0=[B|S1].

rule(13,h(_,_,_,_,chesterfields),h(X1,X2,v,X4,X5),N,B,S0-S1) :-
    N=h(X1,X2,fox,X4,X5),         S0=[B|S1].
rule(14,h(_,japanese,_,_,_),      h(v,X2,X3,X4,X5),N,B,S0-S1) :-
    N=h(purple,X2,X3,X4,X5),      S0=[B|S1].
rule(15,h(_,norwegian,_,_,_),     h(v,X2,X3,X4,X5),N,B,S0-S1) :-
    N=h(blue,X2,X3,X4,X5),        S0=[B|S1].
rule(16,h(_,american,_,_,_),      h(X1,X2,X3,v,X5),N,B,S0-S1) :-
    N=h(X1,X2,X3,water,X5),       S0=[B|S1].
rule(17,h(_,_,_,_,kools),         h(X1,X2,v,X4,X5),N,B,S0-S1) :-
    N=h(X1,X2,horse,X4,X5),       S0=[B|S1].
rule(18,h(_,_,_,_,seven_stars),   h(X1,X2,v,X4,X5),N,B,S0-S1) :-
    N=h(X1,X2,zebra,X4,X5),       S0=[B|S1].
rule(_,_,_,_,_,S0-S1) :- otherwise | S0=S1.
```

The informal specification of the program is given in Figure 8.2.

In truth, this program has a serious practical flaw: it generates too much garbage. The problem stems from the construction of a new b/6 state by the caller to rule,

Procedure: solve(S)
   – S: stream of solutions

Relation: S contains all and only unique solutions to the Zebra problem. A solution is a b/6 structure containing six houses.

Procedure: member(In, I, Out)
   + In: list of partial solutions   – Out: list of partial solutions
   + I: integer (1–18)

Relation: Out contains all member extensions of partial solutions from In satisfying constraint I. Each I corresponds to a rule/6 clause.

Procedure: nextTo(In, I, Out)
   + In: list of partial solutions   – Out: list of partial solutions
   + I: integer (1–18)

Relation: Out contains all next-to extensions of partial solutions from In satisfying constraint I.

Procedure: add(I, B, S)
   + I: integer (1–18)   – S: stream of partial solutions
   + B: partial solution

Relation: S contains all member extensions of partial solution B satisfying constraint I. There can be at most k member extensions per partial solution for a problem with k houses.

Procedure: nadd(I, B, S)
   + I: integer (1–18)   – S: stream of partial solutions
   + B: partial solution

Relation: S contains all next-to extensions of partial solution B satisfying constraint I. There can be at most $2(k-1)$ next-to extensions per partial solution for a problem with k houses.

Procedure: rule(I, H1, H2, H3, B, S)
   +I: integer (1–18)   +H2: house   +B: partial solution
   ?H1: house   –H3: house   –S: stream of partial solutions

Relation: If B satisfies constraint I with H3 replacing H2 then B is sent down stream S. Otherwise S is shorted.

Precondition: B contains house H3, initially unbound.

Figure 8.2
Informal Specification of FGHC Zebra

System	Method	instr	reduct	back/susp	entries	sec	KEPS
Aurora	no unrolling	10916409	1389462	1942586	3332048	61.3	54
	fully unrolled	12048543	198556	1308535	1507091	48.2	31
	unrolled + ordered	5949300	112846	604569	717415	20.0	36
Panda		8236018	404193	2242	406435	24.7	16

Table 8.1
Zebra (4 solutions) High-Level Characteristics on Symmetry (eight PEs)

System	Method	1 PE	2 PE	4 PE	8 PE	12 PE	15 PE
		execution time (seconds)					
Aurora	no unrolling	479.6	237.3	119.5	61.3	42.6	34.7
	fully unrolled	388.5	192.7	96.4	48.2	32.2	25.9
	unrolled + ordered	160.4	79.9	39.8	20.0	13.3	10.8
Panda		144.4	75.2	38.9	24.7	21.0	19.6
		naive speedup					
Aurora	no unrolling	1.0	2.0	4.0	7.8	11	14
	fully unrolled	1.0	2.0	4.0	8.0	12	15
	unrolled + ordered	1.0	2.0	4.0	8.0	12	15
Panda		1.0	1.9	3.7	5.9	6.9	7.4

Table 8.2
Zebra (4 solutions) Performance Characteristics on Symmetry

instead of within **rule** itself. Each failed **rule** (i.e., each **rule** that immediately shorts itself) will have generated seven words of garbage. Dataflow analysis indicates that the fifth argument B of **rule** is either issued down the output stream or discarded in the final clause. Thus the creation of B can be moved into each clause of **rule**. One might expect a very sophisticated source-to-source optimizer to do this translation. For the measurements presented in the next section, this translation was performed by hand.

Discussion

Table 8.1 gives the high-level characteristics (on eight PEs) of the Zebra programs executing on Symmetry. Table 8.2 gives the execution times (in seconds) and speedups of the programs. Figure 8.3 summarizes the measurements.

Three Prolog programs were measured: one with the original ordering of facts and no unrolling, one with the original ordering of facts and full unrolling, and one with the optimized ordering of severe constraints first and full unrolling. Even without unrolling, the Prolog program achieves reasonably good speedup. With full

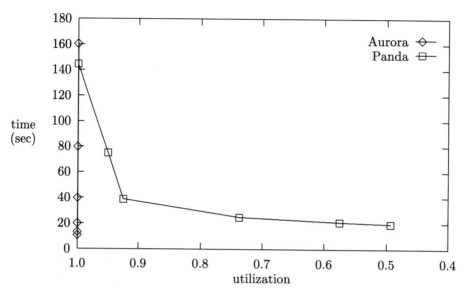

Figure 8.3
Zebra (4 Solutions): Utilization vs. Time (Symmetry)

unrolling, the speedup improved to perfectly linear! In addition, on a single PE, the unrolled program is 24% faster than the standard version. This difference is due to the decreased number of reductions and backtracks. The fully unrolled versions of **nextTo** and **member** require only one reduction per invocation, whereas the standard versions must iterate. In addition, the unrolled versions perform no unnecessary backtracking, whereas the standard versions make one or two superfluous end iterations.

Optimized ordering reduces the Prolog search space as hypothesized — on eight PEs the number of procedure entries is reduced to one-half. Aurora achieves linear speedup (efficiency greater than one is due to measurement variances). Thus, although slower than Panda on a single PE, Aurora overtakes Panda and executes twice as fast on 15 PEs. Panda has relatively poor speedup with lower than 50% efficiency on 15 PEs.

The FGHC program is a good test of a common scheduler weakness in stream-AND parallel architectures. The processes **add** and **nadd** spawn a great number of **rule** goals, which are unit facts. Thus a good scheduling policy is to reduce the entire **add** or **nadd** process on a single PE with no remote spawning. The Panda scheduler treats all goals equally, remotely spawning many **rule** processes;

therefore it achieves poor speedup. This problem is aggravated as the number of PEs increases, because there is less work per PE and soon all that is left to give idle PEs are `rule` goals.

One solution to this scheduling problem is to implement a policy wherein goals for unit facts cannot be remotely spawned. This solution is not sufficiently general — we actually want to avoid remote spawning of a goal that has little computation, i.e., small granularity. Compiler analysis may be able to evaluate goal granularity, either statically or by producing runtime annotations that can be dynamically evaluated for more accurate estimators [130, 39, 40]. The purpose of such schemes is simply to avoid overheads in remotely spawning goals that involve little computation.

As mentioned in the previous chapter (Section 7.1.3), Parlog allows the programmer to annotate body goals as either AND-parallel or sequential. AND-parallel goals are similar to FGHC goals. Sequential goals are not only executed locally, but their order of execution with respect to textually surrounding goals also is guaranteed. The performance advantages of sequential goals can outweigh implementation complexities. For Zebras written in Parlog with sequential body goals in `add` and `nadd`, 75% efficiency was achieved on 15 Symmetry PEs, i.e., a speedup of 11.3. Although we could sequence the `rule` body goals in FGHC by including a dependency variable connecting each consecutive pair of body goals, this strategy still would not guarantee local execution of all body goals on the same PE.

8.2 Salt and Mustard

The following problem by Lewis Carroll was first solved with logic programming by Disz *et al.* [44]:

> Five friends, Barry, Cole, Dix, Lang, and Mill, agreed to meet every day at a certain *table-d'hote*. They devised the following rules, to be observed whenever beef appeared on the table.
>
> 1. If Barry takes salt, then either Cole or Lang takes *one* only of the two condiments, salt and mustard: if he takes mustard, then either Dix takes neither condiment, or Mill takes both.
>
> 2. If Cole takes salt, then either Barry takes only *one* condiment, or Mill takes neither: if he takes mustard, then either Dix or Lang takes both.
>
> 3. If Dix takes salt, then either Barry takes neither condiment or Cole takes both: if he takes mustard, then either Lang or Mill takes neither.
>
> 4. If Lang takes salt, then either Barry or Dix takes only *one* condiment: if he takes mustard, then either Cole or Mill takes neither.

5. If Mill takes salt, then either Barry or Lang takes both condiments: if he takes mustard, then either Cole or Dix takes only *one*.

The problem is to discover whether these rules are *compatible*; and, if so, what arrangements are possible.

[N.B. In this problem it is assumed that the phrase "If Barry takes salt" allows of *two* possible cases, viz. (1) "He takes salt *only*"; (2) "He takes *both* condiments." And so with all similar phrases.

It is also assumed that the phrase, "Either Cole or Lang takes *one* only of the two condiments" allows of *three* possible cases, viz. (1) "Cole takes *one* only, Lang takes both or neither"; (2) "Cole takes both or neither, Lang takes *one* only"; (3) "Cole takes *one* only, Lang takes *one* only." And so with all similar phrases.

It is also assumed that every rule is to be understood as implying the words "and *vice versa*." Thus the first rule would imply the addition "and, if either Cole or Lang takes only *one* condiment, then Barry takes salt."]

There is only one solution to this problem: assigning {Barry, Cole, Dix, Lang, Mill} to the condiments {both, neither, neither, mustard, salt}, respectively.

Prolog Version

The following Prolog program, written by R. Overbeek [44], uses generate & test to filter out the solutions from a total of $4^5 = 1024$ possible combinations of condiments for the men.

```
:- parallel possibility/1.

go(L) :- findall(X,solution(X),L).

solution(X) :- generate(X), test(X).

possibility(both).
possibility(neither).
possibility(salt).
possibility(mustard).

generate([Barry,Cole,Dix,Lang,Mill]) :-
    possibility(Barry),
    possibility(Cole),
    possibility(Dix),
    possibility(Lang),
    possibility(Mill).
```

```
test(X) :-
    constraint1(X),
    constraint2(X),
    constraint3(X),
    constraint4(X),
    constraint5(X).
```

First we define some auxiliary procedures necessary to formulate the constraints. The `iff/2` procedure, although its logic is flawed by the use of "negation as failure," is sufficient for this program.

```
oneof(salt).
oneof(mustard).

took_salt(salt).
took_salt(both).

took_mustard(mustard).
took_mustard(both).

iff(X,Y) :- call(X), !, call(Y).
iff(X,Y) :- \+(call(Y)).
```

With these auxiliaries, the constraints are easily defined as follows. Recall that Prolog's builtin `G1;G2` is the disjunction (OR) of goal `G1` and goal `G2`.

```
constraint1([Barry,Cole,Dix,Lang,Mill]) :-
    iff(took_salt(Barry),(oneof(Cole); oneof(Lang))),
    iff(took_mustard(Barry),(Dix == neither; Mill == both)).

constraint2([Barry,Cole,Dix,Lang,Mill]) :-
    iff(took_salt(Cole),(oneof(Barry); (Mill == neither))),
    iff(took_mustard(Cole),((Dix == both); (Lang == both))).

constraint3([Barry,Cole,Dix,Lang,Mill]) :-
    iff(took_salt(Dix),((Barry == neither); (Cole == both))),
    iff(took_mustard(Dix),((Lang == neither); (Mill == neither))).

constraint4([Barry,Cole,Dix,Lang,Mill]) :-
    iff(took_salt(Lang),(oneof(Barry); oneof(Dix))),
    iff(took_mustard(Lang),((Cole == neither); (Mill == neither))).

constraint5([Barry,Cole,Dix,Lang,Mill]) :-
    iff(took_salt(Mill),((Barry == both); (Lang == both))),
    iff(took_mustard(Mill),(oneof(Cole); oneof(Dix))).
```

FGHC Version

The FGHC program, like the Prolog program, uses a pure generate & test method. Note that the Prolog program can be automatically translated into FGHC using

Ueda's continuation-based method [138]. However, the Prolog program would first have to be rewritten to avoid use of iff/2, i.e., negation and meta-call. In any case, this rewrite was actually done, but the resulting program was slightly larger and slower than the hand-written version presented here.

We wish to generate all possible condiment lists of five elements corresponding to the five men. This list, PeopleList, is generated incrementally as a stream, and filtered, in parallel, by the five constraints, producing an answer list, CondimentList. Recall that the procedure combo/3 generates combinations with replacement, as introduced in Section 4.1.

```
go(CondimentList) :-
    L = [must, salt, nthr, both],
    combo(L,5,PeopleList),
    filter(PeopleList, CondimentList-[]).
```

There are 1024 combinations of condiments in PeopleList. For each element of this stream, a c1/2 process is spawned to check the five constraints. If the constraints are satisfied, the answer is inserted into the answer stream. Otherwise the answer stream is shorted. Note that filter/2 will quickly spawn as many constraint checkers as can be accepted by the process scheduler. If we reverse the first two body goals of the second clause of filter/2, we risk exploiting less parallelism.

```
filter([],     O1-O2) :- O1=O2.
filter([I|Is],O1-O3) :-
    filter(Is,O1-O2),
    c1(I,      O2-O3).
```

As mentioned, the possibilities are of the form: [Barry,Cole,Dix,Lang,Mill]. Each of the five constraints has two subparts. All ten of these subchecks are linked together in such a manner that a possible answer is passed down the pipeline. If the possible answer contradicts a given constraint, then that solution path is shorted immediately.

```
%              [Barry,Cole,Dix,Lang,Mill]
c1(L,S) :- L = [salt,salt,  _,   _,   _] | c1a(L,S).   \
c1(L,S) :- L = [salt,must,  _,   _,   _] | c1a(L,S).   \
c1(L,S) :- L = [both,salt,  _,   _,   _] | c1a(L,S).    \
c1(L,S) :- L = [both,must,  _,   _,   _] | c1a(L,S).     \ true
c1(L,S) :- L = [salt,  _,  _,salt,   _] | c1a(L,S).    /
c1(L,S) :- L = [salt,  _,  _,must,   _] | c1a(L,S).    /
c1(L,S) :- L = [both,  _,  _,salt,   _] | c1a(L,S).   /
c1(L,S) :- L = [both,  _,  _,must,   _] | c1a(L,S).   /
```

System	instr	reduct	back/susp	entries	sec	KEPS
Aurora	148328	31820	7122	38942	3.7	11
Panda	158806	6153	491	6644	3.1	2

Table 8.3
Salt & Mustard High-Level Characteristics (four PEs Multimax)

```
c1(L,S0-S1) :- otherwise,
               L = [salt,   _,    _,    _,    _] | S0=S1.  \
c1(L,S0-S1) :- L = [both,   _,    _,    _,    _] | S0=S1.  \
c1(L,S0-S1) :- L = [    _,salt,   _,    _,    _] | S0=S1.  \  false
c1(L,S0-S1) :- L = [    _,must,   _,    _,    _] | S0=S1.  /
c1(L,S0-S1) :- L = [    _,    _,  _,salt,    _] | S0=S1.  /
c1(L,S0-S1) :- L = [    _,    _,  _,must,    _] | S0=S1.  /
c1(L,S) :- otherwise | c1a(L,S).                          --- true
```

Note that each subconstraint is of the *modus ponens* form $A \Longrightarrow B$. The first group of clauses (before the first `otherwise`) is a disjunctive check for satisfaction of A. If A is satisfied, the constraint is satisfied. Otherwise, the second group of clauses is a disjunctive check for satisfaction of B. Given that A is false, if B is satisfied, then the constraint fails. Otherwise the last clause, given that B is false, represents the constraint's satisfaction.

The above constraint satisfies "If Barry takes salt, then either Cole or Lang takes *one* only of the two condiments, salt and mustard." Recall that this constraint is encoded in the Prolog program as:

```
iff(took_salt(Barry),(oneof(Cole); oneof(Lang)))
```

This implication is translated into `c1/2`. The relationships could be encoded more concisely at a higher level; however, this strategy severely degrades performance by increasing reductions. For a larger problem, an abstract solution is required simply because the encoding given here is too bulky and error-prone. The remainder of the first constraint and the complete second constraint are given in Figure 8.4. The remaining constraints: `c3`, `c3a`, `c4`, `c4a`, `c5`, and `c5a`, are similar. If `c5a(L, S0-S1)` is satisfied, it terminates with `S0=[L|S1]`.

Discussion

Table 8.3 gives the high-level characteristics of the Salt & Mustard programs on Multimax (four PEs). Table 8.4 gives the execution timings and speedups. Figure 8.5 summarizes the measurements.

The Prolog program achieves better speedup at the cost of higher overhead. On six PEs the effects balance and both programs execute in about the same time.

```
c1a(L,S) :- L = [must,    _,nthr,    _,    _] | c2(L,S).
c1a(L,S) :- L = [both,    _,nthr,    _,    _] | c2(L,S).
c1a(L,S) :- L = [must,    _,    _,  _,both] | c2(L,S).
c1a(L,S) :- L = [both,    _,    _,  _,both] | c2(L,S).
c1a(L,S0-S1) :- otherwise,
                    L = [must,  _,    _,    _,    _] | S0=S1.
c1a(L,S0-S1) :- L = [both,   _,    _,    _,    _] | S0=S1.
c1a(L,S0-S1) :- L = [    _,   _,nthr,    _,    _] | S0=S1.
c1a(L,S0-S1) :- L = [    _,   _,    _,  _,both] | S0=S1.
c1a(L,S) :- otherwise | c2(L,S).

c2(L,S) :- L = [salt,salt,    _,    _,    _] | c2a(L,S).
c2(L,S) :- L = [must,salt,    _,    _,    _] | c2a(L,S).
c2(L,S) :- L = [salt,both,    _,    _,    _] | c2a(L,S).
c2(L,S) :- L = [must,both,    _,    _,    _] | c2a(L,S).
c2(L,S) :- L = [    _,salt,    _,  _,nthr] | c2a(L,S).
c2(L,S) :- L = [    _,both,    _,  _,nthr] | c2a(L,S).
c2(L,S0-S1) :- otherwise,
                    L = [salt,  _,    _,    _,    _] | S0=S1.
c2(L,S0-S1) :- L = [must,   _,    _,    _,    _] | S0=S1.
c2(L,S0-S1) :- L = [    _,salt,    _,    _,    _] | S0=S1.
c2(L,S0-S1) :- L = [    _,both,    _,    _,    _] | S0=S1.
c2(L,S0-S1) :- L = [    _,   _,    _,  _,nthr] | S0=S1.
c2(L,S) :- otherwise | c2a(L,S).

c2a(L,S) :- L = [    _,must,both,    _,    _] | c3(L,S).
c2a(L,S) :- L = [    _,both,both,    _,    _] | c3(L,S).
c2a(L,S) :- L = [    _,must,  _,both,    _] | c3(L,S).
c2a(L,S) :- L = [    _,both,  _,both,    _] | c3(L,S).
c2a(L,S0-S1) :- otherwise,
                    L = [    _,must,    _,    _,    _] | S0=S1.
c2a(L,S0-S1) :- L = [    _,both,    _,    _,    _] | S0=S1.
c2a(L,S0-S1) :- L = [    _,   _,both,    _,    _] | S0=S1.
c2a(L,S0-S1) :- L = [    _,   _,    _,both,    _] | S0=S1.
c2a(L,S) :- otherwise | c3(L,S).
```

Figure 8.4
Salt & Mustard: Remainder of First and Complete Second Constraints

System	1 PE	2 PE	4 PE	6 PE
execution time (seconds)				
Aurora	13.4	6.9	3.7	2.8
Panda	7.7	5.5	3.1	2.5
speedup				
Aurora	1.0	1.9	3.6	4.8
Panda	1.0	1.4	2.5	3.1

Table 8.4
Salt & Mustard: Total Seconds and Speedup (Multimax)

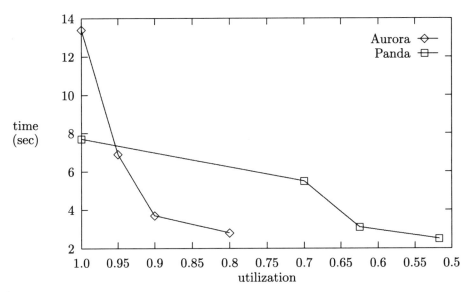

Figure 8.5
Salt & Mustard: Utilization vs. Time (Multimax)

Aurora would apparently outperform Panda on larger numbers of PEs (assuming the Multimax did not have a hardware bottleneck), because of the high efficiency of OR-parallel search.

A more striking result from analyzing the Salt & Mustard Problem is related not to performance, but to ease of programming. The Prolog program consists of 42 source lines. The constraints are implemented in five clauses consisting in total of 15 lines. The FGHC program consists of 130 source lines. The constraints are implemented in ten clauses consisting in total of 122 lines. The difference is primarily due to lack of deep guards in flat languages such as FGHC. Parlog would be better suited for such a problem.

8.3 Summary

Aurora achieves efficiencies of 99% and 80% for Zebra (on 15 Symmetry PEs) and Salt and Mustard (on six Multimax PEs), respectively. Panda achieves efficiences of 49% and 51% respectively. Looking at raw execution time, Aurora is 81% faster than Panda on 15 Symmetry PEs for Zebra and (amazingly!) Panda is 12% faster than Aurora on six Multimax PEs for Salt & Mustard. However, note that Panda is actually *faster* by 11% than Aurora on a single Symmetry PE for Zebra. The raw time for Prolog Salt & Mustard is not entirely fair, however, because the Prolog program is much higher-level than the FGHC program. Thus implementation of iff/2 is quite inefficient and could be obviated, at some cost to program size.

The performance gap for Zebra is entirely due to Panda's indiscriminate remote spawning of leaf processes. We had mentioned similar behavior for the Triangle problem in the previous chapter. The Zebra case is technically easier to fix because the compiler or programmer can spot where to serialize the program to avoid spawning. In the case of Triangle, an oracle is needed to determine when a goal is approaching the leaves of the search tree.

The "programmability" gap for Zebra and especially Salt & Mustard is more profound than the performance differences. Committed-choice languages such as FGHC simply do not have the power to facilitate programming this type of logic problem. There appear to be two issues. First, Prolog enforces the logical constraints by simply backtracking (hence rebinding the variables in question) if a wrong choice is made. Committed-choice languages simulate this action with structure copying. This simulation impacts not only performance (by way of memory consumption) but also programmability. Second, FGHC has no meta-level constructs or deep guards to ease the programmer's burden. As discussed in Section

2.2.5, other committed-choice languages do implement some of these extensions; however, these constructs often are difficult to assign clean semantics, or difficult to implement efficiently, or both.

OR-Prolog can sometimes finesse problems with meta-logical predicates, because its semantics are essentially sequential. For example, there is no worry about the parallel semantics of cut and negation in iff/2, because these predicates are executed completely in the private, sequential portion of the OR-tree. Salt & Mustard exploits OR-parallelism in the generate portion of the generate & test. However, OR-Prolog is schizophrenic, offering in addition "cavalier" meta-logical constructs that do *not* obey sequential semantics. These constructs are sometimes easier to implement efficiently than the strict constructs, and usually allow more efficient algorithms.

Clearly the results of this chapter illustrate Prolog's aptitude for solving logic problems. This type of problem is characterized by the instantiation of many logically interrelated variables. We saw that Panda, with some scheduling corrections, can compete with Aurora in performance. However, FGHC, and many other committed-choice languages, cannot yet compete with Prolog in ease of programming.

Exercises

Exercise 80 In the FGHC Zebra program, write more general versions of the add/3 and nadd/3 that are independent of the number of houses. Try to serialize the invocations of rule to prevent remote spawning. Can you achieve good speedups on eight or more PEs?

Exercise 81 Write a lazy Zebra program in FGHC.

Exercise 82 Modify the non-unrolled Prolog Zebra program to decrease the number of dynamic reductions of nextTo. Measure the performance effect on a sequential Prolog system. We made a change that decreased reductions by 158,000, but unfortunately increased executed WAM instructions by 891,000. How can this be?

Exercise 83 Complete the FGHC program for Salt & Mustard. If the committed-choice system you are using has sufficiently powerful meta-logical predicates, recode the constraints as in Prolog.

Exercise 84 (The Rowers Problem) As a rowing coach, you need to choose six members from the team to make up a crew. The potential members all have the

1	Al	71 kg	6	Fung	75 kg	11	Kevin	64 kg
2	Brad	80 kg	7	Greg	65 kg	12	Lee	63 kg
3	Cal	66 kg	8	Hal	68 kg	13	Mel	82 kg
4	Dave	79 kg	9	Ian	73 kg	14	Ned	67 kg
5	Ed	77 kg	10	Joe	72 kg	15	Owen	70 kg

Table 8.5
Personnel Data for Rowers Problem

same strength and ability, however certain people do not get along well together and
you risk losing the race if they row together. You also want to minimize the weight
of the crew. Write OR-parallel Prolog and FGHC programs to find a minimum-
weight crew from among the team members given in Table 8.5. People who will
fight if rowing with one another are: Brad and Owen, Dave and Hal, Greg and Lee,
Fung and Ian, Kevin and Mel, Cal and Ed, Al and Joe, Ned and Owen.

Exercise 85 (The Shoppers Problem) Solve this logic problem in OR-parallel
Prolog. There are group of twelve married couples who buy several items at a
department store. A couple is defined as:

    couple(Order,Husband,Wife,Family,Purchases)

where

    Purchases = [Gloves,Book,Perfume,Pearls,Sweater,Handbag]

Each item above is either purchased or not purchased by the couple. We are
initially given a scramble of information concerning these people. From these facts,
the proper husband, wife, and family names must be matched to their purchases. In
addition, the order in which the couples are served must be determined; however,
we can choose this one dimension as fixed, i.e., we want to fill in the following
table:

    [[couple(1, _, _, _, [_,_,_,_,_,_]),
      couple(2, _, _, _, [_,_,_,_,_,_]),
      couple(3, _, _, _, [_,_,_,_,_,_]),
      ...
      couple(12, _, _, _, [_,_,_,_,_,_])]]

The clues are as follows.

The Craigs, who bought a handbag, were waited on before the Murphys, who
were not waited on last. The Collins bought gloves, a sweater, a handbag,
and perfume. Couples 8 and 10 bought books. Five consecutive couples are:
the Smiths, Gary and his wife, the couple that bought a book and handbag,
the Swains, and Bill and his wife. Geraldine and her husband did not buy
a sweater nor a handbag. Couple 12 did not buy pearls. Tom and his wife

bought a book. The Marshalls did not buy perfume nor pearls. Evelyn bought gloves, but not perfume. Five consecutive couples are: Martha and her husband, Jack and his wife, the couple that bought gloves, perfume, a book, and a handbag, the couple that did not buy pearls nor a book, and Margaret and her husband. The first five couples bought perfume. Chuck did not buy gloves. Couples 1,2, and 4 did not buy sweaters. Eleanor did not buy perfume. Allen did not buy gloves nor a handbag. The Anthonys did not buy gloves. Allen and the Anthonies are in distinct couples. Cheryl was not 10th or 12th, and bought a sweater and a handbag. John bought a sweater and a handbag. John and Cheryl are in different couples. Couple 9 is the Douglases, and they did not buy gloves nor a sweater. Two consecutive couples are: Adam and his wife and the Days. Adam did not buy a handbag. Steve bought pearls, a book and a sweater. The last three couples did not buy gloves. The Jones did not buy a sweater. Susan bought pearls. George bought a sweater. The following four couples are distinct. Dorothy and her husband did not buy gloves. The Craigs did not buy gloves. Joe and his wife did not buy gloves. Rosalyn and her husband did not buy gloves nor a sweater. The O'Connors bought perfume and a sweater. Two consecutive couples are: Sandra and her husband and Cathleen and her husband. Sandra did not buy a sweater. One husband is Bob, one wife is Elizabeth, and one surname is Stanton.

The wording of these clues requires a bit of clarification. When we say "Sandra did not buy a sweater," we mean that neither Sandra *nor her husband* bought a sweater. When we say "A and B are consecutive couples," we mean that A is served immediately before B is served. Notice that if a naive generate & test were used, there are too many possible solutions to be checked.[4] We need a fused generator, where each constraint either further instantiates the solution with additional information, or rejects a solution as incompatible. Such a pipeline of filter-generators has the same basic structure in both Prolog and FGHC (see the Zebra Problem in Section 8.1).

Exercise 86 Discuss the pragmatics of solving the Shoppers Problem in a committed-choice language. Sketch out one or two algorithms and accurately estimate the expected garbage produced. If you have access to a robust system with sufficiently powerful data structures and/or garbage collector, implement Shoppers and compare its performance to your Prolog version.

---

[4]$(12!)^3 \cdot 2^{72} = 2,262,021,101,080,932,648,792,725,913,600$. Obviously, that is not the way to approach the problem.

9 Instant Insanity and Turtles

This chapter discusses two constraints problems that are similar to the N-Queens problem of Chapter 5. N-Cubes (also called Instant Insanity) is a group of colored cubes that must be stacked so that no color appears twice within a given side of the stack. Turtles is a group of decorated cards that must be placed in the shape of a larger square or rectangle. Two cards with abutting edges must form a complete picture of a monochromatic turtle.

These constraints problems are characterized as having relatively few pieces and a relatively small "board." For example, N-Queens has N pieces and $N \times N$ board cells. As we shall discuss, N-Cubes has $24 \times N$ pieces and N board cells. $M \times N$ Turtles has $4 \times M \times N$ pieces and $M \times N$ board cells. Essentially the "pieces" are unique orientations. Since a queen is one-dimensional, it has only one orientation. A Turtle card is a two-dimensional square, so it has four orientations. A three-dimensional cube has 24 orientations. The problems also have different constraints. A queen is constrained by all $N - 1$ other queens on the board. A turtle card is constrained by four abutting cards (or fewer if it is a border). A cube is constrained by the four visible faces of all $N - 1$ other cubes. In the next chapter, we will explore richer constraint problems that involve irregular orientations of pieces and more complex constraints.

The solutions of these problems reiterate the programming techniques introduced in Chapter 5: fused generate & test, candidates/noncandidates, pipelined filters, and layered streams. In addition, we introduce techniques in FGHC to constrain parallelism, to be used when system resources are swamped by overly parallel programs. Two methods are discussed: serialization by short-circuit chains and bounded-buffer communication.

9.1 Instant Insanity

A game, marketed under the name "Instant Insanity" in the United States at least fifteen years ago, consists of four cubes. Each cube is colored with four colors (red, blue, green and white), as shown in Figure 9.1. The idea is to stack the cubes in a column four high, so that each side of the column displays each of the four colors. As can be seen, this is an ancient, primitive precursor to "Rubik's Cube" (see Exercise 94).

We define a solution to the problem as a list of the visible faces of the four cubes. A cube description is q(N,S,E,W), where N is the Northern color, S is the Southern color, and so on. There are eight solutions to the problem:

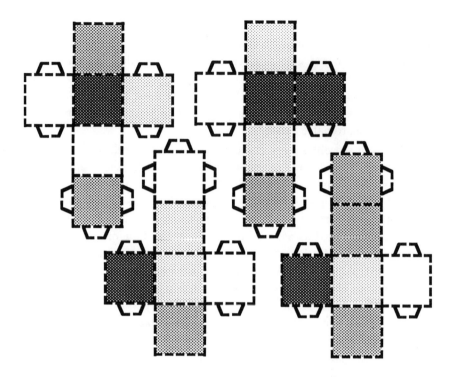

Figure 9.1
Cut Along the Dotted Lines to Make Your Own Four Cubes

```
[q(g,w,r,b),q(b,r,b,w),q(r,g,w,g),q(w,b,g,r)]
[q(g,w,b,r),q(b,r,w,b),q(r,g,g,w),q(w,b,r,g)]
[q(w,g,r,b),q(r,b,b,w),q(g,r,w,g),q(b,w,g,r)]
[q(w,g,b,r),q(r,b,w,b),q(g,r,g,w),q(b,w,r,g)]
[q(r,b,g,w),q(b,w,b,r),q(w,g,r,g),q(g,r,w,b)]
[q(r,b,w,g),q(b,w,r,b),q(w,g,g,r),q(g,r,b,w)]
[q(b,r,g,w),q(w,b,b,r),q(g,w,r,g),q(r,g,w,b)]
[q(b,r,w,g),q(w,b,r,b),q(g,w,g,r),q(r,g,b,w)]
```

Note that, in a solution, all Northern colors are different, etc.

All programs presented describe a cube as three pairs of opposite faces. There are 24 possible orientations of a single cube within the stack. We can choose any two pairs to be visible (three choices) among either the North-South or East-West axis (two choices) and we can exchange the North-South (East-West) faces of each pair (four choices). The programs presented are written in general for any number of cubes. The performance measurements are discussed for the seven cubes shown below (the seven colors are encoded as integers):

```
cubes(C) :-
    C=[q(p(5,1),p(0,5),p(3,1)),
       q(p(2,3),p(1,4),p(4,0)),
       q(p(3,6),p(0,0),p(2,4)),
       q(p(6,4),p(6,1),p(0,1)),
       q(p(1,5),p(3,2),p(5,2)),
       q(p(5,0),p(2,3),p(4,5)),
       q(p(4,2),p(2,6),p(0,3))].
```

Note that, since the third cube has an opposite pair of faces with the same color, then in fact eight of the 24 orientations have duplicate visible faces. We decline to filter away these and other duplicates because they actually represent different solutions (the nonvisible faces are rotated).

Prolog Version

9.1.1   Fused Generate & Test

In a naive generate & test algorithm, the number of possible stacks is 24^N for N cubes. Thus the complexity order is also $\sim O(24^N)$, because each combination must be fully generated and tested (a further discussion of complexity is given in Section 9.1.8). To reduce this complexity, a fused generate & test algorithm is developed wherein each newly-generated cube is tested for compatibility with the previously-placed cubes. The program is largely comprised of the generator. The tester is `check/2`, which checks that all corresponding faces of two cubes have different colors. The generator is composed of nondeterminate `rotate/2` and `exchange/3` procedures. The 24 possible orientations of a single cube are generated. Note that this could be replaced by a simpler table lookup with 24 entries.

```
:- parallel set/2, rotate/3.

go(Rs) :- cubes(Cs), findall(X,solve(Cs,[],X),Rs).

solve([],Rs,Rs).
solve([C|Cs],Ps,Rs) :-
    set(C,P),
    check(Ps,P),
    solve(Cs,[P|Ps],Rs).

check([],_).
check([q(A1,B1,C1,D1)|Ps],P) :-
    P = q(A2,B2,C2,D2),
    A1 =\= A2, B1 =\= B2, C1 =\= C2, D1 =\= D2,
    check(Ps,P).

set(q(P1,P2,P3),P) :- rotate(P1,P2,P).
set(q(P1,P2,P3),P) :- rotate(P2,P1,P).
set(q(P1,P2,P3),P) :- rotate(P1,P3,P).
set(q(P1,P2,P3),P) :- rotate(P3,P1,P).
set(q(P1,P2,P3),P) :- rotate(P2,P3,P).
set(q(P1,P2,P3),P) :- rotate(P3,P2,P).

rotate(p(C1,C2),p(C3,C4),q(C1,C2,C3,C4)).
rotate(p(C1,C2),p(C3,C4),q(C1,C2,C4,C3)).
rotate(p(C1,C2),p(C3,C4),q(C2,C1,C3,C4)).
rotate(p(C1,C2),p(C3,C4),q(C2,C1,C4,C3)).
```

The informal specification of the program is given in Figure 9.2.

FGHC Versions

The backtracking mechanism of Prolog lends itself most elegantly to the generate & test method. In fact, at the outset it is hard to envision another way to solve the problem in Prolog: for both a single solution and all solutions. In committed-choice languages, however, there are several choices. Naive generate & test (a pipeline of combinators), fused generate & test (a pipeline of filters), candidates and noncandidates, and layered streams are some of the options open to us. Instant Insanity is a *degenerate* constraint problem, because the vertical position of the cubes within the stack is not constrained. Thus these programs illustrate simplified forms of the various paradigms.

Procedure: `solve(Cs, Ps, Rs)`
   + `Cs`: list of cubes   − `Rs`: list of orientations
   + `Ps`: list of orientations

Relation: `Rs` is a complete extension of partial solution `Ps`, including the additional placement of the cubes in `Cs`. An "orientation" is a `q/4` structure of visible faces of the cube when placed in the stack of cubes.

Preconditions: Initially `Ps` is empty.

Procedure: `set(C, P)`
   + `C`: cube   − `P`: orientation

Relation: `P` is one of 24 orientations of cube `C`. Even if any of these orientations have identical visible faces, backtracking over this procedure will produce all these redundant answers.

Procedure: `rotate(P1, P2, P)`
   +`P1`: pair of faces   +`P2`: pair of faces   −`P`: orientation

Relation: `P` is one of six orientations of the two pairs of opposite faces of the cube, `P1` and `P2`. Even if any of these orientations have identical visible faces, backtracking over this procedure will produce all these redundant answers.

Procedure: `check(Ps, P)`
   + `Ps`: list of orientations   + `P`: orientation

Relation: None of the visible faces of the cubes in `Ps` conflict with `P`.

Figure 9.2
Informal Specification of Prolog Cubes (Fused Gen & Test)

9.1.2   Naive Generate & Test

Developing a naive generate & test program is an interesting exercise because it
illustrates the problems encountered when generating a massive stream of data. We
run out of heap space not only for data (which is mainly garbage), but also because
too many goals are spawned at once. Techniques of bounded-buffer communication
and forced serialization via short-circuit chains are introduced to overcome these
problems.

First we introduce a naive solution to the problem. The program shown below
uses a modification of the combination procedure introduced in Section 4.1. For
example,

```
?- combo([[a,b],[1,2]],Out).
   Out = [[a,1],[a,2],[b,1],[b,2]]
```

Procedure combo(L,Out) generates all combinations of length N from N lists (in
L), selecting one element from each list.

```
combo(L,Out) :- combo(L,[[]],Out).

combo(    [],In,Out) :- Out=In.
combo([L|Ls],In,Out) :-
    add(In,L,T),
    combo(Ls,T,Out).

add([],_,O1) :- O1=[].
add([I|Is],L,O1) :-
    combo1(L,I,O1-O2),
    add(Is,L,O2).

combo1([],_,O1-O2) :- O1=O2.
combo1([C|Cs],I,O1-O3) :-
    O1 = [[C|I]|O2],
    combo1(Cs,I,O2-O3).
```

The top-level procedure of the Instant Insanity program generates a list of the 24
orientations of each cube. The entire list of N orientation lists, Orients, is used by
combo/2 to spawn a pipeline of N add/3 processes. These processes generate the
full-stack combinations in stream S. The tester then filters the S stream, producing
the answers A.

```
go(A) :- gen(S),test(S,A).

gen(S) :-
    cubes(Cubes),
    gen(Cubes,Orients),
    combo(Orients,S).
```

```
gen([],C) :- C=[].
gen([Q|Qs],C) :-
    C = [L|Ls],
    set(Q,L),
    gen(Qs,Ls).

set(q(P1,P2,P3),S0) :-
    rotate(P1,P2,S0-S1),
    rotate(P2,P1,S1-S2),
    rotate(P1,P3,S2-S3),
    rotate(P3,P1,S3-S4),
    rotate(P2,P3,S4-S5),
    rotate(P3,P2,S5-[]).

rotate(p(C1,C2),p(C3,C4),S0-S1) :-
    S0=[q(C1,C2,C3,C4),
        q(C1,C2,C4,C3),
        q(C2,C1,C3,C4),
        q(C2,C1,C4,C3)|S1].
```

The challenge in writing the tester is to reduce the overhead of checking if a generated combination is correct. We use a type of hash function here. Assume that each of the N colors is represented as a unique integer. We need to choose integers so that the sum of the N different colors is not equal to the sum of any other combination of N colors. This can be accomplished by choosing integer powers of some radix. For instance, picking radix two gives the colors: $1, 2, 4, 8, 16, 32, 64$. Essentially the colors are encoded as bit positions, and a sum of $2^8 - 1 = 1111111_2 = 127$ encodes one of each color.

```
cubes(C) :-
    C=[q(p(32, 2),p( 1,32),p( 8, 2)),
       q(p( 4, 8),p( 2,16),p(16, 1)),
       q(p( 8,64),p( 1, 1),p( 4,16)),
       q(p(64,16),p(64, 2),p( 1, 2)),
       q(p( 2,32),p( 8, 4),p(32, 4)),
       q(p(32, 1),p( 4, 8),p(16,32)),
       q(p(16, 4),p( 4,64),p( 1, 8))].

test([],Out) :- Out=[].
test([A|As],Out) :-
    check(A,Status),
    test(Status,A,As,Out).

test(yes,A,S,Out) :- Out=[A|Os], test(S,Os).
test( no,_,S,Out) :- test(S,Out).

check(Qs,Status) :- check(Qs,0,0,0,0,Status).
```

```
check([cube(N,E,S,W)|Qs],Pn,Pe,Ps,Pw,Status) :-
    Pn < 127, Pe < 127, Ps < 127, Pw < 127 |
    Sn is N+Pn, Se is E+Pe, Ss is S+Ps, Sw is W+Pw,
    check(Qs,Sn,Se,Ss,Sw,Status).
check([],127,127,127,127,Status) :- Status=yes.
check(_,_,_,_,_,Status) :- otherwise | Status=no.
```

The informal specification of the program is given in Figure 9.3.

9.1.3 Serialization by Short-Circuit Chain

The immediate problem with the previous program is that the generator spawns
thousands of goals. Note that creation of the combinations is not constrained in
any way. There simply isn't enough storage in the system to contain all the goal
records produced! We fix this problem by *serializing* the generator with a *short-
circuit chain*. The modified generator is listed below.

```
combo(L,Out) :- combo(L,[[]],Out).

combo(     [],In,Out) :- Out=In.
combo([L|Ls],In,Out) :-
    add(done,In,L,T),
    combo(Ls,T,Out).

add(done,[],_,O1) :- O1=[].
add(done,[I|Is],L,O1) :-
    combo1(L,I,O1-O2,D-done),
    add(D,Is,L,O2).

combo1([],_,O1-O2,D0-D1) :- O1=O2,D0=D1.
combo1([C|Cs],I,O1-O3,D) :-
    O1 = [[C|I]|O2],
    combo1(Cs,I,O2-O3,D).
```

Note that **add** will suspend until its new first argument is bound to **done**. The
recursive call to **add** is passed the D flag, which is the head of the sequencing chain
(D-list) D-done. When **combo1** finishes computation, the chain is shorted (first
clause), and the recursive call to **add** can resume. In this example, the sequencing
chain is trivial, but in more complex applications the chain may be wired through
several processes. Only when *all* the processes have terminated and shorted the
chain will the initial D flag be bound.

Another approach to solve over-eager goal spawning, as taken in Parlog, is to
allow the programmer to annotate the body goals as either AND-parallel or sequential. AND-parallel goals are similar to FGHC goals. Sequential goals are not
only executed locally, but their order of execution with respect to textually sur-

Procedure: gen(Cs, Fs)
  + Cs: list of cubes   − Fs: list of orientation lists

Relation: Fs contains lists of all orientations of each cube in Cs. All redundant orientations (same visible faces) are produced.

Procedure: set(C, Fs)
  + C: cube   − Fs: list of orientations

Relation: Fs contains all 24 orientations of cube C. All redundant orientations (same visible faces) are produced.

Procedure: rotate(P1, P2, Fs)
  + P1: pair of faces   − Fs: stream of orientations
  + P2: pair of faces

Relation: Fs contains all six orientations of the two pairs of opposite faces of the cube, P1 and P2. All redundant orientations (same visible faces) are produced.

Procedure: combo(Fs, As)
  + Fs: list of orientation lists   − As: list of stacks

Relation: As contains all possibles stacks of the N cubes described in predicate cubes/1, formed by combining the orientations of each cube in Fs.

Procedure: test(As, Ss)
  + As: list of stacks   − Ss: list of stacks

Relation: Ss contains all stacks from As that have no repeated integer within any column of visible faces.

Procedure: check(Qs, Pn, Pe, Ps, Pw, Status)
  +Qs: list of orientations   +Pe: integer   +Pe: integer
  +Pn: integer   +Ps: integer   −Status: atom

Relation: Given the checksum (Pn, Pe, Ps, Pw) of the previous cubes in the stack, if the remaining orientations in Qs are consistent, then Status = yes. Otherwise Status = no.

Precondition: Initially all checksums are zero.

Figure 9.3
Informal Specification of FGHC Cubes (Naive Gen & Test)

rounding goals also is guaranteed. The JAM-Parlog architecture [37] is necessarily more complex than Panda because, to guarantee sequentiality of arbitrary goals, a goal queue does not suffice: a *tree* of AND-goals is required. The performance advantages of sequential goals can outweigh implementation complexities (e.g., the Zebra Problem in the previous chapter [131]). In addition, the programmer does not have to muck around with running a short-circuit chain throughout every desired-sequential procedure. Sequential goals also can be used to execute builtins with side-effects, such as I/O. Although this programming style is not recommended, such tricks are useful when debugging because they are fast and require only local modification of code.

Serialization by the short-circuit method rids us of over-eager goal spawning, but another problem arises. The generator is still consuming too much heap space for data. This happens if the tester is not scheduled frequently enough to rapidly convert potential solutions into garbage (so that the garbage collector can reclaim the space). The tester indirectly converts a potential solution into garbage in the second clause of test/4 by discarding the last pointer to the second argument. The Panda scheduler, however, is biased towards depth-first reduction, and will almost exclusively execute the generator without scheduling the tester.

One (ineffective) idea to solve this problem is to parallelize the tester, in the hope that more check processes will be spawned. The previous tester is sequential, however, it is easy to spawn a check/2 process for each potential solution and collect the results in a D-list. Unfortunately, this modification does not solve our heap overflow problem. The scheduler may *still* favor reducing the generator instead of the tester. One must somehow *couple* the generator and tester so that the former will suspend if the latter is not scheduled. This suspension can be accomplished with *bounded buffers*.

9.1.4 Bounded-Buffer Communication

The general idea is to place a buffer (see Section 2.2.4) between the generator and the tester. Thus, when the generator fills up the buffer, the generator will suspend, waiting for the tester to empty the buffer. We need more than a single buffer, however, because our generator is built up from N levels of subgenerators, any one of which can potentially overflow the heap.

Recall that a buffer is implemented as a difference list. Although each slot in the buffer is a logical variable that can be written only once, we can append new slots to the tail of the difference list. Thus, when a consumer reads from the buffer, the consumer must also append a new empty slot to the tail. The producer writes to empty slots and, assuming that the consumer can consume data faster than the producer writes data, the buffer will never suspend. However, if the producer writes faster than the consumer reads, the buffer eventually will fill up, and no empty slots will remain. In this case, the producer suspends. A buffer implemented in this manner emulates a fixed-length FIFO queue at the expense of space complexity $O(n)$ where n is the number of items written (*not* the maximum size of the queue!).

The new top-level of the Cubes program is similar to the old program, except that a buffer B of length K is now produced by the generator. Buffers have been inserted between each level of the generator. The new program is given in Figure 9.4. Refer to Section 4.1.3 for the informal specification of a similar program.

This final program, although it executes with no memory problems, does not exploit much parallelism. To reduce the goal spawning and garbage production on the heap, we sequentialized the generator and inserted buffers. The program will execute correctly if the sum of the buffer sizes does not exceed the storage space of the system.

The buffer size will not significantly affect the total amount or frequency of garbage collection because most garbage is from discarded combinations, the same for any buffer size. The buffer size only affects the active memory requirement. For example, in the PDSS system [65], with buffers of 100 words each, the active heap is only about 3000 words for the 4-Cubes problem. With buffers of 1000 words each, the active heap is about 12,000 words. An important point is that *the very use of buffers* reduces the data storage requirement from exponential to linear order.

> Explicit control of system resources is not without penalty. The method of serialization by a short-circuit chain to prevent runaway goal spawning removes parallelism completely. The method of bounded-buffer communication to constrain memory usage increases suspensions, reducing the amount of exploitable parallelism. However these techniques provide the difference between a program that runs and a program that runs out of memory.

9.1.5 Pipelined Filters

The problem with the naive generate & test program is that combinations are created in full before any partial testing is done. To remedy this problem we now use a fused generate & test where instead of separate **add** and **test** processes in the pipeline, there are **filter** processes, i.e., they test and either add to the partial solution or filter away the partial solution.

```
go(K,A) :- generate(K,B),test(B,A).

generate(K,B) :-
    cubes(Cubes),
    gen(Cubes,Orients),
    combo(Orients,K,B).

combo(L,K,Bout) :-
    Bin = [[],stop]/_,
    top(L,K,Bin,Bout).

top([],_,Bin,Bout) :- Bout=Bin.
top([L|Ls],K,Bin,Bout) :-
    combo1(K,L,Bin,Buff),
    top(Ls,K,Buff,Bout).

combo1(K,L,Bin,Bout) :-
    Bout = OutBuff/_,
    buffer(K,Bout),
    add(done,Bin,L,OutBuff).

add(done,[stop|_]/_,_,[B|_]) :- B=stop.
add(done,[I|Is]/InEnd,L,Buff) :- I \= stop |
    InEnd = [_|NewInEnd],
    combo2(L,I,Buff,NewBuff,done,D),
    add(D,Is/NewInEnd,L,NewBuff).

combo2([],_,B0,B1,D0,D1) :- B0=B1,D0=D1.
combo2([C|Cs],L,[B|B0],B1,D0,D1) :-
    B = [C|L],
    combo2(Cs,L,B0,B1,D0,D1).

buffer(0,B/E) :- B=E.
buffer(N,B/E) :- N>0 | N1 is N-1, B=[_|T], buffer(N1,T/E).

test([stop|_]/_,Out) :- Out=[].
test([A|As]/E,Out) :- A \= stop |
    E = [_|Es],
    check(A,Status),
    test(Status,A,As/Es,Out).
```

Figure 9.4
N-Cubes with Bounded Buffers

At the top-level, for each cube we spawn a column of filters via **spawn/3** and **column/3**. Procedure **set/2**, from the previous program, is used to create a list of all orientations of a cube. Procedure **column/3** then spawns a **filter** process, sharing the same input In as the other filters in the column, and linked into the output stream.

```
go(A) :- cubes(Q), spawn(Q,[[]],A).

spawn([],S0,S1) :- S0=S1.
spawn([Q|Qs],S0,S2) :-
    set(Q,L),
    column(L,S0,S1),
    spawn(Qs,S1,S2).

column([],_,S) :- S=[].
column([C|Cs],In,S0) :-
    filter(In,C,S0-S1),
    column(Cs,In,S1).
```

One filter corresponds to each orientation of each cube in the stack (e.g., for seven cubes, there are $7 \times 24 = 168$ filters). A filter checks incoming partial solutions for correctness. The check is not as clever as the previous naive tester — a checksum cannot be used because the order of the cubes in the stack is not known. Instead, each face of each cube in the partial solution is compared against the filter's cube. If there is a match (**check** clause 3), then the partial solution is discarded. If all cubes pass this test (**check** clause 1), then the filter's cube is prepended to the partial solution.

```
filter([],_,S0-S1) :- S0=S1.
filter([P|Ps],Q,S0-S2) :-
    filter(Ps,Q,S1-S2),
    check(P,Q,P,S0-S1).

check([],Q,P,S0-S1) :- S0=[[Q|P]|S1].
check([q(A1,B1,C1,D1)|Qs],q(A2,B2,C2,D2),P,S) :-
    A1 =\= A2, B1 =\= B2, C1 =\= C2, D1 =\= D2 |
    check(Qs,q(A2,B2,C2,D2),P,S).
check(_,_,_,S0-S1) :- otherwise | S0=S1.
```

The informal specification of this program is given in Figure 9.5.

One serious inefficiency of the program is that, in the second clause of **check**, the data structure q(A2,B2,C2,D2) may be copied for the recursive call. A sophisticated compiler may avoid copying by saving a pointer to the structure when decomposing the structure in the head. The structure pointer can be used when setting up the arguments for the recursive call. One might try to help the compiler with the following coding style:

Procedure: spawn(Qs, In, Out)
    + Qs: list of cubes   − Out: list of stacks
    + In: list of stacks

Relation: Out contains all completions of partial solutions from In, extended
    with cubes in Qs. A stack is a list of orientations. An orientation is a q/4
    structure containing visible faces of a cube. All redundant orientations
    (same visible faces) are produced in Out.

Preconditions: Initially In = [[]] and Qs is described by predicate cubes/1.

Procedure: set(C, Fs)
    + C: cube   − Fs: list of orientations

Relation: Fs contains all 24 orientations of cube C. All redundant orientations
    (same visible faces) are produced.

Procedure: column(Fs, In, Out)
    + Fs: list of orientations   − Out: list of stacks
    + In: list of stacks

Relation: Out contains all consistent extensions of partial solutions from In,
    extended with orientations in Fs.

Procedure: filter(In, C, Out)
    + In: list of stacks   − Out: stream of stacks
    + C: orientation

Relation: Out contains all consistent extensions of partial solutions from In,
    extended with orientation C.

Procedure: check(P, C, A, Out)
    + P: list of orientations   + A: list of orientations
    + C: orientation   − Out: stream of stacks

Relation: If the remaining partial solution P is consistent with orientation C
    then the complete partial solution A is extended by C and issued down
    stream Out. Otherwise Out is shorted.

Figure 9.5
Informal Specification of FGHC Cubes (Pipelined Filters)

```
check([],Q,P,S0-S1) :- S0=[[Q|P]|S1].
check([q(A1,B1,C1,D1)|Qs],Q,P,S) :-
    Q = q(A2,B2,C2,D2),
    A1 =\= A2, B1 =\= B2, C1 =\= C2, D1 =\= D2 |
    check(Qs,Q,P,S).
check(_,_,_,S0-S1) :- otherwise | S0=S1.
```

The check is formulated with Q decomposed in the guard instead of directly in
the head. Thus Q can be passed directly to the tail-recursive call. Unfortunately,
even with this explicit hint, the Panda compiler is not smart enough to avoid
rebuilding the data structure! This problem is a general one with the version of the
Panda compiler used for the measurements presented in this book. Thus garbage
production is somewhat inflated in cases where structures are decomposed in the
guard and then later reused.

Another way to implement the check is slightly more readable, because there are
no guards, but is significantly slower:

```
check([],Q,P,S0-S1) :- S0=[[Q|P]|S1].
check([q(X,_,_,_)|_],q(X,_,_,_),_,S0-S1) :- S0=S1.
check([q(_,X,_,_)|_],q(_,X,_,_),_,S0-S1) :- S0=S1.
check([q(_,_,X,_)|_],q(_,_,X,_),_,S0-S1) :- S0=S1.
check([q(_,_,_,X)|_],q(_,_,_,X),_,S0-S1) :- S0=S1.
check([_|Qs],Q,P,S) :- otherwise | check(Qs,Q,P,S).
```

Here there is no garbage production problem, but check now must fail in the
head of clauses 2–5 before the final clause can commit. The ability of a source-to-
source optimizer to translate this version into the previous version of check appears
doubtful.

The pipelined-filters program not only illustrates the structure of a fused generate
& test, but also forms the basis for the layered-stream program given next. The
problem with the pipelined filters approach is that a pipeline is linear, so parallelism
is limited. Parallelism in this program is exploited in two areas. First, each of the
24 orientations per cube computes in parallel, given the same input stream. Second,
data is streamed through the pipe, allowing parallel processing of all N cubes once
the pipe fills.

It may be unclear, when looking at performance statistics alone (Section 9.1.9),
how the scheduler allocates processes to PEs during execution. A natural way to
allocate the processes in this program is to put each column of filters on a separate
PE. This allocation has two minor problems, however. First, if the number of
columns and the number of PEs are unequal, some tailoring is necessary. Second,
some PEs may remain idle during filling and flushing the pipeline. If goal allocation
can be controlled by user annotations, then this type of mapping is easy, even if

the number of PEs is not known *a priori*.

As a simple example, consider Strand, where a *topology declaration* can be given indicating that the PEs are organized as a ring, torus, mesh, etc. Depending on the topology, goals can be allocated with directional commands, such as *left* and *right* for a ring. Without knowing the number of PEs, columns of filters in Cubes can be allocated to PEs around the ring. If the number of PEs is less than the number of columns, then some PEs are given more than one column, i.e., the mapping *wraps around*.

To execute the program on a multiprocessor with a drastically different topology would require different annotations to achieve the best speedup. For example, if we had a torus (doughnut) machine, it would be best to allocate a column of filters per cross-section of the torus, and allocate the filters within the column along the cross-section. If the number of filters in a column does not exactly match the physical dimensions of the torus, then the mapping will wrap around the cross-section.

Although the initial goal allocation for Cubes fits very nicely onto this topology framework, subsequent filter spawning will form trees that do not map particularly well onto either a ring or a torus. It is not clear what annotations (if any) should be given to those goals. We do not annotate goals for scheduling purposes in this book both because annotation is not supported by Panda, and because we consider it purely the system's responsibility to schedule processes, not the programmer's responsibility.[1]

9.1.6 Layered Streams

The FGHC program discussed in this section, written by A. Okumura [94], uses layered streams in a pipeline of filters, instead of simple streams as in the previous program. Here we also initially create $24 \times 7 = 168$ `filter` processes to represent the cubes in each orientation. The initial spawning of the filters, in `spawn/3`, is identical to that of the previous program. One modification is that the initial seed of the layered stream is `begin`. In addition, the filter first issues its value as a partial solution down the layered stream before spawning a `filter1` process for actual filtering.

---

[1] This is an extremely puritanical stance to take. See for example Fox *et al.* [50] for an approach to parallel programming "regular" problems (e.g., fluid dynamics, matrix operations) where the programmer is responsible for explicit spawning of processes. Explicit control is very efficient, and not exceedingly burdensome for the programmer in such problems, where a process is usually mapped directly onto a portion of a regular data structure such as an array. However, the mapping becomes increasing difficult, and necessarily dynamic, as the problem becomes "irregular" (e.g., constraint problems, complex search problems).

```
go(A) :- cubes(Q), spawn(Q,begin,Out), fromLStoL(Out,A).

filter(In,C,S0-S1) :- S0=[C*Out|S1], filter1(In,C,Out).

filter1(   [],_,Out) :- Out=[].
filter1(begin,_,Out) :- Out=begin.
filter1([Q*Ts|Is],C,Out) :-
    Q = q(A1,B1,C1,D1),
    C = q(A2,B2,C2,D2),
    A1 =\= A2, B1 =\= B2, C1 =\= C2, D1 =\= D2 |
    Out=[Q*O1|Os],
    filter1(Is,C,Os),
    filter1(Ts,C,O1).
filter1([_|Is],C,Out) :- otherwise | filter1(Is,C,Out).
```

Procedure filter1(In,C,Out) accepts an input layered stream of potential, partial solutions In, and produces a layered stream Out of those solutions that do not conflict with the cube defined by C. Each potential, partial solution assumes the form of a layered stream element H*T, where H is a cube description and T is a layered stream of all potential, partial solutions that can form a solution with H.

To filter a partial solution in filter1, if the solution is [] or begin, then such a potential solution is passed onto the output stream. The empty list, [], is the final tail of an invalid (incomplete) layered stream. The atom begin is the final tail of a valid (complete) layered stream. The initial seed to the layered stream is begin, thus every complete layered stream will have begin at its innermost level. An incomplete layered stream with all tails filtered away (at some layer) will end in []. For the N-Cubes problem, a complete layered stream will have N layers.

If the head of the solution, q(A1,B1,C1,D1), contains colors that are different from the corresponding faces of the filter's cube, C, then the head of the partial solution is compatible, and the list of potential tails, Ts, must be checked further. A new filter is spawned to check the tail, creating stream O1. We also continue to check the remainder of the original input stream, Is, by a tail-recursive filter1 call, creating a stream Os. Streams O1 and Os are wired together in an obvious way to form Out, the filter's output stream. Otherwise (if some adjacent faces have the same color) the partial solution is filtered away, i.e., the partial solution is not passed onto the output stream.

Note that head of the potential solution, C, is sent to the output stream immediately, before calls to the filter1 goals. This is one advantage of layered streams: filters further down the pipeline can receive this partially constructed solution and begin checking it, even before O1 has any value.

An interesting aspect of layered-stream programming is the composition of the data in the layered stream. In the program, the layered stream exiting the last filter, for conversion into a real stream, contains a lot of garbage. This garbage takes the form of internal layered streams that end in [], i.e., invalid partial solutions. Note that this is *not* garbage in the sense of a data structure that is not pointed to directly or indirectly by output variables. Thus a garbage collector cannot reclaim the space taken by these invalid partial solutions.

As discussed for N-Queens, the garbage here can be avoided by a *nil check*. The nil check is further illustrated below in a modification of the third clause of filter1.

```
filter1([Q*Ts|Is],C,Out) :-
    Q = q(A1,B1,C1,D1),
    C = q(A2,B2,C2,D2),
    A1 =\= A2, B1 =\= B2, C1 =\= C2, D1 =\= D2 |
    filter1(Ts,C,O1),
    send(O1,Q,Out,Os),
    filter1(Is,C,Os).

send( [],_,S0-S1) :- S0=S1.
send(Out,Q,S0-S1) :- Out\=[] | S0=[Q*Out|S1].
```

The job of send/3 is to issue a layered stream, Out, down the output stream, O-Os, *only if the layered stream is not empty*. Surprisingly, the synchronization in send/3 does *not* affect the execution speed of the program, although this may not be the case in all constraint problems. The positive effect of the new filter is reduction of the size of the layered stream. For a typical execution of the original version of the 4-Cubes problem, the final layered stream has 816 cubes, i.e., q(N,S,E,W). In the new version, only the solutions remain, i.e., $8 \times 4 = 32$ cubes.

As a final note, consider the order of the last two (recursive) goals in the third clause of filter1/3. The order shown significantly *increases* suspensions compared to a version where the goals are reversed (not shown). For 7-Cubes on Symmetry, a performance improvement of 4–5% was measured for the version with reversed goals. Intuitively, one would think that processing the top layer of the layered stream before processing lower layers will reduce suspensions, because lower layers may not be instantiated yet. This behavior is highly dependent on the scheduling policy, however. Both Panda and JAM-Parlog, each with somewhat similar depth-first schedulers, displayed performance improvement when the goals were reversed.

9.1.7 Degenerate Candidates & Noncandidates

In an effort to exploit parallelism beyond that of a linear pipeline, we look to a tree process structure. The candidate/noncandidate paradigm (Section 5.2.1) gives us just that — a tree with a branching factor equal to the number of orientations and a depth equal to the number of cubes. Recall that this process tree corresponds directly to the OR-tree built by Aurora when executing the fused generate & test Prolog program.

In the case of Instant Insanity, the candidates/noncandidates scheme is degenerate because there are no constraints among placing cubes within the column. Therefore a noncandidate list is unnecessary and the program becomes a simple tree search.

```
go(A) :- cubes(Q),gen(Q,Os),select(Os,A).

select(L,A) :- select(L,[],A-[]).

select([],A,S0-S1) :- S0=[A|S1].
select([P|Ps],A,S) :- check(P,Ps,A,S).

check([],_,_,     S0-S1) :- S0=S1.
check([Q|Qs], Ps,As,S0-S2) :-
    check(Qs, Ps,As,S1-S2),
    check(A,Q,Ps,As,S0-S1).

check([],Q,Ps,As,S) :- select(Ps,[Q|As],S).
check([q(A1,B1,C1,D1)|Qs],Q,Ps,As,S) :-
    Q = q(A2,B2,C2,D2),
    A1 =\= A2, B1 =\= B2, C1 =\= C2, D1 =\= D2 |
    check(Qs,Q,Ps,As,S).
check(_,_,_,_,S0-S1) :- otherwise | S0=S1.
```

The check here is similar to that of the pipelined-filters program. The informal specification of this program is given in Figure 9.6. The timings presented in the next section confirm the increase in exploited parallelism over pipelines: on 12 Symmetry PEs the speedup of the pipeline and tree programs are 5.9 and 10.9 respectively.

9.1.8 Complexity

In this section we explore methods of analyzing the time complexity of programs written in Prolog and committed-choice languages. The Instant Insanity Problem is simple enough to require only minimal mathematics. The analysis given here also can be applied to other all-solutions search programs.

The naive generate & test programs generate $O(24^n)$ potential solutions for n

<u>Procedure</u>: gen(Cs, Ps)
  + Cs: list of cubes   − Ps: list of orientation lists

<u>Relation</u>: Ps contains lists of all orientations of each cube in Cs. All redundant orientations (same visible faces) are produced.

<u>Procedure</u>: select(Ps, A, Out)
  + Ps: list of orientation lists   − Out: stream of stacks
  + A: stack

<u>Relation</u>: Out contains all consistent completions of partial solution A extended by the cubes described in Ps.

<u>Precondition</u>: Initially A is empty.

<u>Procedure</u>: check(P, Ps, A, Out)
  + P: list of orientations   + A: stack
  + Ps: list of orientation lists   − Out: stream of stacks

<u>Relation</u>: Out contains all consistent completions of partial solution A extended first by the orientations in P, then by Ps.

<u>Procedure</u>: check(Qs, Q, Ps, As, Out)
  + Qs: stack   + As: stack
  + Q: orientation   − Out: stream of stacks
  + Ps: list of orientation lists

<u>Relation</u>: If orientation Q is consistent with the remaining partial solution Qs then Out contains all consistent completions of the partial solution As extended first by Q, then by Ps. Otherwise Out is shorted.

<u>Precondition</u>: Initially Qs = As.

Figure 9.6
Informal Specification of FGHC Cubes (Non/Candidates)

cubes. Each of the potential solutions must be checked by comparing each of the n cubes with its preceding cubes, until a failure occurs. This check is $O(n^2)$, giving the total complexity $O(n^2 24^n)$.

To analyze the fused generate & test algorithm,[2] assume that the search space of the program is an OR-tree of height n. A partial solution at height k is a list of length k. Consider attempting to extend a partial solution at height k into a set of partial solutions at height $k+1$. We wish to calculate the time complexity of this extension and all extensions it engenders, C_k.

There are 24 orientations with which to extend the partial solution. For each orientation, there are two outcomes: the orientation is either compatible or incompatible with the partial solution. Assume that the probability of the former is P_k and thus the probability of the latter is $1 - P_k$.

If the check succeeds then we expended k reductions to perform the check (assuming one reduction per comparing two cubes, as in the program). In addition, we engender all reductions performed at level $k+1$ and beyond. This workload is in fact the complexity C_{k+1}.

If the check at level k does not succeed, then it costs some number of reductions bounded by k. Let's call this work $k\alpha_k$ where α_k is expected number of checks until failure. Thus our total complexity is:

$$C_k = 24(P_k k + (1 - P_k)k\alpha_k + P_k C_{k+1})$$

We can recursively combine all C_k for $1 \leq k \leq n$ to give the total complexity:

$$\sum_{k=1}^{n} k(P_k + (1 - P_k)\alpha_k) \underbrace{24^k \prod_{j=1}^{k} P_j}_{G_k}$$

The last two factors inside the sum represent the average number of nodes in the tree at height k. This representation will prove useful later, so we name it G_k. The first two factors represent the average work performed at a single node. The important point to note is that the complexity has been reduced to a sum of terms of the form $24^k H_k$ where $H_k < 1$. Rewriting the previous equation:

$$\sum_{k=1}^{n} 24^k \underbrace{k(P_k + (1 - P_k)\alpha_k) \prod_{j=1}^{k} P_j}_{H_k}$$

---

[2]The fused generate & test, pipelined filters and candidates/noncandidates programs all have the same execution time complexity order, although their potential parallelism differs.

N	solutions	T (sec)	T_N/T_4
fused gen. & test			
4	8	41.8	1.0
5	24	167.0	4.0
6	64	687.8	16.5
layered streams			
4	8	11.8	1.0
5	24	32.5	2.8
6	64	167.7	14.2

Table 9.1
Instant Insanity: N-Cubes on Panda (single Multimax PE)

As k increases, H_k decreases exponentially because of the product term of the probabilities.

Although analytical solutions are nice, without accurate estimations of P_k and α_k, this equation will produce no useful results. Assuming a uniform random distribution of n colors on the $6 \times n$ faces of the n cubes, the calculation of these parameters can be simplified. We proceed no further in evaluating this model, but instead jump straight to empirical data from Panda. Table 9.1 shows the execution time (in seconds) of the FGHC fused generated & test and layered-streams programs running on a single PE on Multimax. Three problem sizes were measured for four, five, and six cubes. For fused generate & test, execution time increases fourfold with each additional cube. Note that the algorithm is still of exponential order, although greatly reduced from the naive algorithm.

We now use the analytical model of the fused generate & test algorithm to derive the layered-streams complexity. A layered stream H*Ts can be viewed as a tree where H is a node and Ts are the children branching from that node. In fact, this view corresponds directly to the OR-tree in the fused generate & test program. Extending a partial solution at height k in the OR-tree is equivalent to extending the layered stream at the kth layer (depth k). The critical difference is the *direction* of the compatibility check.

In the OR-tree, a node at height k must check all nodes on a path to the root. This factor k played a critical role in deriving the complexity of fused generate & test. In the layered stream, a filter process at layer k must check a layered stream consisting of k layers, from the top, down. Assuming a perfectly balanced layered stream with branching factor g_k in each layer, there are a maximum of g_k^{k+1} reductions necessary, i.e., there are g_k^{k+1} nodes in the tree, and each represents a cube that needs to be checked.

Consider that $G_k = g_k{}^k$ under the (optimistic) assumption of a balanced tree! The maximum number of checks performed by the fused generate & test algorithm at height k is kG_k, whereas the maximum number of checks performed by the layered streams algorithm at layer k is g_kG_k. Thus we can reuse the previous analytical model, simply replacing k with g_k:

$$\sum_{k=1}^{n} g_k(P_k + (1 - P_k)\alpha_k)24^k \prod_{j=1}^{k} P_j$$

where

$$g_k = \sqrt[k]{G_k} = 24 \sqrt[k]{\prod_{j=1}^{k} P_j}.$$

Note that we can now calculate the relative performance gain offered by layered streams, as the ratio of the two complexities. The equations are the same except for the first term inside the summation. Thus an approximation to the speedup of layered streams over fused generate & test for N-Cubes is the ratio N/g_N. We examine the accuracy of this approximation in the next section.

9.1.9   Discussion

Table 9.2 gives the execution times and speedups of the 7-Cubes programs on Sequent Symmetry. Table 9.3 shows the high-level execution characteristics of the programs on eight PEs. Figure 9.7 summarizes the measurements for Panda.

The 7-Cubes problem has 48 solutions, 24 of which have unique combinations of visible faces. In these measurements, we computed all 48 solutions. The Panda programs were executed with sufficient memory to avoid significant GC overheads, except where indicated for the pipelined filters program. Up to 28% of the pipelined filters execution time was due to GC on 8–12 PEs. As in the N-Queens version of pipelined filters (Section 5.2.4), GC time is highly variable. The poor speedup and slow performance of the pipelined-filters program is due to the sequential nature of the pipeline, the frequent synchronizations of the streams, and the massive garbage produced by stream communication.

Candidates is also extremely slow, but achieves good speedup, in fact the best of the FGHC programs. One inefficiency in the program is the recursive method of creating a "branchpoint" with check/5. This procedure recurses 24 times to spawn all orientations of the cube. An optimization is to unroll check/5 (see Exercise 91), reducing the overhead. For 8x unrolling, so that three recursions remain, procedure entries decrease by 37%, instructions executed decrease by 8%, and speed increases by 9%, with respect to the candidates statistics shown.

System	Method	1 PE	2 PE	4 PE	8 PE	12 PE	15 PE
		raw execution time/GC (seconds)					
Aurora	fused gen & test	306.7	151.9	76.3	38.3	25.7	20.8
Panda	pipelined filters	579.9	308.5	174.1	119.5	99.2	104.5
	GC	5.0	8.2	10.6	33.3	27.9	7.5
	candidates	582.6	295.7	151.9	79.1	53.6	42.2
	layered streams‡	143.9	74.0	39.3	20.9	15.1	12.0
	layered streams†	100.0	50.6	26.1	13.5	9.3	7.6
		speedup					
Aurora	fused gen & test	1.0	2.0	4.0	8.0	12	15
Panda	pipelined filters	1.0	1.9	3.3	4.9	5.8	5.5
	candidates	1.0	2.0	3.8	7.4	10.9	14
	layered streams‡	1.0	1.9	3.7	6.9	9.5	12
	layered streams†	1.0	2.0	3.8	7.4	10.8	13

‡ without nil-check   † with nil-check

Table 9.2
Instant Insanity (7-Cubes): Total Execution/GC Time and Speedup (Symmetry)

System	Method	instr	reduct	back/susp	entries	sec	KEPS
Aurora	fused gen & test	29796501	1293371	503265	1796636	38.3	47
Panda	pipelined filters	39593029	1643205	132	1643337	119.5	14
	candidates	40722733	1686742	4	1686746	79.1	21
	layered streams‡	10810768	395156	121870	517026	20.9	25
	layered streams†	7168952	291196	4343	295539	13.5	22

‡ without nil-check   † with nil-check

Table 9.3
Instant Insanity (7-Cubes): High-Level Characteristics (eight PEs Symmetry)

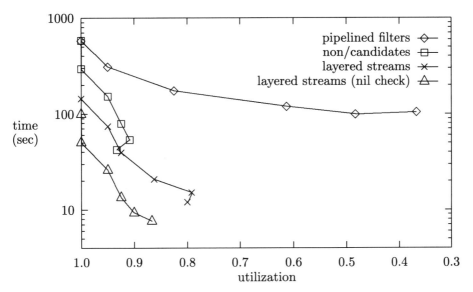

Figure 9.7
7-Cubes: Utilization vs. Time (Multimax)

Layered streams with and without the nil check display opposite behavior than in the N-Queens programs. Here we find that the nil check achieves consistently *better* speedup than no nil check. The reason for this difference is unclear.

Concerning the analytical complexity model given in the previous section for N-Cubes, we can grossly verify the model from the measurements presented in Table 9.3. The model estimates complexity in terms of reductions. Consider 7-Cubes, where the analytical model predicts $N/g_N = 7/g_7 = 3.2$, given the exact values of P_k and α_k for the seven cubes measured.

The fused generate & test Prolog program executes 1,293,371 reductions in Aurora. The FGHC layered-stream program with nil check executes 291,196 reductions in Panda. Thus the ratio is 4.4, not far from the prediction. The fused generate & test complexity model is also valid for the candidates program. However, candidates incurs overhead in **check/4** for spawning a branchpoint recursively. To alleviate this overhead, **check/4** can be unrolled, giving 1,062,647 reductions for 7-Cubes. Thus the ratio is 3.6, even closer to the prediction of 3.2.

Observing the form of the speed-up, N/g_N, we note that for a given problem, the advantage of layered streams (with the nil check) increases as problem size, N, increases, and as the probability of satisfying constraints, P_k, decreases.

9.2   Turtles

The Turtle problem consists of nine square cards as illustrated in Figure 9.8. Each card is labeled on its four edges with a h(ead) or t(ail) of color g(reen), p(ink), b(lue) or o(range). The problem is to rearrange the cards so that the abutting edges form complete turtles, i.e., each with a head and tail of the same color. Note that twelve complete turtles will be formed in a solution, with an additional nine half turtles crawling on/off the grid. The problem has four solutions, as shown below:

```
[[2-ho,9-hb,1-tg,6-hp,4-hp,7-tb,3-ho,5-hg,8-tg],
 [2-tp,7-tp,8-to,9-to,4-to,5-tp,1-tg,6-tb,3-tb],
 [9-to,4-to,5-tp,1-tg,6-tb,7-tb,3-tb,8-tg,2-tg],
 [9-to,4-to,5-tp,2-tg,6-tb,7-tb,3-tb,8-tg,1-tg]]
```

Here each card is represented by its number followed by the edge facing the top. Each solution lists the cards within the larger square from left-to-right and top-to-bottom. For example, in the first solution, square number two is placed in the upper left-hand corner, with the orange head at the top. In the last solution, square number one is placed in the lower right-hand corner with the green tail at the top.

Prolog Version

9.2.1   Fused Generate & Test

The following Prolog program, written by E. Lusk, uses a fused generate & test algorithm to place turtle cards compatible with those cards already placed. We begin by defining the edges necessary to complete turtles of each color:

```
flip(tg,hg).  flip(tp,hp).  flip(to,ho).  flip(tb,hb).
flip(hg,tg).  flip(hp,tp).  flip(ho,to).  flip(hb,tb).
```

Next, we define each of the nine cards and its permutations. Each card, except for the first, has four rotations. The first four arguments of **perm/5** are the top, right, bottom and left edges of the card. The final argument is the card number. The first card has only one allowable rotation to fix the puzzle's orientation (reducing the number of solutions by a factor of four — any card's orientation may be fixed to accomplish this). Nondeterminate **perm/5** is declared **parallel** because, as we shall see, it is from this branchpoint that the parallelism unfolds.

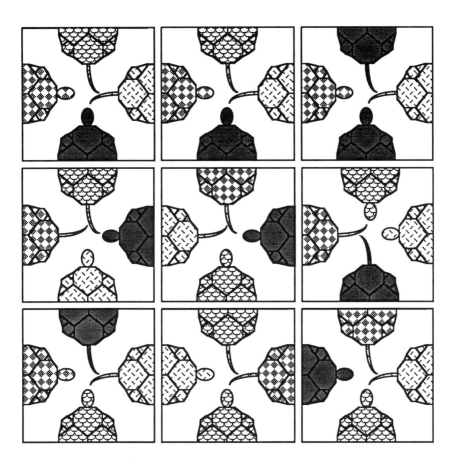

Figure 9.8
3x3 Turtle Cards

```
:- parallel perm/5.

perm(tg,tp,hb,ho,1). perm(tg,tp,hb,ho,2). perm(tp,hb,ho,tg,2).
perm(hb,ho,tg,tp,2). perm(ho,tg,tp,hb,2). perm(tb,tp,hb,ho,3).
perm(tp,hb,ho,tb,3). perm(hb,ho,tb,tp,3). perm(ho,tb,tp,hb,3).
perm(tg,hb,hp,to,4). perm(hb,hp,to,tg,4). perm(hp,to,tg,hb,4).
perm(to,tg,hb,hp,4). perm(to,hb,hg,tp,5). perm(hb,hg,tp,to,5).
perm(hg,tp,to,hb,5). perm(tp,to,hb,hg,5). perm(hg,hp,tb,to,6).
perm(hp,tb,to,hg,6). perm(tb,to,hg,hp,6). perm(to,hg,hp,tb,6).
perm(tb,tp,hg,ho,7). perm(tp,hg,ho,tb,7). perm(hg,ho,tb,tp,7).
perm(ho,tb,tp,hg,7). perm(tg,to,hg,hp,8). perm(to,hg,hp,tg,8).
perm(hg,hp,tg,to,8). perm(hp,tg,to,hg,8). perm(to,tp,hg,hb,9).
perm(tp,hg,hb,to,9). perm(hg,hb,to,tp,9). perm(hb,to,tp,hg,9).
```

The `flip/2` and `perm/5` facts are used as constraints with which to formulate the
problem.

```
go(L) :- findall(Z,turtles(Z),L).

turtles([N1-T1,N2-T2,N3-T3,N4-T4,N5-T5,N6-T6,N7-T7,N8-T8,N9-T9]):-
    functor(Cards,cards,9),
    perm(T5,R5,B5,L5,N5), arg(N5,Cards,5), flip(T5,B2),
    perm(T2,R2,B2,L2,N2), arg(N2,Cards,2), flip(R5,L6),
    perm(T6,_, B6,L6,N6), arg(N6,Cards,6), flip(R2,L3), flip(T6,B3),
    perm(T3,_, B3,L3,N3), arg(N3,Cards,3), flip(L5,R4),
    perm(T4,R4,B4,_, N4), arg(N4,Cards,4), flip(T4,B1), flip(L2,R1),
    perm(T1,R1,B1,_, N1), arg(N1,Cards,1), flip(B5,T8),
    perm(T8,R8,_, L8,N8), arg(N8,Cards,8), flip(B4,T7), flip(L8,R7),
    perm(T7,R7,_, _, N7), arg(N7,Cards,7), flip(R8,L9), flip(B6,T9),
    perm(T9,_, _, L9,N9), arg(N9,Cards,9).
```

The `turtles/1` procedure consists of several constraints. The `perm/5` constraints
are used to select cards for placement. The `flip/2` constraints are used to ensure
that abutting edges form complete turtles. The `arg/3` constraints ensure that no
card is chosen twice. Notice the order in which the squares are satisfied. The order
is chosen to maximize the satisfaction of constraints early in the search, i.e., near
the top of the OR-tree. Thus each new square is constrained by at least one edge,
if not two. The informal specification of the program is given in Figure 9.9.

FGHC Versions

Three FGHC programs are presented in this section. The first uses the (non)candi-
dates method of all-solutions OR-parallel search. The second version uses pipelined
filters implementing a fused generate & test algorithm. This version leads directly
to the third version, which uses an optimization of layered streams within the
pipeline. We have previously introduced these techniques for the N-Queens and
Instant Insanity problems.

Figure 9.9
Informal Specification of Prolog Turtles

    Procedure: `turtles(Cs)`
      ? `Cs`: list of cards

    Relation: All the adjacent cards in `Cs` form "legal" turtles, i.e., turtles with
    a head and tail of the same color.

    Procedure: `perm(Top, Right, Bottom, Left, N)`
      ? `Top`: atom   ? `Bottom`: atom   ? `N`: integer
      ? `Right`: atom   ? `Left`: atom

    Relation: `Top`, `Right`, `Bottom`, and `Left` are the half turtles of an orientation
    of card `N`.

    Preconditions: Each card has four orientations, except for card #1 which is
    fixed. In 3x3 Turtles, `N` ranges from 1–9.

    Procedure: `flip(X, Y)`
      ? `X`: atom   ? `Y`: atom

    Relation: Together, half turtles `X` and `Y` form a legal turtle.

9.2.2 Candidates & Noncandidates

The first FGHC program is based on the candidates/noncandidates paradigm of
all-solutions search with an OR-process tree. In fact, this problem is quite similar
to the Puzzle problem (Chapter 10). In each we are given a number of pieces
with which to pack a space. In Puzzle, the pieces are three-dimensional shapes
for packing a solid rectilinear box. The constraints are simply to fit all the small
pieces perfectly within the box. Here the pieces are flat squares for packing a larger
square. The constraints are that two abutting small pieces must form a complete
turtle.

First we define the set of all nine cards. Each card has four orientations in
two-dimensional space. However, as previously mentioned, one card is arbitrarily
constrained to have only one orientation, in order to prevent each solution from
having four orientations. The `pieces/1` procedure generates the list of 33 orientations.

```
cards(Cards) :-
    Cards=[[tg,tp,hb,ho],[tg,tp,hb,ho],[tb,tp,hb,ho],
          [tg,hb,hp,to],[to,hb,hg,tp],[hg,hp,tb,to],
          [tb,tp,hg,ho],[tg,to,hg,hp],[to,tp,hg,hb]].
```

```
pieces(P) :- cards(C),pieces(C,P).

pieces([[T,R,B,L]|Cs],P) :-
    P = [1-[c(T,R,B,L)]|Ps],      % first is fixed...
    pieces(Cs,2,Ps).

pieces([],_,P) :- P=[].
pieces([C|Cs],N,P) :-
    N1 is N+1,
    P = [N-Cards|Ps],
    rotate(C,Cards),
    pieces(Cs,N1,Ps).

rotate([T,R,B,L],C) :-
    C=[c(T,R,B,L),c(R,B,L,T),c(B,L,T,R),c(L,T,R,B)].
```

The top-level query, go/1, invokes select/2 which performs the candidate/non-candidate selection process of building an OR-tree. The final filter is needed to convert the answer stream, S, into a list of answers compatible with those of the Prolog program. Recall that each answer is a list of the nine card positions, in order of scanning the puzzle from left-to-right, top-to-bottom.

```
go(A) :- pieces(P),select(P,S),final(S,A).

select(P,S) :- select(P,[],[],0,S-[]).

select([],[],          As, _,  S0-S1) :- S0=[As|S1].
select([],[_|_],           _, _,  S0-S1) :- S0=S1.
select([N-P|Ps],    NonC, As, D,  S0-S2) :-
    D1 is D+1,
    check(P,Ps,      NonC,N,As, D1, S0-S1),
    select(Ps,[N-P|NonC], As, D1, S1-S2).
```

For a complete description of the candidate/noncandidate method, see Section 5.2.1 concerning Kumon's N-Queens program. In contrast to N-Queens, where a binary OR-process tree is built, Turtles (and Puzzle) build $(n+1)$-way branching OR-trees. The branching factor n is determined by the number of orientations of each piece. The $(n+1)^{st}$ branch finds solutions *without* that piece placed in the current location. N-Queens is actually just a degenerate case where a queen is a one-dimensional piece and thus has only one orientation (therefore a binary tree is formed).

In review, check/7 searches for all solutions with card N placed at the current position. The orientations of card N are given in list P. A child select process is spawned to search for all solutions *without* card N placed at the current position.

Procedure `check/7` will spawn further **select** processes for each orientation that is consistent with the current partial solution.

```
check([],_,_,_,_,_,S0-S1) :- S0=S1.
check([O|Os],Ps,NonC,N,As,D,S0-S2) :-
    chk(D,As,O,Status1,Status2),
    spawn(Status1,Status2,Ps,NonC,N,O,As,D,S0-S1),
    check(Os,Ps,NonC,N,As,D,S1-S2).

spawn(yes,yes,Ps,NonC,N,c(F1,F2,F3,F4),As,D,S) :-
    append(Ps,NonC,Unused),
    select(Unused,[],[card(N,F1,F2,F3,F4)|As],D,S).
spawn(_,_,_,_,_,_,_,_,S0-S1) :- otherwise | S0=S1.
```

Consistency is enforced in `chk/5` by checking that any abutting edges of the newly placed piece form complete turtles with previously placed pieces. Procedure `chk(D, As, O, S1, S2)` has a partial solution `As` composed of D-1 orientations. Status variables `S1` and `S2` are both bound to **yes** if the new orientation `O` is consistent with `As`.

```
chk(1,_,                      _,         S1,S2) :- S1=yes,        S2=yes.
chk(2,[card(_,T,_,_,_)],
                          c(_,_,B,_),S1,S2) :- flip(T,B,S1), S2=yes.
chk(3,[_,card(_,_,R,_,_)],
                          c(_,_,_,L),S1,S2) :- flip(R,L,S1), S2=yes.
chk(4,[card(_,T,_,_,_),card(_,_,R,_,_)|_],
                          c(_,_,B,L),S1,S2) :- flip(R,L,S1), flip(T,B,S2).
chk(5,[_,_,_,card(_,_,_,_,L)|_],
                          c(_,R,_,_),S1,S2) :- flip(R,L,S1), S2=yes.
chk(6,[card(_,T,_,_,_),_,_,card(_,_,_,_,L)|_],
                          c(_,R,B,_),S1,S2) :- flip(R,L,S1), flip(T,B,S2).
chk(7,[_,_,_,_,_,card(_,_,_,B,_)|_],
                          c(T,_,_,_),S1,S2) :- flip(T,B,S1), S2=yes.
chk(8,[card(_,_,_,_,L),_,card(_,_,_,B,_)|_],
                          c(T,R,_,_),S1,S2) :- flip(R,L,S1), flip(T,B,S2).
chk(9,[_,card(_,_,R,_,_),_,_,_,card(_,_,_,B,_)|_],
                          c(T,_,_,L),S1,S2) :- flip(R,L,S1), flip(T,B,S2).
```

Each abutting edge is checked with `flip/3`, similar to the Prolog program.

```
flip(tg,hg,Z) :- Z=yes.
flip(tp,hp,Z) :- Z=yes.
flip(to,ho,Z) :- Z=yes.
flip(tb,hb,Z) :- Z=yes.
flip(hg,tg,Z) :- Z=yes.
flip(hp,tp,Z) :- Z=yes.
flip(ho,to,Z) :- Z=yes.
flip(hb,tb,Z) :- Z=yes.
flip( _, _,Z) :- otherwise | Z=no.
```

The last piece of the program is the output filter, to rearrange the solutions for compatibility with the Prolog program solutions.

```
lastfilter([],    Out) :- Out=[].
lastfilter([A|As],Out) :- Out=[R|Out1],
    rearrange(A,R),lastfilter(As,Out1).

rearrange(A,B) :- rearrange1(A,C),rearrange2(C,B).

rearrange1([],R) :- R=[].
rearrange1([card(N,T,_,_,_)|Cs],R) :- R=[N-T|Rs],rearrange1(Cs,Rs).

rearrange2([M5,M2,M6,M3,M4,M1,M8,M7,M9],R) :-
    R=[M1,M2,M3,M4,M5,M6,M7,M8,M9].
```

Candidates/noncandidates programs, when formulated in this manner, generally suffer from inefficiencies in spawning the alternative branches for all orientations of a piece. In Turtles, a card has four orientations, so check/7 recurses four times to spawn each orientation. One method of removing this overhead is to *unroll* the loop (as mentioned in Section 9.1.9 for N-Cubes), a method similar to unrolling a branchpoint in Aurora Prolog.

```
check([O1,O2,O3,O4],                Ps,NonC,N,   As,D,S0-S4) :-
    chk(D,As,O1,G1,G2), spawn(G1,G2,Ps,NonC,N,O1,As,D,S0-S1),
    chk(D,As,O2,G1,G2), spawn(G1,G2,Ps,NonC,N,O2,As,D,S1-S2),
    chk(D,As,O3,G1,G2), spawn(G1,G2,Ps,NonC,N,O3,As,D,S2-S3),
    chk(D,As,O4,G1,G2), spawn(G1,G2,Ps,NonC,N,O4,As,D,S3-S4).
check([O1],                         Ps,NonC,N,   As,D,S) :-
    chk(D,As,O1,G1,G2), spawn(G1,G2,Ps,NonC,N,O1,As,D,S).
```

The second clause of check/7 is necessary because card #1 only has one orientation. For the 4x3 Turtles Problem measured in a later section, this optimization makes about 18% fewer reductions and executes about 10% faster than the previous version.

9.2.3 Pipelined Filters

We know quite well from N-Queens and N-Cubes (measurements given later in this chapter) that pipelined filters with streams are generally lacking in parallelism. Still we find it easier to derive a layered-stream version of Turtles by first developing a stream pipelined filters program.

At the top-level, spawn/4 is invoked to create a pipeline of filters according to a plan described by constraints/1. Each card filter is assigned a constraint list that describes the card's relationship with previously-bound squares. The constraint lists implicitly indicate the order assigned to the squares. In other words, we will assign

square five, then two, etc., in an attempt to satisfy the most severe constraints
first. For example, the constraint list [t] for square two indicates that the t(op) of
square five (the previously assigned square) must be compatible with the bottom
of square two.

```
go(A) :-
    cards(C),
    constraints(D),
    seed(S),
    spawn(D,C,S,Out),
    final(Out,A).

constraints(D) :-
    D=[[],
       [t],
       [x,r],
       [t,r,x],
       [x,x,x,l],
       [t,x,x,l,x],
       [x,x,x,x,x,b],
       [l,x,b,x,x,x,x],
       [x,r,x,x,x,b,x,x]].

seed(S) :- S=[[]].

final(S0,S1) :- lastfilter(S0,S1).
```

The 'x' constraint indicates a "don't care." Even if a position is not constrained at
all, it must be checked to ensure that the same card has not been reused. In the
previous candidates/noncandidates program, this check was unnecessary, because
duplicates were not generated.

For each of the nine squares, an **orient** process is spawned, as indicated in the
code below. Lastly, a **final** filter is created to convert the garbled solutions back
into normal form. The final clause of **orient** is not strictly necessary, but is used
to fix card #1 to a single orientation.

```
spawn([],    _,S0,S1) :- S0=S1.
spawn([D|Ds],C,S0,S2) :- orient(1,D,C,S0,S1),spawn(Ds,C,S1,S2).

orient(_,_,[],_,S) :- S=[].
orient(I,D,[C|Cs],In,S) :- I>1 |
    I1 is I+1,
    rotate(I,D,C,In,S-S1),
    orient(I1,D,Cs,In,S1).
orient(1,D,[[T,R,B,L]|Cs],In,S) :-
    filter(In,card(1,T,R,B,L),D,S-S1),
    orient(2,D,Cs,In,S1).
```

For each card other than #1, `rotate` is called, spawning four `filter` processes corresponding to the four orientations (`orient` clause 2). The filters are all wired together with an output solution stream. Procedure `filter/4` checks an incoming partial solution against its own `Card`.

```
rotate(I,D,[T,R,B,L],In,S0-S4) :-
    filter(In,card(I,T,R,B,L),D,S0-S1),
    filter(In,card(I,R,B,L,T),D,S1-S2),
    filter(In,card(I,B,L,T,R),D,S2-S3),
    filter(In,card(I,L,T,R,B),D,S3-S4).

filter([],_,_,S0-S1) :- S0=S1.
filter([P|Ps],Card,D,S0-S2) :-
    filter(Ps,Card,D,S1-S2),
    check(D,P,Card,P,S0-S1).
```

The `check/5` process iterates through the partial solution to determine if the solution is consistent with the filter's card. The constraint list is used as a template for controlling the check. There is a chance that the filter's card already appears in the solution, in which case the solution must be discarded (`check/5` clause 2).

```
check([],_,Card,P,S0-S1) :- S0=[[Card|P]|S1].
check(_,[card(I,_,_,_,_)|_],card(I,_,_,_,_),_,S0,S1) :- S0=S1.
check([x|Ks],[card(I,_,_,_,_)|Cs],Card,P,S) :- Card=card(J,_,_,_,_),I=\=J |
    check(Ks,Cs,Card,P,S).
check([t|Ks],[card(I,T,_,_,_)|Cs],Card,P,S) :- Card=card(J,_,_,B,_),I=\=J |
    flip(T,B,Status),
    check1(Status,Cs,Card,P,Ks,S).
check([r|Ks],[card(I,_,R,_,_)|Cs],Card,P,S) :- Card=card(J,_,_,_,L),I=\=J |
    flip(R,L,Status),
    check1(Status,Cs,Card,P,Ks,S).
check([b|Ks],[card(I,_,_,B,_)|Cs],Card,P,S) :- Card=card(J,T,_,_,_),I=\=J |
    flip(B,T,Status),
    check1(Status,Cs,Card,P,Ks,S).
check([l|Ks],[card(I,_,_,_,L)|Cs],Card,P,S) :- Card=card(J,_,R,_,_),I=\=J |
    flip(L,R,Status),
    check1(Status,Cs,Card,P,Ks,S).

check1(no,_,_,_,_,S0-S1) :- S0=S1.
check1(yes,Cs,Card,P,Ks,S) :- check(Ks,Cs,Card,P,S).
```

This method of checking by iteration down a constraint list is elegant yet inefficient. A method similar to that used in the candidates/noncandidates program could have been used here. However, the purpose of developing the pipelined filters is to lead to the layered-streams program discussed next. As we shall see, layered streams must check the constraints one card at a time. Our hope is that layered streams can sufficiently reduce the complexity order to overcome this high constant overhead.

9.2.4 Layered Streams

The Turtles Problem offers us a classic opportunity to use layered streams, building the program from the previous pipelined-filters program. There are nine cards, eight of which have four rotations, giving 33 possible card instances. For each of the nine squares to fill, each of these 33 card instances is initially a valid candidate. Thus we plan to spawn $9 \times 33 = 297$ filter processes. Each filter will be responsible for checking that incoming layered streams represent consistent partial solutions, i.e., if a card-instance in the stream borders the filter's square, then the abutting edges form a complete turtle.

The program code is almost identical to the pipelined-filters program with the following modifications. The seed for the layered stream is **begin**. The final transformation of the layered stream back into a list involves `fromLStoL/2`. Finally, the `filter/4` process initially issues the value of its corresponding card down the partial-solution layered stream and then spawns a `filter1` process.

```
seed(S) :- S=begin.

final(S0,S2) :- fromLStoL(S0,S1),lastfilter(S1,S2).

filter(In,Card,D,S0-S1) :- S0=[Card*Out|S1], filter1(In,Card,D,Out).

filter1(_,[],_,O) :- O=[].
filter1(_begin,_,O) :- O=begin.
filter1(D,      [C1*_ |Is],C2,O) :-
    C1=card(X,_,_,_,_),C2=card(X,_,_,_,_) |
    filter1(D,Is,C2,O).
filter1([x|Ds],[C1*Ts|Is],C2,O) :-
    C1=card(X,_,_,_,_),C2=card(Y,_,_,_,_), X =\= Y |
    filter2(yes,C1,C2,Is,Ts,x,Ds,O).
filter1([t|Ds],[C1*Ts|Is],C2,O) :-
    C1=card(X,T,_,_,_),C2=card(Y,_,_,B,_), X =\= Y |
    flip(T,B,Status),
    filter2(Status,C1,C2,Is,Ts,t,Ds,O).
filter1([r|Ds],[C1*Ts|Is],C2,O) :-
    C1=card(X,_,R,_,_),C2=card(Y,_,_,_,L), X =\= Y |
    flip(R,L,Status),
    filter2(Status,C1,C2,Is,Ts,r,Ds,O).
filter1([b|Ds],[C1*Ts|Is],C2,O) :-
    C1=card(X,_,_,B,_),C2=card(Y,T,_,_,_), X =\= Y |
    flip(B,T,Status),
    filter2(Status,C1,C2,Is,Ts,b,Ds,O).
filter1([l|Ds],[C1*Ts|Is],C2,O) :-
    C1=card(X,_,_,_,L),C2=card(Y,_,R,_,_), X =\= Y |
    flip(L,R,Status),
    filter2(Status,C1,C2,Is,Ts,l,Ds,O).
```

Procedure `filter1` is much like the **check** procedure of the previous program. Each filter corresponds to an orientation of a card. The incoming layered stream is checked by `filter1` according to a *template* or *roadmap* of constraints D.

> The roadmap technique is useful when a layered-stream filter must perform a complex check among several discontiguous elements of a partial solution. In general the roadmap is built from static information about the problem structure. The template order corresponds to the nesting depth of the layered stream.

In N-Queens the layered-stream filter needs only to check each element in the partial solution; thus no roadmap is necessary. Here we need to skip over those cards that do not abut the filter's card. This information is present in the search order of the cards. In the Waltz algorithm (see Section 10.2), each filter must check to determine if its element is already represented somewhere in the partial solution; if so, it must test that the two values are equal. For Waltz, the roadmap can be built from information present in the problem input.

A roadmap can be inefficient, however, as mentioned in the previous section. The constraint check has been decomposed to allow eager layered-stream construction. Consider the Prolog program and the candidates/noncandidates FGHC program where the constraint check is done in one reduction — a great savings compared to iterating through the partial solution by roadmap.

The layered-stream `filter2` process performs the classic filter split: one filter to check the nested layered stream and one filter to check the remaining partial solutions at the current level. Note the management of the constraint template. When checking the sub-layered stream, the tail of the template, `Ds`, is used. When checking remaining elements at the current level, the entire template, `[D|Ds]`, is used.

```
filter2(no,_,Card2,I,_,D,Ds,O) :- filter1([D|Ds],I,Card2,O).
filter2(yes,Card1,Card2,I,T,D,Ds,O) :-
    O=[Card1*O1|Os],
    filter1(Ds,T,Card2,O1),
    filter1([D|Ds],I,Card2,Os).
```

With a nil check inserted the filter appears as follows:

```
filter2(no,_,Card2,I,_,D,Ds,O) :- filter1([D|Ds],I,Card2,O).
filter2(yes,Card1,Card2,I,T,D,Ds,O) :-
    filter1(Ds,T,Card2,O1),
    send(O1,Card1,O,Os),
    filter1([D|Ds],I,Card2,Os).
```

System	Method	instr	reduct	back/susp	entries	sec	KEPS
Aurora	generate & test	1041808	35542	299968	335510	3.8	88
	pipelined filters	49100571	2727264	24993	2752257	159.9	17
Panda	candidates	22831018	1229530	369	1229899	44.8	27
	layered streams	20415250	1178395	3461	1181856	46.0	26

Table 9.4
Turtles (4x3) High-Level Characteristics on Symmetry (eight PEs)

System	Method	1 PE	2 PE	4 PE	8 PE	12 PE	15 PE
		total execution (seconds)					
Aurora	generate & test	30.5	15.0	7.6	3.8	2.6	2.1
	pipelined filters	790.1	407.4	276.4	159.9	155.2	160.1
Panda	candidates	322.9	165.2	85.7	44.8	31.1	25.8
	layered streams	326.1	166.9	90.0	46.0	32.5	26.3
		speedup					
Aurora	generate & test	1.0	2.0	4.0	8.0	12	15
	pipelined filters	1.0	1.9	2.9	4.9	5.1	4.9
Panda	candidates	1.0	2.0	3.8	7.2	10	13
	layered streams	1.0	2.0	3.6	7.1	10	12

Table 9.5
Turtles (4x3) Performance Characteristics on Symmetry

```
send([],_,S0,S1) :- S0=S1.
send( T,H,S0,S1) :- T\=[] | S0=[H*T|S1].
```

Recall that the advantage of checking for [] is that the size of the layered stream and the amount of speculative work are drastically reduced by incrementally discarding incomplete solutions. The advantage of *not* checking for [] is that subsequent filters can immediately begin working on this new datum, without first synchronizing on the subfilter. This means increased parallelism. In Turtles (as in the Waltz algorithm), without the nil check the generated layered stream becomes very large, as analyzed in the next section.

9.2.5 Discussion

Table 9.4 gives the high-level performance characteristics of a 4x3 Turtles Problem executing on eight Symmetry PEs. Table 9.5 gives the raw execution time (in seconds) and speedups on Symmetry. Figure 9.10 summarizes the measurements for Panda.

The 4x3 problem consists of twelve cards and has eight solutions (see Exercise

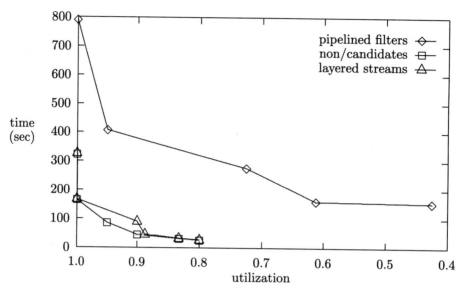

Figure 9.10
Turtles (4x3): Utilization vs. Time (Multimax)

92). The programs are essentially identical to those given, with appropriate modifications to constrain twelve cards instead of nine. The candidates program referred to in the above tables has an unrolled `check/7`, forming the branchpoint in the OR-tree. The layered-streams program has a nil check. Later in this section we discuss the performance results without the nil check.

Although the search order in all of the programs is the same, we find in Table 9.4 that the fastest FGHC programs are still executing more than 3.5 times more procedure entries than the Prolog program. This overhead has a few sources.

First, the FGHC programs are simulating backtracking in a sense. Consider the candidates method: the creation of a "branchpoint" involves reductions of `select`, `check` (if unrolled, this counts as 1/4 reduction), `chk`, `flip`, `spawn`, and `append`. Prolog requires the reduction of only `perm`, `arg`, and `flip`. Thus the difference is mainly `append`, which recurses. Layered streams, although not directly simulating the OR-tree, also has overheads in creating its process structure. The Aurora architecture is designed around an OR-tree, so it is not surprising that overheads encountered in spawning the tree are less than those found when simulating it at the language level in FGHC.

Second, checking constraints is more expensive in FGHC than in Prolog. Considering instructions executed, `chk` is much more costly than the Prolog check. The reason is that all constraints are checked in the context of one Prolog environment for `turtles`. Thus all constraints are available at the minimal cost of binding array overheads. In FGHC, a similar capability is managed by structure copying at much greater overhead.

The layered-streams complexity order is in fact lower than that of the Prolog program. However, the cost of checking has increased further. Now the check requires daisy-chain recursion of `filter1` and `filter2`. The net result is that layered streams executes slightly fewer instructions and reductions than candidates. But with respect to Prolog, the program is over ten times slower.

The 4x3 Turtles problem has abundant parallelism, which is indicated by the ability of the OR-tree search programs (Prolog generate & test and FGHC candidates/noncandidates) to achieve 97% efficiency on 15 PEs. Layered streams, with lower complexity order, is slightly slower than candidates because of overheads. Pipelined filters, although closely related to the layered-streams program, has two major problems: it is very slow and it gets poor speedup! These problems result from the "left-to-right" stream communication through the pipeline. The output stream of any given column of filters is composed in a D-list. Therefore the subsequent column of filters cannot proceed until the previous column's topmost filter completes its computation, and so on. This serialization incurs a high suspension rate.

The kind of stream communication in the pipelined filters program creates tremendous amounts of garbage. Pipelined filters is essentially a fused generate & test process structure. A given column of filters inputs a stream of all previously-created partial solutions, and either extends or discards them. Each extended partial solution is inserted into the output stream. The column's input stream *itself* is the major source of garbage, not the discarded items! By this we mean that, after all filters in a given column read the head of their shared input stream, the stream's *tail pointer cell* is no longer referenced and becomes garbage.

To understand this concept more fully, consider the candidates/noncandidates process structure. Herein all the nodes in the OR-tree share a single output stream. A given node in the OR-tree receives a *single* partial solution, not a stream of partial solutions. The node will either extend or discard the partial solution. If discarded, the partial solution becomes garbage just as in the other programs. However, in either case, no garbage *tail pointer cells* are created from reading an input stream. The candidates paradigm avoids excess stream communication by spawning a process for each node in the all-solutions search space. Each process is responsible for a single solution only. The pipelined filters program avoids excess process spawning by requiring more communication bandwidth between filter processes.

A final point is in order about the nil check in layered-stream programs. The advantages of including a nil check in the FGHC layered-stream program are illustrated for the simpler 3x3 Turtles problem. Without nil checks, the number of reductions increased from 162K to 1642K, more than ten times! The number of suspensions increased (on eight PEs) from 19,332 to 28,960, an increase of 50%. The execution time, which is directly related to the reduction count, was about ten times slower. Speedup improved significantly without the nil check: 7.5 speedup on eight PEs compared to 6.6 with the check. These statistics support the classic behavior of layered streams.

The programmer must choose a programming paradigm with which to solve a particular problem. We have found that for all-solutions search problems, candidates/noncandidates is applicable to a larger number of problems than is layered streams. Consider the view of a constraint problem, as given in the introduction to this chapter, as a "board" to be filled with certain "pieces" according to some constraints.

Layered streams is ideal for constraints problems where the number of potential "pieces" is small. As the range of values that a constrained variable can attain increases linearly, the number of possible objects (pieces) built from such variables increases exponentially. If the number of unique pieces becomes too large, layered streams encounters resource limitations in the number of goals spawned and memory used for communication between goals.

Consider trying to solve the Zebra problem with layered streams. In the case of N houses and M attributes per house, there are N^M unique pieces (house combinations). For the given case of $N = 6$ and $M = 5$, this number is 7776, which would swamp most systems in terms of excess goals and memory usage (remember there are N houses, thus initially $6 \times 7776 = 46,656$ goals would be spawned in a layered-stream program). Theoretically only $(N - 1)^M = 3125$ unique combinations are left for the second house given that the first house has been chosen. However, the layers in the layered stream must be seeded independently at the beginning of the computation, so this reduction cannot be achieved. Thus to solve Zebras we chose pipelined filters, which can realize the reduction in choices for each subsequent house (at the price of parallelism).

Interestingly, the complexity results for N-Cubes (derived in Section 9.1.8) indicate that layered-streams performance increases, with respect to fused generate & test, with increasing numbers of pieces. This result is counterbalanced by our previous observation that space complexity also increases with increasing numbers of pieces!

In general, all algorithms described here have exponential time complexity. Layered-stream programs have a more dampened exponential, but pay the price of exponential space complexity. The nil check can significantly damp this complexity, but not to the extent of less eager algorithms. For example, fused generate & test and the related candidates/noncandidates have further dampened exponential space complexities because there is no speculation.

9.3   Summary

In this chapter we reiterated the programming techniques for all-solutions search introduced in earlier chapters: fused generate & test, candidates/noncandidates, pipelined filters, and layered streams. The problems of pipelined filters and the optimization afforded by layered streams were reevaluated for two constraints problems: N-Cubes and Turtles. The utility of the nil check in layered-streams programs was also analyzed. In addition, we introduced the techniques of serialization by short-circuit chain and bounded buffer communication, to reduce the dynamic system requirements of FGHC programs.

An interesting aspect of the N-Cubes and Turtles problems is the ratio of Aurora/Panda execution times. For N-Cubes, Panda is about three times faster than Aurora. For Turtles, Aurora is about 12 times faster than Panda. In the case of N-Cubes, the factor of three is largely due to the reduction in algorithmic complexity achieved by the layered-stream paradigm. Just as in N-Queens, layered streams outperforms fused generate & test, *all other factors being equal*. It should be possible to implement layered streams in Prolog (theoretically, any committed-choice program can be translated into Prolog), although Aurora will be unable to exploit any potential AND-parallelism.

Consider 9-Queens, where the complexity reduction of layered streams is not as significant as in 7-Cubes — FGHC layered streams outperformed Prolog fused generate & test by only 13% on a single Symmetry PE (Section 5.4, Table 5.6). This result is because there is little *sharing* of subsolutions among the 352 solutions to 9-Queens, as signified by the average solution size of 25 data words, compared to 20 data words for fused generate & test. In 7-Cubes, there is much sharing among the solutions — the average layered-streams solution size is 28 data words, compared to 51 data words for fused generate & test. The amount of sharing is important not in terms of space reduction, but because a lot of sharing implies that the layered stream is well-balanced, maximally reducing the number of checks. As we saw in Section 9.1.8, the analytical models based on a perfectly-balanced layered stream indicate great reduction in complexity.

In Turtles, however, all other factors are *not* equal. The FGHC programs have an inherent handicap — the programs are significantly more complex and use more memory than the streamlined Prolog program. Prolog exploits backtrackable assignment within a single environment to achieve very high performance. This constitutes a *super-fused* generate & test: the ratio of backtracks to reductions is 8.4. We have also seen super fusion in Triangle, with a ratio of 16.5. In such situations, Panda cannot compete with Aurora.

Exercises

Exercise 87 Rewrite the FGHC stack and queue managers in Section 3.4 with fixed-length buffer size. One way to implement this program is to have two input streams: one for pushes and one for pops. If a push message arrives at a full buffer then the manager waits for a pop message. If a pop message arrives at an empty buffer then the manager waits for a push.

Exercise 88 Assume we are given a sequential '&' operator as in Parlog, e.g., a body "G1 & G2" executes goal G1 followed by goal G2. Subgoals within G1 and G2 are *not* serialized (unless they too contain '&' operators). Make the *minimum* modification to the FGHC N-Cube program in Section 9.1.2 to serialize the generator. If you have access to a Parlog system, confirm that parallelism in the generator has been throttled.

Exercise 89 Modify the FGHC N-Cubes program with the naive generate & test (Section 9.1.4) to find one and only one solution. Be careful how you terminate the generator when the tester finds a valid solution. Hint: the buffers may cause a slight problem.

Exercise 90 Write a lazy N-Cubes program in FGHC for finding any M solutions. Time your program for different M to illustrate approximately where the eight solutions reside in the OR-tree for 4-Cubes:

```
cubes(C) :-
    C=[q(p(0,2),p(3,0),p(1,3)),
       q(p(0,1),p(2,2),p(1,3)),
       q(p(0,1),p(3,2),p(2,0)),
       q(p(0,1),p(3,3),p(2,3))].
```

Exercise 91 Unroll the `check/5` procedure in the candidates/noncandidates version of N-Cubes, as described in Section 9.1.9. The method is similar to the Turtles optimization given in Section 9.2.2. Measure the performance improvement.

Exercise 92 Generalize the Turtles programs to solve MxN arrays of cards. The input data for the programs should be a simple list of cards. Be sure first to create a *plan* specifying the order in which to select the squares. The plan should maximize constraint satisfaction as early in the search as possible. Test your programs with the 4x3 problem (eight solutions):

```
cards(Cards) :-
    Cards=[[tg,tp,hb,ho],[tg,tp,hb,ho],[tb,tp,hb,ho],
           [tg,hb,hp,to],[to,hb,hg,tp],[hg,hp,tb,to],
           [tb,to,hg,ho],[tg,to,hg,hp],[to,tp,hg,hb],
           [hp,tb,hg,tp],[ho,hb,to,tg],[ho,hp,tg,tb]].
```

Exercise 93 Write an OR-parallel Prolog version of Turtles with hexagonal cards. For the *same size* of problem, do you expect square cards or hexagonal cards to contain more exploitable parallelism, and why? Confirm your hypothesis by measurement. Be careful how you define problem size.

Exercise 94 (Rubik's Cube) Write an OR-parallel Prolog or FGHC program to find a single solution to an NxNxN Rubik's Cube. The cube can be viewed as a stack of NxN squares. Each square in the stack can be rotated (into four positions) independently of the other squares. In addition, the entire cube can be rotated (into three positions) redefining the stack. Since there are N squares per stack, there are 4^{3N} possible transformations. However, a great number of these transformations are equivalent.

Each face of a "virgin" cube is a unique color. To "shuffle" the cube, a series of transformations is performed to disperse the colors over the faces. Given a shuffled cube, a solution entails the series of transformations needed to monochromatically color each face, i.e., regain virginity (it is about that difficult).

Initially define the transformations declaratively and experiment with shuffling a cube randomly. For solving the cube, avoid generate & test algorithms, which are seriously inefficient even for $N = 2$. Hint: color a single face first.

Exercise 95 Carefully examine the use of the nil check in the layered-streams programs in this chapter. Why doesn't the nil check remove *all* incomplete solutions? Can you modify the check to guarantee total removal? If so, is all parallelism also removed? Explain.

10 Puzzle and Waltz

"The matrix is an abstract representation of the relationships between data systems. Legitimate programmers jack into their employers' sector of the matrix and find themselves surrounded by bright geometries representing the corporate data. Towers and fields of it ranged in colorless nonspace of the simulation matrix, the electronic consensus-hallucination that facilitates the handling and exchange of massive quantities of data. Legitimate programmers never see the walls of ice they work behind, the walls of shadow that screen their operations from others, from industrial espionage artists and hustlers..."

William Gibson
Burning Chrome
Grafton Books 1988

This chapter introduces two constraint problems of a more irregular nature than the N-Queens, N-Cubes, and Turtles problems discussed previously. Puzzle is a solid-packing problem wherein a 5x4x3 solid is filled with seven small irregularly shaped pieces. Waltz's algorithm concerns the interpretation of line drawings of three-dimensional solids. Each arc of the drawing must be assigned a consistent interpretation from among: concave, convex, clockwise border, or counterclockwise border. For each of these problems we search for all solutions.

These problems are more irregular than previous constraints problems, so our solutions cannot avoid additional complexity. From our arsenal of programming tools, we select fused generate & test in Prolog, and in FGHC a disguised form of candidates/noncandidates (corresponding almost directly to the Prolog fused generate & test) and layered streams. Interestingly, both problems display parallelism that Panda can exploit (87% efficiency for Puzzle on 15 Symmetry PEs and 64% efficiency for Waltz on 4 PEs), whereas Aurora can exploit Puzzle (85% efficiency on 15 PEs) but not Waltz (41% efficiency on 4 PEs). However, Aurora significantly outperforms Panda on both problems, by factors of 2.9 and 2.2 on one Symmetry PE. These results characterize the ability of Prolog to execute irregular constraint problems efficiently by backtracking over logical variables. Such programming style has less parallelism than that offered by committed-choice languages. This is best illustrated for Waltz, where the speed disadvantage of 2.2 on a single PE reverses to an advantage of 20% on 12 PEs.

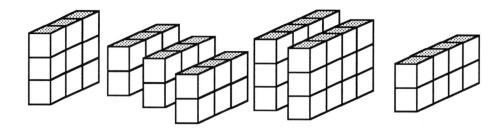

Figure 10.1
The Small 5x4x3 Puzzle Pieces

10.1   Puzzle

The Prolog and FGHC versions of a variant of F. Basket's famous Puzzle program
are presented in this section. Puzzle has been implemented in many different languages including 'C', Pascal, Lisp, and Prolog. It entertains some notoriety as a
symbolic computation benchmark. The Puzzle problem presented here has been
reduced in size from the original sequential benchmark. Figure 10.1 shows a group
of seven puzzle pieces that must be constructed into a 5x4x3 solid with a chip
removed from any corner.

The original Puzzle problem (e.g., see Gabriel [53]) requires that a *particular*
solution be found. This restriction is meant to ensure that all implementations
use the same search algorithm for calibration. For parallel systems, calibration is
not so easy because in the course of search for solutions in parallel, two systems
(with different data structures, database search strategies, and schedulers) may find
different solutions. Therefore the only fair way to write this application in parallel
is to find all solutions. Unfortunately, the original 5x5x5 puzzle has a very large
number of solutions, and so a smaller 3x4x5 puzzle is introduced here.

Prolog Versions

Two Prolog programs for Puzzle are presented in this section. Both use the same
fused generate & test control scheme; however, the programs represent the pieces
and the board differently.

10.1.1   List Representation: Board Copying in Prolog

The first program uses a simple representation of the board: a list of 120 elements. Elements instantiated to 'z' represent boundary walls in the positive X, Y, and Z directions.[1] Unbound elements represent cells as yet empty within the solid. The second program uses a much more complex representation for the board, as described later.

```
make_board( [z,_,_,_,_,z,
             _,_,_,_,_,z,
             _,_,_,_,_,z,
             _,_,_,_,_,z,
             z,z,z,z,z,z,

             _,_,_,_,_,z,
             _,_,_,_,_,z,
             _,_,_,_,_,z,
             _,_,_,_,_,z,
             z,z,z,z,z,z,

             _,_,_,_,_,z,
             _,_,_,_,_,z,
             _,_,_,_,_,z,
             _,_,_,_,_,z,
             z,z,z,z,z,z,

             z,z,z,z,z,z,
             z,z,z,z,z,z,
             z,z,z,z,z,z,
             z,z,z,z,z,z,
             z,z,z,z,z,z] ).
```

This is a 5x4x3 puzzle where one corner cube is missing, i.e., there are only 59 cubes in the solid. The program collects all 65 solutions in the form of a list of lists. A solution list contains seven pairs corresponding to the pieces, e.g.,

$$[[321|2],[123|5],[133|7],[413|14],[413|20],[412|31],[312|38]]$$

A pair, [A|B], is defined as: B is the cell number within the solid where the shape is placed (its "origin"), and A is an integer representing the shape and its orientation. The integer code consists of three digits corresponding to the X, Y, and Z dimensions of the piece. The cell number can be interpreted as $B = X + 6Y + 30Z$, where X, Y, and Z are cell coordinates beginning at 000 for the missing corner.

We build this program from the top down, assuming four piece procedures (p321, p431, p331, and p421) that nondeterministically return instances of the four different

---

[1]The first z represents a chip taken from the origin — this is to reduce the solution space of the puzzle by removing the symmetry of the solid.

types of pieces. The procedures are named to indicate the dimensions of the pieces. These procedures are defined as follows: p431(Color,Id,Board) where Color is input as an atom with which to fill in the board, Id is returned as a unique identifier representing a given orientation and type of piece, and Board is the game board (used as both input and output). Declaratively, p431(Color,Id,Board) is true when piece Id can be successfully placed within Board with color Color. The color is needed to differentiate the pieces: each piece is a unique color.

```
:- parallel fill/4, p321/3, p431/3, p331/3, p421/3.

go(A) :-
    make_board(Board),
    initialize(Board, Pieces),
    findall(Game, play(Board, Pieces, Game, 0), A).

initialize(_, [[a,b,c], [d,e], [f], [g]]).

play([],_,[],_).                      % game over
play([V|Rest],Pieces,Ns,N) :-         % spot already filled
    nonvar(V),!,
    N1 is N+1,
    play(Rest,Pieces,Ns,N1).
play(Board,Pieces,[[L|N]|Ns],N) :-
    fill(Board,L,Pieces,NewPieces), % spot empty - try to fill
    N1 is N+1,
    Board = [_|Rest],               % at least current origin filled
    play(Rest,NewPieces,Ns,N1).

fill(Board,Id,[[Color|P1]|T],[P1|T]) :-
    p321(Color,Id,Board).
fill(Board,Id,[P1,[Color|P2]|T],[P1,P2|T]) :-
    p431(Color,Id,Board).
fill(Board,Id,[P1,P2,[Color|P3]|T],[P1,P2,P3|T]) :-
    p331(Color,Id,Board).
fill(Board,Id,[P1,P2,P3,[Color|P4]|T],[P1,P2,P3,P4|T]) :-
    p421(Color,Id,Board).
```

The pieces, each with a different color, are initialized as a list of four sublists (one per piece type). The assignment of a unique color (a–g) to each piece will guarantee that two pieces cannot be placed *overlapping* one another.

All that remains is to define the pieces in their various orientations. Pieces are placed at a given *origin* within the solid. By convention, with no loss of generality, a piece is placed *into* the positive X, Y, and Z directions. Although the 4x2x1 and 4x3x1 pieces have six orientations, only four of these can fit in the given solid because the Z-dimension of the solid is too short. The 4x2x1 piece definition is listed below. Other pieces are similarly constructed.

```
p421(M, 421, [M,M,M,M,_,_,
              M,M,M,M|_]).

p421(M, 241, [M,M,_,_,_,_,
              M,M,_,_,_,_,
              M,M,_,_,_,_,
              M,M|_]).

p421(M, 142, [M,_,_,_,_,_,
              M,_,_,_,_,_,
              M,_,_,_,_,_,
              M,_,_,_,_,_,
              _,_,_,_,_,_,
              M,_,_,_,_,_,
              M,_,_,_,_,_,
              M,_,_,_,_,_,
              M|_]).

p421(M, 412, [M,M,M,M,_,_,
              _,_,_,_,_,_,
              _,_,_,_,_,_,
              _,_,_,_,_,_,
              _,_,_,_,_,_,
              M,M,M,M|_]).
```

The informal specification of the program is given in Figure 10.2.

10.1.2 Structure Representation: Constraints in Prolog

The second Prolog version of the Puzzle problem follows. The main difference is the data structure representation of a piece and the board. The board is a list of 60 structures of the form s(M,P1,P2,P3). The variable M plays the same role as in the first implementation: if it is ground, the square is filled; if it is unbound, the square is not filled. The additional three elements are pointers, instantiated when the board is created. These pointers point to the squares in the positive X, Y, and Z directions. This trick allows very fast unification of pieces with the board.

```
make_board(Board) :-
    make_level( Board-Level1, Level1),
    make_level(Level1-Level2, Level2),
    make_level(Level2-[],      [z,z,z,z,z,
                                z,z,z,z,z,
                                z,z,z,z,z,
                                z,z,z,z,z]).
```

Procedure: play(Board, Pieces, Solution, Cell)
    + Board: list of cells   − Solution: list of pairs
    + Pieces: list of color lists   + Cell: integer

Relation: Board can be filled with Pieces in the manner described by
    Solution, a list of pairs: a cell location associated with each piece orien-
    tation.

Preconditions: Cell is the cell location associated with the head of Board.
    All pieces in Board and Pieces have unique colors. Initially Cell=0 and
    Board has unbound cells except for borders.

Postconditions: Board fully instantiated.

Procedure: fill(Board, Id, Pieces, NewPieces)
    + Board: list of cells   + Pieces: list of color lists
      Id: integer   − NewPieces: list of color lists

Relation: A piece with orientation Id can be chosen from Pieces leaving
    NewPieces such that the piece can be placed at the head of Board, ex-
    tending into the rest of Board.

Preconditions: Head of Board is unbound. All pieces in Board and Pieces
    have unique colors.

Postconditions: Head of Board and other cells instantiated.

Procedure: p421(Color, Id, Board)
    + Color: atom   − Id: integer
    + Board: list of cells

Relation: Color piece orientation Id can be placed at the head of Board,
    extending into the rest of Board.

Preconditions: Head of Board is unbound.

Postconditions: Head of Board and other cells instantiated with Color.

Figure 10.2
Informal Specification of Prolog Puzzle

```
make_level([C00,C10,C20,C30,C40,
            C01,C11,C21,C31,C41,
            C02,C12,C22,C32,C42,
            C03,C13,C23,C33,C43|K]-K,

            [Z00,Z10,Z20,Z30,Z40,
            Z01,Z11,Z21,Z31,Z41,
            Z02,Z12,Z22,Z32,Z42,
            Z03,Z13,Z23,Z33,Z43|L]-L) :-

       C00 = s(_,C10,C01,Z00),    C01 = s(_,C11,C02,Z01),
       C10 = s(_,C20,C11,Z10),    C11 = s(_,C21,C12,Z11),
       C20 = s(_,C30,C21,Z20),    C21 = s(_,C31,C22,Z21),
       C30 = s(_,C40,C31,Z30),    C31 = s(_,C41,C32,Z31),
       C40 = s(_,  z,C41,Z40),    C41 = s(_,  z,C42,Z41),
       C02 = s(_,C12,C03,Z02),    C03 = s(_,C13,  z,Z03),
       C12 = s(_,C22,C13,Z12),    C13 = s(_,C23,  z,Z13),
       C22 = s(_,C32,C23,Z22),    C23 = s(_,C33,  z,Z23),
       C32 = s(_,C42,C33,Z32),    C33 = s(_,C43,  z,Z33),
       C42 = s(_,  z,C43,Z42),    C43 = s(_,  z,  z,Z43).
```

As seen below, the program structure is the same as in the previous version. Here we initialize the board by unifying a chip (z) in its corner.

```
go(A) :-
    make_board(Board),
    initialize(Board, Pieces),
    findall(Game, play(Board, Pieces, Game, 0), A).

% chip-off corner to remove symmetry...
initialize([s(z,_,_,_)|_],[[a,b,c], [d,e], [f], [g]]).

play([],_,[],_).                       % game over
play([s(V,_,_,_)|Rest],Pieces,Ns,N) :-  % spot already filled
    nonvar(V),!,
    N1 is N+1,
    play(Rest,Pieces,Ns,N1).
play([Spot|Rest],Pieces,[[L|N]|Ns],N) :-
    fill(Spot,L,Pieces,NewPieces),      % spot empty - try to fill
    N1 is N+1,
    play(Rest,NewPieces,Ns,N1).

fill(Spot,Id,[[Color|P1]|T],[P1|T]) :-
    p321(Color,Id,Spot).
fill(Spot,Id,[P1,[Color|P2]|T],[P1,P2|T]) :-
    p431(Color,Id,Spot).
fill(Spot,Id,[P1,P2,[Color|P3]|T],[P1,P2,P3|T]) :-
    p331(Color,Id,Spot).
fill(Spot,Id,[P1,P2,P3,[Color|P4]|T],[P1,P2,P3,P4|T]) :-
    p421(Color,Id,Spot).
```

The 4x2x1 piece definition is given in Figure 10.3. Other pieces are similarly constructed. Note that counting positions within the solid differs between the two versions presented. In the newer version, counting is based on a 5x4x3 solid. In the previous version, counting is based on a 6x5x3 solid (the "walls" are counted). For instance, the new version gives the following answer corresponding to the answer previously shown:

$$[[321|2],[123|5],[133|6],[413|12],[413|17],[412|21],[312|27]]$$

Timings (on SICStus Prolog) show that the simple implementation runs slower than the second version by at least a factor of two.

10.1.3   Board Copying in FGHC

The FGHC program is similar to the first Prolog program described in Section 10.1.1. The board is represented by a list of atoms. Borders are represented, as in the Prolog program, by 'z' elements. Empty cells, corresponding to unbound logical variables in the Prolog program, are represented by 'v' elements. Elements with other values (a–g) represent filled-in cells. The initial board is created with the following procedure.

```
makeBoard(X) :-
    X = [z,v,v,v,v,z,
         v,v,v,v,v,z,
         v,v,v,v,v,z,
         v,v,v,v,v,z,
         z,z,z,z,z,z,

         v,v,v,v,v,z,
         v,v,v,v,v,z,
         v,v,v,v,v,z,
         v,v,v,v,v,z,
         z,z,z,z,z,z,

         v,v,v,v,v,z,
         v,v,v,v,v,z,
         v,v,v,v,v,z,
         v,v,v,v,v,z,
         z,z,z,z,z,z,

         z,z,z,z,z,z,
         z,z,z,z,z,z,
         z,z,z,z,z,z,
         z,z,z,z,z,z,
         z,z,z,z,z,z] .
```

```
p421(M,   421, s(M,
                  s(M,
                     s(M,
                        s(M,_,
                           s(M,_,_,_),
                           _),
                        s(M,_,_,_),
                        _),
                     s(M,_,_,_),
                     _),
                  s(M,_,_,_),
                  _)).

p421(M,   142, s(M,_,
                  s(M,_,
                     s(M,_,
                        s(M,_,
                           _,
                           s(M,_,_,_)),
                        s(M,_,_,_)),
                     s(M,_,_,_)),
                  s(M,_,_,_))).

p421(M,   241, s(M,
                  s(M,_,_,_),
                  s(M,
                     s(M,_,_,_),
                     s(M,
                        s(M,_,_,_),
                        s(M,
                           s(M,_,_,_),
                           _,
                           _),
                        _),
                     _),
                  _)).

p421(M,   412, s(M,
                  s(M,
                     s(M,
                        s(M,_,
                           _,
                           s(M,_,_,_)),
                        _,
                        s(M,_,_,_)),
                     _,
                     s(M,_,_,_)),
                  _,
                  s(M,_,_,_))).
```

Figure 10.3
4x2x1 Piece (Prolog)

Given a board and a list of pieces, we define the **play/3** procedure to return a
list of answers (each one a packing list). The pieces issued to the **play** procedure
correspond to three 3x2x1, two 4x3x1, one 3x3x1, and one 4x2x1.

```
go(Answer) :-
    makeBoard(Board),
    Pieces = [[a,b,c], [d,e], [f], [g]],
    play(Board, Pieces, Answer).

play(Board, Pieces, Answer) :-
    play(Board, Pieces, Answer-[], 0, []).
```

Procedure **play(Board,Pieces,S,Move,Answer)** is similar to **play/4** in the Prolog
program. Argument **Board** is the list of cells remaining to be searched on the board
(preceding cells are guaranteed to be filled in with pieces). Argument **Pieces** is a
list of sublists, each corresponding to a different type of piece. Argument **S** is the
answer stream (each answer is a list), **Move** is the current number of pieces that have
been placed on the board, and **Answer** is the answer currently under construction.

```
play([],_,S0-S1,_,A) :- S0=[A|S1].
play(Board, Pieces,      S0-S4, N, A) :- Board = [v|_] |
    fill1(Pieces, Board, S0-S1, N, A),
    fill2(Pieces, Board, S1-S2, N, A),
    fill3(Pieces, Board, S2-S3, N, A),
    fill4(Pieces, Board, S3-S4, N, A).
play([_|Rest], Pieces, S, N, A) :- otherwise |
    N1 is N+1,
    play(Rest, Pieces, S, N1,A).
```

If the board has no remaining cells (clause 1), then all the pieces have been successfully placed and the current answer **A** is sent down the answer stream. If the
first remaining board cell is empty (clause 2), we try to fill in pieces of the different
types (in this case, four of them). Each **fill** goal will attempt to extend the search
space by first placing a piece at the current origin. The solutions generated by this
four-way split are managed in the D-list **S0-S4**. Finally, if the first remaining board
cell is *not* empty (clause 3), we skip over the filled cell and continue searching for
an empty cell.

   Each **fill** procedure spawns a group of processes corresponding to the number of
orientations for that type of piece. Again, solutions are managed by linked D-lists.
For example, six orientations of each 3x2x1 piece correspond to goals **p321**, **p213**,
p132, **p231**, **p312**, and **p123**. The job of each goal is to try to match the piece **M**
onto the current position in the **Board**. If the match succeeds, then the search will
continue (via a continuation); otherwise the answer stream will be shorted.

```
fill1([[M|P1], P2, P3, P4], Board, S0-S6, N, A) :-
    Pieces = [P1,P2,P3,P4],
    p321(Board, M, Pieces, S0-S1, N, A),
    p213(Board, M, Pieces, S1-S2, N, A),
    p132(Board, M, Pieces, S2-S3, N, A),
    p231(Board, M, Pieces, S3-S4, N, A),
    p312(Board, M, Pieces, S4-S5, N, A),
    p123(Board, M, Pieces, S5-S6, N, A).
fill1([[],_,_,_],_,S0-S1,_,_) :- S0=S1.

fill2([P1, [M|P2], P3, P4], Board, S0-S4, N, A) :-
    Pieces = [P1,P2,P3,P4],
    p431(Board, M, Pieces, S0-S1, N, A),
    p143(Board, M, Pieces, S1-S2, N, A),
    p341(Board, M, Pieces, S2-S3, N, A),
    p413(Board, M, Pieces, S3-S4, N, A).
fill2([_,[],_,_],_,S0-S1,_,_) :- S0=S1.

fill3([P1, P2, [M|P3], P4], Board, S0-S3, N, A) :-
    Pieces = [P1,P2,P3,P4],
    p331(Board, M, Pieces, S0-S1, N, A),
    p313(Board, M, Pieces, S1-S2, N, A),
    p133(Board, M, Pieces, S2-S3, N, A).
fill3([_,_,[],_],_,S0-S1,_,_) :- S0=S1.

fill4([P1, P2, P3, [M|P4]], Board, S0-S4, N, A) :-
    Pieces = [P1,P2,P3,P4],
    p421(Board, M, Pieces, S0-S1, N, A),
    p142(Board, M, Pieces, S1-S2, N, A),
    p241(Board, M, Pieces, S2-S3, N, A),
    p412(Board, M, Pieces, S3-S4, N, A).
fill4([_,_,_,[]],_,S0-S1,_,_) :- S0=S1.
```

To understand how the pieces are matched onto the board, consider four orientations of the 4x2x1 piece: 4x2x1, 2x4x1, 1x4x2, and 4x1x2. Templates for matching these orientations are shown below:

```
[v,v,v,v,_,_,      [v,v,_,_,_,_,      [v,_,_,_,_,_,      [v,v,v,v,_,_,
 v,v,v,v|_]         v,v,_,_,_,_,       v,_,_,_,_,_,       _,_,_,_,_,_,
                    v,v,_,_,_,_,       v,_,_,_,_,_,       _,_,_,_,_,_,
                    v,v|_]             v,_,_,_,_,_,       _,_,_,_,_,_,
                                       _,_,_,_,_,_,       _,_,_,_,_,_,
                                       v,_,_,_,_,_,       v,v,v,v|_]
                                       v,_,_,_,_,_,
                                       v,_,_,_,_,_,
                                       v|_]
```

For example, the first template matches four empty cells, followed by any two cells (empty or otherwise), followed by four empty cells, followed by anything. The

first cell of the template corresponds to the current position on the board. If the
template matches, then we wish to copy that section of the board corresponding to
the template, filling in the empty cells.

An abstract representation can make the piece descriptions more concise. Templates, instead of being directly encoded, can be meta-interpreted. Assume a codeword vsssss2 represents the constraint that the next 12 board elements must be:

```
[v,_,_,_,_,_,v,_,_,_,_,_]
```

and a codeword ssssss1 represents the constraint that the next six board elements
can be anything:

```
[_,_,_,_,_,_]
```

Then we can represent the 1x4x2 template with five codewords:

```
[vsssss2,vsssss2,ssssss1,vsssss2,vsssss2]
```

We momentarily postpone defining how to interpret these codewords and first look
at the declarative definitions of the pieces. A given piece type is defined with a
number of procedures corresponding to its orientations. Shown below are the four
procedures p421, p142, p412, and p142 for the 4x2x1 piece. Two styles of description are illustrated. Procedures p421 and p241 use direct encoding of the template.
Procedures p142 and p412 use meta-interpretation of a template description.

```
p421(     [v,v,v,v,X1,X2,
             v,v,v,v      |R], M, Pieces, S, N, A) :- N1 is N+1,
       play([       X1,X2,
             M,M,M,M      |R], Pieces, S, N1, [[421|N]|A]).
p421(_,_,_,S0-S1,_,_) :- otherwise | S0=S1.

p241(     [v,v,X1,X2,X3,X4,
             v,v,X5,X6,X7,X8,
             v,v,X9,Xa,Xb,Xc,
             v,v              |R], M, Pieces, S, N, A) :- N1 is N+1,
       play([   X1,X2,X3,X4,
             M,M,X5,X6,X7,X8,
             M,M,X9,Xa,Xb,Xc,
             M,M              |R], Pieces, S, N1, [[241|N]|A]).
p241(_,_,_,S0-S1,_,_) :- otherwise | S0=S1.

p412(Board, M, Pieces, S, N, A) :-
    match([vvvvss1,
           ssssss2,
           ssssss2,
           vvvvss1],
           Board,NewBoard,M,c(NewBoard,Pieces,S,N,A,412)).
```

```
p142(Board, M, Pieces, S, N, A) :-
    match([vsssss2,
           vsssss2,
           ssssss1,
           vsssss2,
           vsssss2],
          Board,NewBoard,M,c(NewBoard,Pieces,S,N,A,142)).
```

Note that, in the directly encoded templates, the board is copied and play is resumed when the match is a success. If the match is unsuccessful, the answer stream is shorted. For the meta-interpreted templates, a continuation c/6 is passed to match/5. If the codewords can be successfully interpreted, then the continuation is invoked and play resumes (clause 8 of match). Otherwise the answer stream within the continuation is shorted (last clause of match).

```
match([vvsss1|R],[ v, v,X1,X2,X3,X4|Xs],B,M,Cont) :-
    B =           [ M, M,X1,X2,X3,X4|Bs],       match(R,Xs,Bs,M,Cont).
match([vvvsss1|R],[ v, v, v,X1,X2,X3|Xs],B,M,Cont) :-
    B =           [ M, M, M,X1,X2,X3|Bs],       match(R,Xs,Bs,M,Cont).
match([vvvvss1|R],[ v, v, v, v,X1,X2|Xs],B,M,Cont) :-
    B =           [ M, M, M, M,X1,X2|Bs],       match(R,Xs,Bs,M,Cont).
match([ssssss1|R],[X1,X2,X3,X4,X5,X6|Xs],B,M,Cont) :-
    B =           [X1,X2,X3,X4,X5,X6|Bs],       match(R,Xs,Bs,M,Cont).
match([ssssss2|R],[X1,X2,X3,X4,X5,X6,
                   X7,X8,X9,Xa,Xb,Xc|Xs],B,M,Cont) :-
    B =           [X1,X2,X3,X4,X5,X6,
                   X7,X8,X9,Xa,Xb,Xc|Bs],       match(R,Xs,Bs,M,Cont).
match([vsssss2|R],[ v,X1,X2,X3,X4,X5,
                    v,X6,X7,X8,X9,Xa|Xs],B,M,Cont) :-
    B =           [ M,X1,X2,X3,X4,X5,
                    M,X6,X7,X8,X9,Xa|Bs],       match(R,Xs,Bs,M,Cont).
match([vsssss3|R],[ v,X1,X2,X3,X4,X5,
                    v,X6,X7,X8,X9,Xa,
                    v,Xb,Xc,Xd,Xe,Xf|Xs],B,M,Cont) :-
    B =           [ M,X1,X2,X3,X4,X5,
                    M,X6,X7,X8,X9,Xa,
                    M,Xb,Xc,Xd,Xe,Xf|Bs],       match(R,Xs,Bs,M,Cont).

match([], Board, Rest, _, c(NewBoard,Pieces,S,N,A,Code)) :-
    N1 is N+1,
    Rest = Board,
    play(NewBoard, Pieces, S, N1, [[Code|N]|A]).
match(_,_,_,_,c(_,_,S0-S1,_,_,_)) :- otherwise | S0=S1.
```

We have chosen to implement seven codewords here. The informal specification of the program is given in Figure 10.4.

Note that this FGHC implementation of the Puzzle problem requires pattern matching and copying (for each template portion of the board). Whether the

Procedure: play(Board, Pieces, Stream, Cell, Partial)
     + Board: list of cells   + Cell: integer
     + Pieces: list of color lists   + Partial: list of pairs
     − Stream: difference list

Relation: Stream holds all solutions to packing a board part of which has
     been partially filled with pieces described in Partial, a list of pairs: a
     cell location associated with each piece orientation. The remaining Board
     can be filled with Pieces.

Preconditions: Cell is the cell location associated with the head of Board.
     All pieces in Board and Pieces have unique colors. Initially Board cells
     are bound to v except for borders.

Postconditions: All solutions in Stream are extensions of Partial.

Procedure: fill4(Pieces, Board, Stream, Cell, Partial)
     + Pieces: list of color lists   + Cell: integer
     + Board: list of cells   + Partial: list of pairs
     − Stream: difference list

Relation: Stream holds all solutions to packing a board part of which has
     been partially filled with pieces described in Partial, where the head of
     Board is filled with all orientations of a 4x2x1 piece. If no 4x2x1 pieces
     remain in Pieces then Stream is empty.

Preconditions: Head of Board is v. All pieces in Board and Pieces have
     unique colors.

Postconditions: All solutions in Stream are extensions of Partial.

Procedure: p421(Board, Color, Pieces, Stream, Cell, Partial)
     + Board: list of cells   − Stream: difference list
     + Color: atom   + Cell: integer
     + Pieces: list of color lists   + Partial: list of pairs

Relation: Stream holds all solutions to packing a board part of which has
     been partially filled with pieces described in Partial, where the head
     of Board is filled with a 4x2x1 orientation Color piece. If the 4x2x1
     orientation does not fit then Stream is empty.

Preconditions: Head of Board is v. All pieces in Board and Pieces have
     unique colors.

Postconditions: All solutions in Stream are extensions of Partial.

Figure 10.4
Informal Specification of FGHC Puzzle

System	Method	instr	reduct	back/susp	entries	sec	KEPS
Aurora	lists	2627899	78099	83566	161665	9.9	16
	structures	1925855	61658	83306	144964	8.7	17
Panda	board copying	5712756	283422	18	283440	26.1	11

Table 10.1
Puzzle (65 solutions) High-Level Characteristics (Four PEs Symmetry)

System	Method	1 PE	2 PE	4 PE	8 PE	12 PE	15 PE
		execution time (seconds)					
Aurora	lists	39.7	19.6	9.9	5.0	3.8	3.0
	structures	34.5	17.2	8.7	4.4	3.2	2.7
Panda	board copying	101.6	51.7	26.1	13.5	9.1	7.6
		speedup					
Aurora	lists	1.0	2.0	4.0	7.9	10	13
	structures	1.0	2.0	4.0	7.8	11	13
Panda	board copying	1.0	2.0	3.9	7.5	11	13

Table 10.2
Puzzle (65 solutions) Execution Time (Seconds) and Speedup (Symmetry)

template is directly encoded or meta-interpreted from codewords, the amount of structure copying is approximately equal. In contrast, the Prolog version requires only pattern matching (logical variables are used to represent empty cells so that copying is unnecessary). Neither program requires making lookups *within* the board — the current piece is always placed starting at the first empty cell remaining in the board.

10.1.4   Discussion

Table 10.1 gives the high-level execution characteristics of the programs on four Symmetry PEs. Table 10.2 gives the execution times (in seconds) and naive speedups on Symmetry. As is shown, the programs exhibit excellent parallelism, efficiently exploited by both Aurora and Panda. The variances in speedups on more than eight PEs for the different programs is likely due to the low execution time, making accurate measurements difficult. More significant is that the Prolog programs run about three times faster than the FGHC program, mainly because of Prolog's efficient method of implementing the piece constraints with logical variables.

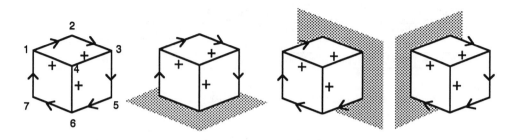

Figure 10.5
Four Clockwise Border Interpretations of a Simple Cube

10.2   Waltz

The programs described in this section implement Waltz's algorithm for interpreting line drawings of three-dimensional solids [146]. An interpretation is a label assignment to each line segment in the drawing. There are four possible labels (+, -, <, >) for each segment representing whether the segment is "out of the page" (convex, +), "into the page" (concave, -), or a border (< or >). A border can have one of two directions — consider one walking around the border of the line-drawing in either a clockwise or counter-clockwise direction. A valid interpretation must have no segment labels that contradict our sense of a real three-dimensional picture, e.g., adjoining border segments running in opposite directions is illegal.

Consider a picture of a simple cube with seven junctions and nine edges. If none of the borders are fixed, then there are eight valid interpretations of the cube: four with clockwise borders and four with counterclockwise borders. Figure 10.5 shows the clockwise interpretations. Note that the leftmost interpretation is a "floating" cube while the other three interpretations constrain one of the hidden sides of the cube to be flat against an imaginary wall.

The classic line-drawing interpretation problem is given a picture description with the borders clearly defined. This description corresponds to a three-dimensional solid floating in space, and has a single valid interpretation. However, this constraint can be relaxed by *not* presupposing which line segments are borders. There may then be multiple interpretations with somewhat abstract meanings. If an interpretation labels the bottom line segments of the picture as concave, we can envision this as if the solid were resting on a table. The table must recede infinitely into the

arrow   el   fork   tee

Figure 10.6
Necessary Junction Types of Line Drawings of 3-D Objects

background and there is no visible horizon; however, grossly we can imagine this. It is this relaxed problem that we solve here with Waltz's classic algorithm.

Generally speaking, junctions (also called vertices or nodes) in any line drawing can be classified into nine types. However, four types suffice to classify all objects under the assumptions that

1. there are no cracks nor shadows.

2. all of the junctions are made with just three planes.

3. the properties of junctions of any line drawing are not changed when the viewpoint is moved.

The derivation of the three assumptions is given fully in Winston [146]. The four necessary junction types are illustrated in Figure 10.6. For instance, the arrow corresponds to the bottommost point of the cube previously shown. Each of the four types has multiple interpretations, e.g., an arrow can have the outer line segments convex and the inner concave, or vice versa. The arrow also can have the outer line segments be borders (as in the cube example).

The Waltz algorithm selects interpretations for the individual junctions and ensures that neighboring junctions have matching interpretations of shared line segments. For example, in the cube, two neighboring junctions (corners of the cube) must agree that their shared line segment (edge of the cube) is either concave, convex, a clockwise border, or a counterclockwise border. The programs presented here produce interpretations with clockwise borders only. This interaction is accomplished with careful crafting of the constraints, as will be shown.

As another example of interpreting line drawings, consider the picture in Figure 10.7. One of eight valid interpretations with clockwise borders is shown for a picture with 13 junctions and 17 arcs. Note that arcs connecting nodes 11–12 and 3–12 are labeled as borders, although they *do not outline* the figure. These borders are also clockwise.

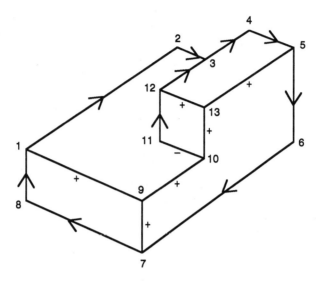

Figure 10.7
Another Example of Line Drawing Interpretation

Prolog Version

10.2.1   Logical Constraints

An example of a picture description is given below. A picture is a list of junctions, each of the form:

```
junct(Node, Type, [LeftNode, MidNode, RightNode])
```

where **Node** is the junction number, **Type** is one of the four junction shapes (arrow (a), fork (f), el (l), tee (t)), and the final list refers to the neighboring junctions (in order) that comprise the shape. The example below is a three-dimensional cube with seven junctions (three arrows, three el's, and one fork) and nine edges. For instance, the fork connects junctions one, three, and six.

```
data([junct(1,a,[7,4,2]),
      junct(2,l,[3,1]),
      junct(3,a,[2,4,5]),
      junct(4,f,[1,3,6]),
      junct(5,l,[6,3]),
      junct(6,a,[5,4,7]),
      junct(7,l,[1,6])]).
```

The input picture description is translated into an internal form that facilitates processing. The internal picture consists of a list of junctions of the form:

```
node(Type, LeftLine, MidLine, RightLine),
```

where the `LeftLine`, `MidLine`, and `RightLine` are logical variables corresponding to the edges of the graph. The translation procedure, `trans/3`, produces, in addition to the translated picture, a list of the logical variables corresponding to the picture's edges, i.e., what the answer will be after instantiation.

```
trans(In, Out, Lines) :-
    trans(In, Out, [], Lines),

trans([], [], Lines, Lines).
trans([junct(Node, Type, Junction)|Js], [N|Ns], L0, Lines) :-
    (Junction = [L,M,R] ->
        getLine(Node, L, LL, L0, L1),
        getLine(Node, M, ML, L1, L2),
        getLine(Node, R, RL, L2, L3)
    ;Junction = [L,R] ->
        getLine(Node, L, LL, L0, L1),
        getLine(Node, R, RL, L1, L3)
    ),
    N = node(Type, LL, ML, RL),
    trans(Js, Ns, L3, Lines).

getLine(Node, L, LL, Lines, Lines) :-
    Node =< L, member(edge(Node, L, LL), Lines), !.
getLine(Node, L, LL, Lines, Lines) :-
    Node > L, member(edge(L, Node, LL), Lines), !.
getLine(Node, L, LL, Lines, [edge(Node, L, LL) | Lines]).

member(X, [X|_]) :- !.
member(X, [_|Xs]) :- member(X, Xs).
```

For example, the cube is translated into the structure `Pict`, with the edges collected in solution list `Lines`.

```
Lines = [edge(6,7,E1),edge(5,6,E2),edge(4,6,E3),
         edge(3,5,E4),edge(3,4,E5),edge(2,3,E6),
         edge(1,2,E7),edge(1,4,E8),edge(1,7,E9)]

Pict = [node(a,E9,E8,E7),
        node(l,E6, _,E7),
        node(a,E6,E5,E4),
        node(f,E8,E5,E3),
        node(l,E2, _,E4),
        node(a,E2,E3,E1),
        node(l,E9, _,E1)]
```

Boundary interpretation of the solutions is subtle. For example, one of the solutions
of the cube is (second from the right in Figure 10.5):

```
[edge(6,7,>),edge(5,6,>),edge(4,6,+),
 edge(3,5,-),edge(3,4,+),edge(2,3,-),
 edge(1,2,>),edge(1,4,+),edge(1,7,<)]
```

We interpret a line `edge(N1,N2,>)` as a border going away from N1 towards N2.
Likewise `edge(N1,N2,<)` is a border going away from N2 towards N1. Thus the
above solution forms a clockwise border intersected by an imaginary plane.

   We now define the program from the top-down. Given the input data, we wish
to find all solutions (line interpretations of the graph). A graph interpretation is
generated with `dispatch/4` by choosing successive interpretations for each vertex.
Since the edges are linked by virtue of their implementation with logical variables,
inconsistent interpretations cause backtracking. The algorithm terminates (a solution has been found) when all the vertices have been successfully interpreted in
`waltz/1`.

```
go(A) :- data(D), findall(X, waltz(D,X), A).

waltz(Data,Ans) :-
    trans(Data,New,Ans),
    waltz(New).

waltz([]).
waltz([node(Type,X,Y,Z)|Ns]) :-
    dispatch(Type,X,Y,Z),
    waltz(Ns).
```

The parallel nature of the algorithm falls on the shoulders of `dispatch/4`. Here we
give a set of rules for each of the four shapes. Some of the rules are defined in terms
of subconstraints on borders, `sv/1` and `sc/1`. Procedure `sv/1` can be interpreted as
a border moving *away from* the junction, and `sc/1` can be interpreted as a border
moving *into* the junction (or vice versa).

```
:- parallel dispatch/4.

dispatch(a, X, +, Z) :- sc(X), sv(Z).
dispatch(a, -, +, -).
dispatch(a, +, -, +).

dispatch(l, X, _, Z) :- sv(X), sc(Z).
dispatch(l, X, _, Z) :- sc(X), sv(Z).
dispatch(l, X, _, +) :- sc(X).
dispatch(l, +, _, Z) :-        sv(Z).
dispatch(l, X, _, -) :- sv(X).
dispatch(l, -, _, Z) :-        sc(Z).
```

```
dispatch(f, +, +, +).
dispatch(f, -, -, -).
dispatch(f, X, -, Z) :- sc(X), sv(Z).
dispatch(f, X, Y, -) :- sv(X), sc(Y).
dispatch(f, -, Y, Z) :- sv(Y), sc(Z).

dispatch(t, X, +, Z) :- sv(X), sc(Z).
dispatch(t, X, -, Z) :- sv(X), sc(Z).
dispatch(t, X, Y, Z) :- sv(X), sv(Y), sc(Z).
dispatch(t, X, Y, Z) :- sv(X), sc(Y), sc(Z).
```

Note that the constraints are crafted quite subtly. By specifying the constraints as
they are, interpretations with only clockwise borders are produced. The definition
of the sv/1 and sc/1 procedures is tricky because, whereas concave or convex
interpretations by different junctions must agree exactly, border directions chosen
by neighboring junctions *must be opposite*. Thus, if a junction chooses < for a line
segment, then a junction sharing this line segment must choose > to be compatible.

```
sc(X) :- var(X), !, X = <.
sc(>).
sv(X) :- var(X), !, X = >.
sv(<).
```

The informal specification of the program is given in Figure 10.8.

FGHC Version

10.2.2 Layered Streams

The FGHC program is based on a layered-streams version written by A. Okumura.
The input picture description is the same as data/1 in the Prolog program. The
FGHC program must also translate the picture description to facilitate processing,
although in a different manner than the Prolog program. In this case, the translation is integrated with the actual Waltz algorithm, so the two must be explained
together. The top-level query is similar to that of the Prolog program, except
that waltz/4 produces a layered stream, not a list. Thus a conversion procedure,
fromLStoL/2, is required. Our converter is nonstandard and also will be described
in this section.

```
go(A) :-
    data(Junctions),
    waltz(Junctions,[],begin,LS),
    fromLStoL(LS,A).
```

The preparation phase of the computation is carried out by waltz/4, which reads
the input data. The data describes the picture in terms of a junction list. A filter

Procedure: trans(Data, Pict, Lines)
  + Data: list of junct/3 – Lines: list of edge/3
  – Pict: list of node/4

Relation: Pict is translated line drawing Data with edges described in Lines, where each edge connecting two vertices is assigned an unbound label.

Preconditions: Junctions in Data are numbered from 1–N in any order.

Postconditions: Every edge label in Interp is shared by *two* nodes in Pict.

Procedure: waltz(Pict)
  + Pict: list of node/4

Relation: All edge labels in Pict are assigned consistently.

Preconditions: Initially edge labels in Pict are unbound.

Postconditions: Pict fully instantiated.

Procedure: dispatch(Type, Left, Mid, Right)
  + Type: atom (junction) ? Mid: atom (label)
  ? Left: atom (label)   ? Right: atom (label)

Relation: The edges of this Type node can be labeled consistently as Left, Mid and Right. If middle edge nonexistent than Mid remains unbound.

Figure 10.8
Informal Specification of Prolog Waltz

is spawned for each edge and node in the list. Since each edge appears twice in the description, two filters in fact are spawned for each edge. To ensure that these two filters compute an identical interpretation of that edge, a *roadmap* between the two filters is created (review Section 9.2.4 for background about roadmaps in layered-streams programs). One filter in each pair must check that its interpretation is identical to the other filter, as indicated by its roadmap. The details of this check are described later in this section. Here we look at how the roadmap is created.

```
waltz([],_,LS0,LS1) :- LS1=LS0.
waltz([junct(NodeID,Type,Neighbors)|Junctions],EdgeStack0,LS0,LS3) :-
    map(Type,List),
    genEdges(Neighbors,List,NodeID,EdgeStack0,EdgeStack,  LS0,LS1),
    node(Type,                                            LS1,LS2),
    waltz(Junctions,EdgeStack,                            LS2,LS3).

genEdges([],[],_,ES0,ES1,LS0,LS1) :- ES0=ES1,LS0=LS1.
genEdges([N1|Ns],[T|Ts],NodeID,EdgeStack0,EdgeStack,LS0,LS2) :-
    genMap(EdgeStack0,NodeID-N1,0,Map),
    edge(T,Map,NodeID,N1,LS0,LS1),
    genEdges(Ns,Ts,NodeID,[N1-NodeID|EdgeStack0],EdgeStack,LS1,LS2).
```

Procedure **genMap** is given an edge stack listing all the edges encountered so far in the picture description. The edge-stack entries correspond one-to-one with the nested order of elements in the layered-stream solutions. Therefore, to create a roadmap, **genMap** searches for the current edge in the edge stack. For each edge-stack entry that doesn't match, the map value is incremented (clause 3). If the edge-stack entry matches, i.e., a filter for that edge exists, the map is completed (clause 2). If, however, a filter for that edge does *not yet exist*, then the map is given a zero value (clause 1) because it is simply not needed.

```
genMap([],_,_,Map) :- Map=0.
genMap([E|_],E,M,Map) :- M1 is M+1, Map=M1.
genMap([_|Es],E,M,Map) :- otherwise | M1 is M+1, genMap(Es,E,M1,Map).
```

Each junction corresponds by type to one of four node filters. Each of the node filters spawns an appropriate number of **nFilter** processes to check all possible interpretations of the junction. For example, the tee junction has four possible interpretations represented by the constraint lists: [>,+,<], [>,-,<], [>,>,<] and [>,<,<]. Each of the **nFilter** procedures share the same input layered stream and are linked together via their output layered stream.

```
node(a,In,Out) :-
    nFilter([<,+,>],In,Out,L1),
    nFilter([-,+,-],In,L1,L2),
    nFilter([+,-,+],In,L2,[]).
```

```
node(1,In,Out) :-
    nFilter([>,<],In,Out,L1),
    nFilter([<,>],In,L1,L2),
    nFilter([<,+],In,L2,L3),
    nFilter([+,>],In,L3,L4),
    nFilter([>,-],In,L4,L5),
    nFilter([-,<],In,L5,[]).

node(f,In,Out) :-
    nFilter([+,+,+],In,Out,L1),
    nFilter([-,-,-],In,L1,L2),
    nFilter([<,-,>],In,L2,L3),
    nFilter([>,<,-],In,L3,L4),
    nFilter([-,>,<],In,L4,[]).

node(t,In,Out) :-
    nFilter([>,+,<],In,Out,L1),
    nFilter([>,-,<],In,L1,L2),
    nFilter([>,>,<],In,L2,L3),
    nFilter([>,<,<],In,L3,[]).
```

The node filter, nFilter, matches the constraint list as its first argument against the incoming layered stream. The two or three constraints in the list correspond directly to the next two or three layers of the stream. Each is an arc leading into the node. If all the constraints match, the lower layers of the stream are passed through (clause 1). If the input layered stream empties, then the output stream is shorted (clause 2). For each matching constraint (clause 3), the constraint is sent out immediately on the output stream and the two subfilters are spawned. The first subfilter checks the remaining lower incoming layers against the remaining constraints. The second subfilter checks the remaining incoming partial solutions at the same level within the layered stream. Finally, if a constraint does *not* match (clause 4), then the partial solution is discarded and the remaining incoming solutions are checked.

```
nFilter([],In,S,_) :- S=In.
nFilter( _,[],S,T) :- S=T.
nFilter([L|Ls],[edge(N1,N2,L)*In|Ins],S,T) :-
    S = [edge(N1,N2,L)*Out|M],
    nFilter(Ls,In,Out,[]),
    nFilter([L|Ls],Ins,M,T).
nFilter(Ls,[_|Ins],S,T) :- otherwise |
    nFilter(Ls,Ins,S,T).
```

The layered stream is seeded, by edge/6 and spawn/7, with initial partial solutions for each arc entering a node. If the arc has not yet been encountered, i.e., M=0, then no filter is needed. However, if a filter for the opposite node has already been spawned, we need an arc filter, `efilter`, to ensure consistency. For example, each arc entering an arrow junction is constrained to be of a certain type. The leftmost arc can be either a clockwise border, convex or concave (`[>,+,-]`). The middle arc cannot be a border, and so on. These constraints are formulated in `map/2`. The `efilters` are spawned according to the plan outlined by `map/2`. Again, the arc filter is needed only to ensure consistency with a previously-spawned node filter.

```
edge([],_,_,_,_,_,S) :- S=[].
edge([T|Ts],M,N1,N2,In,S0) :-
    spawn(M,T,N1,N2,In,S0,S1),
    edge(Ts,M,N1,N2,In,S1).

spawn(0,T,N1,N2,In,S0,S1) :-
    S0=[edge(N1,N2,T)*In|S1].
spawn(M,T,N1,N2,In,S0,S1) :- M>0 |
    S0=[edge(N1,N2,T)*Out|S1],
    opp(T,U),
    efilter(M,U,In,Out).

map(t,L) :- L=[[<],[>,<,+,-],[>]].
map(l,L) :- L=[[>,<,+,-],[>,<,+,-]].
map(f,L) :- L=[[>,<,+,-],[>,<,+,-],[>,<,+,-]].
map(a,L) :- L=[[>,+,-],[+,-],[<,+,-]].

opp(+,U) :- U = +.
opp(-,U) :- U = -.
opp(<,U) :- U = >.
opp(>,U) :- U = <.
```

A partial solution is initially created, in `spawn/7`, on the output stream, corresponding to each possible interpretation. Note, however, that the partial solution issued for a clockwise border is in fact a counterclockwise border and vice versa. This opposition allows the border labels to be checked, much the same way as in `sc/1` and `sv/1` in the Prolog program.

The `efilter` procedure ensures that a previous node filter spawned for the same arc is labeled consistently. Each decrement of the map corresponds to a layer in the partial solution (clause 2). Since these layers are independent of the arc in question, these layers are immediately issued down the output stream. When the map reaches `M=1`, the corresponding layer is the same as the arc in question. If that layer of the partial solution matches the edge filter's label, then the partial solution is consistent and processing continues (clause 3). Otherwise, if that layer of the partial solution does not match, then the partial solution is discarded (clause 4).

```
efilter(_,_,[],Out) :- Out=[].
efilter(M,Label,[X*In1|Ins],Out) :- M>1 |
    M1 is M=1,
    Out = [X*Out1|Outs],
    efilter(M1,Label,In1,Out1),
    efilter(M,Label,Ins,Outs).
efilter(1,Label,[edge(N1,N2,Label)*Out1|Ins],Out) :-
    Out = [edge(N1,N2,Label)*Out1|Outs],
    efilter(1,Label,Ins,Outs).
efilter(1,Label,[_|In],Out) :- otherwise |
    efilter(1,Label,In,Out).
```

The astute reader will no doubt wonder: if we detect the pre-existence of a labeled
arc in the partial solution (clause 2 of **spawn**), why do we check that it is consistent
and then issue a redundant label to be checked again by **node/3**? The reason is
that, although some arcs adjoining the new node may have already been labeled,
others may not. Therefore node filters are necessary to check the consistency of the
new node. The easiest method to check node consistency is with **node/3**, which
assumes that all the arcs are on *adjacent layers* in the partial solution. To avoid
redundancies we would have to write a complex version of **nFilter/4** that could
check the consistency among arbitrary layers.

The remaining piece of the program is a converter to translate from a layered
stream into a list of solutions. The converter, listed below, is nonstandard because
it removes redundant edges from the raw solutions to create normal-form solutions.

```
fromLStoL(LayeredStream,List) :-
    fromLStoS(LayeredStream,[],List-[]).

fromLStoS(begin,           Stack,L0-L1) :- L0=[Stack|L1].
fromLStoS([],                  _,L0-L1) :- L0=L1.
fromLStoS([edge(N1,N2,A)*LS1|Rest],Stack,L0-L2) :- N1 > N2 |
    fromLStoS(LS1,[edge(N1,N2,A)|Stack], L0-L1),
    fromLStoS(Rest,Stack,      L1-L2).
fromLStoS([_*LS1|Rest],Stack,L0-L2) :- otherwise |
    fromLStoS(LS1,Stack,       L0-L1),
    fromLStoS(Rest,Stack,      L1-L2).
```

The informal specification of the program is given in Figure 10.9.

As with all layered-streams programs, filters can be rewritten incorporating the
nil check to improve the efficiency of the code. For instance, the first phase of the
node filter is rewritten with **send/4**:

```
send([],S0,_,S1) :- S0=S1.
send( Y,S0,X,S1) :- Y\=[] | S0=[X*Y|S1].
```

Procedure: waltz(Junct, Edges, In, Out)
+ Junct: list of junctions   + In: layered stream
+ Edges: list of edges   − Out: layered stream

Relation: Out contains all interpretations of picture, part of which has been partially labeled by solutions in In, where Junct is the remaining picture to be labeled and Edges are the arcs labeled so far.

Preconditions: Nodes in Junct are numbered from 1–N in any order. Initially In is begin and Edges is empty.

Postconditions: A solution in Out has two redundant labels for each edge.

Procedure: genEdges(Nodes, Labels, Node, Ein, Eout, In, Out)
+ Nodes: list of integers   − Eout: list of edges
+ Labels: list of atom lists   + Ein: list of edges
+ Node: integer   − Out: layered stream
+ In: layered stream

Relation: Out contains all partial interp. from In, extended by all potentially consistent Labels for the arcs of Node, excluding those that contradict labels assigned to identical arcs within solutions in In. The only arcs that can be excluded in this manner are those emanating from Node.

Preconditions: Initially In = begin.

Procedure: node(Type, In, Out)
+ Type: atom (junction)   − Out: layered stream
+ In: layered stream

Relation: Out contains all partial interp. from In that are consistent with a Type junction. Any interp. that are inconsistent do not appear in Out.

Procedure: nFilter(Labels, In, Out)
+ Labels: list of atom lists
+ In: layered stream   − Out: difference list

Relation: Out contains all partial interp. from In that have assignments Labels for the topmost arcs. Any deviant interp. do not appear in Out.

Procedure: eFilter(M, Label, In, Out)
+ M: integer (M ≥ 1)   + In: layered stream
+ Label: atom   − Out: layered stream

Relation: Out contains all partial interp. from In that have assignment Label for the Mth topmost arc. Any deviant interp. do not appear in Out.

Figure 10.9
Informal Specification of FGHC Waltz

System	instr	reduct	back/susp	entries	sec	KEPS
Aurora	224381	27059	14154	41213	4.6	9
Panda	1134051	66226	8396	74622	6.7	11

Table 10.3
Waltz (288 Solutions): High-Level Characteristics (four Symmetry PEs)

System	1 PE	2 PE	4 PE	8 PE	12 PE	15 PE
execution time (seconds)						
Aurora	7.6	5.1	4.6	—	—	—
Panda	17.0	10.3	6.7	4.5	3.8	—
speedup						
Aurora	1.0	1.5	1.7	—	—	—
Panda	1.0	1.7	2.5	3.8	4.5	—

Table 10.4
Waltz (288 Solutions): Execution Time and Speedup (Symmetry)

```
nFilter([],In,S,_) :- S=In.
nFilter( _,[],S,T) :- S=T.
nFilter([L|Ls],[L*In|Ins],S,T) :-
    nFilter(Ls,In,Out,[]),
    send(Out,S,L,M),
    nFilter([L|Ls],Ins,M,T).
nFilter(Ls,[_|Ins],S,T) :- otherwise |
    nFilter(Ls,Ins,S,T).
```

The **efilter** must also be modified in this manner. In addition, the [H|T] notation
is used (in the programs measured) for layered streams instead of H*T. For the Waltz
algorithm interpreting any non-trivial picture, the nil check proves indispensable
for reducing garbage.

10.2.3   Discussion

Table 10.3 gives the high-level characteristics of Waltz programs executing on four
Symmetry PEs. Table 10.4 shows the execution times (in seconds) and speedups of
the programs. The '—' statistics represent no improvement in execution speed with
increasing numbers of PEs. Figure 10.10 summarizes the timing measurements.
The measurements were taken of the picture given in Figure 10.11. The picture
has 38 junctions, 51 arcs, and produces 288 clockwise interpretations, assuming we
do not fix the borders. The nil check, used in the FGHC layered-streams program,
successfully removed most garbage collection. Without the nil check pictures of

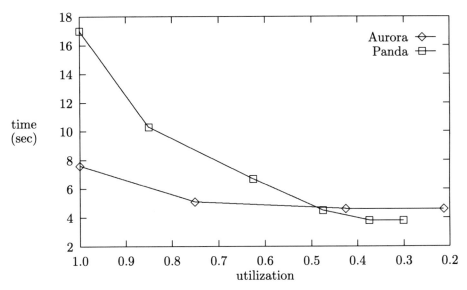

Figure 10.10
Waltz (288 Solutions): Utilization vs. Time (Symmetry)

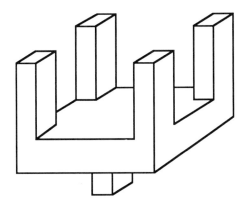

Figure 10.11
Test Picture for Waltz Algorithm: 288 Interpretations

this size are simply too large to interpret.

On a single Symmetry PE, the FGHC program executes 1.6 times more procedure entries (no suspensions occur on one PE) and runs 2.2 times slower than the Prolog program. A large percentage of the gap is due to the layered-stream conversion in the FGHC program, which executes in 4.4 seconds on one Symmetry PE. Without conversion, the FGHC program runs in 12.6 seconds, or 1.6 times slower than the Prolog program.

Aside from conversion, the main difference in the programs' performance is in the efficiency of enforcing constraints with logical variables in Prolog. The layered-streams FGHC algorithm actually has a lower complexity order than the Prolog algorithm when searching for all solutions. However, the constant overhead of the algorithm is greater for the problem sizes examined. Enforcing each constraint in FGHC involves some number of goal reductions, whereas in Prolog the constraints are satisfied essentially "for free." The Turtles programs illustrated this same deficiency with layered streams as compared to solving constraints in Prolog with generate & test. Note however that, unlike Turtles, Panda Waltz overtakes Aurora by virtue of its speedup. On eight PEs the two systems are equally fast and Panda can gain a bit more improvement up to 12 PEs.

In general, however, neither system can achieve good speedup on multiple PEs because limited parallelism is inherent in the data. No matter how large an input picture we examine, each junction still has at most six potential interpretations, and most of these will be immediately discarded. The performance measurements confirm that the search is highly constrained — both systems lose efficiency rapidly on increasing numbers of PEs.

10.3 Summary

In the irregular constraint problems discussed in this chapter, Prolog performed significantly better than FGHC because of Prolog's ability to backtrack over unification. Even with superior parallelism, Panda could not come close to Aurora's performance. FGHC's greedy memory-bandwidth requirement is its Achilles' Heel. It is critical to develop sophisticated architectures that can dynamically (or even statically!) and inexpensively determine if a data object is no longer referenced and, if so, reuse its storage immediately.

Incremental garbage collection (GC) is critically important for these systems. Panda cannot do this, nor can most other current parallel logic programming architectures. MultiPsi/V2 KL1 is one of the first committed-choice architectures

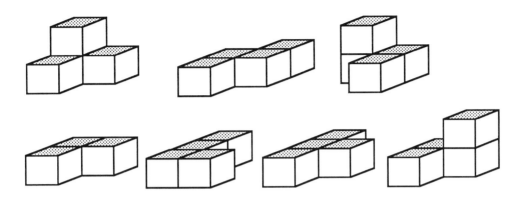

Figure 10.12
SOMA Cube Pieces

that allows limited incremental GC (based on the MRB method [66]). Much additional research and experimentation is needed in this area.

In the next chapter, we concentrate on Aurora's Achilles' Heel — solving problems with no (apparent) OR parallelism. Because this is characteristic of the problem, in fact no architectural cure exists short of implementing AND-parallelism in Aurora (and this has in fact been done, for precisely these reasons, in Andorra [58]). However, in the next chapter we remain at the source-code level, introducing some programming techniques that help achieve better performance given a general lack of parallelism.

Exercises

Exercise 96 The SOMA cube is a 3x3x3 puzzle similar to the Puzzle problem described in this chapter. There are seven unique pieces in the puzzle, as illustrated in Figure 10.12. Write a Prolog program to pack the SOMA cube (there are two rather inefficient programs given in Coelho [31]). How many solutions are there?

Exercise 97 The original Puzzle problem [53] defined a 5x5x5 cube to be packed with 18 pieces: 13 (4x2x1), 3 (3x1x1), 1 (2x2x1), and 1 (2x2x2). Modify the given Prolog program to solve this problem. How many solutions are there? (Do not attempt this problem unless you have *a lot* of computer time!)

Exercise 98 Rewrite the FGHC puzzle program so that the code is independent of the types and orientations of the pieces, i.e., generalize `fill1/6`, `fill2/6`, etc.

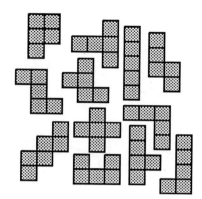

Figure 10.13
Pentamino Puzzle Pieces

Exercise 99 Write an FGHC version of Puzzle based on an array representing the board. In most logic programming languages, an array can be simulated with a structure. You may wish to refer to the LISP version of Puzzle given by Gabriel [53]. Measure the performance of the array version and compare it on multiple PEs to the board-copying version given here.

Exercise 100 Write OR-parallel Prolog and FGHC programs to find all solutions to the Pentamino puzzle. We wish to pack a 10x6 board with 12 unique shapes, each composed of five squares. The 12 shapes are illustrated in Figure 10.13. Both parallel Prolog and parallel 'C' versions of this problem are given in Lusk *et al.* [77].

Exercise 101 Recall from Exercise 29 that the Grep Problem is a procedure `grep(String,Pattern,N)` to find N occurrences of `Pattern` within `String`, executed in mode `grep(+,+,-)`. A string is represented by a list of characters. Simple patterns are defined as strings. Write OR-Prolog and FGHC Grep programs that exploit parallelism efficiently. It is difficult to measure the speedups of these programs unless we grep very large files of data, in which case the I/O costs may far outweigh the computation cost. Give an argument, preferably supported by performance measurements (of synthesized data), about the effectiveness of the parallel execution of your programs.

Exercise 102 Implement the Waltz algorithm in FGHC with a paradigm other than layered streams. Can you achieve better performance than the given layered-stream program?

Exercise 103 (Definite Clause Grammars) Another type of constraint problem, similar in a very broad sense to the interpretation of line drawings, is the parsing of natural language. An analogy can be drawn (argghh...) between a line drawing and its interpretation and a sentence and its *parse tree*. For example, the English sentence "John loves the girl who sings" can be parsed as:

```
s(np(pn(john)),
    vp(tv(loves),
        np(det(the),
            n(girl),
            rel(who,
                vp(iv(sings))))))
```

where s is the sentence root, np is a noun phrase, vp is a verb phrase, pn is a proper noun, tv is a transitive verb, det is a determiner, iv is an intransitive verb, n is a noun, and rel is an optional relative clause.

A simple nondeterminate parser can be written easily in Prolog with a difference list to represent the sentence. The following code is similar to that in Pereira and Shieber [98].

```
s(S0-S2) :- np(S0-S1), vp(S1-S2).
np(S0-S3) :- det(S0-S1), n(S1-S2), optrel(S2-S3).
np(S0-S1) :- pn(S0-S1).
vp(S0-S2) :- tv(S0-S1), np(S1-S2).
vp(S0-S1) :- iv(S0-S1).
optrel(S0-S1) :- S0=S1.
optrel(S0-S2) :- S0=[who|S1], vp(S1-S2).

pn( S0-S1) :- S0 = [john |S1].
tv( S0-S1) :- S0 = [loves|S1].
det(S0-S1) :- S0 = [the   |S1].
n( S0-S1) :- S0 = [girl |S1].
iv( S0-S1) :- S0 = [sings|S1].
```

The first set of clauses defines the complex parse rules. The second set of clauses defines the lexicon, basically a word dictionary of nouns, verbs, and determiners. Only the words needed in the previous example are given, but other words can easily be added by including more rules in the program. Examples of queries to this program are:

```
?- s([john,loves,the,girl,who,sings]).
    yes
?- s([john,loves,the,girl,who,loves,john]).
    yes
?- s([john,loves]).
    no
```

The final query fails because we did not define "loves" as an intransitive verb. Most Prolog systems, Aurora included, define a special syntax for implementing definite clause grammars (DCGs) of this type. The previous code can be rewritten more succinctly as:

```
s --> np, vp.
np --> det, n, optrel.
np --> pn.
vp --> tv, np.
vp --> iv.
optrel --> [].
optrel --> [who], vp.

pn  --> [john].
tv  --> [loves].
det --> [the].
n   --> [girl].
iv  --> [sings].
```

The system translates this syntax into standard Prolog by including the difference lists and incorporating the terminals (in square brackets).

As described DCGs would be of little use. Their key importance lies in the ability to include additional arguments that are unified in the standard Prolog manner. For example, to force nouns and verbs to *agree in number*, we add a new argument that the word in the lexicon binds to either **singular** or **plural**:

```
s --> np(N), vp(N).
np(N) --> det(N), n(N), optrel.
np(N) --> pn(N).
vp(N) --> tv(N), np(_).
vp(N) --> iv(N).

pn(singular)   --> [john].
tv(singular)   --> [loves].
tv(plural)     --> [love].
det(singular)  --> [the].
det(plural)    --> [the].
n(singular)    --> [girl].
n(plural)      --> [girls].
iv(singular)   --> [sings].
iv(plural)     --> [sing].
```

Examples of queries to this new program are:

```
?- s([the,girls,who,sing,love,john]).
   yes
?- s([john,loves,the,girls,who,loves,john]).
   no
```

Additional arguments can be introduced for other purposes as well, for instance to create parse trees.

In this exercise, we wish to explore the potential for speedup of single-sentence parsing in the OR-parallel execution of DCGs. Extend the simple DCG given to enforce verb-noun agreement in person (first, second, or third person), and enlarge the lexicon to permit elaborate sentences. What is the best way to execute this program in OR-parallel? Invent a correct (but very long!) sentence to illustrate that the program can achieve speedup on two PEs.

Exercise 104 Write a parallel parser in FGHC and compare its performance with the previous Prolog parser. One idea is a "bottom-up" parser, as described by Y. Matsumoto [83].

Exercise 105 Implement Waltz's algorithm in OR-parallel Prolog as a DCG. Measure the speedups of the program on multiple PEs for the test data shown in Figure 10.11.

Exercise 106 Solve the famous calculation ciphers shown below in Prolog and OR-parallel Prolog. Each letter represents a unique decimal digit in each cipher

```
      S  E  N  D              D  O  N  A  L  D
   +  M  O  R  E           +  G  E  R  A  L  D
   ───────────             ──────────────────
   M  O  N  E  Y           R  O  B  E  R  T
```

(the two problems are independent). Is there any exploitable OR-parallelism when searching for a single solution? How about when searching for all solutions? A CHIP program is given in Van Hentenryck [140], and a Prolog-III program is given in Colmerauer [32].

Exercise 107 Generalize the techniques you developed in Exercises 106 and 109 to solve general calculation ciphers. Solve the two multiplication problems shown below. Each letter represents a unique decimal digit in each cipher, and '0' is zero. The two problems are independent. Is there any exploitable parallelism? Can you attain real speedups?

```
          D  C  A                     C  E  D  B
       *  E  D  B                  *  G  0  H  A
       ──────────                  ─────────────
       D  D  0  A                  C  G  F  0  C
       C  B  0                     A  F  I  H
    F  E  A                  I  C  D  B  E
    ────────────            ───────────────────
    H  0  G  0  A            I  C  F  0  E  E  H  C
```

Exercise 108 Solve the SEND + MORE = MONEY problem in FGHC with the layered-stream method. Can you obtain reasonable speedups?

Exercise 109 Solve the SEND + MORE = MONEY problem in FGHC with a paradigm other than layered streams. Can you achieve better performance than the layered-stream program?

Exercise 110 (Simple Image Processing) We have not discussed "regular" problems in this book because such algorithms have been analyzed extensively in the literature (e.g., Fox *et al.* [50]). In addition, regular problems involving arrays can benefit greatly from destructive assignment or, to put it another way: without *very* efficient garbage collection, parallel logic programming systems cannot manipulate large arrays without severe overheads. This exercise, derived from Winston and Horn [147], concerns regular array manipulations in image processing that offer a great deal of parallelism because of the independence of the subtasks. We explore both the formulation of the problem in parallel logic programs and the memory management overheads.

Consider a two-dimensional binary array P that depicts an image. For simplicity we assume P is square, with m rows and m columns and a total size of m^2 bits. $P_{i,j}$ denotes the bit in row i and column j of array P. We define the row, column and diagonal projections of the image as:

$$r_j = \sum_{i=1}^{m} P_{i,j}$$

$$c_j = \sum_{i=1}^{m} P_{j,i}$$

$$d_k = \sum_{i=1}^{k-1} P_{i,k-i} = \sum_{i=1}^{k-1} P_{k-i,i}$$

where index $1 \leq j \leq m$ and $2 \leq k \leq 2m$. These projections are vectors characterizing the weight in each row, column, and diagonal in the image. The total "weight" of the image is therefore

$$w = \sum_{i=1}^{m} r_i = \sum_{i=1}^{m} c_i = \sum_{k=2}^{2m} d_k.$$

The center of the image, (i_0, j_0), can then be calculated as

$$i_0 = \frac{1}{w} \sum_{i=1}^{m} i r_i$$

$$j_0 = \frac{1}{w} \sum_{i=1}^{m} i c_i.$$

The axis along which the image has the least inertia is called the image's *orientation*. Intuitively the orientation corresponds to the lengthwise axis in an elongated image. The orientation can be characterized by the angle of inclination θ_0 of the axis of least inertia. We can use the projections and the center coordinates to calculate the orientation quite efficiently (a derivation of these formula is given in Winston and Horn):

$$\theta_0 = \frac{1}{2} arctan(\frac{c}{a-b})$$

where

$$a = \sum_{i=1}^{m} i^2 r_i - w{i_0}^2$$

$$b = \sum_{i=1}^{m} i^2 c_i - w{j_0}^2$$

$$c = 2\sum_{k=2}^{2m} k^2 d_k - a - b - 2w i_0 j_0.$$

Write Prolog and FGHC programs to calculate (i_0, j_0, a, b, c) characterizing an image. Use `bigfunctor/3` and `bigarg/3`, defined in Section 12.1, to manage a large image array, where each element is either '0' or '1'. Measure the speedup of your programs on multiple PEs for various images of single objects.

11 Semigroup and Pascal's Triangle

Kappa mo kawanagare.
(Even a kappa sometimes drowns.)

old Japanese proverb

Some problems apparently have no exploitable parallelism. For example, determinate problems often have little (or no) OR-parallelism. Some types of constraint propagation problems (such as Waltz's algorithm) are rather sequential because constraints propagate via nearest neighbors. Simulation problems often require a discrete time step wherein all updates to the state are synchronized, thus reducing parallelism. The list goes on and on. It is important to face up to these problems and attempt to squeeze parallel solutions out of them. This exercise is not academic: the techniques devised can then be used to enhance the performance of munificently parallel applications.

In this chapter we tackle two determinate problems; each has a single solution. The Semigroup Problem computes a large group of vectors from an initial small group of vectors by repeated piecewise multiplication and comparison. Pascal's Triangle is composed of the coefficients of $(x + y)^n$ for $n \geq 0$. The binomial coefficients of degree n are computed by adding successive pairs of coefficients of degree $n - 1$. Although these problems are somewhat artificial, they illustrate how things can go wrong with parallelism and how to fix things when they do go wrong.

We present two programming techniques that prove useful in improving the speedup of parallel logic programs: *granularity collection* in OR-parallel systems and *removal of synchronization points* in AND-parallel systems. Although parallel Prolog is meant to hide parallel execution worries from the programmer, if the *natural* granularity of the program is too small, performance suffers greatly. By rearranging code to allow the efficient placement of a branchpoint, e.g., via a `parallel` procedure call, we can alleviate some of this overhead, achieving real speedup.

Removal of synchronization points in a committed-choice language is the recoding of a problem to allow streams to flow freely without causing suspensions. This recoding increases the throughput of the processes comprising the program, thus increasing speed and speedup. Removal of synchronization points, like granularity collection, is very much a programming art.

•	1	2	3	4	5
1	1	1	1	1	1
2	1	2	1	4	1
3	1	1	3	1	5
4	1	1	4	1	2
5	1	5	1	3	1

Table 11.1
Multiplication Rule Used in the Semigroup Problem

11.1 Semigroup

A semigroup, S, is computed from a binary operation; let's call it multiplication •
over a set of generators G. The basic idea is to initialize the semigroup to the set of
generators and then perform all pairwise multiplications within the semigroup to
produce new products. All as-yet-unseen products are appended to the semigroup.
All pairwise multiplications are again performed, and so on. When no new products
are calculated, the semigroup is complete.

The programs discussed in this section use the multiplication rule given in Table 11.1 [44] (integers are used to represent the elements). For example, if $G =
\{(32)(44)\}$, then one product of these generator tuples is $(32) • (44) = (11)$. Mul-
tiplying in the other direction: $(44) • (32) = (41)$. Other pairwise multiplications
within G are $(32) • (32) = (32)$ which already exists and $(44) • (44) = (11)$ which
has just been computed. Thus two new products have been computed: (11) and
(41). To cut a long story short, only one remaining product creates a new tuple:
$(32) • (44) = (14)$. Thus the semigroup of G has five tuples.

As noted by N. Ichiyoshi [132], the above algorithm can be improved in two ways.
First, pairwise multiplications need only be performed in *one direction* (even if the
operator is not commutative!). Second, the initial set of generators forms a basis
for the group, so that as-yet-unseen products need not be multiplied by *all* current
members of the semigroup, but *only by the set of generators*.

Initially let $S := G$ and $R := G$. The cross-product of R and G is calculated:
$T := R \times G$.[1] T is filtered so that only as-yet-unseen (in S) products remain. Now
T is appended to S, and $R := T$. Again, we calculate the cross-product of R and
G, and so on. When T is empty after filtering, the computation has terminated.

In the programs presented, we begin with a set of four generator tuples, each
forty elements in length:

---

[1]R and G are sets of tuples so that this cross-product implies multiplication (•) of all pairs
selected one from each set.

```
{1,1,1,1,1,2,2,2,2,2,3,3,3,3,3,4,4,4,4,4,
 5,5,5,5,5,3,3,3,3,3,5,5,5,5,5,4,4,4,4,4}

{1,2,3,4,5,1,2,3,4,5,1,2,3,4,5,1,2,3,4,5,
 1,2,3,4,5,1,2,3,4,5,1,3,2,4,5,1,2,3,4,5}

{1,1,1,1,1,2,2,2,2,2,3,3,3,3,3,5,5,5,5,5,
 4,4,4,4,4,2,2,2,2,2,4,4,4,4,4,3,3,3,3,3}

{1,2,3,5,4,1,2,3,5,4,1,2,3,5,4,1,2,3,5,4,
 1,2,3,5,4,1,2,3,4,5,1,2,3,5,4,1,2,3,5,4}
```

Thus the fundamental multiplication operation involves forty binary operations, each of which is a multiplication-table look-up. There are 309 generated tuples in this semigroup, plus the initial kernel of four generators, giving 313 tuples in the solution.

Prolog Versions

The Prolog programs presented here are based on the original code written by R. Overbeek [44]. The sequential version of this program was in fact written *after* the parallel version. However, the sequential version is simpler, thus better to explain first. One could actually write this program first and evolve it into the parallel version with a method of granularity collecting, as discussed later in this section.

All of the programs use the following *hash list* representation of the initial generators:

```
kernel(K) :-
    K = [[1833472791, 1,1,1,1,1,2,2,2,2,2,3,3,3,3,3,4,4,4,4,4,
                      5,5,5,5,5,3,3,3,3,3,5,5,5,5,5,4,4,4,4,4],
         [-590019130, 1,2,3,4,5,1,2,3,4,5,1,2,3,4,5,1,2,3,4,5,
                      1,2,3,4,5,1,2,3,4,5,1,3,2,4,5,1,2,3,4,5],
         [1084198104, 1,1,1,1,1,2,2,2,2,2,3,3,3,3,3,5,5,5,5,5,
                      4,4,4,4,4,2,2,2,2,2,4,4,4,4,4,3,3,3,3,3],
         [1154844798, 1,2,3,5,4,1,2,3,5,4,1,2,3,5,4,1,2,3,5,4,
                      1,2,3,5,4,1,2,3,4,5,1,2,3,5,4,1,2,3,5,4]]].
```

The first argument in each tuple is a hash key calculated from the subsequent tuple elements. This key permits a fast comparison between two tuples, a necessary operation when determining if a newly-produced tuple is already in the partial semigroup.

11.1.1   Sequential Prolog

The top-level goal, `go/1`, returns the list of semigroup tuples. First, two data structures are initialized: `Kernel`, the list of initial tuples, and `Tree`, the 2–3 tree

corresponding to these tuples. Initially, the tuples to be processed are the kernel
tuples. The initial 2–3 tree is created by **extendTree/3** which incrementally adds
each tuple to a **nil** tree with **add23/3**, defined later in this section. The main
workhorse is **loop/6**, which computes the solution in **Ans**.

```
go(Ans) :-
    initial(Kernel,Tree),
    loop(Kernel,[],Tree,Kernel,Ans,Kernel).

initial(Kernel,Tree) :-
    kernel(Kernel),
    extendTree(Kernel,nil,Tree).

extendTree([],T,T).
extendTree([E|Es],T0,T2) :-
    add23(T0,E,T1),
    extendTree(Es,T1,T2).
```

Procedure **loop(Cand,Sos,Tree,Hbg,Ans,Kernel)** returns the final semigroup in
Ans given a set of generators in **Kernel**. Argument **Cand** is the list of candidate
tuples that need to be multiplied by the kernel (but have already been appended to
the partial semigroup). Initially **Cand** is set to **Kernel**. Argument **Sos** is a second
set of candidates similar to **Cand** (in fact, **Sos** is not strictly necessary, and can
be avoided by adding new candidates directly to the tail of **Cand**). Initially **Sos**
is empty. Argument **Hbg** is the partial semigroup (list) and **Tree** is the 2–3 tree
corresponding to **Hbg**; both are initialized with the kernel.

The semigroup is complete when both candidate lists are empty. If only the first
candidate list is empty, the first list is replaced by the second candidate list and
computation continues. Otherwise, the next tuple is chosen from the candidate list
and multiplied by the kernel in **loop2/8**. The remaining candidate tuples are then
processed.

```
loop([],[],_,F,F,_) :- !.
loop([],Sos,Tree,Hbg,F,K) :-
    loop(Sos,[],Tree,Hbg,F,K).
loop([E|Es],Sos,Tree,Hbg,F,K) :-
    loop2(K,E,Tree,Tree1,Sos,Sos1,Hbg,Hbg1),
    loop(Es,Sos1,Tree1,Hbg1,F,K).
```

Procedure **loop2/8** multiplies the kernel by a single tuple. Each product tuple, **M**,
is checked for inclusion in the partial semigroup. The check is performed on the 2–3
tree (for speed) with **acc23/2**. If the product tuple already exists, then the copy is
discarded and computation continues. If the product is new, it is inserted into the
2–3 tree with **add23/3** and into the new candidate list and partial semigroup list.

```
loop2(    [],_,Tree,Tree, Sos,Sos, Hbg,Hbg).
loop2([K|Ks],E,Tree,TreeF,Sos,SosF,Hbg,HbgF) :-
    mult(K,E,M),
    (acc23(Tree,M) ->
        loop2(Ks,E,Tree,TreeF,Sos,SosF,Hbg,HbgF)
    ;
        add23(Tree,M,Tree1),
        loop2(Ks,E,Tree1,TreeF,[M|Sos],SosF,[M|Hbg],HbgF)
    ).
```

The multiplication procedure is given below. Procedure `mult(W1,W2,P)` multiples tuples W1 and W2 to produce tuple P. An informal specification of the program is given in Figure 11.1.

```
mult([_|X],[_|Y],[Key|Zs]) :-
    mult(X,Y,Zs,0,0,Key).

mult([], [], [], Key, I, A) :- A is I+Key*3.
mult([X|Xs], [Y|Ys], [Z|Zs], Key, I, A) :-
    NewKey is I+Key*3,
    m(X, Y, Z),
    mult(Xs, Ys, Zs, NewKey, Z, A).

m(2,1,1):-!. m(3,1,1):-!. m(4,1,1):-!. m(5,1,1):-!. m(1,1,1):-!.
m(2,2,2):-!. m(3,2,1):-!. m(4,2,1):-!. m(5,2,5):-!. m(1,2,1):-!.
m(2,3,1):-!. m(3,3,3):-!. m(4,3,4):-!. m(5,3,1):-!. m(1,3,1):-!.
m(2,4,4):-!. m(3,4,1):-!. m(4,4,1):-!. m(5,4,3):-!. m(1,4,1):-!.
m(2,5,1):-!. m(3,5,5):-!. m(4,5,2):-!. m(5,5,1):-!. m(1,5,1):-!.
```

The hash key is calculated by the equation:

$$H_0 = 0$$
$$H_i = E_i + 3H_{i-1}$$

where E_i is element i of the tuple. This hash function is a nice one for the given data, giving only five synonyms in 313 tuples. The hash key is placed as the first argument for a good reason. The 2–3 tree code below compares tuples when searching and inserting them into the 2–3 tree. Tuple comparison requires pairwise comparison of elements *in order*. Thus if we can create a unique integer as the first argument of `tuple`, tuple comparison becomes very efficient, with *no* changes necessary to the following 2–3 tree algorithm.

The 2–3 tree is not strictly necessary — it is used simply to speedup tuple lookups. A hash table could be used as an alternative, or the `Hbg` list could be scanned each time. The 2–3 tree is interfaced through `add23/3` and `acc23/2`. The code shown in Figure 11.2 is taken from Bratko [16], where its derivation is carefully discussed.

Procedure: `go(Ts)`
  − Ts: list of tuples

Relation: `Ts` contains all tuples in the semigroup generated by the initial tuples specified by `kernel/1`. A tuple is a list of integer elements, where the first element is a hash key.

Procedure: `add23(Tin, E, Tout)`
  + Tin: 2–3 tree of tuples   + E: tuple   − Tout: 2–3 tree of tuples

Relation: If `Tin` does not contain tuple `E` then `Tout` is tree `Tin` extended with E. Otherwise this call fails.

Procedure: `acc23(Tin, E)`
  + Tin: 2–3 tree of tuples   + E: tuple

Relation: If tree `Tin` does not contain `E` then this call fails.

Procedure: `loop(Cand, Sos, Tree, Hbg, Ans, Kernel)`
  + Cand: list of tuples   + Hbg: list of tuples
  + Sos: list of tuples   + Ans: list of tuples
  + Tree: 2–3 tree of tuples   + Kernel: list of tuples

Relation: `Ans` is the semigroup created by extending `Hbg` by the as-yet-unseen products of `Kernel` with candidates in both `Cand` and `Sos`.

Preconditions: Initially Sos is empty, `Cand=Hbg=Kernel`, the set of generators specified by `kernel/1`. Tree holds the same tuples as in `Hbg`, but in 2–3 tree form.

Procedure: `loop2(Kernel, E, Tree, Tree1, Sos, Sos1, Hbg, Hbg1)`
  + Kernel: list of tuples   + Sos: list of tuples
  + E: tuple   − Sos1: list of tuples
  + Tree: 2–3 tree of tuples   + Hbg: list of tuples
  − Tree1: 2–3 tree of tuples   − Hbg1: list of tuples

Relation: All as-yet-unseen products of E with tuples in `Kernel` are added to `Tree`, `Sos` and `Hbg`, to form `Tree1` `Sos1` and `Hbg1`.

Procedure: `mult(T1,T2,T3)`
  + T1: tuple   + T2: tuple   − T3: tuple

Relation: `T3` is the product of `T1` and `T2` according to multiplication rules given in `m/3`.

Figure 11.1
Informal Specification of Prolog Semigroup (Sequential)

```
acc23(l(X),              X) :-           !.
acc23(n2(T1,M,_),        X) :- M @> X, !, acc23(T1,X).
acc23(n2(_,_,T2),        X) :-           !, acc23(T2,X).
acc23(n3(T1,M2,_,_,_),X) :- M2 @> X, !, acc23(T1,X).
acc23(n3(_,_,T2,M3,_),X) :- M3 @> X, !, acc23(T2,X).
acc23(n3(_,_,_,_,T3), X) :-              acc23(T3,X).

add23(Tree,X,Tree1) :-
    ins(Tree,X,Tree1).
add23(Tree,X,n2(T1,M2,T2)) :-
    ins(Tree,X,T1,M2,T2).

ins(nil,X,l(X)) :- !.
ins(n2(T1,M,T2),X,n2(NT1,M,T2)) :- M @> X,
    ins(T1,X,NT1).
ins(n2(T1,M,T2),X,n3(NT1a,Mb,NT1b,M,T2)) :- M @> X, !,
    ins(T1,X,NT1a,Mb,NT1b).
ins(n2(T1,M,T2),X,n2(T1,M,NT2)) :- X @> M,
    ins(T2,X,NT2).
ins(n2(T1,M,T2),X,n3(T1,M,NT2a,Mb,NT2b)) :- X @> M, !,
    ins(T2,X,NT2a,Mb,NT2b).
ins(n3(T1,M2,T2,M3,T3),X,n3(NT1,M2,T2,M3,T3)) :- M2 @> X, !,
    ins(T1,X,NT1).
ins(n3(T1,M2,T2,M3,T3),X,n3(T1,M2,NT2,M3,T3)) :- X @> M2, M3 @> X, !,
    ins(T2,X,NT2).
ins(n3(T1,M2,T2,M3,T3),X,n3(T1,M2,T2,M3,NT3)) :- X @> M3,
    ins(T3,X,NT3).

ins(l(A),X,l(A),X,l(X)) :- X @> A, !.
ins(l(A),X,l(X),A,l(A)) :- A @> X, !.
ins(n3(T1,M2,T2,M3,T3),X,n2(NT1a,Mb,NT1b),M2,n2(T2,M3,T3)) :- M2 @> X, !,
    ins(T1,X,NT1a,Mb,NT1b).
ins(n3(T1,M2,T2,M3,T3),X,n2(T1,M2,NT2a),Mb,n2(NT2b,M3,T3)) :-
    X @> M2, M3 @> X, !,
    ins(T2,X,NT2a,Mb,NT2b).
ins(n3(T1,M2,T2,M3,T3),X,n2(T1,M2,T2),M3,n2(NT3a,Mb,NT3b)) :- X @> M3,
    ins(T3,X,NT3a,Mb,NT3b).
```

Figure 11.2
2–3 Tree Access Code (modified from Bratko)

The version here differs only in that cuts have been added to remove all unnecessary choicepoints. The @>/2 builtin compares two Prolog terms, given an ordering. We don't really care what the ordering is, only that we use it to sort the tuples.

We experimented with two versions of the sequential program: with and without acc23 in loop2. The acc23 call is unnecessary, because add23 will *fail* if the item to be added is already in the tree. Thus, with minor modification to loop2, acc23 can be eliminated. However, eliminating acc23 increases execution time by 14%! The reason is that add23 is an expensive way to check for membership because of its two nondeterminate clauses (see Bratko for discussion).

11.1.2 Granularity Collection

The parallel program top level is derived from the sequential version. Note that, in the sequential program, all the multiplications are performed in procedure loop2. Procedure loop2 is serialized, however, doing one multiplication per iteration. Our goal is to collect the granularity inherent in loop2 into a single chunk of work that can be executed in OR-parallel.

We begin the parallel derivation with loop/5. Procedure loop(Sos,Tree,Hbg, F, Kernel) is given inputs Kernel, the kernel tuples and Sos, the list of candidate tuples (they are now ready to be included in the semigroup, but have not yet been used to generate further candidate tuples). Argument Tree is the 2–3 tree holding the current semigroup tuples, Hbg is the current (partial) list of semigroup tuples, and F is the final output list of semigroup tuples.

If the candidate list is empty, then the current list of semigroup tuples is the *complete* list of tuples. Otherwise, the state, Sos, Tree, and Hbg, must be reduced to a further state, NewSos, NewTree, and NewHbg. The reduction is guaranteed to terminate, as explained below.

```
go(Ans) :-
    initial(Kernel,Tree),
    loop(Kernel,Tree,Kernel,Ans,Kernel).

loop([], _, Hbg, Hbg, _) :- !.
loop(Sos, Tree, Hbg, F, Kernel) :-
    findall(Tuple, newTuple(Sos, Kernel, Tree, Tuple), L),
    filter(L, Tree, NewTree, [], NewSos, Hbg, NewHbg),
    loop(NewSos, NewTree, NewHbg, F, Kernel).
```

The state is reduced by first calculating all the tuples generated by the "cross-product" of the candidate tuples, Sos, and the kernel tuples, Kernel. The new candidates, L, are filtered by checking them against the current (partial) semigroup tuples (Tree and Hbg) in filter/7. Procedure filter/7 creates the new state,

`NewSos`, `NewTree`, and `NewHbg`.

The cross-product is calculated by doing a `findall/3` on `newTuple/4`. Procedure `newTuple/4` uses `member/2` to force OR-parallel execution. Tuples from the candidate list and kernel list are selected, multiplied, and checked against the current (partial) semigroup tree.

```
newTuple(L,K,Tree,New) :-
    member(E1,L),
    member(E2,K),
    mult(E2,E1,New),
    \+ acc23(New,Tree).
```

Any product already in the tree is rejected by failing and backtracking. Note, however, that the test uses Prolog negation, i.e., the tree is not modified. We do not choose to insert into the tree here, even if the new product is *not* presently in the tree, because two identical products may be computed concurrently. Thus we still need a filtering phase, as described next. One may think of AND-parallelism wherein processes computing these tuples can lock the tree, add a tuple, and then unlock the tree. This protocol would obviate the need for a subsequent filtering phase. However, the OR-parallel mechanism available to us here is a group of independent processes that cannot share the tree. Thus `newTuple` simply checks the tree, without modifying it.

Procedure `filter/7` tests the new candidates against the partial-semigroup tree to determine valid semigroup tuples. At this stage, if a new candidate is not in the tree, the new candidate is inserted. Procedure `filter(L, Tree, Tree1, Sos, Sos1, Hbg, Hbg1)` has the arguments: L is the list of new candidate tuples to be possibly added to the queue; `Sos`, `Tree`, and `Hbg` are the current state; and `Sos1`, `Tree1`, and `Hbg1` are the next state, after the new candidates L are added. If the new candidate list is empty, then tree and candidate queue remain the same. This is the end of the computation, because the old candidate queue is always empty. If the new candidate list L is not empty, we try to add the head tuple H to the tree. If H can be added (doesn't exist already), then `Tree1` is the new tree and H is added to `Sos0` to get a new candidate list. Otherwise, if H cannot be added because it exists already, then the new tree and candidate list are simply the old tree and candidate list. The final new tree and candidate list are computed recursively.

```
filter(   [], Tree, Tree,  Sos, Sos,  Hbg, Hbg).
filter([H|T], Tree, TreeF, Sos, SosF, Hbg, HbgF) :-
    add23(Tree,H,Tree1), !,
    filter(T, Tree1, TreeF, [H|Sos], SosF, [H|Hbg], HbgF).
filter([_|T], Tree,  TreeF, Sos, SosF, Hbg, HbgF) :-
    filter(T, Tree,  TreeF, Sos, SosF, Hbg, HbgF).
```

That concludes the main body of the program. Note that, if the `findall` (in `loop/5`) returns its list of solutions (new candidates) in an unknown order, then the 2–3 tree may be constructed differently for different runs of the program, or on different numbers of PEs. Thus the reduction count of the program may also differ. An informal specification of the program is given in Figure 11.3. Procedures borrowed from the sequential program are not specified here.

Several factors affect the amount and efficiency of the parallelism exploited by this program. Tuple size affects efficiency: large tuples require large granularity multiplications, therefore parallelism is efficient, i.e., overhead is small. The two calls to `member` that split the OR-parallel branchpoint affect the amount of parallelism. When we unroll these branchpoints, potential parallelism increases with the splitting factor, although exploitable parallelism normally does not increase proportionally because of overheads. An unrolled version of `member` is shown below. Further unrolling does not decrease execution time for this example.

```
:- parallel member/2.

member(H,[H|_]).
member(H,[_,H|T]).
member(H,[_,_,H|T]).
member(H,[_,_,_,H|T]).
member(H,[_,_,_,_|T]) :- member(H,T).
```

In fact, the benefit of unrolling *both* `member`s is unclear. A completely different approach is to avoid `member` altogether and unroll `newTuple` directly, as shown below.

```
:- parallel newTuple/4.

newTuple([E|_],     [K|_],      Tree,New) :- mult(K,E,New),\+acc23(Tree,New).
newTuple([E|_],     [_,K|_],    Tree,New) :- mult(K,E,New),\+acc23(Tree,New).
newTuple([E|_],     [_,_,K|_],Tree,New) :- mult(K,E,New),\+acc23(Tree,New).
newTuple([E|_],     [_,_,_,K],Tree,New) :- mult(K,E,New),\+acc23(Tree,New).
newTuple([_,E|_],   [K|_],      Tree,New) :- mult(K,E,New),\+acc23(Tree,New).
newTuple([_,E|_],   [_,K|_],    Tree,New) :- mult(K,E,New),\+acc23(Tree,New).
newTuple([_,E|_],   [_,_,K|_],Tree,New) :- mult(K,E,New),\+acc23(Tree,New).
newTuple([_,E|_],   [_,_,_,K],Tree,New) :- mult(K,E,New),\+acc23(Tree,New).
newTuple([_,_,E|_],[K|_],      Tree,New) :- mult(K,E,New),\+acc23(Tree,New).
newTuple([_,_,E|_],[_,K|_],    Tree,New) :- mult(K,E,New),\+acc23(Tree,New).
newTuple([_,_,E|_],[_,_,K|_],Tree,New) :- mult(K,E,New),\+acc23(Tree,New).
newTuple([_,_,E|_],[_,_,_,K],Tree,New) :- mult(K,E,New),\+acc23(Tree,New).
newTuple([_|Es],    K,          Tree,New) :- newTuple(Es,K,Tree,New).
```

Generally both of the two lists, `Sos` and `Kernel`, can be unrolled any number of times, in an effort to boost the productivity of the branchpoint. Note however

Procedure: go(Ts)
    – Ts: list of tuples

Relation: Ts contains all tuples in the semigroup generated by the initial
    tuples specified by kernel/1. A tuple is a list of integer elements, where
    the first element is a hash key.

Preconditions: kernel/1 describes a non-empty list of initial tuples.

Procedure: loop(Cand, Tree, Hbg, Ans, Kernel)
    + Cand: list of tuples   + Hbg: list of tuples
    + Tree: 2–3 tree of tuples   + Ans: list of tuples
                                  + Kernel: list of tuples

Relation: Ans contains the semigroup created by extending Hbg by the as-
    yet-unseen products of Kernel with Cand.

Preconditions: Initially Cand=Hbg=Kernel, the set of generators specified by
    kernel/1. Tree holds the same tuples as in Hbg, but in 2–3 tree form.

Procedure: newTuple(Ts1, Ts2, Tree, Tout)
    + Ts1: list of tuples   + Tree: 2–3 tree of tuples
    + Ts2: list of tuples   – Tout: tuple

Relation: Tout is the product of some pair of tuples chosen from Ts1 and
    · Ts2. If Tout is already in Tree then this call fails.

Procedure: filter(Ts, Tree, TreeF, Sos, SosF, Hbg, HbgF)
    + Ts: list of tuples   + Sos: list of tuples
    + Tree: 2–3 tree of tuples   – SosF: list of tuples
    – TreeF: 2–3 tree of tuples   + Hbg: list of tuples
                                      – HbgF: list of tuples

Relation: Each as-yet-unseen tuple in Ts is added to Tree, Sos and Hbg to
    form TreeF, SosF and HbgF.

Precondition: Initially Sos is empty and Tree holds the same tuples as in
    Hbg, but in 2–3 tree form.

Figure 11.3
Informal Specification of Prolog Semigroup (Granularity Collection)

that, unlike an OR-tree search problem, here the branches are just stubs (each a tuple multiplication) with or without unrolling. Thus extensive unrolling, as shown above, does not significantly affect performance.

FGHC Versions

Three FGHC versions of the Semigroup program are presented in this section. The first version introduces the method of *pipelined filters*, similar in concept to that used in the Sieve of Eratosthenes (Section 3.5) to gather prime numbers. The pipeline here is more complex because the generator is part of the pipeline itself, i.e., the pipe output feeds the pipe input. This pipeline requires a special "book-end" method to detect termination of the algorithm. The second program presented corrects the inefficiencies of the first program by increasing the throughput of the pipeline, i.e., decreasing its sequentiality. The bookend method is further optimized. Finally, no matter how efficient the pipeline becomes, its performance is fundamentally limited by the linear complexity of checking each tuple in line. The third program alleviates this drawback by introducing a *binary tree filter* that has logarithmic complexity.

The FGHC programs use the same tuple representation, `kernel/1`, as the Prolog programs. The multiplication procedure `mult/3` and lookup table `m/3` are also similar.

11.1.3 Pipelined Generator/Filters

The first program is a modified version of the original written by N. Ichiyoshi [122]. The basic idea of the program is to create a pipeline of filters, with `gen_g/5`, one filter corresponding to each new tuple in the semigroup. Initially this pipeline has four tuples corresponding to the generators. In addition, a group of messages, created by `gen_gen`, is sent through the pipeline stream.

```
go(Out) :-
    kernel(Gens),
    gen_g(Gens, Gin, Fin, Gout, Fout),
    gen_gen(Gens, Gin-NGin),
    connect(Gout, Fin),
    ends(Fout, _, _, NGin, Gens, Out-[]).

gen_g([X|Xs], G0, F0, G, F) :-
    g(G0, F0, G1, F1, X),
    gen_g(Xs, G1, F1, G, F).
gen_g([], G0, F0, G, F) :- G0=G, F0=F.
```

Each tuple in the pipeline begins as a `g/5` process — during this phase, the tuple multiplies itself by tuples received as messages. The message stream holds the new semigroup tuples, delimited by two bookends: **begin** and **end**. When the new group ends, the **g/5** process has done its job and changes into an **f/3** filter process. The **f/3** filter remains until program termination, simply checking oncoming product tuples for a match (in which case the oncoming tuple is discarded).

```
g([gen(X,P-P0)|Gin1], Fin, Gout, Fout, E) :-
    mult(E, X, EX),
    P0 = [EX|P1],
    Gout = [gen(X,P,P1)|Gout1],
    g(Gin1, Fin, Gout1, Fout, E).
g([begin|Gin1], Fin, Gout, Fout, E) :-
    Gout = [begin|Gout1],
    g(Gin1, Fin, Gout1, Fout, E).
g([end|Gin1], Fin, Gout, Fout, E) :-
    Gout = [end|Gin1],
    f(Fin, Fout, E).

f([],F1,_) :- F1=[].          % die and kill others...
f([E|F0],F1,E) :- f(F0,F1,E).
f([X|F0],F1,E) :- otherwise | F1 = [X|F2], f(F0,F2,E).
```

Note that the **otherwise** in the last clause of **f/3** is included to improve execution performance. The second clause tests whether the filter's tuple is the same as the incoming message tuple. Although general unification is used, unification will usually terminate after comparing the hash keys. The **otherwise** avoids performing the unification twice. It is likely that a sophisticated compiler could remove the second test automatically, obviating the need for the user to use **otherwise** explicitly.

The messages sent through the pipeline always correspond to the generator tuples. In addition to being delimited by **begin** and **end** messages, each tuple is wrapped in a **gen/3** structure. Structure **gen(Tuple,S)** contains the tuple hash list, **Tuple**, and a difference list, **S**, containing the products formed by multiplying this tuple by the pipeline tuples (in **g/5**). Procedure **gen_gen/2** generates the messages from the generator tuples.

```
gen_gen(Gens, G0-G) :-
    G0 = [begin|G1],
    gen_gen1(Gens, G1-G).

gen_gen1([X|Xs], G0-G) :-
    G0 = [gen(X,P-P)|G1],
    gen_gen1(Xs, G1-G).
gen_gen1([], G0-G) :-
    G0 = [end|G].
```

All the new products are included together as elements of a single stream with connect/2. Procedure connect/2 appends the series of difference lists in the gen/2 structures in the manner given in Section 2.1.5 — by binding the tail of each to the subsequent difference list. The process of connecting the products serializes the computation. For instance, if connect/2 is not scheduled in a timely manner, the new products cannot be filtered back through the pipeline as fast as they are created.

```
connect([gen(_,P0-P)|Gs],F)  :- F=P0,           connect(Gs,P).
connect([begin          |Gs],F)  :- F=[begin|Fs], connect(Gs,Fs).
connect([end            |Gs],F)  :- F=[end|Gs].
```

The last and most mysterious procedure to be described is end/6, which feeds the output of the pipe, via connect/2, back into its input. One end/6 process sits at the end of the pipeline monitoring the stream of filtered messages. If end/6 receives two bookends back-to-back (first clause), then it initiates program termination because the pipeline is complete.

```
ends([begin,end|_],_,_,Gin,OGin,_,O1-O2) :-  Gin=[],OGin=[],O1=O2.
ends([begin,X|Fout2],_,_,OGin,Gens,Out) :- X \= end |
    gen_gen(Gens,NGin0-NGin),
    ends([X|Fout2],NGin0,NGin,OGin,Gens,Out).
ends([end|Fout1],Gout,Gin,OGin,Gens,Out) :-
    connect(Gout,OGin),
    ends(Fout1,_,_,Gin,Gens,Out).
ends([X|Fout1],Gout,Gin,OGin,Gens,O1-O3) :- otherwise |
    O1=[X|O2],
    g(Gout,Fout1,NewGout,NewFout,X),
    ends(NewFout,NewGout,Gin,OGin,Gens,O2-O3).
```

The second and third clauses of end/6 deal with the bookkeeping that becomes necessary when encountering a begin or end singleton, respectively. For a begin, a new message stream, NGin0-NGin, is created with gen_gen/3, but not immediately used. For an end, a new connect/2 is spawned to attach the pipeline output (consisting of new products that haven't been filtered yet) back into the pipeline's input.

Tuple messages are processed in the last clause of end/6. For each message, now a new addition to the partial semigroup, a g/5 process is created between the end of the pipeline and the end/6 process. This addition allows subsequent candidates to be filtered by previous products *in the same group*. The new message list (of the generators), created previously when a begin message was seen, is fed through the *first* inserted g/5 process. The new g/5 processes have linked D-lists, Gout-NewGout, so the message stream will pass through all of them, generating a new set of candidate products.

This program is interesting in many aspects, not the least of which is its difficulty to understand! Subsequent versions of the program show improvement, not only in performance, but also in clarity. We defer giving an informal specification of the program until the final revision is explained.

11.1.4 Improving the Pipeline Throughput

As mentioned, one problem in the above program is the unnecessary serialization or synchronization points. We now lessen the serialization by carefully rewriting the code to allow each candidate tuple immediately to flow directly to the filters. Procedure gen_gen/3 is no longer needed—we pass the raw tuples directly down the stream. By issuing the new products directly into the tail of spawn/3's input stream, we obviate the need for connect/2. Note also that the g/3 and f/3 processes are spawned together, avoiding unnecessary synchronization. The strange binding of S0 in the fourth clause of spawn/3 is to skip four slots in the candidate stream for the four kernel products. This removes any synchronization with the recursive call to spawn. The code can (should) be generalized to skip as many slots as kernel elements.

```
go(Out) :-
    kernel(K),
    append([begin|K],[end|R],S),
    spawn(S,R,Out-[]).

spawn([begin,end|_], S0, T0-T1) :- T0=T1, S0=[].
spawn([begin,X|Xs],  S0, T) :- X \= end |
    S0 = [begin|S1],
    spawn([X|Xs],S1,T).
spawn([end|Xs],S0,T) :-
    S0=[end|S1],
    spawn(Xs,S1,T).
spawn([X|Xs0],S0,T0-T2) :- otherwise |
    kernel(K),
    T0 = [X|T1],                    % send output
    S0 = [_,_,_,_|S1],              % skip kernel elements
    g(K,X,S0),
    f(Xs0,Xs1,X),
    spawn(Xs1,S1,T1-T2).

g([],_,_).
g([K|Ks],E,[P|Ps]) :-
    g(Ks,E,Ps),
    mult(K,E,P).
```

We can simplify the optimized program while noticing that only one bookend is really necessary. Instead of checking for begin followed immediately by end, we

use only **end** and a flag to indicate if two **ends** fall back-to-back. This modification
does not increase speed, but is prettier. The new, entire program is listed below.

```
go(Out) :-
    kernel(K),
    append(K,[end|R],S),
    spawn(S,R,Out-[],_).

spawn([end|Xs],S0,T,tuple) :-
    S0=[end|S1],
    spawn(Xs,S1,T,end).
spawn([end|Xs],S0,T0-T1,end) :- T0=T1, S0=[].
spawn([X|Xs0],S0,T0-T2,_) :- otherwise |
    kernel(K),
    T0 = [X|T1],
    S0 = [_,_,_,_|S1],
    g(K,X,S0),
    f(Xs0,Xs1,X),
    spawn(Xs1,S1,T1-T2,tuple).
```

In the single-bookend version, a flag is set as **tuple** or **end**, depending on whether
the previous message was a tuple or a bookend, respectively. When an **end** message
is received, if the flag is set as **tuple**, then we continue processing. Otherwise, if
the flag is set as **end** and an **end** message is received, the algorithm terminates.

This program still suffers from the handicap of a long pipeline of filters. On a
single processor the pipeline requires a linear number of checks, whereas the 2–3
tree in Prolog requires only a logarithmic number of checks. This observation is
confirmed by execution timings for the given data, where Prolog's advantage on
one PE is a factor of 6.7 in speed; but this advantage decreases to only 4.0 on eight
PEs. Ideally we would like a 2–3 tree in the FGHC program also; however, we
settled for a binary tree filter and it proved quite sufficient.

11.1.5 Binary Hash Tree Filter

The tree filter introduced in this section is an unbalanced binary tree containing
the tuples. Measurements presented in the next section show that even this simple
data structure is a great improvement over the previous pipeline filter. First we
slightly modify the definition of a tuple. Here a tuple is K-T where K is the hash
key and T is a list of elements.

The unbalanced binary hash tree code is given in Figure 11.4. A node, containing
a bucket B of tuples and its hash key X, is comprised of one of four types of processes:
leaf (no children), right-child only, left-child only, and with both right and left
children. A node process responds to four types of messages: []—kill yourself,
m(Y,C,S)—check/insert tuple C with hash key Y, out(S0,S)—output your value,

```
% leaf node (node with no child nodes)
t([],_,_).
t([m(Y,C,S) |T],X,B) :- X =:= Y | insertBucket(B,B,C,B1,S), t(T,X,B1).
t([m(Y,C,S) |T],X,B) :-   X < Y | gen(C,S), tr(T,X,B,R), t(R,Y,[C]).
t([m(Y,C,S) |T],X,B) :-   Y < X | gen(C,S), t(L,Y,[C]), tl(T,X,B,L).
t([out(S0,S)|T],X,B) :- send(B,S0-S), t(T,X,B).
t([end(S0,S)|T],X,B) :- S0=[end|S], t(T,X,B).


% node with right child only
tr([],_,_,R) :-  R = [].
tr([m(Y,C,S) |T],X,B,R) :- X =:= Y | insertBucket(B,B,C,B1,S), tr(T,X,B1,R).
tr([m(Y,C,S) |T],X,B,R) :-   X < Y | tr(T,X,B,R1), R = [m(Y,C,S)|R1].
tr([m(Y,C,S) |T],X,B,R) :-   Y < X | gen(C,S), t(L,Y,[C]), tlr(T,X,B,L,R).
tr([out(S0,S)|T],X,B,R) :- send(B,S0-S1),  tr(T,X,B,R1), R = [out(S1,S)|R1].
tr([end(S0,S)|T],X,B,R) :- S0=[end|S], tr(T,X,B,R).


% node with left child only
tl([],_,_,L) :-  L = [].
tl([m(Y,C,S) |T],X,B,L) :- X =:= Y | insertBucket(B,B,C,B1,S), tl(T,X,B1,L).
tl([m(Y,C,S) |T],X,B,L) :-   X < Y | gen(C,S), tlr(T,X,B,L,R), t(R,Y,[C]).
tl([m(Y,C,S) |T],X,B,L) :-   Y < X | L=[m(Y,C,S)|L1], tl(T,X,B,L1).
tl([out(S0,S)|T],X,B,L) :- L=[out(S0,S1)|L1], tl(T,X,B,L1), send(B,S1-S).
tl([end(S0,S)|T],X,B,L) :- S0=[end|S], tl(T,X,B,L).


% node with both left and right children
tlr([],_,_,L,R) :-  L = [], R = [].
tlr([m(Y,C,S) |T],X,B,L,R) :- X =:= Y |
                             insertBucket(B,B,C,B1,S),tlr(T,X,B1,L,R).
tlr([m(Y,C,S) |T],X,B,L,R) :-   X < Y | tlr(T,X,B,L,R1), R = [m(Y,C,S)|R1].
tlr([m(Y,C,S) |T],X,B,L,R) :-   Y < X | L = [m(Y,C,S)|L1], tlr(T,X,B,L1,R).
tlr([out(S0,S)|T],X,B,L,R) :- L=[out(S0,S1)|L1], tlr(T,X,B,L1,R1),
                             send(B,S1-S2), R=[out(S2,S)|R1].
tlr([end(S0,S)|T],X,B,L,R) :- S0=[end|S], tlr(T,X,B,L,R).

insertBucket([],     B,C,B1,S)    :- B1=[C|B],gen(C,S). % new element
insertBucket([C|_], B,C,B1,S0-S1) :- B1=B, S0=S1.       % already in bucket
insertBucket([_|Cs],B,C,B1,S)     :- otherwise | insertBucket(Cs,B,C,B1,S).

send([],    S0-S1) :- S0=S1.
send([T|Ts],S0-S2) :- S0=[T|S1], send(Ts,S1-S2).
```

Figure 11.4
Unbalanced Binary Hash Tree (FGHC)

340   Chapter 11. Semigroup and Pascal's Triangle

`end(S0,S)`—pass bookend through.

To check/insert the new tuple, the hash key is used to route the message to the appropriate node in the tree. Note that general unification of the entire tuple is avoided until the final bucket check in `insertBucket`. If that tuple already exists, the stream S is shorted (clause 2). If that tuple is new, it is inserted into the tree, and `gen(C,S)` is used to generate the cross-product with the kernel (clause 1). These product tuples are sent down the S stream.

Given the tree code, the new semigroup program, shown below, is even simpler than the previous pipeline program. Again we use a single-bookend termination method. In this case, `spawn` no longer spawns anything, but simply checks for termination. Spawning generators and filters is replaced by sending the tuples as m/3 messages into the tree. The crux of the biscuit is the stream argument of the check/insert message, R0-R1, in the last clause of `spawn`. Similar to the original program, we issue the new products, via R0-R1, into the tail of `spawn`'s own input stream.

```
go(Out) :-
    kernel(K),
    append(K,[end|R],T),
    t(T1,0,[]),
    spawn(T,T1,sawelement,R,Out).

spawn([end|T],T1,sawelement,R0,Out) :-
    T1=[end(R0,R1)|Ts],
    spawn(T,Ts,sawend,R1,Out).
spawn([end|_],T1,sawend,_,Out) :- T1=[out(Out,[])].
spawn([X-Y|T],T1,_,R0,Out) :-
    T1=[m(X,Y,R0-R1)|Ts],
    spawn(T,Ts,sawelement,R1,Out).

gen(X,S) :- kernel(K), g(K,X,S).

g([],_,S0-S1) :- S0=S1.
g([K|Ks],E,S0-S2) :-
    S0=[P|S1],
    g(Ks,E,S1-S2),
    mult(K,E,P).

mult(_-X,Y,Out) :- Out=Key-R, mult(X,Y,R,0,Key,0).
```

The informal specification of the program is given in Figure 11.5 (many of the hash tree process specifications are left as an Exercise).

This final FGHC program is quite elegant and efficient. It matches Prolog for succinctness and surpasses OR-Prolog for exploitable parallelism. Almost all syn-

Procedure: go(Ts)
    − Ts: stream of tuples

Relation: Ts is the semigroup generated from the kernel/1 tuples.

Procedure: t(S, Key, Bucket)
    +S: stream of messages   +Bucket: list of tuples
    +Key: integer

Relation: t/3 is a leaf node in a binary hash tree, acting on the following messages on S: []—terminate, m/3— accept an incoming tuple, out/2—output local value, end/2—pass bookend through stream.

Preconditions: Initially the binary hash tree is created as t(S,0,[]), where S is a stream into the root of the tree.

Procedure: insertBucket(Cs, Bin, E, Bout, S)
    +Cs: list of tuples   +E: tuple   −S: stream of tuples
    +Bin: list of tuples   −Bout: list of tuples

Relation: If E is contained in bucket Cs then Bout=Bin and S is shorted. Otherwise E is prepended to Bin to form Bout, and all products of E with the kernel tuples are sent down S.

Preconditions: Initially Cs=Bin.

Procedure: spawn(Q, S, Flag, R, Out)
    + Q: stream of candidates   −R: tail of candidate stream
    + S: stream of messages   −Out: stream of tuples
    + Flag: atom

Relation: For each candidate tuple on Q, an m/3 message is sent down S into the root of the hash tree. If the candidate is 'end' and Flag = sawelement, then an end/2 message is send down S and Flag is toggled. If Flag = sawend then an out/2 message is send down S and this process is terminated.

Preconditions: Initially Flag = sawelement.

Procedure: gen(E, S)
    +E: tuple   −S: stream of tuples

Relation: S contains the products of E with tuples in kernel/1.

Figure 11.5
Informal Specification of FGHC Semigroup

System	Method	1 PE	2 PE	4 PE	8 PE	12 PE	15 PE
	execution time (seconds)						
Aurora	sequential	34.2					
	granule collect	35.6	20.2	12.7	9.1	8.0	7.5
	+ hash keys	171.2	92.7	59.0	35.6	32.9	30.0
Panda	+ synch. removal	163.6	87.1	45.9	27.4	19.7	18.6
	+ binary tree	37.5	19.1	10.1	5.8	4.2	3.6
	speedup						
Aurora	granule collect	1.0	1.8	2.8	3.9	4.5	4.7
	+ hash keys	1.0	1.8	2.9	4.8	5.2	5.7
Panda	+ synch. removal	1.0	1.9	3.6	6.0	8.3	8.8
	+ binary tree	1.0	2.0	3.7	6.5	8.9	10

Table 11.2
Semigroup (313 Members) Execution Time and Speedup (Symmetry)

System	Method	instr	reduct	back/susp	entries	sec	KEPS
Aurora	sequential		118200	28893	147093	34.2	4
	granule collect	1525955	125869	34169	160038	9.1	18
Panda	binary tree	2106112	123175	3411	126586	5.8	22

Table 11.3
Semigroup (313 Members) High-Level Characteristics (eight PEs Symmetry)

chronization points in the original FGHC code have been systematically removed.

11.1.6   Discussion

Table 11.2 gives the execution times (in seconds) and speedups of the Semigroup programs on Symmetry. Table 11.3 summarizes the high-level characteristics of the optimized versions of Semigroup in each language. Figure 11.6 summarizes the measurements. All programs calculate the 313-member semigroup given by the four generators shown previously. All the programs use lists to represent tuples (structures are another alternative, but we have found only slight timing differences).

With the inclusion of granularity collection, the sequential program achieves steady speedups up to 4.7 on 15 PEs. This poor efficiency is primarily due to the sequential nature of the 2–3 tree lookup. The FGHC programs, however, all achieve higher speedups. The optimizations afford a continuous range of performance improvement. Removal of synchronization points gives a speedup of 30% on eight PEs. More significantly, the tree filter gives a speedup of 4.7.

Comparing the speeds of the fastest Prolog and FGHC programs, we find them

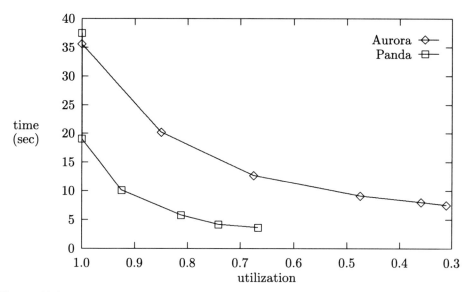

Figure 11.6
Semigroup (313 Members): Utilization vs. Time (Symmetry)

comparable on one PE but, on 15 PEs, FGHC overtakes Prolog by about a factor of two in speed. This result is partially because the binary-tree lookup in FGHC runs in parallel whereas the 2–3 tree lookup in Prolog is sequential. The Prolog program is working with large parallel granules composed of calls to the 2–3 tree, whereas the FGHC program can parallelize *through* calls to the binary tree.

> In general, the programming techniques of granularity collection and synchronization point removal are general tools that prove useful in an imperfect world where linear speedups cannot be produced automatically by smart compilers and schedulers. The ability to parallelize *all* parts of a computation is seen to be very important.

row

```
0                           1
1                        1     1
2                     1     2     1
3                  1     3     3     1
4               1     4     6     4     1
...          1     a     b    ...    a     1
          1    1+a   a+b   ...   ...  a+1   1
```

Figure 11.7
Pascal's Triangle

11.2   Pascal's Triangle

The binomial theorem states:

$$(x+y)^r = \sum_k \binom{r}{k} x^k y^{r-k}$$

for $r \geq 0$. The coefficients of $(x+y)^r$ are called *binomial coefficients of degree r*.
For example

$$(x+y)^3 = x^3 + 3x^2y + 3xy^2 + y^3$$

has the coefficients (1,3,3,1). Pascal's Triangle is the composed of the binomial
coefficients of increasing degree [73].

We define the previous set of coefficients to be the *third* set or row in Pascal's
Triangle. The zero row is (1), the first row is (1,1) and so on, as illustrated in
Figure 11.7. In general, row n has $n+1$ coefficients. In addition, the coefficients
are symmetric around the vertical axis of the triangle. Any row can be calculated
easily, albeit naively, from the previous row by adding pairs of successive coefficients.
It is this naive algorithm we wish to study in this section as a litmus test of how
well these systems behave in adverse (very fine-grained) conditions.

The first coefficient of each row is always one. The complexity of the algorithm
mainly depends on the number of additions performed. To calculate the nth row
from the previous row, $O(n)$ additions are needed. If n is even, the number of
additions is $n/2$. If n is odd, the number of additions is $(n-1)/2$. Thus the
complexity of the algorithm is as follows. If $n = 2k$ (even):

$$\sum_{i=1}^{k} \frac{2i}{2} + \sum_{i=1}^{k} \frac{(2i-1)-1}{2} = k^2$$

If $n = 2k + 1$ (odd):

$$\sum_{i=1}^{k} \frac{2i}{2} + \sum_{i=1}^{k+1} \frac{(2i-1)-1}{2} = k^2 + k + 2$$

Thus, in both cases, the complexity order is $O(k^2)$.

Infinite precision ("bignum") addition must be used because the coefficients grow large, e.g., the middle (maximum) coefficient of row 100 has 30 decimal digits. The bignum definition we are using here is based on a radix $R = 10^5$. A bignum is a list

$$[X_0, X_1, ..., X_{j-1}, X_j]$$

with the intended value

$$X_0 + X_1 R + ... + X_{j-1} R^{j-1} + X_j R^j.$$

All programs presented use **mod**, a modulus operator and **//**, an integer division operator.

Prolog Versions

Three Prolog versions of this problem are described in this section. First a sequential version is presented. Second, an OR-parallel version is presented which uses a clever method for nondeterminately selecting pairs of coefficients to add. Third, an AND-in-OR parallel version and related granularity collection optimizations are described.

11.2.1   Sequential Prolog

The sequential Prolog program computes left-half rows of Pascal's Triangle in makeRows/4 and then expands the final half row into a full row in fillout/3. The first half row is empty and each new half row is generated in makeRow/3.

```
go(N,Row) :- N>0, makeRows(1,N,[],Row).

makeRows(N,N,HalfRow,Row) :- !,
    Odd is N mod 2,
    fillout(Odd,[[1,0]|HalfRow],Row).
makeRows(K,N,HalfRowK,Row) :-
    K1 is K+1,
    Odd is K mod 2,
    makeRow([[1,0]|HalfRowK],Odd,HalfRowK1),
    makeRows(K1,N,HalfRowK1,Row).
```

```
makeRow([_],0,[]).
makeRow([X],1,[S]) :- !, bigPlus(S,X,X).
makeRow([X1,X2|Xs],Odd,[S|Ss]) :-
    bigPlus(S,X1,X2),
    makeRow([X2|Xs],Odd,Ss).

fillout(0,HalfRow,Row) :-
    rev(HalfRow,[_|Rev]),
    append(HalfRow,Rev,Row).
fillout(1,HalfRow,Row) :-
    rev(HalfRow,Rev),
    append(HalfRow,Rev,Row).
```

Procedure makeRow/1 takes advantage of the symmetry of the triangle to avoid recomputation of the second half of each row. Note that the inefficiency of reversing and appending in fillout/3 is insignificant with respect to the complexity of the algorithm. The bignum integer addition procedure is listed below. The informal specification of the program is given in Figure 11.8.

```
bigPlus(X,X,[]) :- !.
bigPlus(Y,[],Y) :- !.
bigPlus([Z|Zs],[X|Xs],[Y|Ys]) :-
    S is X+Y,
    (S < 100000 ->
        Z is S,
        bigPlus(Zs,Xs,Ys)
    ;
        Z is S mod 100000,
        R is S // 100000,
        bigPlus(Xs1,Xs,[R]),
        bigPlus(Zs,Xs1,Ys)
    ).
```

The previous Prolog program is correct but can quickly run out of memory because of profligate garbage production. Since the algorithm is determinate, the normal Prolog storage reclamation backtracking mechanism is not invoked and, unless the system has a general garbage collector, each row calculated will fill up available memory.

As a precursor to our OR-parallel Prolog program, anticipating that the Aurora system measured here has no garbage collector, we introduce "home brew" garbage collection for this sequential code. Instead of passing the current half row as a recursive argument, the half row is asserted into the database as a fact, halfRow/1. Only one halfRow fact is present at any time, corresponding to the last row calculated. By saving the program state in the database, we can exploit Prolog's automatic garbage collection upon failure, as described below.

<u>Procedure</u>: go(N, Row)
   +N: integer   −Row: list of integers

<u>Relation</u>: Row contains the coefficients of the Nth row of Pascal's Triangle.

<u>Procedure</u>: makeRows(K, N, HalfRow, Row)
   + K: integer   + HalfRow: list of integers
   + N: integer   − Row: list of integers

<u>Relation</u>: HalfRow, the left-hand coefficients of the Kth row, are expanded into Row, all the coefficients of the Nth row.

<u>Preconditions</u>: Initially K=1 and HalfRow is empty.

<u>Procedure</u>: makeRow(HalfRow, Odd, NewHalfRow)
   + HalfRow: list of integers   −NewHalfRow: list of integers
   + Odd: integer (0 or 1)

<u>Relation</u>: The kth HalfRow is expanded into the $(k + 1)^{st}$ NewHalfRow, by adding all successive pairs. If k is Odd then NewHalfRow has one extra coefficient.

<u>Procedure</u>: fillout(Odd, HalfRow, Row)
   + Odd: integer (0 or 1)   −Row: list of integers
   + HalfRow: list of integers

<u>Relation</u>: Row is the full row of coefficients corresponding to HalfRow.

<u>Procedure</u>: bigPlus(Z, X, Y)
   −Z: bignum   +X: bignum   + Y: bignum

<u>Relation</u>: Z is the sum of X and Y. A bignum is a list of integers representing radix 10^5 digits.

Figure 11.8
Informal Specification of Prolog Pascal

	no GC		GC	
n	T_n (sec.)	T_n/T_{100}	T_n (sec.)	T_n/T_{100}
100	2.9	1.0	3.9	1.0
200	21.1	7.3	26.4	6.8
300	69.5	24.0	85.6	21.9

Table 11.4
Pascal's Triangle on One Symmetry PE (SICStus Prolog)

```
go(N,Row) :- N > 0,
    assert(halfRow([])),
    makeRows(1,N,Row).

makeRows(N,N,Row) :- !,
    retract(halfRow(HalfRow)),
    Odd is N mod 2,
    fillout(Odd,[[1,0]|HalfRow],Row).
makeRows(K,N,Row) :-
    Odd is K mod 2,
    makeRow(Odd),
    K1 is K + 1,
    makeRows(K1,N,Row).

makeRow(Odd) :-
    retract(halfRow(HalfRowK)),
    makeRow([[1,0]|HalfRowK],Odd,HalfRowK1),
    assert(halfRow(HalfRowK1)),
    fail.
makeRow(_).
```

To calculate a new row, the previous row is retracted from the database and the new row is asserted. Garbage collection is then implemented by *failing*. Failure, in addition to cleaning up the heap and stack, causes execution of the second clause of makeRow/1 which succeeds, allowing continuation of the algorithm. Granted this is a hack, but it is simply necessary to execute the program for large n.

Timings of the sequential version of Pascal's Triangle (with and without home-brew garbage collection) on SICStus Prolog running on a single Symmetry PE are interesting. The amount of computation required as a function of the row number is given in Table 11.4. We saw that the algorithm has addition complexity order $O(N^2)$. However, the complexity of *each* addition grows with N because bignums are in use. As shown in the table, home-brew garbage collection (GC) *reduces* time complexity slightly by increasing memory locality. In any case, for $n = 300$, instead of a nine times increase in execution with respect to $n = 100$, execution time increases over 20 times!

11.2.2 Pairwise Addition

One idea that immediately comes to mind to parallelize the sequential Prolog program is to select pairs of elements nondeterminately to add in parallel in makeRow/3 from the previous program. Recall that makeRow/3 calculates half of row $k+1$ from the previous row k. The key to the new definition of this procedure is pair/3, which adds pairs of adjacent coefficients. Procedure makeRow/3 uses a findall to calculate these additions in parallel. First we write the code, assuming that findall does *not* guarantee any order of solutions (in Sums). Thus pair returns an *entire half-row list* for each new coefficient. The solutions to pair appear as:

```
[S1|_]
[_,S2|_]
[_,_,S3|_]
...
[_,_,...,_,Sn]
```

where S1, S2, etc. are the new coefficients. These lists are cleverly unified in unify/2, thus creating a complete half row containing all the new coefficients.

```
:- parallel pair/3.

makeRow(HalfRowK,Odd,HalfRowK1) :-
    findall(Sum,pair([[1,0]|HalfRowK],Odd,Sum),Sums),
    unify(Sums,HalfRowK1).

pair([_],0,[]).
pair([X],1,[S]) :- bigPlus(S,X,X).
pair([X1,X2|_],_,[S|_]) :- bigPlus(S,X1,X2).
pair([_|Xs],Odd,[_|Ss]) :- pair(Xs,Odd,Ss).

unify([],_).
unify([Row|Rows],Row) :- unify(Rows,Row).
```

If findall is implemented to guarantee the same order (of the solutions in its third argument) as in sequential Prolog, then the following, simplified procedure can be used. Here pair/3 returns a new coefficient that is guaranteed to be placed in the proper order by findall.

```
:- parallel pair/3.

make_row(HalfRowK,Odd,HalfRowK1) :-
    findall(Sum,pair([[1,0]|HalfRowK],Odd,Sum),HalfRowK1).

pair([X],1,S) :- bigPlus(S,X,X).
pair([X1,X2|_],_,S) :- bigPlus(S,X1,X2).
pair([_|Xs],Odd,Ss) :- pair(Xs,Odd,Ss).
```

The overhead of **unify** in the non-ordered **findall** is significant. On Symmetry for a single PE (for $n = 200$), the ordered **findall** runs about three times faster than the non-ordered **findall** for small numbers of PEs. Before analyzing the performance characteristics in detail, let us consider ways to speed up the program.

One idea to speed things up is to unroll **pair/3**. This method requires the use of **unify/2** to piece together the groups of sums without appending. An example of unrolling (one addition into three additions) follows:

```
pair([X1,X2,X3,X4|_],_,[S1,S2,S3|_])  :- bigPlus(S1,X1,X2),
                                          bigPlus(S2,X2,X3),
                                          bigPlus(S3,X3,X4).
pair([_,_,_|Xs],Odd,[_,_,_|Ss])        :- pair(Xs,Odd,Ss).
pair([_],         0,[]).
pair([X],         1,[S])               :- bigPlus(S,X,X).
pair([X1,X2],     0,[S])               :- bigPlus(S,X1,X2).
pair([X1,X2],     1,[S1,S2])           :- bigPlus(S1,X1,X2),
                                          bigPlus(S2,X2,X2).
pair([X1,X2,X3],0,[S1,S2])             :- bigPlus(S1,X1,X2),
                                          bigPlus(S2,X2,X3).
pair([X1,X2,X3],1,[S1,S2,S3])          :- bigPlus(S1,X1,X2),
                                          bigPlus(S2,X2,X3),
                                          bigPlus(S3,X3,X3).
```

In the unrolled **pair/3**, the first clause is the large granule of three bignum additions. The second clause is the recursive calculation of the remainder of the half row. The final six clauses handle the end cases when less than four coefficients remain in the previous half row.

Table 11.5 compares the 3x unrolled unordered-**findall** program with the previous programs. By unrolling we actually reduce the number of recursive calls to **pair/3**, thereby significantly decreasing the execution time on a single PE. In fact, unrolling makes the unordered-**findall** program competitive with the ordered program. Still, high overheads make speedup difficult. Only on four PEs do the programs break even and achieve real speedup.

11.2.3   AND-in-OR Parallelism

This OR-parallel Prolog version of Pascal's Triangle is directly based on the sequential version. Again, the key notion is to perform the additions of a single row in parallel. Since this is AND-parallelism, it must be simulated with the OR-parallel mechanism available to us. If we hypothesize a procedure **and(G1,G2)** that somehow executes the goals **G1** and **G2** in parallel, then we might, for instance, place the **and** around the two goals of the last clause of **makeRow/3** in the sequential program. However, if **and/2** has some significant overhead, such exploitation of

Program	1 PE	2 PE	4 PE
execution time (seconds)			
sequential	55.2		
unordered	221.4	201.9	196.6
ordered	79.4	74.2	51.0
3x unrolling	81.5	60.5	48.0
naive speedup			
unordered	1.0	1.1	1.1
ordered	1.0	1.1	1.6
3x unrolling	1.0	1.3	1.7
real speedup			
unordered	0.25	0.28	0.28
ordered	0.70	0.74	1.1
3x unrolling	0.68	0.91	1.2

Table 11.5
Pascal's Triangle ($n = 200$): Pairwise Addition in Prolog (Aurora/Symmetry)

fine-grain parallelism (attempting to execute *each* addition in parallel) will surely be inefficient (as we shall see). Thus two implementation problems must be tackled: how to simulate AND-in-OR parallelism, and how to collect work into large granules that can be efficiently executed in parallel. We will discuss the first issue in this section and continue with the latter in the next section.

A scheme for simulating AND-in-OR parallelism in Prolog was developed by M. Carlsson *et al.* [20]. A variation of the method is given here, however, it is optimized for the specific case of two-way determinate parallelism.

```
:- parallel gather/3.

and(Goal1,Goal2) :-
    findall(Sol, gather(Sol,Goal1,Goal2), Sols),
    (Sols = [s1(Goal1),s2(Goal2)] ;
     Sols = [s2(Goal2),s1(Goal1)]),!.

gather(s1(Goal1),Goal1,_) :- call(Goal1).
gather(s2(Goal2),_,Goal2) :- call(Goal2).
```

The `and/2` procedure works as follows. The `findall` collects all solutions to `gather/3`, which executes two independent, determinate goals in parallel. It is important to realize that each goal returns only one answer. Thus, if the `findall` is unordered, then the solution list, of length two, can be either `[s1(Goal1), s2(Goal2)]` or `[s2(Goal2),s1(Goal1)]`. The variables `Goal1` and `Goal2` contain the output bindings from the execution of the goals.

Note that `findall/3` does *not* instantiate any unbound logical variables in its second argument. To receive the set of answers, the returned list, `Sols`, must be decomposed and reunified with the input goals. This appears rather strange and magical because `findall` is extra-logical: it renames all free variables in its second argument before collecting answers.

Lastly, we add a final cut to ensure that the disjunction does not leave a choice-point. Note that, if we had a `findall` that guaranteed order, then `and/2` could be defined as:

```
:- parallel gather/3.

and(Goal1,Goal2) :-
    findall(Sol, gather(Sol,Goal1,Goal2), [Goal1,Goal2]).

gather(Goal1,Goal1,_) :- call(Goal1).
gather(Goal2,_,Goal2) :- call(Goal2).
```

The versions of `and/2` defined above work quite nicely for any two determinate goals because each goal can produce only one answer. In general, `and/2` must be rewritten to work with nondeterminate goals, i.e., goals that return more than one answer. Assuming that the `findall` returns an unordered list:

```
:- parallel gather/3.

and(Goal1,Goal2) :-
    findall(Sol,gather(Sol,Goal1,Goal2),Sols),
    member(s1(Goal1),Sols),
    member(s2(Goal2),Sols).

member(X,[X|_]).
member(X,[_|L]) :- member(X,L).
```

In this implementation, each `member` will extract any number of instances of the two goals within the solution list `Sols`.

To implement parallel conjunctions of more than two goals, we can nest calls to `and/2`:

```
?- and(Goal1,and(Goal2,Goal3)).
```

This looks prettier when defined as an infix operator `&/2`:[2]

```
?- Goal1 & Goal2 & Goal3.
```

More efficient implementations of multiple conjunctions can be written. Even for as few as three determinate goals, the large number of possible solution lists requires the use of `member`.

---

[2]not to be confused with the Parlog operator of the same name, which has the opposite effect!

```
:- parallel gather/4.

and(Goal1,Goal2,Goal3) :-
    findall(Sol,gather(Sol,Goal1,Goal2,Goal3),Sols),
    member(s1(Goal1),Sols),
    member(s2(Goal2),Sols),
    member(s3(Goal3),Sols).
```

With respect to Pascal's Triangle, our first attempt at utilizing AND-in-OR parallelism is in the final clause of makeRow/3.

```
makeRow([X1,X2|Xs],Odd,[S|Ss]) :-
    and(bigPlus(S,X1,X2),
        makeRow([X2|Xs],Odd,Ss)).
```

This method, however, proves too costly to achieve speedups. For example, on a single Symmetry PE for $n = 200$, this naive AND-in-OR program executes in 91.6 seconds compared to 9.3 seconds for the sequential Prolog version! The two branches of and/2 are unbalanced — the left branch is a short stub (one bignum addition) and the right branch is the summation of the rest of the row. To improve the situation, we must increase the granularity of the left branch, as described next.

11.2.4 Granularity Collection

Granularity collection refers to the combination of many lightweight goals (i.e., with little computation) into a single goal. Specifically, we use it to increase the computational weight of a branch extending from a parallel branchpoint in OR-parallel Prolog. By increasing the computation of a branch, the relative overhead of creating and managing the branchpoint becomes lower and speedup improves.

The new Prolog program is based on the sequential version. An input argument G is added, relating to the granule size. In this program, we chose to divide each row of Pascal's Triangle into G chunks. Thus granules actually increase in size as the computation progresses.

```
go(N,G,Row) :- N > 0,
    assert(halfRow([])),
    makeRows(1,N,G,Row).

makeRow(Odd,H,Q) :-
    retract(halfRow(HalfRowK)),
    makeRow(H,[[1,0]|HalfRowK],Odd,HalfRowK1,Q),
    assert(halfRow(HalfRowK1)),
    fail.
makeRow(_,_,_).
```

```
makeRows(N,N,_,Row) :- !,
    retract(halfRow(HalfRow)),
    Odd is N mod 2,
    fillout(Odd,[[1,0]|HalfRow],Row).
makeRows(K,N,G,Row) :-
    Odd is K mod 2,
    H is K//2,
    Q is H//G + 1,
    makeRow(Odd,H,Q),
    K1 is K + 1,
    makeRows(K1,N,G,Row).
```

Each chunk is spawned in AND-parallel, with the remaining portion of the row to be processed. The end of the row, i.e., the leftovers, is sequentialized. The main factor limiting execution speed is home-brew GC, implemented by a fail. Since GC is invoked for each row calculation, parallelism cannot overlap row calculations.

We make row N in `makeRow(N,PrevRow,Odd,NewRow,Q)`, where input `PrevRow` is half-row N-1, output `NewRow` is half-row N, `Odd` indicates if N is odd or even, and `Q` is the granularity, in terms of chunks per row. Instead of calculating one pair of additions per iteration, we calculate a chunk per iteration. When less than a chunk remains, the fourth clause of `makeRow/5` finishes up the additions.

```
makeRow(0,[_],0,[],_) :- !.
makeRow(0,[X],1,[S],_) :- !,bigPlus(S,X,X).
makeRow(N,In,Odd,Out,Q) :- N > Q,!,
    N1 is N-Q,
    and(rest(N1,In,Odd,Out,Q),
        work(Q,In,Out)).
makeRow(N,[A,B|Rest],Odd,[AB|R],Q) :-
    N1 is N-1,
    bigPlus(AB,A,B),
    makeRow(N1,[B|Rest],Odd,R,Q).
```

The chunks are executed within `and/2`. The `rest` procedure recurses back to `makeRow/5`. The `work` procedure does the actual additions.

```
rest(N,In,Odd,Out,Q) :-
    prepare(Q,In,Rest,Out,R),
    makeRow(N,Rest,Odd,R,Q).

prepare(0,R,R,S,S) :- !.
prepare(N,[_|Is],Rest,[_|S],R) :-
    N1 is N-1,
    prepare(N1,Is,Rest,S,R).
```

n	G	1 PE	2 PE	4 PE
100	seq	9.3		
	2	15.2	10.2	10.4
	3	18.0	13.8	11.7
	4	22.2	16.2	14.0
140	seq	23.7		
	2	34.6	24.3	24.4
	3	42.3	31.7	26.6
	4	49.2	37.5	31.5

Table 11.6
Pascal's Triangle: Execution Time (seconds) on Symmetry

```
work(0,_,_) :- !.
work(N,[A,B|Rest],[AB|R]) :-
    N1 is N-1,
    bigPlus(AB,A,B),
    work(N1,[B|Rest],R).
```

There is a serious bottleneck in rest. Simply recursing back to makeRow/5 is impossible without first preparing its arguments. Note that the coefficients are *not known*, but simply placed correctly so computation of the remainder of the row can proceed. Unfortunately, this placement requires a loop, because we do not know the granularity size *a priori*. Thus we see that, in general, exploiting AND-parallelism involves decoupling the AND goals. If the granularity size were known, for example G=6, then the third clause of makeRow/5 could be replaced with:

```
makeRow(N,[A,B,C,D,E,F,H|Rest],Odd,[AB,BC,CD,DE,EF,FH|R],_) :-
    N1 is N-6,
    and(makeRow(N1,[H|Rest],Odd,R),
        (bigPlus(AB,A,B),
         bigPlus(BC,B,C),
         bigPlus(CD,C,D),
         bigPlus(DE,D,E),
         bigPlus(EF,E,F),
         bigPlus(FH,F,H))).
```

This clause would be more efficient than the general program outlined previously. However, we wish to parameterize G in order to determine the relationship between granularity and performance.

Table 11.6 shows the effect of G on program performance. The program measured used the ordered-findall implementation of and/2, i.e., it is a best case assumption. Speedups are not shown because real speedup was not attained for any of the experiments conducted. Large granularity is needed (half to a third of

System	Method	1 PE	2 PE	4 PE	8 PE	12 PE	15 PE
execution time (seconds)							
Aurora	sequential	55.2					
	pairwise (unrolled)	81.5	60.5	48.0	37.1	—	—
	AND-in-OR (G=3)	104.4	76.8	64.0	—	—	—
Panda		35.8	18.6	9.4	4.9	3.4	2.8
naive speedup							
Aurora	pairwise (unrolled)	1.0	1.3	1.7	2.2	—	—
	AND-in-OR (G=3)	1.0	1.4	1.6	—	—	—
Panda		1.0	1.9	3.8	7.3	11	13

Table 11.7
Pascal's Triangle ($n = 200$): Execution Time and Speedup (Symmetry)

System	Method	reduct	back/susp	entries	sec	KEPS
Aurora	sequential (PE=1)	227079	48641	275720	55.2	5
	pairwise (unrolled)	263865	72772	336637	48.0	7
	AND-in-OR (G=3)	248131	206212	454343	64.0	7
Panda		154281	4469	158750	9.5	17

Table 11.8
Pascal's Triangle ($n = 200$): High-Level Characteristics (four PEs Symmetry)

the additions comprising a row calculation) to gain optimal performance. However, increasing the number of PEs beyond four did not improve performance. This result is because *more* granules are needed to exploit more PEs but, as we see, for problem sizes of $n = 100$ and $n = 140$, granules smaller than a certain critical size cannot be efficiently executed. There is hardly any difference in the characteristics of $n = 100$ and $n = 140$, indicating that speedups will improve only for significantly larger programs. We would have expected $n = 140$, which involves about twice the computation as $n = 100$, to fare better on four PEs.

The FGHC code, shown in Figure 11.9, is similar to the original sequential Prolog program. The bignum integer addition procedure in FGHC is also listed.

11.2.5   Discussion

Table 11.7 gives the raw timing of execution and speedups of the Pascal's Triangle programs for $n = 200$ on Symmetry. The '—' statistics represent no improvement in execution speed with increasing numbers of PEs. Table 11.8 gives the high-level characteristics on four PEs. Figure 11.10 summarizes the measurements. The pairwise addition and AND-in-OR Prolog programs both assume an ordered `findall`,

```
go(N,Row) :- makeRows(1,N,[],Row).

makeRows(N,N,HalfRow,Row) :-
    Odd is N mod 2,
    fillout(Odd,[[1,0]|HalfRow],Row).
makeRows(K,N,HalfRowK,Row) :- K =\= N |
    K1 is K+1,
    Odd is K mod 2,
    makeRow([[1,0]|HalfRowK],Odd,HalfRowK1),
    makeRows(K1,N,HalfRowK1,Row).

makeRow([_],0,A)  :- A=[].
makeRow([X],1,A)  :- A=[S], bigPlus(S,X,X).
makeRow([X1,X2|Xs],Odd,A) :-
    A=[S|Ss],
    bigPlus(S,X1,X2),
    makeRow([X2|Xs],Odd,Ss).

fillout(0,HalfRow,Row) :-
    rev(HalfRow,[_|Rev]),
    append(HalfRow,Rev,Row).
fillout(1,HalfRow,Row) :-
    rev(HalfRow,Rev),
    append(HalfRow,Rev,Row).

bigPlus(A,X,Y) :- bigp(X,Y,A,0).

bigp([X|Xs],[Y|Ys],A,C) :-
    T is X+Y+C,
    setc(T,A1,C1),
    A = [A1|As],
    bigp(Xs,Ys,As,C1).
bigp([],[Y|Ys],A,C) :-
    T is Y+C,
    setc(T,A1,C1),
    A = [A1|As],
    bigp([],Ys,As,C1).
bigp([X|Xs],[],A,C) :-
    T is X+C,
    setc(T,A1,C1),
    A = [A1|As],
    bigp([],Xs,As,C1).
bigp([],[],A,0) :- A=[].
bigp([],[],A,C) :- C>0 | A=[C].

setc(T,A,C) :- T < 100000  | C=0, A=T.
setc(T,A,C) :- T >= 100000 | C=1, A is T-100000.
```

Figure 11.9
Pascal's Triangle with Integer Bignums (FGHC)

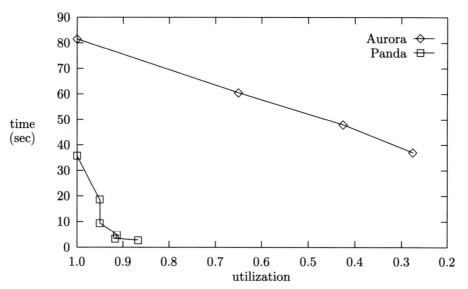

Figure 11.10
Pascal's Triangle ($n = 200$): Utilization vs. Time (Symmetry)

i.e., a best-case assumption for Prolog. The pairwise-addition program measured was unrolled three times, as shown previously. Measurements of the non-unrolled pairwise-addition program and naive AND-in-OR program are not given because these programs are extremely inefficient, as discussed in previous sections.

The large numbers of backtracks performed by the Prolog programs may be puzzling because the Pascal's Triangle algorithms are determinate. These backtracks are shallow, for example, the backtrack incurred with the bignum procedure when determining if the sum of two bignum digits is less than the radix. Note that shallow backtracks require far less computation than reductions; however, we calculate procedure entries as the sum of all backtracks and reductions, hence the KEPS statistic is misleading. Although Panda executes five times faster than Aurora on four PEs, Panda's KEPS measure is less than three times that of Aurora.

The statistics do clearly show the inefficiency of exploiting small granularity OR-parallelism in Aurora. Maximum real speedup of 1.5 (naive speedup of 2.2) on eight PEs was achieved by the unrolled pairwise-addition program. Exploiting such fine-grained AND-in-OR parallelism is almost impossible. The best that granularity collection could achieve was a naive speedup of 1.6 on four PEs. This perceived speedup is in reality a slowdown with respect to the sequential program. However,

System	Method	1 PE	2 PE	4 PE	8 PE	12 PE	15 PE
execution time (seconds)							
Aurora	Semigroup	35.6	20.2	12.7	9.1	8.0	7.5
	Pascal	81.5	60.5	48.0	37.1	—	—
Panda	Semigroup	37.5	19.1	10.1	5.8	4.2	3.6
	Pascal	35.8	18.6	9.4	4.9	3.4	2.8
ratio	Semigroup	0.95	1.1	1.3	1.6	1.9	2.1
	Pascal	2.3	3.2	5.1	7.6	11	13
real speedup							
Aurora	Semigroup	0.96	1.7	2.7	3.8	4.3	4.6
	Pascal	0.68	0.91	1.2	1.5	—	—
Panda	Semigroup	1.0	2.0	3.7	6.5	8.9	10
	Pascal	1.0	1.9	3.8	7.3	11	13

Table 11.9
Semigroup and Pascal's Triangle Summary: Execution Time and Speedup
(Symmetry)

the granularity collection can be considered successful in that at least naive speedup
was displayed!

On the other hand, FGHC does quite well, achieving a speedup of 12.8 on 15 PEs.
FGHC's main advantage is the ability to parallelize across row computations, since
explicit garbage collection is unnecessary. In addition, Panda efficiently supports
this type of fine-grain AND-parallel computation.

11.3 Summary

First a word about the proverb at the beginning of this chapter. A *kappa* is a
mythical creature from medieval Japan. It is a small half-human, half-fish creature
that lives near rivers and is a natural swimmer. Without water in a bowl-like
indentation in the top of its head, the *kappa* loses its power. Although the *kappa*
has been romanticized over the years, it was originally a nasty beast, like a troll. In
any case, we feel that the *kappa* is a metaphor (in some perverse sense) for Aurora
in this chapter.

Table 11.9 shows the performance timings of the fastest Prolog and FGHC versions of both the Semigroup (313 member solution) and Pascal's Triangle ($n = 200$)
problems. Execution time (in seconds), the ratio of Aurora to Panda execution time,
and the *real* speedups on Symmetry are given. The most striking characteristic is
that Aurora cannot achieve good speedups for these problems. Panda, however,

can exploit the fine-grained AND-parallelism quite nicely.

The natural granularity of the problems are indicated by the ratio of the speedups achieved by the systems. For Semigroup and Pascal on eight Symmetry PEs, Panda achieves 1.7 times and 3.3 times the naive speedup of Aurora, respectively. On 15 PEs, the ratios increase to 2.2 times and 5.8 times. Semigroup has larger natural granularity — the multiplication of two vectors, as compared to a single bignum integer addition in Pascal's Triangle. To be fair to Aurora, as the natural granularity or collectible granularity increases with problem size, Prolog will perform better. Panda performance will also improve somewhat, but probably not as significantly as Aurora. For example, computing a semigroup with 100 element tuples and an initial generator of ten tuples, or computing the 500th row of Pascal's Triangle, Aurora would perform significantly better. Unfortunately, we cannot report the results of such large problems here because the Aurora system measured has memory management limitations that prevent very large OR-trees from being built.

The Prolog programs represented — granularity collection for Semigroup and unrolled pairwise addition for Pascal's Triangle — require explicit user-programming techniques to achieve their limited speedup. The FGHC Semigroup program also needed refinement (the programming technique of removing synchronization points) to achieve its speedup. Pascal's Triangle in FGHC was different, requiring no recoding and yet achieving the highest efficiency among the programs at 85% on 15 PEs. We do not think the explicit recoding for parallel efficiency in OR-Prolog is excessive. Clearly Aurora's goal of completely implicit, parallel execution is not met for these "degenerate" programs. Still Aurora does surprisingly well given such unfriendly lack of OR-parallelism.

Exercises

Exercise 111 Write an AND-in-OR parallel Prolog program to calculate the total years each house of the British monarchy reigned (use the Prolog database developed in Exercise 8).

Exercise 112 Create large enough input data (with a large set of generators) for the Semigroup Problem to achieve good speedup. Measure the performance of the Prolog and FGHC programs for these data.

Exercise 113 The fastest version given of the Prolog Semigroup program lags behind the fastest FGHC version by a significant margin. Can this difference be partially corrected by replacing Prolog's 2–3 tree with a simple unbalanced binary

tree, as in the FGHC program? One hypothesis is that this will speed up the
sequential access to the tree without great penalty for unbalancing. Test this hypothesis by implementing an unbalanced binary tree within Prolog Semigroup and
measuring speedups.

Exercise 114 M. Carlsson wrote a significantly faster Prolog Semigroup program
based on the following idea. Since the tuple multiplications always involve at least
one generator tuple, and the generators are known *a priori*, these multiplications
can be "compiled." For example, one can define a procedure g1(+,-) that returns
the product of an input tuple with the first generator. Similarly g2/2, etc. can
be coded quite efficiently. Implement this scheme and measure its performance,
comparing it to the previously-discussed programs for large input data (Exercise
112). We suggest you first write a program that compiles the input tuples into
multiplier procedures g1/2, g2/2, etc.

Exercise 115 Write succinct informal specifications for FGHC procedures tr/4,
tl/4, and tlr/5 to complete the specification of the binary hash tree. This exercise should convince you that writing declarative descriptions of message-passing
programs is not easy!

Exercise 116 Solve the following linear algebra problem in both OR-parallel Prolog and FGHC. Given a set of tuples, each a vector of n integers, consider all the
possible $n \times (n + 1)$ matrices containing the tuples as columns. Given k tuples in
the set, a total of k^{n+1} such matrices exist. We wish to partition these matrices
into equivalence classes. Two matrices P_1 and P_2 are said to be equivalent if there
exists some manipulation matrix R such that $P_1 = RP_2$.
    Since the P matrices are $n \times (n + 1)$, they can be decomposed as $P_1 = [G_1 T_1]$
and $P_2 = [G_2 T_2]$ where T_1 and T_2 are tuples and G_1 and G_2 are square matrices.
Thus if $P_1 = RP_2$ then $G_1 T_1 = R[G_2 T_2] = [RG_2 RT_2]$. Therefore $G_1 = RG_2$ and
$T_1 = RT_2$. We solve the first of these equations for $R = G_1 G_2^{-1}$, where G_2^{-1} is the
inverse of square matrix G_2. If $T_1 = RT_2$, then in fact P_1 and P_2 are equivalent.
If any of these conditions does not hold then the two matrices belong to different
equivalence classes.
    Experiment with input data of approximately $n = 3$ and $k = 6$. Partition all the
generated tuples into equivalence classes.

Exercise 117 In the Prolog and FGHC Pascal programs define a `granule/4` procedure:

```
granule(C,X,Y,Z) :- bigPlus(Z,X,Y), spin(C).

spin(0) :- !.
spin(I) :- I1 is I-1, spin(I1).
```

Incorporate C as an input to the new top-level query. For sufficiently large N, plot the *real* speedup of the parallel programs (i.e., with respect to a sequential version) as a function of number of PEs for a family of C curves. Show a few values of C that allow the program to achieve efficiencies between 0.0 and 1.0. Given large enough C, which Prolog program performs better: pairwise additions or AND-in-OR parallel? Does large enough C calibrate the Prolog and FGHC programs?

Exercise 118 (The Game of Life) The Game of Life consists of a two-dimensional grid or torus of cells, called the "world." A cell has a binary state of *alive* or *dead*. The game is a discrete time simulation wherein for each time cycle the state of the grid is updated. To update the grid, each cell is locally updated as a function of its eight nearest neighbors, *independently* from other updates. If a cell is currently alive and two or three neighboring cells are alive, then the cell lives. If a cell is currently alive and less than two or greater than three neighboring cells are alive, then the cell dies. If a cell is currently dead and three neighboring cells are alive, then the cell is reborn. Otherwise the cell remains dead.

Implement the Game of Life in OR-parallel Prolog. Try to develop an OR-parallel algorithm for updating the state, collecting the granularity to improve efficiency. How does the serial overhead between cycles affect the attainable speedup?

Exercise 119 Implement the Game of Life in FGHC. One method is to spawn a process corresponding to each cell in the world. How does the forced synchronization at the end of each cycle affect the attainable speedup?

Exercise 120 Write a Prolog or FGHC program to solve simple substitution ciphers. For example:

"Kzb wg z egsrsgg pzggwyb." — Gzhas

can be decoded as:

"Man is a useless passion." — Sarte

The following facts [150] should help in developing decoding strategies. The most frequently used letters are 'e', 't', 'n', 'o', 'a', 'i', and 'r', in that order. Common

act	all	any	and	are	can	day
did	for	had	has	her	him	his
its	man	may	men	new	how	not
now	one	old	our	saw	say	see
she	six	ten	the	try	two	was
who	was	you	able	been	bill	book
both	does	done	call	city	days	down
fact	five	four	from	gave	give	gone
goes	half	have	high	into	last	love
many	meet	more	next	nine	over	said
says	sees	seem	send	sent	some	such
take	than	that	them	they	this	time
took	upon	very	what	whom	with	will
when	your	wait	went	were	year	about
above	adopt	after	along	among	aware	being
below	books	calls	could	eight	facts	first
given	gives	large	loved	loves	might	money
other	place	reach	since	seems	seven	shall
sleep	slept	takes	their	think	three	times
trade	tries	tried	under	water	which	waits
which	whose	would	woman	women	years	

Table 11.10
Dictionary of 146 Common English Words

short words are: a, I, am, an, at, be, by, do, go, he, if, in, is, it, me, my, no, of, on, or, so, to, up, us, we. In addition, one can develop larger dictionaries of other common words, to help guess given the following statistical fact. If one knows 15 or 100 of the most common English words, one can respectively understand on average 25% and 60% of most text. That is to say, if we can't match 60% or more of the words in the text in the 100-word dictionary, then at least one of the decoded letters is wrong. But which one? A word that doesn't match anything in the dictionary is a good candidate as containing an incorrectly decoded letter.

A good program will make frequent use of these heuristics and avoid blind backtracking over all permutations of the alphabet. See Yang [150] for a more detailed discussion, references to the literature, and the sketch of a decoder written in Andorra. Table 11.10 gives Yang's original dictionary of common words. These words were not derived statistically as *most common*, so to be conservative, we might use the 146 words listed here to enforce the 60% rule. Similarly, the previous list of 25 short words could be used to enforce the 25% rule.

12 BestPath

"Feeling in need of a rest after our strenuous efforts we entered the hut and found it full of cheerful schoolgirls, looking a good deal fresher than we did. After lunch we pushed on into the mist and despite some difficulty in knowing which path to take we finally reached the large cross indicating the summit. Heavy fog restricted our view so we scribbled our names in a large book thoughtfully provided on top and made our plans for the descent. We decided to pioneer a little so ignored the many broad paths leading off the summit and plunged instead down an ill-defined track that lead into an easy rock gully supplied with a wire rope to hinder the climber. We then glissaded down some easy slopes for several thousand feet and finally emerged below the clouds. To our chagrin we discovered that instead of traversing the mountain we were still on much the same side and the same group of giggling schoolgirls was only a short distance away."

Edmund Hillary
Nothing Venture, Nothing Win
Hodder and Stoughton Ltd 1975

In previous chapters we have analyzed problems that are well suited to both OR-parallel Prolog and committed-choice languages. Irregular constraint problems were efficiently solved in Prolog but not in FGHC. Problems with fine-grain parallelism were efficiently solved in FGHC but not in OR-parallel Prolog. In this chapter we introduce a problem that is not conducive to *either* paradigm. Like Waltz, this problem has little parallelism, and efforts to solve it in parallel are instructive.

The *single-source bestpath problem* is a simple search problem concerning a graph. The graph is constructed of nodes and nondirected edges. Each edge connects two nodes and a node is connected to at least one edge. The edges each have a non-negative cost. A path is a route from one node to another, through an arbitrary number of edges. The cost of the path is the sum of the costs of the edges on the path. The single-source bestpath problem is to find all *minimum-cost paths* for a given starting node to all other nodes. An example is shown in Figure 12.1. Consider a typical query `bestpath(N,S,L)` where input N is the number of nodes, S is the starting node, and output L is the list of all bestpaths to each node. Sample queries and solutions are:

```
?- bestpath(6,1,X).
   X = [0-[1],2-[2,1],5-[3,2,1],1-[4,1],2-[5,4,1],4-[6,5,4,1]]

?- bestpath(6,2,X).
   X = [2-[1,2],0-[2],3-[3,2],2-[[4,1,2],[4,5,2]],2-[5,2],4-[6,5,2]]
```

For example, in the first query, solution 5-[3,2,1] is a path from 3 to 1 via 2, with cost five. Note that in the same minimum-cost path, no node can be visited twice,

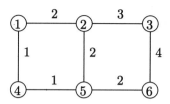

Figure 12.1
A Simple Graph

nor can any edge be traversed twice. Further note that although multiple bestpaths may exist for the same pair of nodes, as in the above example, the algorithms we describe in this chapter find only a single bestpath per node, for simplicity. Graphs are defined in the same manner in all the programs presented here. A graph is a collection of nodes:

```
edge(Node1,[NodeA*CostA,NodeB*CostB,...])
```

where the list contains all connected nodes and the costs of the connecting edges. The previous graph is encoded as follows:

```
edge(1,N) :- N=[4*1,2*2].
edge(2,N) :- N=[1*2,5*2,3*3].
edge(3,N) :- N=[2*3,6*4].
edge(4,N) :- N=[1*1,5*1].
edge(5,N) :- N=[4*1,2*2,6*2].
edge(6,N) :- N=[5*2,3*4].
```

The form of the solutions is also important. All of the algorithms we describe here produce path solutions in the form of an intermediate data structure consisting of one entry per node. This entry contains the total cost of the bestpath to that node and the previous node within the bestpath. It must be the case that the bestpath (from the start) of any node is composed of the bestpaths (from the start) of all nodes *comprising that path*. Thus the bestpath of a node can be denoted as the bestpath of one of its neighbors plus the edge connecting the two nodes. For example the solution to the above graph is:

```
?- bestpath(6,1,X).
   X = [0-none,2-1,5-2,1-1,2-4,4-5]
```

The last entry indicates that a path extends from node 6 to node 5 with total cost 4. We see from the next-to-last entry that a path extends from node 5 to node 4 with total cost 2. Finally a path extends from node 4 to node 1 (the start) with cost 1. From this information we can imply the edge costs of the bestpaths also.

The bestpath problem is important because it is one of many problems that allow *distributed* algorithms. A distributed algorithm involves a group of semi-autonomous processes that communicate locally as they compute a solution. A popular example is a relaxation algorithm for calculating solutions to partial differential equations [50]. Distributed algorithms are quite naturally implemented in committed-choice languages. However, the time and storage complexity of these programs are sometimes difficult to analyze because of scheduling nondeterminacy.

As previously mentioned, the single-source best-path problem is also valuable because it does *not* allow efficient parallel algorithms for low-connectivity (sparse) graphs, i.e., few edges per node. The sequential Johnson-Dijkstra algorithm [70] is so efficient, $O(N \log N)$ asymptotic complexity for N nodes,[1] that parallel programs have trouble competing for sparse graphs. We chose sparse graphs as representative of realistic map applications. In this chapter we describe Prolog and FGHC algorithms and analyze their performances searching a 1237-node graph of Tokyo streets.

12.1 Johnson-Dijkstra in Prolog

The Prolog program presented is an implementation of the Johnson-Dijkstra sequential algorithm [70]. We do not present an OR-parallel Prolog algorithm because the fine granularity of the problem precludes an efficient implementation. See, however, Exercise 129 for the description of a viable algorithm. We begin here by describing Dijkstra's original algorithm [42].

Consider beginning the bestpath search at a start node. By definition no cost is required to arrive at the start. All edges extending from the start are labeled with a positive cost. In fact the edge among these with the minimal cost defines a bestpath! Consider this: if the minimum-cost edge from the start was *not* a bestpath then another path must exist that has less cost. Yet every other edge extending from the start has *higher* cost. Thus there can be no cheaper path than that defined by the minimum edge. Note that if there are more than one edge with the *same* minimum cost then these edges are *all* bestpaths.

Thus in our first step we have successfully found a (very short) bestpath extending

---

[1]There has been much research in algorithmic improvements to Dijkstra's original algorithm [42] with advanced data structures. See Ahuja *et al.* [8] for the latest of these advances. In this chapter we do not concern ourselves with further reducing the asymptotic complexity, but rather with parallelization.

from the start node to some neighboring node called the *pivot*. In the next step
consider extending the path through the pivot node by collecting all of the pivot's
neighboring nodes. The start node, which is also a neighbor, need not be considered
because its bestpath is known. We also still have the nodes neighboring the start
node that we didn't use yet. This total group of nodes is called the *boundary*. A
boundary node is necessarily a neighbor of a node for which a bestpath is known,
and the cost of the boundary node is the cost of this known bestpath plus the
edge cost connecting the two neighbors. The minimum-cost boundary node defines
yet another bestpath! The reasoning is similar to the first step, although we must
consider the possibility of paths first going from the start to the first pivot, since
that is a proven minimal-cost path.

Intuitively we are incrementally (and unfortunately sequentially) creating the
boundary — each step of the algorithm extends the boundary by one new node,
i.e., the pivot. As soon as the pivot is itself extended, the pivot is removed from the
boundary because it has been solved. Thus the complexity order of the algorithm
is linear in the total number of nodes with the overhead of finding the pivot from
among the boundary nodes. Since the new pivot is the minimum-cost boundary
node, this overhead will be the expense of keeping the boundary sorted.

Several sorted data structures are available, ranging from simple lists to trees to
heaps, offering lower access time complexity at the cost of higher insertion time
complexity and implementation complexity. Dijkstra originally used a list, whereas
Johnson improved upon this with a prioritized heap [126].

The heap used here is an ordered binary tree where every node is guaranteed
to have a value less than or equal to the values of its children. At the top level,
the bestpath table `Array` is initialized in `bestpath/3`. In addition, the heap is
also initialized, to the starting node. Given the initial `Heap`, `find/3` collects all
bestpaths in `Array`.

```
bestpath(N,Start,Array) :-
    functor(Array,t,N),
    heapIn(void,a(Start,0,none),Heap),
    find(N,complete(Heap),Array).
```

Procedure `bestpath(N,Start,Array)` calculates all bestpaths from node `Start` in
the N node graph specified by `edge/2`. To implement the bestpath `Array` we use
structures, as discussed further at the end of this section. The kth element of `Array`
corresponds to node k, and is of the form `Cost-Prev`, where `Cost` is the cost of the
minimum path, and `Prev` is the previous node in the minimum-cost path.

The heap is accessed via two procedures: `heapIn/3` and `heapOut/3`. Procedure
`heapIn(Hin,Node,Hout)` inserts `Node` into heap `Hin` producing heap `Hout`. Pro-

cedure `heapOut(Hin,Root,Hout)` removes the `Root` node of heap `Hin` producing heap `Hout`.

A node in the heap is defined either as `void` (empty) or `node(Left,Value,Right)` where `Left` and `Right` are the children nodes. The node value is defined as `a(Node,Cost,Prev)` where `Node` is the node number, `Cost` is the current minimum-cost, and `Prev` is the previous node in the current minimum-cost path.

The heap, accessed by its root, can be in one of two possible states. A heap `complete(node(L,V,R))` represents a standard heap with root value `V` and children `L` and `R`. As an optimization we also allow an incomplete heap `partial(L,R)` with an empty root value and children `L` and `R`.

Procedure `find/3` is the main procedure, and iterates until all nodes have been selected as pivots, i.e., a bestpath has been found for each node. First, the heap is read with `heapOut/3`, producing a candidate, `Node`, for the new pivot. If `Node` is already in the bestpath array, then it has already been a pivot so it is discarded and `find/3` recurses. Otherwise `Node` is a new pivot and its `Edges` are inserted into the heap, with `insertall/6`.

```
find(M,Heap,Array) :- M>0,!,
    heapOut(Heap,a(Node,Cost,Prev),NewHeap),
    arg(Node,Array,V),
    (var(V) ->
        V = Prev-Cost,
        M1 is M-1,
        edge(Node,Edges),
        insertall(Edges,Cost,Node,NewHeap,Array,M1)
    ;
        find(M,NewHeap,Array)
    ).
find(0,_,_).
```

When inserting, each neighbor of the pivot is also checked for a previously computed bestpath, and if one exists, the neighbor is discarded. Otherwise the neighbor is inserted into the heap with `heapIn/3`.

```
insertall([],_,_,Heap,Array,M) :- find(M,Heap,Array).
insertall([Edge*Delta|Es],Cost,Node,Heap,Array,M) :-
    arg(Edge,Array,V),
    (var(V) ->
        NewCost is Cost + Delta,
        heapIn(Heap,a(Edge,NewCost,Node),NewHeap),
        insertall(Es,Cost,Node,NewHeap,Array,M)
    ;
        insertall(Es,Cost,Node,Heap,Array,M)
    ).
```

The heap access procedures are built upon two auxiliary procedures: `heapify/2` and `insert/3`. Procedure `heapify(Root,NewRoot)` makes consistent a heap with a possibly inconsistent root value. Consistency is enforced by percolating the root value downwards until the value reaches a node where it is less than or equal to that node's children's values. Procedure `insert(Root,Data,NewRoot)` writes a value `Data` into `Root`, producing `NewRoot`. The method used is similar to heapifying.

```
heapIn(complete(Root),Data,complete(NewRoot)) :-
    insert(Root,Data,NewRoot).
heapIn(partial(L,R),Data,complete(NewRoot)) :-
    heapify(node(L,Data,R),NewRoot).

heapOut(complete(node(L,Data,R)),Data,partial(L,R)).
heapOut(partial(L,R),Data,partial(L1,R1)) :-
    heapify(node(L,a(leaf,999999,leaf),R),node(L1,Data,R1)).
```

To write a value into a complete heap, the value is inserted into root (`heapIn/3` clause 1). To write a value into a partial heap, the value is bound to the empty root and heapified downwards (`heapIn/3` clause 2). To read a value from a complete heap, the root value is returned and the heap becomes partial (`heapOut/3` clause 1). To read a value from a partial heap, an "infinite" value is bound to the root and heapified downwards (`heapOut/3` clause 2). For our purposes, an infinite value is 999,999, guaranteed to be larger than any path cost. As a result of heapifying an infinite value downwards, the infinite value will come to rest at the leaves, or above other infinite values.

The code for `insert/3` and `heapify/2` is given in Figures 12.2 and 12.3. We do not include a detailed explanation, as the code is quite declarative. The heap is termed "passive" because it is implemented as a pure data structure, with a manager that modifies it by traversal and structure copying. In Section 12.3 we introduce an "active" heap that is implemented as a group of communicating processes.

An interesting part of the passive heap manager is the last clause of `insert/3`, representing the case when the current value can be inserted either into the left or right child with equal validity. To approximate tree balancing, the decision to insert left or right is made by whether the sum of two costs (the value to be inserted and the current node value) is even or odd.

In this bestpath program, the `functor/3` and `arg/3` builtins are frequently used. Most Prolog systems put a limit on the maximum structure size, enforced by these builtins. In the Aurora system the limit is 255 elements. In the procedures given below, up to 65,025 element structures can be accommodated. The Prolog performance measurements presented in this chapter utilize these routines.

```
insert(void,Data,node(void,Data,void)) :- !.
insert(node(Left,A0,void),A,
        node(Left,Top,node(void,Bot,void))) :- !,
    A0 = a(N0,C0,P0), A = a(N,C,P),
    (C0 =< C ->
        Top = A0, Bot = A
    ;
        Top = A, Bot = A0
    ).
insert(node(void,A0,Right),A,
        node(node(void,Bot,void),Top,Right)) :- !,
    A0 = a(N0,C0,P0), A = a(N,C,P),
    (C0 =< C ->
        Top = A0, Bot = A
    ;
        Top = A, Bot = A0
    ).
insert(node(Left,A0,Right),A,New) :-
    A0=a(N0,C0,P0), A=a(N,C,P),
    (C =< C0 ->
        Top = A, Bot = A0
    ;
        Top = A0, Bot = A
    ),
    (0 is (C0+C) mod 2  ->   % either branch is ok...
        New = node(Left,Top,NewRight),
        insert(Right,Bot,NewRight)
    ;
        New = node(NewLeft,Top,Right),
        insert(Left,Bot,NewLeft)
    ).
```

Figure 12.2
Passive Heap Manager in Prolog: insert/3

```
heapify(Heap,New) :-
    Heap = node(node(L1,A1,R1),A0,void),
    A0=a(N0,C0,P0), A1=a(N1,C1,P1),
    (C0 > C1 ->
        New = node(Left,A1,void),
        heapify(node(L1,A0,R1),Left)
    ;
        New = Heap
    ).
heapify(Heap,New) :-
    Heap = node(void,A0,node(L2,A2,R2)),
    A0=a(N0,C0,P0), A2=a(N2,C2,P2),
    (C0 > C2 ->
        New = node(void,A2,Right),
        heapify(node(L2,A0,R2),Right)
    ;
        New = Heap
    ).
heapify(node(node(L1,A1,R1),A0,Right),New) :-
    Right=node(L2,a(N2,C2,P2),R2),
    A0=a(N0,C0,P0), A1=a(N1,C1,P1),
    C0 > C1, (C0 =< C2 ; C1 =< C2), !,
    New = node(NewLeft,A1,Right),
    heapify(node(L1,A0,R1),NewLeft).
heapify(node(Left,A0,node(L2,A2,R2)),New) :-
    Left=node(L1,a(N1,C1,P1),R1),
    A0=a(N0,C0,P0), A2=a(N2,C2,P2),
    C0 > C2, (C0 =< C1 ; C2 < C1), !,
    New = node(Left,A2,NewRight),
    heapify(node(L2,A0,R2),NewRight).
heapify(New,New).
```

Figure 12.3
Passive Heap Manager in Prolog: `heapify/2`

```
bigfunctor(V,N,Arity) :-
    H is Arity//255,
    M is Arity mod 255,
    H1 is H+1,
    functor(V,N,H1),
    loop(H,V),
    (M>0 -> functor(G,t,M),arg(H1,V,G) ; true).

loop(0,_) :- !.
loop(K,V) :-
    K1 is K-1,
    functor(G,t,255),
    arg(K,V,G),
    loop(K1,V).

bigarg(I,A,E) :-
    H is ((I-1)//255)+1,
    M is ((I-1) mod 255)+1,
    arg(H,A,G),arg(M,G,E).
```

There are at least two problems with the heap manager given. First, by frequently heapifying infinite values, the heap grows large, filled with mostly dummy nodes by the end of the algorithm. This problem can be fixed by removing infinite leaves, but at some overhead. Second, the heap is a "passive" structure, so the algorithm is sequentialized. We shall see how to fix this problem in FGHC.

FGHC Versions

In this section we describe five alternative FGHC solutions to the bestpath problem. The first program is included as a bit of humor — a Todai student's contribution of how *not* to program in FGHC. The second program is an "active heap" version of the Johnson-Dijkstra algorithm. The next two programs represent two important concurrent programming styles: a *monitor*-controlled data-structure approach (sometimes called a "blackboard") and a process-structure approach. The final program is variant of Moore's algorithm [84]: a hybrid between the monitor and process-structure schemes.

The modification of the passive heap in Prolog to an active heap in FGHC allows the exploitation of parallelism by overlapping heap accesses with each other and with other computation. The heap is represented by a binary tree of processes and messages are used to communicate heapify and insert operations. Once a message passes down the left branch of a node, other messages are free to pass down the right branch, i.e., concurrent accesses.

The blackboard program encodes the bestpath information in a table whose access is controlled by a *monitor* process. Other search processes explore the graph, creating new potential bestpaths that are sent to the evaluator for inspection. The evaluator replies to each searcher query, causing the searcher to either continue or abandon that path. Termination occurs "naturally" when all the searchers have each terminated independently. At this point the message stream to the evaluator closes indicating that the current table of bestpaths is the final answer.

The process-structure program distributes the bestpath information among the nodes of the graph, each of which corresponds to a process. The node processes communicate with each other, each sending messages containing extensions to its current bestpath. A node process discards a message with higher cost than its current bestpath, and accepts a message with lower cost, as a new bestpath. Eventually each node contains a final bestpath and all communication ceases. To terminate, a *short-circuit technique* is required.

The partitioned-Moore program splits the graph into partitions, and allocates a monitor for each partition. In this sense, it is a distributed form of the blackboard program. From another view, it is a higher-granularity form of the process-structure program, since each process now corresponds to a group of graph nodes. The resulting program has both lower complexity than the previous alternatives, and achieves better speedup.

The performance of these programs is analyzed in Section 12.8.

12.2   How Not to Program in FGHC

The following FGHC program is unique in that, for a small 152-node graph on a single PE, it runs over 100 times slower than our implementation of Dijkstra's algorithm. On 15 PEs, this program is over 200 times slower than the FGHC algorithms we describe next. The program achieves a speedup of 1.3 on two PEs but slows down with increasing numbers of PEs. And on top of all this, the program manages to do this without consuming memory. On the bright side, the program is the *shortest* logic programming implementation we have seen of bestpath!

```
go(Start,N,Paths) :-
    init(1,N,State),
    process(Start,0,none,999999,State,Paths).

update(1,[_|Cs],CP,T) :- T=[CP|Cs].
update(N,[C|Cs],CP,T) :- N>1 | N1 is N-1,
    T=[C|Ts], update(N1,Cs,CP,Ts).
```

```
lookup(N,[ _|Ts],S) :- N>1 | N1 is N-1, lookup(N1,Ts,S).
lookup(1,[C-_|_],S) :- S=C.

init(I,N,A) :- I > N | A=[].
init(I,N,A) :- I =< N | I1 is I+1, A=[999999-_|As], init(I1,N,As).
```

Like the Prolog programs, this program also manipulates a bestpath table. In this case, the table is implemented as a list, State. List element i corresponds to node i. Initially each entry, Cost-Prev, has Cost=999,999, a suitably large number, and the previous node in the bestpath, Prev, is undetermined. There are two access procedures for the state: lookup/3 and update/4. Procedure lookup(N,S,C) returns the cost C of the current bestpath of node N in state S. Procedure update(N,S0,CP,S1) replaces the information of node N in state S0 with new information CP, creating a new state S1. One reason the program is concise but slow is that the state is implemented with a list.

Procedure process(N,C,P,Cost,S0,S1) is given a node N with a potential improved-cost path represented by cost C and previous node P, the currently known minimum cost to the node, Cost, and the current state S0. If the new path cost C is not less than the known minimum cost, then that branch of the search is terminated and the output state S1 is equal to the input state S0 (process/6 clause 1). If a new minimum-cost path has been found (process/6 clause 2), the state is updated with this information and the search is extended among the edges of the node, with send/5.

```
process(_,C,_,Cost,S0,S1) :- C >= Cost | S0=S1.
process(N,C,P,_,S0,S2) :- otherwise |
    update(N,S0,C-P,S1),
    edge(N,Nodes),
    send(Nodes,C,N,S1,S2).
```

The algorithm proceeds by extending the search for bestpaths in process send/5. For each edge extending from a node, the extended path cost, C2, is computed. The known cost of the neighboring node, Cost, is looked up in the state. These two costs are compared in process/6, where the search is recursively extended if the extended path has minimal cost.

```
send([],_,_,S0,S1) :- S1=S0.
send([N*C1|Ns],C,P,S0,S2) :-
    C2 is C+C1,
    lookup(N,S0,Cost),
    process(N,C2,P,Cost,S0,S1),
    send(Ns,C,P,S1,S2).
```

The program is sequential because the update of state information synchronizes the searching of each of the nodes extending from a parent node. State S1 synchronizes the last two body goals in the second clause of **send/5**. One solution to this problem is to introduce an impartial process, often called a *monitor*, to manage the state.

However, the algorithm has a much more serious problem: its time complexity is very high. No comparisons are made among the edges of a node to select the best edge to follow next. The algorithm may easily start out following a high-cost edge, generating presumed bestpaths throughout the graph, only to discover later (when alternative edges from the start node are finally explored) that all the work was in vain.

12.3   Dijkstra's Algorithm with an Active Heap

The Johnson-Dijkstra algorithm with a passive heap, as implemented in Prolog, suffers from heap accesses sequentializing the control flow. To retain the low complexity of the algorithm, one idea is to relax the heap implementation to allow multiple, concurrent accesses. This can be accomplished with an "active" data structure, i.e., a heap constructed of communicating processes.

The following FGHC program is a direct translation of the sequential Prolog program previously given, with two exceptions: both the heap and bestpath table have been reimplemented. The bestpath table is implemented here as a binary tree because Panda is not powerful enough to support efficient accesses to large structures.

The top level, **bestpath/3**, is similar to the previous programs. The bestpath **Table** is initially empty and the heap is initialized with the starting node. Procedure **find(N,Ms,Table)** finds all bestpaths from the start node in an N-node graph specified by **edge/2**, given a stream **Ms** into the root of the heap.

```
bestpath(N, Start, Table) :-
    init(N, Table),
    node(Ms, a(Start,0,none)),
    find(N, Ms, Table).
```

Procedure **find/3** and its auxiliary procedure **insertall/6** are quite similar to the Prolog code. To access the heap, **read/3** and **write/3** messages are sent down the stream to its root. The bestpath table is accessed with **lookup/4**. It is imperative to synchronize the bestpath table **lookup** with **find1**, to ensure that **find1** checks the table entry and does not eagerly execute (in which case the second clause of **find1** may erroneously commit, even if the table entry is bound). Note that when **find** has collected all bestpaths, the message stream to the heap is closed, terminating the heap processes.

```
find(M, Ms, Table) :- M > 0 |
    Ms = [read(a(Node,Cost,Prev))|Ms1],
    lookup(Node,Table,V,Synch),
    find1(Synch,V,Node,Prev,Cost,M,Ms1,Table).
find(0, Ms, _) :- Ms = [].

find1([],P-C,_,_,_,M,Ms,Table) :-
    find(M,Ms,Table).
find1([],V,Node,Prev,Cost,M,Ms,Table) :-
    M1 is M-1,
    V = Prev-Cost,
    edge(Node,Edges),
    insertall(Edges,Cost,Node,Ms,Table,M1).
```

Procedure `find1` is written with the assumption that the clauses are attempted in
their textual order. If this is not the case, then a builtin `var/1` predicate must
be used in the guard of the second clause. Procedure `insertall/6` inserts the
neighbors of the pivot in the heap if the neighbors do not already have a known
bestpath. Insertion is performed with `write/3` messages into the heap root. Again,
`insertall1/10` assumes that the two clauses are attempted in their textual order.

```
insertall([],_,_,Ms,Table,M) :-
    find(M,Ms,Table).
insertall([Edge*Delta|Es],Cost,Node,Ms,Table,M) :-
    lookup(Edge,Table,V,Synch),
    insertall1(Synch,V,Delta,Edge,Es,Cost,Node,Ms,Table,M).

insertall1([],P-C,_,_,Es,Cost,Node,Ms,Table,M) :-
    insertall(Es,Cost,Node,Ms,Table,M).
insertall1([],_,Delta,Edge,Es,Cost,Node,Ms,Table,M) :-
    NewCost is Cost + Delta,
    Ms = [write(a(Edge,NewCost,Node))|Ms1],
    insertall(Es,Cost,Node,Ms1,Table,M).
```

Although the client of a heap, for instance the code above, communicates with only
`read`, `write`, and `[]` messages, there are an additional two types of messages used
internally to the heap. The semantics of all the message types, as received at a
given node, are now defined.

The `[]` message terminates the node. Message `cost(X)`, which is seen only by
interal nodes, returns the value of the node in `X`. Message `read(X)`, which is seen
only by the root, returns the value of a complete root in `X`, and the root becomes
partial. If the root is already partial then an "infinite" value must be heapified
downwards with `replace/1` messages.

Messages `replace/1` and `write/1` perform the actions of heapification and insertion. Message `replace(Vin)`, which is seen only by internal (complete) nodes,

replaces the value of the node with `Vin` if the node's children have greater values. Otherwise the value `Vin` is further heapified downwards, and the value of the node is replaced with one of the children's values.

Message `write` has the dubious distinction of appearing at both partial and complete nodes, since it can be received by both the root and internal nodes. When `write(Vin)` appears at a complete node with one or no children, a new child is created. Value `Vin` is compared with the node's value, and the values in the new child and node are bound accordingly. When `write(Vin)` appears at a complete node with two children, the tree balancing is approximated by routing the message according to whether the sum of two costs is odd or even (**node/4** clause 4). When `write(Vin)` appears at a partial root, `Vin` is heapified downwards in the usual manner.

The FGHC code corresponding to the heap processes is now given. A **partial** root process, of which there can be only one, has from 1–3 arguments depending on the number of children. A complete **node** process has from 2–4 arguments, also depending on the number of children. These processes use four auxiliary procedures that are defined afterwards.

Nodes with no children follow:

```
partial([]).
partial([write(Vin)|Ms]) :- node(Ms,Vin).

node([],                 _).
node([cost(X)      |Ms],V) :- X=V, node(Ms,V).
node([read(X)      |Ms],V) :- X=V, partial(Ms).
node([replace(Vin)|Ms],_) :- node(Ms,Vin).
node([write(Vin)   |Ms],V) :-
    switch(Vin, V, Vpar, Vchild),
    node(Ms, Vpar, Ls),
    node(Ls, Vchild).
```

Nodes with only one child follow:

```
partial([],Ls) :- Ls=[].
partial([read(V)|Ms],L0) :-
    L0 = [cost(Vc)|L1],
    compare(Vc, a(leaf,999999,leaf), V, L1, L2),
    partial(Ms, L2).
partial([write(Vin)|Ms],L0) :-
    L0 = [cost(Vc)|L1],
    compare(Vc, Vin, V, L1, L2),
    node(Ms, V, L2).
```

```
node([],            _,Ls) :- Ls=[].
node([cost(X)|Ms],V,Ls) :- X=V, node(Ms,V,Ls).
node([read(X)|Ms],V,Ls) :- X=V, partial(Ms,Ls).
node([replace(Vin)|Ms],_,L0) :-
    L0 = [cost(Vc)|L1],
    compare(Vc, Vin, V, L1, L2),
    node(Ms, V, L2).
node([write(Vin)|Ms], V, Ls) :-
    switch(Vin, V, Vpar, Vchild),
    node(Ms, Vpar, Ls, Rs),
    node(Rs, Vchild).
```

Nodes with two children follow:

```
partial([],L,R) :- L=[], R=[].
partial([read(V)|Ms],L,R) :-
    L = [cost(Vl)|L1], R = [cost(Vr)|R1],
    compare(Vl, Vr, a(leaf,999999,leaf), V, L1, L2, R1, R2),
    partial(Ms, L2, R2).
partial([write(Vin)|Ms],L,R) :-
    L = [cost(Vl)|L1], R = [cost(Vr)|R1],
    compare(Vl, Vr, Vin, V, L1, L2, R1, R2),
    node(Ms, V, L2, R2).

node([],             _,L,R) :- L=[], R=[].
node([cost(X)    |Ms],V,L,R) :- X=V, node(Ms,V,L,R).
node([read(X)    |Ms],V,L,R) :- X=V, partial(Ms,L,R).
node([write(Vin) |Ms],V,L,R) :-
    Vin = a(_,C0,_), V = a(_,C1,_),
    Even is (C0+C1) mod 2,
    insert(Even, Vin, V, Vnew, L, R, Ls, Rs),
    node(Ms, Vnew, Ls, Rs).
node([replace(Vin)|Ms],_,L,R) :-
    L = [cost(Vl)|L1], R = [cost(Vr)|R1],
    compare(Vl, Vr, Vin, V, L1, L2, R1, R2),
    node(Ms, V, L2, R2).
```

Procedure insert/8 is used to route a heap insertion to one of two children, where either child is acceptable. The first argument is a pseudo-random binary number meant to approximate tree balancing.

```
insert(0, Ain, Aold, Anew, L, R, Ls, Rs) :- Ls = L,
    R = [write(Anext)|Rs],
    switch(Ain, Aold, Anew, Anext).
insert(1, Ain, Aold, Anew, L, R, Ls, Rs) :- Rs = R,
    L = [write(Anext)|Ls],
    switch(Ain, Aold, Anew, Anext).
```

Values A0 and A1 are exchanged as a function of their costs in switch(+,+,-,-).

```
switch(A0,A1,Top,Bot) :-
    A0 = a(_,C0,_), A1 = a(_,C1,_), C0 =< C1 |
    Top = A0, Bot = A1.
switch(A0,A1,Top,Bot) :- otherwise | Top = A1, Bot = A0.
```

Procedure compare(+,+,-,+,-) is used by a parent node with a single child, during heapification. The heapification terminates in the first clause because the parent has a lesser value. The heapification continues in the second clause by issuing a replace/1 message to the child.

```
compare(a(_,Cr,_), Ain, Aout, R, Rs) :- Ain = a(_,Cin,_), Cin =< Cr |
    Aout = Ain, Rs = R.
compare(Ar, Ain, Aout, R, Rs) :- otherwise |
    Aout = Ar, R = [replace(Ain)|Rs].
```

Procedure compare(+,+,+,-,+,-,+,-) is used by a parent with two children. The following code is annotated.

```
% parent cost is less than both child costs: stop heapification
compare(Al, Ar, Ain, Aout, L, Ls, R, Rs) :-
    Ain = a(_,Cin,_), Al = a(_,Cl,_), Ar = a(_,Cr,_),
    Cin =< Cl, Cin =< Cr |
    Aout = Ain, Rs = R, Ls = L.
% parent cost exchanged with left child: heapify down left branch
compare(Al, Ar, Ain, Aout, L, Ls, R, Rs) :-
    Ain = a(_,Cin,_), Al = a(_,Cl,_), Ar = a(_,Cr,_),
    Cl =< Cr, Cl < Cin |
    Aout = Al, L = [replace(Ain)|Ls], Rs = R.
% parent cost exchanged with right child: heapify down right branch
compare(Al, Ar, Ain, Aout, L, Ls, R, Rs) :-
    Ain = a(_,Cin,_), Al = a(_,Cl,_), Ar = a(_,Cr,_),
    Cl > Cr, Cl < Cin |
    Aout = Ar, R = [replace(Ain)|Rs], Ls = L.
% parent cost exchanged with right child: heapify down right branch
compare(Al, Ar, Ain, Aout, L, Ls, R, Rs) :-
    Ain = a(_,Cin,_), Al = a(_,Cl,_), Ar = a(_,Cr,_),
    Cr =< Cl, Cr < Cin |
    Aout = Ar, R = [replace(Ain)|Rs], Ls = L.
% parent cost exchanged with left child: heapify down left branch
compare(Al, Ar, Ain, Aout, L, Ls, R, Rs) :-
    Ain = a(_,Cin,_), Al = a(_,Cl,_), Ar = a(_,Cr,_),
    Cr > Cl, Cr < Cin |
    Aout = Al, L = [replace(Ain)|Ls], Rs = R.
```

The remaining piece of the program is how the bestpath table is implemented. Unfortunately, Panda is not sophisticated enough to allow constant-time updates of a structure, even in a write-once fashion. Here the bestpath table is implemented as a balanced binary tree.

```
init(N,Tree) :- N1 is N+1, make(1,N1,Tree).

make(E,E,_).
make(E1,E2,Tree) :- otherwise |
    R  is E2-E1,
    H  is R//2,
    M  is H+E1,
    M1 is M+1,
    Tree = t(M,_,Left,Right),
    make(E1,M,Left),
    make(M1,E2,Right).

lookup(Key,t(Key,Value,_,_),V,S) :- V=Value, S=[].
lookup(Key,t(Key1,_,Left,_),V,S) :- Key < Key1 |
    lookup(Key,Left,V,S).
lookup(Key,t(Key1,Value,_,Right),V,S) :- otherwise |
    lookup(Key,Right,V,S).
```

Overlapped heap accesses achieve only 45% efficiency on four Symmetry PEs, and no speedup thereafter, as discussed in Section 12.8. In fact, computation pipelining, achieving similar performance, can be achieved with both the passive heap and even a simple list implementation of the priority queue! In any of these data structures, FGHC can schedule subsequent iterations as soon as the root of the queue is bound. Therefore even with structure copying during management, pipelining can take effect.

12.4 Monitor Evaluation

This program is based on an original version written by K. Taki [122]. The top-level procedure arguments are similar to those of the other programs. Initially a single **search** process is spawned with the edges emanating from the starting node. Also the evaluator process, **eval**, is spawned with an initial message instructing it to generate an (empty) table of bestpaths. Note the message stream **Ms** connecting the initial searcher with the evaluator.

```
bestpath(N,Start,Paths) :-
    edge(Start,Edges),
    search(Edges,0,[Start],Ms),
    eval([init(Start,N)|Ms],_,Paths).
```

Procedure **search(Edges,Cost,Path,Ms)** attempts to extend path **Path** with cost **Cost** by iterating on the edges in list **Edges**. For each edge, a new cost is calculated and both **merge** and **check** processes are spawned. The binary **merge** wires together the message streams to the evaluator.

```
search([Node*NodeCost|Edges],PathCost,Path,P0) :-
    NewPathCost is PathCost+NodeCost,
    search(Edges,PathCost,Path,P2),
    merge(P1,P2,P0),
    check(Path,Node,NewPathCost,Path,P1).
search([],_,_,P) :- P=[].
```

The check/5 procedure simply checks that the current node has not been encountered yet in the path (check/5 clause 1). If the node *has* been encountered then this search path is terminated (check/5 clause 2). Otherwise we attempt to extend the search by querying the evaluator about the validity of this new bestpath (check/5 clause 3). The evaluator replies by binding Status. If Status=yes then the new bestpath is the minimal path to this node found so far. In this case the path is extended through the current node and the search continues. If Status=no then the new bestpath is an imposter and this branch of the search is discontinued.

```
check([N|Ns],Node,NewPathCost,Path,P0) :- N =\= Node |
    check(Ns,Node,NewPathCost,Path,P0).
check([N|_],N,_,_,P0) :- P0=[].
check([],Node,NewPathCost,Path,P0) :-
    P0=[query(Node,NewPathCost,Path,Status)|P1],
    cont(Status,Node,Path,NewPathCost,P1).

cont(yes,Node,Path,NewPathCost,Out) :-
    edge(Node,Edges),
    search(Edges,NewPathCost,[Node|Path],Out).
cont(no,_,_,_,Out) :- Out=[].
```

The evaluator eval/3 responds to two types of messages. A query/4 message (clause 1) requests confirmation about a potential new bestpath. The bestpath table information for that node is accessed, and if the new path is of lower cost than the current path in the table, the table is updated. The Status flag is used to indicate if in fact a new bestpath was found.

An init/2 message (clause 2) indicates that a new bestpath table should be initialized by the evaluator. This encapsulates the implementation of the table. Finally, if the message stream is empty (clause 3) then the evaluator knows that the search has terminated, and the current bestpath table is bound to A, the final answer.

```
eval([query(Node,NewCost,NewPath,Status)|Ms],Table,A) :-
    lookup(Node,NewCost-NewPath,Table,NewTable,Status),
    eval(Ms,NewTable,A).
eval([init(Start,N)|Ms],_,A) :-
    init(N,Start,Table),eval(Ms,Table,A).
eval([],Table,A) :- A=Table.
```

The implementation of the bestpath table given here is a binary tree similar to the one used in the previous program. The code here is more complex because this bestpath table must be updated, whereas in Dijkstra's algorithm, the bestpath table is written only once.

```
init(N,Start,Tree) :-
    N1 is N+1,
    make(1,N1,T),
    lookup(Start,0-[],T,Tree,_).

make(E,E,_).
make(E1,E2,Tree) :- otherwise |
    R  is E2-E1,
    H  is R//2,
    M  is H+E1,
    M1 is M+1,
    Tree = t(M,999999-_,Left,Right),
    make(E1,M,Left),
    make(M1,E2,Right).

lookup(Key,New,t(Key,Old,Left,Right),T,S) :-
    T = t(Key,Value,Left,Right),
    insert(New,Old,Value,S).
lookup(Key,New,t(Key1,Old,Left,Right),T,S) :- Key < Key1 |
    T = t(Key1,Old,NewLeft,Right),
    lookup(Key,New,Left,NewLeft,S).
lookup(Key,New,t(Key1,Old,Left,Right),T,S) :- Key > Key1 |
    T = t(Key1,Old,Left,NewRight),
    lookup(Key,New,Right,NewRight,S).

insert(NewCost-NewPath,OldCost-_,Value,S) :- NewCost < OldCost |
    S = yes,
    Value = NewCost-NewPath.
insert(_,Old,Value,S) :- otherwise | S=no, Value=Old.
```

Improving the Search

The previous program performs an inefficient search. Many of the edges in **search** will not be extended, yet a **merge** is spawned for each. There is great overhead in spawning **merges** that will be immediately closed. To avoid this we rewrite the relevant section of the code:

```
search([Node*NodeCost|Edges],PathCost,Path,P0) :- otherwise |
    NewPathCost is PathCost+NodeCost,
    search(Edges,PathCost,Path,P2),
    check(Path,Node,NewPathCost,Path,P2,P0).
search([],_,_,P) :- P=[].
```

```
check([N|Ns],Node,NewPathCost,Path,P2,P0) :- N =\= Node |
    check(Ns,Node,NewPathCost,Path,P2,P0).
check([N|_],N,_,_,P2,P0) :- P0=P2.
check([],Node,NewPathCost,Path,P2,P0) :-
    P0=[query(Node,NewPathCost,Path,Status)|P1],
    cont(Status,Node,Path,NewPathCost,P2,P1).

cont(yes,Node,Path,NewPathCost,[],P) :-
    edge(Node,Edges),
    search(Edges,NewPathCost,[Node|Path],P).
cont(yes,Node,Path,NewPathCost,P2,P0) :-
    merge(P1,P2,P0),
    edge(Node,Edges),
    search(Edges,NewPathCost,[Node|Path],P1).
cont(no,_,_,_,P2,P0) :- P0=P2.
```

Two optimizations are included. First, we delay the spawning of the `merge` until
`cont/6` when we know for certain that the path can be extended along that edge.
Second, we avoid spawning the `merge` for the last edge (`cont/6` clause 1).

12.5 Distributed Nearest Neighbors

This program is based on a version written by N. Ichiyoshi [122]. The idea is to
spawn a process structure corresponding to the graph as in the FGHC implementation of Dijkstra's algorithm given in Section 12.3. The node processes communicate
with their nearest neighbors, sending messages containing extensions to their current bestpath. A node process discards a message with higher cost than its current
bestpath and accepts a message with lower cost, as a new bestpath. Eventually
each node contains a final bestpath and all communication ceases. To terminate
such an algorithm we use a short-circuit chain.

The top-level arguments of the program are similar to those of the previous
programs. The input graph is first transformed by `data/2` into an edge list. The
process structure is generated with `genNodes/4`.

```
bestpath(N,Start,Paths) :-
    data(N,Edges),
    genNodes(N,Start,Edges,Paths).
```

The list of edges has entries of the form `e(M-N,C,F-T)` where neighboring nodes `M`
and `N` communicate over streams `F` (M to N) and `T` (N to M), with edge cost `C`. For
example the edge list of the simple six node graph shown previously is as follows:

```
[e(1-2,2,A-B), e(1-4,1,C-D), e(2-1,2,B-A), e(2-3,3,E-F),
 e(2-5,2,G-H), e(3-2,3,F-E), e(3-6,4,I-J), e(4-1,1,D-C),
 e(4-5,1,K-L), e(5-4,1,L-K), e(5-2,2,H-G), e(5-6,2,M-N),
 e(6-5,2,N-M), e(6-3,4,J-I)]
```

The code generating the edge list is given in Figure 12.4. The details of the procedures are rather messy — it suffices to say that the code has much lower time complexity than simplistic methods with $O(N^2)$ [122]. Procedure genNodes/4 generates the process structure corresponding to the graph.

```
genNodes(N,Start,Edges,Paths) :-
    genNodes(1,N,Edges,_,Paths-[],Start).

genNodes(K,N,_,_,R0-R,_) :- K > N | R0=R.
genNodes(K,N,E0,End,R0-R,S) :- K =< N |
    K1 is K+1,
    genNode(K,E0,E1,[],[],[],End,R0-R1,S),
    genNodes(K1,N,E1,End,R1-R,S).
```

An answer stream is routed between the nodes for collection of the final paths upon termination. A termination variable End is passed to every node process. The starting node is initialized with an additional seed message in its input stream. This message, cp(0,[],End-end) means that it requires zero cost to arrive at the start with no previous node in the path. The final argument is the short-circuit chain. All messages sent during the computation are of this form. Each holds a link to the short-circuit chain and when all links have been shorted, End is bound to the atom end and all processes are terminated.

```
genNode(N,[e(N-_,Cost,Self-Other)|E0],E1,Ins,Outs,Costs,End,RR,S) :-
    Ins1 = [merge(Self)|Ins],
    Outs1 = [Other|Outs],
    Costs1 = [Cost|Costs],
    genNode(N,E0,E1,Ins1,Outs1,Costs1,End,RR,S).
genNode(N,[],_,Ins,Outs,Costs,End,RR,S) :- N =\= S |
    merger(Ins,In),
    node(In,Outs,999999,_,End,RR,Costs,N).
genNode(N,[],_,Ins,Outs,Costs,End,RR,N) :-
    merger([[cp(0,[],End-end)]|Ins],In),
    node(In,Outs,999999,_,End,RR,Costs,N).
genNode(N,E0,E1,Ins,Outs,Costs,End,RR,N) :- otherwise |
    E1 = E0,
    merger([[cp(0,[],End-end)]|Ins],In),
    node(In,Outs,999999,_,End,RR,Costs,N).
genNode(N,E0,E1,Ins,Outs,Costs,End,RR,S) :- N =\= S |
    E1 = E0,
    merger(Ins,In),
    node(In,Outs,999999,_,End,RR,Costs,N).
```

```
data(N,Edges) :- data(1,N,[],Edges).
data(K,N,S,E) :- K > N | E=S.
data(K,N,S0,E0) :- K =< N |
    K1 is K+1,
    edge(K,E),
    add(E,K,S0,S1,[],L,E0,E1),
    mergesort(S1,L,S2),
    data(K1,N,S2,E1).

add([],_,S0,S1,L0,L1,E0,E1) :- E1=E0, S1=S0, L1=L0.
add([N*_|Ns],M,[e(M-K,C,Com)|S0],S1,L0,L1,E0,E2) :- M >= N |
    E0 = [e(M-K,C,Com)|E1],
    add(Ns,M,S0,S1,L0,L1,E1,E2).
add([N*C|Ns],M,S0,S1,L0,L2,E0,E2) :- M < N |
    E0 = [e(M-N,C,From-To)|E1],
    mergesort(L0,N,e(N-M,C,To-From),L1),
    add(Ns,M,S0,S1,L1,L2,E1,E2).

mergesort(E,[],S) :- S = E.
mergesort([],L,S) :- S = L.
mergesort([e(M-K0,C0,D0)|Es],[e(N-K1,C1,D1)|Ls],S) :- M < N |
    S = [e(M-K0,C0,D0)|Ss],
    mergesort(Es,[e(N-K1,C1,D1)|Ls],Ss).
mergesort([E|Es],[L|Ls],S) :- otherwise | S = [L|Ss],
    mergesort([E|Es],Ls,Ss).

mergesort([],_,E,S) :- S = [E].
mergesort([e(M-K,C,Com)|Es],N,E,S) :- M < N |
    S = [e(M-K,C,Com)|Ss],
    mergesort(Es,N,E,Ss).
mergesort([E1|Es],_,E0,S) :- otherwise | S=[E0,E1|Es].
```

Figure 12.4
Creating the Edge List in Ichiyoshi's Distributed BestPath

Node processes respond to one type of message: `cp/3`. If the message's cost is not less than the known cost, the message is discarded after shorting its short-circuit link (`node/8` clause 1). If the message's cost is less than the known cost, then the node is updated and all its neighbors are informed of the new bestpath, via `send/6` (`node/8` clause 2). If End is bound to end then the node process terminates. The node process first sends its node number, current cost path, and previous node number on the output stream. The streams to all of the node's neighbors are closed by broadcasting a nil with `closeOuts`.

```
node([cp(Cost,Path,T0-T)|In],Outs,C,P,End,R,Cs,N) :- Cost >= C |
    T0=T,
    node(In,Outs,C,P,End,R,Cs,N).
node([cp(Cost,Path,T0-T)|In],Outs,C,P,End,R,Cs,N) :- Cost < C |
    send(Outs,Cs,Cost,[N|Path],T0-T,NewOuts),
    node(In,NewOuts,Cost,Path,End,R,Cs,N).
node(_,Outs,C,P,end,R0-R,_,N) :-
    R0=[p(N,C,P)|R],
    closeOuts(Outs).

closeOuts([]).
closeOuts([Out|Outs]) :- Out=[], closeOuts(Outs).
```

Note that `send/6` is the core of the algorithm because it constitutes most of the program's execution. The overhead involved in simply sending a message from one node to another is quite high. The stream for each neighbor must be pulled from the `Outs` list and the new stream, `Out1` must be added to the `NewOuts` list. The short-circuit chain must be wired through the message. The code below can be rewritten to reduce garbage slightly but the bottom line is that issuing each message down a separate stream is costly in terms of time and garbage produced. Finally, the message will be routed through some number of merges before arriving at its destination.

```
send([],_,_,_,T0-T,NewOuts) :- T0=T, NewOuts=[].
send([Out|Outs],[C|Cs],Cost,NewPath,T0-T,NewOuts) :-
    NewCost is Cost+C,
    Out = [cp(NewCost,NewPath,T0-T1)|Out1],
    NewOuts = [Out1|NewOuts1],
    send(Outs,Cs,Cost,NewPath,T1-T,NewOuts1).
```

For the 1237-node graph analyzed in a later section, this algorithm terminated only after some nodes received between 500 and 600 messages! During this computation there are only three types of processes reducing: **node**, **send**, and some kind of merger. As mentioned, **send** can probably be sped up slightly. We discuss the design of fast mergers in the next section. The sparse graphs we studied have few neighbors per node, thereby lessening the advantage of merge trees and the like over simple chains of binary merges. Finally there isn't much that can be done to optimize **node**. In any case, speeding up the mechanics of the program will not help reduce the complexity of the algorithm! The problem is that messages are eagerly sent without any regard for how close to the minimum cost they are. Messages with high costs can propagate throughout the graph creating tremendous traffic.

This algorithm was in fact implemented on the MultiPsi/V2 multiprocessor which offers the full KL1 language, including goal priorities (see Section 2.2.5). A KL1 goal can be assigned a dynamic priority at runtime and will be scheduled accordingly. Chikayama's optimization to this distributed bestpath algorithm in KL1 is to assign a priority to messages with low cost [142]. This is accomplished by issuing the message via a procedure invocation prioritized with the cost. Thus low-cost messages are sent beforc high-cost messages! As a result, graph areas containing low-cost nodes (near the boundary) will be favored over graph areas with high cost (speculative parallelism far from the boundary). Utilizing goal priorities in this manner can successfully throttle speculative parallelism and drastically reduce the complexity of the program.

Panda does not have priorities, although one idea to simulate them is to ensure that the **Outs** list is sorted by increasing costs. One might imagine that if **send/6** issues its low-cost messages first, then depth-first scheduling may help favor computation near the boundary. In truth this is not the case — the dynamics and dependencies of the algorithm and graph are too intricate to ensure that no branches of the search reach out into the speculative region of the graph. We examine a feasible way of simulating priorities after the next section.

12.6   Mergers Revisited

Recall from Section 4.2 that a naive n-way merger can be constructed from a chain of binary **merge** processes:

```
merger([],Out) :- Out=[].
merger([merge(S)|Ms],Out) :-
    merger(Ms,T),
    merge(S,T,Out).
merger([M|Ms],Out) :- otherwise |
    Out = [M|Os],
    merger(Ms,Os).
```

In the bestpath problem we see, for perhaps the first time, that mergers are *critical* to committed-choice languages. Any type of distributed programming involves frequent communication of messages via streams. Unfortunately streams are defined from difference lists, and therefore all data are ordered. This inadvertent ordering stifles most parallelism in a program with pure streams. We have seen this again and again in all-solutions search with pipelined filters.

Alleviating the problem requires creating a new abstract data type that lessens or removes the ordering of stream items. One such scheme is *layered streams* where we relax the ordering with structure sharing. In a layered stream, the order of items can be reconstructed with a simple translation filter. Another scheme is *mergers* that combine streams nondeterministically. In this case, order is completely lost. There are more advanced schemes also, such as *channels* which partially order stream items [135]. We do not discuss these further because they cannot be implemented with the machinery available to committed-choice languages such as FGHC, Parlog, and Strand.

The concept of an unordered stream is so critical, for performance reasons, that most present-day systems offer builtin mergers of some flavor or another. In some cases, the builtins are nothing more than a fast binary merge and macros for the source-level constructions we show here. In other cases, the builtins are implemented at the lowest architectural level, even in micro-code [66]. As pragmatists we find nothing wrong with these solutions. There are those who find the very necessity of merging distasteful and push for unordered streams to become first-class data types. This would be nice; however, there is still a lot we can do even with the simple technology we now have.

A balanced binary tree of **merge** processes gives an $O(\log n)$ n-way merger. For simplicity, we remove the feature of including individual data in the input stream to **merger**. The binary tree can then be constructed as follows:

```
merger(Ms,Out) :-
    merger1(Ms,Ts),
    cont(Ts,Out).

cont([merge(S)],Out) :- Out=S.
cont(Ms,Out) :- otherwise | merger(Ms,Out).

merger1([],Ts) :- Ts=[].
merger1([merge(S)],T) :- T=[merge(S)].
merger1([merge(S0),merge(S1)|Ms],T) :-
    T = [merge(M)|Ts],
    merge(S0,S1,M),
    merger1(Ms,Ts).
```

In the above implementation the second level of the binary tree (from the leaves) is initiated as soon as creation of the first level **merge**s begins. For less delay we can

imagine trees with higher branching factors, using custom-built merge components.
For example with a trinary merge:

```
merge([W|Ws], Xs, Ys, Z) :- Z = [W|Zs], merge(Ws, Xs, Ys, Zs).
merge(Ws, [X|Xs], Ys, Z) :- Z = [X|Zs], merge(Ws, Xs, Ys, Zs).
merge(Ws, Xs, [Y|Ys], Z) :- Z = [Y|Zs], merge(Ws, Xs, Ys, Zs).
merge([], X, Y, Z) :- merge(X,Y,Z).
merge(W, [], Y, Z) :- merge(W,Y,Z).
merge(W, X, [], Z) :- merge(W,X,Z).
```

we can build a balanced trinary tree in a similar manner. Reduction in delay is
offset in these schemes by the increasing complexity of the implementation. Still,
decreasing the number of reductions wins. Recall once again that *Panda has no
builtin support for mergers or binary merge in any form at all.* Thus the measurements of Ichiyoshi's nearest-neighbor program are overly pessimistic.

12.7 Partitioned Moore

The partitioned-Moore algorithm is based on dividing the graph into a small set
of partitions, each with an associated worker process. The worker consists of two
pieces: a bestpath cost table, and a priority queue. In the FGHC implementation,
the partitioning function is simple yet effective, and the cost table is a binary tree.
Prioritization of cost messages is simulated by queuing them in sorted lists. In
fact, the sorted lists can be viewed as a software implementation of the firmware
priority queues in the MultiPsi. The algorithm is also related to Quinn's multiqueue
variation of Moore's algorithm [100]. The program described here was originally
implemented by P. Adamson [3].

The algorithm behaves like a hybrid of both the monitor-based and process-based
paradigms described in previous sections. Each worker acts like a monitor, i.e., the
cost-table access bottleneck in Taki's algorithm is split across several workers. The
high complexity of Ichiyoshi's fully-distributed algorithm is reduced by grouping
several nodes per worker. The resulting performance characteristics are quite en-
couraging: the program achieves real speedups and is the fastest implementation
we have analyzed.

The top-level predicate, `bestpath(N,Start,P,Paths)`, has one argument, P, in
addition to those in the other programs discussed. The graph is divided into P
equal partitions, each group managed with its own priority queue. A node number
K is mapped into partition number K mod P, i.e., consecutively numbered nodes
are split across the partitions. This mapping works well if neighboring nodes are
numbered consecutively, thereby distributing the search quickly and evenly among

the partitions. We discuss the performance characteristics as a function of the
number of partitions and PEs in the next section.

```
bestpath(N,Start,P,Paths) :-
    init(P,N,Tables),
    build_streams(P,Outs,Ins),
    spawn(0,P,Start,Tables,Outs,Ins,_,Paths).
```

Procedure `bestpath/4` creates P initial bestpath `Tables` in `init/3`. In general,
`build_streams(P,Outs,Ins)` transforms the graph into a set of merge networks
connecting the P partitions. List `Ins` is a set of input streams, one per partition,
each merging all messages sent to that partition. List `Outs` is a set of output
stream lists, one list per partition, each list for routing the output messages of the
associated partition. A message is sent (via `send/4`, discussed below) to node K
via the $(K \bmod P)^{th}$ element of the output stream list.

Procedure `spawn/8` creates the `worker` processes, one per partition, that execute
the algorithm. Each `worker` is outfitted with an input stream, `In`, connected to a
priority queue. The priority queue is created by `getQueue/5`. The `worker` has a
bestpath cost `Table`, a list of output streams `Out`, a termination flag `End`, and a
final answer D-list, `F0-F1`.

```
spawn(K,K,_,_,_,_,_,F) :- F=[].
spawn(K,P,Start,[Table|Tables],[Out|Outs],[In|Ins],End,F0) :- K < P |
    K1 is K+1,
    Partition is Start mod P,
    getQueue(Partition, K, Start, In, End),
    worker(K, P, Table, Out, End, F0-F1),
    spawn(K1, P, Start, Tables, Outs, Ins, End, F1).

getQueue(Part, Part, Start, In, End) :-
    queue(In, [a(Start,0,0,End-end)], []).
getQueue(Part0, Part1, _, In, _) :- Part0 =\= Part1 |
    queue(In, [], []).
```

Procedure `getQueue/5` creates the priority queue for each partition. The elements
in the queue, representing paths, are of the form `a(Node,Cost,Prev,Chain)`. The
path terminates at `Node` with previous node `Prev` and total cost `Cost`. The D-list
`Chain` is a short-circuit chain wired between all `a/4` paths.

The partition containing the starting node `Start` (`getQueue/5` clause 1) receives
a queue initialized to `a(Start,0,0,End-end)`. Here the short-circuit chain consists
of the termination flag `End` and the atom `end`. When the chain is fully shorted,
`End=end` and the algorithm terminates. Partitions not containing the starting node
(`getQueue/5` clause 2) receive an empty queue.

Procedure `worker/6` concludes its computation when the termination flag is bound to `end` (clause 1). The local bestpath table is sent out on the answer stream F0 and the output streams are closed with `closeOuts/1`. In the normal mode of operation (clause 2), the next minimum path V is extracted from the local priority queue and checked with `check/7`.

```
worker(_,_,Table,Outs,end,F0-F1) :-
    F0=[Table|F1],
    closeOuts(Outs).
worker(Id,P,Table,Outs,End,F) :-
    send(Id,extract(V),Outs,NewOuts),
    check(V,Id,P,Table,NewOuts,End,F).

closeOuts([]).
closeOuts([Out|Outs]) :- Out=[], closeOuts(Outs).
```

First, `check/7` must check for termination, in which case the bestpath cost table is output and the streams are closed (`check/7` clause 1). Otherwise, the minimum path is accessed in the cost table (`check/7` clause 2). The access function of the table, `lookup/5`, is defined at the end of Section 12.4.

```
check(_,_,_,Table,Outs,end,F0-F1) :-
    F0=[Table|F1],
    closeOuts(Outs).
check(a(Node,Cost,Prev,Chain),Id,P,Table,Outs,End,F) :-
    lookup(Node,Cost-Prev,Table,NewTable,Flag),
    check(Flag,Node,Cost,Prev,Chain,Id,P,NewTable,Outs,End,F).

check(no,_,_,_,D0-D1,Id,P,Table,Outs,End,F) :- D0=D1,
    worker(Id,P,Table,Outs,D,F).
check(yes,Node,Cost,Prev,Chain,Id,P,Table,Outs,End,F) :-
    edge(Node,Edges),
    extend(Edges,Node,Cost,Prev,Chain,Id,P,Table,Outs,End,F).
```

If the path does not represent a real minimum (because the table has a lower cost alternative), then the `worker` continues after shorting the chain within the false minimum path (`check/11` clause 1). If the path is in fact a new minimum (`check/11` clause 2), then its edges are expanded in `extend/11`.

Procedure `extend/11` issues an insertion message to each partition corresponding to the nodes neighboring a new minimum path node (clause 3). Note the wiring of the short-circuit chain through every message to ensure proper termination. The `worker` process continues after the messages are sent (clause 1). The following implementation has a further optimization (clause 2) wherein a message is not sent to the previous node in the current best path.

```
extend([],_,_,_,D0-D1,Id,P,Table,Outs,End,F) :- D0=D1,
    worker(           Id,P,Table,Outs,D,  F).
extend([Prev*_|Rest],Last,Cost,Prev,Chain,Id,P,Table,Outs,End,F) :-
    extend(     Rest, Last,Cost,Prev,Chain,Id,P,Table,Outs,End,F).
extend([Node*Delta|Rest],Last,Cost,Prev,D0-D2,Id,P,Table,Outs,End,F) :-
    Node =\= Prev |
    NewCost is Cost + Delta,
    Part is Node mod P,
    send(Part,insert(a(Node,NewCost,Last,D0-D1)),Outs,NewOuts),
    extend(Rest,Last,Cost,Prev,D1-D2,Id,P,Table,NewOuts,End,F).
```

Procedure send(P,M,Outs,NewOuts) issues a message M to partition P via the associated stream in list Outs. The tail of that stream is incorporated into a new stream list, NewOuts. Unlike send/6 in Section 12.5, here we send a message to a single process (representing a group of nodes). However, the procedure is invoked repeatedly when extending a node, in extend/11. An expanded version of the definition below is necessary for more than six partitions.

```
send(0,M,[A         |Ss],S) :- A=[M|Ms], S=[         Ms|Ss].
send(1,M,[A,B       |Ss],S) :- B=[M|Ms], S=[A,       Ms|Ss].
send(2,M,[A,B,C     |Ss],S) :- C=[M|Ms], S=[A,B,     Ms|Ss].
send(3,M,[A,B,C,D   |Ss],S) :- D=[M|Ms], S=[A,B,C,   Ms|Ss].
send(4,M,[A,B,C,D,E |Ss],S) :- E=[M|Ms], S=[A,B,C,D, Ms|Ss].
send(5,M,[A,B,C,D,E,F|Ss],S) :- F=[M|Ms], S=[A,B,C,D,E,Ms|Ss].
```

The remaining pieces of the program are auxiliary functions: transforming the graph into a merge network, implementing the priority queues, and implementing the bestpath cost tables. The graph transformation code is given in Figure 12.5. Procedure queue(Ms,List,Q) manages the priority list, List, executing the commands on stream Ms. The two commands are extract/1 and insert/1. The manager is more complex than the program given in Section 3.4 because this queue is sorted. The sort is performed by procedure find/3.

```
queue([],_,_).
queue([extract(X)|Ms],[],    Q)  :- queue(Ms,[],[X|Q]).
queue([extract(X)|Ms],[H|T],Q)  :- X=H, queue(Ms,T,Q).
queue([insert(X) |Ms],T,    []) :- find(X,T,Tnew), queue(Ms,Tnew,[]).
queue([insert(X) |Ms],T,[Q|Qs]) :- Q=X, queue(Ms,T,Qs).

find(a(E1,C1,P1,D1),[a(E2,C2,P2,D2)|Rest],A) :- E1 =\= E2, C1 > C2 |
    A = [a(E2,C2,P2,D2)|As],
    find(a(E1,C1,P1,D1),Rest,As).
find(a(E1,C1,P1,D1),[a(E2,C2,P2,D2)|Rest],A) :- C1 =< C2 |
    A = [a(E1,C1,P1,D1),a(E2,C2,P2,D2)|Rest].
find(a(E,C1,_,D1),[a(E,C2,P2,D2)|Rest],A) :- C1 >= C2 | D0=D1,
    A = [a(E,C2,P2,D2)|Rest].
find(Item,[],A) :- A=[Item].
```

```
build_streams(N,Outs,Ins) :-
    build_matrix(N,N,Matrix,MergeList),
    transpose(Matrix,Outs),
    domerges(MergeList,Ins).

build_matrix(0,_,A,M) :- A=[], M=[].
build_matrix(N,P,Matrix,MergeList) :- N > 0 |
    N1 is N-1,
    Matrix = [Streams|Mxs],
    MergeList = [Mlist|Ms],
    col(P,Streams,Mlist),
    build_matrix(N1,P,Mxs,Ms).

col(0,Col,Mergelist) :- Col=[], Mergelist=[].
col(N,Col,Ml) :- N > 0 |
    N1 is N-1,
    Col = [ThisStream|Cs],
    Ml = [mymerge(ThisStream)|Ms],
    col(N1,Cs,Ms).

transpose([[]|_],A) :- A=[].
transpose([H|T],A) :- H \= [] |
    A = [Col|As],
    take_first([H|T],Remainder,Col),
    transpose(Remainder,As).

take_first([],N,A) :- N=[], A=[].
take_first([[H|T]|Rest],New,A) :-
    A = [H|As],
    New = [T|Ns],
    take_first(Rest,Ns,As).

domerges([],S) :- S=[].
domerges([Mlist|Rest],StreamList) :-
    StreamList = [S|Ss],
    merger(Mlist,S),
    domerges(Rest,Ss).
```

Figure 12.5
Creating the Stream Lists in Partitioned-Moore BestPath

This queue also has the ability to borrow against future insertions. If an **extract(X)** message arrives when the queue is empty, then **X** is pushed onto a secondary queue, **Q**. When an **insert(Y)** arrives and **Q** is non-empty, an element is popped from **Q** and bound to **Y**. In this case, **Y** is not inserted into the priority queue. This mechanism prevents deadlock from occurring. Note that a **worker** will suspend when an **extract** message is not answered. Thus multiple **extracts** cannot originate from the same **worker**. In fact, **queue/3** is more general than is required by the bestpath program because a worker can issue **extract** requests to its own queue only. Therefore **Q** can be just a single logical variable.

The implementation of the bestpath table given here is a set of binary trees, each similar to the tree defined in Section 12.5. We use trees because Panda does not support constant-time structure updates. Procedure **init(P,N,TreeList)** creates P trees in a list, **TreeList**, each of approximate size N/P. Each tree holds a mutually exclusive subset of the graph node numbers. The tree is defined as **t(Key,Cost-Prev,Left,Right)**, where **Key** is the lookup key, **Cost-Prev** is the bestpath cost and previous node, and **Left**, **Right** are subtrees. Leaves are represented with the atom **nil**. Procedure **make/5** is analogous to **make/3** in Section 12.4; however, the calculation of the key is more complex. Initially, all cost values are 999,999, a sufficiently high value.

```
init(P,N,TreeList) :-
    Size is N//P + 2,
    trees(0,P,Size,TreeList).

trees(P,P,_,T) :- T=[].
trees(K,P,Size,T) :- K < P | K1 is K+1,
    T = [Tree|Ts],
    make(0,Size,P,K,Tree),
    trees(K1,P,Size,Ts).

make(Start,Fin,_,_,Tree) :- Start > Fin | Tree = nil.
make(Fin,Fin,P,Offset,Tree) :-
    N is Fin*P + Offset,
    Tree = t(N,999999-_,nil,nil).
make(Start,Fin,P,Offset,Tree) :- Start < Fin,
    Size  is Fin - Start,
    Split is Size // 2,
    Key   is Start + Split,
    M1    is Key-1, M2 is Key+1,
    Kval  is Key*P + Offset,
    Tree = t(Kval,999999-_,Left,Right),
    make(Start,M1, P,Offset,Left),
    make(M2,   Fin,P,Offset,Right).
```

Language	Origin	Method
Prolog	Dijkstra	passive heap
		sequential but low complexity
FGHC	Dijkstra	active heap
		retains low complexity, poor speedup
	Taki	monitor-based search: single monitor manages
		OR-parallel path search, damping complexity
	Ichiyoshi	fully distributed: local communication has
		high complexity and very good speedup
	Moore	partitioned, with prioritized list
		low complexity and very good speedup

Table 12.1
Summary of BestPath Algorithms

12.8   Discussion and Summary

The performance measurements of a 1237-node graph are discussed in this section.
The graph derives from a digitized street map of part of Shimooma, a suburb of
Tokyo. The nodes are actual street intersections and the edge costs are the length
of the streets between two intersections. The graph is sparse, i.e., relatively few
edges per vertex. Sparse graphs offer less opportunity for parallel search than
high-connectivity graphs because the boundary remains limited in size. In a street
map, the boundary grows as the square of the distance from the starting node. A
three-dimensional grid would grow the boundary as the cube, and so on.

The algorithms described in the chapter are summarized in Table 12.1. Table
12.2 and Table 12.3 give the performance statistics for the 1237-node graph. The
'—' statistics represent no improvement in execution speed with increasing numbers
of PEs. Figure 12.6 summarizes the Panda measurements. Note the utilizations
greater than one, indicating superlinear speedup. These anomalies are explained
below.

The most significant characteristic is the successively decreasing complexity from
the fully-distributed algorithm, to the monitor algorithm, to the Johnson-Dijkstra
(essentially sequential) algorithm, and finally to the partitioned Moore algorithm.
Compared to Prolog, none of the FGHC programs can achieve real speedup, except for partitioned Moore. We would expect, however, that an implementation of
Dijkstra's algorithm (with either a priority list or passive heap) in FGHC would be
competitive with the Prolog program (see Exercise 126).

The measurements presented for partitioned Moore in Tables 12.2 and 12.3 have

System	Method	1 PE	2 PE	4 PE	8 PE	12 PE	15 PE
		execution time (seconds)					
Aurora	Dijkstra (passive)	23.5					
Panda	Ichiyoshi (distr)	569.9	266.3	127.2	72.7	47.9	41.0
	Taki (monitor)	315.3	189.7	82.8	74.9	43.0	50.8
	Dijkstra (active)	47.0	32.6	26.6	—	—	—
	Moore (list)	43.8	22.3	8.1	5.7	5.0	—
		naive speedup					
Panda	Ichiyoshi (distr)	1.0	2.1	4.5	7.8	12	14
	Taki (monitor)	1.0	1.7	3.8	4.2	7.3	6.2
	Dijkstra (active)	1.0	1.4	1.8	—	—	—
	Moore (list)	1.0	2.0	5.4	7.7	8.8	—

Table 12.2
Bestpath (1237-Nodes): Execution Time (seconds) on Symmetry

System	Method	instr	reduct	back/susp	entries	sec	KEPS
Aurora	Dijkstra (PE=1)		70194	56847	127041	23.5	5
Panda	Ichiyoshi (distr)	23668267	1264420	494251	1758671	72.7	24
	Taki (monitor)	18804210	1365508	171738	1537246	74.9	21
	Dijkstra (active)	2517053	133496	56842	190338	26.6	7
	Moore (list, 8 part)	1432668	71008	21652	92660	5.9	16

Table 12.3
Bestpath (1237-Nodes): High-Level Characteristics (eight PEs Symmetry)

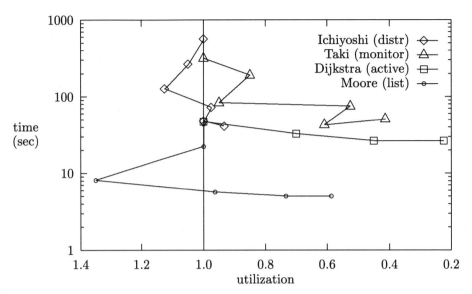

Figure 12.6
Bestpath (1237-Nodes): Panda Utilization vs. Time (Symmetry)

the number of partitions set to minimize execution time. Table 12.4 gives a more
in-depth look at the relationship between execution time, number of PEs, and
number of partitions (the variance gets increasingly larger with the number of
partitions — these measurements are minimum observed values). The columns
without measurements represent *very* lengthy computations. When the number of
partitions is less than the number of PEs, performance is poor because the `worker`
processes are split across PEs. The statistics suggest that a performance-optimal
number of partitions is approximately equal to the number of PEs. Intuitively,
the fastest execution occurs when each PE executes some small number of `worker`
processes, possibly time-sharing between them. The on-demand Panda scheduler
manages best with an equal number of partitions and PEs. There is no explicit
mapping of `worker` processes to PEs, although these measurements indicate such a
binding. In contrast, we note that the JAM Parlog scheduler [38] operates fastest
when the number of partitions is half the number of PEs, for the same program.

   Both Ichiyoshi's algorithm and the partitioned-Moore program achieved naive
superlinear speedup on small numbers of PEs because of nondeterminate process
scheduling. In other words, the search complexity is reduced by a lucky arrival
sequence of messages. These measurements depend on the labeling of the graph

# Partitions	# Processors					
	1	**2**	**4**	**8**	**12**	**15**
1	43.8	31.7	22.6	20.2	20.5	21.3
2	40.8	22.3	15.1	13.4	12.8	12.5
4		120.3	9.5	8.2	7.6	7.5
8			8.1	5.9	5.0	5.1
12			10.3	5.7	5.0	4.9

Table 12.4
Partitioned Moore (1237-Nodes): Execution Time (seconds) on Symmetry

and the modulus mapping we used — another labeling and mapping will no doubt produce different characteristics.

Considering real speedup with respect to the sequential Prolog execution time, partitioned Moore achieved a speedup of 4.7 on 12 PEs, or 39% efficiency. This comparison is unfair however, because the Prolog program uses an write-once array for the bestpath cost table, whereas the partitioned-Moore program uses a non-destructive binary tree. On a single PE, partitioned Moore reduces to Dijkstra's algorithm, yet their execution time ratio is 1.9. The extra 90% derives from the inability to destructively update the cost table.

Exercises

Exercise 121 Write efficient procedures in OR-parallel Prolog and FGHC to convert the node array representation of bestpaths into the actual paths. For example,

```
?- convert([0-none,2-1,5-2,1-1,2-4,4-5],X).
   X = [0-[1],2-[2,1],5-[3,2,1],1-[4,1],2-[5,4,1],4-[6,5,4,1]]
```

Can this be parallelized?

Exercise 122 Modify the monitor evaluation FGHC program for the BestPath problem to *avoid* using merge. Instead use a stream to communicate with the evaluator. Measure the performance and speedups, and compare to the merge version given. What conclusions can you draw about the utility of communication via mergers?

Exercise 123 In the nearest-neighbor message-passing FGHC program for the BestPath problem, the procedure sendOuts/6 is not very smart. Suppose node

B receives a message from a neighbor, node A. If the message contains a new minimum cost for node B, node B then proceeds to send messages to all its neighbors (with the connecting edge costs added in), via `sendOuts/6`. Node B will also send a message back to node A. Such a message will surely *not* be a new minimum cost for A (the path traveled from A to B and then back). We can avoid such messages by sending the node identifier in the message. For each node, not only must we save the edge costs and channels, but also the node identifiers corresponding to these edges. Then `sendOuts/6` can avoid sending a message to a node who just sent it a message. Does performance improve with this optimization?

Exercise 124 Test the nearest-neighbor message-passing FGHC program for the BestPath problem with an improved `merger` (see Exercise 32). Develop an input graph that illustrates the improvement in performance.

Exercise 125 Rewrite the balanced binary tree n-way merger to include the feature of accepting individual data items on the input stream.

Exercise 126 Write Dijkstra's sequential algorithm in FGHC with the priority queue implemented both as a list and as a passive heap. Compare the performances with the Prolog passive heap program and the FGHC active-heap program given. Show that parallelism can still be exploited by overlapping accesses, even with these simple data structures. In what situations or applications would an "active" data structure display significant performance benefits?

Exercise 127 Implement the active-heap Johnson-Dijkstra and partitioned-Moore algorithms in a logic programming system with efficient structure access. Rewrite the bestpath table manager to use a write-once array and compare the performances with the given versions.

Exercise 128 An innovative idea for an FGHC implementation of the Bestpath Problem, also based on Dijkstra's algorithm, represents the boundary as a comparator tree. As pivots are chosen from within the graph, their neighbors are added to the boundary. Consider a boundary wherein the nodes are merged with a tree of binary merge/comparators. A merge/comparator will save the minimum value seen on its inputs and filter away all inputs with a greater value. In this manner the root of the comparator tree will have the minimum cost, i.e., the new pivot!

If the comparator tree is balanced, a new pivot can be produced in $O(\log N)$ delay where N is the boundary size. In addition, the comparator tree can overlap comparisons, computing multiple pivots simultaneously. Implement this scheme in FGHC and measure its performance, comparing it to the active heap version. Comment on the overheads and bottlenecks in this scheme.

Exercise 129 Consider the following OR-parallel bestpath algorithm suggested by R. Overbeek. The boundary in Dijkstra's algorithm is incrementally built by extending it at the pivot, i.e., the node with the shortest path (from the start). The neighbors of the pivot are added to the boundary. It is not necessarily true that the next pivot will come from these new boundary nodes. It is in fact *improbable* because often the boundary is extended along a "wavefront." If two successive pivots are not related as neighbors, then selection of both pivots can proceed concurrently. In general, multiple pivots can be extended in parallel.

In this scheme, the entire boundary is extended, to some depth, in OR-parallel. The collected nodes are thus not all true members of the boundary — some of them may be "false" extensions. The candidates must therefore be sorted and filtered (only the minimum-cost instance of each node retained) to guarantee their membership in the boundary. For those new boundary members, all of whose neighbors are also in the boundary, the minimum cost is known. These nodes (analogous to pivots) are not extended again.

Implement this algorithm in OR-parallel Prolog and measure its performance.

Exercise 130 Empirically analyze the performance of the various algorithms discussed in this chapter with respect to the degree of graph connectivity. Artificially generate graphs of arbitrary connectivity and size for your measurements. Do your results indicate better algorithms for highly-connected graphs?

Exercise 131 Write a program to find the set of all spanning trees for a connected graph. A spanning tree is a group of edges with no cycles that includes every node in the graph. A fantastically inefficient Prolog program for this problem may be found in Bratko [16]. A reasonable Strand program may be found in Foster [49]. We suggest that for this and the next three exercises, you experiment with very small graphs!

Exercise 132 Write a program to find the set of all *minimum-cost* spanning trees for a connected graph. A discussion of an appropriate algorithm and a Flat Concurrent Prolog implementation can be found in Shafrir and Shapiro [115].

Exercise 133 Write a program to find the set of all Hamiltonian paths from a given start node to every node in a connected graph. A Hamiltonian path is an acyclic path that includes every node. Note that a pair of nodes may *not* have a Hamiltonian path.

Exercise 134 Write a program to find the set of all *minimum-cost* Hamiltonian paths from a given start to every node in a connected graph.

Exercise 135 Write a program to travel from a given start node to a finish node, passing through every node, with minimum cost. The difference between this and the previous exercise is that here we allow cycles, guaranteeing that such a path exists for each node in the graph. The inclusion of cycles makes the search difficult to conduct. For example consider a graph shaped like a four-leaf clover, i.e., four subgraphs joined together at a single "bridge" node. We must cross the bridge at least three times to pass through all nodes.

Exercise 136 Write a program to navigate through a maze. A maze is a planar graph with fixed start and exit nodes. At first write an algorithm that guarantees discovery of the exit in a finite number of moves (from node to node). Then rewrite your algorithm with heuristics that reduce the number of moves.

Exercise 137 (24 Hours of Le Mans) Write a discrete-time simulator to navigate through a rectilinear maze in a simple car. Nodes in a rectilinear maze have at most four edges, grouped in two pairs. Assume the edges are labeled with their integer lengths.

Initially the car has zero speed and is located at the start node. The car must finish at the exit node at any speed. Each time step of the simulation the car can accelerate by five units or decelerate by two units. The car can pass through a node via edges of the same pair at any speed. However, to pass through the node via edges of different pairs (i.e., to turn left or right) the car must first decelerate to a dead stop. If the driver miscalculates the proper deceleration so that the speed is positive at a junction node, there are two possibilities. If the car's incoming edge is a member of a pair, i.e., the road continues straight, then the car will overshoot the turnoff. However, if the road does not continue (either it is a "T" or "L") then the car crashes. A crash delays the car 20 time steps while it gets repairs.

Modularize your program so that the details of the maze implementation and layout are hidden from the driver procedure. At any given position, the driver can only see the upcoming node and its outgoing edges. The state of the car at any given time consists of its speed and relative location within some edge. Of course, the driver can be implemented to store any or all of the maze that it has seen.

Experiment with different mazes to develop a first-class driving course. Experiment with different driving strategies to reduce the number of time steps necessary to complete the course. Organize a competition between programs over the same course.

Exercise 138 (The Japanese Game of Life) Committed-choice languages are very good for simulations of all kinds. Implement the Japanese Game of Life with a discrete-time step simulator written in FGHC.

Initially there are L Dietmen, M geishas and N angry wives, randomly located in the Tokyo subway system. The individuals in our story travel according to the following rules. A geisha randomly flits about, with a strong bias towards Ginza where she will go shopping. A geisha has a scent (most likely an expensive perfume) and thus leaves a trail which can be detected by others. A Dietman travels in a drunken stupor (Brownian motion) until he detects the scent of a geisha. He then follows her path (the path is *not* directional, so half the time he follows the path *in the wrong direction*). The Dietman also has a scent (freshly printed Y10,000 notes and whiskey). An angry wife generally travels in spirals, hoping to catch scent of a Dietman, whom she will try to follow.

If a Dietman meets a Dietman, they immediately exit the subway for the nearest bar. If a wife meets a lone Dietman, together they take the next train home, to Denenchofu.

If a Dietman meets up with a geisha, they travel together, making all due haste for Akasaka. However, together they give off such an overpowering scent that angry wives from nearby can determine where they are! The wives attempt to get to them before they can escape from the system. If a wife catches a Dietman with a geisha, she kills them both immediately.

Illustrate the correctness of your simulator for various numbers and initial locations of Dietmen, geishas and wives. Clearly state all assumptions.

13 Summary and Conclusions

"The whole magical thing about our painting, Mrs Berman, and this was old stuff in music, but it was brand new in painting: it was pure *essence of human wonder*, and wholly apart from food, from sex, from clothes, from houses, from drugs, from cars, from news, from money, from crime, from punishment, from games, from war, from peace—and surely apart from the universal human impulse among painters and plumbers alike toward inexplicable despair and self-destruction!"

Kurt Vonnegut
BlueBeard
Dell 1987

In this final chapter, a review of parallel logic programming techniques is given, along with a critique of their utility. We summarize the empirical performance results of the previous chapters, comparing all the programs at once. When the programs are studied piecemeal, one easily loses sight of certain trends and characteristics. Here we wish to "tie up loose ends" by taking a wider view of parallel logic programming. We look at all the programs with the question in mind: "How easy was it to write these programs?" This question leads to some philosophizing about the future of parallel logic programming, from both language and architecture viewpoints.

13.1 Programming Techniques

13.1.1 OR-Parallel Prolog

All parallelism in OR-Parallel Prolog is exposed with the **parallel** declaration. This declaration is made for nondeterminate procedures that promise to split the computation space into independent chunks of work. The larger the chunks, the more efficient the program execution. One extreme of maximum granularity leading to linear speedup is illustrated by the N-Cubes program. Here nondeterminate **set** and **rotate** procedures are declared parallel. The procedures respectively split the OR-tree into six and four roughly equal chunks for each invocation. The other extreme of minimum granularity leading to dismal speedup is illustrated by Pascal's Triangle. Here the nondeterminate **pair** procedure is declared parallel. A **findall** invokes **pair** to add all adjacent pairs of integers in a vector. The amount of work per parallel branch is too low to achieve good speedup.

The **parallel** declaration is used in conjunction with a **findall** or similar builtin to collect multiple solutions in parallel. We exclusively used **findall** in this book because it has the least overhead of the aggregation operators and has sufficient power for our needs. Note that, depending on system implementation, `findall` may be defined to return its solutions in the sequential Prolog order or in a non-specified order, i.e., out-of-order. The former is helpful if we need to reconstruct the solutions into a single data structure, as in Pascal's Triangle where we reconstruct the sums into a new vector. If an unordered `findall` is used, a secondary phase of sorting the solutions may be necessary. For instance, we saw (Section 11.2.3) how AND-in-OR parallelism can be simulated with `member` to sort solutions generated by an unordered `findall`.

Parallel procedures are executed by creating a branchpoint representing the existence of multiple clauses that can potentially succeed. Depending on many dynamic factors, the system will spawn parallel branches from the branchpoint. A branch can be executed by a worker, i.e., processor. When a worker becomes idle, it traverses the OR-tree looking for a suitable branchpoint from which to execute a branch. One useful heuristic for selecting the branchpoint is that any other workers executing its branches are doing significant enough computation (i.e., must be deep enough in the OR-tree) to warrant more parallel exploration.

Often the procedure we declare to be `parallel` is recursive, like most Prolog procedures. The standard two-clause definition of `member` is a good example. The recursion limits the efficiency of the branchpoint because the tail recursion causes a reduction and the creation of another branchpoint. Even if the space occupied by the previous branchpoint can be reused, the management overhead is still high. To increase the *pregnancy* of the choicepoint, we can *unroll* the procedure to increase the number of potential branches per recursion. Again, `member` is a good example of this practice — unrolled `member` is used in several of the programs in this book.

A beneficial byproduct of unrolling is that, even in sequential execution, the number of reductions decreases. A disadvantage of unrolling is that it can confuse otherwise declarative procedures, making them difficult to understand, debug, and extend. In the best of all possible worlds, unrolling would be done automatically by an optimizing compiler.

Related to unrolling is a more general technique of *granularity collection* for efficiently exploiting large-grain parallelism. The idea is to collect as much work as possible into chunks that can be executed independently in OR-parallel. A well-written sequential program often will distribute these chunks of work around many recursive loops, thus increasing modularity and minimizing reductions. The program can be restructured so that the independent work is collected, often in the form of lists or other data structures, to be issued to a `findall` that can execute in parallel. An example of this restructuring is the Semigroup program, where we collected two vectors with the purpose of calculating their cross-product (Section 11.2.4). The vectors were passed to `newTuple` and evaluated by two parallel, unrolled `members` and a vector multiplication procedure.

For problems that contain only AND-parallelism, such as computing a determinate solution with no nondeterminate subcomponents, OR-parallel Prolog is at a loss. With no `parallel` declarations, the OR-Prolog programs execute efficiently under Aurora, losing some small percentage due to overheads on a single processor. However, the real problems occur when one attempts to exploit parallelism on multiple PEs when there just isn't that much parallelism there. In such cases, Aurora has a tendency to thrash — the main culprit is the scheduler we measured [17]. For example, the AND-in-OR technique can only work for very large-grain tasks. When we tried to use it for Pascal's Triangle, performance suffered greatly. By granularity collection we managed to achieve naive speedups, but could not achieve real speedups (with respect to the sequential algorithm). Current research in OR-parallel scheduling for Aurora has already produced one scheduler [18] superior to the version we measured here, and more are on the way [15, 12]. In addition, other OR-parallel systems (e.g., Muse [6]) use different schedulers. However, we don't expect any of these to do extremely well either in cases of very small granularity.

In summary, parallel Prologs can use as many programming paradigms as can Prolog. Implicit parallelism is exploited with no need for significant help from the programmer. Applications performing large-grain all-solutions searches can exploit OR-parallelism most efficiently. However, all nondeterminate programs can benefit, such as parsers, deductive databases, and planners [72].

13.1.2 AND-Parallel FGHC

We categorize committed-choice languages as "concurrent" because programs in these languages have a "process reading" in addition to the standard procedural and declarative semantics of Horn-clause programs. The process reading is an interpretation of the program wherein goals are processes that communicate via shared logical variables.

A variety of communication methods are used. The simplest is when a producer process binds a logical variable that is read by a consumer process. If the consumer attempts to read the variable before it is bound, then the consumer will suspend. Thus synchronization is implemented hand-in-hand with communication. FGHC implements synchronization by suspending if an output unification is attempted in the head or guard of a clause. Other committed-choice languages differ only slightly in their synchronization mechanisms.[1]

More powerful communication methods can be built on top of binding a single variable. The variable may be bound to a structure containing another unbound variable meant to hold an answer binding (Foster [49] compares this to including a self-addressed stamped envelope inside a letter). In fact, the internal variable may be used either for a return binding or for a further message from the producer process. The latter methodology is often specialized to list form: [M|Ms] where M is the current message and Ms is a list of all subsequent messages. This list, of course, is a stream. Writing a message M to a stream is a bit more difficult. We need to use a difference list (D-list), S0-S, and bind S0 = [M|S1], giving a new D-list S1-S.

We noted throughout the book that streams implemented as D-lists have several advantages as well as problems. D-lists can be compiled efficiently, they are easy to manipulate, they can be appended in constant time, and they are declarative. However, D-lists are also inherently ordered, which can remove most of the potential parallelism in a program. D-lists can grow without limit (as can lists), making eager evaluation of a producer dangerous in terms of sucking up system resources. Solutions to these two major problems come in the form of more advanced communication structures built on top of streams: layered streams, mergers, and buffers.

A layered stream is a list of elements H*Ts where Ts is a layered stream containing all the possible tails of a list with head H. The elements in a layered stream are still ordered, but structure sharing relaxes synchronization constraints, thus allowing more parallelism. We analyzed many layered streams programs in this book and achieved quite good performance and speedups. Data sharing reduced the algorithmic complexity of constraint problems and facilitated parallel execution. The main disadvantages of layered streams are that their applications are limited and programming with them is rather difficult.

There is no data structure in FGHC or similar committed-choice languages that allows communication with absolutely no order imposed on the messages. However, we can remove the order with mergers that nondeterminately join multiple streams. Some systems offer mergers as builtins, efficiently implemented even at as low a level as microcode. In the Panda system described here, mergers are implemented in FGHC itself, as trees of merge processes. Such an implementation is a high price to pay to remove stream ordering — each message sent causes a series of reductions

---

[1]The type of synchronization described is weak because the largest data structure that can be atomically bound is a simple logical variable. Therefore emulation of a complex object whose state must be atomically updated is very messy. As summarized in Section 2.2.5, some committed-choice languages incorporate *atomic unification* which alleviates some but not all of this problem.

and suspensions in the merge tree. We saw that, for distributed algorithms that do a lot of communication, this overhead is simply not tolerable.

The other problem with D-lists mentioned above is their potential for unlimited growth. On the face of it, such growth does not seem disadvantageous since, like most languages utilizing dynamic data structures, we do not wish to statically fix the size of data structures. However, sometimes we do wish to fix the length of a stream (at any given time) in order to limit the computation performed by a producer communicating its output on that stream. We described two similar methods of limiting the producer: bounded buffers and lazy evaluation.

A bounded buffer is a D-list of fixed size. The size is enforced by reading and writing rules that must explicitly be obeyed by the producer and consumer communicating via the buffer. As with a stream, the consumer can read a message only when the buffer is not empty, otherwise the consumer suspends. When the consumer reads a message, it creates a new "slot" (unbound logical variable) in the buffer's tail. The producer can write a message only if a free unbound slot exists, otherwise the producer suspends. This method of communication prevents the producer from "running away" and calculating more data than is needed by the consumer.

A similar method is data-driven computation or lazy evaluation. Here the program structure is itself modified so that the output stream connecting the consumer and producer is initially bound by the consumer, not the producer. The consumer binds the stream to a series of slots, each to hold a datum generated by the producer. The producer is then rewritten so that its computation is synchronized on each such slot. Committed-choice programs are normally written as eager evaluators, i.e., standard stream communication between a producer supplying a consumer with data. Rewriting an eager program to a lazy program is often not trivial.

During the course of program development, if too many system resources are being spent on some producer, that section of the code must be rewritten. We may choose to modify the code with bounded-buffer communication or with lazy evaluation. Lazy evaluation has the benefit of enabling a search of a given number of the solutions in a multiple-solution problem. Other methods of limiting resource usage with short-circuit chains are unreliable if the scheduler is not fair.

The above discussion summarizes the basic communication mechanisms in stream-AND-parallel committed-choice languages, specifically FGHC. If performance were not a concern, then even the previously mentioned layered streams, buffers, and lazy evaluation would be unnecessary. However, performance is very much our concern and we now summarize a few more techniques developed in the book.

For all-solutions search problems, such as Zebra and Turtles, an OR-parallel search can be simulated with a committed-choice language in several ways. We analyzed the performance of automatic translation, pipelined filters, layered streams, and (non)candidates. Automatic translation from Prolog with Ueda's continuation method can be used when all passed arguments are ground data structures. With optimization, this method's performance is not quite as good as the candidates paradigm. In any case, its applicability is limited because of the restriction to ground structures. Pipelined filters were introduced primarily as an introduction to the process structure required by layered-streams programs. The dismal performance of pipelined filters can be attributed to lack of parallelism in a pipeline-process structure and excessive garbage production due to stream communication. Layered streams alleviated these problems by exploiting data sharing. The candidates paradigm takes a different approach: a complete OR-tree is built as a process structure. A tree affords much parallelism, but has the disadvantage of the same computational complexity as fused generate & test. In other words, each branch of the tree is independent and thus independently duplicates the same work as other branches logically sharing pieces of the partial solution.

For single-result computations, such as Semigroup and Bestpath, execution speed is often limited by synchronization points that remove parallelism. As previously mentioned, a key synchronization point is anyplace where output streams are appended together from multiple producers to a consumer. Even if the consumer does not care about the order of the data, the order is built into the stream, so that computation cannot proceed unless the first producer has bound its output, then the second producer, and so on. In this case, we might rewrite the program to use a merger to join the output streams, allowing the consumer to freely process messages from whichever producer first starts producing data. In general, this example illustrates synchronization-point removal.

We saw other examples of synchronization-point removal in the text. For instance, in one Semigroup program (Section 11.1.4), a producer binds an output stream to some logical variables as answer slots before actually instantiating the variables. This binding allows the computation to proceed because the values were not immediately needed. We also used a pipeline of filters wherein the input stream was fed directly from the pipeline's output (termination was guaranteed by a book-end method). The stream feedback required no overhead processing (as in an original version of the program) i.e., synchronization points were removed.

Another performance-related programming method is granularity collection. We introduced granularity collection mainly from an OR-parallel perspective because OR-Prolog exploits large-grain parallelism much more efficiently than small-grain. Thus granularity collection is a more critical optimization in OR-Prolog programs.

However, granularity collection can even be used in small-grain languages such as FGHC. Granularity is collected in a committed-choice language by explicitly serializing a section of the computation. A group of sequential goals usually has larger granularity than the same group of concurrent goals. Assuming that the overhead of enforced serialization does not outweigh the benefits of scheduling the larger granule, performance will improve. Although Panda does not support sequential goals, the Triangle program was given as an example of how Parlog (for instance) could increase granularity with explicit serialization. Note that, although goals can be serialized in Panda with a short-circuit chain, such a method does not guarantee that serialized goals are scheduled on the same PE. In this respect, *logical serialization* is different than the sequential '&' operator offered by Parlog.

In summary, committed-choice languages can be used in a rich variety of programming styles. Several methods of all-solutions search, lazy evaluation, data-oriented programming with managers, and distributed process-oriented programming were discussed here. Other paradigms, such as systolic programming and event-driven simulation, are also possible [116].

13.2   How Easy Was it to Write These Programs?

It is never as easy to write a program as it may appear when viewing the final product. Nor does it help when there is no programming environment or debugger! Still with fortitude we can press on and develop fairly elaborate parallel logic programs. Considering the effort to write parallel programs at lower levels (Section 1.1), the programming languages introduced here seem a joy. Glancing at the FORTRAN programs given in Babb [10] or Fox *et al.* [50] one reminisces about the hum of key punches, and that would probably be one of the *best* remembrances one could conjure... However, let us be honest in this section and criticize parallel logic programming fairly.

Attempts to translate AND-in-OR and OR-in-AND parallelism failed. AND-in-OR parallelism only works for very-large-grain goals. OR-in-AND parallelism via automatic translation has limited applicability. The promise of Prolog programs translated into committed-choice programs is still a dream.

In general, it was easy to write all of the programs in Prolog. However, it was difficult to rewrite problems without OR-parallelism to run efficiently under Aurora. It was difficult to implement logic problems, such as Zebra and Salt & Mustard, in FGHC. This difficulty occurred because we lacked meta-logical builtins in Panda, but moreover because backtracking over logical variables must be simulated. Such difficulty is also seen when comparing the coding effort to implement complex constraints — Prolog was significantly easier than FGHC, as shown in Turtles and layered-stream programs in general.

FGHC has no inherent limit to the *parallelism* that it can exploit when collecting all solutions in an OR-tree search, even though it is primarily an AND-parallel language. But searching for fewer than all solutions can be implemented with lazy evaluation or other techniques. In Aurora we can search either for all solutions or for a single solution. In addition, lazy evaluation is impossible in OR-Prolog.

FGHC *is* inherently limited in the *speed* that it can achieve because structure copying and reduction of small granularity goals creates a high-memory-bandwidth requirement. This requirement also impacts garbage collection by increasing its frequency. Aurora does not have heap-garbage problems as does Panda, but it does frequently experience branchpoint-stack overflow. Again, there is no method of implementing lazy algorithms in OR-Prolog, and therefore problems that are too large cannot be throttled so that they still execute.

Debugging OR-parallel Prolog for correctness is no more difficult than debugging sequential Prolog. However, debugging OR-parallel Prolog for performance is more difficult than advertised. Performance bottlenecks often arise mysteriously because the overheads of managing branchpoints and the complex scheduler heuristics are mysteries to the programmer. Debugging FGHC requires fortitude and patience. Given equal debugger technology, e.g., at the level of Byrd's box model for Prolog [101], from which most current Prolog debuggers have derived, FGHC is far more difficult to debug than Prolog.

Given more advanced technology, e.g., trace-driven animation, graphics, and execution movies, debugging concurrent languages will become easier. We often feel like plumbers when writing FGHC programs, constantly welding together D-lists, streams via mergers, short-circuit chains, layered streams, and buffers. Debugging for correctness is like checking for leaks in the final hairy mess of pipes. Debugging for performance is like checking for water pressure in the pipes, trying to find where the bottlenecks are. Stretching the metaphor a bit further, the constant buildup of garbage is like corrosion building up inside the pipes, requiring periodic purging with strong chemicals (GC). A plumber has a distinct advantage over today's FGHC programmers: a plumber can, in one glance, *see* and touch the mess of pipes in three-dimensional space. A programmer can only turn on the input faucet, desperately trace the torrent of information circulating in the pipes, and hope to see a trickle of somewhat correct results at the point of output.

Program	Size of Problem	# Sol.	Paradigm	Notes
Aurora				
Queens	10x10	724	constraints	Bratko with structures
NAND Gates	2–1 MUX	2		no intelligent backtracking
Triangle	15 pegs	133		structure representation
MasterMind	4 pegs	860	generate & test	naive (3 colors, 3 guesses)
Zebra	6 houses	4	generate & test	fused, fully unrolled
Cubes	7 cubes	48	generate & test	fused
Turtles	4x3 cards	8	generate & test	super fused
Puzzle	5x4x3 cells	65		pieces are structures
Waltz	38 nodes	288	constraints	
Semigroup	4x40-tuples	1		313 tuples in semigroup
Pascal	200 rows	1	AND-in-OR	unrolled + ordered `findall`
Panda				
Queens	10x10	724	layered streams	with nil check
NAND Gates	2–1 MUX	2		
Triangle	15 pegs	133		
MasterMind	4 pegs	860	generate & test	naive (3 colors, 3 guesses)
Zebra	6 houses	4	pipelined filters	
Cubes	7 cubes	48	layered streams	with nil check
Turtles	3x4 cards	8	non/candidates	
Puzzle	5x4x3 cells	65		board copying
Waltz	38 nodes	288	layered streams	with nil check
Semigroup	4x40-tuples	1	pipeline	313 tuples in semigroup
Pascal	200 rows	1		

Table 13.1
Best Program Summary

13.3 Empirical Results

Table 13.1 summarizes the fastest OR-Prolog and FGHC programs of selected problems in this book. Refer to the preceding chapters for the details of the input data sets used for these measurements. High-level statistics are given in Table 13.2. Measurements presented here are the instructions per reduction, reductions per backtrack (or suspension), and the thousands of procedure entries per second (KEPS) on eight Sequent Symmetry PEs. The Prolog programs show biased statistics towards few reductions per backtrack typical of all-solutions search programs. The mean reductions per suspension for the FGHC programs is an unreliable statistic because the programs vary a great deal with respect to this measure. We would

Aurora							
Program	**instr**	**reduct**	**back**	**entries**	$\frac{instr}{reduct}$	$\frac{reduct}{back}$	**sec**	**KEPS**
9-Queens	604	45	24	69	13	1.9	2.6	27
NAND Gates	2053	111	151	262	19	0.73	9.7	27
Triangle	5497	34	553	587	160	0.061	8.6	68
MasterMind	8894	927	534	1461	10	1.7	25.0	58
Zebra	5949	113	605	717	53	0.19	20.0	36
7-Cubes	29797	1293	503	1797	23	2.6	38.3	47
4x3 Turtles	1042	36	300	336	29	0.12	3.8	88
5x4x3 Puzzle	1926	62	83	145	31	0.74	4.4	33
Waltz	224	27	14	41	8	1.9	4.6	9
Semigroup	1526	126	34	160	12	3.7	9.1	18
Pascal	*	264	73	337	*	3.6	37.1	9
average †					24	1.7		34

Panda							
Program	**instr**	**reduct**	**susp‡**	**entries**	$\frac{instr}{reduct}$	$\frac{reduct}{supend}$	**sec**	**KEPS**
9-Queens	1480	99	7523	106	15	13	3.2	33
NAND Gates	2287	142	2811	145	16	51	4.5	32
Triangle	13174	601	1	601	22	600000	25.7	23
MasterMind	25676	1510	15495	1525	17	97	39.5	39
Zebra	8236	404	2242	406	20	180	24.7	16
7-Cubes	7169	291	4343	296	25	67	13.5	22
4x3 Turtles	22831	1230	369	1230	19	3300	44.8	27
5x4x3 Puzzle	5713	283	18	283	20	16000	13.5	21
Waltz	1134	66	8396	75	17	8	4.5	17
Semigroup	2106	123	3411	127	17	36	5.8	22
Pascal	2539	154	4469	159	16	35	4.9	32
average †					19	2000		25

* statistics unavailable

† The arithmetic mean of the benchmarks, discounting the min and max values.

‡ raw count of suspensions (cf., **instr**, **reduct**, **back**, and **entries** in thousands)

Table 13.2
Best Program Summary: High-Level Characteristics (eight PEs Symmetry)

expect a lower ratio for the class of applications using meta-interpreters [7] that is not represented here. The averages of 19 and 24 abstract instructions per reduction for the two systems have less variance and are consistent with the high-level WAM-based instruction sets used in both systems (see Appendix A).

Table 13.3 lists the execution timings, from the Symmetry, for the best programs. A '—' statistic indicates that the execution time did not decrease with increasing numbers of PEs. Table 13.4 gives the naive speedups of these programs. In cases where the actual measurement exceeds the theoretically possible linear speedup (because of measurement variance), the speedup statistic was truncated, e.g., Aurora's Triangle on two PEs. The measurements are plotted in Figures 13.1 and 13.2, showing PE utilization vs. execution time. Note that programs with linear speedups are not listed in these plots (such curves would all fall along the y-axis). Also, the curves are smoothed, producing relatively monotonic behavior (c.f., Figure 7.3).

Table 13.5 gives the ratios of execution times and real speedups, derived from the raw data in the previous two tables. The ratios are always greater than or equal to one. A '+' indicates that the ratio is calculated as Panda divided by Aurora, otherwise vice versa. Thus a '+' in the execution time ratios indicates that Aurora is faster than Panda, whereas a '+' in the speedup ratios indicates that Panda had higher speedup than Aurora. For example, Zebra executes equally fast on four PEs in both systems. The programs are arranged in the table to emphasize two distinct groups: the programs for which Aurora achieves superior speed, and the programs for which Panda achieves superior speed. The programs divide evenly between the two groups.

The superior Aurora programs are the all-solutions-search problems, all with constraints except for MasterMind. Zebra is exceptional because it falls between the two groups, switching over on four PEs. As discussed in Section 8.1, the switchover occurs because Panda begins to spawn unit facts remotely, instead of throttling this source of potential parallelism. In a system such as JAM-Parlog, this mistake can be avoided by declaring certain body goals to be sequentialized.

Three of the Aurora-superior programs display increasing execution time ratios, whereas the other three are decreasing. This difference is directly related to the speedups of the programs. For example, Prolog MasterMind is faster than FGHC MasterMind, but FGHC achieves better speedup, therefore the execution time ratio is decreasing.

The superior Panda programs are single-solution computations (Semigroup and Pascal) and all-solutions-search problems with degenerate OR-trees (the NAND-gate circuit designer). N-Cubes is exceptional because it is an all-solutions logical-constraint problem, like Turtles, but it executes very slowly on Aurora. One reason

Program	1 PE	2 PE	4 PE	8 PE	12 PE	15 PE
Aurora						
10-Queens	58.5	30.9	17.3	10.4	8.3	7.4
NAND Gates	42.6	22.4	13.0	9.7	7.0	7.1
Triangle	68.1	33.6	16.9	8.6	5.9	4.8
MasterMind	155.9	86.8	45.0	25.0	19.6	17.5
Zebra	160.4	79.9	39.8	20.0	13.3	10.8
7-Cubes	306.7	151.9	76.3	38.3	25.7	20.8
4x3 Turtles	30.5	15.0	7.6	3.8	2.6	2.1
5x4x3 Puzzle	34.5	17.2	8.7	4.4	3.2	2.7
Waltz	7.6	5.1	4.6	—	—	—
Semigroup	35.6	20.2	12.7	9.1	8.0	7.5
Pascal	81.5	60.5	48.0	37.1	—	—
Panda						
10-Queens	86.7	45.7	27.8	13.4	9.1	7.5
NAND Gates	33.4	17.1	9.1	4.5	3.1	2.6
Triangle	184.2	98.5	52.8	25.7	21.2	16.6
MasterMind	307.9	157.1	79.3	39.5	26.6	21.0
Zebra	144.4	75.2	38.9	24.7	21.0	19.6
7-Cubes	100.0	50.6	26.1	13.5	9.3	7.6
4x3 Turtles	322.9	165.2	85.7	44.8	31.1	25.8
5x4x3 Puzzle	101.6	51.7	26.1	13.5	9.1	7.6
Waltz	17.0	10.3	6.7	4.5	3.8	—
Semigroup	37.5	19.1	10.1	5.8	4.2	3.6
Pascal	35.8	18.6	9.4	4.9	3.4	2.8

Table 13.3
Best Program Summary: Execution Time in Seconds (Symmetry)

Program	1 PE	2 PE	4 PE	8 PE	12 PE	15 PE
Aurora						
10-Queens	1.0	1.9	3.4	5.6	7.0	7.9
NAND Gates	1.0	1.9	3.3	4.4	6.1	6.0
Triangle	1.0	2.0	4.0	7.9	12	14
MasterMind	1.0	1.8	3.5	6.2	8.0	8.9
Zebra	1.0	2.0	4.0	8.0	12	15
7-Cubes	1.0	2.0	4.0	8.0	12	15
4x3 Turtles	1.0	2.0	4.0	8.0	12	15
5x4x3 Puzzle	1.0	2.0	4.0	7.8	11	13
Waltz	1.0	1.5	1.7	—	—	—
Semigroup	1.0	1.7	2.7	3.8	4.3	4.6
Pascal	1.0	1.3	1.7	2.2	—	—
Panda						
10-Queens	1.0	1.9	3.1	6.5	9.5	12
NAND Gates	1.0	2.0	3.7	7.4	11	13
Triangle	1.0	1.9	3.5	7.2	8.7	11
MasterMind	1.0	2.0	3.9	7.8	12	15
Zebra	1.0	1.9	3.7	5.8	6.9	7.4
7-Cubes	1.0	2.0	3.8	7.4	11	13
4x3 Turtles	1.0	2.0	3.8	7.2	10	13
5x4x3 Puzzle	1.0	2.0	3.9	7.5	11	13
Waltz	1.0	1.7	2.5	3.8	4.5	—
Semigroup	1.0	2.0	3.7	6.5	8.9	10
Pascal	1.0	1.9	3.8	7.3	11	13

Table 13.4
Best Program Summary: Naive Speedup (Symmetry)

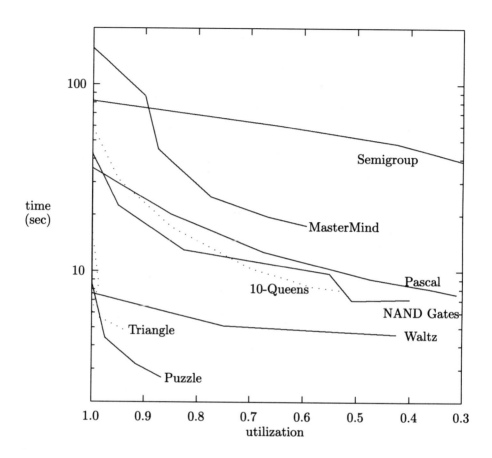

Figure 13.1
Best Program Summary: Aurora Utilization vs. Time (Symmetry)

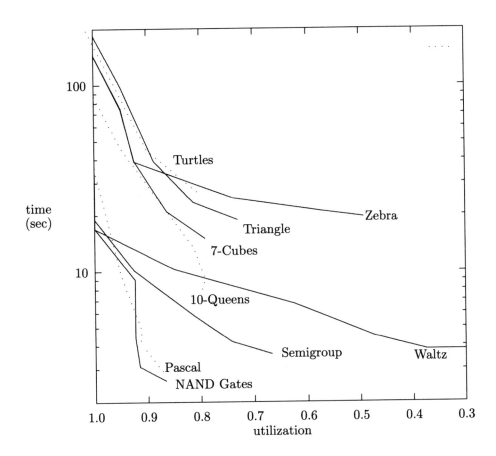

Figure 13.2
Best Program Summary: Panda Utilization vs. Time (Symmetry)

Program	1 PE	2 PE	4 PE	8 PE	12 PE	15 PE
ratio of execution times						
4x3 Turtles	+11	+11	+11	+12	+12	+12
5x4x3 Puzzle	+2.9	+3.0	+3.0	+3.1	+2.8	+2.8
Triangle	+2.7	+2.9	+3.1	+3.0	+3.6	+3.5
Mastermind	+2.0	+1.8	+1.8	+1.6	+1.4	+1.2
10-Queens	+1.5	+1.5	+1.6	+1.3	+1.1	+1.0
Zebra	1.1	1.1	1.0	+1.2	+1.6	+1.8
Waltz	+2.2	+2.0	+1.5	1.0	1.0	1.0
Semigroup	+1.1	1.1	1.3	1.6	1.9	2.1
NAND Gates	1.3	1.3	1.4	2.2	2.3	2.7
7-Cubes	3.1	3.0	2.9	2.8	2.8	2.7
Pascal	2.3	3.3	5.1	7.6	11	13
ratio of speedups						
Zebra	1.0	1.0	1.1	1.4	1.7	2.0
Triangle	1.0	1.1	1.1	1.1	1.3	1.3
4x3 Turtles	1.0	1.0	1.1	1.1	1.1	1.2
7-Cubes	1.0	1.0	1.0	1.1	1.1	1.1
5x4x3 Puzzle	1.0	1.0	1.0	1.0	1.0	1.0
10-Queens	1.0	+1.0	1.1	+1.2	+1.4	+1.5
Mastermind	1.0	+1.1	+1.1	+1.3	+1.5	+1.7
NAND Gates	1.0	+1.0	+1.1	+1.7	+1.8	+2.1
Semigroup	1.0	+1.2	+1.4	+1.7	+2.1	+2.3
Waltz	1.0	+1.1	+1.5	+2.3	+2.7	+2.7
Pascal	+1.5	+2.1	+3.3	+4.9	+7.1	+8.6

'+' means that the ratio is Panda/Aurora;
otherwise the ratio is Aurora/Panda.

Table 13.5
Best Program Summary: Execution Time and Speedup Ratios (Symmetry)

is that the complexity order of the Prolog algorithm, a fused generate & test, is larger than that of the FGHC algorithm, which uses layered streams. All the superior Panda programs display increasing execution time ratios except N-Cubes. This is due to Prolog's superior speedup for the program.

The speedup ratios also form two distinct groups: the programs in which Aurora achieves superior speedup and the programs in which Panda achieves superior speedup. In both groups, the ratio increases with increasing numbers of PEs, indicating that the speedup curves are not linear.[2] In other words, poor speedups almost always degrade nonlinearly with increasing numbers of PEs. The first five programs (in the bottom half of Table 13.5) form the Aurora-superior group — these are all-solutions-search logical-constraint problems. The OR-trees are large enough to exhibit large granularity that Aurora can exploit efficiently. Interestingly, the ratio increases slowly, indicating that the poor Panda speedups are almost linear. Except for Zebra, the ratio is always less than 20% in favor of Aurora.

The final seven programs (in Table 13.5) form the Panda-superior group. These are a disparate bunch of programs. Semigroup and Pascal are single-solution computations. The NAND-gate circuit designer also is an essentially single-solution computation (recall that it generates a large number of duplicate solutions that are all filtered away). N-Queens and Mastermind are all-solutions-search problems with degenerate OR-trees, preventing Aurora from achieving good speedups. Panda can still achieve excellent speedups because it is not exploiting OR-tree granularity, but rather fine-grain AND-parallelism.

Interestingly, Mastermind program performance is almost the same in both Prolog and FGHC. The search space is such that OR-branches are short, taxing Aurora with high overhead for parallel spawning. Unlike the first group, this second group shows a rapidly increasing speedup ratio with increasing numbers of PEs. This implies that the poor Aurora speedup curves are far from linear, i.e., they are rapidly degrading. One can summarize that, whereas Panda can achieve some speedup on just about any program, Aurora cannot. The BestPath programs, not included in the summary above, confirm this difference. No OR-parallel algorithm can efficiently exploit parallelism searching sparse graphs, whereas Panda exhibited real speedups on up to 12 PEs.

---

[2]By "linear" we mean a curve $y = kx$ for some $0 < k \leq 1$. We do *not* necessarily mean $k = 1$ in this case!

Program	entries	solutions	$\frac{entries}{solution}$	speedup
Bratko's 9-Queens	69,089	352	196	5.2
MasterMind	1,460,550	860	1698	6.2
5x4x3 Puzzle	144,964	65	2230	7.8
Triangle	586,925	133	4413	7.9
7-Cubes	1,796,636	48	37430	8.0
4x3 Turtles	335,510	8	41939	8.0
Zebra	717,415	4	179353	8.0

Table 13.6
Correlation Between Entries/Solution and Speedup for Aurora (8 PEs Symmetry)

> Generalizing, a stream AND-parallel architecture can exploit parallelism
> in just about any problem, whereas an OR-parallel architecture cannot.
> From another viewpoint, we can usually write a fairly efficient AND-
> parallel program to simulate an all-solutions search, but we can rarely
> write an OR-parallel program to simulate AND-parallel computation,
> because AND-parallel computation often requires communication.

Further discussion of the seemingly impossible speedups attained by Aurora on
Triangle, Zebra, N-Cubes, Turtles, and Puzzle is worthwhile. One reason for the
speedups is because of the high ratio of procedure entries to solutions, indicating
a light load on `findall`. Table 13.6 summarizes several Prolog programs that use
a single top-level `findall` to collect all solutions. The statistics were collected on
Symmetry, running on eight PEs. There is a direct correlation between the ratio
of entries to solutions and the speedup. The correlation is far from linear. For
large numbers of solutions, as in 9-Queens, the `findall` is overloaded and speedup
is poor. For sparse solutions, as in 7-Cubes, the `findall` is essentially unloaded
and speedup excels. Between these two extremes lies the normal operating range of
`findall`, wherein some overhead gives speedups of about 6–8 on eight PEs. Many
other variables affect speedup, such as excessive storage requirements, executing
complex builtins, etc. However, these other factors are for the most part absent
from the previous programs.

Interestingly, Panda achieved seemingly impossible superlinear speedup on the
BestPath problem. Recall that the partitioned Moore algorithm had a naive speedup of 5.4 on four PEs. The nondeterminate nature of the search enables four PEs
to find a solution more than four times faster than a single PE. Also note that the
real speedup is not superlinear!

Analyzing the extremes among the benchmarks, we see that Turtles and Triangle are best suited for OR-Prolog and worst suited for FGHC, whereas Pascal's Triangle and BestPath are best suited for FGHC and worst suited for OR-Prolog. The evidence is strong in both execution-time ratios and speedup ratios. Better-crafted systems, i.e., engines, schedulers, compilers, and builtin support functions, will probably close the gap between the extremes. However, fundamental incompatibilities exist between these problems and the systems on which they misbehave. The granularity of Pascal's Triangle is too small for OR-Prolog. The satisfaction of Turtle constraints in Prolog exploits super fusion of generator and tester, i.e., within a single environment. FGHC cannot search for all solutions, nor satisfy constraint problems, with such ease.

We can conclude from these extremes that neither language offers us the ultimate programming panacea. In the next and final section we briefly examine future parallel logic programming languages that promise to improve upon OR-parallel Prolog and FGHC, and their architectures Aurora and Panda.

13.4   Directions in Parallel Logic Programming

In this section we first review the genealogy of parallel logic programming and then discuss areas of future research. Prehistoric influence on the development of parallel logic programming include Dijkstra's guarded commands [43], Hoare's Communicating Sequential Processes (CSP) [63], occam [67], and (sequential) Prolog [108]. At this time dawned the so-called Golden Age of parallel logic programming.

Prolog first begat IC-Prolog [28] and Concurrent Prolog [116].[3] IC-Prolog begat the Relational Language [27] and Parlog [26]. Concurrent Prolog (CP) begat Flat Concurrent Prolog (FCP) and Guarded Horn Clauses (GHC) [137]. GHC begat Flat GHC (FGHC), KL1 [65], FLENG [89] and FLENG++ [124]. Parlog begat an illustrious Parlog family, including Flat Parlog [48] and Flat Guarded Definite Clauses (FGDC) [105]. Flat Parlog begat Strand [49]. Prolog, living to a ripe old age, begat (in alphabetical order) Aurora [78, 21], Delta Prolog [99], Epilog [148], Muse [6], parallel NU-Prolog [87], OPAL (the AND-OR Process Model) [34], PEPSys [104, 23], P-Prolog [149], RAP (Restricted AND parallel Prolog) [41, 62], ROPM (the Reduced-OR Process Model) [103], and countless other parallel children.

Prolog also begat sequential constraint languages such as Prolog II, Prolog III [32], and CLP(X) [68]. The CLP schema begat a number of languages includ-

---

[3]We loosely mention these names meaning both the language and underlying architecture. In reality, each language corresponds to a family of different implementation architectures.

ing CLP(R) [69], CHIP [140], and CAL [109]. The CLP paradigm was lifted to
concurrency in ALPS [79] which begat Herbrand [110].

Such was the Golden Age of parallel logic programming, part of which this book
holds testament. At this time dawned the New Age of parallel logic programming.
Previously designed AND- and OR-parallel languages were cross-fertilized. Aurora
and P-Prolog begat Andorra [58]. Parlog and Andorra begat Pandora [11]. FGHC
and Andorra begat AND-OR-II [123]. FGHC and Actors [4] begat $\mathcal{A}'\mathcal{UM}$ [153].
Previously designed concurrent constraint languages were implemented in parallel,
such as CHIP within PEPSys [141]. Herbrand begat Janus [111]. Herbrand and
CAL begat Guarded Definite Clauses with Constraints (GDCC) [60].

Various research groups are busily implementing these new languages. The New
Age heralds an increased perception that dependent-AND parallelism, nondeterminism, and constraints need to be exploited in high-performance parallel logic
programming architectures. We conclude this book by giving a short introduc-
tion to some of these bright stars on the horizon: $\mathcal{A}'\mathcal{UM}$, Pandora, and Andorra.
$\mathcal{A}'\mathcal{UM}$ joins committed-choice languages with objects. Pandora and Andorra join
together committed-choice and strict Horn-clause logic languages.

13.4.1   A'UM

$\mathcal{A}'\mathcal{UM}$, designed by K. Yoshida [153], is a concurrent programming language based
on stream communication. To introduce the language, we present an N-Queens
algorithm similar to Kumon's Queens in Section 5.2.1. Although this example does
not illustrate the full richness of the language, it suffices to give a taste of the
programming style. The only algorithmic difference between this program and the
FGHC version is that collection of all solutions with a difference list is obviated by
$\mathcal{A}'\mathcal{UM}$'s truly nondeterministic streams.

$\mathcal{A}'\mathcal{UM}$ is "object-oriented" in the sense that objects communicate with messages
via directional streams. There are two main types of objects: *classes* and *instances*.
A class defines a template of its instances, similar to processes of a certain type
of procedure. An object consumes messages from a single incoming stream. Each
consumption defines a new *generation* of the object. The messages that can be
acted upon, and the actions taken upon those messages, are described in a *method*
for the object. Like most object-oriented languages, $\mathcal{A}'\mathcal{UM}$ supports multiple-class
inheritance.

We review $\mathcal{A}'\mathcal{UM}$ syntax first because it differs considerably from that of Horn-
clause programs. The following class, test, defines methods top/2 and go/2, each
with two arguments. For example, both arguments of go are defined on inlets
(stream terminals toward objects), as denoted by the carat. Variable ^N is the

number of queens and ^S is a bag into which solutions are collected.

```
class test.
:top(^N, B$2) ->
    #bag = ^B,
    :go(N, B$1).

:go(^N, ^S) ->
    #util:gen(N, ^Cs),
    #column:queen(Cs, [], S).
end.
```

Method go/2 calculates solutions to the N-Queens problem with two sub-methods: the gen/2 object in class util and the queen/3 object in class column. Note that gen(N,^Cs) accepts its input N from go/2 and sends its output ^Cs to queen/3.

The top/2 method has a purpose similar to wrapping a nondeterminate Prolog procedure in a findall builtin. Streams B$1 and B$2 empty into a bag (an instance of class bag — we do not present this definition here), where the postscripts mean that the two streams are appended in the specified order. This forces all solution messages on B$1, from go/2, to be sent to the bag before retrieval-request messages on B$2, from the caller of top/2, are sent to the bag.

The N-Queens program consists of four classes: test, util, column, and row. Class test contains the top-level query to find all solutions. Class util contains methods for generating a list of consecutive integers and appending two lists. Class column is for testing every possible candidate for each column. Class row is for testing every possible candidate for each row of a column. The variable names in the program have been kept as close as possible to the original Kumon's Queens, to accentuate the similarities.

Class util is given below. Method gen/2 is functional in style. Note that the output list of consecutive integers is built up by self-recursion. The meaning of the conditionals in gen and append are self-evident. The term Xs:car(^X):cdr(^Xs1) is a rather formal way of getting the head and tail of Xs, by sending car and cdr messages to Xs. Method append terminates its recursion when Xs empties, i.e., Xs becomes an atom, [].

```
class util.
:gen(^N, Cs) ->
    (N > 0) ? (
    :'true -> [N|Cs1] = ^Cs,
              :gen(N-1, ^Cs1) ;
    :'false -> [] = ^Cs
    ).
```

```
      :append(^Xs, ^Ys, Zs) ->
          (class_of Xs) ? (
          :list -> Xs:car(^X):cdr(^Xs1),
                   [X|Zs1] = ^Zs,
                   :append(Xs1, Ys, ^Zs1) ;
          :atom -> Ys = ^Zs
          ).
      end.
```

Class `column` has an exported method `queen(Cs,L,S)`, where `Cs` are the candidate positions yet to be placed, L is a partial solution, and S is the bag of solutions. A sub-method `queen/4` is invoked in order to initialize the noncandidates. Note the `add/1` message for sending a completed solution L to bag S when `Cs` empties (`add` is a method of the bag not defined here).

```
      class column.
      :queen(^Cs, ^L, ^S) ->
          (class_of Cs) ? (
          :list -> :queen(Cs, [], L, S) ;
          :atom -> S:add(L)
          ).

      :queen(^Cs, ^NCs, ^L, ^S) ->
          (class_of Cs) ? (
          :list -> Cs:car(^C):cdr(^Cs1),
                   #row:check(C, Cs1, NCs, L, S),
                   :queen(Cs1, [C|NCs], L, S);
          :atom ->
          ).
      end.
```

Those classes which are substantially sequential are implemented with self-recursion (sending messages to itself, e.g., `:queen/4` in class `column`). Those classes which should be executed in parallel are implemented creating independent objects (e.g., creating an instance of class `row` within a loop of `:queen` in class `column`). Programmer control over parallelism in this manner is clean and quite useful.

Method `check(C,Cs,NCs,L,S)` is similar to that in Kumon's queens. First a subordinate method is invoked: `check/7` containing the column difference D. The recursion is conditional on the false disjunction of the three arithmetic comparisons. If the recursion reaches the terminus of `Ps`, then `check` has succeeded and the new candidate list `Rs` is constructed with `append` from the noncandidate list `NCs` and the remainder of the candidate list `Cs`. Then `#column:queen/3` is invoked with the extended partial solution, `[C|L]`.

```
    class row.
    :check(^C, ^Cs, ^NCs, ^L, ^S) ->
        :check(L, C, 1, NCs, Cs, L, S).

    :check(^Ps, ^C, ^D, ^NCs, ^Cs, ^L, ^S) ->
        (class_of Ps) ? (
        :list -> Ps:car(^P):cdr(^Ps1),
            (C == P) \/ (P-C == D) \/ (C-P == D) ? (
            :'true  -> ;
            :'false -> :check(Ps1, C, D+1, NCs, Cs, L, S)
            ) ;
        :atom -> #util:append(NCs, Cs, ^Rs),
                #column:queen(Rs, [C|L], S)
        ).
    end.
```

The difference between FGHC and $\mathcal{A}'\mathcal{UM}$ looks great but, if one goes along from FGHC to FLENG to FLENG++ to $\mathcal{A}'\mathcal{UM}$, the slight differences accumulated become clear. The object-oriented abstraction of $\mathcal{A}'\mathcal{UM}$ may be its strongest contribution, enabling it to bridge both MIMD and SIMD computation models [153].

13.4.2 Pandora

Pandora, designed by R. Bahgat and S. Gregory [11], is a logic programming language that combines stream AND-parallelism in a committed-choice setting with nondeterminate procedures. A program consists of committed-choice ("don't care") procedures similar to those in Parlog, in addition to nondeterminate ("don't know") procedures similar to those in Prolog.

Each goal ready for execution can be categorized as either determinate or nondeterminate. A goal that corresponds to a committed-choice procedure invocation is determinate. A goal that corresponds to a nondeterminate procedure wherein only one clause can possibly match is also considered determinate. However, if multiple clauses can potentially succeed, that goal is categorized as nondeterminate.

The execution model is quite simple: execution proceeds as in FGHC, with the suspension of any invocation of a nondeterminate. At any point, the group of suspended goals consists of some determinate and some nondeterminate goals. As in any committed-choice language, deadlock occurs when no executable goals remain, i.e., all goals have suspended. For a language like FGHC, deadlock implies a program flaw and is fatal.

Pandora, however, has a card up its sleeve: to break deadlock, a nondeterminate goal can be resumed and its reduction attempted. A branchpoint is created for the goal and all or some of the clauses are attempted in parallel. If a clause unifies successfully, then the body goals (either determinate or nondeterminate) are added to the goal queue (no execution order is enforced). In addition, successful unification might bind variables that trigger resumption of other suspended goals. Thus the deadlock is broken by the generation of executable goals. Execution proceeds by reducing determinate goals and suspending nondeterminate goals until another deadlock, and so on.

Pandora executes in this two-step manner in order to explore the search space as lazily as possible. Nondeterminate goals consist of disjunctive choices that represent speculative parallelism (unless all solutions are required). Andorra (described in the next section) is a related language with the same two-step execution model, although based on Prolog rather than Parlog. To further understand the model, let us examine Bahgat's active constraints N-Queens Pandora program shown below. [4]

```
:- nondeterminate cell/8.

cell(I, J, J, I, I, I, begin-end, begin-end).
cell(_, _, _, _, _, _, Hc-Hc,      Vc-Vc).

queens(N,V) :-
    board(0,N,V,L,R,D).
    init(D).

init([]-[]).
init([B|Bs]-[E|Es]) :- B=begin, E=end, init(Bs-Es).

board(N, N, _,  _,  _,  V0-V1) :- V1=V0.
board(K, N, Cs, Lt, Rs, V0-V2) :- K < N |
    K1 is K+1,
    Rs = [_|Rt],
    row(K1, 0, N, _, Cs, [L|Lt], Rs, begin-end, V0-V1),
    board(K1, N, Cs, [L|Lt], RT, V1-V2).

row(_, N, N, _, Cs, _, _, H0-H1, D) :-
    Cs=[], H0=H1, D=[]-[].
row(I, J, N, H, Cs, Ls, Rs, H0-H2, D) :- J < N |
    J1 is J+1,
    Cs=[C|Ct], Ls=[L|Lt], Rs=[R|Rt], D=[X|Xt]-[Y|Yt],
    cell(I,J1,  H, C, L,  R,  H0-H1, X-Y),
    row( I,J1,N, H, Ct, Lt, Rt, H1-H2, Xt-Yt).
```

The key to understanding the program is the definition of `cell`, a nondeterminate procedure. A cell represents a square in the chess board. A cell has a state denoted by its first two arguments, giving the column and row numbers of the square. The next four variables enforce the constraints between different squares. These constraints (in left-to-right order) link all rows in a column, link all columns in a

---

[4]The dialect of Pandora given here is based on FGHC to familiarize the reader.

row, link all squares in a left-top to right-bottom diagonal, and link all squares in a right-top to left-bottom diagonal. These variables are shared among cells in a manner similar to Kondo's algorithm in Section 5.1.3.

If any cell attempts to satisfy this procedure call, reduction against the first clause will be tried. The reduction can succeed if the arguments unify, as in Prolog. In other words, reduction will succeed if the four constraint variables linking the cells are compatible and/or unbound. Success of the first clause may cause bindings of the constraint variables (which are trailed, enabling backtracking).

If some other cell has already bound a constraint variable, making the first clause inconsistent, then unification will fail and the second clause will be attempted. The second clause "shorts" the final arguments, essentially removing the cell from among the placement choices within its row and column.

The last two `cell` arguments are difference lists guaranteeing that one and only one queen is placed within each row and column, respectively. When a given cell becomes determinate, i.e., its first clause fails, there are two possible outcomes: either the second clause succeeds or it fails. If the second clause succeeds, then shorting the final two chains removes this cell from competing for placement in the corresponding row and column.[5]

If all but one of the cells for a given row or column are shorted, then the chain at the remaining cell becomes bound to `begin-end`. If the remaining cell can succeed in its first clause, then in fact the cell is determinate (because `begin-end` cannot unify with `Hc-Hc` or `Vc-Vc` in the second clause) and so it may be reduced. Intuitively this is as we expect: by eliminating all choices but one, the choice has essentially been made!

However, if all cells but one are eliminated and the remaining cell *cannot* satisfy the first clause, then the second clause will *also* fail. Thus the `cell` invocation fails. Intuitively we know that this happens when previous choices make it impossible to place a consistent queen anywhere within a given row or column. When a nondeterminate procedure fails, that branch of the search space is discontinued. If all branches emanating from a branchpoint fail, then the branchpoint itself fails, and so on. Live branchpoints, i.e., with untried alternatives, are represented by suspended nondeterminate goals, allowing the alternative branches to be examined upon deadlock.

The N-Queens program (procedures `board` and `row`) does little more than generate the N^2 `cell` processes comprising the board. The cells for 4-Queens are

---

[5]N-Queens requires that every row contain a queen. By symmetry we also know that every column must also contain a queen since the board is square. There is no requirement however that every diagonal also contain a queen.

shown below. Note that the initialization of the column chains to **begin** and **end** is performed by **init/1**.

```
cell(1,1, H1, C1, L3, _,  begin-Z0,  begin-T0)
cell(1,2, H1, C2, L2, R1,    Z0-Z1,  begin-U0)
cell(1,3, H1, C3, L1, R2,    Z1-Z2,  begin-V0)
cell(1,4, H1, C4, _,  R3,    Z2-end, begin-W0)

cell(2,1, H2, C1, L4, R1, begin-Y0,  T0-T1)
cell(2,2, H2, C2, L3, R2,    Y0-Y1,  U0-U1)
cell(2,3, H2, C3, L2, R3,    Y1-Y2,  V0-V1)
cell(2,4, H2, C4, L1, R4,    Y2-end, W0-W1)

cell(3,1, H3, C1, L5, R2, begin-X0,  T1-T2)
cell(3,2, H3, C2, L4, R3,    X0-X1,  U1-U2)
cell(3,3, H3, C3, L3, R4,    X1-X2,  V1-V2)
cell(3,4, H3, C4, L2, R5,    X2-end, W1-W2)

cell(4,1, H4, C1, _,  R3, begin-S0,  T2-end)
cell(4,2, H4, C2, L5, R4,    S0-S1,  U2-end)
cell(4,3, H4, C3, L4, R5,    S1-S2,  V2-end)
cell(4,4, H4, C4, L3, _,     S2-end, W2-end)
```

Since the cells are nondeterminate, they suspend until generation and initialization have completed. At that point, only the suspended **cell** goals remain and deadlock ensues. The second phase of execution is triggered and a single **cell** goal is selected for reduction.

By binding any choice for the selected cell, all other cells in that row, column, and left and right diagonals will be resumed, because these goals were suspended on constraint variables that are now bound. In 4-Queens, suppose that we conditionally bind a queen in cell (1,1). The binding will trigger resumption of cells (1,2), (1,3), (1,4), (2,1), (3,1), (4,1), (2,2), (3,3), and (4,4). The constraint variables causing the resumptions are H1, C1, and L3 (no right diagonal exists).

These goals will be successfully reduced because they have become determinate, i.e., their first clauses no longer can succeed. As a result, by making one choice we have removed nine other possibilities from the search space of 16. Of the remaining six choices, one nondeterminate **cell** goal again is chosen for conditional reduction, and so on.

For 4-Queens, the choice of placement in (1,1) is erroneous. Eventually, failure of some sequence of **cell** invocations will cause backtracking to this initial choice. Redoing this **cell** invocation is simple: the alternative is *not* to place a queen at (1,1), i.e., match the second clause. Eventually a valid solution is found when all goals terminate.

There are numerous interesting aspects of Pandora. The use of *active constraints*, as in the previous N-Queens programs, can significantly reduce the execution time complexity of constraint-satisfaction algorithms [140]. The ability to backtrack over logical variables and still exploit stream AND-parallelism is precisely what our empirical analysis of Aurora and Panda suggests is needed. Implementing Pandora also poses great challenges. Most significant is making the runtime test of determinism as cheap as possible [133] and making the best decision as to which branchpoint to reinstate upon deadlock. As in Prolog, intelligent backtracking can save work, but it is difficult to implement with low overhead.

13.4.3 Andorra

Andorra-I[6] [58, 36, 151] is an older relative of Pandora, built around the foundation of Prolog instead of a committed-choice language. Its architecture can generally be thought of as Aurora fused with the capability of exploiting stream AND-parallelism. The execution model is almost the same as that of Pandora: determinate goals are reduced while nondeterminate goals are suspended. However, unlike Pandora, upon deadlock Andorra must evaluate the nondeterminate goal *leftmost in the OR-tree* to make a branchpoint. This strategy adheres to strict Prolog semantics.

Most Prolog programs given in this book are also Andorra programs by default. However, Andorra programs have alternative procedure definitions similar to "don't care" (Parlog-like) procedures in Pandora (more about this later). The semantics of meta-logical builtins such as `var/1` are strict; alternative "cavalier" versions are supported. A strict meta-logical goal that is not determinate is suspended until it is leftmost in the OR-tree. Aurora finesses builtins with side effects in a similar manner, by suspending the OR-branch containing the problematic goal until it is leftmost. Other unaffected OR-branches can continue executing. In Andorra, suspending a nondeterminate body goal will not prevent subsequent body goals from attempting execution.

Andorra and Pandora make the same essential runtime determinancy checks to allow reduction, although Pandora does this only for a declared "don't know" subset of the program, whereas Andorra does it for all procedures. We now illustrate an Andorra program with L. Pereira's fused generate & test N-Queens (identical to the Prolog code in Section 5.1.2). All of the Aurora N-Queens programs can be run as Andorra programs with little or no modification. We chose this example because of its simplicity.

---

[6]We refer to this language and architecture simply as Andorra in this section. Other variations of the model exist.

```
queen(N,A) :- gen(N,L), queen(L,[],A).

gen(0,[]) :- !.
gen(N,[N|X]) :- M is N-1, gen(M,X).

queen([],R,R).
queen([H|T],R,P) :-
    del(A,[H|T],L),
    safe(R,A,1),
    queen(L,[A|R],P).

:- parallel del/3.
del(X,[X|Y],Y).
del(X,[Y|Z],[Y|W]) :- del(X,Z,W).

safe([],_,_).
safe([H|T],U,D) :-
    H-U=\=D,
    U-H=\=D,
    D1 is D+1,
    safe(T,U,D1).
```

Let us trace through the reduction sequence for the second clause of **queen/3**, the key to understanding Andorra. Successful unification of the head of **queen/3** leads to the attempted reduction of the three body goals. The first goal, **del/3**, will suspend, because it is invoked in a nondeterminate manner, with only the second argument bound. The other body goals also attempt to reduce. Goal **safe/3** can reduce because its first argument is bound, therefore it is determinate. However, the arithmetic body goals within **safe/3** will suspend because the second argument U is unbound. The last body goal of **queen/3**, the recursive call, suspends because its first argument is not yet bound, therefore it is nondeterminate.

When all active goals suspend, **del/3**, as the leftmost suspended goal, will be forced to resume. A branchpoint is created for **del/3**, as in Aurora, creating two branches of computation. If sufficient workers (processors) are available, each of these branches will execute in parallel. Along each, the arithmetic goals and **queen/3** goal will be resumed in a manner similar to Pandora or any committed-choice language.

The resumption of goals via binding their suspended variables also allows us to write the active constraints N-Queens program in Andorra. Similarly, procedures like stream merge can be written in Andorra by declaring them as "don't care" procedures and declaring their argument modes explicitly. In addition, all procedures can have *sequential* body goals, explicitly indicated as in Parlog.

In summary, Andorra is a combination of Prolog and committed-choice languages.

The programmer can specify Prolog-like procedures and Parlog-like procedures, managed by the implicit execution rule that all determinate goals are reduced before any nondeterminate goals. Andorra and Pandora promise to deliver the programming advantages of backtracking and stream communication, as well as the combined algorithmic performance that these paradigms enable.

A Aurora and Panda Instruction Sets

In this appendix, the abstract instruction sets of the Aurora and Panda systems are described. The unifying example of Kumon's N-Queens program (Section 5.2.1) is given for each. The FGHC version of this program is shown in Figure A.1. The expositions of the architectures given here are only sketches to whet the reader's appetite. We strongly suggest reading the original WAM document by Warren [143] followed by the KL1-B paper by Kimura and Chikayama [71].

A.1 Aurora's Abstract Machine

Aurora's abstract instruction set is based on the Warren Abstract Machine (WAM). Aurora (Delta version) uses an old version of the SICStus Prolog compiler and emulator, which implement a modified version of the original WAM. The following assembly listings are slightly simplified versions of actual output from the SICStus Prolog compiler. Simplifications were made to avoid cluttering the assembly code with irrelevant details and to avoid a discussion of advanced optimizations that are beyond the scope of this text. The assembler syntax has been changed to clarify the code. Many WAM instructions are two-address instructions specifying a source operand and a destination operand. We always list the source operand first. The rightmost field of the assembler listings are comments indicating the corresponding source code.

It is unimportant that the code shown was generated by a particular compiler. In fact, high-performance systems do not emulate an instruction set at this level, but rather the compiler generates machine code. Understanding this instruction set is important for understanding the execution characteristics of Aurora.

We begin with the top-level procedure go/2.

```
go:    allocate           2             go(N,
       get_variable       X1,Y1            A) :-
       put_variable       Y0,X1         gen(N,L
       call               gen                 ),
       put_unsafe_value   Y0,X0         queen(L,
       put_constant       [],X1                  [],
       put_value          X1,X2                       [],
       put_value          Y1,X3                            A,
       put_value          X1,X4                       []
       deallocate
       execute            queen                            ).
```

The `allocate` and `deallocate` instructions create and remove a continuation called an *environment*. A stack is reserved for these environments (as well as other types

```
go(N,A)  :- gen(N,L),queen(L,[],[],A,[]).

queen([C|Cs],NCs,L,S0,S2) :-
    check(L,C,1,NCs,Cs,L,S0,S1),
    queen(Cs,[C|NCs],L,S1,S2).
queen([],[],L,S0,S1)  :- S0=[L|S1].
queen([],[_|_],_,S0,S1)  :- S1=S0.

check([],C,_,NCs,Cs,L,S0,S1) :-
    append(NCs,Cs,Ps),
    queen(Ps,[],[C|L],S0,S1).
check([P|Ps],C,D,NCs,Cs,L,S0,S1) :-
    P-C =\= D,  C-P =\= D |
    D1 is D+1,
    check(Ps,C,D1,NCs,Cs,L,S0,S1).
check(_,_,_,_,_,_,S0,S1)  :- otherwise | S0=S1.

gen(0,X)  :- X=[].
gen(N,X)  :- N>0 | N1 is N-1, X=[N|Xs], gen(N1,Xs).

append([],L1,L2)  :- L1=L2.
append([X|L1],L2,L4)  :- L4=[X|L3], append(L1,L2,L3).
```

Figure A.1
Kumon's N-Queens Program in FGHC

of objects) in the WAM storage model. Information needed for subsequent calls to body goals is stored in an environment. The information primarily consists of a code pointer to the next body goal to execute and the variables referenced in the subsequent body goals. Variables stored in an environment are called *permanent* variables because they must survive across user-defined procedure calls. Other variables are called *temporary* variables and are not guaranteed to survive across user-defined procedure calls.

In the case of go/2, there are two permanent variables. One is a parameter, A, and the other is the variable L. The passed parameter N is temporary. All variables present in a clause could be permanently allocated in an environment, but this allocation would be wasteful in terms of stack size and memory operations needed to access the variables. Temporary variables are short-lived and need not be stashed away in an environment. Instead, temporaries are allocated in registers, as discussed below.

A clause is compiled into a head portion followed by code segments for each body goal. All body goals except the final goal are invoked with **call** instructions. The final goal is invoked with an **execute** instruction which inherits the return address from its parent (via a state register called the *continuation pointer*). Thus in the above code, if **queen** succeeds it returns to the caller of **go**. The **deallocate** is executed *before* the **execute** to implement *tail-recursion* or *last-call optimization*. This optimization allows reuse of the current environment (in this case, the go/2 environment) within the final goal (**queen** or one of its descendants).

The head portion of go/2 consists of only one instruction: **get_variable Xi,Yj** which loads the value of register Xi into the permanent variable Yj (i.e., the variable in the current environment at index j). By convention we denote registers (holding temporary variables) as X and permanent variables as Y, both numbered from 0,1,2,... The passed parameters are allocated initially in the X registers. The beginning of a clause is usually a sequence of **get_**... instructions that save all passed parameters needed beyond the first body goal, i.e., those that are permanent.

The set-up code for the call to gen/2 consists of only one instruction: **put_variable Yi,Xj** which creates an unbound permanent variable Yi and loads a pointer to that variable into register Xj. The first argument for the call to gen/2 is already set up correctly from the call to go/2. Before each procedure call is a sequence of **put_**... instructions that load the X registers with the arguments for that call.

The set-up code for the call to queen/5 consists of five instructions. Instruction **put_constant C,Xi** writes the immediate constant C into register Xi. Instruction **put_value Vi,Xj** transfers the contents of Vi into register Xj, where Vi is either a register or a permanent variable. **put_unsafe_value Yi,Xj** is similar to put_value Yi,Xj except that it is used in the case that Yi *might exist only as an unbound variable in the current environment*. Although not the case in the above code segment, since gen/2 binds L, this condition cannot be determined by the compiler (without mode analysis). If Yi is in fact an unbound variable in the current environment, then Yi is copied onto a storage area called the *heap*. In this and all other cases the put_unsafe_value instruction proceeds as does put_value Yi,Xj. Note that the operation of making a permanent variable *safe* by globalizing it on the heap is needed to implement last-call optimization. The heap is also used for storing data structures, as discussed below.

The code for queen/5 is listed in Figure A.2. Here we see an additional level of code complexity: the introduction of multiple clauses and indexing. In general a multiple-clause procedure is compiled into a group of code segments, one per clause, preceded by an indexing block. In the case of queen, the three clause blocks are located at labels L10, L11, and L12. The indexing block consists of eight instructions. The switch_on_term Lv,Lc,Ll,Ls instruction performs a four-way branch on the *type* of the first argument passed to the procedure, in register X0. Control passes to label Lv if X0 is unbound; to label Lc if X0 is a constant; to label Ll if X0 is a list; to label Ls if X0 is a structure.

Since there is only one clause indexed by a list, Ll=L10 is a direct label of that clause block. Since no clauses are indexed by a structure, Ls=L6 labels a fail instruction (more on failure in a moment). The remaining two argument types (unbound variable and constant) cause branches to labels L8 and L7, which define additional indexing instructions.

The L8 block corresponds to an unbound input argument. The try instruction creates a *choicepoint* for the subsequent instruction and then executes the code at label L10. A choicepoint is implemented in Aurora as a frame on the *control stack*. The frame contains the current values of the state[1] and argument (X) registers. The purpose of a choicepoint is to summarize the state of computation so that subsequent *failure* can precisely restore the state. We have encountered only one instruction that can fail, namely the fail instruction! Shortly we will meet instructions that fail more subtly.

State restoration upon failure, via a choicepoint, is called *backtracking*. Backtracking always selects the recentmost choicepoint to restore. A choicepoint that is used to spawn OR-parallel tasks is called a *branchpoint*. A branchpoint contains extra bookkeeping information (with respect to a choicepoint) that is used by the Aurora scheduler.

---

[1] Examples of state registers are the instruction counter, the current environment pointer, etc. WAM defines about eight of these.

```
queen:  switch_on_term        L8,L7,L10,L6
L8:     try                   L10
        retry                 L11
        trust                 L12
L6:     fail
L7:     switch_on_constant    [[[],L9]]
L9:     try                   L11
        trust                 L12

L10:    get_list              X0            queen([
        allocate              6
        unify_variable        Y1                      C|
        unify_variable        Y0                        Cs],
        get_variable          X1,X3                         NCs,
        get_variable          X2,X0                             L,
        get_variable          X3,X6                               S0,
        get_variable          X3,Y2
        get_variable          X0,Y3
        get_variable          X4,Y5                                      S2) :-
                                            check(L,      NCs,      S0,
        put_constant          1,X2                              1,
        put_value             Y1,X1                     C,
        put_value             Y0,X4                               Cs,
        put_value             X0,X5                                 L,
        put_variable          Y4,X7                                       S1
        call                  check                                         ),
        put_list              X1            queen(    [
        unify_value           Y1                          C|
        unify_value           Y2                            NCs],
        put_value             Y0,X0                   Cs,
        put_value             Y3,X2                             L,
        put_unsafe_value      Y4,X3                               S1,
        put_value             Y5,X4                                 S2
        deallocate
        execute               queen                                           ).

L11:    get_constant          X0,[]         queen([],
        get_constant          X1,[]                   [],L,S0,S1) :-
        get_list              X3            S0=[
        unify_value           X2                  L|
        unify_value           X4                    S1].
        proceed

L12:    get_constant          X0            queen([],
        get_list              X1                    [_|_],_,S0,S1) :-
        get_value             X4,X3         S1=S0.
        proceed
```

Figure A.2
WAM Code for queen/5

Suppose that, after the execution of the **try** instruction, a subsequent instruction fails and the recentmost choicepoint is the one created by the **try**, i.e., no intervening instructions created their own choicepoints. This failure causes restoration of the choicepoint, meaning (among other things) that the instruction counter is reset to point to the **retry** instruction.

The **retry** modifies the instruction pointer saved in the choicepoint to point to the instruction *following* the **retry** instruction (in this case, **trust**). The **retry** instruction then executes the code at label L11. In a similar manner, failure can again cause backtracking to the choicepoint and execution of the **trust** instruction. The **trust** removes the choicepoint and then executes the code at label L12.

At label L7 we encounter a new indexing instruction: **switch_on_constant** H, where H is a hash list. The first argument, X0, is hashed into the hash list to produce a branch label. A branch is taken to the label. If there is no matching hash key, the instruction fails. In this code segment, if the first argument is [], a **try** block is executed, attempting the second and third clauses at labels L11 and L12.

A new control instruction, **proceed**, is introduced at the end of the second and third clauses. This instruction is a procedure return via the continuation pointer. [2] The compiler generates a **proceed** at the end of each unit clause, corresponding to the complete reduction of a goal.

When examining the code blocks, we encounter many new head matching instructions. Instruction **get_variable** Xi,Xj transfers the contents of register Xi into register Xj. Instruction **get_constant** Xi,C checks if the value of register Xi can unify with the immediate constant C. If register Xi has value C, then the instruction succeeds.[3] If register Xi is *unbound*, then Xi is bound to C and *trailed* if necessary.[4] Otherwise the instruction fails.

---

[2]The continuation pointer is loaded with the address following each **call** instruction, and is saved in the environment of a clause with multiple body goals. This implies that an environment is created for every non-unit clause, even those without permanent variables.

[3]Register Xi may have an *indirect value*, i.e., a pointer to a data cell on the stack or heap. In fact, any data cell may have an indirect value, but eventually all pointer chains must terminate with a concrete value (possibly unbound). Therefore, to determine the value of register Xi, it must be *dereferenced* to its concrete value. Dereferencing may involve any number of indirect memory references, but empirically we know it is usually zero or one.

[4]Trailing involves saving the address and new value of the unbound variable on a special stack called the trail. In the case of backtracking a certain portion of the trail is popped and the memory location at each address therein is reset to unbound. It is not always the case that a binding needs to be trailed, although we will not go into the details of this optimization.

The binding value is saved in the trail entry to enable the Aurora scheduler to *load* a computation state of an independent OR-parallel task. When a processor becomes idle, its scheduler will backtrack to the most recent, active branchpoint and load the computation state of one of its parallel branches. Loading the state involves examining the trail, and the memory location at each address therein is bound to the saved binding value.

Instruction `get_value Xi,Xj` unifies the value of register `Xi` with the value of register `Xj`. The actions taken on success and failure of the unification are similar to those in `get_constant`. The difference is that `get_value` performs a *general unification* that may entail any number of bindings. Each binding must be trailed if necessary. In typical Prolog programs, general unification as performed in this instruction is not *deep*, i.e., unification rarely must traverse deeply into two structures — top-level bindings usually satisfy unification.

Instruction `get_list Xi` is similar to `get_constant`, except that `get_list` has a side effect of initializing a *structure pointer* to the heap and a *mode bit* (to either *read mode* or *write mode*). The operation of subsequent `unify` instructions depends on the structure pointer and mode. In read mode, the `unify` instructions will attempt to match the head and tail of the list (referred to by the structure pointer) against given registers. This attempt may result in failure. In write mode, the `unify` instructions will write the values of their given registers into the heap locations referenced by the structure pointer. In write mode the `unify` instructions cannot fail. Both the structure pointer and mode bit are state registers in the WAM architecture.

Instruction `unify_value Xi` attempts unification against a bound temporary variable in register `Xi`. This instruction performs general unification between `Xi` and the value referenced by the structure pointer. Instruction `unify_value Yi` is similar except that the operand is a permanent variable. Instruction `unify_variable Yi` attempts unification against an unbound permanent variable. This instruction always succeeds by binding `Yi` to the value (on the heap) referenced by the structure pointer.

To allocate registers efficiently, a `get_list` instruction may be separated from its subsequent `unify` instructions by a sequence of `allocate` and `get` instructions. In addition, procedure arguments need not be read in or set up in left-to-right order. The compiler may choose to match arguments in a jumbled order, thereby minimizing temporary register and permanent variable usage.

In the assembly code for `check/8` (Figure A.3), there is one new `unify` instruction and some builtin arithmetic, comparison, and cut instructions. Instruction `unify_variable Xi` is similar to `unify_variable Yi` except that unification is attempted against an unbound *temporary* variable. This instruction always succeeds by binding `Xi` to the value (on the heap) referenced by the structure pointer.

The arithmetic and comparison instructions are two-address operations. For example, `subtract Xi,Xj` means `Xj := Xj-Xi`. If either operand is unbound, then an error condition occurs, similar in severity to a divide-by-zero event in a conventional architecture. Register `Xi` and `Xj` are both dereferenced to integer values, and

```
check:    switch_on_term       L13,L15,L16,L14
L13:      try                  L17
          retry                L18
          trust                L19
L16:      try                  L18
          trust                L19
L14:      fail
L15:      switch_on_constant   [[[],L17]]

L17:      get_constant         X0,[]              check([],
          allocate             5
          get_variable         X1,Y1                          C,_,
          get_variable         X3,X0                             NCs,
          get_variable         X4,X1                               Cs,
          get_variable         X5,Y2                                 L,
          get_variable         X6,Y3                                  S0,
          get_variable         X7,Y4                                   S1) :-
          put_variable         Y0,X2                     append(NCs,Cs,Ps
          call                 append                              ),
          put_constant         [],X1             queen(    [],
          put_list             X2                                [
          unify_value          Y1                                 C|
          unify_value          Y2                                  L],
          put_unsafe_value     Y0,X0                        Ps,
          put_value            Y3,X3                                S0,
          put_value            Y4,X4                                 S1
          deallocate
          execute              queen                               ).

L18:      get_list             X0                check([
          unify_variable       X9                       P|
          unify_variable       X0                        Ps],C,D,NCs,Cs,L,S0,S1) :-
          put_value            X9,X8
          subtract             X1,X9
          not_eq               X2,X9                  P-C =\= D,
          put_value            X1,X9
          subtract             X8,X9
          not_eq               X2,X9                  C-P =\= D,
          put_constant         1,X8
          cut                                         !,
          add                  X8,X2             D1 is D+1,
          execute              check             check(Ps,C,D1,NCs,Cs,L,S0,S1).

L19:      get_value            X6,X7             check(_,_,_,_,_,_,S0,S1) :- S0=S1.
          proceed
```

Figure A.3
WAM Code for check/8

register Xj is overwritten with the difference. Dependent on the underlying host, other instruction formats and semantics may be more appropriate for arithmetic.

The register allocation for the first clause of **check/8** is nonoptimal because it uses five permanent variables. However, as we shall soon see, **append** uses only four temporary registers, implying that enough temporary registers remain to store the five variables needed for the last call to **queen**. Such register allocation requires analysis across procedure-call boundaries.

The code above pessimistically assumes that all temporary registers may be destroyed across any user-defined procedure call. With global register allocation, we could compile the first clause of **check/8** into the code shown below. No permanent variables are needed, obviating environment management and all data memory references. This allocation affords great savings in execution time.

```
L17:    get_constant      X0,[]           check([],
        get_variable      X1,X8                  C,_,
        get_variable      X3,X0                      NCs,
        get_variable      X4,X1                         Cs,L,S0,S1) :-
        put_variable      X2,X9           append(NCs,Cs,Ps
        call              append                        ),
        put_value         X9,X0           queen(Ps,
        put_constant      [],X1                 [],
        put_list          X2                        [
        unify_value       X8                         C|
        unify_value       X5                          L],
        put_value         X6,X3                         S0,
        put_value         X7,X4                          S1
        execute           queen                         ).
```

The assembly code for **append/3** is shown below. As noted previously, **append/3** uses registers 0–3 only.

```
append: switch_on_term    L3,L1,L2,L4
L3:     try               L1
        trust             L2
L4:     fail

L1:     get_constant      X0,[]           append([],L1,L2) :-
        get_value         X1,X2                  L1=L2.
        proceed
L2:     get_list          X0              append([
        unify_variable    X3                      X|
        unify_variable    X0                       L1],L2,L4) :-
        get_list          X2              L4=[
        unify_value       X3                   X|
        unify_variable    X2                    L3],
        execute           append          append(L1,L2,L3).
```

Many Prolog implementors quote performance in terms of determinate **append** MLIPS (millions of logical inferences per second). For the WAM, a single **append** logical inference is the execution of the `switch_on_term` instruction followed by the seven instructions beginning at label L2. The execution time is the product of the machine cycle time and the number of cycles incurred in the seven instructions. For **append**, MLIPS can be particularly misleading for a few reasons. Cycle time is dependent on many factors, of which logic programming architecture may not be the most significant. For example, one system may execute twice the MLIPS of another system, simply due to faster memory. Also, these seven instructions do not represent the mix of operations in an "average" logical inference.

A.2   Panda's Abstract Machine

The FGHC instruction set, called KL1-B, was designed by Y. Kimura and T. Chikayama [71]. The instructions are based on the WAM and the similarities will become clear as we step through the N-Queens example. The major difference between KL1-B and the WAM is that KL1-B is a *goal-stacking* architecture. This term means that, in a query $A := B_1, B_2, ..., B_n$, we first create a goal record[5] for B_n and push it onto the stack, then create a goal record for B_{n-1}, etc. Finally we load the arguments of B_1 directly into the register set and begin its execution. Recall that the WAM does just the opposite: it first creates a *continuation* for goals $B_2, ..., B_n$, consisting of little more than a code pointer, and then immediately executes B_1.

To give some historical background, D. H. D. Warren actually designed a goal-stacking architecture for Prolog in 1983 [144], shortly before the WAM. This approach then lay dormant until 1987, when Kimura and Chikayama realized its potential for committed-choice languages. For Prolog, or for any sequential, procedural, or functional language for that matter, goal-stacking is inefficient because the stack fills up with goals. For Prolog, this inefficiency is particularly disadvantageous because backtracking might make the stacked goals obsolete. For FGHC, however, there is no waste because all goals will eventually be executed. The space requirement is still as severe, but the payoff is the exposure of the goals on the stack for spawning on multiple PEs. Continuations reduce stack size to a minimum, especially when exploiting last-call optimization, but hide all potential parallelism!

The KL1-B instruction set described here implements simple goal-stacking. A

---

[5]Unlike a WAM environment, a KL1-B goal record stores all arguments passed to a body goal, in addition to some bookkeeping information.

goal invocation is reduced into a group of body goals that share no environment. The total necessary computation state required by a body goal is contained in its goal record. As mentioned, this approach is wasteful in terms of memory usage, and is limited because it forces all goals to be potentially parallel! To solve both problems, an interesting idea is to implement continuations *in addition to* individual goals. In fact, JAM Parlog does just that, with the primary motivation of supporting user-defined sequential goals [37].

The KL1-B code discussed in this section is modified output of the Panda compiler used in this study. Simplifications were introduced to avoid a discussion of advanced optimizations. In addition, instruction formats were made to closely resemble those of the WAM previously described, to facilitate comparison.

The assembly of the top-level procedure, go/2, of the N-Queens program is shown below.

```
go:    set_value     X1,Y3          go(N,A) :- queen(        A,
       set_variable  X1,Y0                             L,
       set_constant  [],Y1                                [],
       set_constant  [],Y2                                   [],
       set_constant  [],Y4                                      []
       enqueue_goal  5,queen                                     ),
       execute       2,gen                        gen(N,L).
```

There are five instructions for setting up the arguments inside a new goal record for the recursive call to **queen**. Instruction **set_variable Xi,Yj** creates an unbound variable **Yj** in the goal record (i.e., the variable in the current goal record at index j) and a pointer to this variable in argument register **Xi**. Notice that the KL1-B goal record plays the role of the WAM environment, hence we use the same **Y** notation. Similarly, the **X** registers in both architectures perform the same function as passed arguments and temporaries.

Instruction **set_constant C,Yi** writes a constant **C** in the goal record variable **Yi**. Instruction **set_value Xi,Yj** loads the value of argument register **Xi** into the goal record variable **Yj**. The **enqueue_goal** instruction completes the goal-stacking operation by linking the new goal record into the *goal queue*. In general, we may wish to enqueue and dequeue goals in more flexible ways than a simple LIFO stack; however, in Panda, the goal queue is treated exactly as a stack.

Procedure **gen/2** is directly executed so that instead of creating a goal record, the arguments are loaded directly into registers. The first argument, **N**, is already in place from being passed through **go/2**. The second argument, **L** is loaded by the **set_variable** instruction.

The **queen/5** procedure is shown below. Because there are multiple clauses, a **try_me_else** instruction is generated which points to a *continuation address* (in this case, the **suspend** instruction at label L1). If any subsequent instruction within the procedure fails then execution proceeds at continuation address, which can be changed by another **try_me_else**. As we shall soon see, instruction failure occurs in the head or guard, because of an attempt to export a binding or the inability to satisfy a simple predicate (such as arithmetic comparison).

Note that KL1-B instruction "failure" is much lighter than WAM instruction failure. In FGHC, the program state cannot be modified within a clause head and guard. Therefore failure need only transfer control to the next available clause. If no such clause exists, then the procedure executes a **suspend** instruction. In **go/3** there is no head unification or guard, so the procedure cannot suspend and the **try_me_else** is not needed. Note that the continuation address is analogous to a minimal choicepoint in the WAM.

In **queen/5** (Figure A.4) we see how simple indexing is performed. The **switch_-on_type La,Ll,Ls** instruction is similar to the WAM instruction of the same name. A branch on the type of register X0 is executed. Label **La** is for atoms, **Ll** is for lists, and **Ls** is for structures. If **X0** is unbound, the index instruction will fail, causing transfer to the continuation address.

Input-unification instructions are present in this code segment. Instruction **test_-constant Xi,C** tests if register **Xi** is equal to constant **C**. The next instruction is executed if the test succeeds. If **Xi** is bound and the test fails, then the instruction fails. If **Xi** is unbound, this constitutes an attempted illegal output unification. The address pointed to by register **Xi** is pushed onto a small special stack called the *suspension stack*. The instruction then fails.[6] The purpose of this last operation is to record each potentially suspending variable during attempted procedure reduction.

If any of the clauses in the procedure succeed or if all clauses fail,[7] then the suspension stack is discarded. Otherwise the **suspend** instruction is executed, accessing the suspension stack. Each variable on the stack is "hooked" to a *suspension record* pointing to the goal record corresponding to the procedure call (that goal record subsequently "floats" independently of the goal queue). An unbound variable is hooked by assigning to it a special tag and a pointer to the suspension record. Subsequent binding of that variable will trigger a *resumption* routine in the abstract machine. Resumption restores the linked goal record to the goal queue.[8]

---

[6] switch-on-term acts similarly and pushes X0 onto the suspension stack.

[7] This case rarely occurs in a well-written program.

[8] A subtle but important issue entails whether to restore the resumed goal at the head, tail or intermediate point in the goal queue. More generally, goals might be assigned priorities, either statically or dynamically, and queued with respect to these priorities.

```
queen:   try_me_else     L1
         switch_on_type  L4,L6,L1
L4:      test_constant   X0,[]          queen([],
         try_me_else     L8
L7:      test_constant   X1,[]                        [],L,S0,S1) :-
         put_list        X0             T=[
         write_value     X2               L
         write_value     X4                 |S1],
         get_list_value  X0,X3          S0=T.
         proceed


L8:      try_me_else     L1
         get_list        X1             queen([],[_|_],
         get_value       X3,X4                      _,S0,S1) :- S1=S0.
         proceed


L6:      read_variable   X9             queen([C|
         read_variable   X5                    Cs],
         put_value       X1,X8                      NCs,
         put_value       X2,X0                          L,
         put_value       X3,X6                            S0,S2) :-
         set_value       X5,Y0          queen(Cs,
         put_list        X1                        [
         write_value     X9                         C|
         write_value     X8                           NCs],
         set_value       X1,Y1
         set_value       X0,Y2                            L,
         set_variable    X3,Y7                             S1,
         set_value       X4,Y4                              S2
         enqueue_goal    5,queen                            ),
         put_value       X9,X1          check(L,C,
         put_constant    1,X2                     1,
         put_value       X8,X3                      NCs,
         put_value       X5,X4                         Cs,
         put_value       X0,X5                           L,S0,S1
         execute         8,check                           ).
L1:      suspend         queen
```

Figure A.4
KL1-B Code for queen/5

Instruction `read_variable` requires that the previous instruction executed was `switch_on_term` for the case when X0 is a list. Thus a heap structure pointer has been prepared pointing to the head of the list. Instruction `read_variable` Xi loads the value referenced by the structure pointer into register Xi and increments the structure pointer. Instruction `put_value` Xi,Xj transfers register Xi into register Xj.

Output-unification instructions are also present in the code segment. Instruction `get_value` Xi,Xj unifies the value of register Xj to the value of register Xi. Instruction `put_list` Xi creates a list in the heap, sets the structure pointer to point to the head of the new list, and loads a pointer to the new list into register Xi. Instruction `write_value` Xi writes the value of register Xi into the location pointed to by the structure pointer. Instruction `get_list_value` Xi,Xj unifies a list pointed to by register Xi to the value of register Xj (`get_value` could be used as well, with slightly less efficiency). This sequence of four instructions for creating a list cell has been deliberately generated. When building the new list cell, no locking is required. Locking is needed only within the `get_list_value` instruction; thus locking periods and conflicts are minimized.

The assembly code for `check/8` is given in Figure A.5. We have in fact seen most of the instructions with the exception of arithmetic and the `otherwise` guard. Arithmetic is represented here with instructions similar to the WAM arithmetic instructions. Instruction `subtract` Xi,Xj means Xj := Xj-Xi, loading the difference in register Xj after dereferencing both source values. Unlike Prolog, however, if either source operand is unbound then Panda will *suspend* this clause (recall that Prolog will produce an error exception). Arithmetic instructions are always compiled into the guard instead of becoming separate body goals. This strategy reduces the overall number of suspensions in the program, because most goals that receive the result of an arithmetic calculation cannot proceed without a ground value. Therefore we force synchronization of all arithmetic.

Note that, if the `test` instructions fail, then execution continues at the address specified by the latest `try_me_else` instruction. In this case, the `try_me_else` points not to a `suspend`, but rather to the `otherwise` instruction. The `otherwise` guard is implemented by forcing the procedure call to suspend if any of the clauses preceding the `otherwise` instruction have suspended variables. Thus `otherwise` is implemented by checking the suspension stack. If the stack is empty, then execution proceeds. If the stack is not empty, then a suspension occurs.

The final code segment given is for `append/3`. We have already encountered all of these instructions.

```
check:   try_me_else      L11
         switch_on_type   L10,L12,L11          check([],C,_,NCs,Cs,L,S0,S1) :-
L10:     test_constant    X0,[]                   queen(Ps,
         set_variable     X2,Y0                         [],
         set_constant     [],Y1                              [
         put_list         X0                                 C|
         write_value      X1                                    L],
         write_value      X5
         set_value        X0,Y2                                      S0,
         set_value        X6,Y3                                        S1
         set_value        X7,Y4                                          ),
         enqueue_goal     5,queen                  append(NCs,
         put_value        X3,X0                            Cs,Ps
         put_value        X4,X1                              ).
         execute          3,append

L12:     read_variable    X9                    check([P|
         read_variable    X0                           Ps],C,D,NCs,Cs,L,S0,S1) :-
         put_value        X9,X8
         subtract         X1,X9
         not_eq           X2,X9                    P-C =\= D,
         put_value        X1,X9
         subtract         X8,X9
         not_eq           X2,X9                    C-P =\= D,
         put_constant     1,X8
         add              X8,X2                    D1 is D+1,
         execute          8,check                  check(Ps,C,D1,NCs,Cs,L,S0,S1).

L11:     otherwise        check                 check(_,_,_,_,_,_,S0,S1) :-
         try_me_else      L13
         get_value        X6,X7                    S1=S0.
         proceed
L13:     suspend          check
```

Figure A.5
KL1-B Code for check/8

```
append:  try_me_else      L5
         switch_on_type   L16,L2,L5
L16:     test_constant    X0,[]           append([],L1,L2) :-
         get_value        X1,X2              L2=L1.
         proceed

L2:      read_variable    X3              append([X|
         read_variable    X0                       L1],L2,L4) :-
         put_list         X4                 T=[
         write_value      X3                     X|
         write_variable   X3                       L3],
         get_list_value   X4,X2              L4=T,
         put_value        X3,X2              append(L1,L2,L3
         execute          3,append                          ).
L5:      suspend          append
```

Additional WAM and KL1-B instructions do not appear in the previous programs, but we leave these to the reader to ferret out in the original sources.

A.3 Summary

Aurora and Panda are abstract architectures for OR-parallel Prolog and FGHC, respectively. These architectures are designed specifically for shared-memory multiprocessors, although this does not preclude implementations of these and similar languages on other hosts, such as Aurora on the Butterfly [85], Strand and FCP on the HyperCube [127], and FLENG on the Connection Machine [91]. Throughout this book we present performance measurements taken from Aurora and Panda running on both the Sequent Symmetry and Encore Multimax.

In the literature, Maier and Warren [80] carefully describe how to build logic programming implementations up from propositional logic. Kogge [74] also derives logic programming architectures from first principles and discusses hardware implementations. D.H.D. Warren's original technical report on the WAM [143] is a classic paper on high-level language architecture. Aurora papers include an overview by Lusk *et al.* [78], principles of operations [21], Aurora scheduling [18, 17], and Aurora execution characteristics [121, 129]. The best papers about KL1-B are Kimura and Chikayama [71] and Shinogi et al. [117]. The Panda system and its execution characteristics are described in Sato [113, 112] and Tick [129]. There are several interesting papers about garbage collection in logic programming systems [25, 93, 88, 9, 134, 55, 96].

B Programming Projects

Four large parallel programming projects are outlined in this section. These projects are suggested for either individuals or groups of students. Each problem can be implemented in a parallel logic-programming language of choice. Complexity of the algorithm(s) should be analyzed, correctness of the program should be exhibited, and performance should be measured on a multiprocessor for reasonable-sized input data.

B.1 Dynamic Programming (DP) Matching

Finding the best match between two strings of characters is an important problem in the study of genetics and other applications. Given two strings of length M and N, where $M \leq N$, we wish to change one string into the other string with maximal *fit* or minimal *cost*. The operations allowed in this computation are insertion, deletion, and transformation of characters. The costs of insertion and deletion are usually fixed, independent of where the operation takes place within the string, although not always.

The cost of transforming a character is usually a function of the original and target characters. In genetics, for instance, it is easy to transform *valine* into *leucine* because this entails modifying few amino acids. However, it is very rare (costly) to transform *valine* into *histidine*, because this process involves a complete overhaul of the DNA. In some problems we are simply not allowed to transform characters, so this operation is given infinite cost.

There are many variations on the rules by which DP-matching is played, depending on the application. We present here an example of protein homology, wherein we try to maximize the fit of two strings. We allow either insertion of "blanks" in either string or mutation of two characters in the same string position. The mutations have fixed costs, as outlined in Table B.1 (from Yoshida [152]). An entry along the diagonal corresponds to an exact match of characters giving the highest fit of six. Off-diagonal entries correspond to mutations at lower fits of 0–5. Consider the strings:

```
A = vedqkltskc
B = venkltrpkc
```

The best match, with maximum fit 51, is:

```
A = vedqklt skc
B = ven kltrpkc
```

	c	s	t	p	a	g	n	d	e	q	h	r	k	m	i	l	v	f	y	w
c: systeine	6																			
s: serine	4	6																		
t: threonine	2	5	6																	
p: proline	2	4	4	6																
a: alanin	2	5	5	5	6															
g: glycine	2	5	2	3	5	6														
n: asparagine	2	5	4	2	3	3	6													
d: aspartic acid	1	3	2	2	4	4	5	6												
e: glutamic acid	0	3	3	3	4	4	3	5	6											
g: glutamine	1	3	3	3	3	2	3	4	4	6										
h: histidine	2	3	2	3	2	1	4	3	2	4	6									
r: arginine	2	3	3	3	2	3	2	2	2	3	4	6								
k: lysine	0	3	4	2	3	2	4	3	4	4	3	5	6							
m: mathionine	2	1	3	2	2	1	1	0	1	2	1	2	2	6						
i: isoleucine	2	2	3	2	2	2	2	1	1	1	1	2	2	4	6					
l: leucine	2	2	2	3	2	2	1	1	1	2	3	2	2	5	5	6				
v: valine	2	2	3	3	5	4	2	3	4	2	1	2	3	4	5	5	6			
f: phenylalanine	3	3	1	2	2	1	1	1	0	1	2	1	0	2	4	4	4	6		
y: tyrosine	3	3	2	2	2	2	3	2	1	2	3	1	1	2	3	3	3	5	6	
w: tryptophan	3	2	1	2	2	3	0	0	1	1	1	2	1	3	2	4	3	3	3	6

Table B.1
Protein Homology Mutability Table

Here we inserted two blanks (zero fit) and mutated d-n and s-p (fits five and four respectively). The other characters matched exactly with fit six. Consider an inferior choice:

```
A = vedq k l tskc
B = venkltrpkc
```

This solution has a fit of only 30. It is interesting to note that the critical choice was to mutate q-k instead of inserting a blank as above. Although the mutation was a better *local* fit than the insertion, the subsequent mismatches proved detrimental.

The basic idea of a parallel algorithm for DP-matching is to create an $M \times N$ grid of processes. Envision the horizontal axis of the grid corresponding to the upper string and the vertical axis corresponding to the lower string. A process communicates with six of the eight neighbors surrounding it. The West, Northwest, and North neighbors supply communication input streams. The process supplies output streams to its South, Southeast, and East neighbors.

A process at location (i, j) within the grid will be presented with strings partially matched up to the first $max(i, j)$ characters. The process may receive up to three messages from neighbors, each vying for consideration. A simple decision method is to pick the message with the greatest fit. Once a process decides which of its inputs to choose, it then calculates three possible extensions of the match: a blank inserted in the upper string (communicate this to the East), a blank inserted in the lower string (communicate this to the South), and mutating the characters in place (communicate this to the Southeast).

A complete solution (string match) corresponds to a sequence of processes beginning at the left or top of the grid and terminating at the right or bottom of the grid. Intuitively, solutions beginning at the bottom left correspond to shifting the upper string quite a bit, whereas solutions terminating at the upper right correspond to shifting the lower string quite a bit. Since insertion of blanks have zero fit value, these paths are inferior. The best fits lie along the diagonal, because these paths involve mostly mutations rather than shifts.

Write a parallel logic program implementing DP-matching for a subset of the protein homology given. First write the program to simply dump all the solutions, each consisting of the two matched strings and the fit value. Then write the program to output a reconstruction of the process grid, with indications of the actual pathways chosen. As an example, Figure B.1 [152] illustrates a portion of the grid corresponding to the previous ten-character string match (# represents a blank). Only two paths (solutions) are shown in the figure. Others can easily be included. Note that this graphical representation clearly indicates the critical juncture at

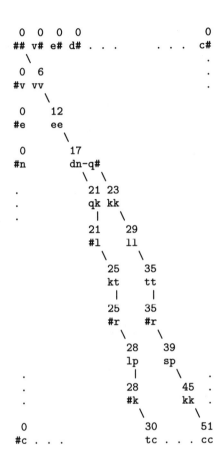

Figure B.1
Part of the Protein Homology Grid

$(i, j) = (3, 3)$ where the path splits. We also easily see that, although the left path made a better local choice, the right path quickly gains because it is better aligned.

B.2   The N-Body Problem

The N-Body problem described here is part of a simulation of the gravitational interaction of galaxies. You are given n stars distributed in some manner in three-dimensional space. Each star has a mass and an initial velocity vector. In one simulation time-step, the gravitational force exerted on each star by all the other stars is calculated. From these forces we easily derive accelerations by Newton's law, and hence can find new velocities and new positions for each star.

Consider n stars: each star i is initially given a state consisting of a location vector $\bar{x}_i$, a mass c_i, and a velocity vector $\bar{v}_i$. Here $\bar{x}_i = (x_i, y_i, z_i)$, the three-dimensional space coordinates of the star. For convenience, we define mass as $c_i = Gm_i$ where G is the gravitational constant. The combined force acting on a given star i is given by Newton's Law and by the law of gravity:

$$\begin{aligned} \bar{F}_i &= m_i \bar{a}_i \\ \bar{F}_i &= G \sum_{j \neq i} \frac{m_i m_j}{r_{ij}^2} \hat{r_{ij}} \end{aligned}$$

where $\hat{r_{ij}}$ is the unit vector pointing from star i to star j. Combining the two force equations,

$$\bar{a}_i = \sum_{j \neq i} \frac{c_i}{r_{ij}^2} \hat{r_{ij}}$$

Note that $\hat{r_{ij}}/r_{ij}^2 = \bar{r_{ij}}/r_{ij}^3$. This formulation is simpler, since

$$\begin{aligned} \bar{r_{ij}} &= (x_i - x_j, y_i - y_j, z_i - z_j) \\ r_{ij}^3 &= ((x_i - x_j)^2 + (y_i - y_j)^2 + (z_i - z_j)^2)^{3/2} \end{aligned}$$

Simulation proceeds in time-steps Δt. At time t, each star i has some state $(\bar{x}_i, c_i, \bar{v}_i)$. For each time-step, for each star i, we calculate:

$$\begin{aligned} \bar{a}_i &= \sum_{j \neq i} \left(\frac{c_i(x_i - x_j)}{r_{ij}^3}, \frac{c_i(y_i - y_j)}{r_{ij}^3}, \frac{c_i(z_i - z_j)}{r_{ij}^3} \right) \\ \Delta \bar{v}_i &= \Delta t \bar{a}_i \\ \Delta \bar{x}_i &= \Delta t \bar{v}_i \end{aligned}$$

Thus the state changes from $(\bar{x}_i, c_i, \bar{v}_i)$ to $(\bar{x}_i + \Delta\bar{x}_i, c_i, \bar{v}_i + \Delta\bar{v}_i)$.

We are not concerned with the simulation *per se*, but with the calculations involved in one time-step. A naive algorithm of $O(N^2)$ is used to actually calculate the force between every pair of stars. However, if a group of stars is sufficiently far away from a given star, their gravitational effect can be approximated as if the group were a single heavier star at the center of the mass of the group. This approximation leads to "tree-code" algorithms [64, 81] with low time complexity. The algorithms represent the stars in an *oct-tree*. An *oct-tree* has an eight-way branching factor at each node. The sub-branches represent the eight quadrants of a three-dimensional subspace. *The key to representing stars in space is to ensure that no two stars share the same leaf subquadrant.*

Given an oct-tree partially filled with stars (at the leaves), we insert a new star by successively traveling deeper into the subquadrants until we either find an empty subquadrant or a star in that position. In the former case, we can simply insert the star. In the latter case, that subquadrant is expanded into eight smaller subquadrants, and so on until the two conflicting stars land in different spaces.

Why use such a complex representation? It allows us to find stars in $O(logN)$ time. It also allows us easily to determine if the aforementioned approximation is appropriate, i.e., how far away one star is from a group of stars. Consider calculating all the forces on a given star. As the oct-tree is traversed, for each node we consider if the subquadrant represented by that node is far enough from the star to warrant the approximation. A subquadrant has an edge size l and a distance from the star d (we will calculate distance from the center of the subquadrant). If l/d is small enough, we can approximate all the stars in the subquadrant as acting from its center. "Small enough" is defined by a parameter θ that controls the accuracy of the calculation.

As a practical consideration, we assume that all stars are of equal mass. Thus all $c_i = Gm_i = K$, a constant that is removed from all computations. The data is in effect scaled by $1/K$. Star position data can be generated with the galaxy-cluster model given by Aarseth *et al.* [1]. This model assumes that each star has equal mass, $1/N$, and that the star distribution forms a uniform spherical mass.[1]

To increase the accuracy of the computation, a constant factor $k = N^{-2/3}$ is

---

[1]Thus the mass as a function of radius (from some origin) is: $M(r) = r^3(1 + r^2)^{-3/2}$ or inversely, $r = (D^{-2/3} - 1)^{-1/2}$. The trick is to uniformly select a random D for each star to determine its radius from the origin. At that point one must randomly pick where the star sits on the sphere defined by that radius. This is done by two additional random numbers as outlined by Aarseth [1].

added to the coordinates when calculating $r_{ij}{}^3$ [82].

$$r_{ij}{}^3 = ((x_i - x_j)^2 + (y_i - y_j)^2 + (z_i - z_j)^2 + k)^{3/2}$$

Note that it is *not* necessary to compute $\sqrt{p}$ for *any* p in this algorithm. We need only compute r^{-1}, i.e., $p = r^2$:

$$\bar{a}_i = \sum_{j \neq i} \frac{(x_i - x_j, y_i - y_j, z_i - z_j)}{r_{ij}^3}$$

$$= \sum_{j \neq i} \frac{(x_i - x_j, y_i - y_j, z_i - z_j)}{r_{ij}^2 \cdot r_{ij}}$$

$$= \sum_{j \neq i} \frac{(x_i - x_j, y_i - y_j, z_i - z_j)}{r_{ij}^2} \cdot \frac{1}{r_{ij}}$$

$$r_{ij}^{-1} = 1 / \sqrt{(x_i - x_j)^2 + (y_i - y_j)^2 + (z_i - z_j)^2 + k}$$

Hut and Makino [64] give a fast iterative approximation algorithm for this case. Let

$$r_0 = (|x_i - x_j| + |y_i - y_j| + |z_i - z_j| + g)/2$$

where $g = k^{1/2} = N^{-1/3}$. Then,

$$a_0 = 2r_0/(r_0{}^2 + r_{ij}{}^2)$$

where

$$r_{ij}{}^2 = (x_i - x_j)^2 + (y_i - y_j)^2 + (z_i - z_j)^2 + k.$$

By iteration on m,

$$a_{m+1} = (3a_m - a_m{}^3 r_{ij}{}^2)/2$$

Four to five iterations are generally sufficient for convergence [82]. Notice that only multiplication and division are used. Let us call this function $r_{ij}^{-1} = h(a_0, r^2)$. Then,

$$\bar{a}_i = \sum_{j \neq i} \frac{h(a_0, r_{ij}{}^2)}{r_{ij}{}^2} \cdot (x_i - x_j, y_i - y_j, z_i - z_j)$$

This equation is the backbone of our (and most other) N-Body algorithms.

We sketch here a possible set of data structures with which to construct the program. A star in the initial data base is represented by its coordinates:

```
star(Xx1,Xy1,Xz1).
star(Xx2,Xy2,Xz2).
...
```

The initial velocity and acceleration are assumed to be zero. Each node in the oct-tree, **node/3**, has eight subtrees, coordinates of its center, and the total number of all stars within it:

        node(o(Xx,Xy,Xz),N,[S1,S2,S3,S4,S5,S6,S7,S8])

A leaf in the oct-tree, **leaf/5**, consists of a position, velocity, and acceleration vectors.

        leaf(o(Xx,Xy,Xz),o(Vx,Vy,Vz),o(Ax,Ay,Az))

B.3   The Maxflow Problem

The Maxflow Problem determines a *maximal flow* through a graph of directed, non-negatively weighted edges. The flow on a given edge cannot exceed its weight and must be non-negative. The flow entering a vertex must exactly equal the flow leaving a vertex. Specially-selected inflow and outflow vertices are chosen for input and output from the graph. Note that *maximal flow* is subtly different from *maximum flow*. A flow is maximal if every path from the input to output vertices contains at least one saturated edge. A saturated edge has a flow equal to its capacity. Maximum flow is precisely the largest flow sustainable through the graph.

One distributed algorithm, given by Hellerstein and Shapiro [61], spawns a process for each vertex in the graph, connected to neighboring vertices by channels (two-way streams) as in the bestpath programs. Initially a large amount of fluid, in quantum chunks, is introduced at the input vertex. The fluid propagates through the edges of the graph. Fluid arriving at the output vertex is tallied and disappears from the system. When a vertex is reached where the offered fluid cannot be sent further, the vertex is marked as blocked. In this case, all or a portion of the offered fluid is sent back. The algorithm terminates when all the initially-offered fluid has left the system via either the input or output.

Hellerstein examined different strategies concerning how best to select outgoing and incoming edges for fluid distribution. One idea is: keep a list of edges for each vertex, and distribute any fluid in strict list order, giving each edge as much fluid as it can accept. This policy is probably a good one for sending fluid to the outgoing edges, because it minimizes the number of messages and keeps the edges filled to capacity. For returning fluid back to the incoming edges, another idea is to return the fluid back to the edge it last came from. This strategy can be implemented with a stack in each vertex.

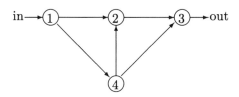

Figure B.2
A Graph that is Not a Layered Network

The trick is that, for certain graphs, the maximum flow problem can be solved by a series of maximal flow problems. These graphs are called *layered networks*. The graph can be labeled so that each vertex has a positive integer "layer number" that is exactly one greater than every vertex it points to. The input vertex has a layer number of zero. The output vertex must therefore have a greater layer number than those of all other vertices.

The simplifying assumption of a layered network will finesse unpleasant graphs such as the one in Figure B.2. Assume that each internal edge of the graph has weight one. Then the *maximum* flow of the graph is two. In this case, the maximum flow can be most easily calculated by taking the minimum cut. However, consider calculating the *maximal* flow. If fluid is sent down path 1-2-4-3, a maximal flow of one is calculated. If fluid is sent down paths 1-2-3 and 1-4-3, then a maximal flow of two is calculated. This graph is not a layered network because node 4 cannot be legally labeled.

Write a parallel logic program to find the maximal flow through a layered network. Test your program on large graphs. Experiment with different strategies to distribute forward and backward flow.

B.4 Event-Driven Circuit Simulation

Event-driven simulation is an important class of problems introduced by this example of digital-circuit simulation given by D. Dure.

Given a network of components and a behavioral model of each of them, most simulators aim to simulate the interaction of the components as time advances. The point is to provide the user of the simulator with an image of the global behavior of the network, whereas only local behavior is known *a priori*. We are interested here in a special category of simulators: event-driven logic simulators, used to debug or evaluate large-scale designs of integrated circuits or board-level systems.

In event-driven simulation, interaction of components is constrained to take place at discrete points in time. Interaction is then modeled naturally by time-stamped messages. The task of the simulator is thus to propagate these messages and to evaluate a local model whenever a message reaches it, in turn causing more messages to be sent, and so on.

An important property that should be satisfied by event-driven simulators is admissibility [154]. Roughly speaking, a simulator is admissible if one can predict the global behavior it exhibits from the network and local equations, simply assuming that events are processed in increasing order of time stamps and that simultaneous events are considered explicitly by local models. In other words, the simulator has correct models and evaluates simultaneous events in a sound fashion.

In logic simulation, parts are restricted to send and accept Boolean values. The Boolean set is usually extended to include 'x' (undetermined value) and 'z' (high impedance). In most cases, parts are connected together through unidirectional ports. One output can be connected to several inputs. If several outputs are connected together, an abstract object, called a *node*, is introduced to resolve conflicts. Resolution can be done pairwise, on inputs to a node, recursively with the following rules of composition between values. For all A,B in [0,1,x,z]:

```
node(A,B) = node(B,A)
node(A,A) = A
node(0,1) = x
node(x,A) = x
node(z,A) = A
```

Time is usually incorporated in local models in the form of delays, rather than in a global form. So, whenever inputs of some local model change, output changes some delay after. A delay can be defined in different ways. In the following exercises, we shall see the different approaches.

Exercise 1: Cycle Simulation

This simple simulation assigns the same delay to all parts and all transitions. The basic algorithm is thus:

1. propagate output values

2. evaluate local models

3. update outputs

4. go to step 1

Restricting yourself to extended Boolean functions (values [0,1,x,z]) of 1–3 inputs, write an FGHC program which takes a network of such functions and the stimuli (lists of Boolean values) to apply, and produces the output response. The basic idea is to associate an FGHC process with each part, connected to other parts via streams. Each part is synchronously waiting for a new value on all inputs, and produces the new output value accordingly. Do not worry about termination of your program. Be careful about termination: the circuit should dissolve itself when the input streams close.

Exercise 2: Optimization of Local Evaluation

In the previous exercise, the most naive implementation involves writing one instance of each predicate for each possible input pattern. For example, a two-input NAND gate operating on the extended Booleans has $4^2 = 16$ rules if listed naively. Depending on the system (e.g., is indexing implemented or not?), the time necessary to address the appropriate rule may grow exponentially with the number of inputs. Devise a way to diminish the number of alternative clauses and observe the change in performance of your program for a logic function with 2–4 inputs.

   The basic idea is to construct a finite-state automaton that considers inputs one by one. To gain more speed, at the expense of memory, the automaton is not stored as a table, but is compiled into a set of predicates (one predicate per state). In some cases, the output may be temporarily independent of some inputs which can be bypassed. This is another source of speed. Inspiration for the construction of finite automata can be found in Aho and Ullman [5]. We highly recommend writing a *program which generates the automata* and minimizes them.

Exercise 3: Transfer-Delay Model

The unit-delay model presented in the previous exercises has some limitations. In particular, it does not allow proper analysis of races between signals or analysis of transient conditions. We now assume that a delay is a positive integer, constant for a given part. In the transfer-delay model, if some input changes occur at time t, then the output change will occur at time $t + d$, where d is the delay. Output transitions are never cancelled. Because input transitions are no longer synchronous, we need to decide when we can evaluate a part. The following criterion is used:

> Assume the part has n inputs, each of them carrying a time/value pair (v'_i, t_i) where $1 \leq i \leq n$. If current input values are v_i, then the part is evaluated for time $t = min(t_i)$, with input values v''_i, where $v''_i = v_i$ if $t_i > t$ and $v''_i = v'_i$ otherwise.

This criterion defines acceptability of input messages [22]. Stated more procedurally, each part will have *current* values associated with each input. New values will appear asynchronously at the input streams, represented as time/value pairs. When at least one such new value pair arrives at each input, their minimum time is calculated. Each new value at the minimum time becomes a current value and is removed from the stream. Each new value at a time greater than the minimum time remains queued in the corresponding input stream. The output of the part is then evaluated from the current values, marked at the minimum time.

Write an FGHC program, with similar inputs as Exercise 1, plus a delay for each part. Once this is working, you can think of some automata to shorten the test for acceptability for parts with two inputs.

Exercise 4: Selective Trace

So far we did not make the distinction between a *useful* input message and a *void* input message. A message is void if it carries the same value as the previous message. Void messages essentially carry no information and cause unnecessary reductions. To limit the number of reductions, benefiting from the natural latency of most circuits, most simulators perform *selective trace*.

We cannot simply remove void messages, because the simulator would deadlock at every feedback loop. A better idea is to include in each message the time of the next "possible" transition. Then, depending on the current state of a part, we may in certain cases suppress void messages.

Here we describe a distributed algorithm for limiting void messages. All values are now triplets of the form (v, t_{now}, t_{next}). Time t_{now} is when the message was generated (the "current" time) and t_{next} is the guaranteed time that the next input will arrive. Thus the input will remain at value v for the period $t_{next} - t_{now}$.

Consider an AND-gate with two inputs. The first input receives the message $(0, 0, 1000)$ and the second input receives the messages $(1, 0, 100)$, $(0, 100, 200)$, ..., $(1, 1000, ...)$. Clearly, since the first input keeps the value zero until time 1000, only one message need be sent from the AND-gate output: $(0, 0, 1000)$.

Modify the previous program to include selective trace. You may want to use automata here also, to increase speed, but be aware that the number of predicates necessary to model a part will grow very quickly with the number of inputs.

Exercise 5: Inertial-Delay Model

The transfer-delay model can be used to observe signal races, but it generates too many transitions. In particular, unharmful transients are propagated and perhaps distorted. In the inertial-delay model, a transition can be cancelled between its start and the time it is released. More formally, if at time t an input message occurs which causes output to change value, then the output message is sent only after all input changes which may change the output value have been taken into account. In other words, all input messages marked between time t and $t + d$ must be processed before any final output message is sent.

Modify the program from the previous exercise to include an inertial-delay capability. Note that it is possible, and realistic, to have different delays according to the type of the output transition. Typically, a 0/1 transition (from 0 to 1) takes more time than a 1/0 transition (from 1 to 0). Find a reasonable way to express delays of transitions including 'x' or 'z' according to 0/1 and 1/0 transition delays.

Attempt to model the following R-S latch with the inertial-delay model. Note that the parts are two-input NAND gates.

Attempt to model the following D flip-flop with the inertial-delay model. Note that the leftmost NAND gate is used to invert input D. Both polarities drive the middle two NANDs which are regulated by the clock pulse CLK. Finally the rightmost two NANDs form an R-S latch.

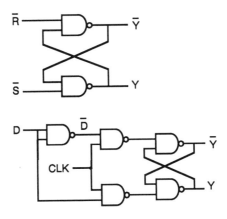

C Glossary

Andorra is an AND/OR parallel language related to Aurora OR-Prolog [58].

Aurora is an OR-parallel Prolog system based on SICStus Prolog [78].

backtrack is the operation of reverting the current failure state of a Prolog computation to an earlier state.

branchpoint is a node of the Aurora OR-tree that represents a procedure (declared `parallel`) invocation with multiple clauses that potentially match. This node can spawn parallel OR-branches.

buffer is a fixed-size stream. The reader (consumer) of a buffer must ensure that its length remains constant, thereby constraining resources allocated to the writer (producer).

cavalier commit is an OR-Parallel Prolog builtin used to prevent undesired backtracking. Cavalier commit accepts the *first* derivation of the procedure containing the commit, and all other derivations are disallowed. See *cut*.

CHIP is Constraint Handling In Prolog, a constraints language [140].

choicepoint is an internal stack object in a Prolog abstract machine that denotes a procedure invocation with multiple clauses that potentially match. A branchpoint is the OR-parallel version of a choicepoint.

commit is the action of selecting a single clause among perhaps multiple choices for procedure reduction. After commitment, the clause selection cannot be undone. Thus if a body goal fails, the entire program fails.

consumer is a process whose computation is data-driven (usually from a stream). See *producer*.

CP is Concurrent Prolog, a committed-choice language [116].

cut is a Prolog builtin used to prevent undesired backtracking. As a goal in a clause of a procedure, cut always succeeds, causing a side effect of disallowing goals textually preceding the cut or subsequent clauses of the procedure to be tried in the event of backtracking.

deadlock ensues when all processes are suspended. In committed-choice programs, deadlock often happens when syntax errors prevent certain instantiations of passed arguments from being recognized in a procedure call. More rarely, the program semantics nondeterminately cause a race wherein two or more processes are suspended, each waiting for a binding (e.g., a message) from another to proceed. See *suspension*.

determinate as used in this book, is a classification given to a Horn-clause procedure if the procedure produces one and only one solution for any inputs. See *nondeterminate*.

difference list or D-list is a structure often noted as H–T where H is a list with an unbound tail T. Appending two D-lists is a constant time operation.

eager evaluation is a computation wherein a producer generates data irrespective of the rate at which consumer(s) use the data. Typical stream-communicating programs in committed-choice languages execute eagerly.

efficiency is the speedup for N PEs divided by N.

FCP is Flat Concurrent Prolog [116, 127].

failure in Prolog is a procedure invocation that cannot successfully unify the head of any clause in a corresponding defined procedure. In FGHC, failure is a procedure invocation that cannot commit to any clause in a corresponding defined procedure because of unsuccessful input unification or unsuccessful guard evaluation.

FGHC is Flat Guarded Horn Clauses [137].

FLENG is a committed-choice language similar to FGHC [89].

GC is garbage collection — for logic programming considerations, see [25, 93, 88, 9, 134, 55].

GHC is Guarded Horn Clauses [137].

guard in committed-choice languages, is a conjunction of goals that must be satisfied before committing to a clause. In flat languages, guards must consist of simple goals that can be evaluated without further reductions, e.g., arithmetic comparison and type checking.

JAM is Jim's Abstract Machine, a Parlog instruction-set architecture [37].

KEPS is thousands of entries per second. An Prolog entry is either a reduction or backtrack. An FGHC entry is either a reduction or suspension.

KLIPS is thousands of logical inferences (goal invocations) per second. Not all logical inferences are equal, because different goal invocations may require different amounts of computation.

KL1-B is the instruction-set architecture of KL1-U [71, 117].

KL1-U is the extended version of FGHC that includes meta-logical builtins [65].

KRPS is thousands of reductions per second (see *KLIPS*).

layered stream is a (possibly empty) list of elements of the form H*Ts where Ts is a layered stream representing the set of all possible tails of head H [94]. For constraints problems, a layered stream can also take the special value begin. All internal layered streams that do not end in begin are considered incomplete.

lazy evaluation is a data-driven computation where the consumer triggers the calculation of each datum from a producer.

merger is a process that joins a set of streams, usually nondeterministically.

MLIPS is millions of logical inferences per second (see KLIPS above).

MultiPsi/V2 is a loosely-coupled multiprocessor comprised of 64 PSI-II machines microcoded to execute KL1-B [66].

nondeterminate as used in this book is a classification given to a Horn-clause procedure if the procedure produces multiple solutions for some set of inputs. This classification is independent of whether the solutions are produced in order or lack thereof. See *determinate* and *nondeterministic*.

nondeterministic process is a process whose behavior cannot be exactly predicted. For example, successive readings of a thermometer constitutes a nondeterministic process.

OR-tree describes both the storage model of OR-parallel Prolog and the search space for nondeterminate all-solutions search problems. Branches from root to leaf represent alternative solutions to a query. Nodes represent subproblems with alternative solutions. See *branchpoint*.

otherwise is a guard in many committed-choice languages that partitions clauses. If all clauses textually preceding the `otherwise` clause fail, then the `otherwise` clause and all subsequent clauses (until the next `otherwise`) are attempted. If any clause textually preceding the `otherwise` clause suspends and no clause succeeds, then the procedure call suspends.

Panda is a shared-memory architecture for FGHC (also called KL1-PS) [113, 112].

Pandora is a committed-choice language extended with nondeterminate execution [11].

Parlog is a committed-choice language [26].

PDSS is the PIMOS Development Support System, a sequential KL1 system running under UNIX [65].

PE is a processing element of a multiprocessor. Also called a "worker."

PIM is the Parallel Inference Machine.

producer is a process that generates data to drive a consumer (usually on a stream). See *consumer*.

Prolog is a sequential logic programming language based on Horn clauses [29, 16, 119].

PSI-II is a Prolog machine using a microcoded WAM emulator.

reduction is a procedure invocation that commits to some clause.

resumption is the operation of restarting a process that has been suspended. In FGHC, a binding that liberates a suspended goal triggers the resumption of that goal, i.e., the goal is made runnable. Depending on the system, a resumed goal may be scheduled immediately or at some future time. See *suspension*.

scheduler is the component of a parallel system that allocates tasks to PEs [18, 17, 113, 15, 12]. The particular Aurora scheduler measured in this book is the Argonne scheduler [17], Delta version.

short-circuit technique is a programming paradigm used to serialize goal execution, terminate distributed algorithms, etc. A difference list X-Y has one "end" initially bound, e.g., X=end. The D-list is strung between messages, processes, etc., to track the proliferation of these objects. An object can "short" its D-list X-Y by unifying X=Y. A short communicates a change of state in the object, e.g., a process has terminated or failed, a message has been discarded. When all the objects in the chain short the binding appears at the other "end" of the initial D-list.

speedup is a performance measure of a multiprocessor. Naive speedup of a given program for N PEs is the execution time of the program on a single PE divided by the execution time of the same program on N PEs. Real speedup of a given program for N PEs is the execution time of the fastest sequential program (in the same language) on a single PE divided by the execution time of the given program on N PEs. In this book, a speedup of close to N is called a *linear speedup*. A speedup of greater than N on N PEs is called *superlinear*. Speedup of less than one is called *slowdown*.

Strand is a committed-choice language similar to Flat Parlog [49].

stream is an incomplete list used for communication between processes. For reading a stream S, S=[M|Ms] returns the message M and the rest of the stream Ms. To write to a stream, a message is sent down the stream's tail. Consider a stream S0 with tail S1, usually denoted by the difference list S0-S1. Bind the tail S1=[M|S2], giving the stream and new tail S0-S2.

suspension is the operation of temporarily halting a process. In FGHC, a procedure invocation suspends when it cannot yet commit to any clause because output bindings are attempted in the heads or guards. If all processes are suspended, the program is deadlocked. See *resumption* and *deadlock*.

WAM is Warren's Abstract Machine, a Prolog instruction-set architecture [143].

Bibliography

[1] S.J. Aarseth, M. Henon, and R. Wielen. A Comparison of Numerical Methods for the Study of Star Cluster Dynamics. *Astronomy and Astrophysics*, 37:183–187, 1974.

[2] P. Adamson. Explorations in Parallel Programming on a Sequent Symmetry, May 1990. Unpublished.

[3] P. Adamson and E. Tick. Partitioned Graph-Search Algorithms. Technical report, University of Oregon, Department of Computer Science, January 1991.

[4] G. A. Agha. *A Model of Concurrent Computation in Distributed Systems*. MIT Press, Cambridge MA, 1986.

[5] A. Aho, R. Sethi, and J. Ullman. *Compilers, principles, techniques, and tools*. Addison-Wesley, Reading MA, 1985.

[6] K. A. M. Ali and R. Karlsson. The Muse Or-Parallel Prolog Model and its Performance. In *North American Conference on Logic Programming*, pages 757–776. Austin, MIT Press, October 1990.

[7] L. Alkalaj, T. Lang, and M. Ercegovac. Architectural Support for the Management of Tightly-Coupled, Fine-Grain Goals in Flat Concurrent Prolog. In *International Symposium on Computer Architecture*, pages 292–301. Seattle, June 1990.

[8] R. K. Anuja et. al. Faster Algorithms for the Shortest Path Problem. *Journal of the ACM*, 37(2):213–223, April 1990.

[9] K. Appleby, M. Carlsson, S. Haridi, and D. Sahlin. Garbage Collection for Prolog Based on WAM. *Journal of the ACM*, 31(6):719–741, June 1988.

[10] R. G. Babb II, editor. *Programming Parallel Processors*. Addison-Wesley Ltd., Wokingham, England, 1988.

[11] R. Bahgat and S. Gregory. Pandora: Non-deterministic Parallel Logic Programming. In *Sixth International Conference on Logic Programming*, pages 471–486. Lisbon, MIT Press, June 1989.

[12] A. Beaumont, S. Muthu Raman, and P. Szeredi. Scheduling Or-Parallelism in Aurora with the Bristol Scheduler. Technical Report TR-90-04, University of Bristol, March 1990.

[13] R. Bisiani *et al.* The Agora Programming Environment. Technical Report, Carnegie-Mellon University, March 1988.

[14] S. H. Bokhari. Multiprocessing the Sieve of Eratosthenes. *IEEE Computer*, pages 50–58, April 1987.

[15] P. Brand. Wavefront Scheduling. Technical Report, Swedish Institute of Computer Science, PO Box 1263, S-16313 Spanga, Sweden, 1988.

[16] I. Bratko. *Prolog Programming for Artificial Intelligence*. Addison-Wesley Ltd., Wokingham, England, 2nd edition, 1986.

[17] R. Butler *et al.* Scheduling OR-Parallelism: an Argonne Perspective. In *Fifth International Conference and Symposium on Logic Programming*, pages 1565–1577. University of Washington, MIT Press, August 1988.

[18] A. Calderwood and P. Szeredi. Scheduling Or-Parallelism in Aurora. In *Sixth International Conference on Logic Programming*, pages 419–435. Lisbon, MIT Press, June 1989.

[19] M. Carlsson. *SICStus Prolog User's Manual*. PO Box 1263, S-16313 Spanga, Sweden, February 1988.

[20] M. Carlsson, K. Danhof, and R. Overbeek. A Simplified Approach to the Implementation of AND-Parallelism in an OR-Parallel Environment. In *Fifth International Conference and Symposium on Logic Programming*, pages 1565–1577. University of Washington, MIT Press, August 1988.

[21] M. Carlsson and P. Szeredi. The Aurora Abstract Machine and its Emulator. Technical Report, Swedish Institute of Computer Science, March 1990.

[22] K. M. Chandy and J. Misra. Asynchronous Distributed Simulation via a Sequence of Parallel Computations. *Communications of the ACM*, 24(11):198–206, April 1981.

[23] J. Chassin, J. Syre, and H. Westphal. Implementation of a Parallel Prolog System on a Commercial Multiprocessor. In *Proceedings of European Conference on Artificial Intelligence*, pages 278–283. Munich, August 1988.

[24] T. Chikayama. Unique Features of ESP. In *International Conference on Fifth Generation Computer Systems*, pages 292–298, Tokyo, 1984. ICOT.

[25] T. Chikayama and Y. Kimura. Multiple Reference Management in Flat GHC. In *Fourth International Conference on Logic Programming*, pages 276–293. University of Melbourne, MIT Press, May 1987.

[26] K. Clark and S. Gregory. PARLOG: Parallel Programming in Logic. In E.Y. Shapiro, editor, *Concurrent Prolog: Collected Papers*, volume 1, pages 84–139. MIT Press, Cambridge MA, 1987.

[27] K. L. Clark and S. Gregory. A Relational Language for Parallel Programming. In *Conference on Functional Programming Languages and Computer Architecture*, pages 171–178. ACM, Portsmouth NH, October 1981.

[28] K. L. Clark, F. G. McCabe, and S. Gregory. IC-Prolog Language Features. In K. L. Clark and S.-A. Tarnlund, editors, *Logic Programming*, APIC Studies in Data Processing No. 16, pages 253–266. Academic Press, London, 1982.

[29] W.F. Clocksin and C.S. Mellish. *Programming in Prolog*. Springer-Verlag, Berlin, 1981.

[30] M. Codish and E. Shapiro. Compiling OR-Parallelism into AND-Parallelism. In *Third International Conference on Logic Programming*, number 225 in Lecture Notes in Computer Science, pages 283–298. Imperial College, Springer-Verlag, July 1986.

[31] H. Coelho and J. C. Cotta. *Prolog By Example*. Symbolic Computation–Artificial Intelligence. Springer-Verlag, 1988.

[32] A. Colmerauer. An Introduction to Prolog-III. *Communications of the ACM*, 33(7):69–90, July 1990.

[33] J. S. Conery. *Parallel Execution of Logic Programs*. Kluwer Academic Publishers, Norwell MA, 1987.

[34] J. S. Conery. Binding Environments for Parallel Logic Programs in Non-shared Memory Multiprocessors. *International Journal of Parallel Programming*, 17(2):125–152, April 1988.

[35] T. Conlon. *Programming in Parlog*. Addison-Wesley, Wokingham, England, 1989.

[36] V. S. Costa, D. H. D. Warren, and R. Yang. Andorra-I: A Parallel Prolog System that Transparently Exploits both And- and Or-Parallelism. Technical report, University of Bristol, September 1990.

[37] J. A. Crammond. *Implementation of Committed-Choice Logic Languages on Shared-Memory Multiprocessors*. PhD thesis, Heriot-Watt University, Endinburgh, May 1988.

[38] J. A. Crammond. Scheduling and Variable Assignment in the Parallel Parlog Implementation. In *North American Conference on Logic Programming*, pages 642–657. Austin, MIT Press, October 1990.

[39] S. K. Debray. A Remark on Tick's Algorithm for Compile-Time Granularity Analysis. Research note, Department of Computer Science, University of Arizona, June 1989.

[40] S. K. Debray, N. Lin, and M. Hermenegildo. Task Granularity Analysis in Logic Programs. Research report, Department of Computer Science, University of Arizona, October 1989. Draft.

[41] D. DeGroot. Restricted AND-Parallelism. In *International Conference on Fifth Generation Computer Systems*, pages 471–478, Tokyo, November 1984. ICOT.

[42] E. W. Dijkstra. A Note on Two Problems in Connexion with Graphs. *Numerical Mathematics*, 1:269–271, 1959.

[43] E. W. Dijkstra. Guarded Commands, Nondeterminacy and the Formal Derivation. *Communications of the ACM*, 18(8):453–457, August 1975.

[44] T. Disz, E. Lusk, and R. Overbeek. Experiments with OR-Parallel Logic Programs. In *Fourth International Conference on Logic Programming*, pages 576–600. University of Melbourne, MIT Press, May 1987. Also available as ANL Technical Report TM-87.

[45] N. A. Elshiewy. *Robust Coordinated Reactive Computing in SANDRA*. PhD thesis, Swedish Institute of Computer Science, 1990. Technical Report D-90-9003.

[46] Encore Computer Corporation. *UMAX 4.2 Programmers Guide*. Marlboro MA 01752, 1985.

[47] B. S. Fagin. *A Parallel Execution Model for Prolog*. PhD thesis, The University of California at Berkeley, November 1987. Technical Report UCB/CSD 87/380.

[48] I. Foster and S. Taylor. Flat PARLOG: A Basis for Comparison. *International Journal of Parallel Programming*, 16(2), 1988.

[49] I. Foster and S. Taylor. *Strand: New Concepts in Parallel Programming*. Prentice Hall, Englewood Cliffs, NJ, 1989.

[50] G. Fox *et al. Solving Problems on Concurrent Processors*, volume 1. Prentice Hall, Englewood Cliffs NJ, 1988.

[51] K. Fuchi and K. Furukawa. The Role of Logic Programming in the Fifth Generation Computer Project. In *Third International Conference on Logic Programming*, number 225 in Lecture Notes in Computer Science, pages 1–24. Imperial College, Springer-Verlag, July 1986.

[52] K. Furukawa, A. Okumura, and M. Murakami. Unfolding Rules for GHC Programs. *New Generation Computing*, 6(2–3):143–157, 1988.

[53] R. P. Gabriel. *Performance and Evaluation of Lisp Systems*. MIT Press, Cambridge MA, 1985.

[54] R. P. Gabriel and J. McCarthy. Queue-Based Multi-Processing Lisp. In *Symposium on Lisp and Functional Programming*, pages 25–44. ACM, 1984.

[55] A. Goto, Y. Kimura, T. Nakagawa, and T. Chikayama. Lazy Reference Counting. In *Fifth International Conference and Symposium on Logic Programming*, pages 1241–1256. University of Washington, MIT Press, August 1988.

[56] A. Goto, A. Matsumoto, and E. Tick. Design and Performance of a Coherent Cache for Parallel Logic Programming Architectures. In *16th International Symposium on Computer Architecture*, pages 25–33. Jerusalem, IEEE Computer Society, May 1989.

[57] S. Gregory. *Parallel Logic Programming in PARLOG: The Language and its Implementation*. Addison-Wesley Ltd., Wokingham, England, 1987.

[58] S. Haridi and P. Brand. Andorra Prolog—An Integration of Prolog and Committed Choice Languages. In *International Conference on Fifth Generation Computer Systems*, pages 745–754, Tokyo, November 1988. ICOT.

[59] B. Hausman. *Pruning and Speculative Work in OR-Parallel PROLOG*. PhD thesis, Royal Institute of Technology, Stockholm Sweden, March 1990. Available in SICS Dissertation Series.

[60] D. Hawley and A. Aiba. Guarded Definite Clauses with Constraints — A Preliminary Report. In *Japan-Italy-Sweden Workshop on Logic Programming and Parallel Processing*, Nynashamn, Sweden, August 1990. Swedish Institute of Computer Science.

[61] L. Hellerstein and E. Shapiro. Implementing Parallel algorithms in Concurrent Prolog: The MAXFLOW Experience. In E.Y. Shapiro, editor, *Concurrent Prolog: Collected Papers*, volume 1, pages 258–290. MIT Press, Cambridge MA, 1987.

[62] M. V. Hermenegildo. *An Abstract Machine Based Execution Model for Computer Architecture Design and Efficient Implementation of Logic Programs in Parallel*. PhD thesis, University of Texas at Austin, August 1986. Technical Report TR-86-20.

[63] C. A. R. Hoare. Communicating Sequential Processes. *Communications of the ACM*, 21(8):666–677, August 1978.

[64] P. Hut and J. Makino. Gravitational N-Body Algorithms: A Comparison between Super-computers and a Highly Parallel Computer. Astrophysics Preprint Series IASSNS-AST 88/56, The Institute for Advanced Study, Princeton, 1988.

[65] ICOT. *PDSS Manual (Version 1.64e)*. 21F Mita Kokusai Bldg, 1-4-28 Mita, Minato-ku Tokyo 108, Japan, February 1989.

[66] Y. Inamura, N. Ichiyoshi, K. Rokusawa, and K. Nakajima. Optimization Techniques Using the MRB and Their Evaluation on the Multi-PSI/V2. In *North American Conference on Logic Programming*, pages 907–921. Cleveland, MIT Press, October 1989.

[67] INMOS, Ltd. *occam 2 Reference Manual*. New York, 1988.

[68] J. Jaffar and J-L. Lassez. Constraint Logic Programming. Technical Report, IBM Thomas J. Watson Research Center, 1986.

[69] J. Jaffar and S. Michaylov. Methodology and Implementation of a CLP System. In *Fourth International Conference on Logic Programming*, pages 196–219. University of Melbourne, MIT Press, May 1987.

[70] D. B. Johnson. Efficient Algorithms for Shortest Paths in Sparse Networks. *Journal of the ACM*, 24:1–13, 1977.

[71] Y. Kimura and T. Chikayama. An Abstract KL1 Machine and its Instruction Set. In *International Symposium on Logic Programming*, pages 468–477. San Francisco, IEEE Computer Society, August 1987.

[72] F. Kluzniak. Developing Applications for Aurora. Technical Report TR-90-17, Department of Computer Science, University of Bristol, August 1990.

[73] D. E. Knuth. *The Art of Computer Programming: Fundamental Algorithms*. Addison-Wesley, Reading MA, 2nd edition, 1973.

[74] P. M. Kogge. *The Architecture of Symbolic Computers*. McGraw-Hill, New York, 1991.

[75] R. A. Kowalski. Predicate Logic as a Programming Language. In *Proceedings IFIPS*, pages 569–574. Stockholm, 1974.

[76] J. W. Lloyd. *Foundations of Logic Programming*. Springer-Verlag, 1984.

[77] E. Lusk et al. *Portable Programs for Parallel Processors*. Holt, Rinehart and Winston, Inc., New York, 1987.

[78] E. Lusk et al. The Aurora Or-Parallel Prolog System. In *International Conference on Fifth Generation Computer Systems*, pages 819–830, Tokyo, November 1988. ICOT.

[79] M. J. Maher. Logic Semantics for a Class of Committed-Choice Programs. In *Fourth International Conference on Logic Programming*, pages 858–876. University of Melbourne, MIT Press, May 1987.

[80] D. Maier and D. S. Warren. *Computing with Logic: Logic Programming with Prolog*. Benjamin/Cummings Publishing Co. Inc., Menlo Park, 1988.

[81] J. Makino. On an O(NlogN) Algorithm for the Gravitational N-Body Simulation and its Vectorization. In *Proceedings of the First Appi Workshop on Supercomputing*, pages 153–168, Tokyo, 1987. Institute of Supercomputing Research. ISR Technical Report 87-03.

[82] J. Makino. personal communication, February 1989.

[83] Y. Matsumoto. A Parallel Parsing System for Natural Language Analysis. In *Third International Conference on Logic Programming*, number 225 in Lecture Notes in Computer Science, pages 396–409. Imperial College, Springer-Verlag, July 1986.

[84] E. F. Moore. The Shortest Path Through a Maze. In *Proceedings of the International Symposium on Theory of Switching*, pages 285–292, Cambridge MA, April 1957. Harvard University Press.

[85] S. Mudambi. Performance of Aurora on NUMA Machines. Technical report, Computer Science Dept., Brandeis University, July 1990.

[86] L. Naish. All Solutions Predicates in Prolog. In *International Symposium on Logic Programming*, pages 73–78. Boston, IEEE Computer Society, July 1985.

[87] L. Naish. Parallelizing NU-Prolog. In *Fifth International Conference and Symposium on Logic Programming*, pages 1546–1564. University of Washington, MIT Press, August 1988.

[88] K. Nakajima. Piling GC: Efficient Garbage Collection for AI Languages. In *IFIP Working Conference on Parallel Processing*, pages 201–204. Pisa, North Holland, May 1988.

[89] M. Nilsson and H. Tanaka. FLENG Prolog—The Language which turns Supercomputers into Parallel Prolog Machines. In E. Wada, editor, *Proceedings of the Logic Programming Conference*, number 264 in Lecture Notes in Computer Science, pages 170–179. Springer-Verlag, June 1986.

[90] M. Nilsson and H. Tanaka. A Flat GHC Implementation for Supercomputers. In *Fifth International Conference and Symposium on Logic Programming*, pages 1337–1350. University of Washington, MIT Press, August 1988.

[91] M. Nilsson and H. Tanaka. Massively Parallel Implementation of Flat GHC on the Connection Machine. In *International Conference on Fifth Generation Computer Systems*, pages 1031–1040. Tokyo, ICOT, November 1988.

[92] N. J. Nilsson. *Problem-Solving Methods in Artificial Intelligence*. McGraw-Hill Inc., New York, 1971.

[93] K. Nishida, Y. Kimura, A. Matsumoto, and A. Goto. Evaluation of MRB Garbage Collection on Parallel Logic Programming Architectures. In *7th International Conference on Logic Programming*, pages 83–95. Jerusalem, MIT Press, June 1990.

[94] A. Okumura and Y. Matsumoto. Parallel Programming with Layered Streams. In *International Symposium on Logic Programming*, pages 224–233. San Francisco, IEEE Computer Society, August 1987.

[95] A. Osterhaug, editor. *Guide to Parallel Programming on Sequent Computer Systems*. Prentice Hall, Englewood Cliffs, NJ, 2nd edition, 1989.

[96] T. Ozawa *et al.* Generation Type Garbage Collection for Parallel Logic Languages. In *North American Conference on Logic Programming*, pages 291–305. Austin, MIT Press, October 1990.

[97] C. M. Pancake and D. Bergmark. Do Parallel Languages Respond to the Needs of Scientific Programmers? *Computer*, 23(12):13–23, December 1990.

[98] F.C.N. Pereira and S.M. Shieber. *Prolog and Natural-Language Analysis*. CSLI Lecture Notes Number 10. Center for the Study of Language and Information, Stanford University, 1987.

[99] L. M. Pereira, L. Monteiro, J. Cunha, and J. N. Aparicio. Delta Prolog: a Distributed Backtracking Extension with Events. In *Third International Conference on Logic Programming*, number 225 in Lecture Notes in Computer Science, pages 69–84. Imperial College, Springer-Verlag, July 1986.

[100] M. Quinn and Y. Yoo. Data Structures for the Efficient Solution of Graph Theoretic Problems on Tightly Coupled MIMD Computers. In *International Conference on Parallel Processing*, pages 431–438, Penn State, August 1984.

[101] Quintus Computer Systems Inc. *Quintus Prolog User's Guide and Reference Manual— Version 6*. 2100 Geng Road, Palo Alto CA 94303, April 1986.

[102] Quintus Computer Systems Inc. *Quintus Prolog Multiprocessing Package Release 1.1*, October 1989.

[103] B. Ramkumar and L. V. Kale. Compiled Execution of the Reduce-OR Process Model on Multiprocessors. In *North American Conference on Logic Programming*, pages 313–331. Cleveland, MIT Press, October 1989.

[104] M. Ratcliffe and P. Robert. PEPSy: A Prolog for Parallel Processing. Technical Report CA-17, ECRC, Munich, April 1986.

[105] G. A. Ringwood. Predicates and Pixels. *New Generation Computing*, 7(1):59–80, 1989.

[106] J. A. Robinson. A Machine Oriented Logic Based on the Resolution Principle. *Journal of the ACM*, 12(23):23–41, January 1965.

[107] J. A. Robinson. *Logic: Form and Function*. North-Holland, New York, 1979.

[108] P. Roussel. Prolog: Manuel de Reference et d'Utilisation. Technical Report, University of d'Aix-Marseille, Groupe de IA, 1975.

[109] K. Sakai and A. Aiba. CAL: A Theoretical Background of Constraint Logic Programming and Its Applications. *Journal of Symbolic Computation*, 8:589–603, 1989.

[110] V. A. Saraswat. *Concurrent Constraint Programming*. Logic Programming. MIT Press, Cambridge MA, 1990.

[111] V. A. Saraswat, K. Kahn, and J. Levy. Janus: A Step Towards Distributed Constraint Programming. In *North American Conference on Logic Programming*, pages 431–446. Austin, MIT Press, October 1990.

[112] M. Sato and A. Goto. Evaluation of the KL1 Parallel System on a Shared Memory Multiprocessor. In *IFIP Working Conference on Parallel Processing*, pages 305–318. Pisa, North Holland, May 1988.

[113] M. Sato *et al.* KL1 Execution Model for PIM Cluster with Shared Memory. In *Fourth International Conference on Logic Programming*, pages 338–355. University of Melbourne, MIT Press, May 1987.

[114] D. De Schreye and M. Bruynooghe. An Application of Abstract Interpretation in Source Level Program Transformation. In *International Workshop on Programming Languages Implementation and Logic Programming*, number 348 in Lecture Notes in Computer Science, pages 35–57. Orleans, France, Springer-Verlag, May 1988.

[115] A. Shafrir and E. Shapiro. Distributed Programming in Concurrent Prolog. In E.Y. Shapiro, editor, *Concurrent Prolog: Collected Papers*, volume 1, pages 318–338. MIT Press, Cambridge MA, 1987.

[116] E.Y. Shapiro, editor. *Concurrent Prolog: Collected Papers*, volume 1,2. MIT Press, Cambridge MA, 1987.

[117] T. Shinogi *et al.* Macro-Call Instruction for the Efficient KL1 Implementation on PIM. In *International Conference on Fifth Generation Computer Systems*, pages 953–961, Tokyo, November 1988. ICOT.

[118] H. Simonis. Test Generation Using the Constraint Logic Programming Language CHIP. In *Sixth International Conference on Logic Programming*, pages 101–112. Lisbon, MIT Press, June 1989.

[119] L. Sterling and E.Y. Shapiro. *The Art of Prolog*. MIT Press, Cambridge MA, 1986.

[120] P. Szeredi. More Benchmarks of Aurora. Dept. of Computer Science, University of Bristol, 1988. Unpublished.

[121] P. Szeredi. Performance Analysis of the Aurora Or-Parallel Prolog System. In *North American Conference on Logic Programming*, pages 713–732. Cleveland, MIT Press, October 1989.

[122] S. Takagi. A Collection of KL1 Programs — Part I. Technical Memo TM-311, ICOT, Japan, May 1987.

[123] A. Takeuchi, K. Takahashi, and H. Shimizu. A Description Language with AND/OR Parallelism for Concurrent Systems and its Stream-Based Realization. Technical Report 229, ICOT, Tokyo, February 1987.

[124] H. Tanaka. A Parallel Object Oriented Language FLENG++ and Its Control System on the Parallel Inference Machine PIE64. In *Proceedings of the Japan/UK Workshop*, September 1989.

[125] A. S. Tanenbaum. *Structured Computer Organization*. Prentice Hall, Englewood Cliffs, NJ, 3rd edition, 1990.

[126] R. E. Tarjan. *Data Structures and Network Algorithms*, volume 44 of *Regional Conference Series in Applied Mathematics*. Society for Industrial and Applied Mathematics, Philadelphia PA, 1983.

[127] S. Taylor. *Parallel Logic Programming Techniques*. Prentice Hall, Englewood Cliffs, NJ, 1989.

[128] E. Tick. *Memory Performance of Prolog Architectures*. Kluwer Academic Publishers, Norwell MA, 1987.

[129] E. Tick. Performance of Parallel Logic Programming Architectures. Technical Report TR-421, ICOT, Tokyo, September 1988.

[130] E. Tick. Compile-Time Granularity Analysis of Parallel Logic Programming Languages. *New Generation Computing*, 7(2):325–337, January 1990.

[131] E. Tick and J. A. Crammond. Comparison of Two Shared-Memory Emulators for Flat Committed-Choice Logic Programs. In *International Conference on Parallel Processing*, volume 2, pages 236–242, Penn State, August 1990.

[132] E. Tick and N. Ichiyoshi. Programming Techniques for Efficiently Exploiting Parallelism in Logic Programming Languages. In *Symposium on Principles and Practices of Parallel Programming*, pages 31–39. Seattle, ACM SIGPLAN, March 1990.

[133] E. Tick and M. Korsloot. A Determinacy Testing Algorithm for Nondeterminate Flat Concurrent Logic Programming Languages. Technical Report CIS-TR-90-18, University of Oregon, Department of Computer Science, November 1990.

[134] H. Touati and T. Hama. A Light-Weight Prolog Garbage Collector. In *International Conference on Fifth Generation Computer Systems*, pages 922–930, Tokyo, November 1988. ICOT.

[135] E. D. Tribble *et al.* Channels: A Generalization of Streams. In E.Y. Shapiro, editor, *Concurrent Prolog: Collected Papers*, volume 1, pages 446–463. MIT Press, Cambridge MA, 1987.

[136] K. Ueda. Making Exhaustive Search Programs Deterministic. In *Third International Conference on Logic Programming*, number 225 in Lecture Notes in Computer Science, pages 270–283. Imperial College, Springer-Verlag, July 1986.

[137] K. Ueda. Guarded Horn Clauses. In E.Y. Shapiro, editor, *Concurrent Prolog: Collected Papers*, volume 1, pages 140–156. MIT Press, Cambridge MA, 1987.

[138] K. Ueda. Making Exhaustive Search Programs Deterministic: Part II. In *Fourth International Conference on Logic Programming*, pages 356–375. University of Melbourne, MIT Press, May 1987.

[139] M. H. van Emden and R. A. Kowalski. The Semantics of Predicate Logic as a Programming Language. *Journal of the ACM*, 23:733–742, October 1976.

[140] P. Van Hentenryck. *Constraint Satisfaction in Logic Programming*. MIT Press, Cambridge MA, 1989.

[141] P. Van Hentenryck. Parallel Constraint Satisfaction in Logic Programming: Preliminary Results on CHIP within PEPSys. In *Sixth International Conference on Logic Programming*, pages 165–180. Lisbon, MIT Press, June 1989.

[142] K. Wada and H. Ichiyoshi. A Study of Mapping Locally Message Exchanging Algorithms on a Loosely-Coupled Multiprocessor. Technical Report 587, ICOT, 1-4-28 Mita, Minato-ku Tokyo 108, Japan, August 1990.

[143] D. H. D. Warren. An Abstract Prolog Instruction Set. Technical Report 309, Artificial Intelligence Center, SRI International, 333 Ravenswood Ave, Menlo Park CA 94025, 1983.

[144] D. H. D. Warren. Prolog Engine. Technical report, Artificial Intelligence Center, SRI International, April 1983. Unpublished.

[145] D. H. D. Warren. The SRI Model for OR-Parallel Execution of Prolog—Abstract Design and Implementation. In *International Symposium on Logic Programming*, pages 92–102. San Francisco, IEEE Computer Society, August 1987.

[146] P. H. Winston. *Artificial Intelligence*. Addison Wesley, Reading MA, 2nd edition, 1984.

[147] P. H. Winston and B. K. P. Horn. *Lisp*. Addison Wesley, Reading MA, 1981.

[148] M. J. Wise. *Prolog Multiprocessors*. Prentice Hall, Englewood Cliffs, NJ, 1987.

[149] R. Yang. *P-Prolog: A Parallel Logic Programming Language*. World Scientific Publishing Co., Singapore, 1987.

[150] R. Yang. Solving Simple Substitution Ciphers in Andorra-I. In *Sixth International Conference on Logic Programming*, pages 111–128. Lisbon, MIT Press, June 1989.

[151] R. Yang and V. S. Costa. Andorra-I: A System Integrating Dependent And-Parallelism and Or-parallelism. Technical Report TR-90-03, University of Bristol, March 1990.

[152] K. Yoshida. personal communication, September 1989.

[153] K. Yoshida. *A'UM: A Stream-Based Concurrent Object-Oriented Programming Language*. PhD thesis, Keio University, March 1990.

[154] B. Zeigler. *Multifaceted Modelling and Discrete Event Simulation*. Academic Press, London, 1984.

Index

2–3 tree, 327

A

A'UM, 424
accumulator, 74, 122
active data structure, 194
active part, 34, 74
aggregation operator, 3
all-solutions search, 15, 280
Amdahl's Law, 96
AND parallelism, 2
 independent, 78, 85, 172
 restricted, 2, 423
 stream, 2, 17, 42
AND-in-OR parallelism, 172, 350, 406, 411
Andorra, 431, 465
anonymous variable, 20
append/3, 71
architecture, 56
 environment-stacking, 435
 goal-stacking, 444
argument, 19
 modes, 22, 38, 47–48, 73–74, 441
 registers, 438, 445
arithmetic, 441, 448
arity, 19
array, 27
 write-once, 27
Aurora, 57, 465
 binding mechanism, 60
 calibration with Panda, 58
 data cell, 63
 instruction-set architecture, 58, 435
 scheduler, 17, 60–61, 120, 163, 199, 407, 438, 440
 storage model, 58

B

backtracking, 2, 23, 60, 438, 465
 intelligent, 181, 197, 431
 shallow, 64, 358
 simulated in FGHC, 222, 278
benchmarks
 append/3, 71
 append/3
  KL1-B code, 448
  WAM code, 443
 BestPath, 365
 del/3, 120
 Instant Insanity (N-Cubes), 241
 MasterMind, 205
 N-Queens, 58, 117
 naive reverse (nrev/2), 75

Pascal's Triangle, 344
 permutations, 91
 Puzzle, 286
 Quicksort, 77
 Salt and Mustard, 229
 Semigroup, 324
 Sieve of Eratosthenes, 84
 Triangle, 197
 Turtles, 266
 Waltz, 300
 Zebra, 219, 280
bigarg/3, 370
bigfunctor/3, 370
binding, 25, 27, 60
 array, 60
 conflict, 2
 undoing a, 60, 440
body of procedure, 20, 34
book-end termination, 335
bounded buffer — see buffer
branch, 59
branchpoint, 59, 129, 438, 465
 unrolling, 131, 221, 263, 272, 332, 350, 406
buffer, 44, 97, 250, 465
 consumer, 44, 250, 409
 producer, 45, 250, 409
builtins, 26, 40
 ;/2, 231
 arg/3, 27
 call/1, 27
 cavalier commit //0, 29, 465
 cut !/0, 26, 465
 findall/3, 3, 26, 65
 functor/3, 27
 is/2, 27, 41
 negate/1, 27
 otherwise/0, 40, 53, 448, 468
 var/1, 26, 55, 105

C

cactus stack, 59
candidates/noncandidates, 129, 269
CHIP, 465
choicepoint, 64, 438, 465
ciphers, 362
clause, 20
 conjunctive, 21
 fact, 20
 mutually-exclusive, 74
 rule, 21
client, 81
combo/3, 92, 209, 232, 246
commit, 34, 465
committed-choice

architecture, 444
language, 3, 45, 423
complexity, 109, 222
execution time, 52, 175, 259
of layered streams, 161
concatenate — see append/3
concurrency, 12
Concurrent Prolog, 48, 465
Flat, 48, 466
conjunction, 21, 34
constraints, 124, 219, 241, 289, 301
constructive parallelism, 39
consumer, 44, 101, 144, 407, 409, 465
continuation, 50, 435
-based translation, 133
pointer in WAM, 437
control stack, 438
criptarithmetic, 114, 319
cross product, 108
cross/3, 108, 174, 185
cut, 26, 77, 465
cavalier, 29, 151, 465
scope of, 151
strict, 151

D

D-list — see difference list
dappend/3, 30, 42
deadlock, 37, 157, 466
declaration
mode, 47
parallel, 29
topology, 256
declarative reading, 3, 21, 34, 72
definite clause grammars, 317
del/3, 91, 120
demand-driven — see lazy
dereference, 440
determinate, 15, 24, 466
die back, 59
difference list, 29, 42, 77, 466
garbage creation, 146
shorted, 42, 468
Dijkstra's bestpath algorithm, 367
disjunction, 21, 231
distributed processes, 139, 367
don't-care variable, 20

E

eager evaluation, 92, 466
efficiency, 10, 466
Encore Multimax, 16, 64
operating system, 4

environment in WAM, 435
exercises
abstract machine emulation, 193–194
binary tree managers, 113
ciphers, 362
circuit simulation, 459
criptarithmetic, 114, 319
definite clause grammars, 317
eager queue, 88
Game of Life, 362
Grep Problem, 111
Hamiltonian paths, 401
Hamming's Problem, 114
Horner's Rule, 113
image processing, 320
Knight's Tour, 167
Latin Squares, 216
layered stream to list conversion, 112
lazy Zebra Problem, 237
lazy append, 112
list permutations, 110
list to layered stream conversion, 112
Magic Series, 216
Mahjong, 217
Maxflow, 458
Maximum Number Problem, 112
maze navigation, 402
N-Bodies, 455
n-way merger, 112
Nim, 216
Ramanujan Numbers, 114
Rowers, 237
Rubik's Cube, 283
Shoppers, 238
shuffling, 111
size of layered stream, 88
sorting, 88
spanning trees, 401
string matching, 451
test-pattern generation, 191
Tiles, 216

F

fact, 20
failure, 23, 60, 438, 446, 466
FGHC, 1, 33, 466
abstract architecture, 444
arithmetic, 41, 448
builtins, 40
code optimization, 134
conjunction, 34
data structures, 33, 37
failure, 36
how not to program in, 374

procedure, 33
reduction, 36
semantics
  declarative, 34
  procedural, 36
  translation from Prolog, 133
  unification, 36
flattened tree, 42
FLENG, 46, 466
folding, 135, 137
free list, 59
functor, 19

G

game playing, 197
garbage
  collection, 62, 64, 99, 466
  creation, 279
gen/2, 47, 119
generate & test
  fused, 122, 209, 220, 251, 266, 286
  naive, 119, 207, 230, 243
  super fusion, 282
goal, 20
  dependent, 78, 85
  pragma, 46
  priority, 46, 155, 388
  queue, 250, 445
  record, 59, 444
  sequential, 229
  thrashing, 204
granularity, 2, 6, 28, 55, 79, 405, 411
  collection, 323, 330, 353, 406, 410
graph, 365
ground term, 22
guard, 34, 466
  deep, 45
  failure, 36
  flat, 34
Guarded Horn Clauses, 45, 466
Guarded Horn Clauses,Flat — see FGHC

H

hash function, 191, 247, 325
head of procedure, 20, 34
heap, 60, 368, 438
hole in Aurora stack, 59
Horn-clause resolution, 24

I

indexing, 40, 58, 438, 446
Instant Insanity, 241
Intel 80386, 16

intelligent backtracking, 181, 197, 431
isomorphic tree, 20, 38, 50, 54, 169

J

JAM Parlog, 10, 17, 58, 466

K

kappa, 359
KEPS, 467
KL1, 33, 46, 57
  architecture (KL1-B), 58, 467
KLIPS, 2, 467
KRPS, 2, 467

L

last-call optimization, 62, 131, 437
layered stream, 43, 147, 256, 275, 305, 467
  conversion to list, 43, 112
  nil check, 150
  seed, 148, 256, 275, 308
  sharing among elements, 281
  size, 88, 150
  suspension rate, 151
  time complexity, 161
lazy evaluation, 99, 156, 467
load balancing, 61
locking, 3, 58, 61, 448
logic programming, 2
  parallel languages, 423
logical inference, 2, 444

M

manager, 81
MasterMind, 205
member/2, 406
  not unrolled, 352
  unrolled, 221
merge, 104, 140
  binary, 105
  customized, 108
  delayed, 154
  demand-driven, 106
  fair, 105
  n-way, 106, 112, 388, 467
meta-logic, 27
MLIPS, 444, 467
monitor, 4, 57, 381
most general unifier, 24
Multiple Reference Bit (MRB), 99, 146
multiprocessor
  bus bandwidth, 56
  Encore Multimax, 16, 64

Sequent Symmetry, 16, 64
shared-memory, 56
topology, 256
MultiPsi/V2, 18, 46, 314, 388, 467

N

N-Cubes, 241
N-Queens, 117
naive reverse (nrev/2), 75
Naoko, v
negation as failure, 231
nil check, 150, 258
noncommitted-choice, 19
nondeterminate, 15, 24, 467
nondeterministic, 15, 467
NS32032, 16

O

OR parallelism, 2
OR-in-AND parallelism, 133, 411
OR-tree, 59, 117, 467
  branching factor, 210
  branchpoint, 59, 129, 438, 465

P

Panda, 57, 468
  binding mechanism, 60
  calibration with Aurora, 58
  data cell, 63
  instruction-set architecture, 58, 444
  scheduler, 61, 155, 163, 204, 228, 250, 258
  storage model, 58
Pandora, 427, 468
Parallel Inference Machine, 57, 468
parallelism, 12
  AND, 2
  AND-in-OR, 172, 350, 406, 411
  constructive, 39
  OR, 2
  OR-in-AND, 133, 411
  pipeline, 144, 334
  speculative, 39, 53, 141, 173
  throttling of, 29, 97, 150, 415
Parlog, 47, 468
  Flat, 48
  JAM, 10, 17, 58, 466
  scheduler, 17
  sequential goals in, 229, 248
Pascal's Triangle, 344
passive data structure, 194
passive part, 74
passive structure, 373
PDSS, 46, 58, 468

PE (processing element), 468
perm/2, 91
permanent variable, 437
permutations, 91
pipeline, 94
  filters, 86, 143, 186, 222, 251, 272
  of constraints, 224
  parallelism, 144, 334
pragma, 46
procedural reading, 23, 36
procedure, 20, 33
  active part, 34, 74
  body, 20, 34
  commit, 34
  evaluation order of clauses in, 40, 53
  folding, 135, 137
  fusing, 76
  goal, 20
  guard, 34
  head, 20, 34
  passive part, 74
process
  -reading, 3, 36
  perpetual, 81, 140
  structure, 37, 384
producer, 101, 144, 407, 409, 468
program specification, 72
Prolog, 2, 19, 468
  abstract architecture, 435
  arithmetic, 27, 441
  builtins, 25–26
  conjunction, 21
  data structures, 19
  disjunction, 21, 231
  failure, 60
  list, 25
  OR-parallel, 1, 28, 405, 465
  procedure, 20
  semantics
    declarative, 21
    procedural, 23
  SICStus, 57, 435
  translation into FGHC, 133
Psi-II, 18, 468

Q

query, 21
queue, 81, 251
Queue-Lisp, 11
Quicksort, 77

R

reduction, 2, 468

reification, 38
resolution, 24
resolvent, 24, 28, 33, 37
resource starvation, 101, 155
resumption, 446, 468
roadmap, 276, 307
rule, 21

S

Salt and Mustard, 229
saturation, 79
scheduling, 39, 46, 53, 61, 163, 255, 409, 468
 Aurora, 17, 60, 120, 199, 407, 438, 440
 eager, 92
 fair, 155
 JAM Parlog, 17
 lazy, 99
 Panda, 155, 204, 228, 250, 258
 self-, 6
scope
 of cut, 151
 of variable, 24
search problems
 all solutions, 15, 280
 fixed number of solutions, 152
search space, 222
seed, 97
 of layered stream, 148, 256, 275, 308
 of pipelined filters, 144
semaphore, 152
Semigroup, 324
Sequent Symmetry, 16, 64
sequentiality, 13
serializing goals, 229, 248, 411
Shoppers Problem, 238
short-circuit
 chain, 155, 248, 468
SICStus Prolog, 57, 435
Sieve of Eratosthenes, 84
single-solution computation, 15
slowdown, 469
specification, 72
speculative parallelism, 39, 53, 141, 173
speedup, 10, 81, 96
speedup!real, 469
speedup!superlinear, 398, 469
speedup
 linear, 469
 naive, 469
 superlinear, 136
splitter, 106
stack!hole, 59
stack
 abstract data type, 81

cactus-, 59
group, 59
in WAM, 435
suspension-, 446
starvation, 101, 155
storage model, 58
Strand, 48, 58, 469
stream, 42, 469
 layered, 43, 147, 256, 275, 467
structure, 19
 active, 194, 376
 copying, 199
 ground, 22
 locking during creation, 61
 passive, 194, 373
 pointer in WAM, 441
suspension, 3, 36, 131, 446, 469
 -record, 59, 446
 -stack, 446
 in layered streams, 151
synchronization points, 323

T

tail-recursion optimization, 62, 131, 437
task switch, 61
temporary variable, 437
term — see structure
termination
 book-end method, 335
 short-circuit method, 468
throttling, 29, 97, 150, 415
trail, 440
tree
 2–3, 327
 binary, 20, 106, 113, 169, 338, 389
 flattened, 31, 42
 isomorphic, 20, 38, 54, 169
 OR-, 59, 117, 467
Triangle, 197
Turtles, 266

U

unification, 2, 24
 atomic, 49
 general, 441
 input, 446
 output, 448
unit clause, 20
unrolling, 111, 120, 131, 221, 227, 263, 272,
  332, 350, 406
utilization — see efficiency

V

variable, 19
 anonymous, 20
 don't-care, 20
 existentially-quantified, 21, 35
 hooked, 446
 locking, 3, 58, 61, 448
 permanent, 437
 read-only, 48
 scope of, 24
 temporary, 437
 universally-quantified, 21, 35
vector, 27

W

Warren Abstract Machine, 58, 435, 469
 arithmetic, 441
 globalizing unsafe variable, 438
 read and write modes, 441
 stack group, 59
worker, 62, 468
write-once array, 27

Z

Zebra, 219

The MIT Press, with Peter Denning as general consulting editor, publishes computer science books in the following series:

ACM Doctoral Dissertation Award and Distinguished Dissertation Series

Artificial Intelligence
Patrick Winston, founding editor
J. Michael Brady, Daniel G. Bobrow, and Randall Davis, editors

Charles Babbage Institute Reprint Series for the History of Computing
Martin Campbell-Kelly, editor

Computer Systems
Herb Schwetman, editor

Explorations with Logo
E. Paul Goldenberg, editor

Foundations of Computing
Michael Garey and Albert Meyer, editors

History of Computing
I. Bernard Cohen and William Aspray, editors

Information Systems
Michael Lesk, editor

Logic Programming
Ehud Shapiro, editor; Fernando Pereira, Koichi Furukawa, Jean-Louis Lassez, and David H. D. Warren, associate editors

The MIT Press Electrical Engineering and Computer Science Series

Research Monographs in Parallel and Distributed Processing
Christopher Jesshope and David Klappholz, editors

Scientific and Engineering Computation
Janusz Kowalik, editor

Technical Communication
Ed Barrett, editor